500 Plates & Chargers

500 Plates & Chargers

Innovative Expressions of Function & Style

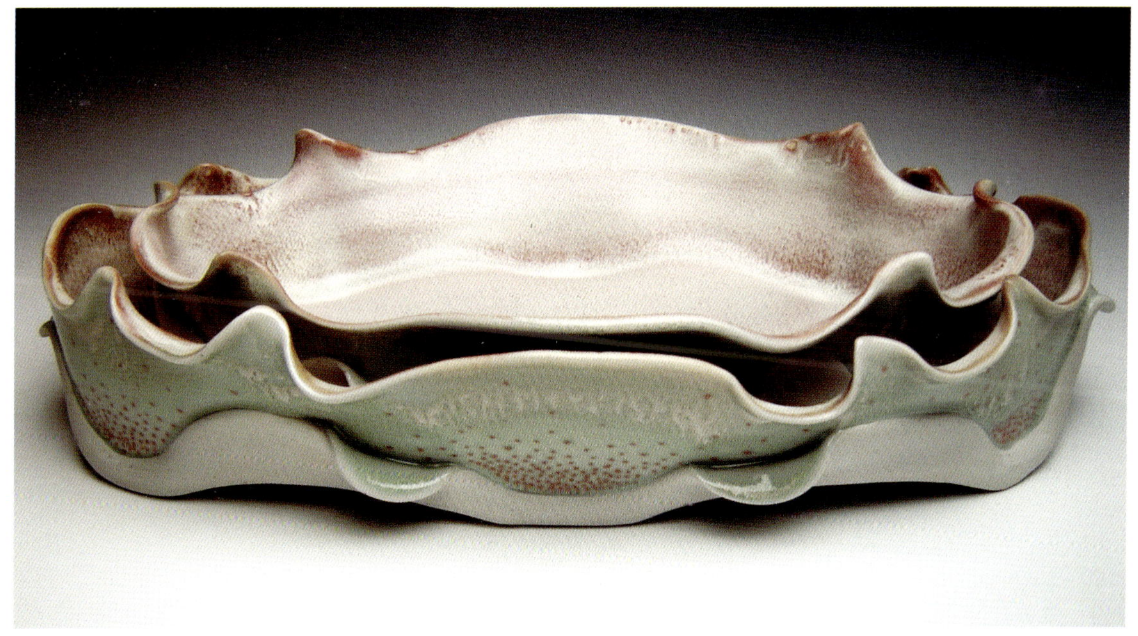

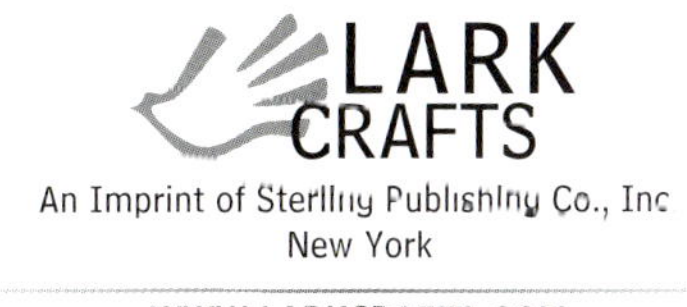

An Imprint of Sterling Publishing Co., Inc
New York

WWW.LARKCRAFTS.COM

DEVELOPMENT EDITOR
Suzanne J.E. Tourtillott

EDITOR
Larry Shea

ART DIRECTOR
Matt Shay

COVER DESIGNER
Cindy LaBreacht

FRONT COVER
Josh DeWeese
Platter, 2007

BACK COVER, FROM TOP LEFT
Maggie Mae Beyeler
Passion Flower Dessert Plates, 2007

Bede Clark
A Window Opens There, 1999

Ronan Kyle Peterson
Square Plates (Gall Decoration), 2006

Mirtha Aertker
Receko, 2007

SPINE
Donna Cole
Red Geometric, 2006

FRONT FLAP, FROM TOP
Clay Leonard
Rippled Plate Set, 2007

Carol Ann Wedemeyer
Smoke Rings Party Tray, 2004

BACK FLAP, FROM TOP
Marko Fields
Dang Deviled Egg Tray Thinks It's Alive; Wants to Go to Las Vegas and Serve Wayne Newton, 2004

Jonathan Barnes
Plates, 2006

PAGE 3
Martha H. Grover
Two Serving Trays, 2007

PAGE 5
Alice Shepherd
Snake Plate, 2006

Library of Congress Cataloging-in-Publication Data

500 plates & chargers : innovative expressions of function & style / development editor, Suzanne J.E. Tourtillott.
p. cm.
Includes index.
ISBN-13: 978-1-57990-688-7 (PB-trade pbk. : alk. paper)
ISBN-10: 1-57990-688-5 (PB-trade pbk. : alk. paper)
1. Plates (Tableware)--United States--Catalogs. 2. Pottery, American--21st century--Catalogs. I. Tourtillott, Suzanne J.E. II. Title: Five hundred plates and chargers.
NK4695.P55A13 2008
738.3'8--dc22

2007050678

10 9 8 7 6 5 4 3

Published by Lark Crafts, An Imprint of Sterling Publishing Co., Inc.
387 Park Avenue South, New York, NY 10016

Distributed in Canada by Sterling Publishing,
c/o Canadian Manda Group, 165 Dufferin Street
Toronto, Ontario, Canada M6K 3H6

Distributed in the United Kingdom by GMC Distribution Services,
Castle Place, 166 High Street, Lewes, East Sussex, England BN7 1XU

Distributed in Australia by Capricorn Link (Australia) Pty Ltd.,
P.O. Box 704, Windsor, NSW 2756 Australia

If you have questions or comments about this book, please contact:
Lark Crafts
67 Broadway
Asheville, NC 28801
828-253-0467

Manufactured in China

ISBN 13: 978-1-57990-688-7

For information about custom editions, special sales, premium and corporate purchases, please contact Sterling Special Sales Department at 800-805-5489 or specialsales@sterlingpub.com

For information about desk and examination copies available to college and university professors, requests must be submitted to academic@larkbooks.com. Our complete policy can be found at www.larkcrafts.com.

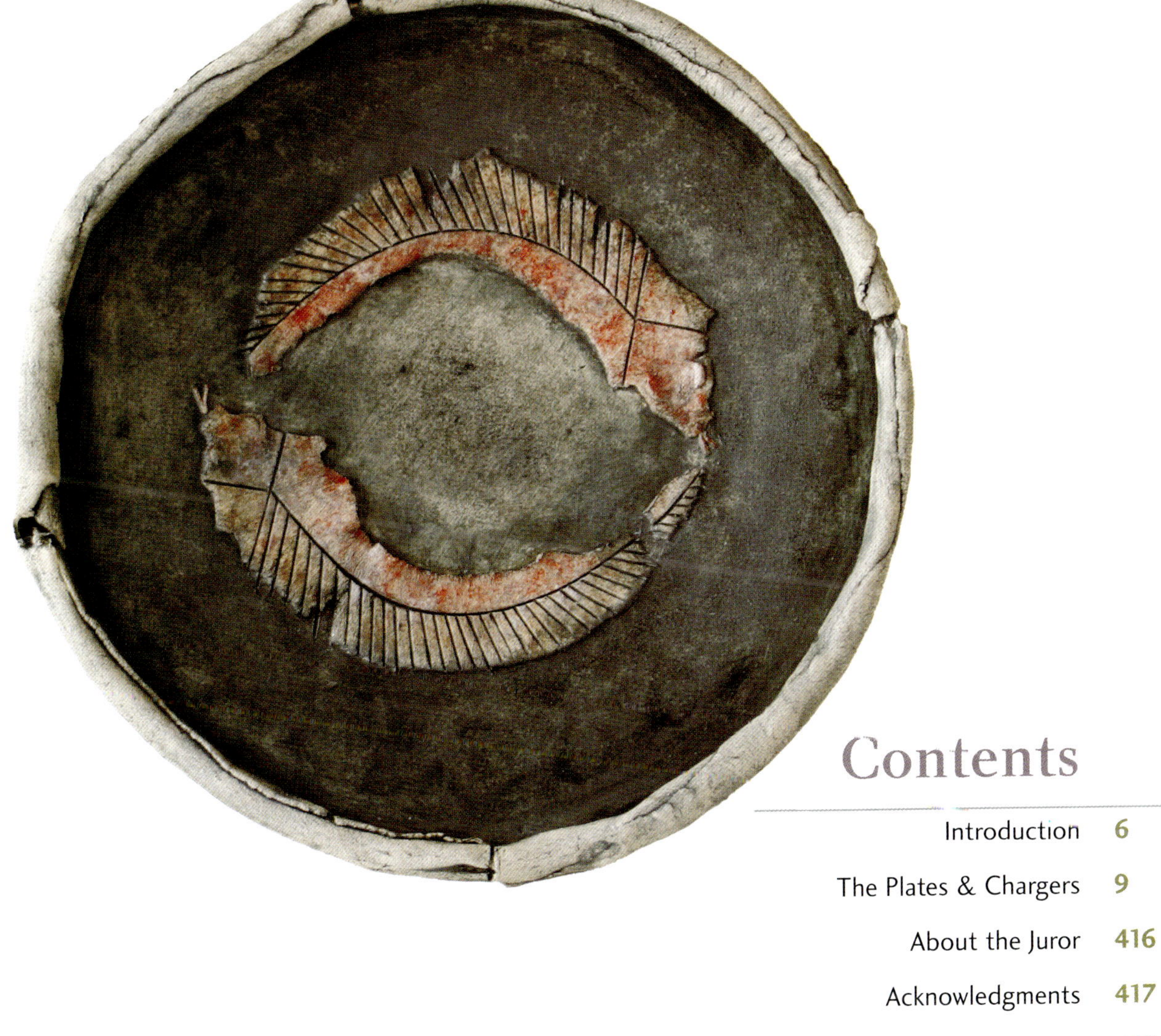

Contents

Introduction

From our earliest memories of family dinners, the plate is a recognizable, friendly reminder of coming together, and of the sensual joys of food and eating. From the lowly paper plate to grandma's special-event china, the plate is a staple in daily life. Plates call us to the table, or frame our cherished thoughts of home.

The artist's plate makes a virtue of the necessity of eating, incorporating far-ranging topics into the dinner hour and rewarding the attention of the diners. Like children telling stories of their day to the family, such plates charm and inform around the dinner table. Going beyond their simple everyday functions, plate forms can also hold a special place as heraldry displayer, frame, and iconic messenger in a domestic setting. Italian Renaissance portrait plates honored the personal image, connecting people to those absent or fixing the image of a place, event, or person in time.

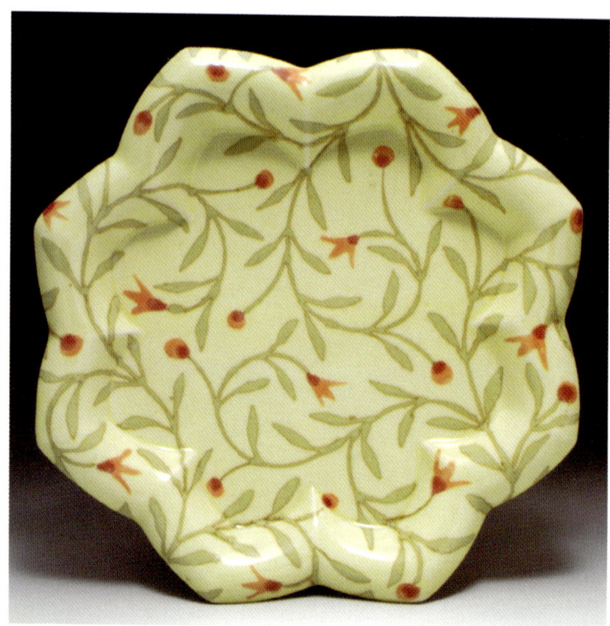

Brenda Quinn
Scalloped Platter | 2007

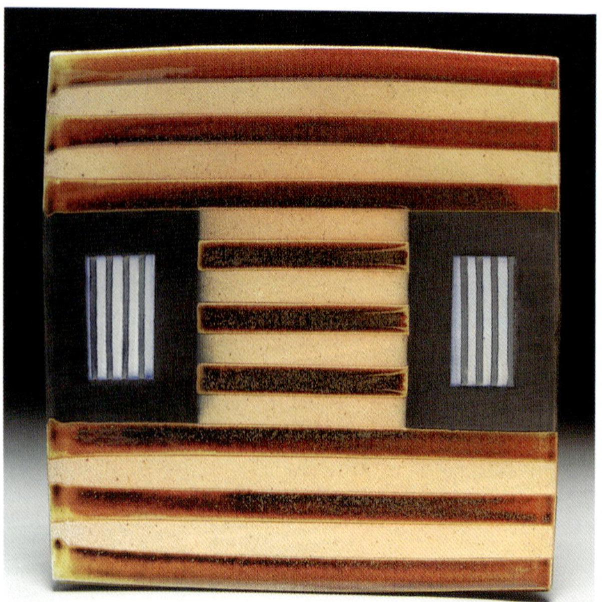

David Crane
Chief Platter—Amber | 2006

The plates included in *500 Plates & Chargers* cover a wide range in purpose and function. Some follow the traditional role of the plate as a purveyor of sustenance that collaborates with the food served (like Catherine Boswell's beautiful, restrained porcelain plate).

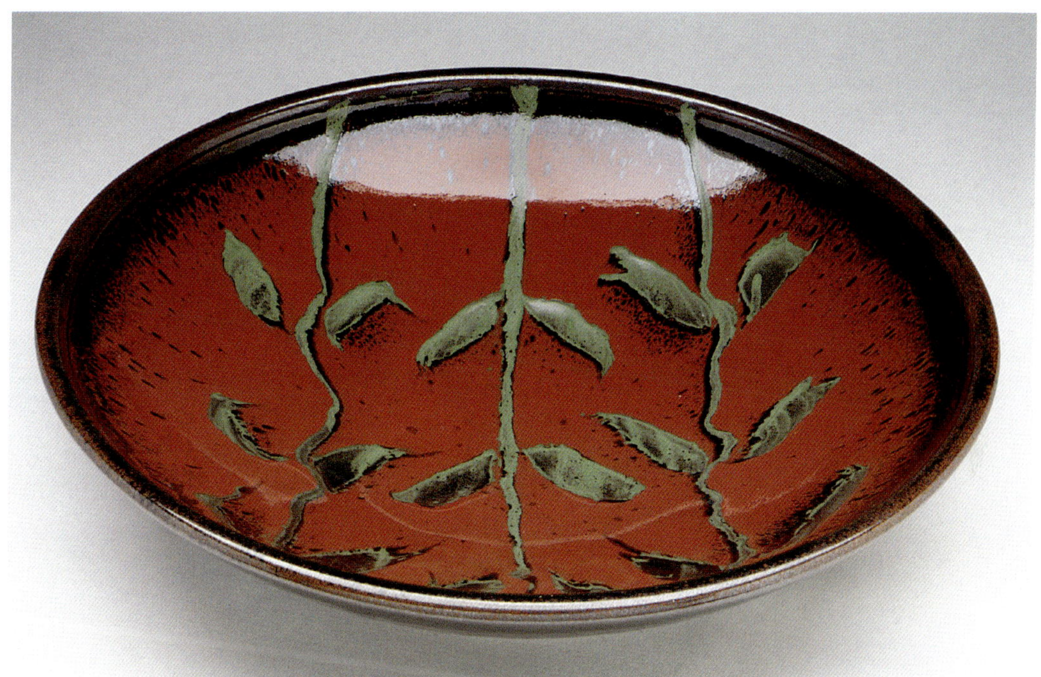

Chris Harford
Vine | 2005

Other plates serve as domestic decoration (Brenda Quinn's actively patterned *Scalloped Platter*) or as a bearer of values (Kelly McKibben's amusing *Going for a Stroll*). With some plates, artists comment on such topics as materiality (Broc Allen's anagama-fired *Koka*), process (Tara Wilson's painterly wood-fired *Small Plate*), or art and design (David Crane's sophisticated *Chief Platter—Amber*). Certain plates—like Peggy Ericson's abstraction, *Dot to Dot Platter and Charger*—work against the concept of function itself.

Angi Curreri's lively *Square Platter with Birds and Fruit*, Chris Harford's beautiful high-fired *Vine*, and Kathryn E. Narrow's elegant porcelain *Sorb Apple Plate* tell us about the richness of nature and the joys to be found there: comfort and beauty from the natural world on the dinner plate (literally and in metaphor). The narratives in George McCauley's briskly painted platter, Sally Campbell's *Plenty*, Bern Emmerichs' provocative *Endeavours with Arthur*, and Laurie Shaman's whimsically domestic *State of Enlightenment* take us away from the tabletop into stories that engage us through the artist's use of drawing and painting to create a highly personal world.

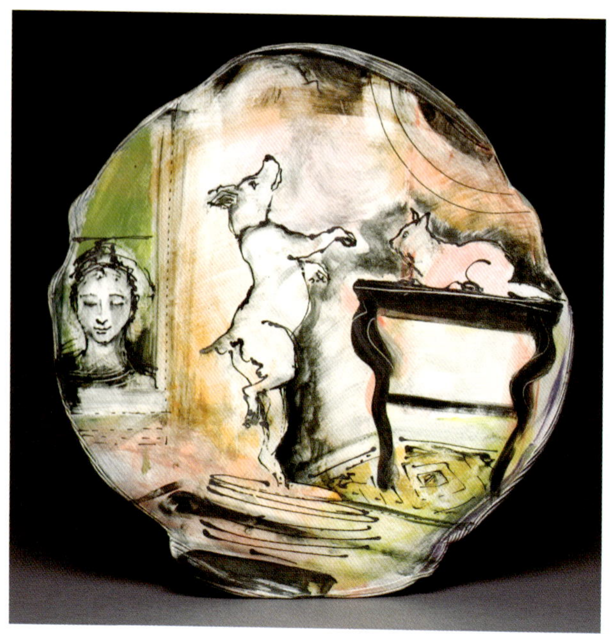

Laurie Shaman
State of Enlightenment | 2006

Unlike the cup, which is held in the hand and touched to the lips, the plate holds a space on a table or display, presenting a desired substance or idea and calling our attention to view its contents. Artists' plates seek to speak through our connection to home, using the common act of eating together to invoke a farther-reaching philosophy or message. It's a subversive move for an artist to try to put his or her values in front of people, where they live, and to ask the owners of the work to spend their personal time with those values. Pieces of art in a domestic environment have to be very special to fit comfortably within the hustle and clutter of everyday life, yet still say something skillfully enough to make repeated readings of the work worthwhile.

Henri Matisse said, "Creativity takes courage." People working in clay are some of the bravest.

—Linda Arbuckle, Juror

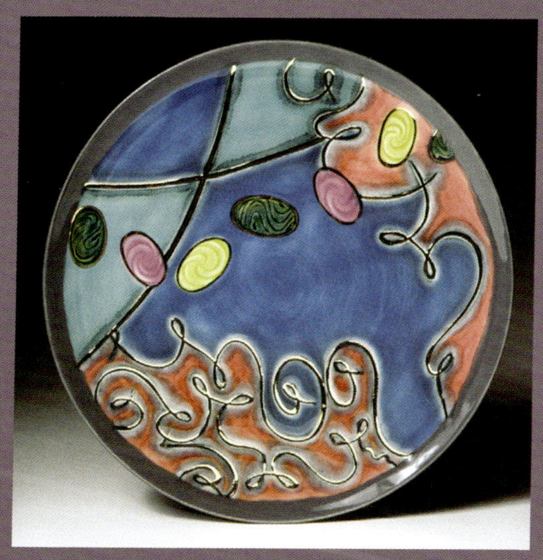

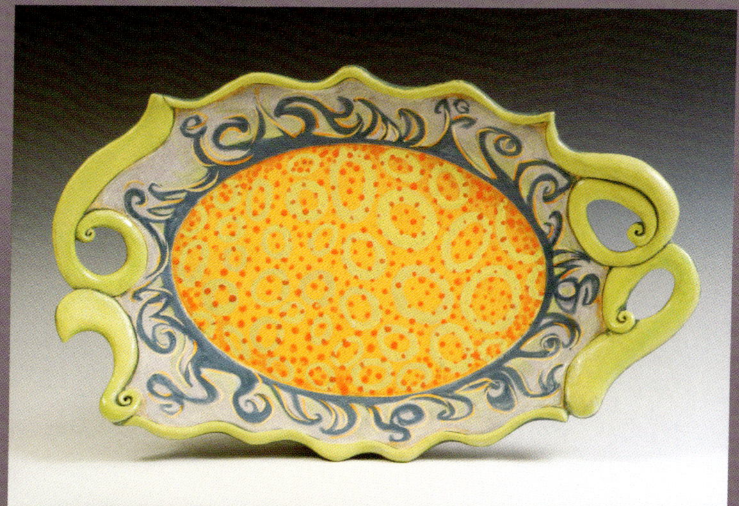

The Plates & Chargers

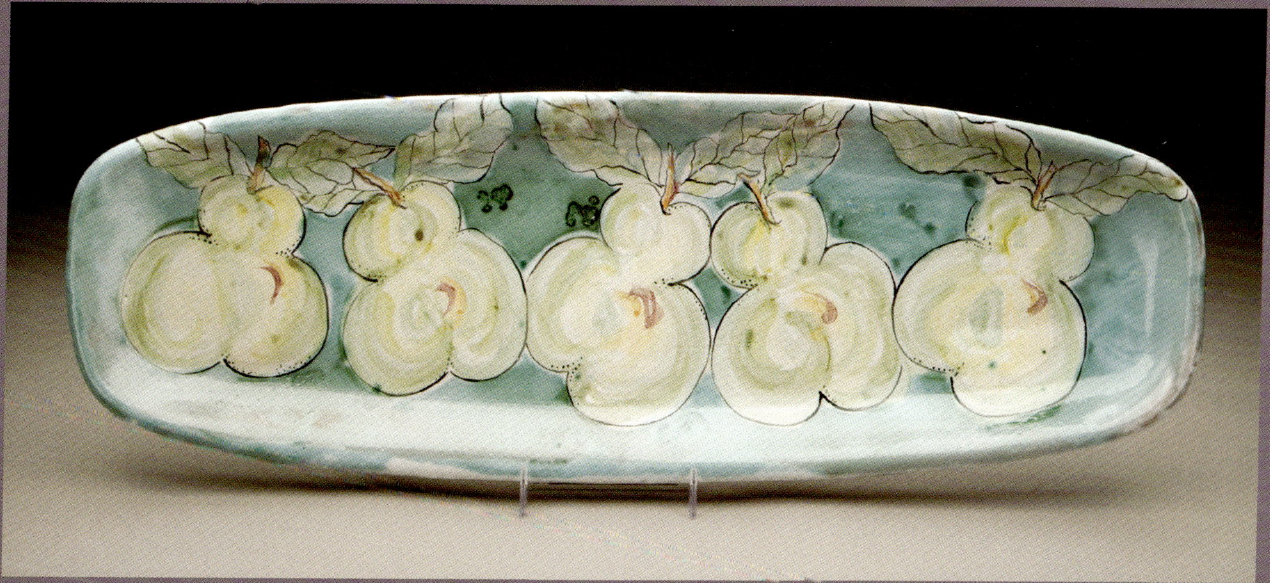

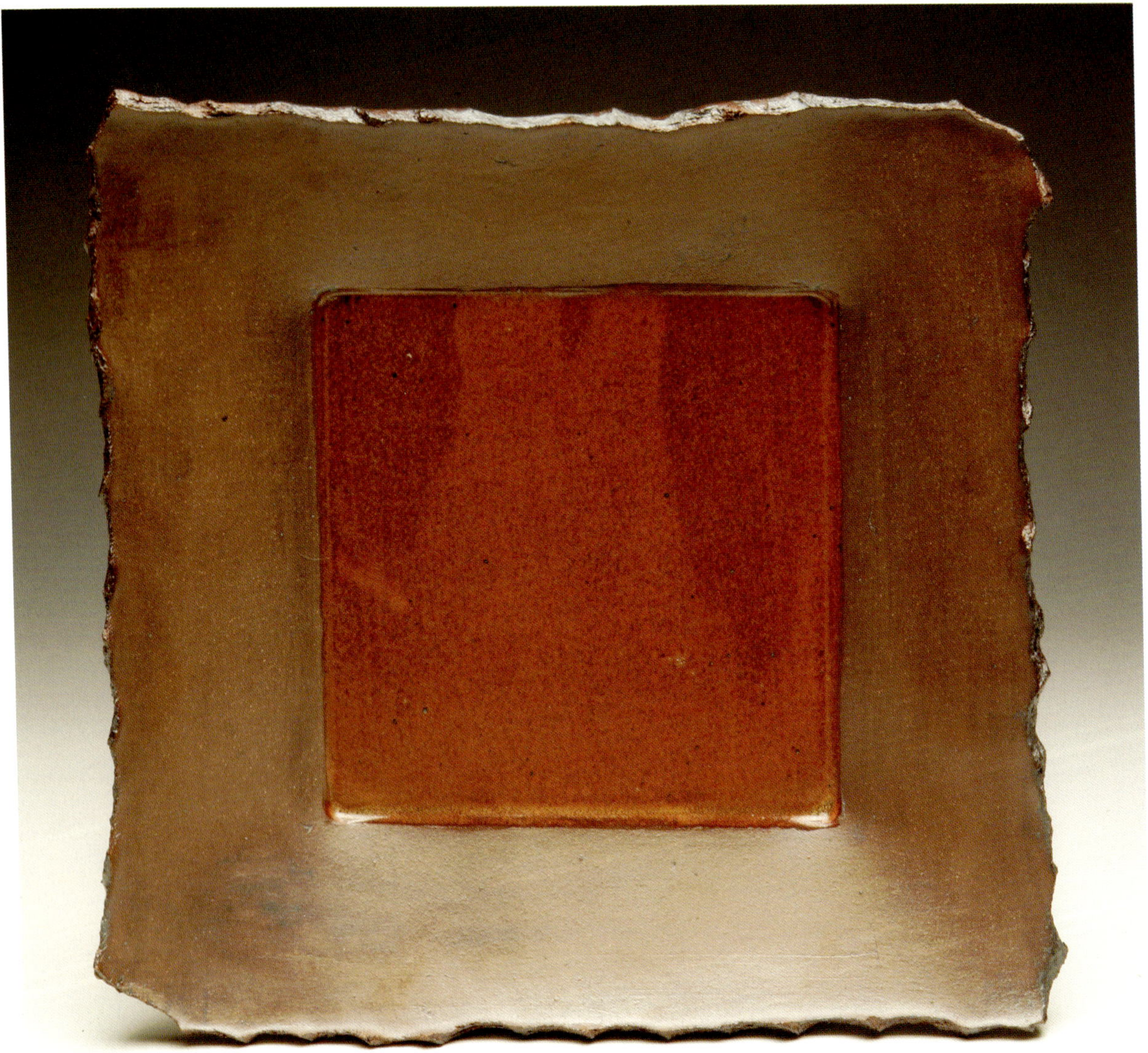

Andrea Gettings

 # 12 Square Plate in Autumn Brown | 2007

11 1/2 X 11 INCHES (29.2 X 27.9 CM)

Hand-built stoneware; cone 06; glaze and oxide rub; cone 10 reduction

PHOTO BY DAN CUNNINGHAM

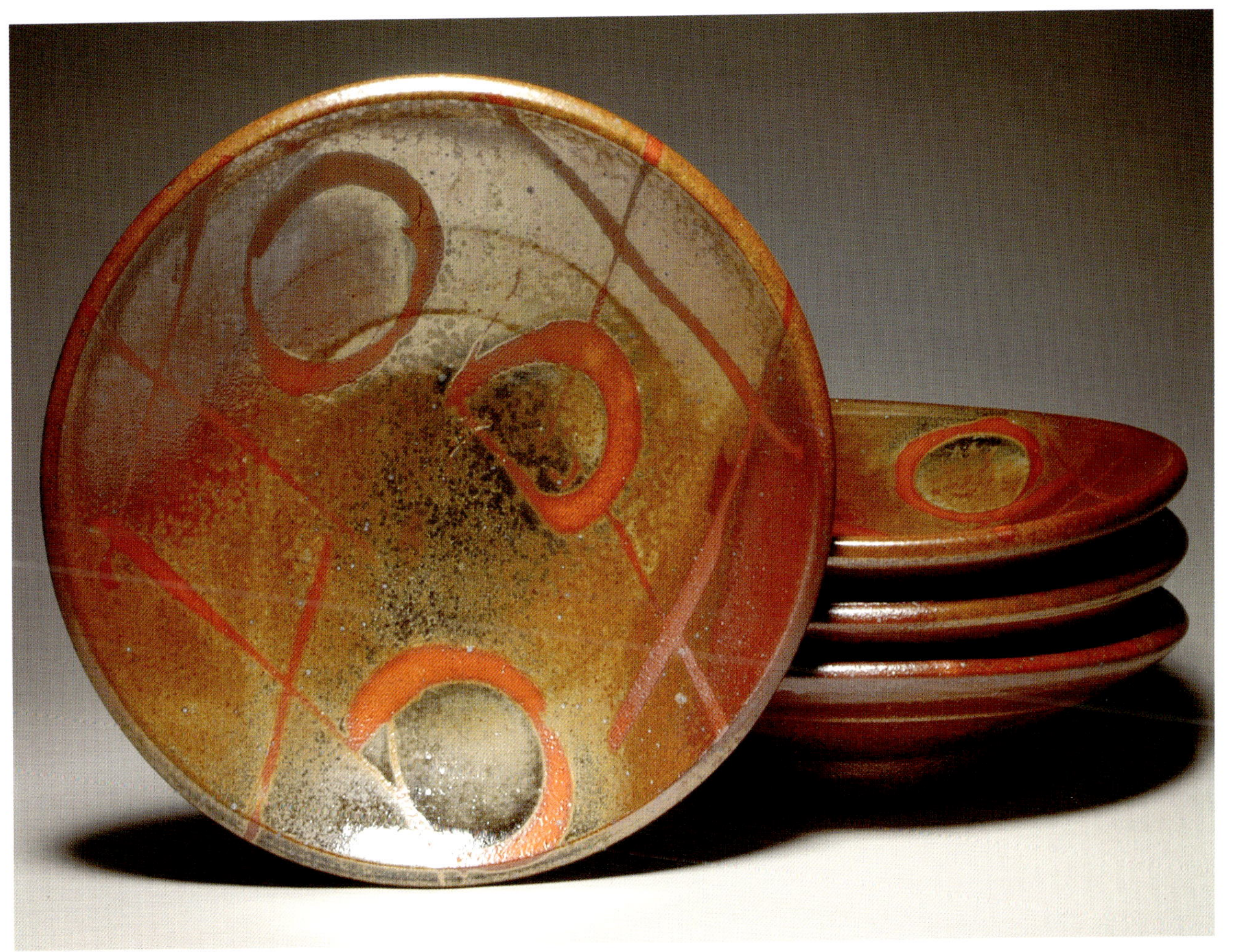

Jonathan Barnes

Plates | 2006

EACH: $2\frac{1}{2}$ X 12 INCHES (6.4 X 30.5 CM)

Wheel-thrown stoneware; shino and wax resist; reduction fired, cone 10

PHOTO BY ARTIST

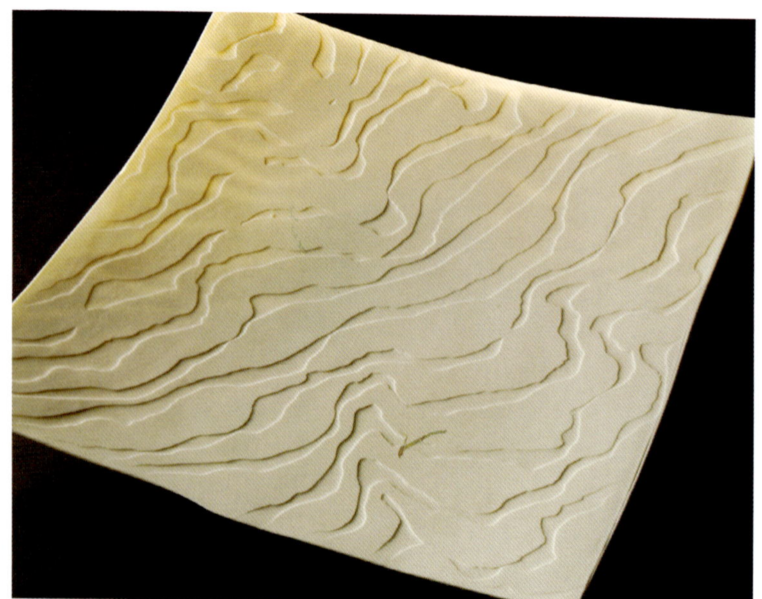

Maiju Altpere-Woodhead

White-on-White | 2006

$1\frac{3}{4}$ X $12\frac{3}{4}$ X $12\frac{3}{4}$ INCHES (4.5 X 32.4 X 32.4 CM)

Slip-cast and hand-built translucent porcelain; carved; gas fired, cones 9–10; polished

PHOTO BY DEREK ROSS

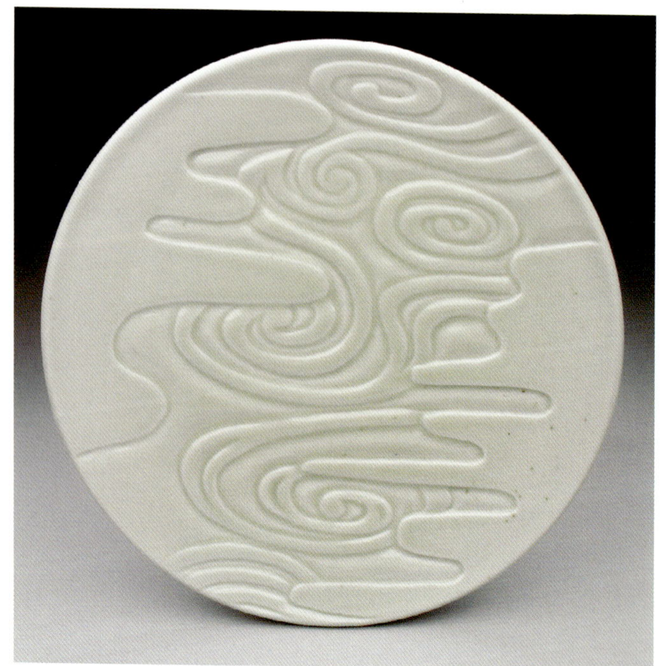

Yoshi Fujii

Plate—Mist Over Waves | 2007

1 X $9\frac{1}{2}$ INCHES (2.5 X 24.1 CM)

Wheel-thrown and hand-carved porcelain; gas fired in reduction, cone 10

PHOTO BY ARTIST

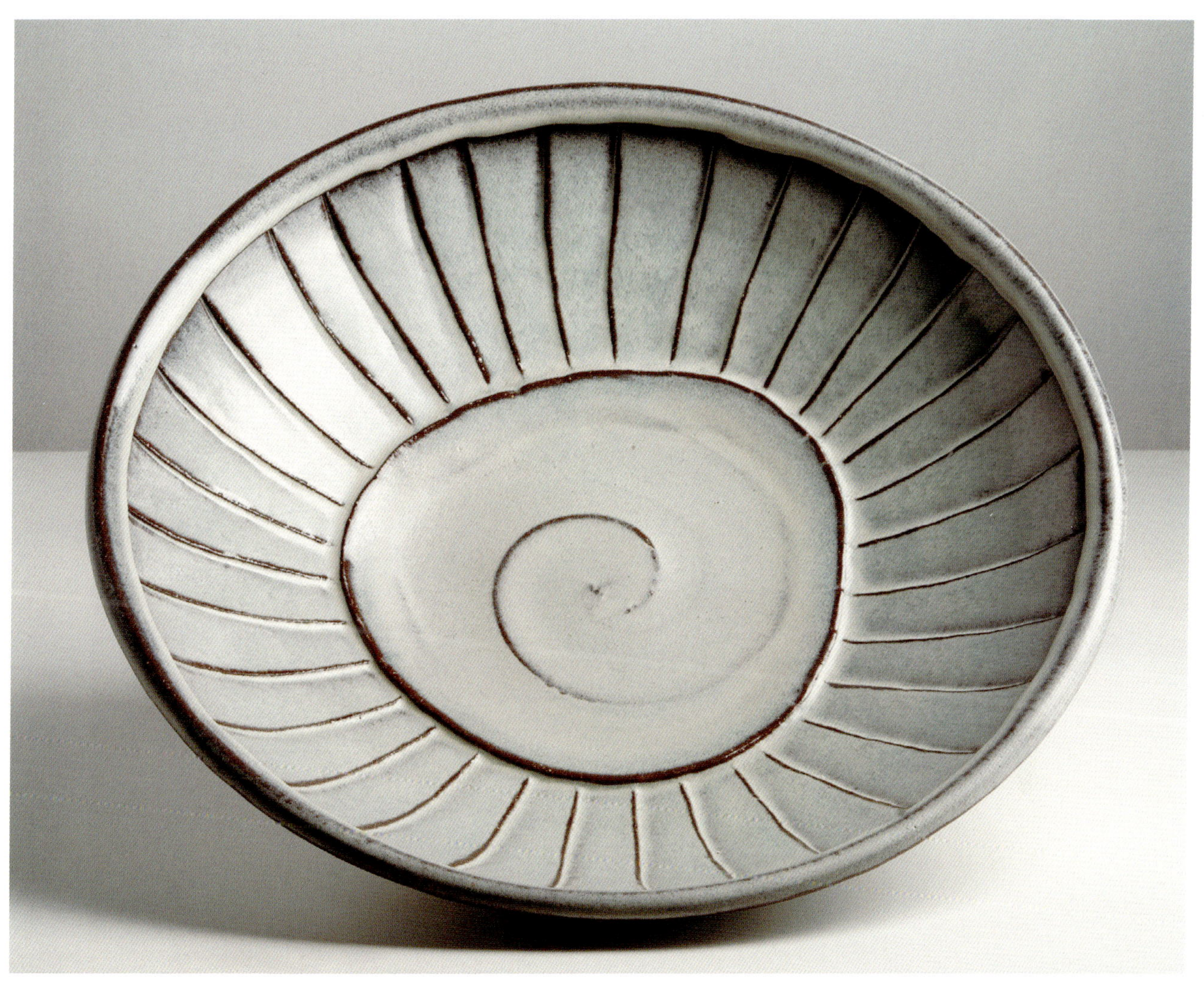

Louise Deroualle

Prato Risca | 2006

3 X 13 1/2 X 13 1/2 INCHES (7.6 X 34.3 X 34.3 CM)

Wheel-thrown and hand-built earthenware; electric fired, cone 03

PHOTO BY MONICA MENDES

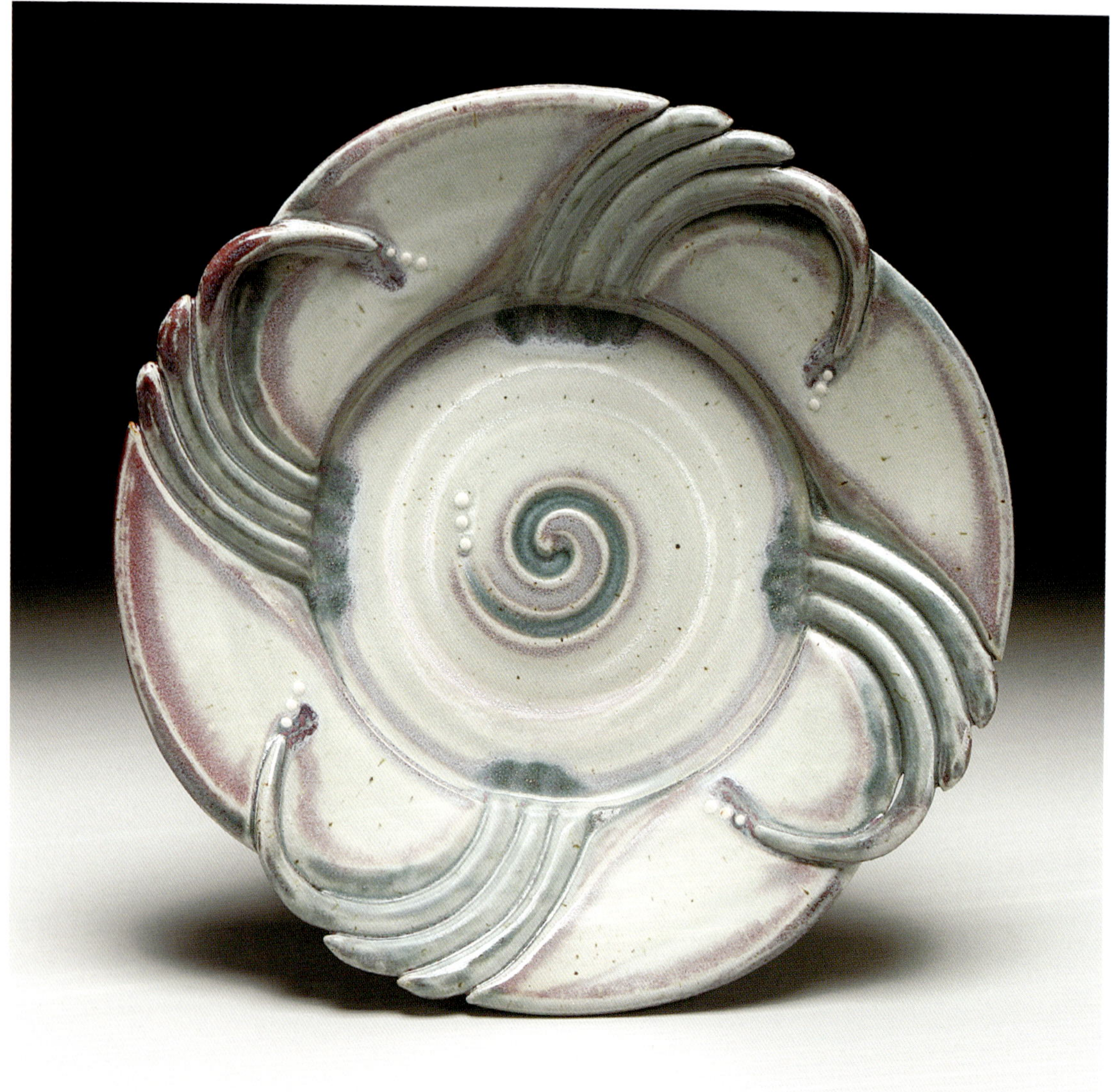

Cat Jarosz

Untitled | 2007

$3\frac{1}{4}$ X 17 INCHES (8.3 X 43.2 CM)

Wheel-thrown and hand-built stoneware with porcelain slip; carved; mamo-based glaze, copper stain overspray; gas fired in reduction, cones 10–11

PHOTO BY TIM BARNWELL

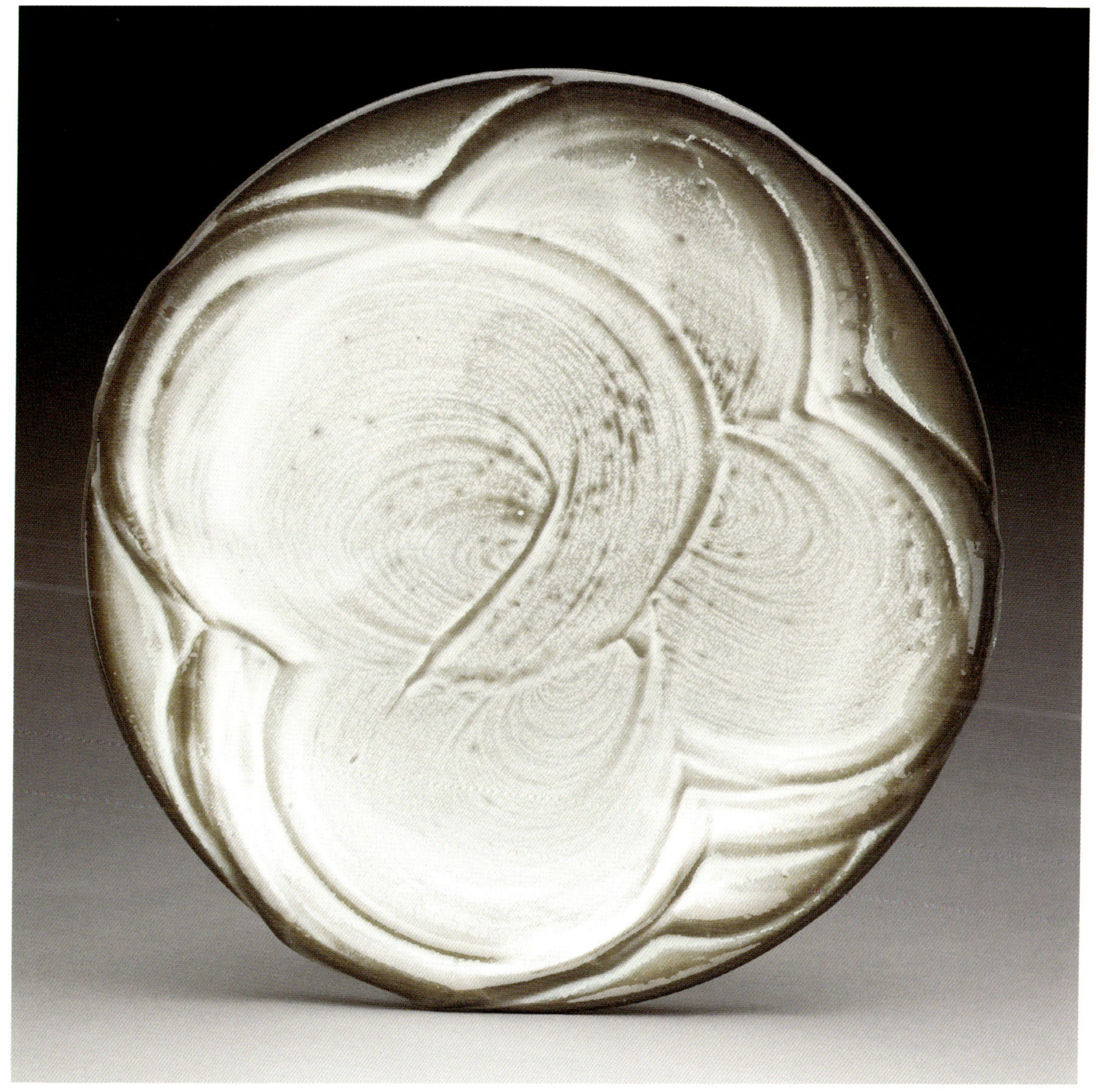

Matt Long

Dessert Plate | 2007

1 X 8½ INCHES (2.5 X 21.6 CM)

Wheel-thrown porcelain; slip; soda fired, cone 11

PHOTO BY STEVE PASZT

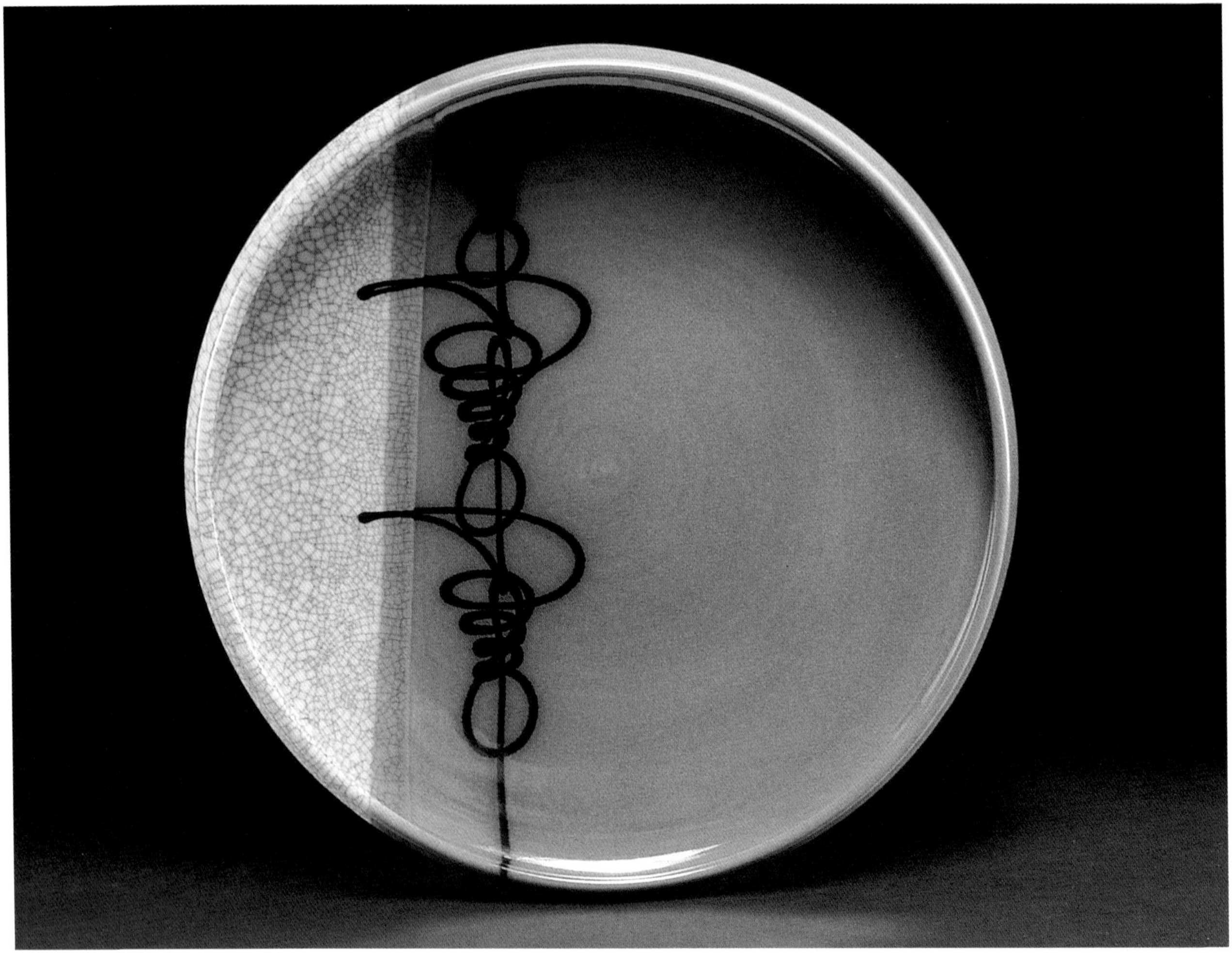

Deborah Shapiro

Platter, Mint Green | 2006

2 1/2 X 16 INCHES (6.4 X 40.6 CM)

Wheel-thrown porcelain; applied glaze, oxidation fired, cone 10; chrome-tin pink flush

PHOTOS BY COURTNEY FRISSE

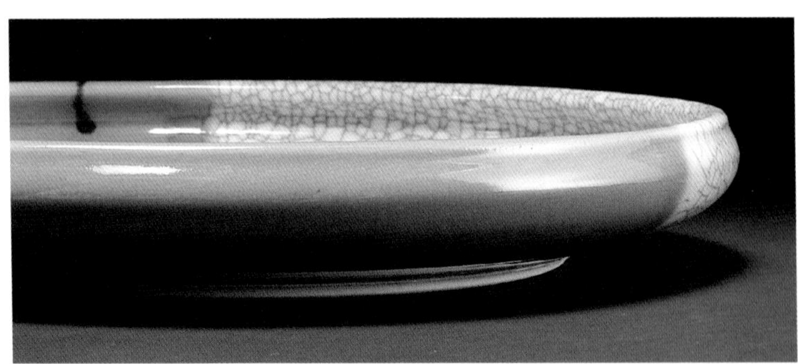

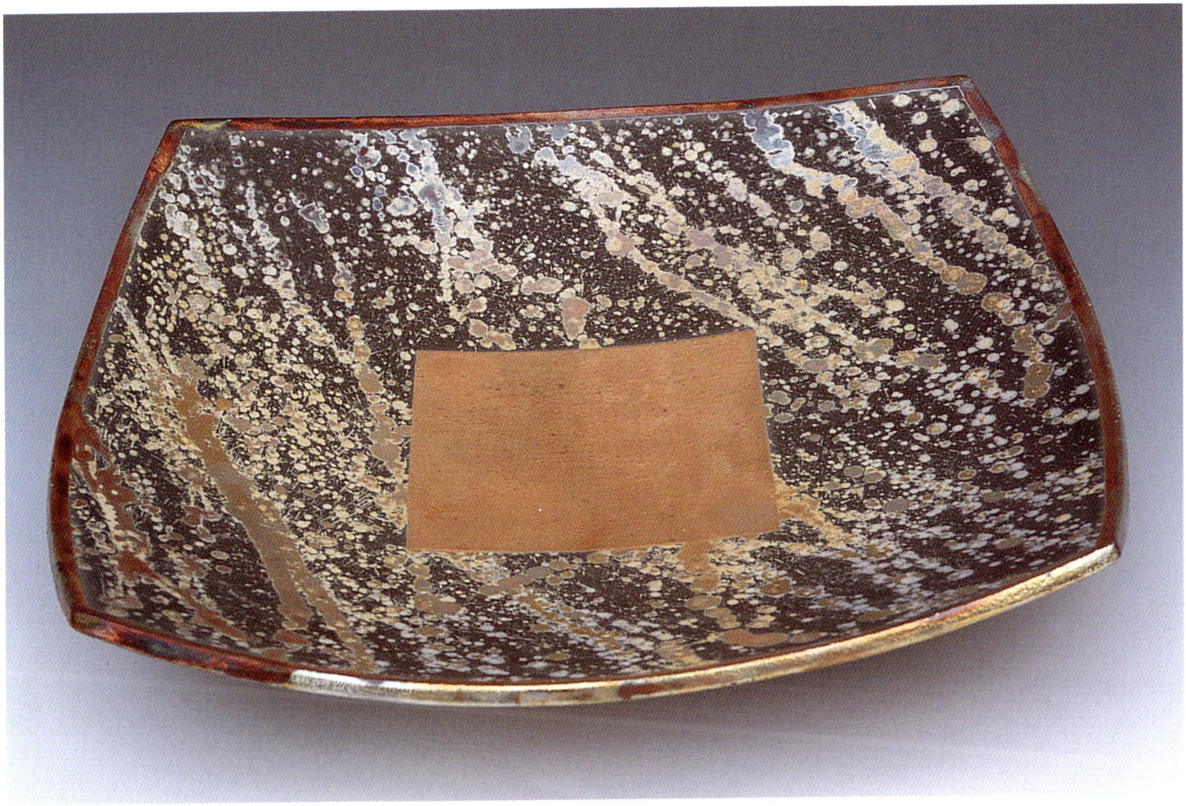

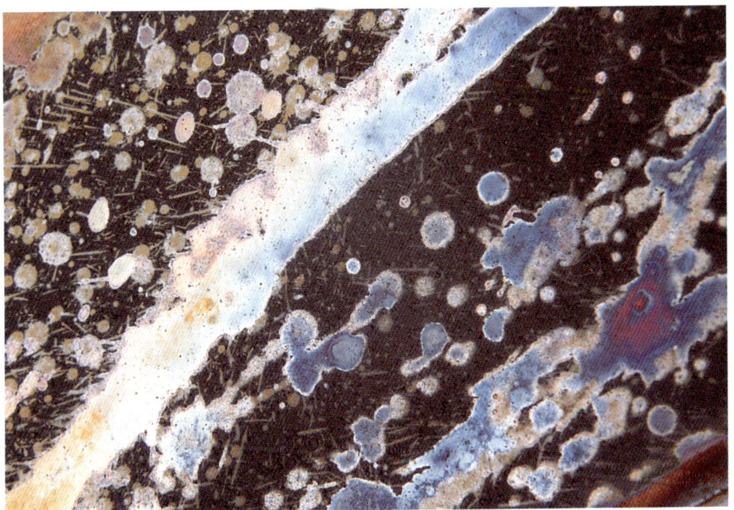

Zsuzsa Monostory

Untitled | 2007

3 X 12 X 12 INCHES (7.6 X 30.5 X 30.5 CM)

Slab-built Thompson raku; raku fired, cone 06

PHOTOS BY CAROL-ANN MICHAELSON

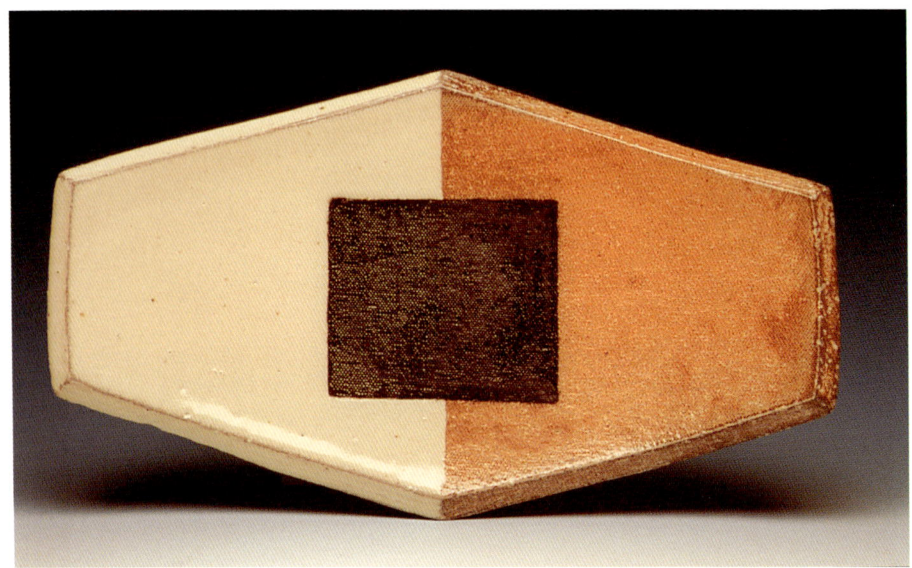

Jason Lachtara

Diamond Plate | 2006

2 X 13 X 6 INCHES (5.1 X 33 X 15.2 CM)

Slab-built stoneware; glazes and flashing slip; soda fired, cone 10

PHOTO BY ARTIST

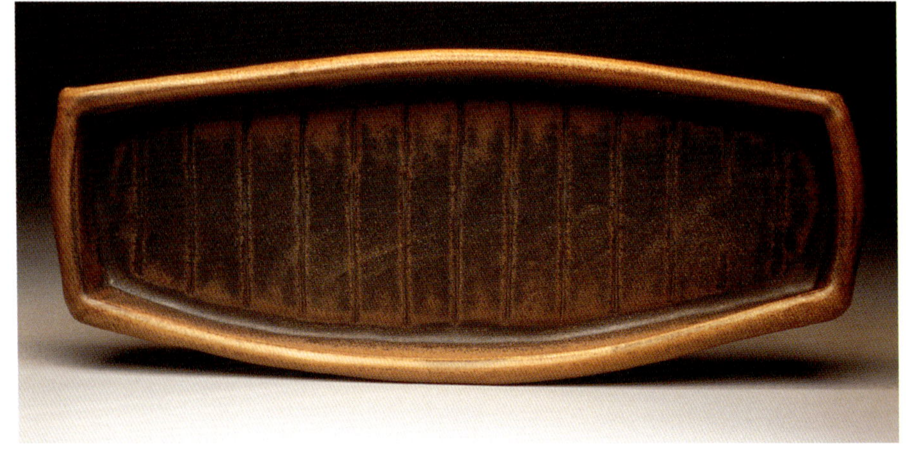

Amy Von Bargen

Oblong Rimmed Platter | 2007

2 X 18 X 7½ INCHES (5.1 X 45.7 X 19.1 CM)

Hand-built stoneware; reduction fired, cone 10; glazes, cone 10

PHOTO BY PETER LEE

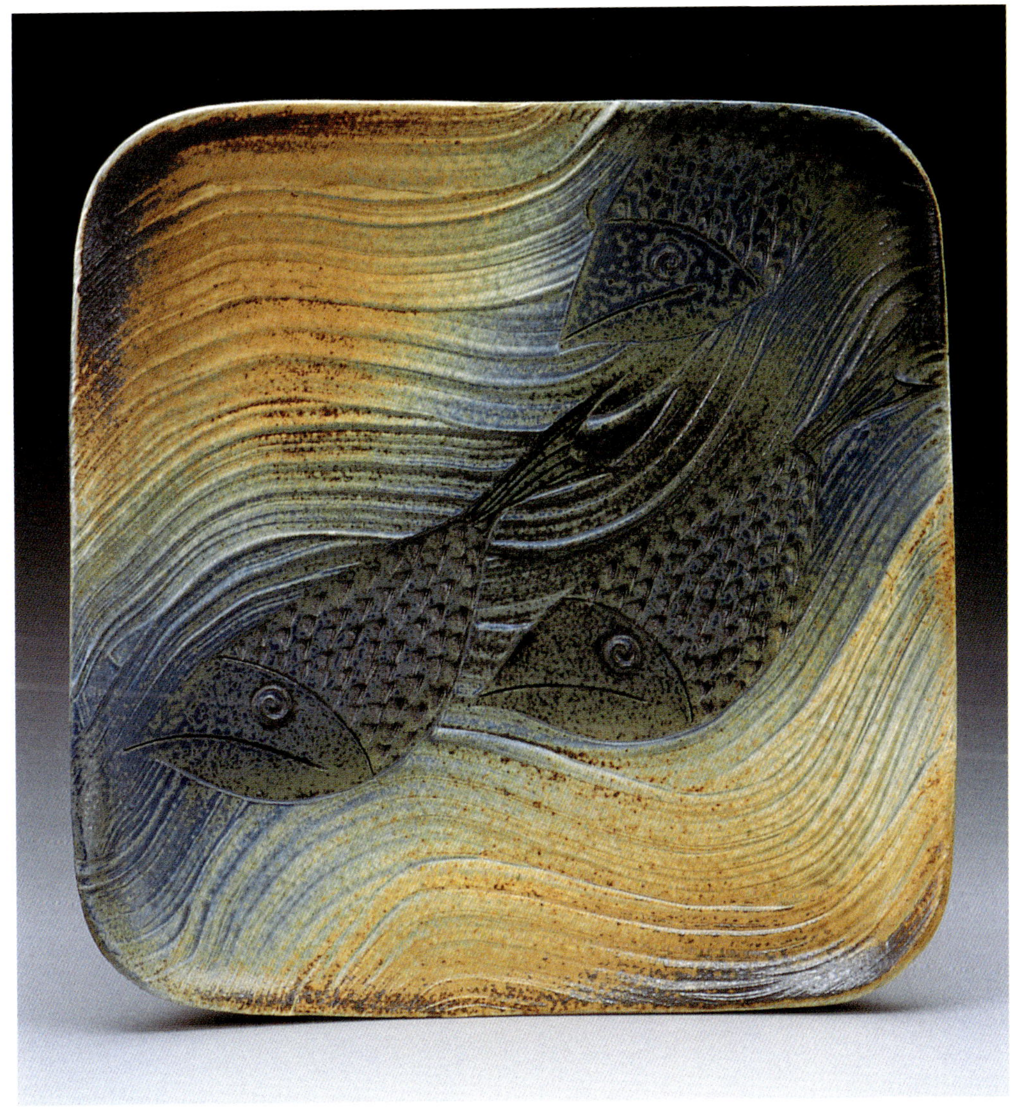

Hsin-Yi Huang

Fish Platter | 2005

2 X 11 1/2 X 11 INCHES (5.1 X 29.2 X 27.9 CM)

Slab-built stoneware; slip decoration; Craig Martell ash glaze; reduction fired, cone 10

PHOTO BY BILL BACHHUBER

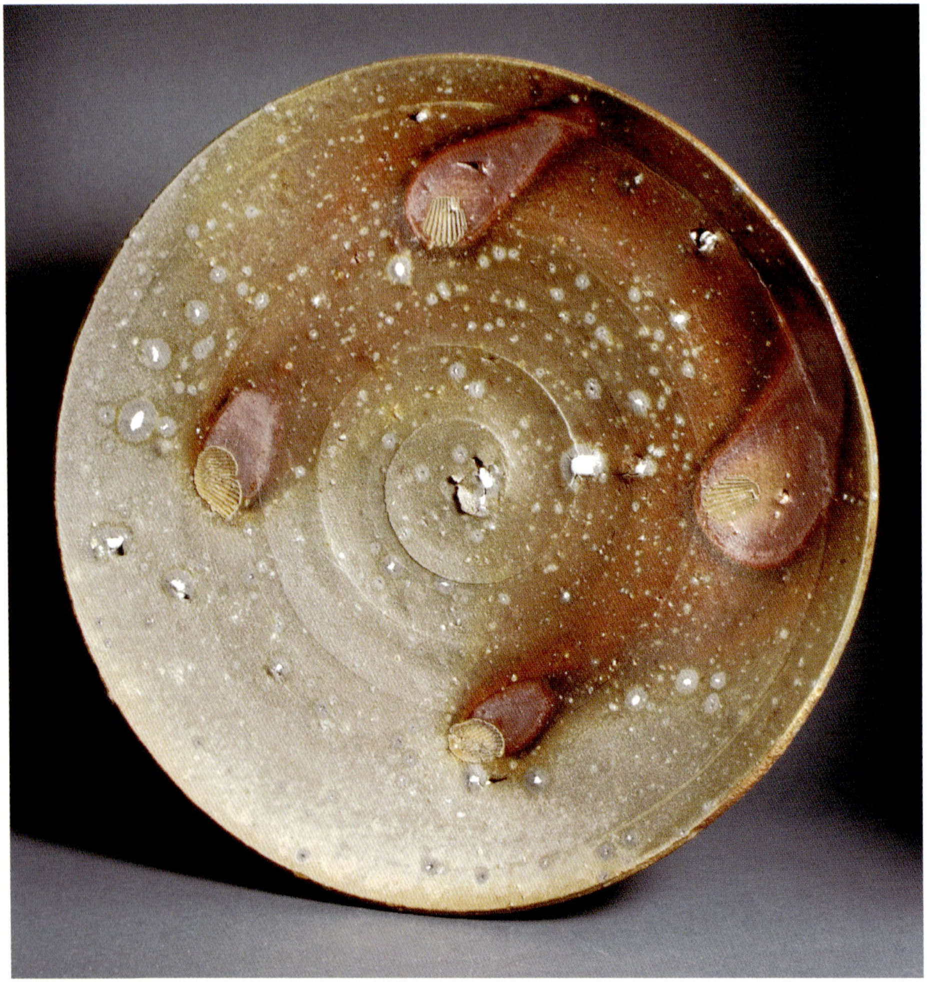

Dale Huffman

Untitled | 2006

2 X $18\frac{1}{8}$ INCHES (5 X 46 CM)

Wheel-thrown stoneware; natural ash glaze, wood fired, cone 12

PHOTOS BY ARTIST

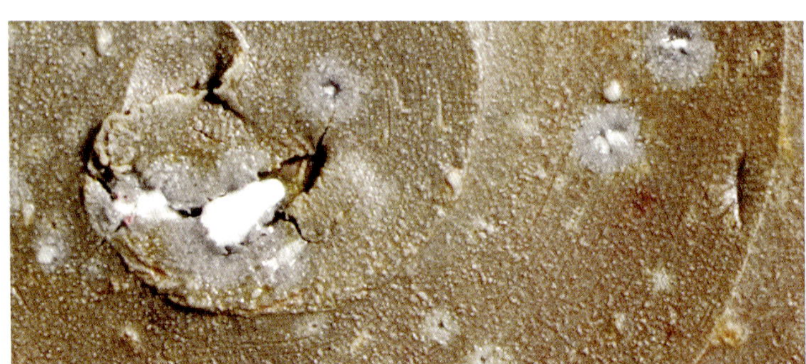

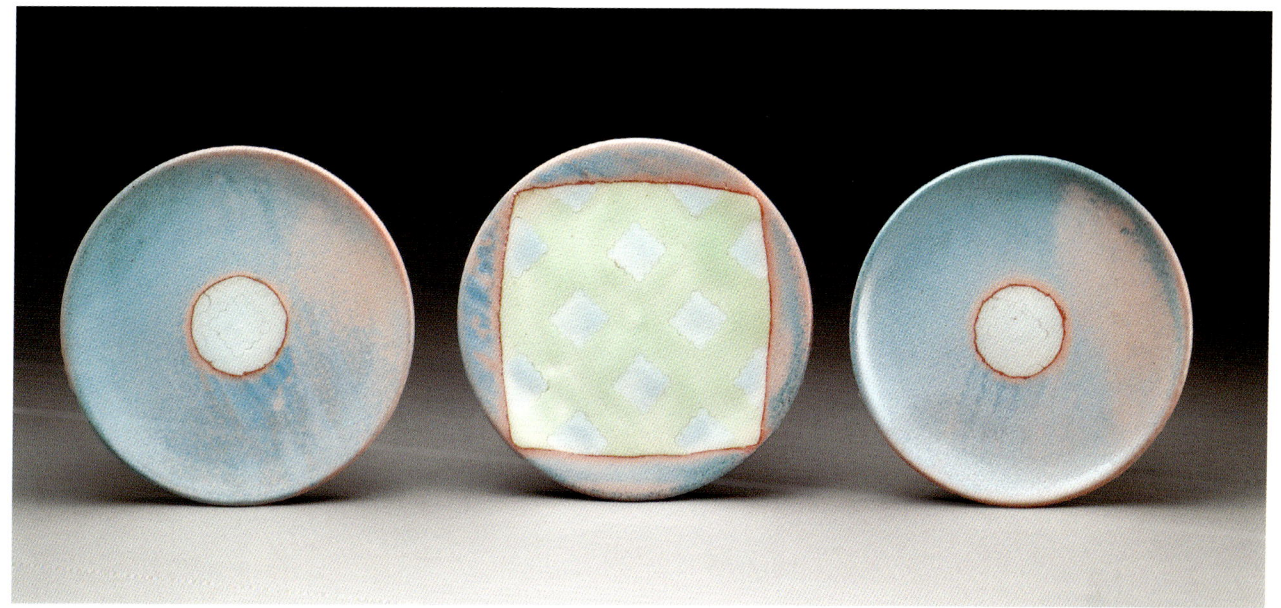

Benjamin Carter

Untitled | 2006

EACH: 1 1/2 X 8 INCHES (3.8 X 20.3 CM)

Wheel-thrown porcelain; glaze inlay with Pete's Strontium Best and Pinnell's Clear; gas fired in reduction, cone 10

PHOTO BY TOM MILLS

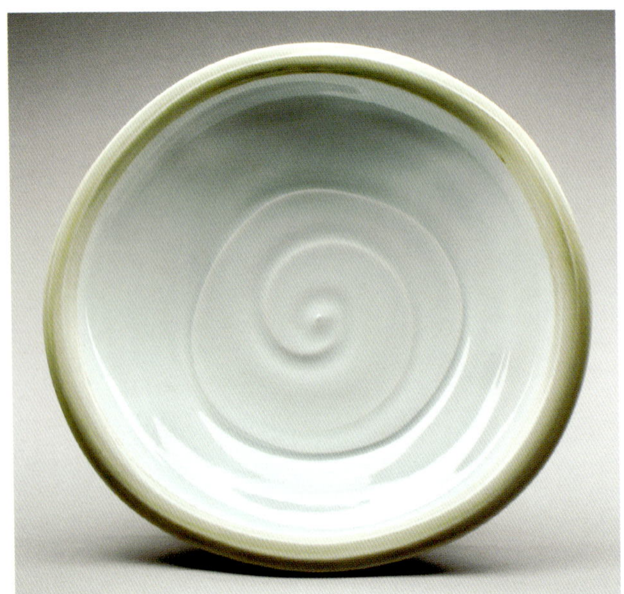

Mike Jabbur

Platter | 2006

4 X 17 INCHES (10.2 X 43.2 CM)

Wheel-thrown porcelain; celadon glazes, reduction fired, cone 10

PHOTO BY ARTIST

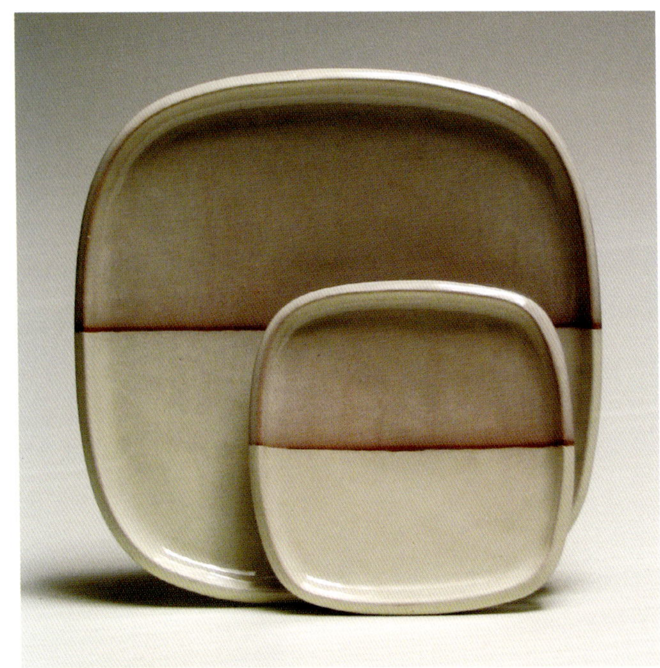

Todd Hayes

Red Line Plate Series | 2006

LARGEST: 1 1/2 X 10 X 10 INCHES (3.8 X 25.4 X 25.4 CM)

Hand-built earthenware; white slip; clear glaze; electric fired, cone 03

PHOTO BY ARTIST

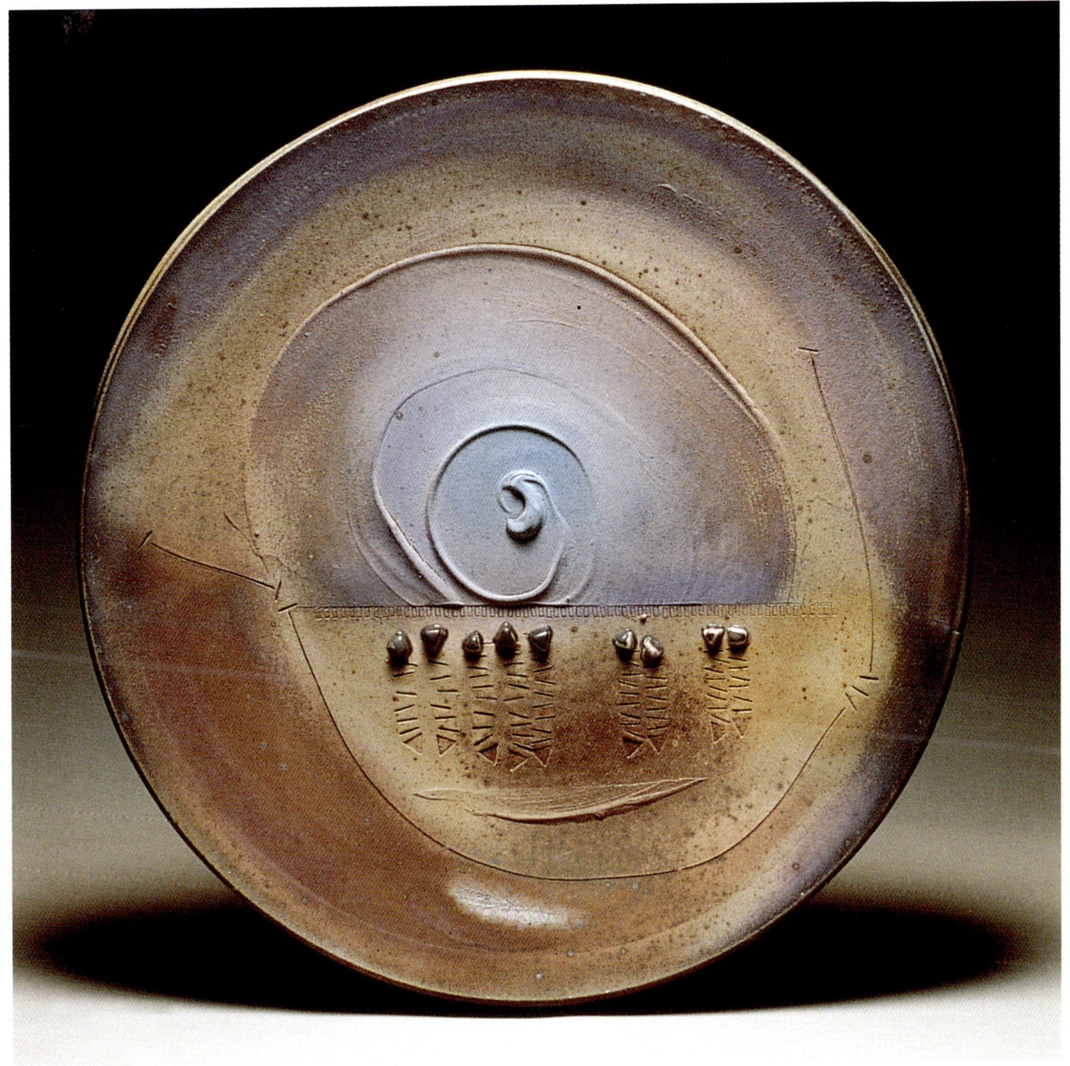

Maishe Dickman

Untitled | 2002

3 1/2 X 23 INCHES (8.9 X 58.4 CM)

Wheel-thrown and altered stoneware; gas fired in salt reduction, cone 10

PHOTO BY JOHN PELVERTS

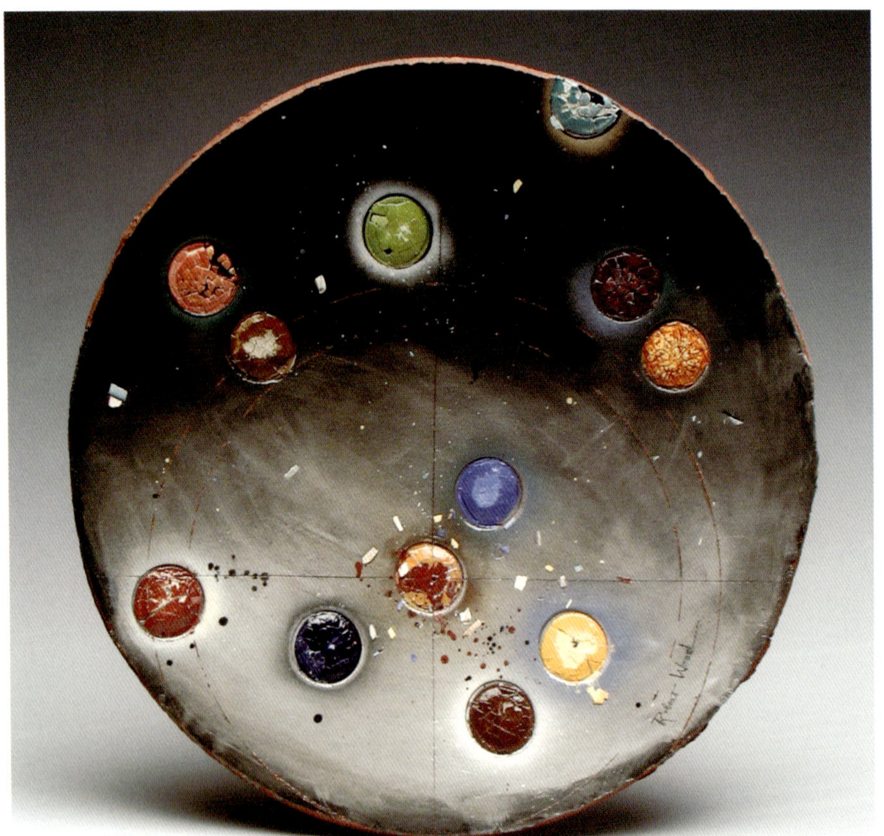

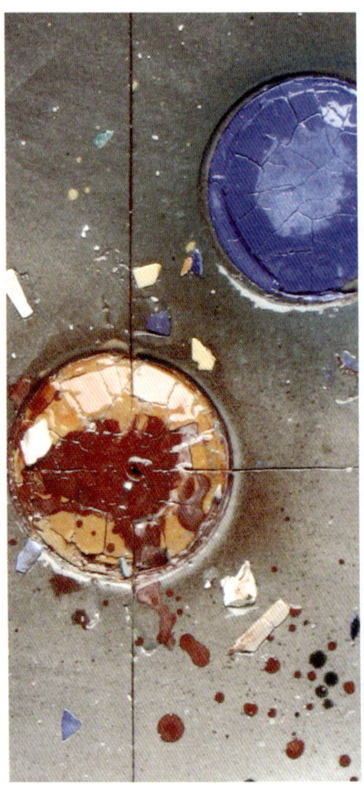

Robert L. Wood

Target | 2006

19 INCHES (48.3 CM) IN DIAMETER

Slump-molded and wheel-thrown earthenware; wet and dry slips; electric fired, cone 1; clear glaze, cone 04

PHOTOS BY ARTIST

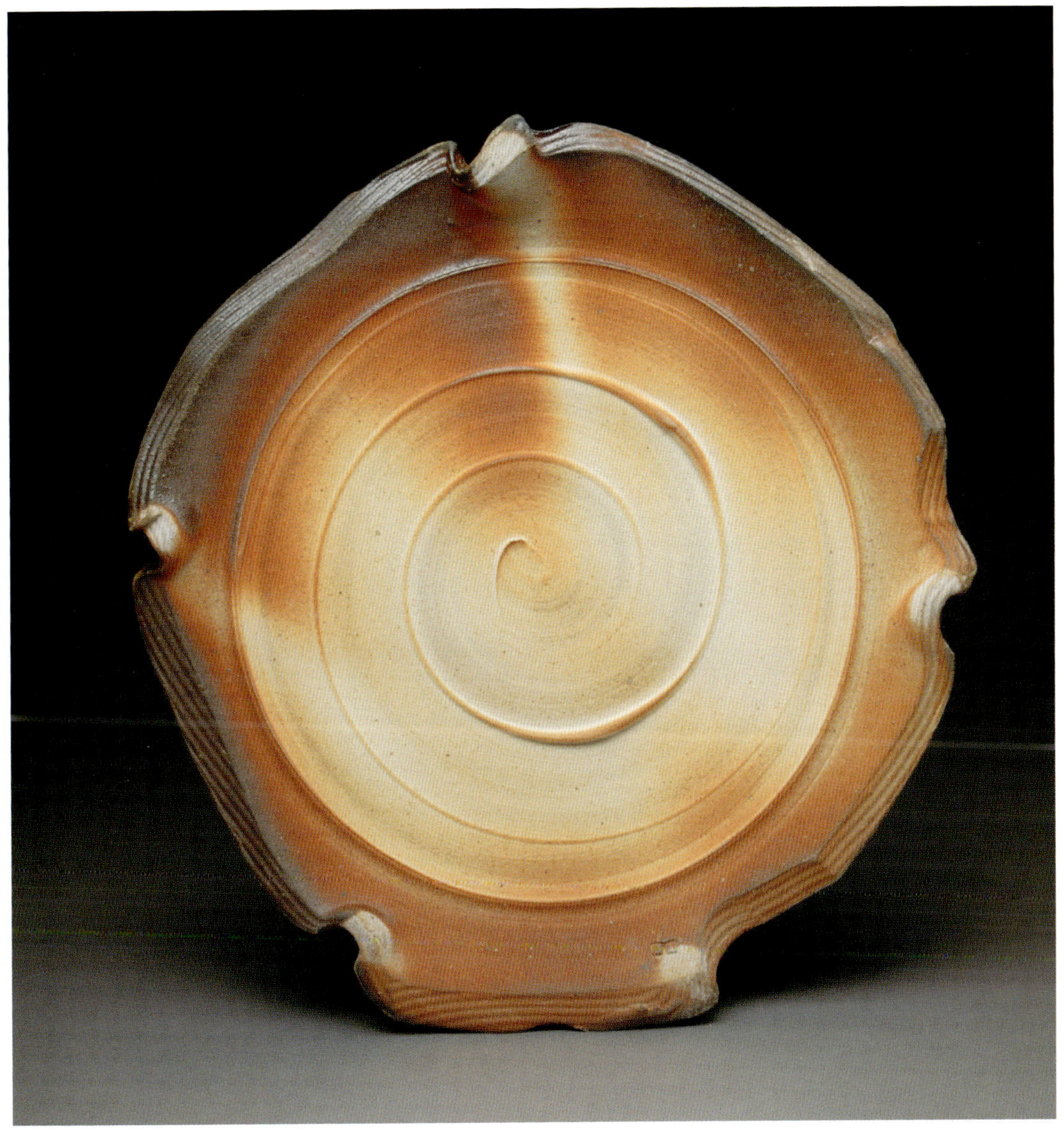

Von Venhuizen
Untitled | 2007
1 X 17 INCHES (2.5 X 43.2 CM)
Wheel-thrown stoneware; porcelain slip; wood fired, cone 11
PHOTO BY ARTIST

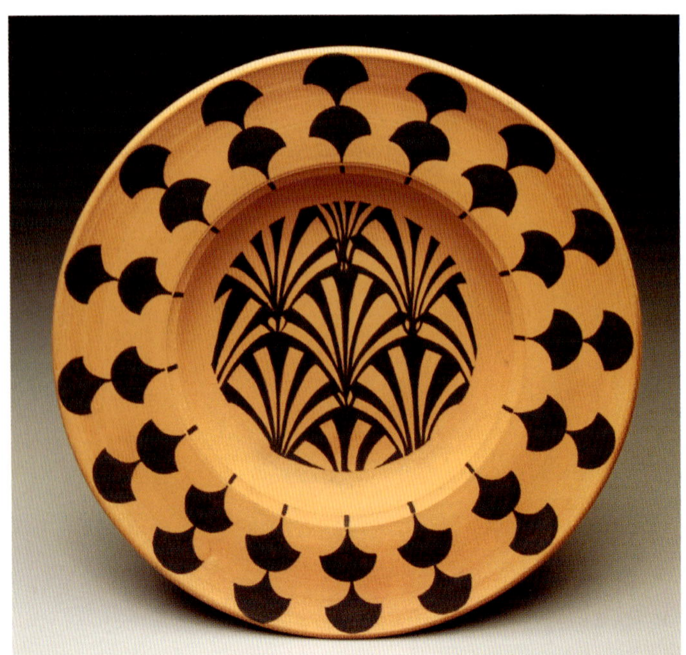

Beverly Fetterman

Scales | 2007

2¾ X 14½ INCHES (7 X 36.8 CM)

Wheel-thrown and hand-painted terra cotta; black underglaze; electric fired, cone 05

PHOTO BY CHRIS GRAY

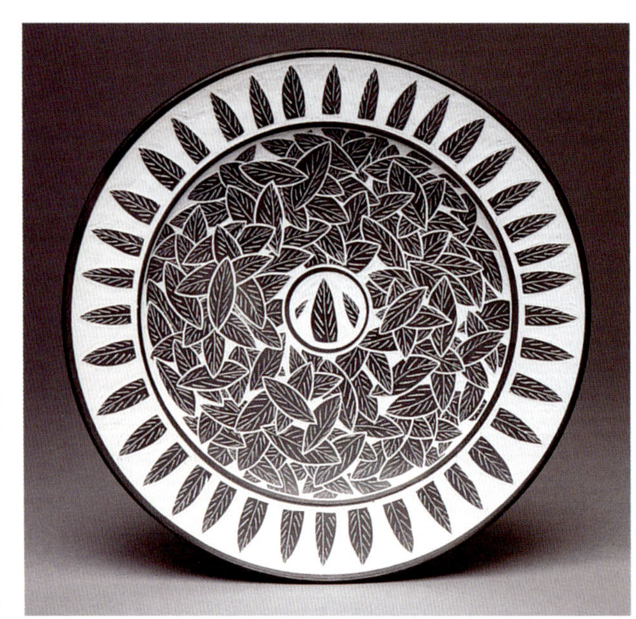

Becky Lloyd
Steve Lloyd

Platter with Leaf Pattern | 2004

3⅛ X 11 13/16 INCHES (8 X 30 CM)

Terra sigillata on English porcelain; sgraffito decoration

PHOTO BY PETER LEE

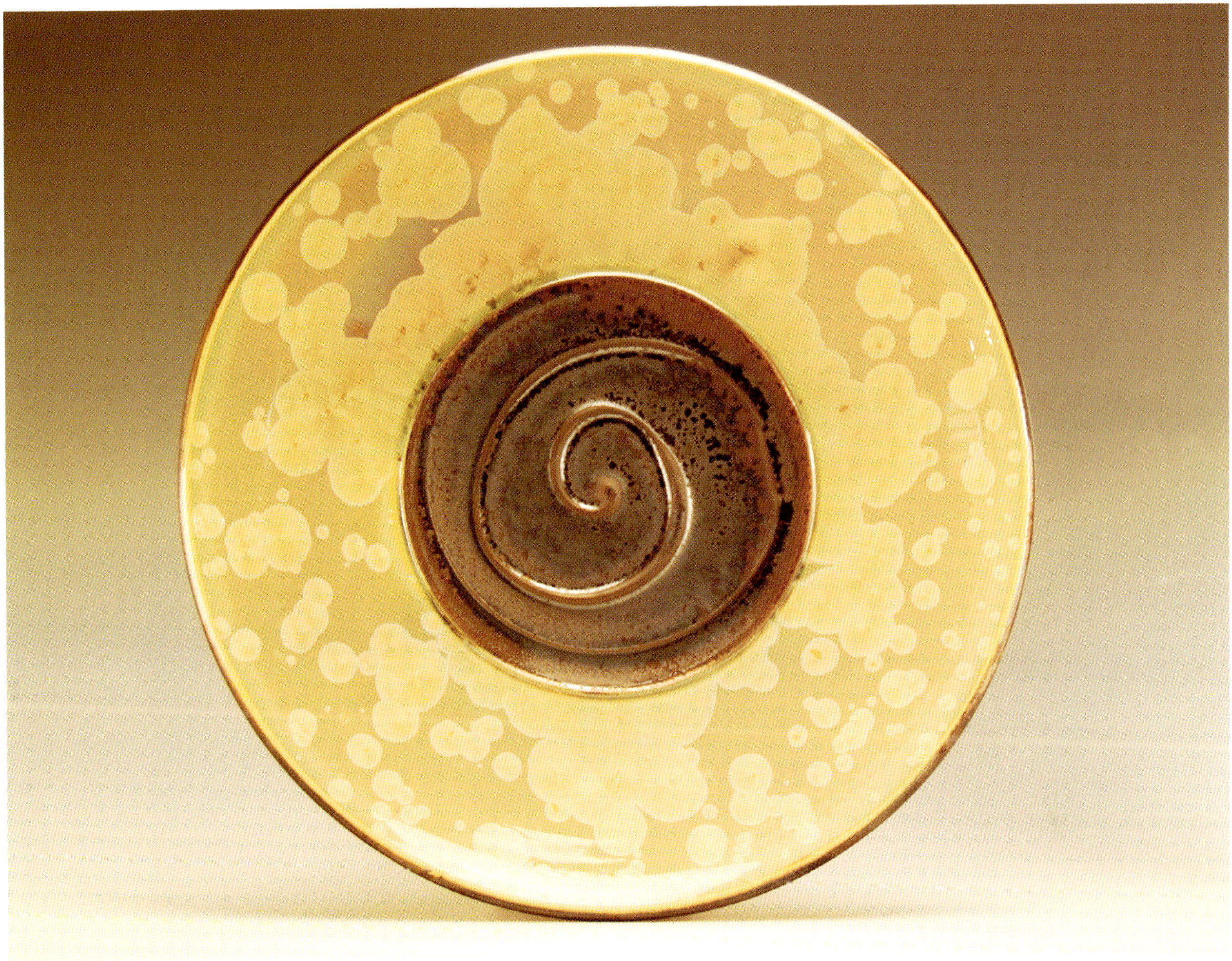

Annette Kirma

Crystalline Platter | 2007

$2\frac{1}{2}$ X 15 INCHES (6.4 X 38.1 CM)

Wheel-thrown porcelain; bronze and crystalline glazes; electric fired, cone 10

PHOTOS BY ARTIST

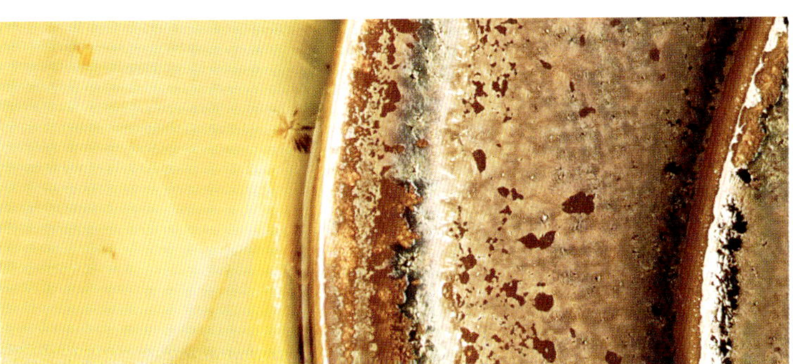

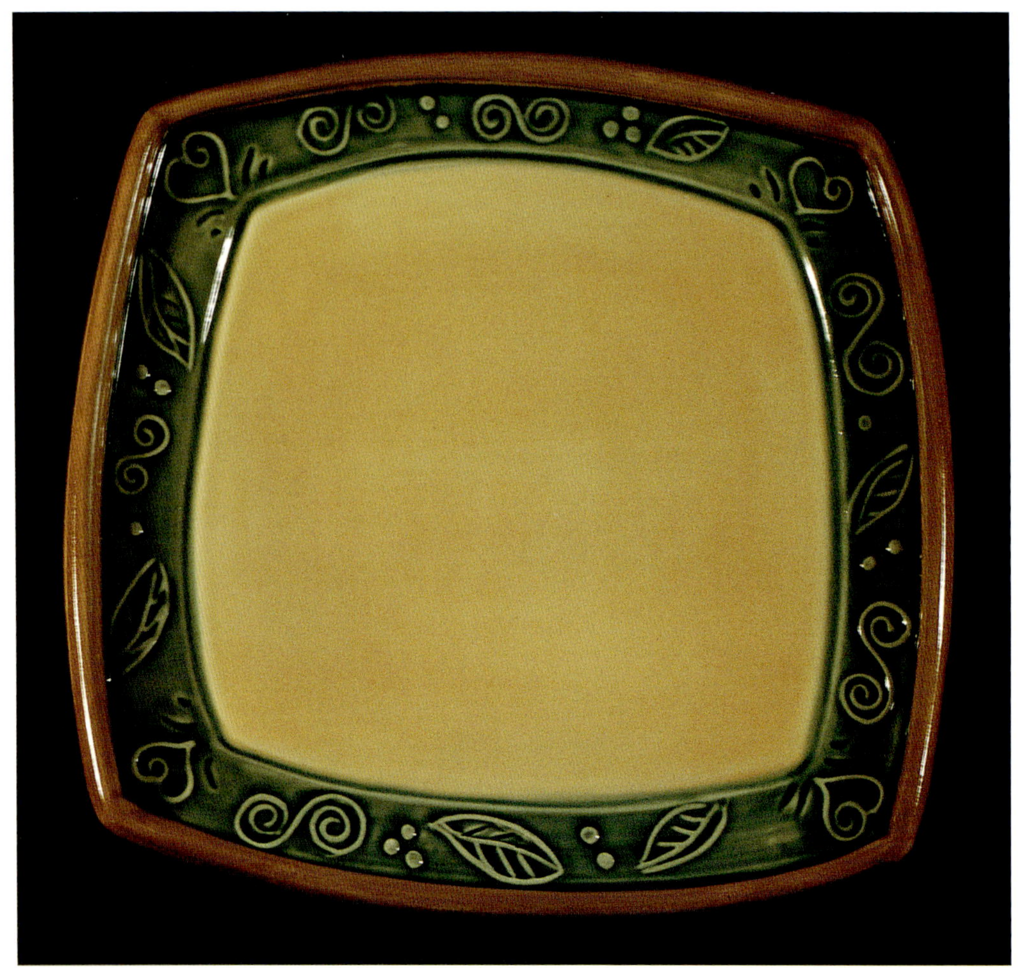

Carol Voyt

Quintessence Series—Dinner Plate, Autumn | 2007

1 1/2 X 11 X 11 INCHES (3.8 X 27.9 X 27.9 CM)

Wheel-thrown and hand-built earthenware; electric fired, cone 03

PHOTO BY ARTIST

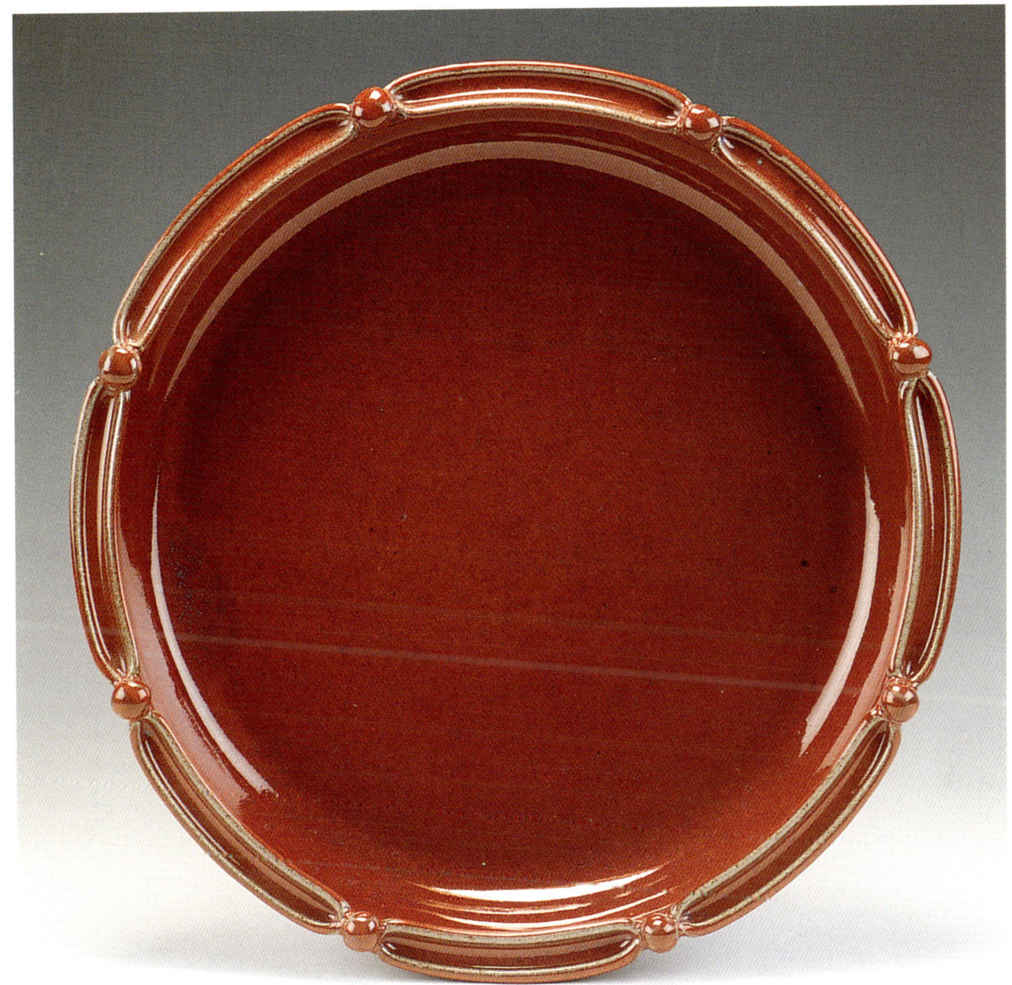

Stephanie Schorr

Copper Red Garland Server | 2006

2 X 20 INCHES (5.1 X 50.8 CM)

Wheel-thrown and altered stoneware; copper red glaze; gas reduction fired, cone 10

PHOTO BY ROB MOORMAN

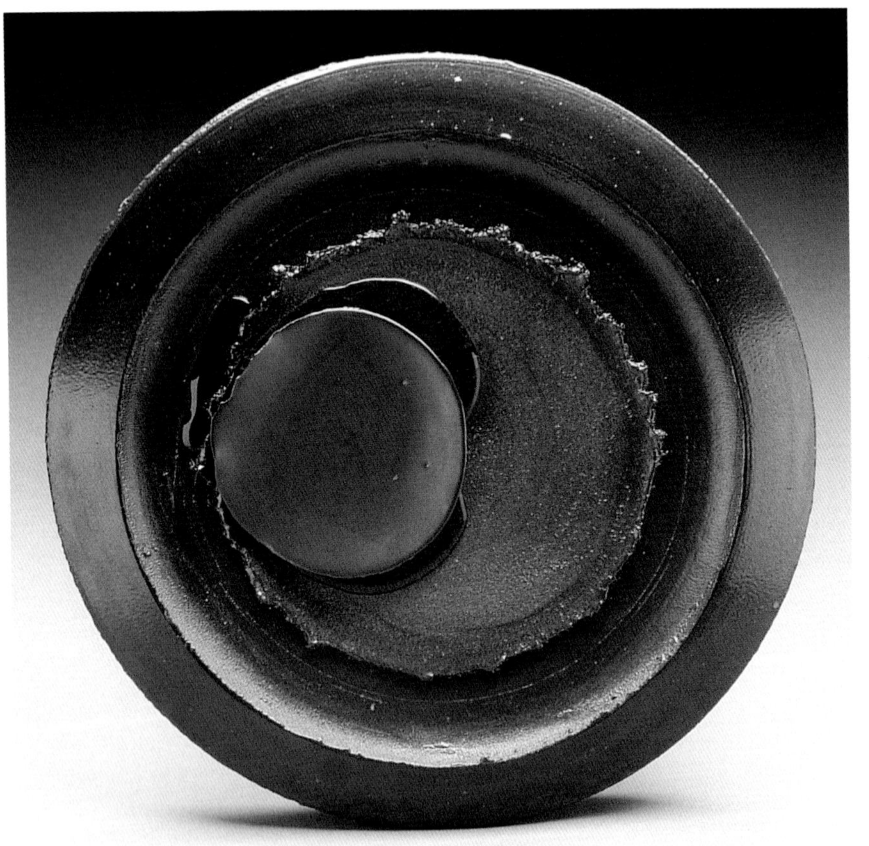

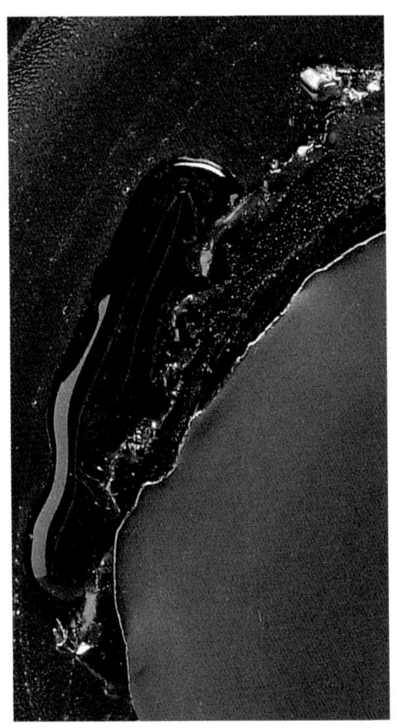

Brad Schwieger
Black Disc | 2005
4 X 26 INCHES (10.2 X 66 CM)
Wheel-thrown stoneware; porcelain disc, fused glass; cone 9; cone 08
PHOTOS BY ARTIST

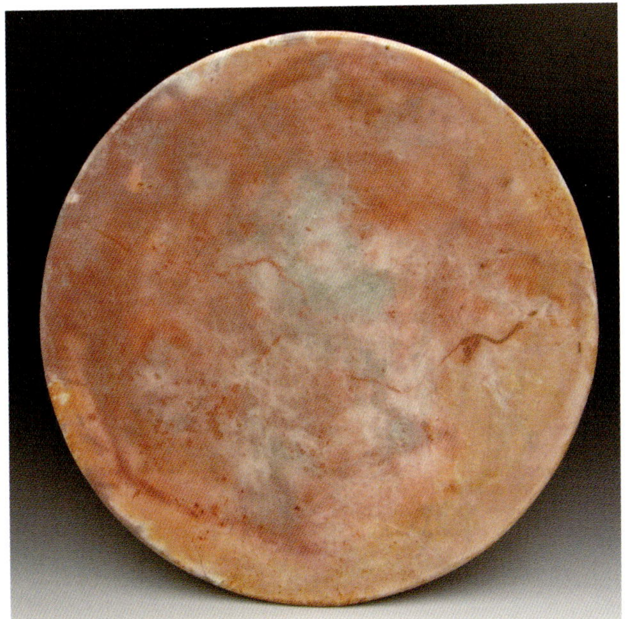

George Tomkins

Yuma Sunset #2 | 2006

3 X 22 INCHES (7.6 X 55.9 CM)

Slab built with thrown foot; bisque fired, cone 04; gas fired in heavy reduction with copper, iron, and salt, cone 010

PHOTO BY ARTIST

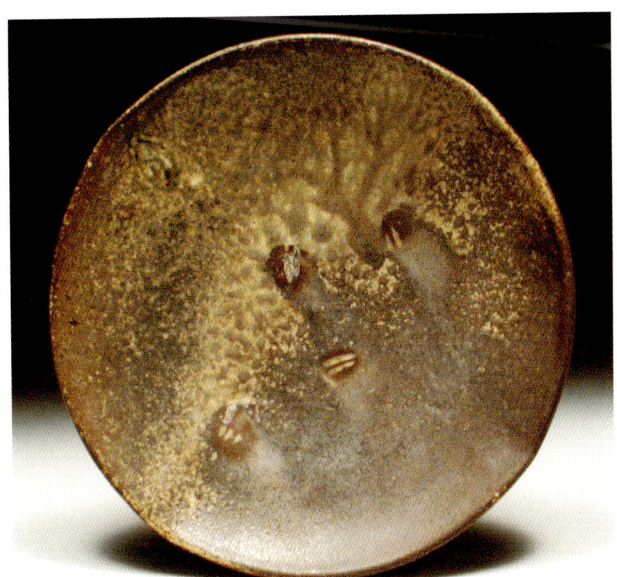

Shawn O'Connor

Untitled | 2007

3 X 17 INCHES (7.6 X 43.2 CM)

Wheel-thrown and altered stoneware; flashing slip; wood fired, cone 11

PHOTO BY ARTIST

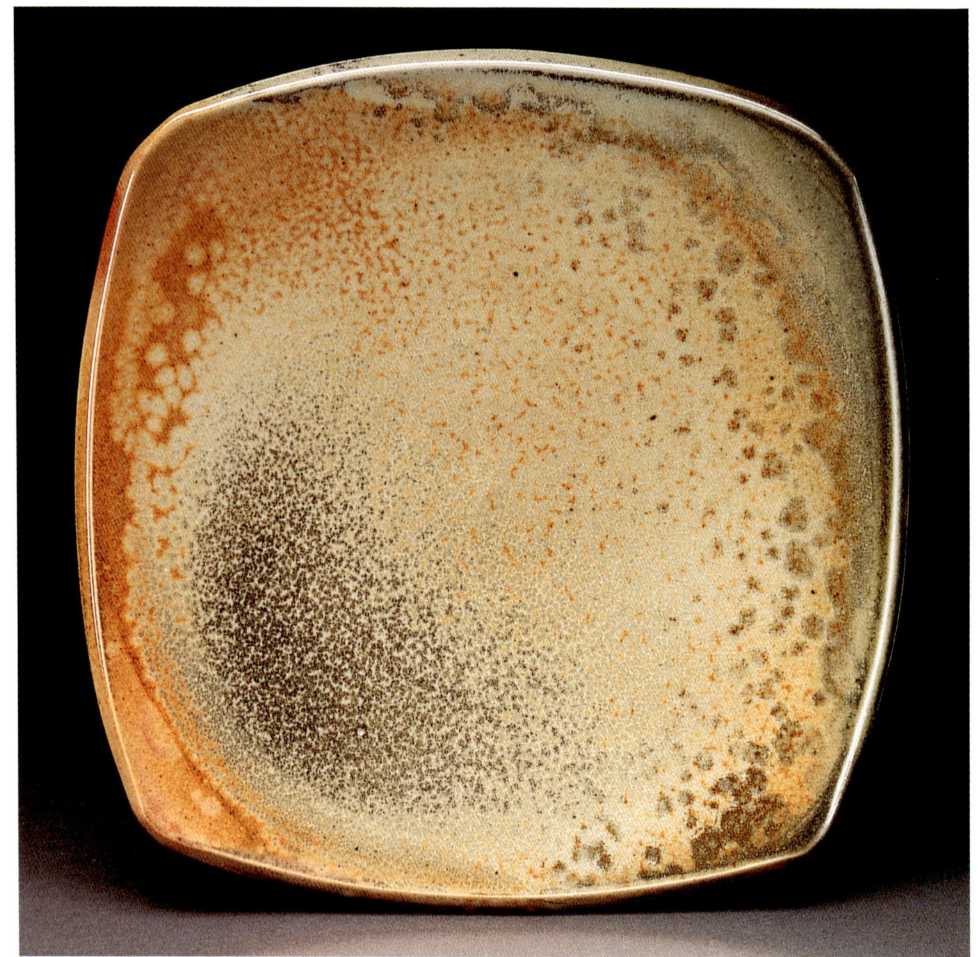

Connie Christensen

Dinner Plate | 2006

1 1/4 X 9 X 9 INCHES (22.9 X 22.9 X 3.2 CM)

Wheel-thrown and altered porcelain; shino glaze; gas fired in reduction, cone 10

PHOTO BY JOHN BONATH

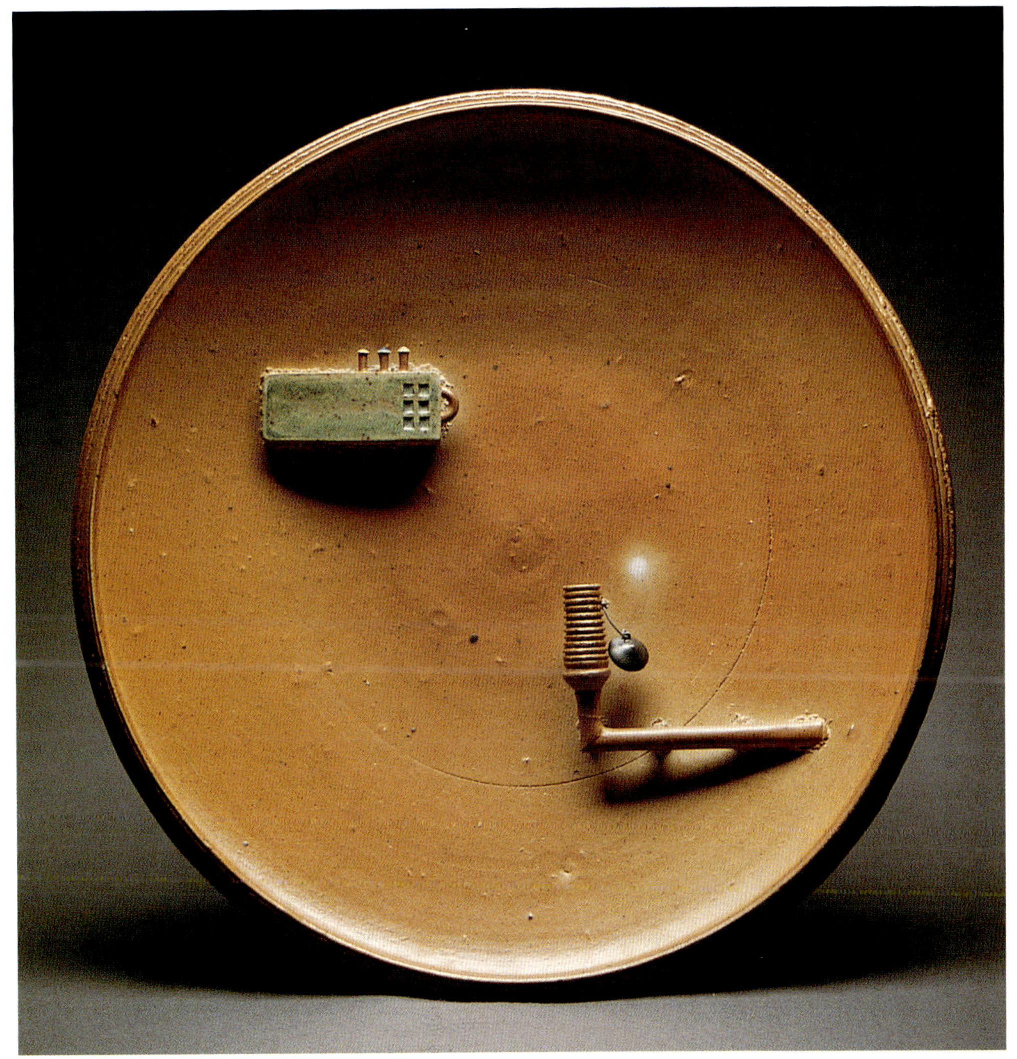

Stephen Heywood

Platter | 2002

3 X 20 INCHES (7.6 X 50.8 CM)

Wheel-thrown stoneware; Baver Orange slip; soda fired, cone 10

PHOTO BY ARTIST

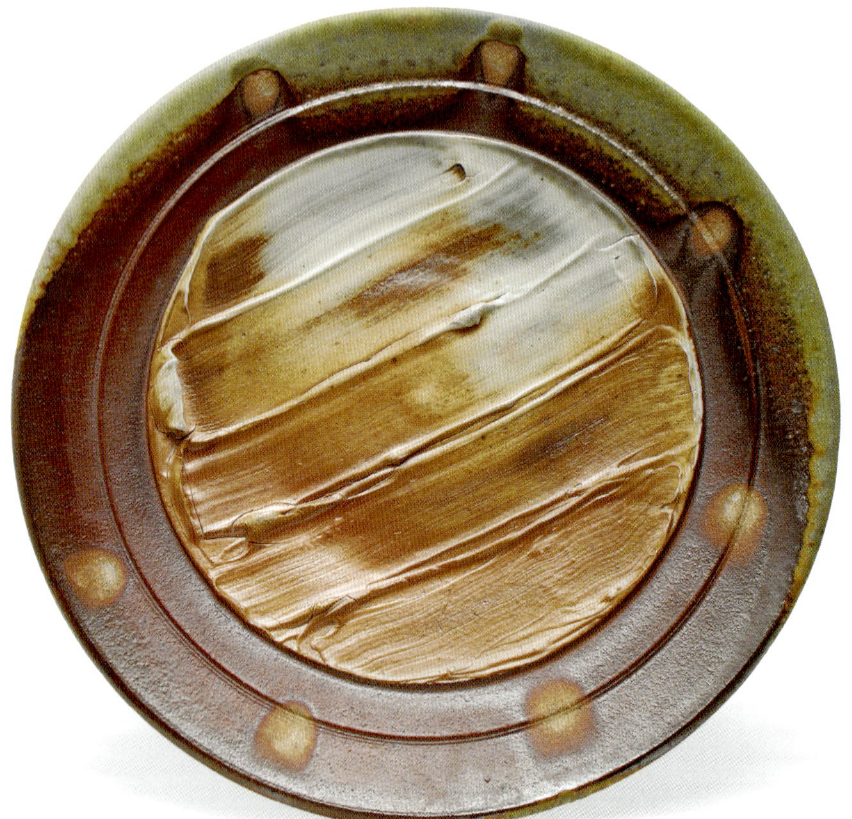

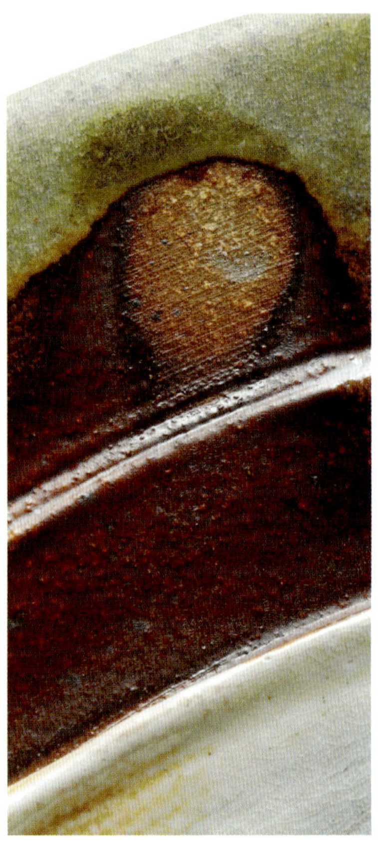

Marion Nehmer

Soda-Fired Platter | 2006

$2\frac{1}{2}$ X $14\frac{1}{2}$ INCHES (6.3 X 37 CM)

Wheel-thrown stoneware; porcelain slip; soda fired, cone 10

PHOTOS BY ADAM ALBRIGHT

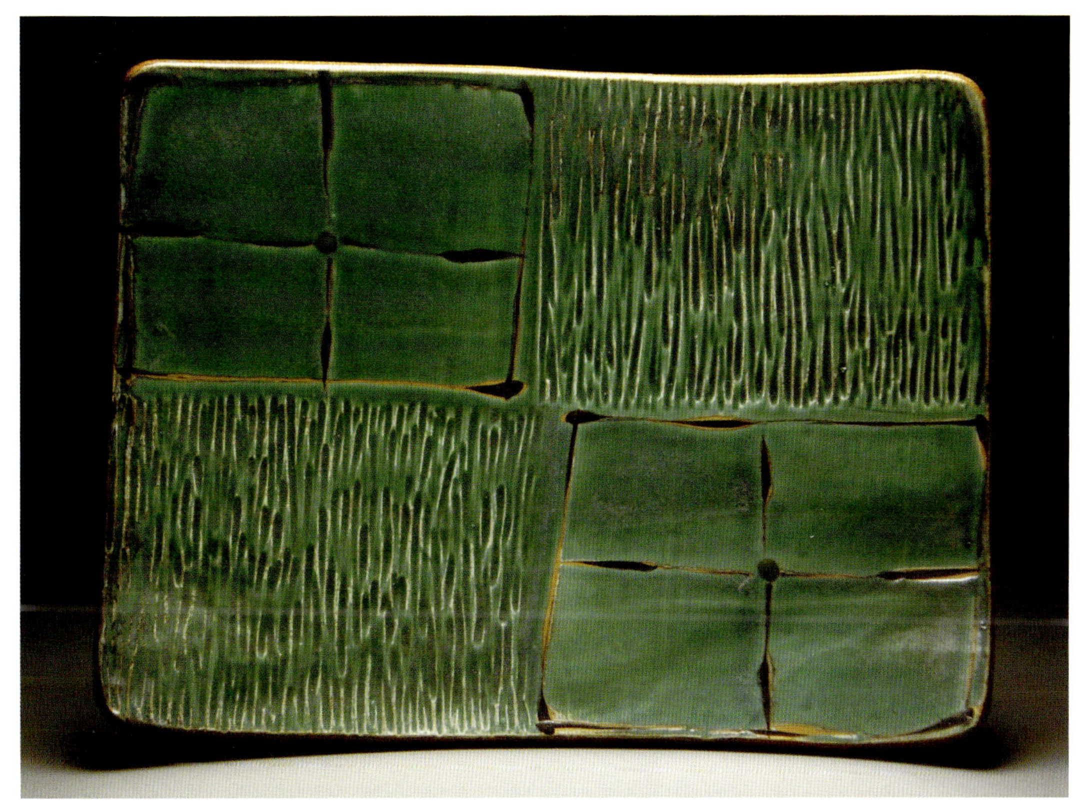

McKenzie Smith
Untitled | 2007
5 X 18 X 14 INCHES (12.7 X 45.7 X 35.6 CM)
Wheel-thrown stoneware;
soda/salt fired, cone 10
PHOTO BY ARTIST

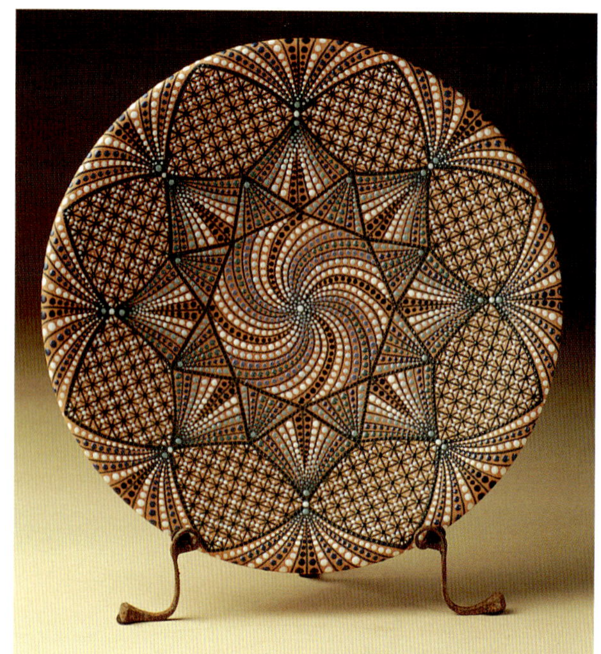

Ricky Maldonado

Kaleidoscope Series #201 | 2005

15 INCHES (38.1 CM) IN DIAMETER

Slab-built earthenware; terra sigillata, slip design; glaze dots, cone 04; electric fired, cone 06

PHOTO BY IMAGINATION

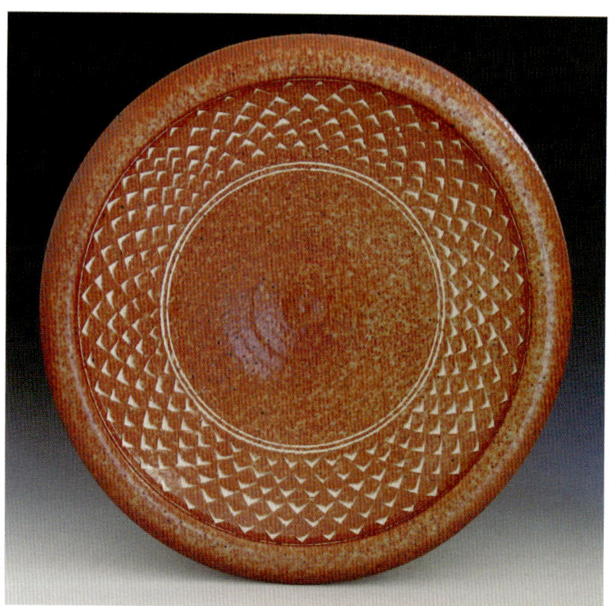

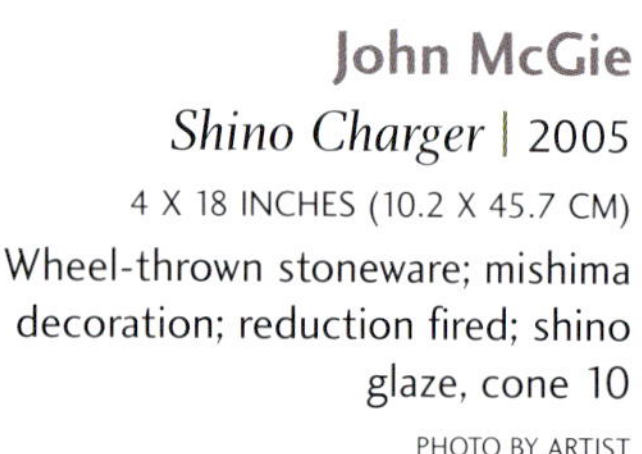

John McGie

Shino Charger | 2005

4 X 18 INCHES (10.2 X 45.7 CM)

Wheel-thrown stoneware; mishima decoration; reduction fired; shino glaze, cone 10

PHOTO BY ARTIST

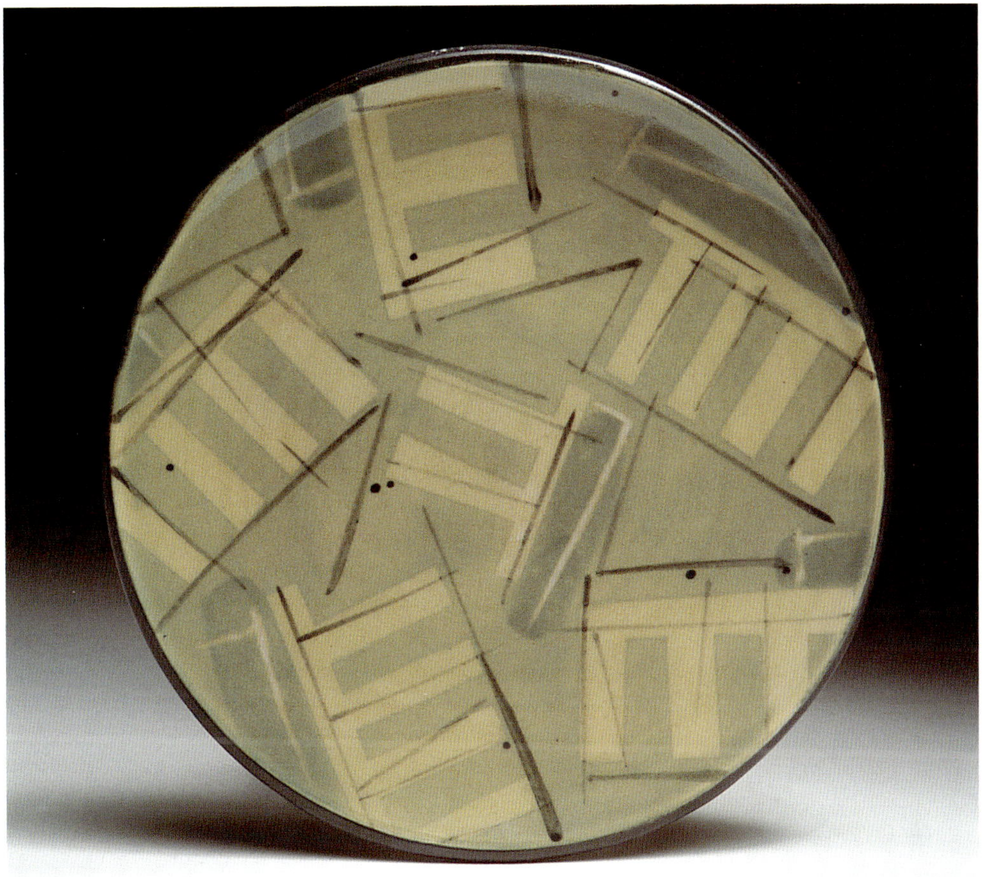

Joan Ulrich

Pi Plate | 2004

3/4 X 6 INCHES (1.9 X 15.2 CM)

Wheel-thrown porcelain; slip decoration and paper resist; electric fired, cone 6

PHOTOS BY D. JAMES DEE

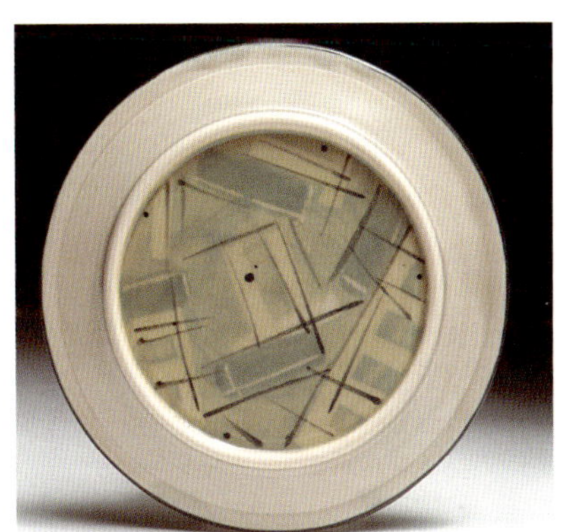

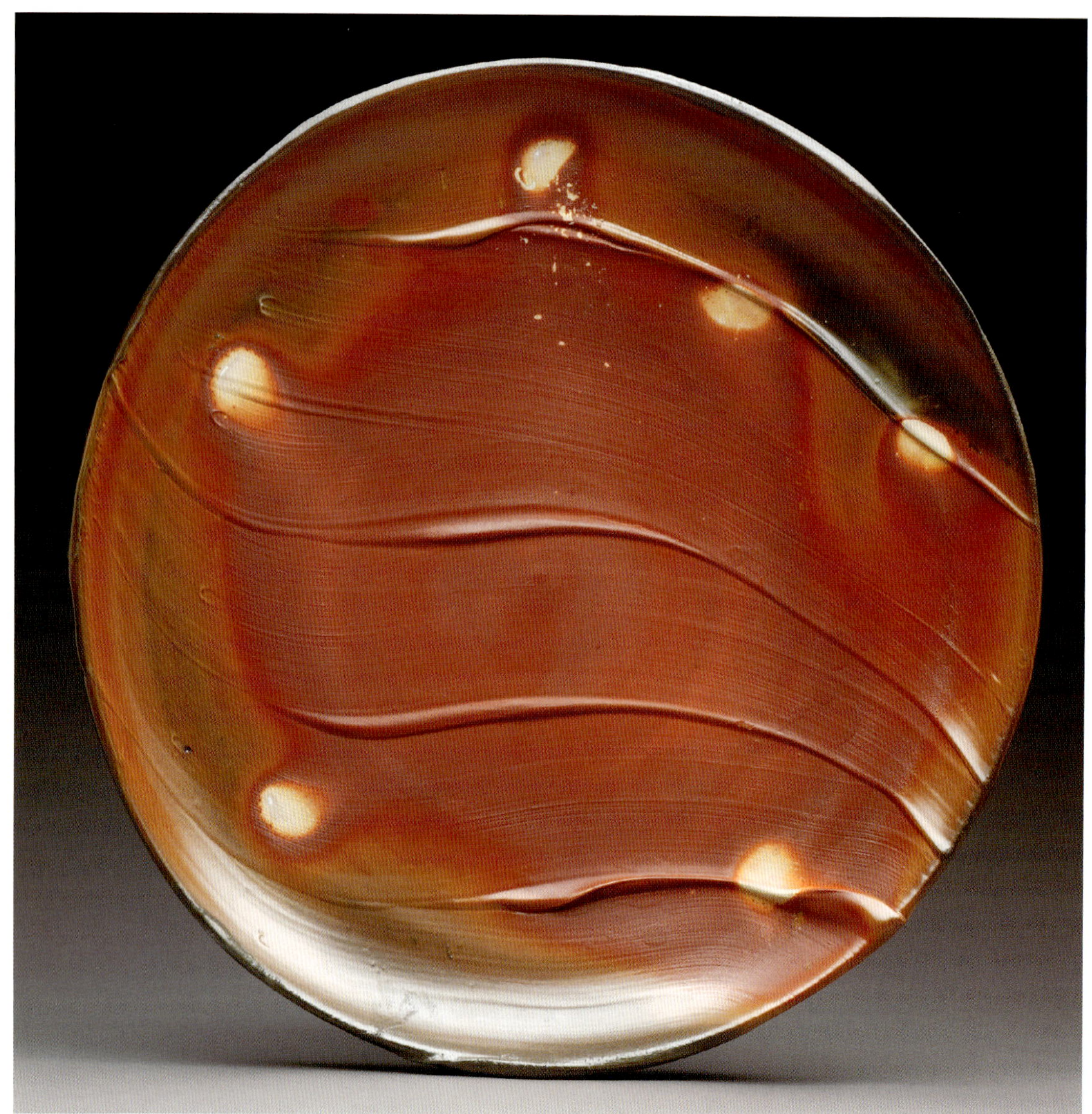

Matt Long
Platter | 2006
3 X 19 INCHES (7.6 X 48.3 CM)
Wheel-thrown porcelain;
slip; soda fired, cone 11
PHOTO BY STEVE PASZT

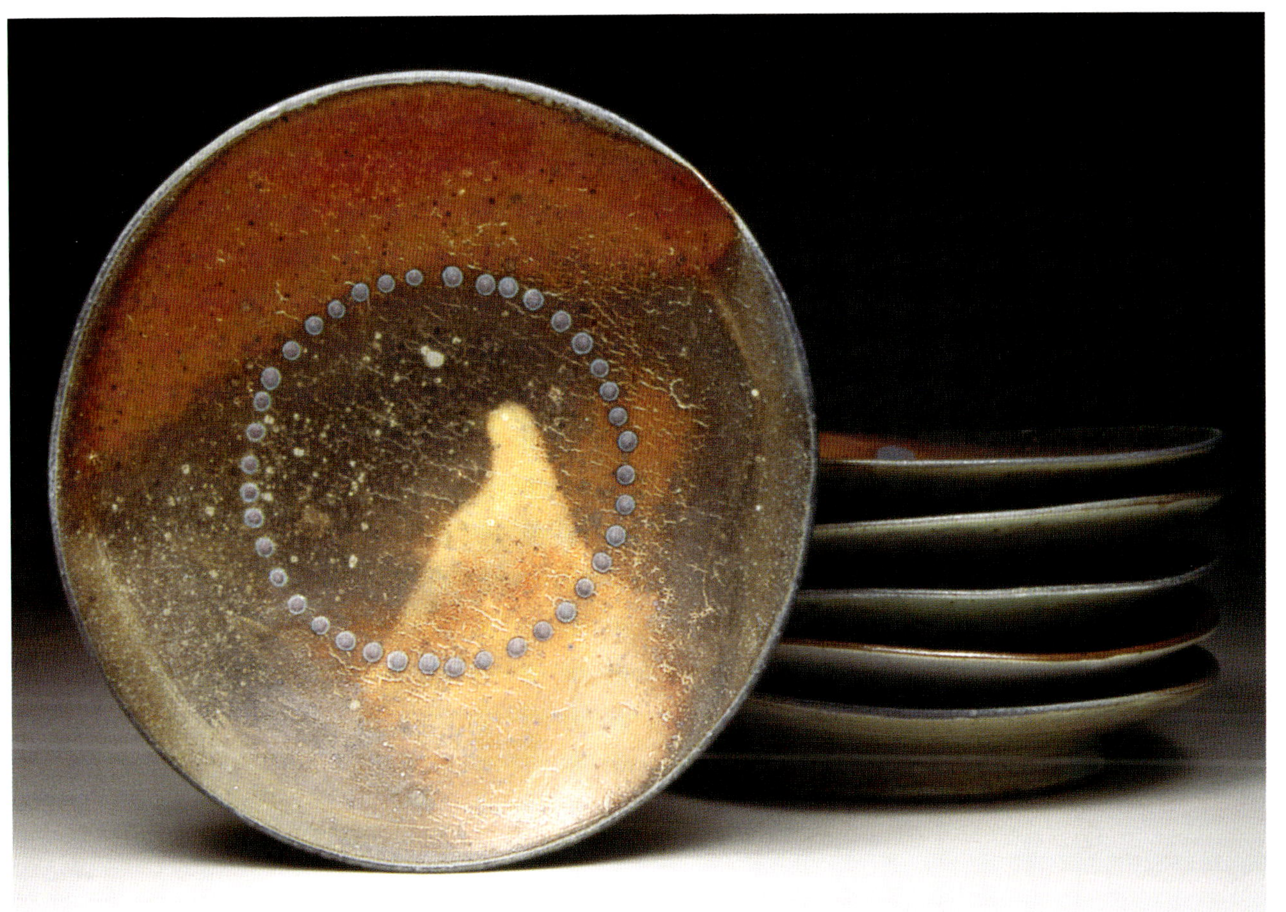

Matt Kelleher

Yellow Mountain—Set of Dinner Plates | 2001

EACH: 1 1/2 X 10 1/2 INCHES (3.8 X 26.7 CM)

Slab-built stoneware over bisque mold; flashing slip; soda fired, cone 10

PHOTO BY ARTIST

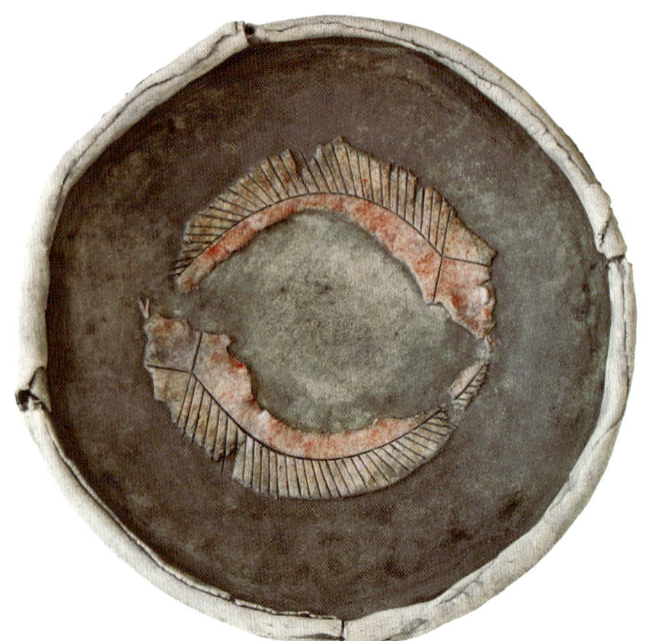

Alice Shepherd

Snake Plate | 2006

9 INCHES (22.9 CM) IN DIAMETER

Press-molded and hand-built stoneware; oxides and slips; electric fired, cone 6; onglaze, cone 017

PHOTO BY KATE BARRY

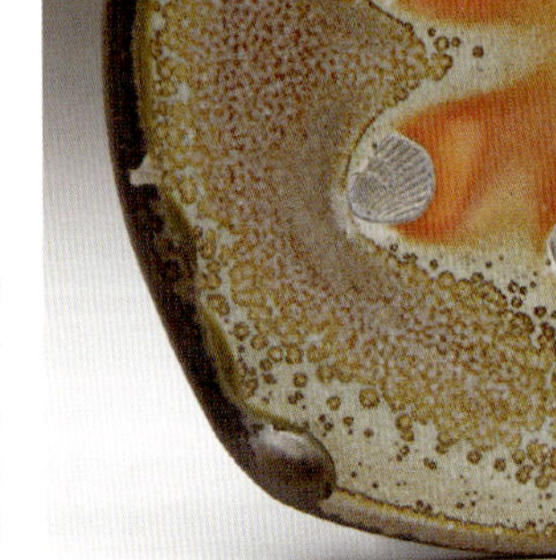

Tara Wilson

Small Plate | 2007

1 X 8 X 8 INCHES (2.5 X 20.3 X 20.3 CM)

Wheel-thrown and altered porcelain; wood fired

PHOTO BY ARTIST

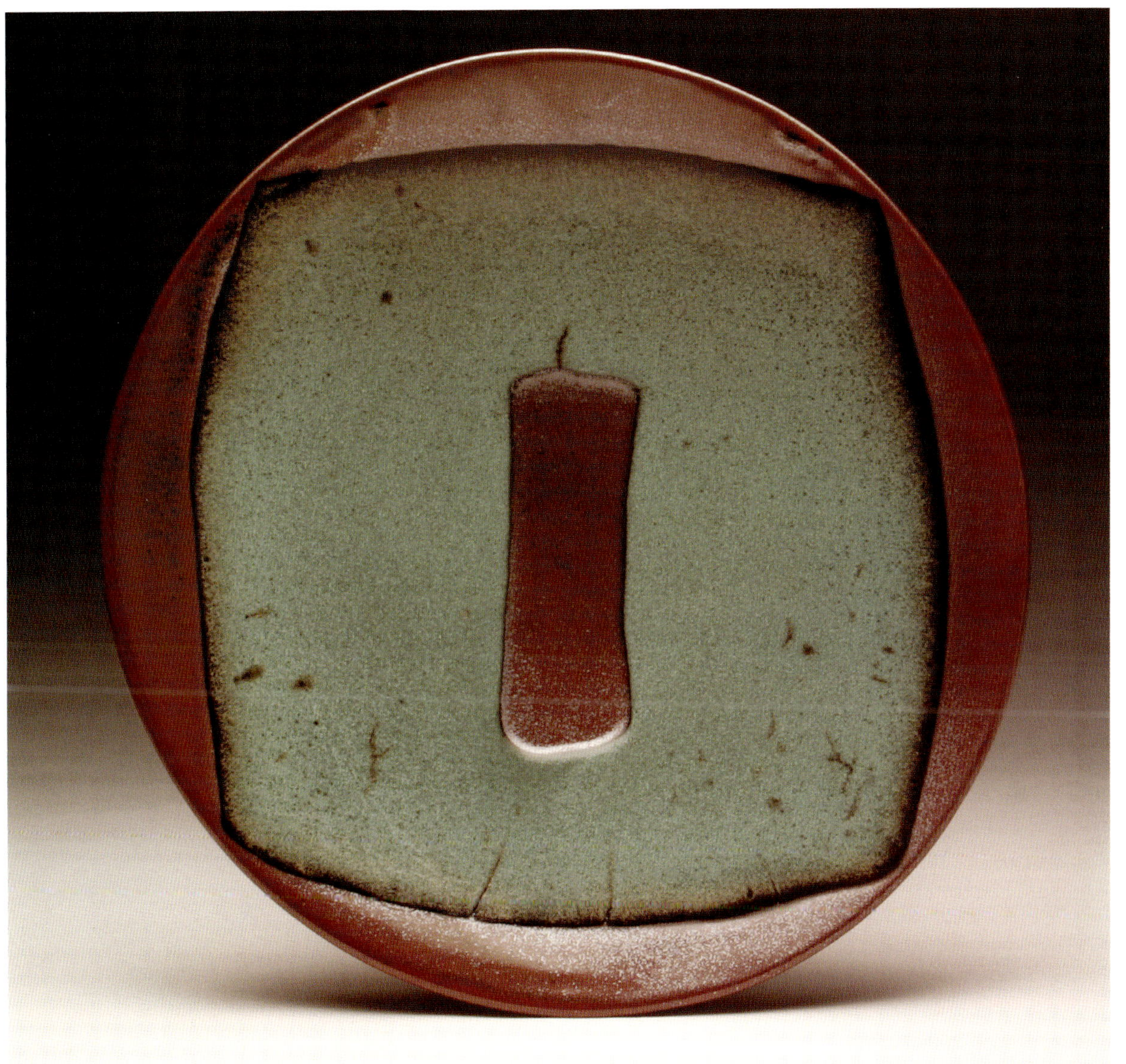

Daphne Roehr Hatcher

Teal Slot | 2007

2 X 11 INCHES (5.1 X 27.9 CM)

Slab-built stoneware with thrown foot; gas fired, cone 12

PHOTO BY GARY C. HATCHER

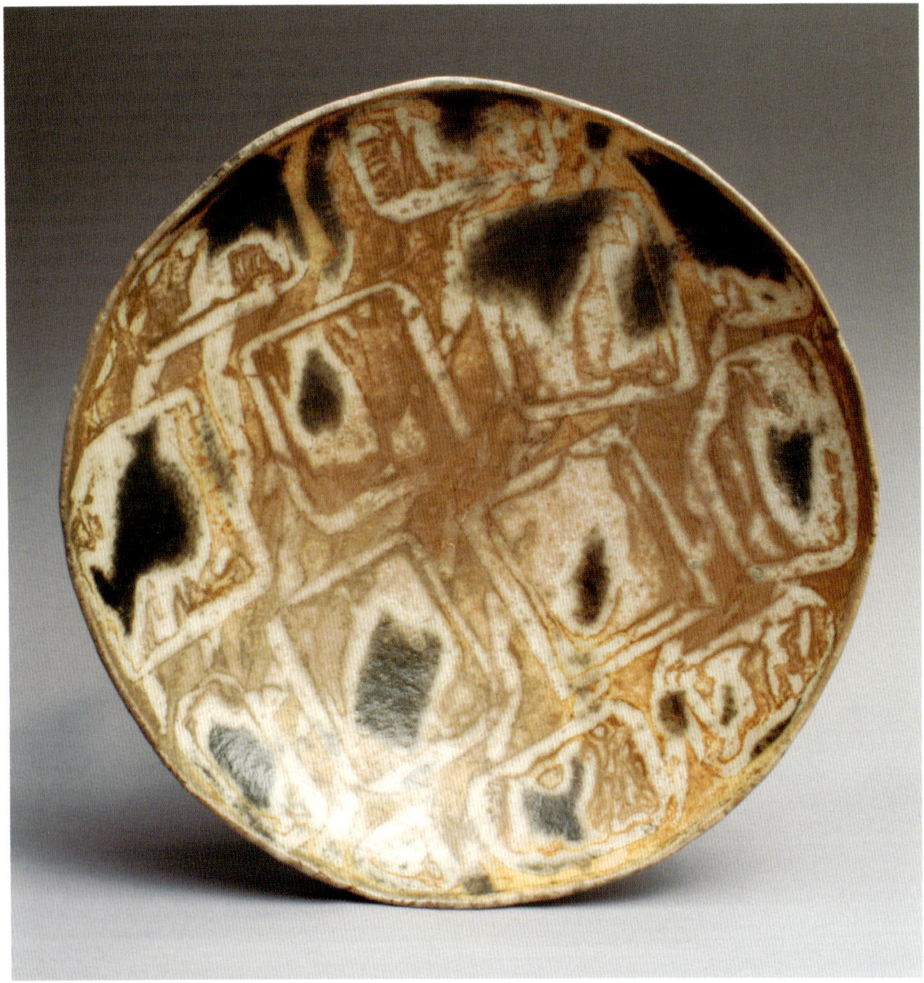

Russel Fouts

There It Begins | 2005

12 INCHES (30.5 CM) IN DIAMETER

Hand-built terra cotta; terra sigillata, paper and soda resist; smoke fired, electric kiln, aluminum foil saggar

PHOTOS BY ARTIST

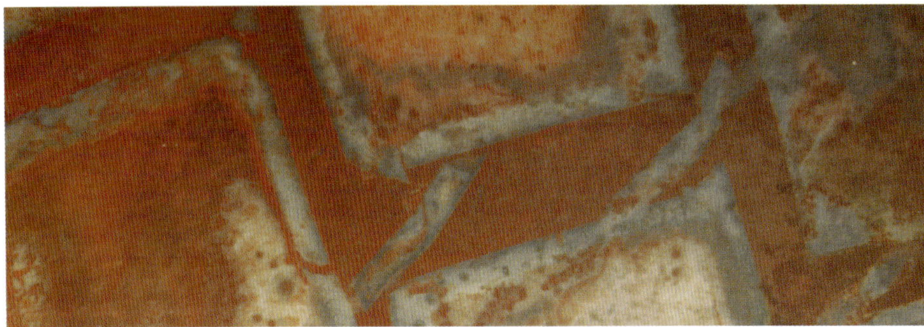

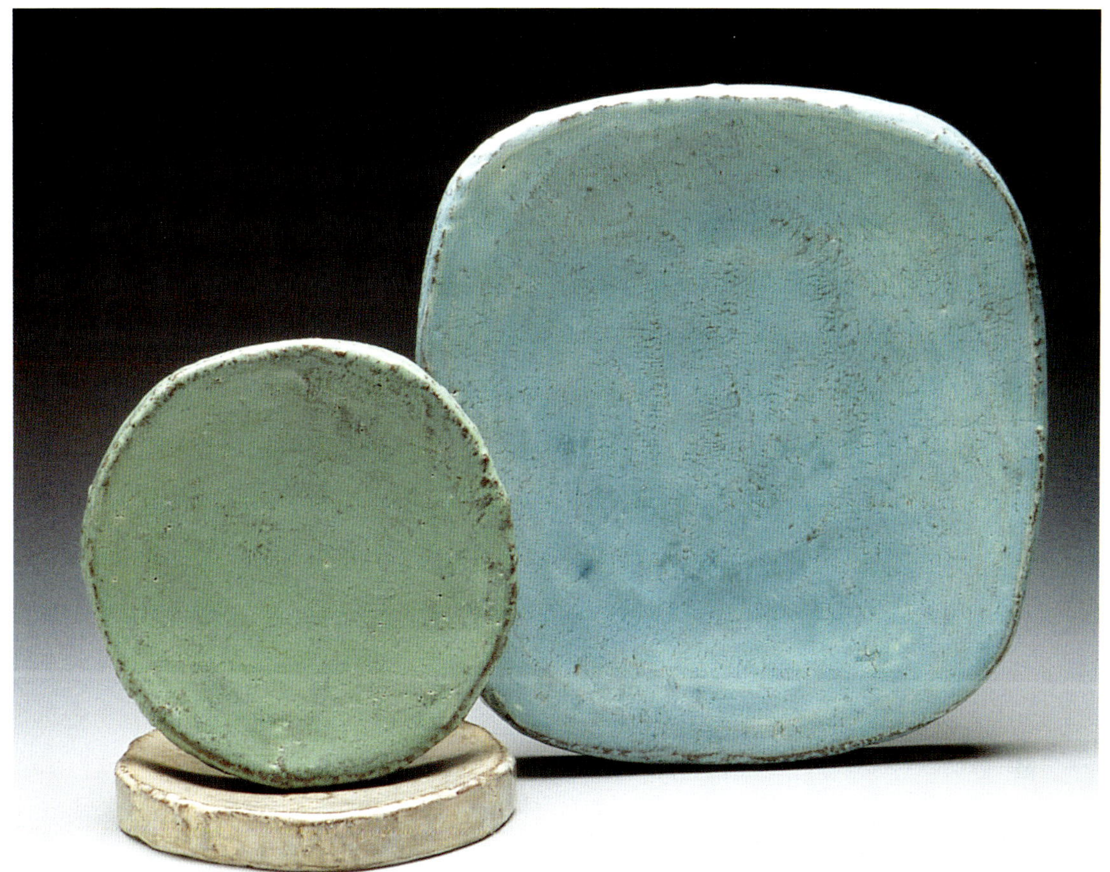

Joseph Pintz

Set of Plates | 2004

LARGEST: 2 X 10 X 10 INCHES (5.1 X 25.4 X 25.4 CM)

Hand-built earthenware;
electric fired, cone 02

PHOTO BY ARTIST

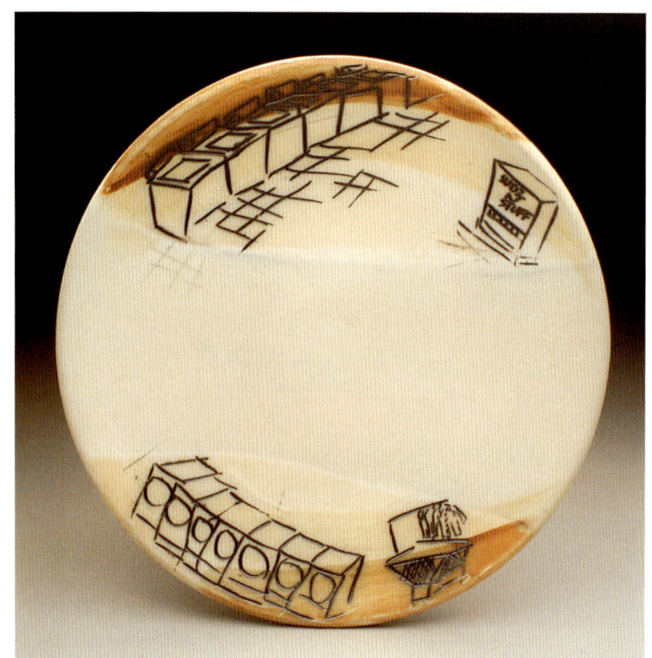

Kowkie Durst

Plate | 2005

1 X 10 INCHES (2.5 X 25.4 CM)

Wheel-thrown porcelain; salt fired, cone 6; sgraffito with terra sigillata and glaze

PHOTO BY ARTIST

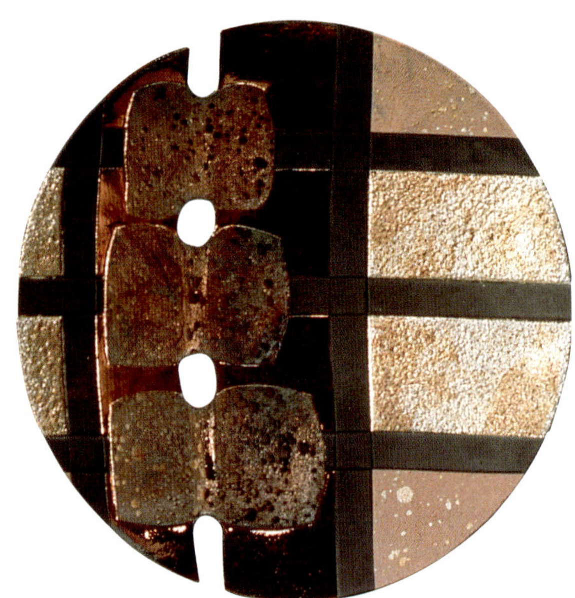

Skip Esquierdo

Untitled | 2006

4 X 24 INCHES (10.2 X 61 CM)

Wheel-thrown and hand-constructed stoneware; bisque fired, cone 06; glazes, raku fired, reduced in combustibles

PHOTO BY LEE FATHEREE

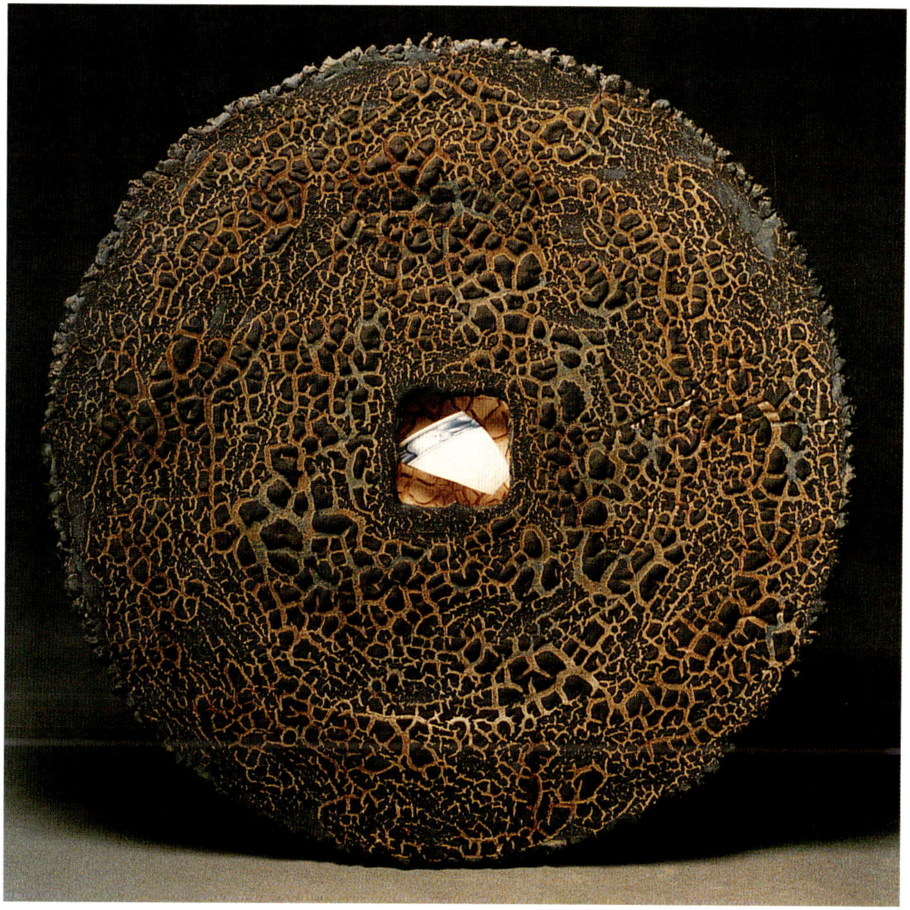

Patrick S. Crabb

Fetish Plate Series | 2004

5 X 28 INCHES (12.7 X 71.1 CM)

Drape-molded stoneware; electric fired, cone 02; glazes, cone 06–04

PHOTOS BY ARTIST

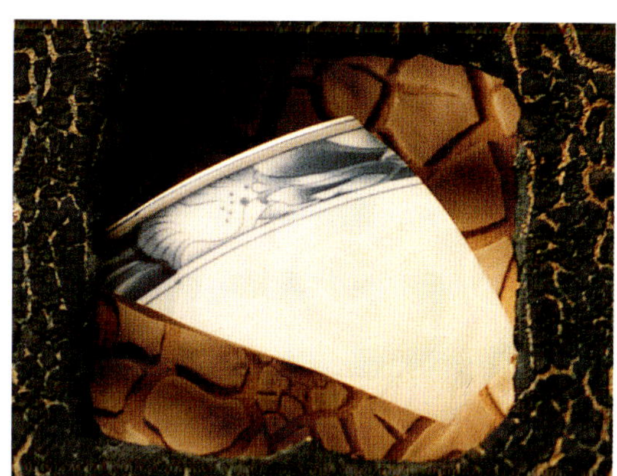

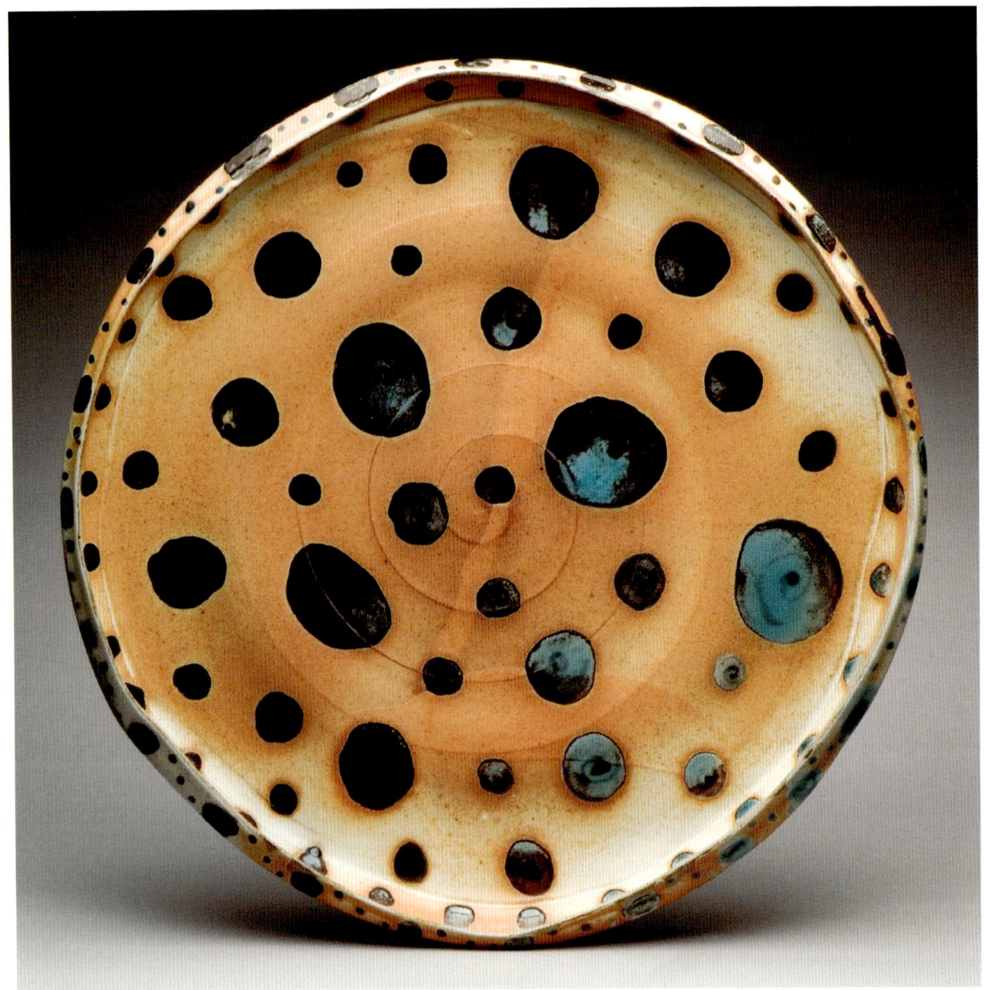

Mark Knott

Untitled | 2006

3 X 26 INCHES (7.6 X 66 CM)

Wheel-thrown stoneware;
soda fired, cone 6

PHOTO BY WALKER MONTGOMERY

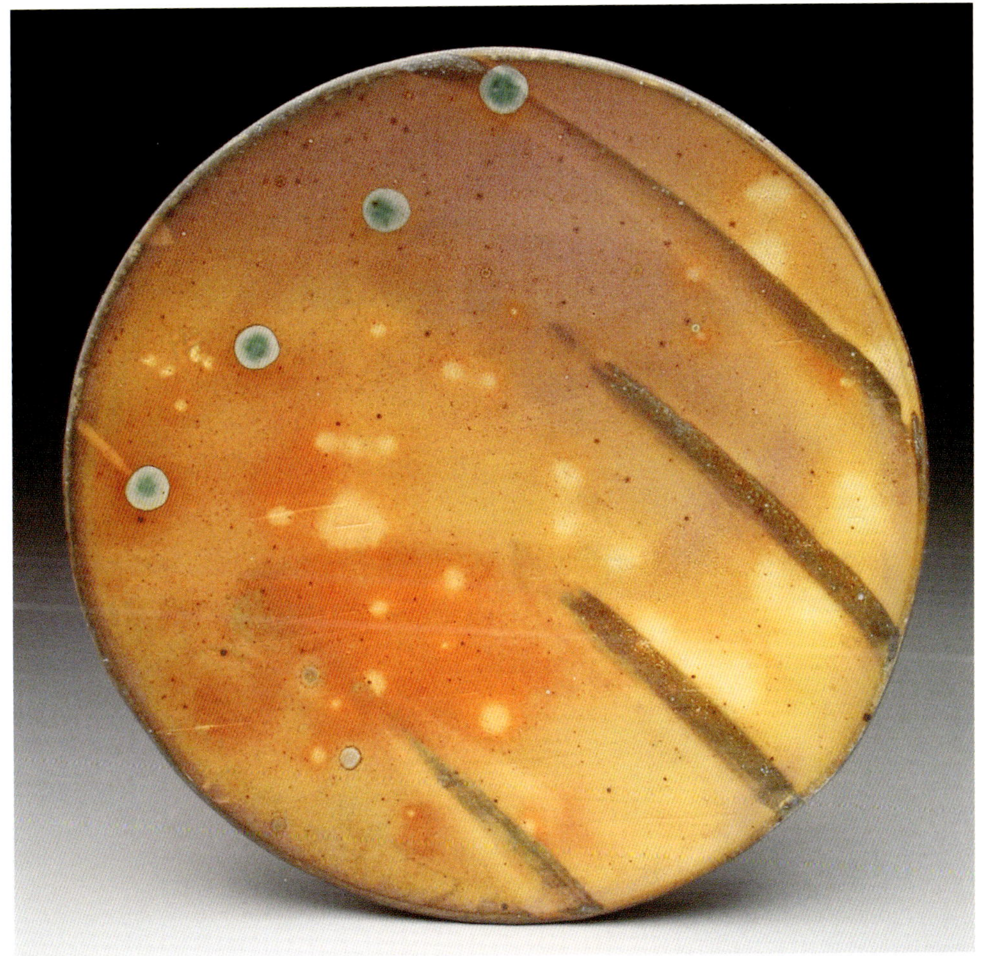

Matt Kelleher

Wall Plate | 2006

1 1/2 X 10 1/2 INCHES (3.8 X 26.7 CM)

Slab-built stoneware over bisque mold; flashing slip; soda fired, cone 10

PHOTO BY ARTIST

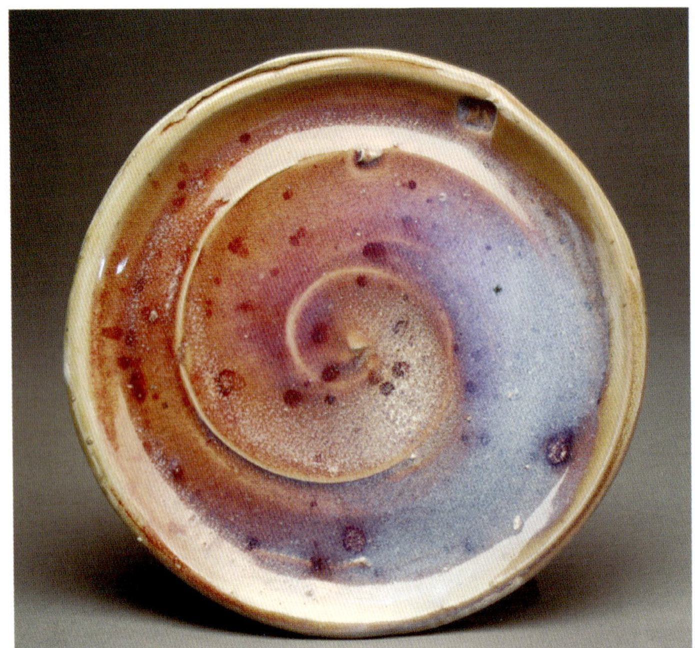

Meredith "Mud" Bailey

Untitled | 2006

3/4 X 7 INCHES (1.9 X 17.8 CM)

Wheel-thrown stoneware; salt fired, cone 10

PHOTO BY ARTIST

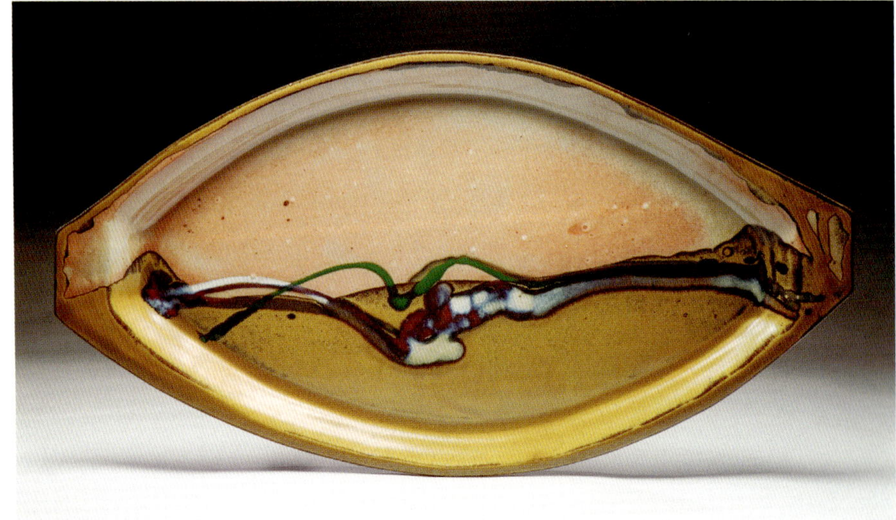

Macy Dorf

Fish Tray | 2007

1 X 23 X 12 INCHES (2.5 X 58.4 X 30.5 CM)

Hand-built stoneware; cone 10

PHOTO BY CHARLIE ROY

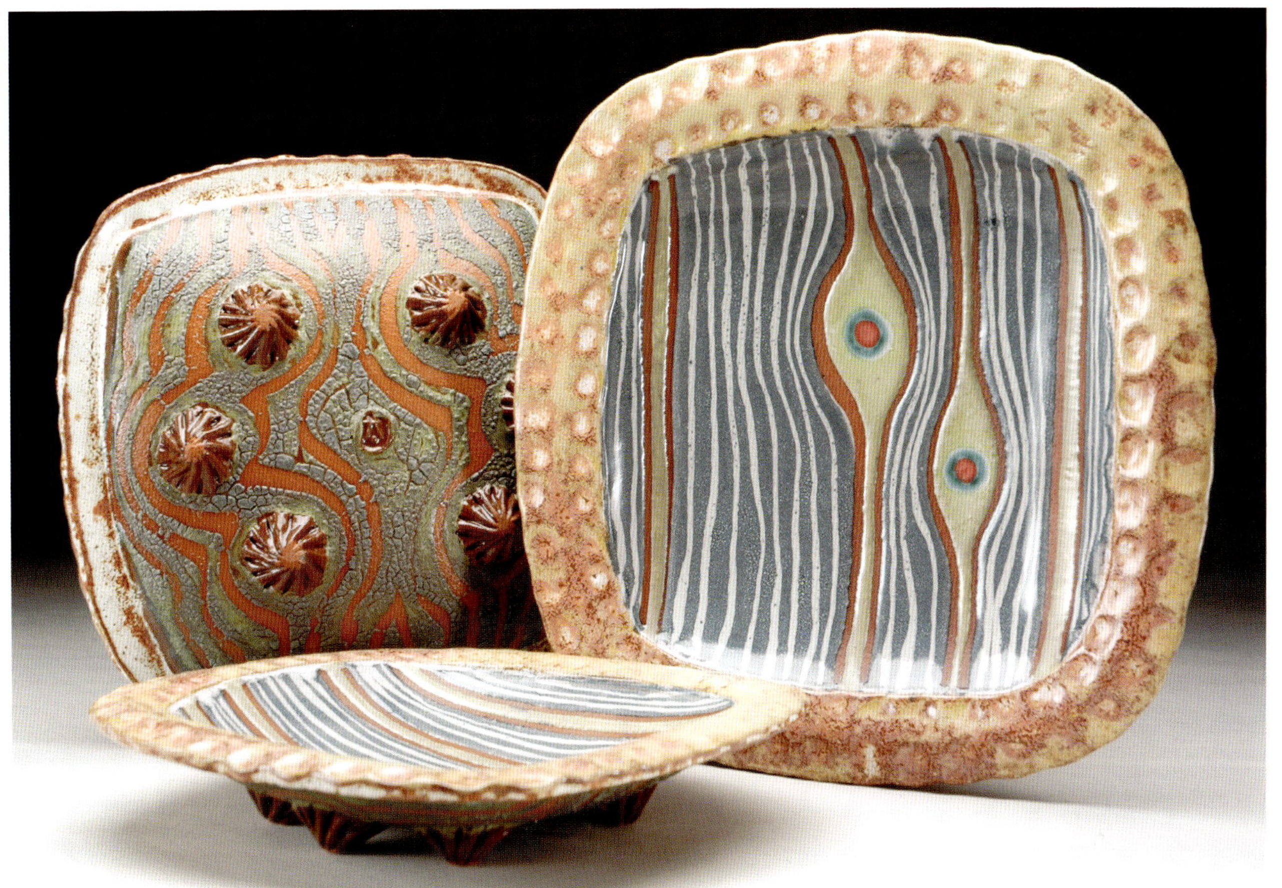

Ronan Kyle Peterson

Square Plates (Gall Decoration) | 2006

LEFT: 2 X 9 X 9 INCHES (5.1 X 22.9 X 22.9 CM); CENTER: 2 X 7 X 7 INCHES (5.1 X 17.8 X 17.8 CM); RIGHT: 2 X 10 X 10 INCHES (5.1 X 25.4 X 25.4 CM)

Hand-built and press-molded earthenware; terra sigallata; electric fired, cone 04; glaze, cone 3; wax resist, glazed, and stained

PHOTO BY NIEL HORA

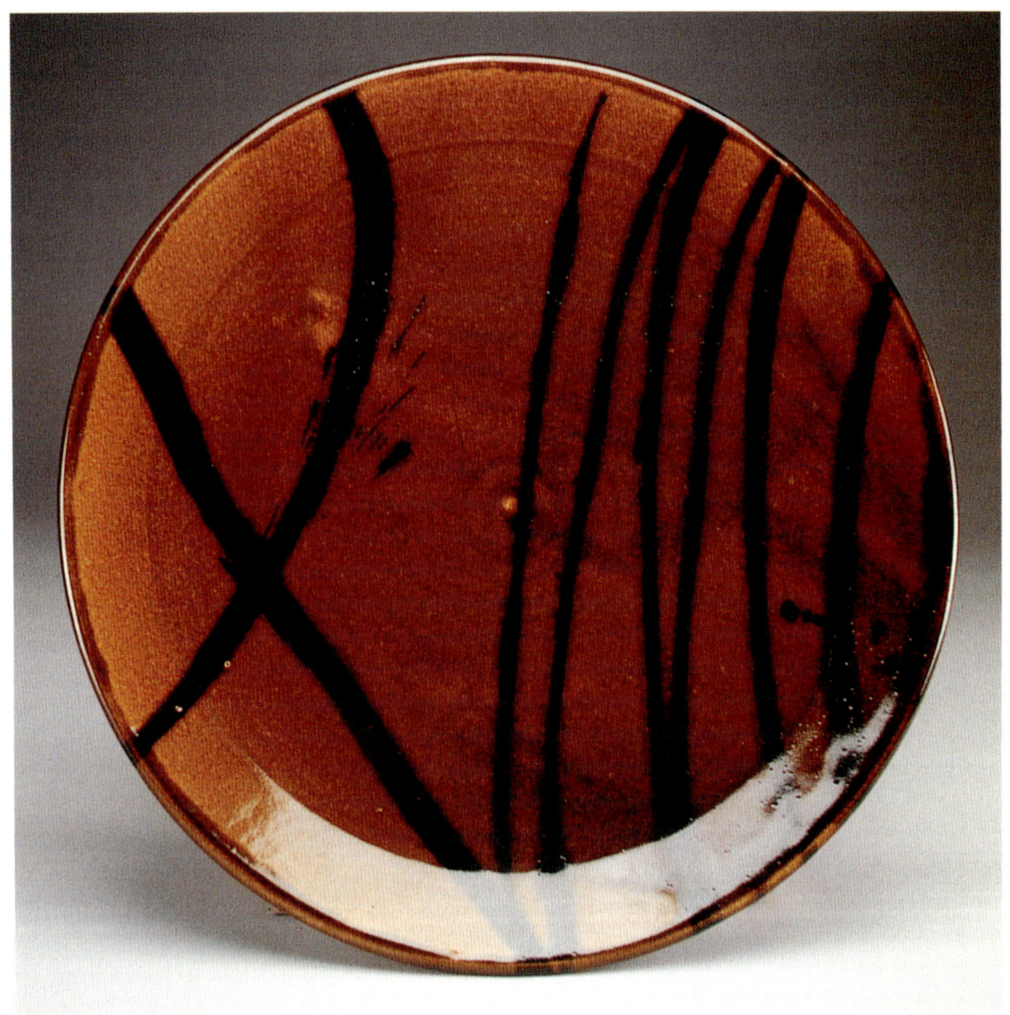

Matthew Whisler

Tiger's Eye | 2006

1 X 13 INCHES (2.5 X 33 CM)

Wheel-thrown stoneware;
electric fired, cone 6

PHOTO BY BRIAN GIALLORETO

Shari Druckman

Celestial Swirl | 2007

½ X 11 INCHES (1.3 X 27.9 CM)

Hand-built stoneware; electric fired, cone 5

PHOTO BY RICHARD NICOL

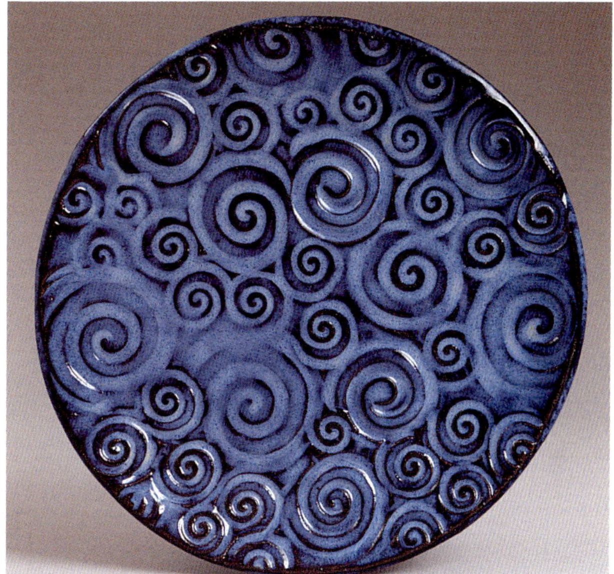

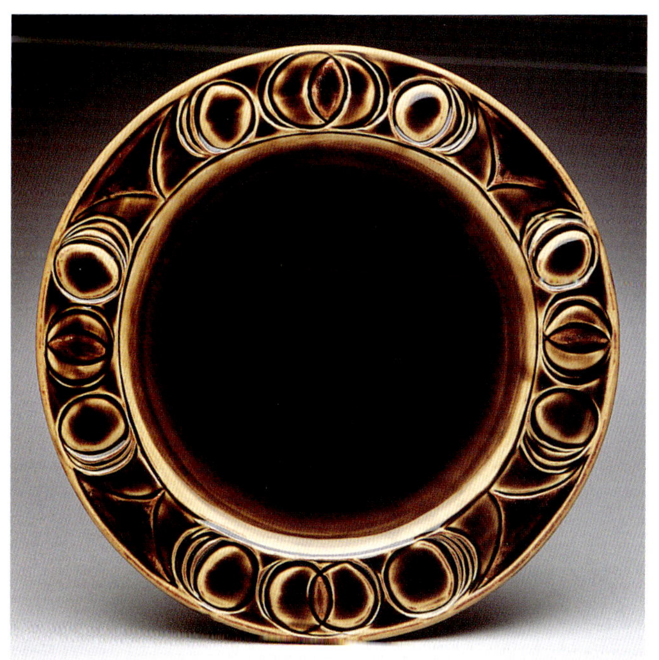

Lora Groton Rust

Plate | 2007

1 X 11 INCHES (2.5 X 27.9 CM)

Wheel-thrown porcelain; geometric texture; yellow celadon glaze; gas fired in reduction, cone 10

PHOTO BY WALKER MONTGOMERY

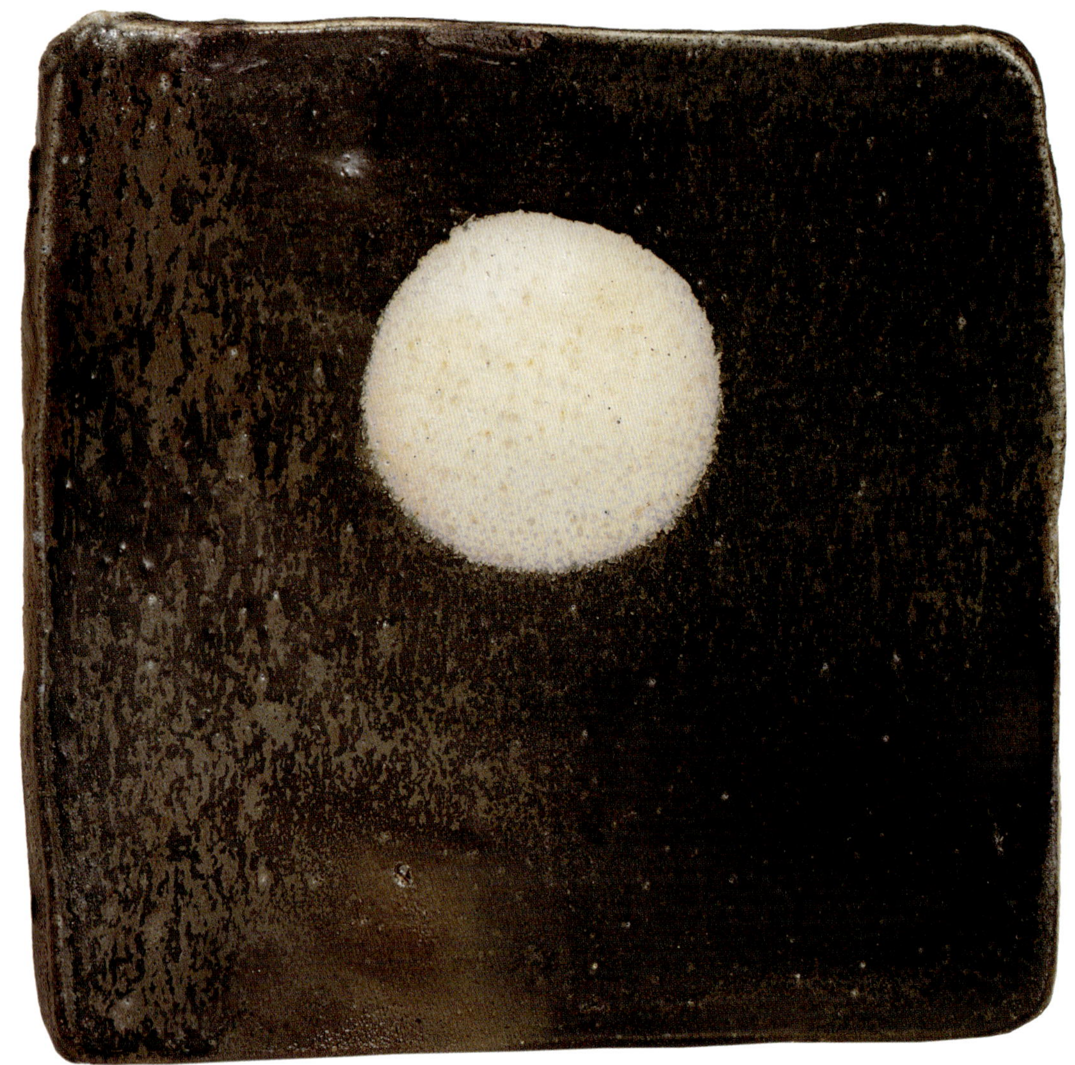

Christopher Staley
Lunar Stillness | 2002
3 X 14 X 14 INCHES (7.6 X 35.6 X 35.6 CM)
Hand-built and thrown stoneware;
glaze, salt fired, cone 8
PHOTO BY DICK ACKLEY

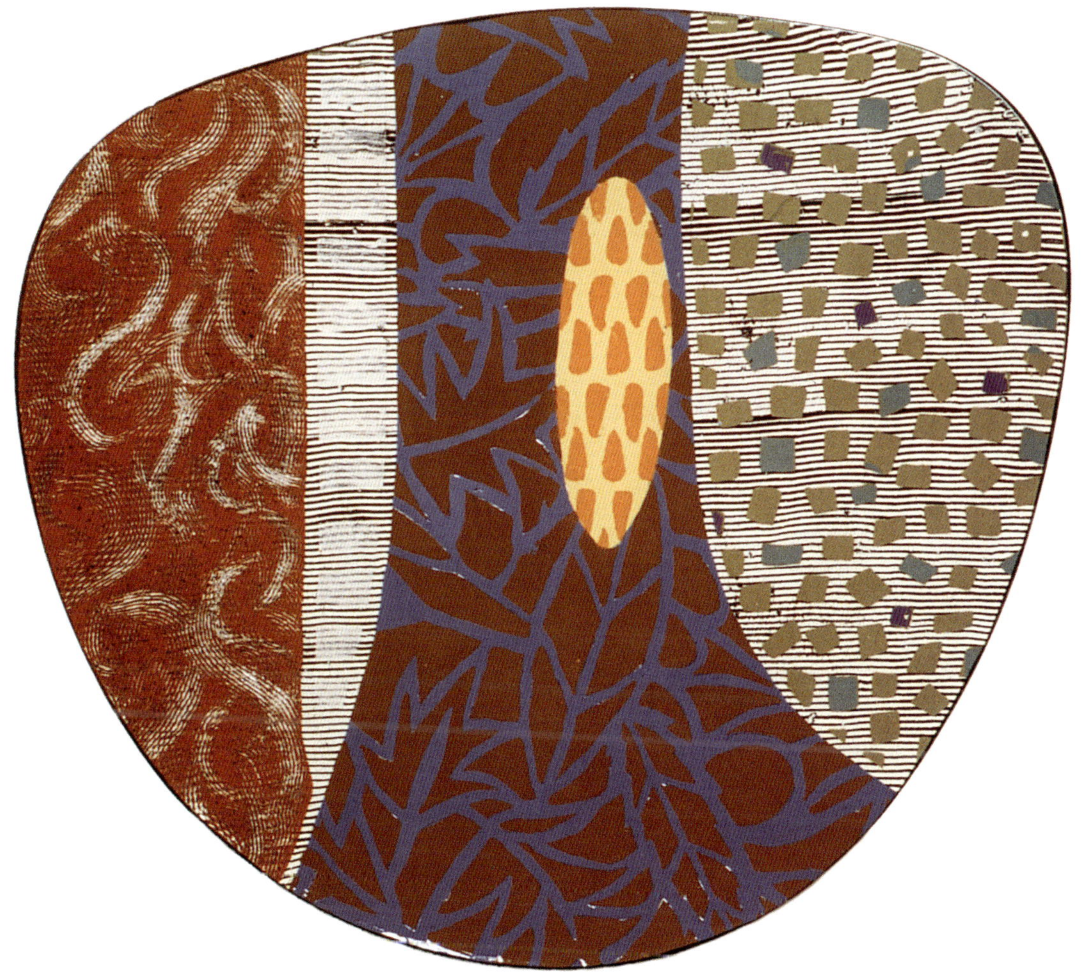

Claudia Reese

Odd Disks | 2006

4 X 24 X 20 INCHES (10.2 X 61 X 50.8 CM)

Slab-built earthenware; slips, inverse inlay; clear glaze, electric fired, cone 03

PHOTO BY CHRIS CASELLI

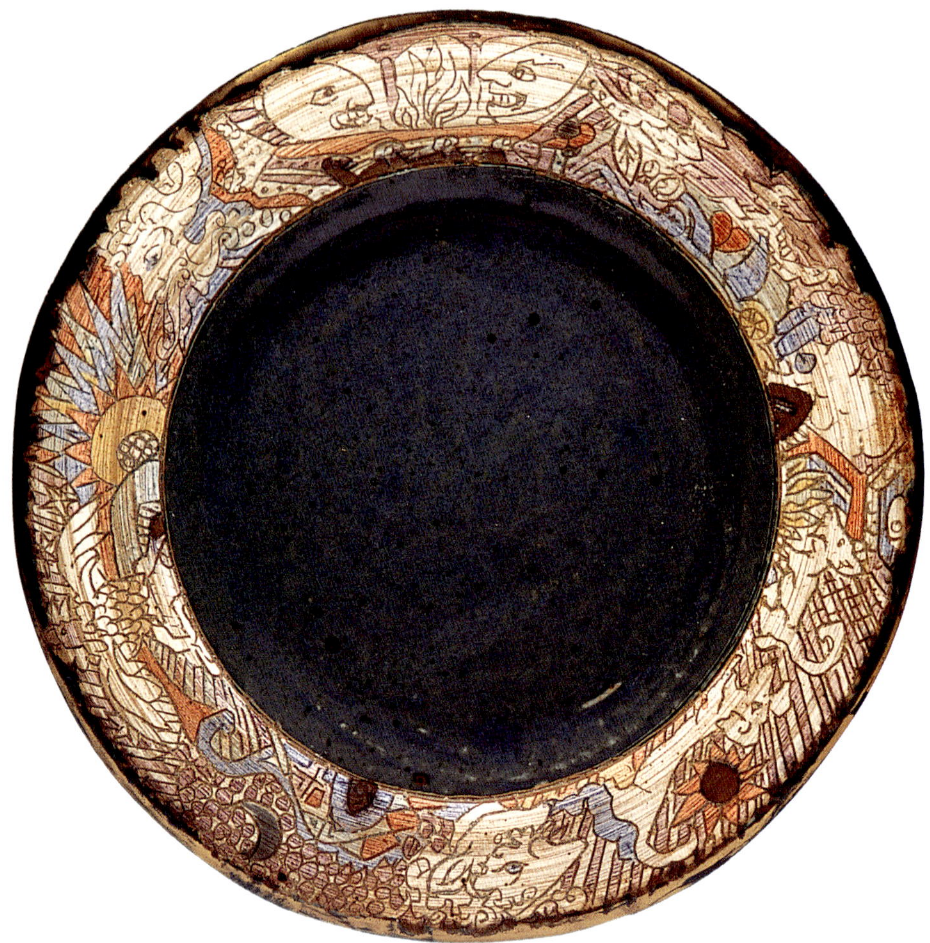

Jerry Chappelle

Faces for Aces | 2003

8 1/2 INCHES (21.6 CM) IN DIAMETER

Pressed stoneware; sgraffito, slip, glaze; reduction fired, cone 10; china paint, gold luster, electric fired, cone 018

PHOTO BY WALKER MONTGOMERY

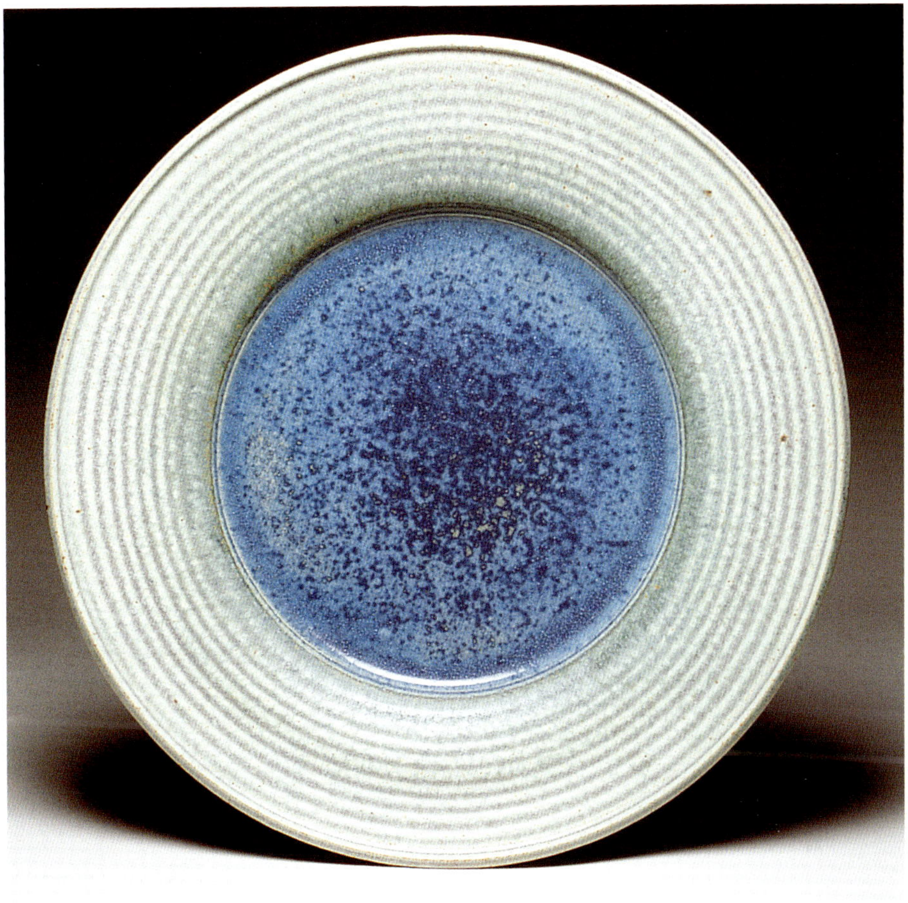

Winthrop Byers

Sage and Turquoise Wide Rimmed Platter | 2006

$2\frac{3}{4}$ X 18 INCHES (7 X 45.7 CM)

Wheel-thrown stoneware; sprayed cobalt, copper, and wood-ash glazes; natural-gas fired in reduction, cone 10

PHOTOS BY SANDRA BYERS

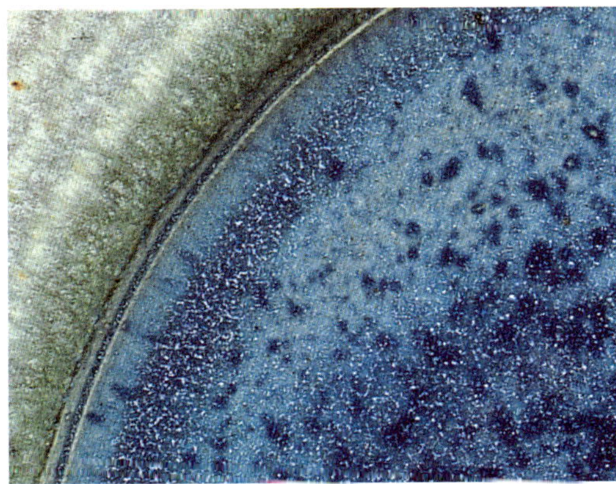

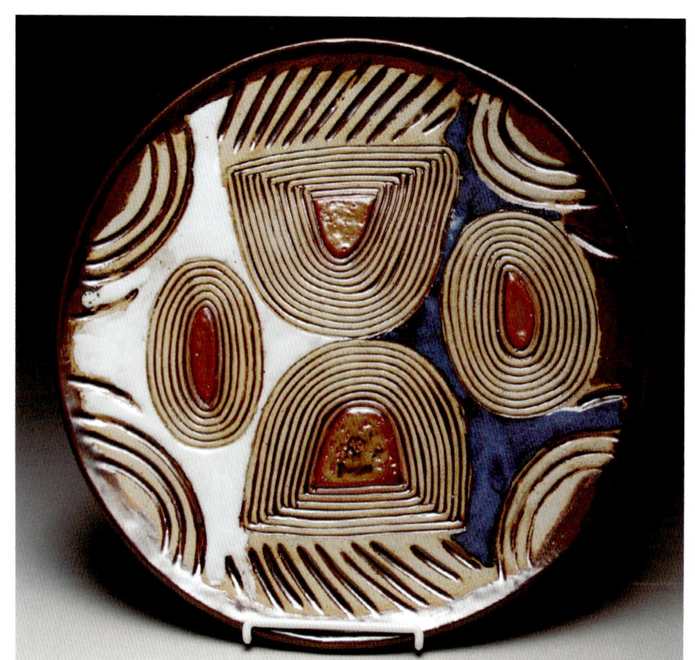

Sam Wallace
Untitled | 2006
2 X 17 INCHES (5.1 X 43.2 CM)
Wheel-thrown and carved white stoneware; various glazes, cone 10 reduction
PHOTO BY MARTINA LANTIN

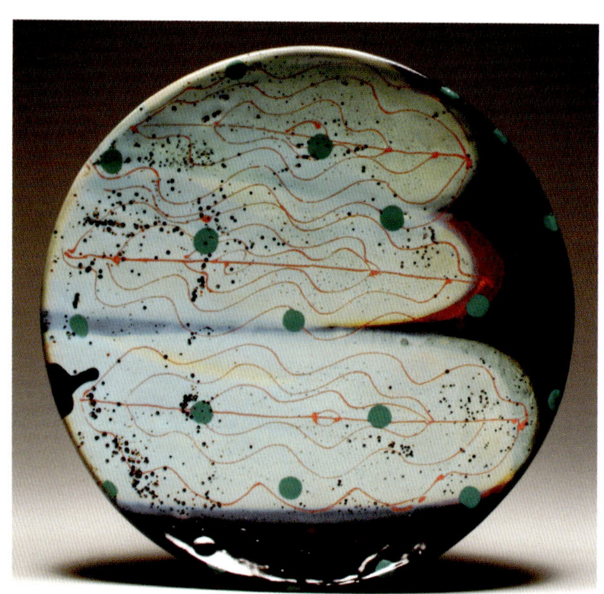

James D. Watral
Untitled | 2006
2¼ X 13 INCHES (5.7 X 33 CM)
Hand-built earthenware; glaze; electric fired, cone 03
PHOTO BY JOHN O. LEWIS

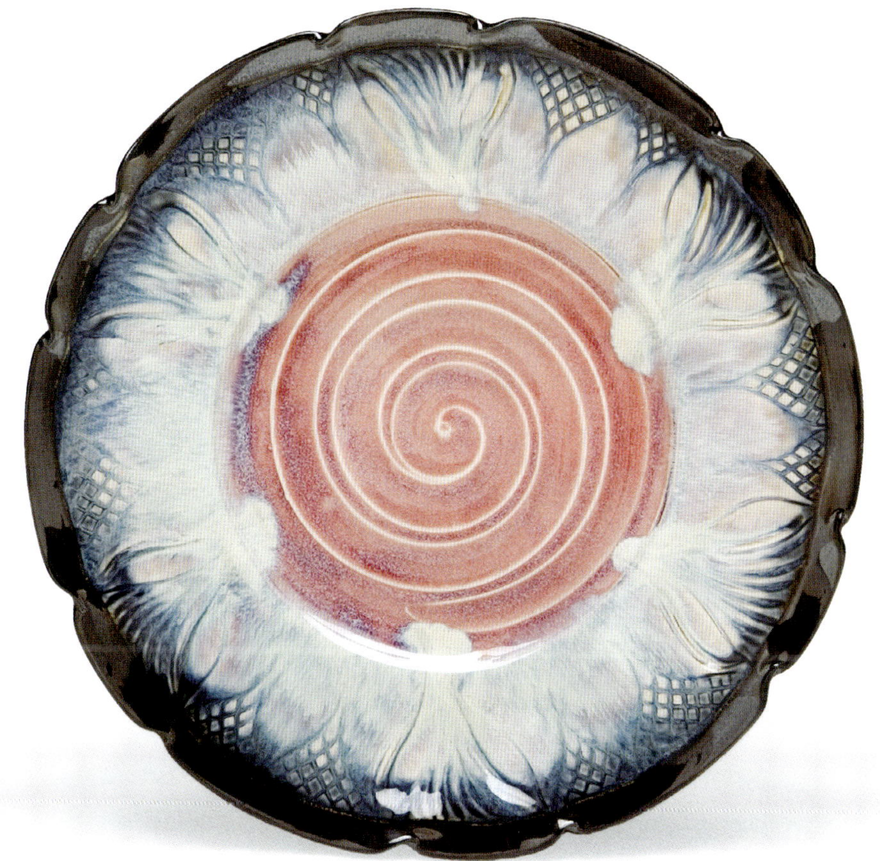

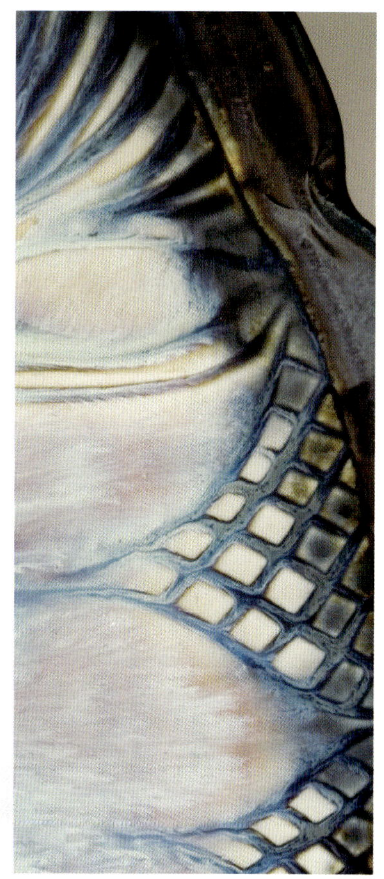

Kathryne Koop

Pink Plate | 2007

1 1/2 X 11 INCHES (3.8 X 27.9 CM)

Wheel-thrown, altered, and carved porcelain; multi-glazed; gas fired in reduction, cone 11

PHOTOS BY BRUCE SPIELMAN

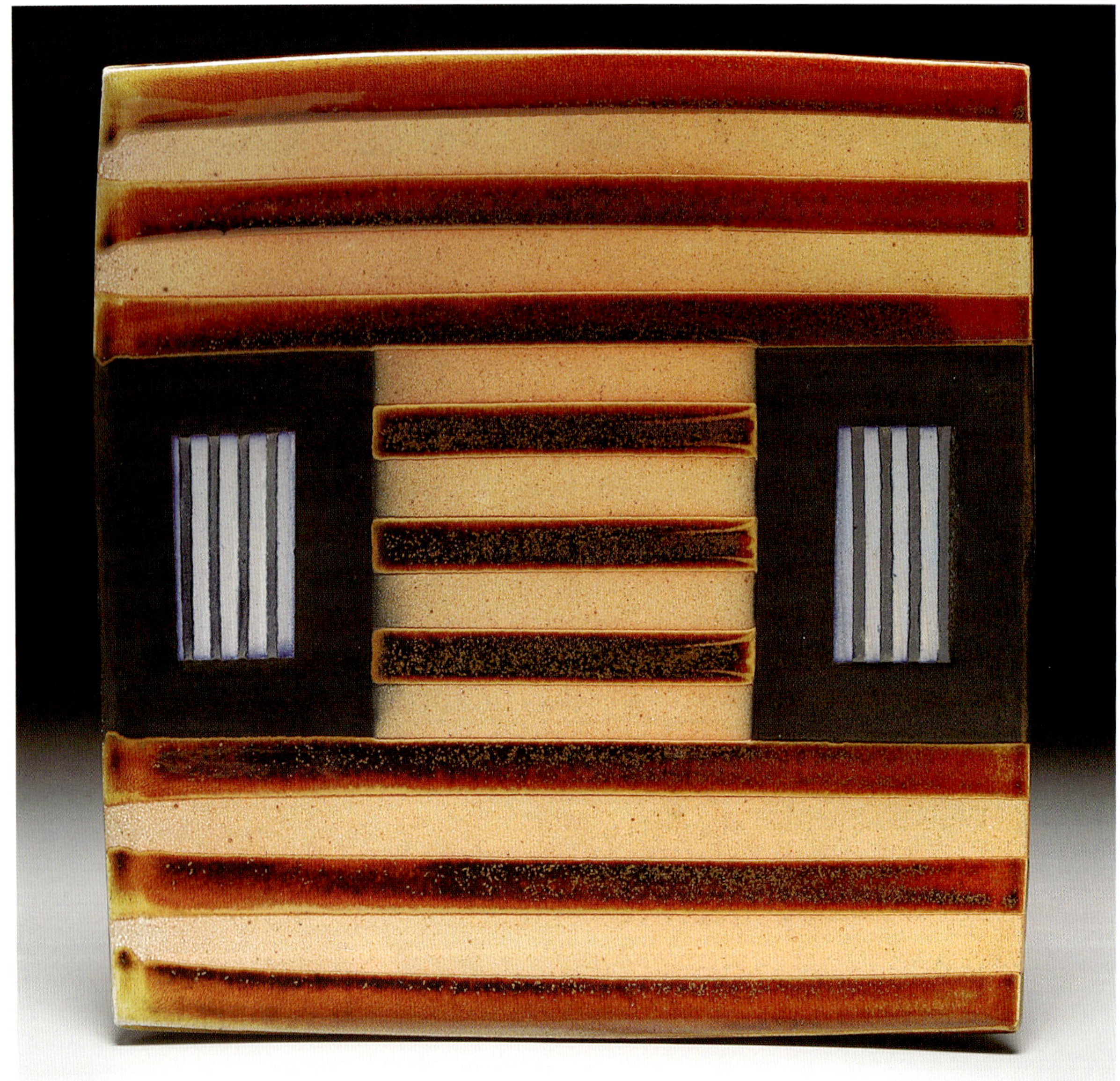

David Crane

Chief Platter—Amber | 2006

2 X 16 X 16 INCHES (5.1 X 40.6 X 40.6 CM)

Slab-built stoneware; high-temp salt fired

PHOTO BY TIM BARNWELL

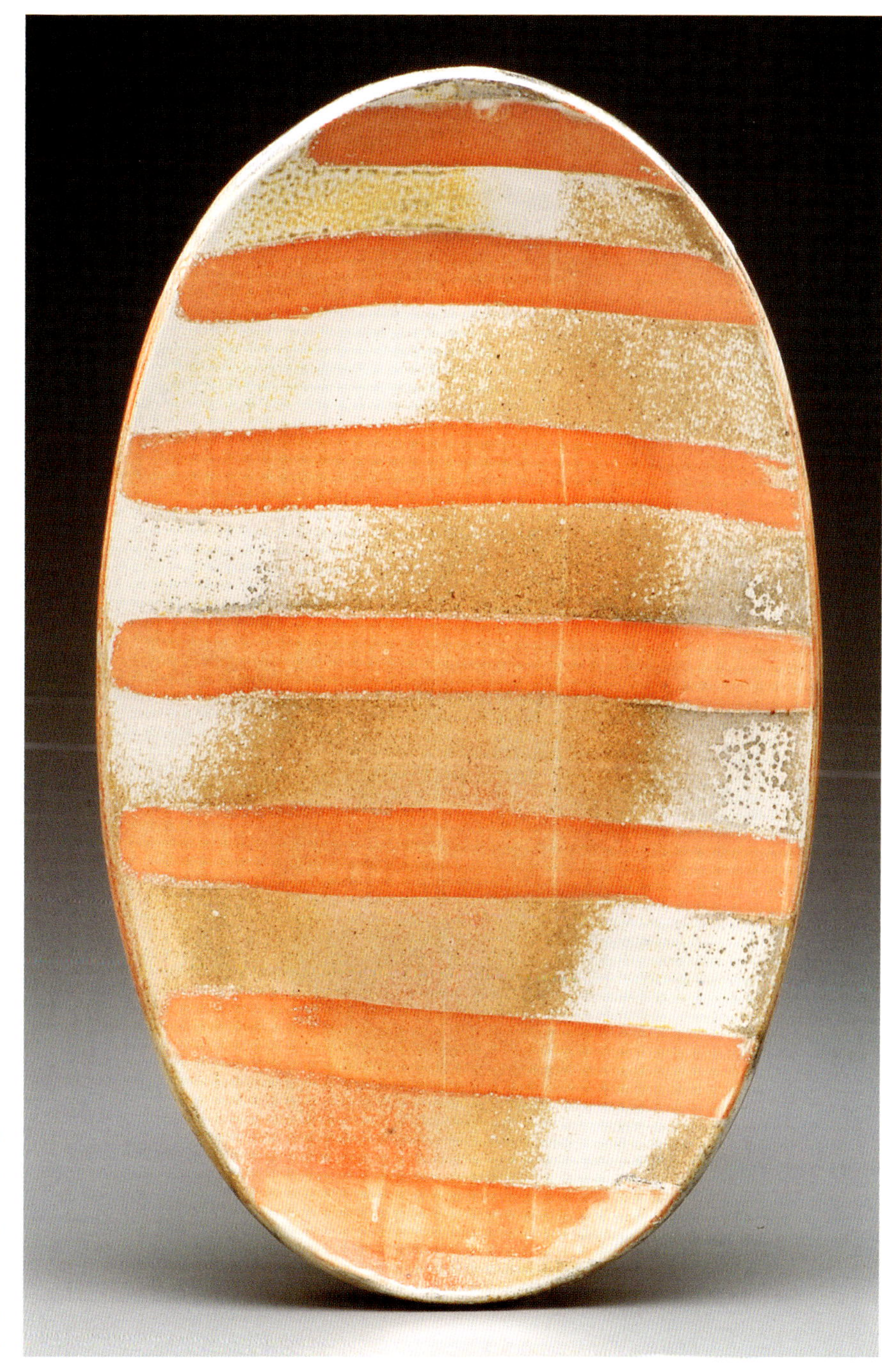

Jenny Swanson

Shino Plate | 2006

$1\frac{1}{2}$ X $9\frac{3}{4}$ X 16 INCHES
(3.8 X 24.8 X 40.6 CM)

Hand-built porcelaneous stoneware; wood ash, shino glaze; gas fired in reduction, cone 10

PHOTO BY LYNN BOHANNON

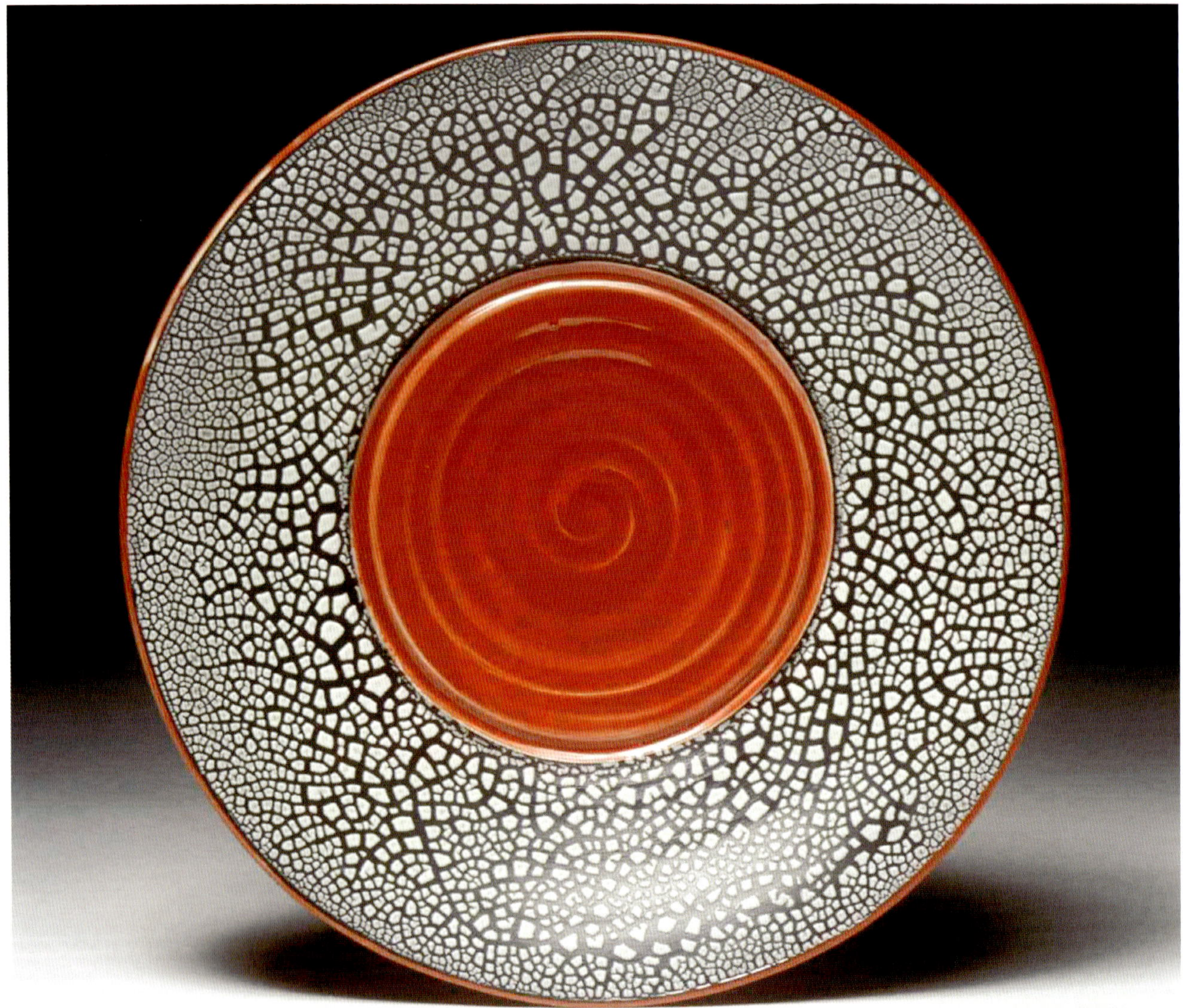

Lois Aronow

Firebird Platter | 2005

15 INCHES (38.1 CM) IN DIAMETER

Wheel-thrown porcelain; reticulating glaze over engobe; oxidation fired, cone 7

PHOTO BY D. JAMES DEE

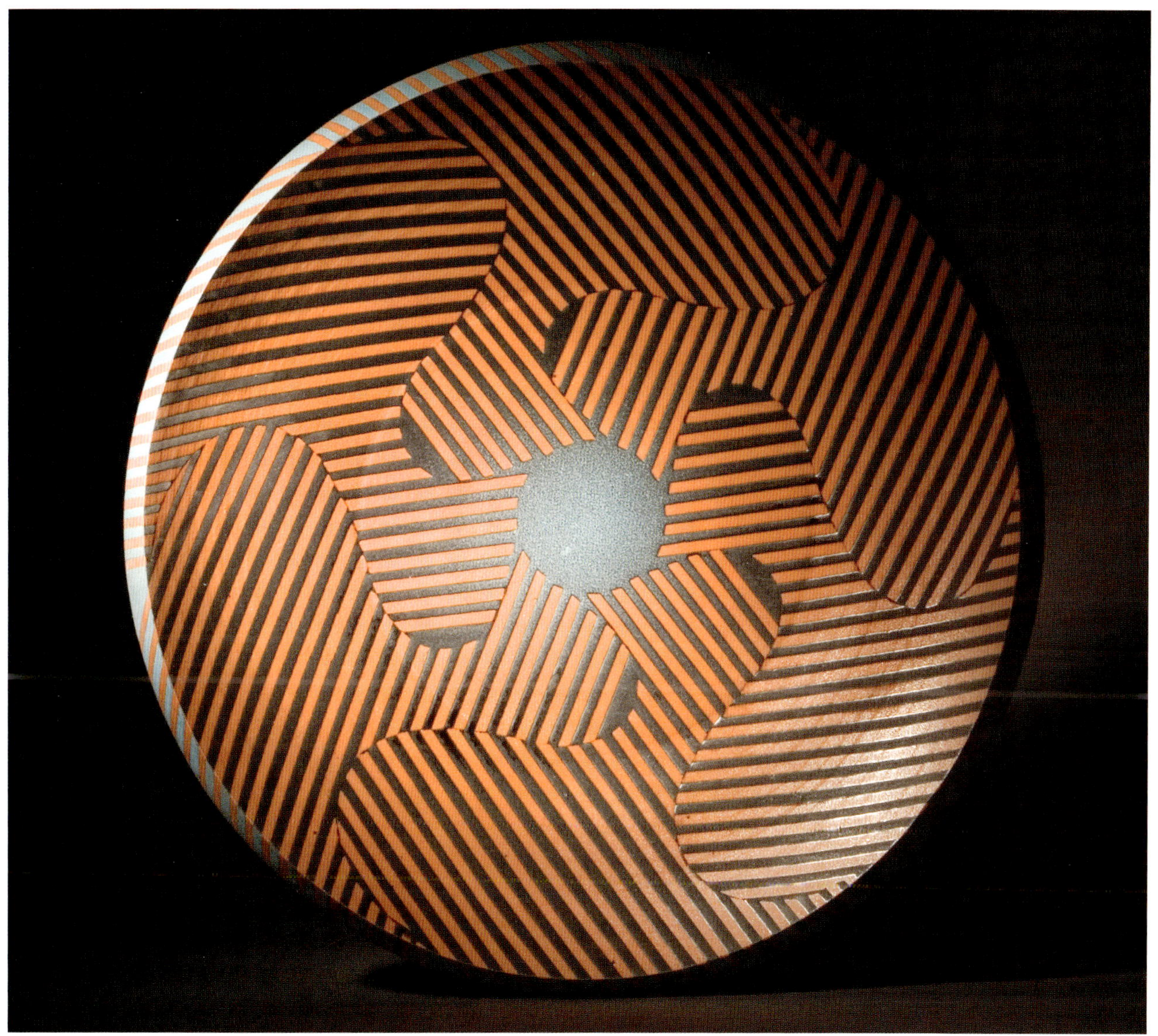

Frank Gaydos

Terra-Cotta Platter | 2007

4 X 22 INCHES (10.2 X 55.9 CM)

Hump-molded terra cotta with thrown rim and foot; electric fired, cone 04; tape resist; black and turquoise glaze

PHOTO BY ART DANEK

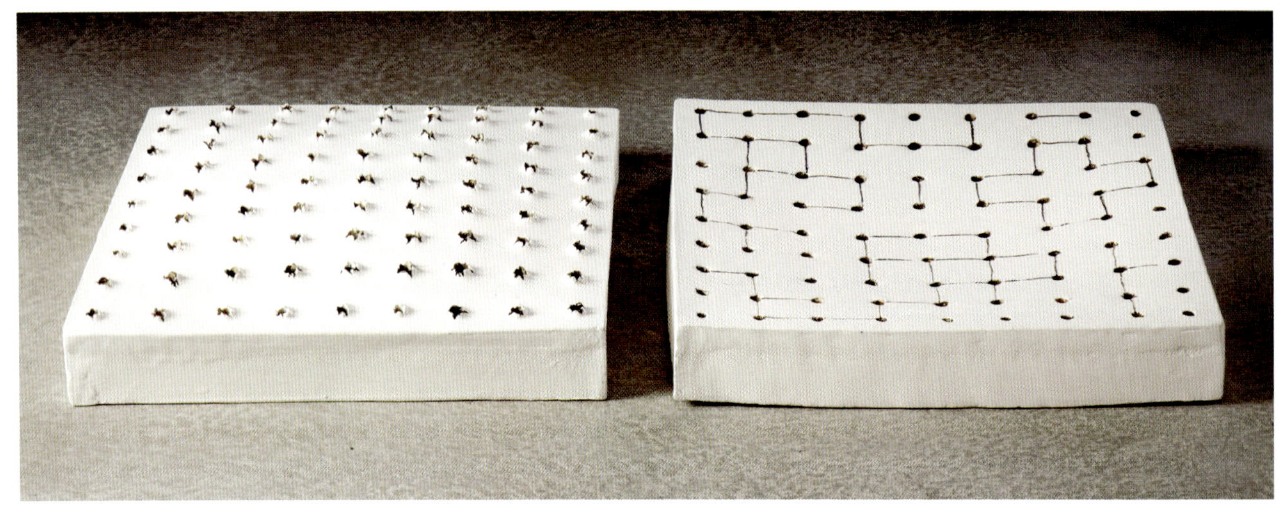

Peggy Ericson

Dot to Dot Platter and Charger | 2007

EACH: 1 1/4 X 8 X 8 INCHES (3.2 X 20.3 X 20.3 CM)

Hand-built, white earthenware paper clay; etched and pierced; manganese dioxide; gas fired, cone 03

PHOTOS BY DUDLEY MEADOWS

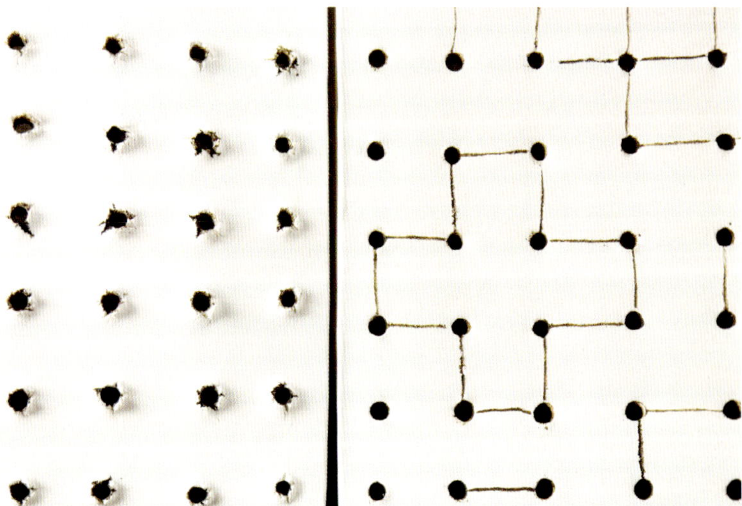

Heath Bultman

Sushi Plate | 2006

2 X 9 X 9 INCHES
(5.1 X 22.9 X 22.9 CM)

Wheel-thrown and hand-built porcelain; stamped; celadon glaze, gas fired in reduction, cone 10

PHOTO BY RICHARD NICOL

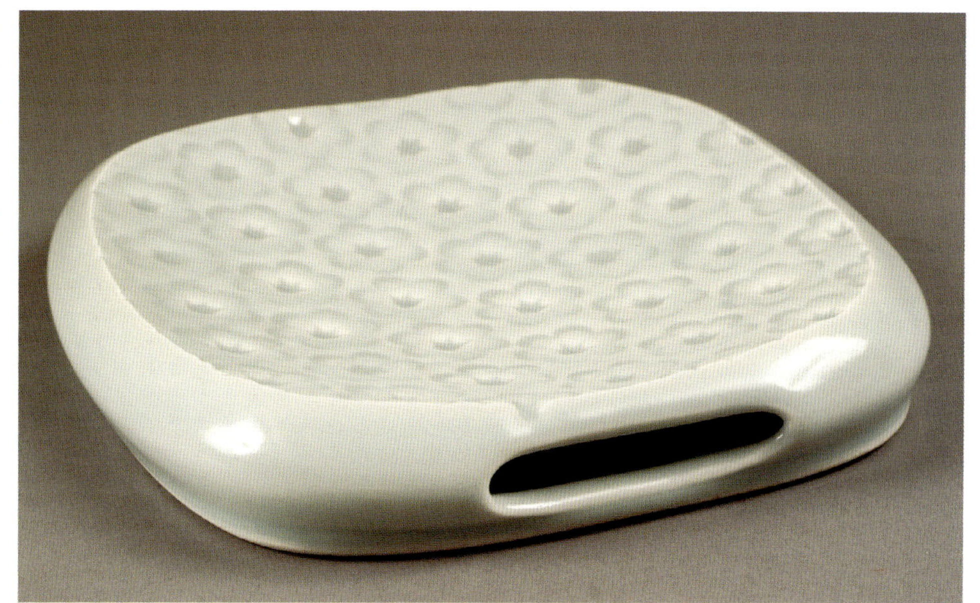

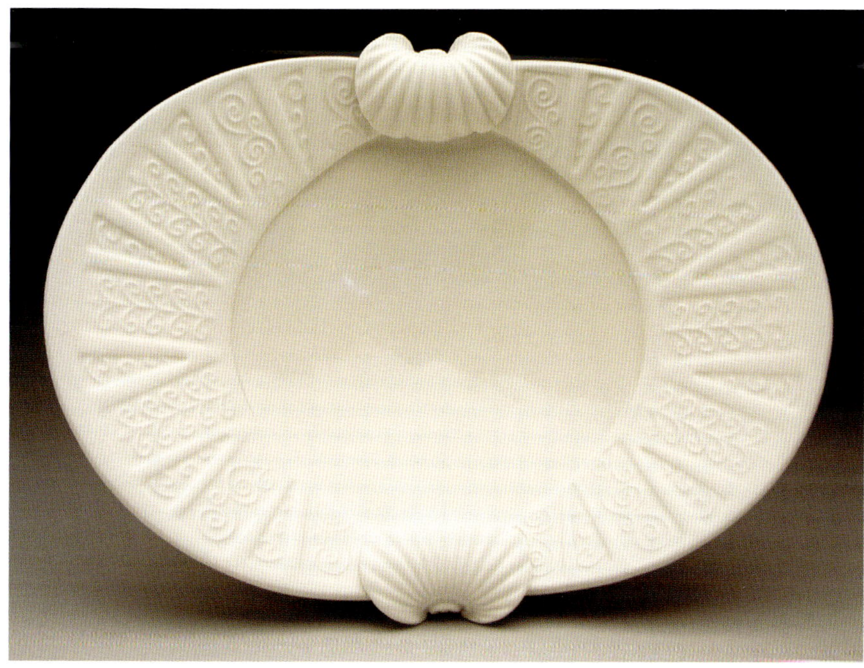

Sandi Pierantozzi

Untitled | 2006

4 X 16 X 10 INCHES (10.2 X 40.6 X 25.4 CM)

Slab-built porcelain; impressed stamps; clear and satin glaze, electric fired, cone 6

PHOTO BY ARTIST

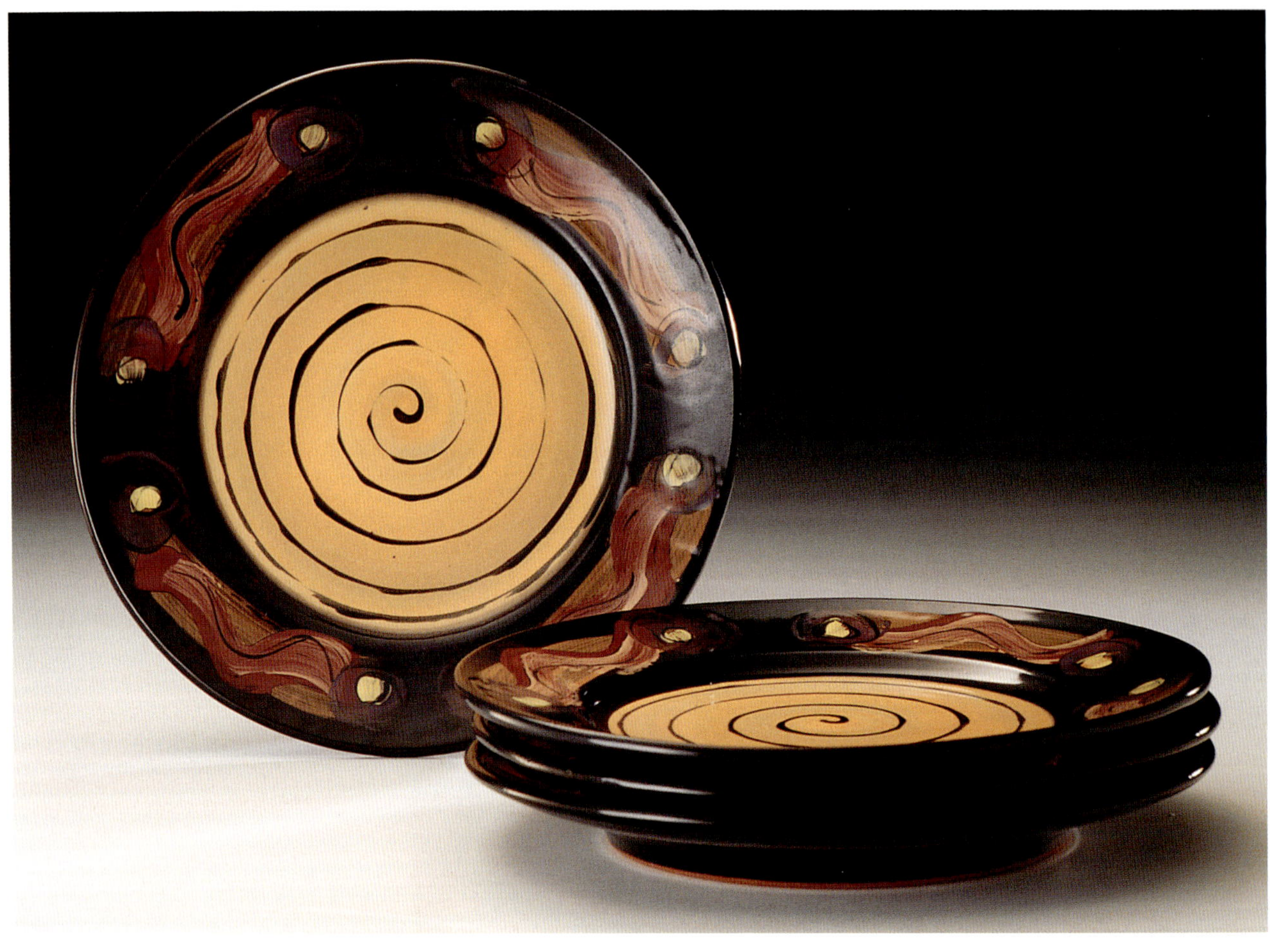

Steve Howell

Dinner Plates | 2006

EACH: 1 X 11 3/4 INCHES (2.5 X 29.8 CM)

Wheel-thrown and hand-built earthenware; electric fired, cone 04; glazes, cones 04–03

PHOTO BY RANDALL SMITH

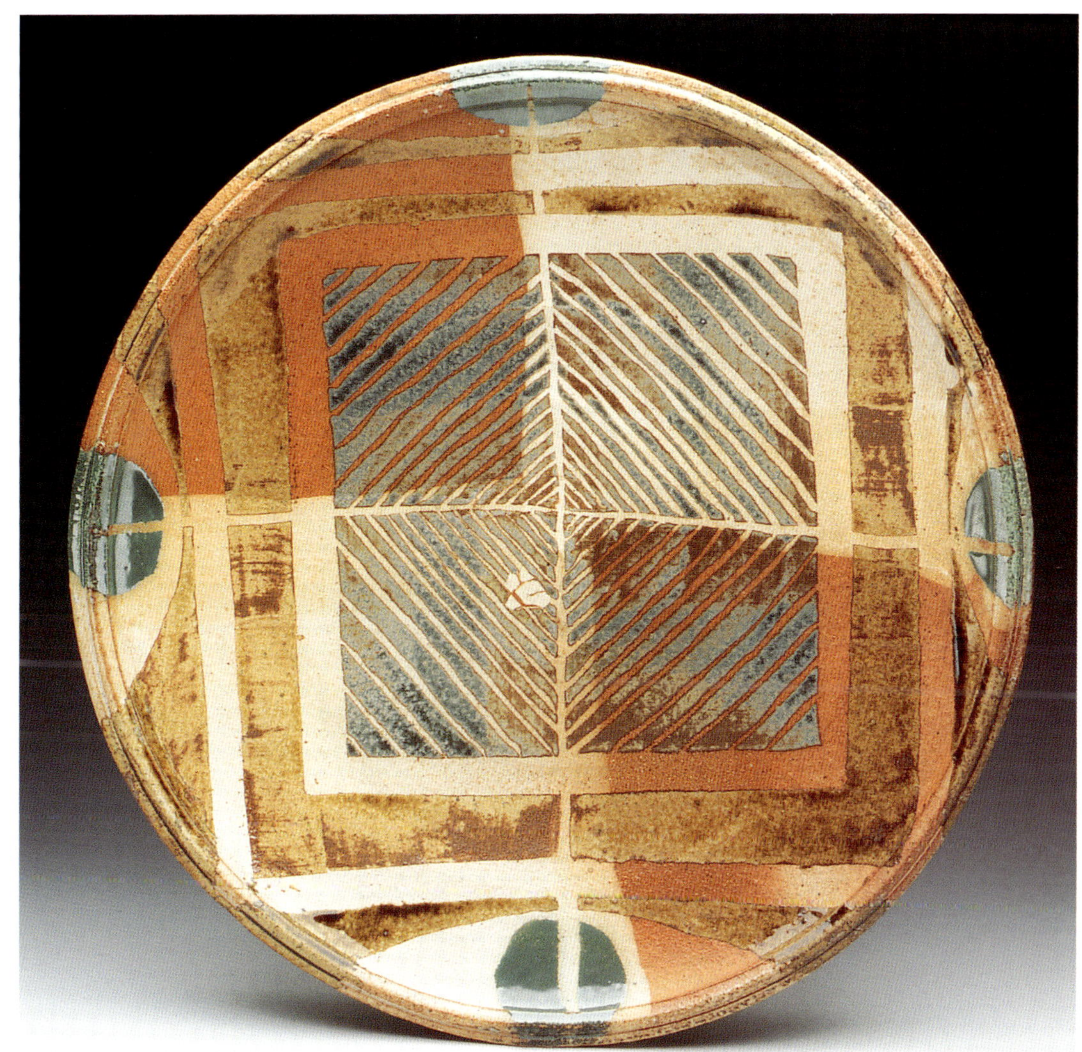

Chris Baskin

Platter | 2006

20 INCHES (50.8 CM) IN DIAMETER

Wheel-thrown stoneware; slips, glazes; soda fired, cone 10

PHOTO BY BOB PAYNE

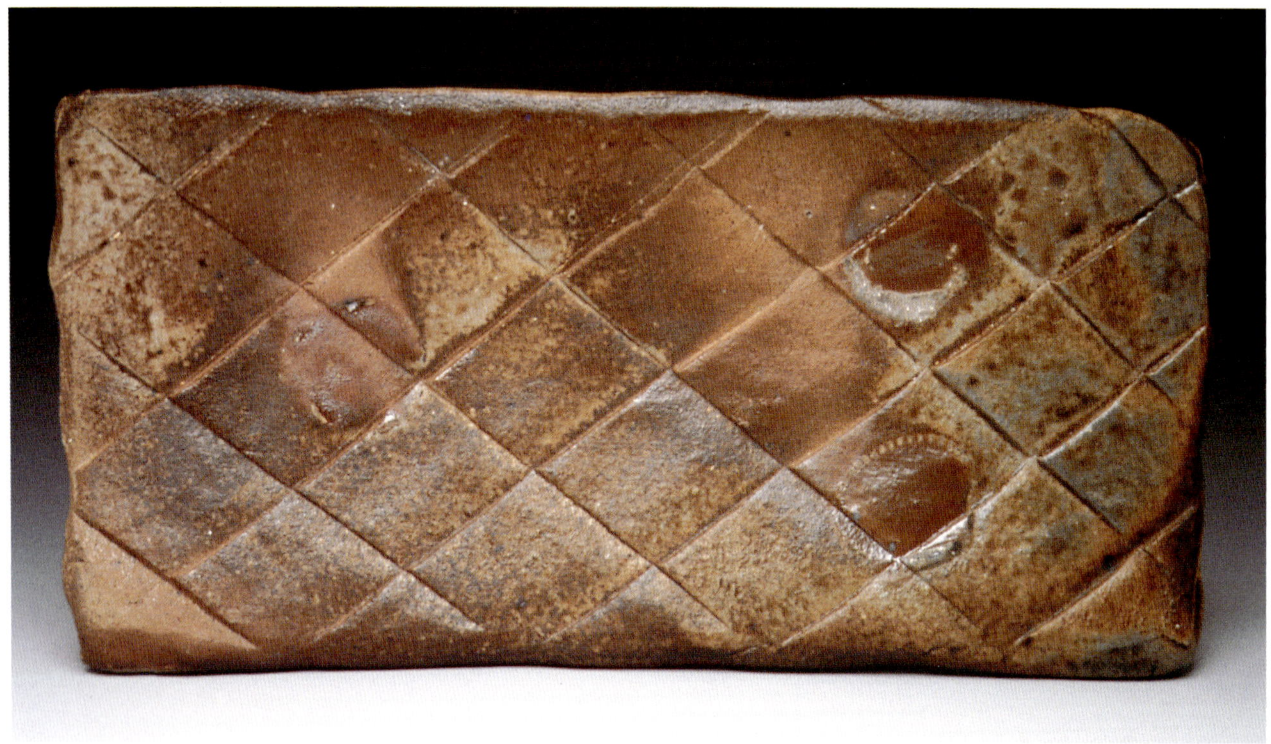

Justin Richert

Quilted Tray | 2005

1 1/2 X 10 X 5 INCHES (3.8 X 25.4 X 12.7 CM)

Slab-built stoneware; flashing slip and shells; wood/salt fired, cone 10

PHOTO BY ARTIST

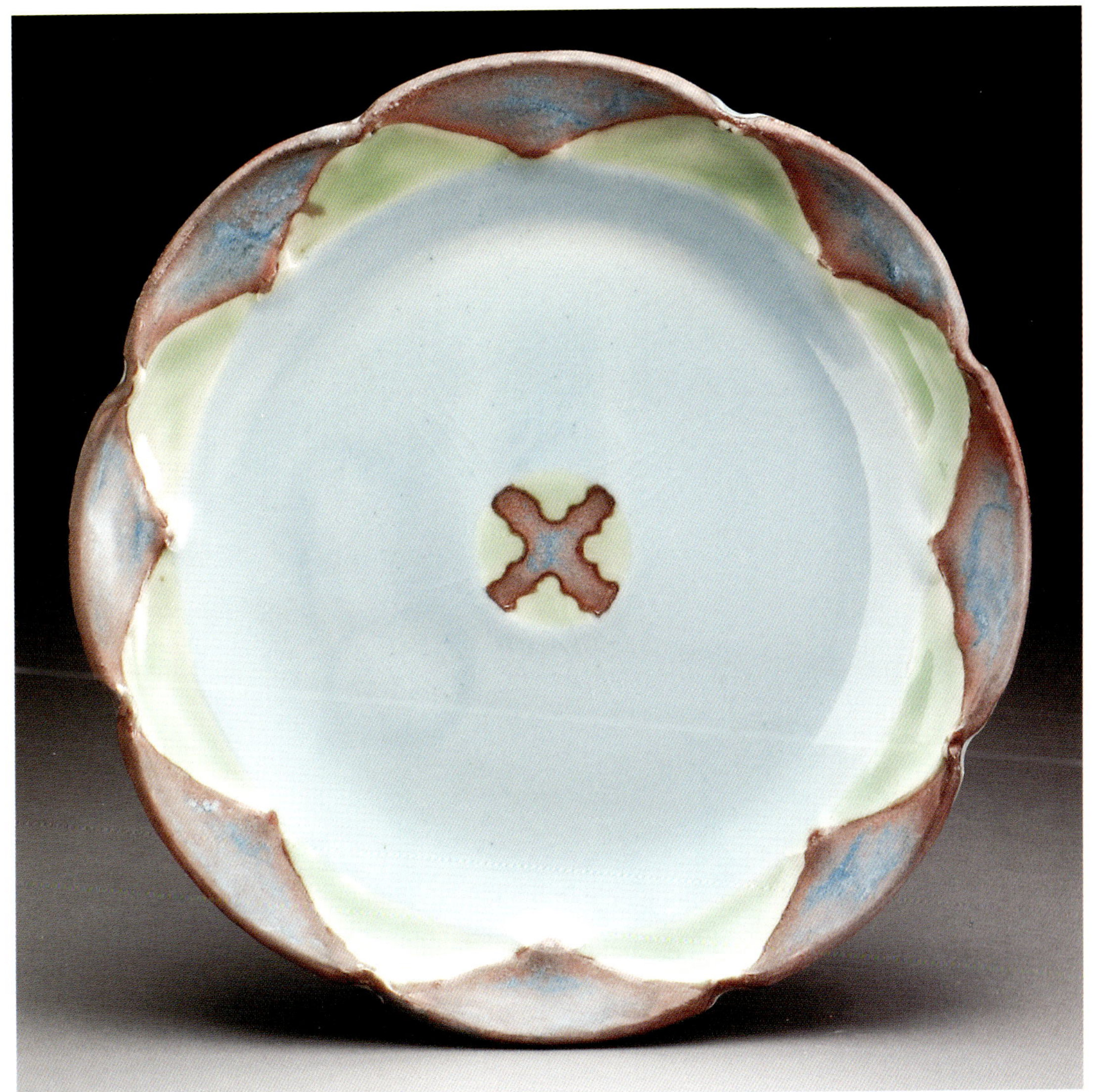

Benjamin Carter

Serving Dish | 2006

2 X 10 INCHES (5.1 X 25.4 CM)

Wheel-thrown porcelain; glaze inlay with Pete's Strontium Best and Pinnell's Clear; gas fired in reduction, cone 10

PHOTO BY TOM MILLS

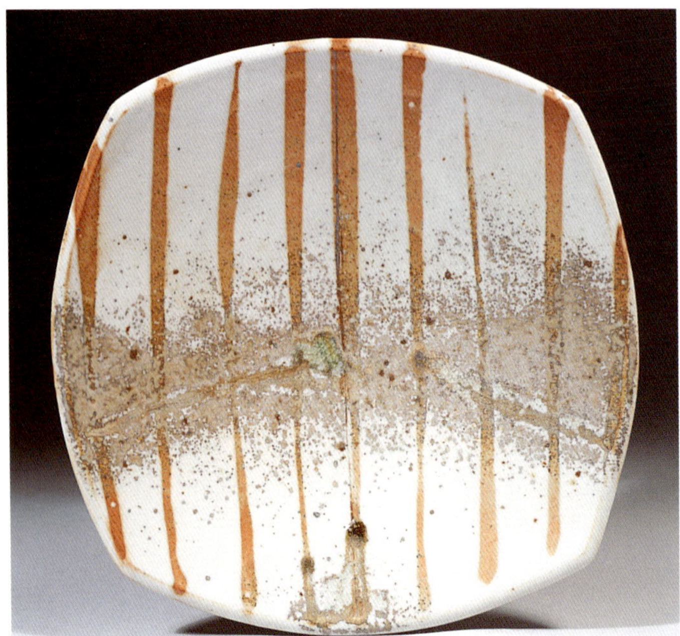

Matthew Hyleck

Field Platter | 2006

3 X 16 X 16 INCHES (7.6 X 40.6 X 40.6 CM)

Wheel-thrown stoneware with iron inlay; gas fired in reduction, cone 10; shino overlay with wood ash

PHOTO BY ARTIST

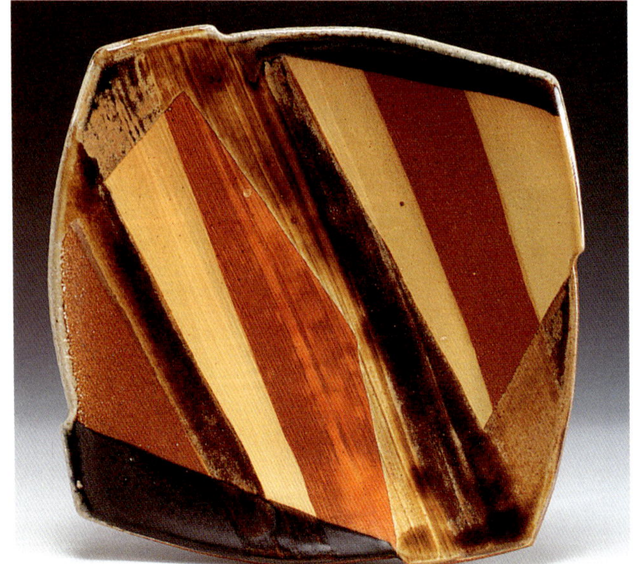

Marcia Paul

Square Plate | 2006

1 X 9 X 9 INCHES (2.5 X 22.9 X 22.9 CM)

Hand-built stoneware; slips and glazes; soda fired, cone 10

PHOTO BY PETRONELLA J. YTSMA

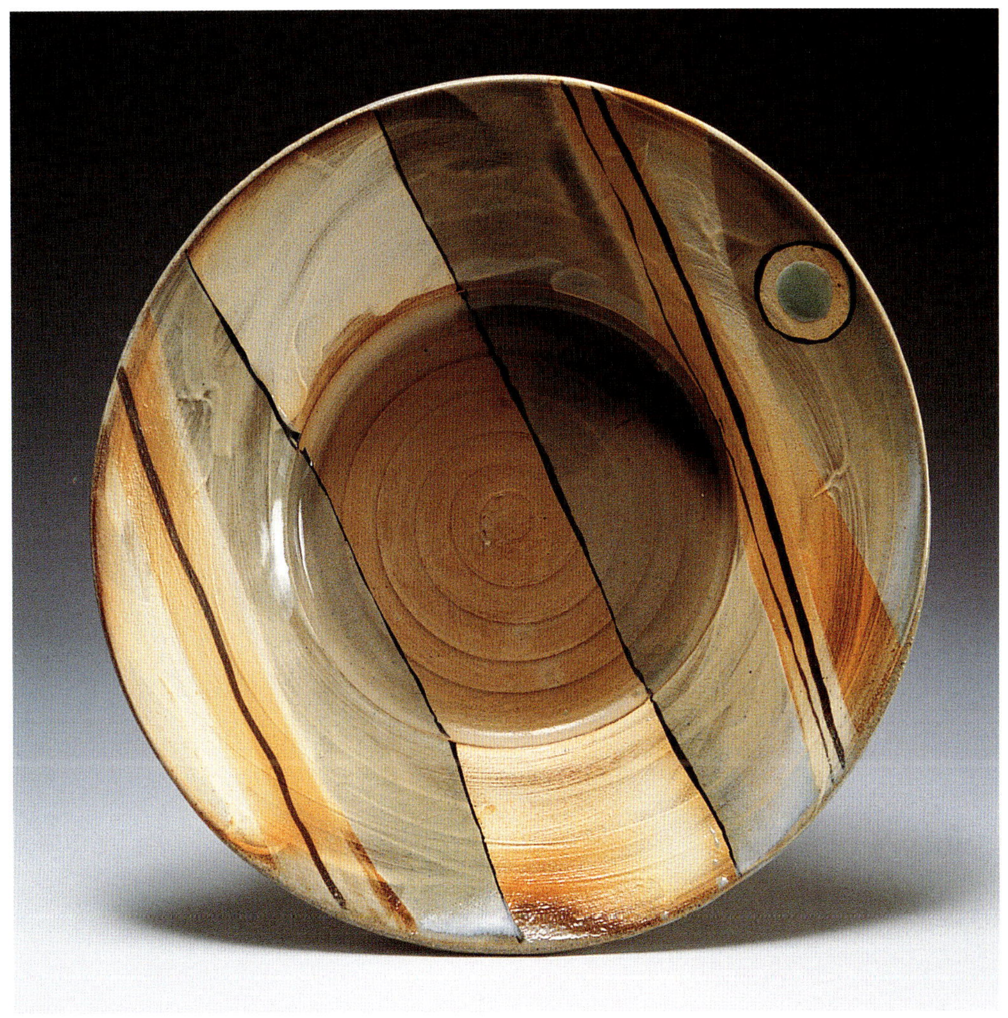

Carolina Niebres

Untitled | 2006

2 3/16 X 12 5/16 INCHES (5.6 X 31.3 CM)

Wheel-thrown stoneware; porcelain and flashing slips; celadon glaze, black underglaze; soda fired, cone 10; wax resist

PHOTO BY PETRONELLA J. YTSMA

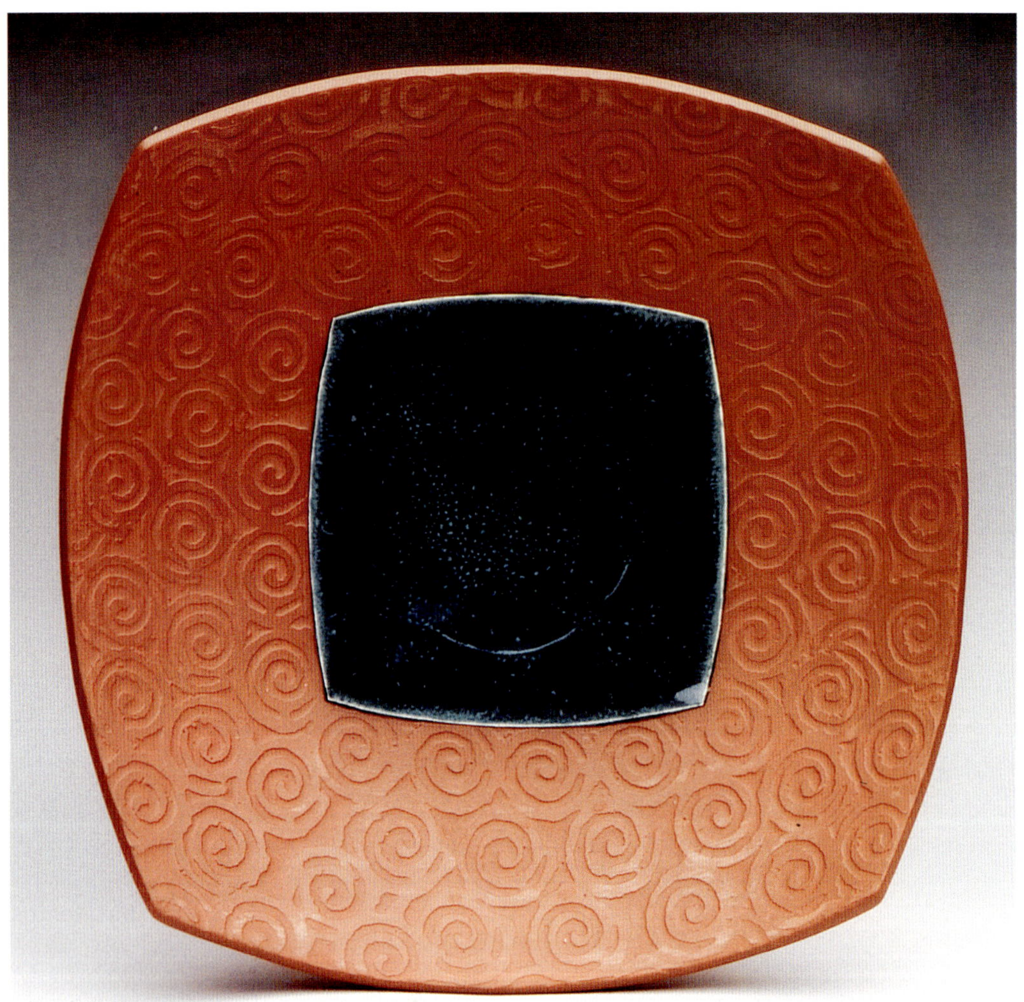

Célia Z. Brandão

Untitled | 2006

$2^{3}/_{8}$ X $11^{1}/_{4}$ X $11^{1}/_{4}$ INCHES (6 X 28.6 X 28.6 CM)

Wheel-thrown slab earthenware; terra sigillatas; glazes; electric fired, cone 06

PHOTO BY DALE RODDICK

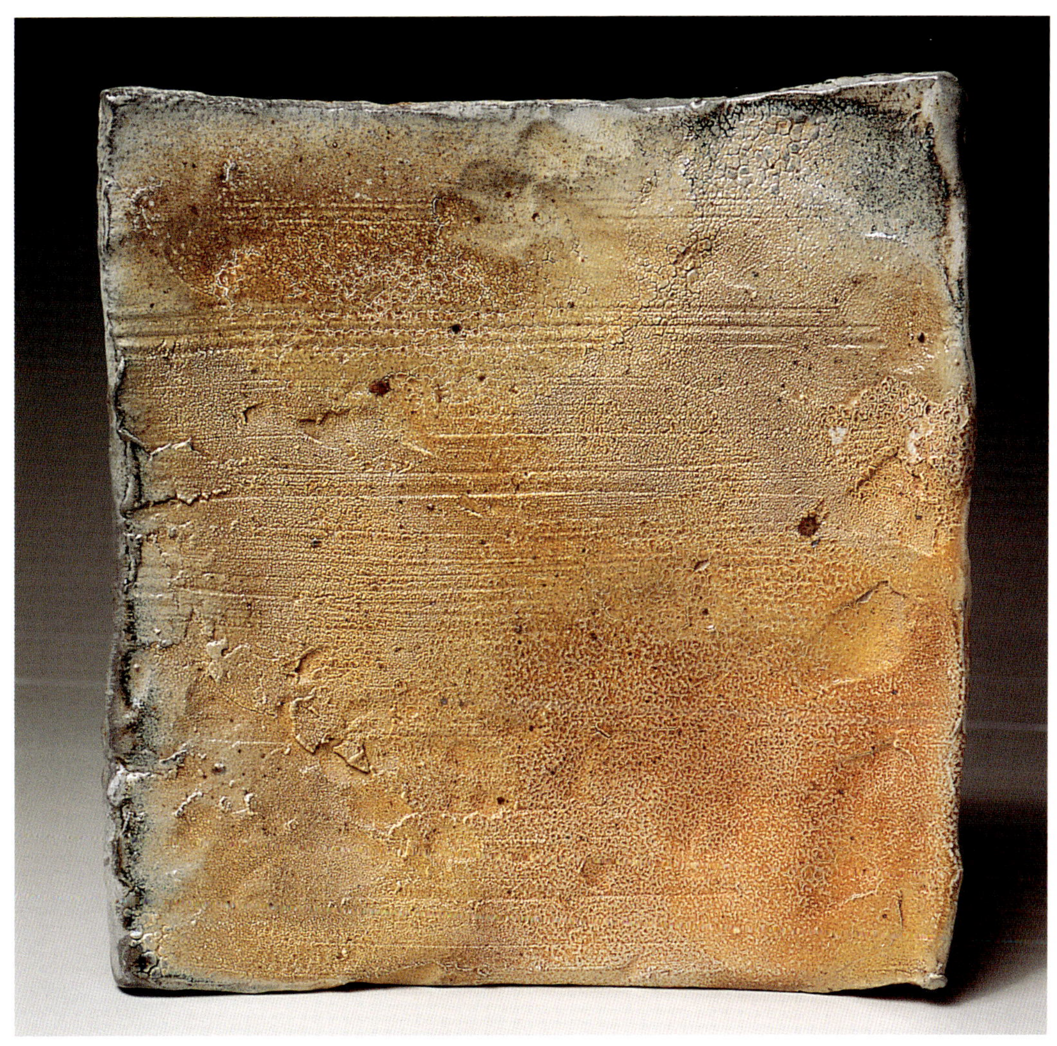

Chris Kranz

Square Plate | 2005

12 INCHES (30.5 CM) IN DIAMETER

Hand-built stoneware;
soda fired, cone 10

PHOTO BY PHYLIS KING

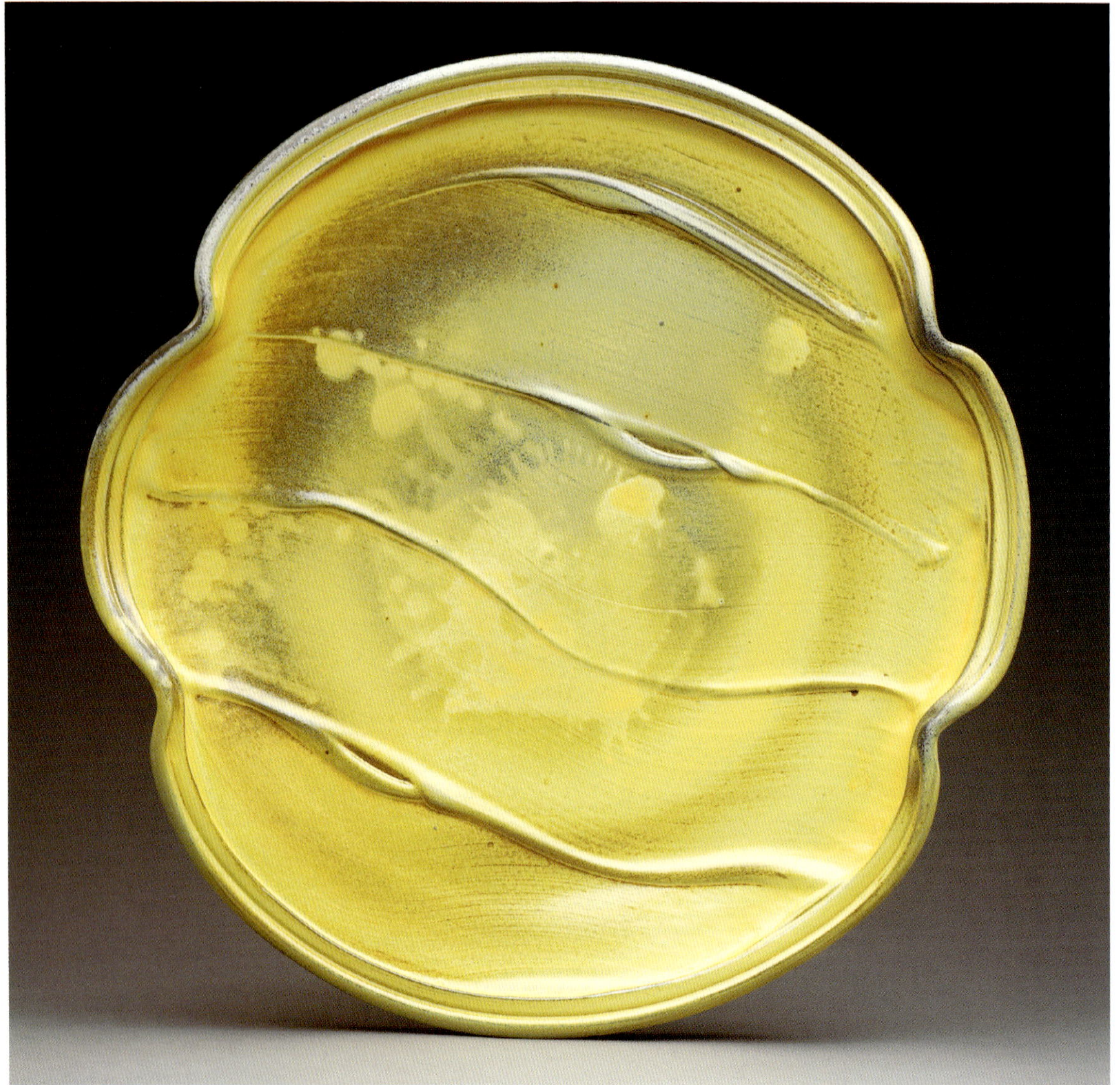

Matt Long

Platter | 2006

3 X 18 1/2 INCHES (7.6 X 47 CM)

Wheel-thrown porcelain; slip; soda fired, cone 11

PHOTO BY STEVE PASZT

Paul Linhares

Platter with Palmettes | 2007

$2\frac{1}{2}$ X 14 X 14 INCHES (6.4 X 35.6 X 35.6 CM)

Wheel-thrown earthenware; white slip with alkaline glaze, stamped; electric fired, cone 2

PHOTO BY ARTIST

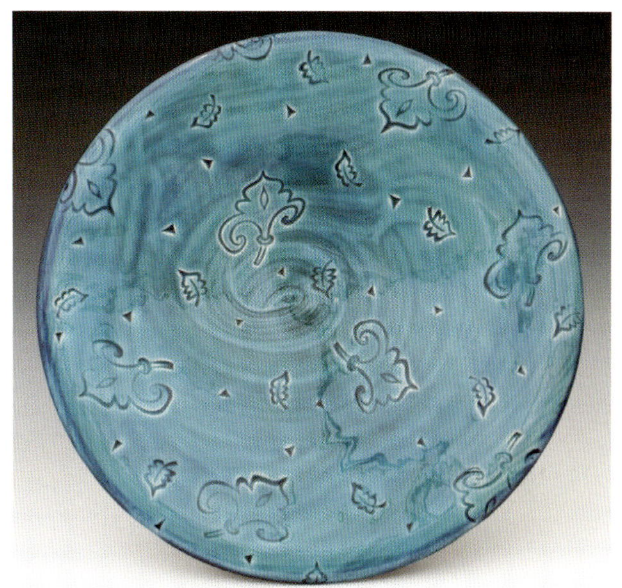

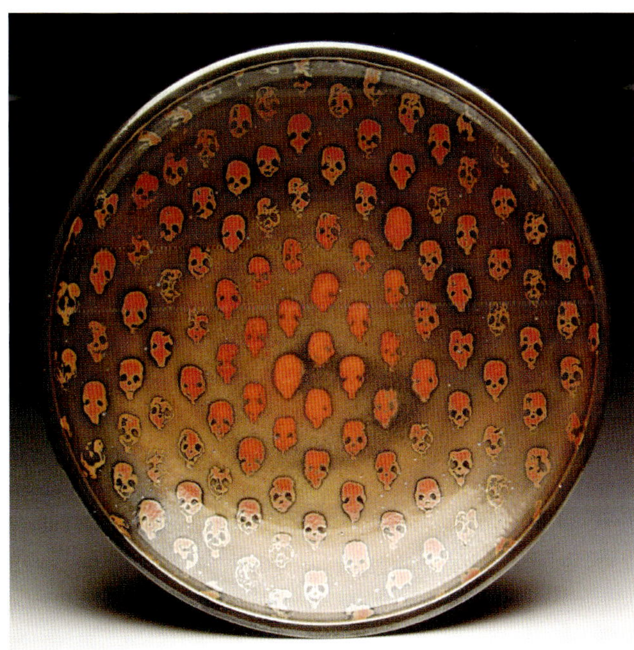

Brian Jensen

Untitled | 2007

4 X 20 INCHES (10.2 X 50.8 CM)

Wheel-thrown stoneware; carbon-trapping shino, cone 10

PHOTO BY ARTIST

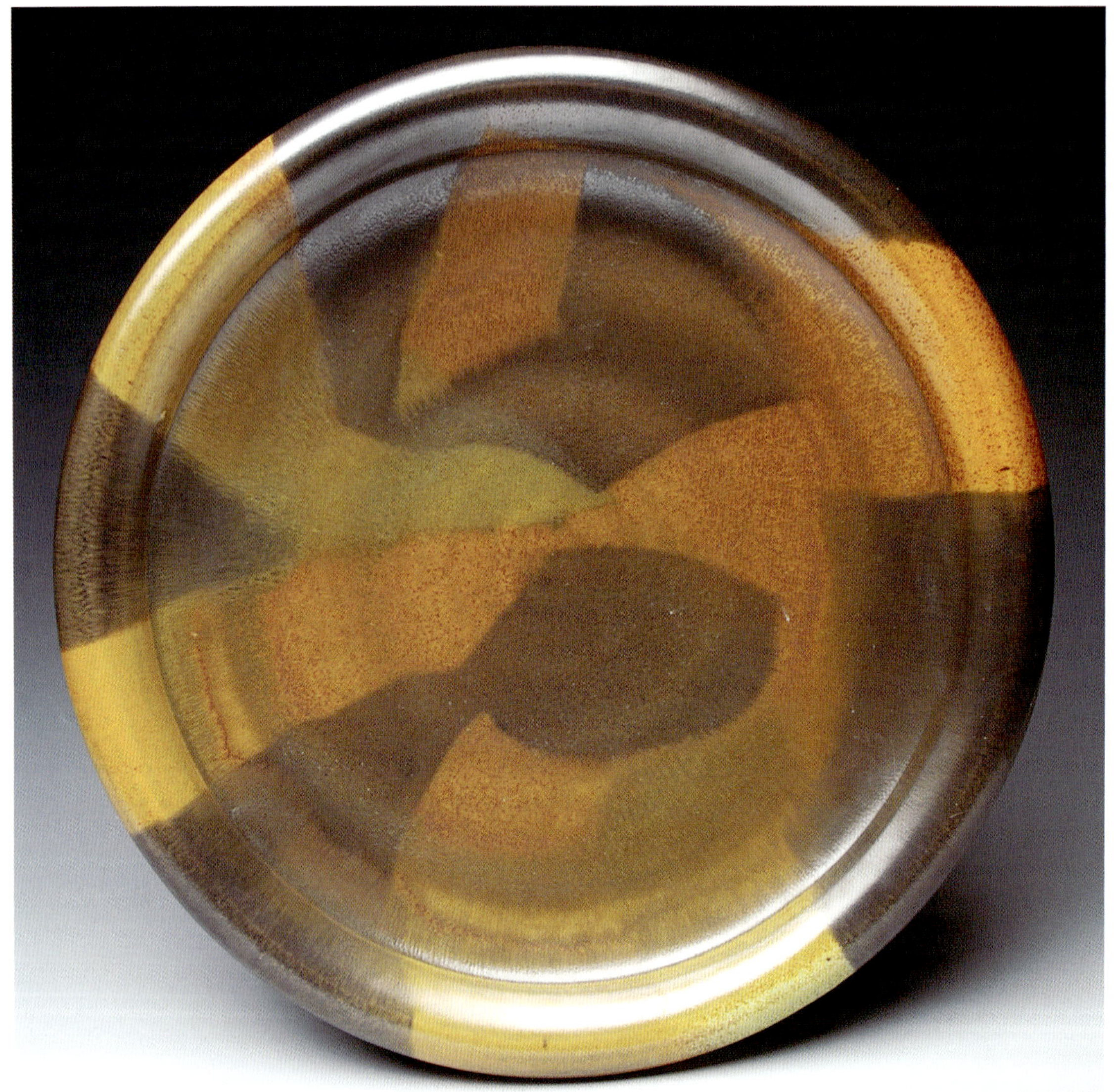

Jake Johnson

Untitled | 2007

3 X 16 INCHES (7.6 X 40.6 CM)

Wheel-thrown stoneware; tape and wax resist, slip; glaze, salt fired, cone 10

PHOTO BY ARTIST

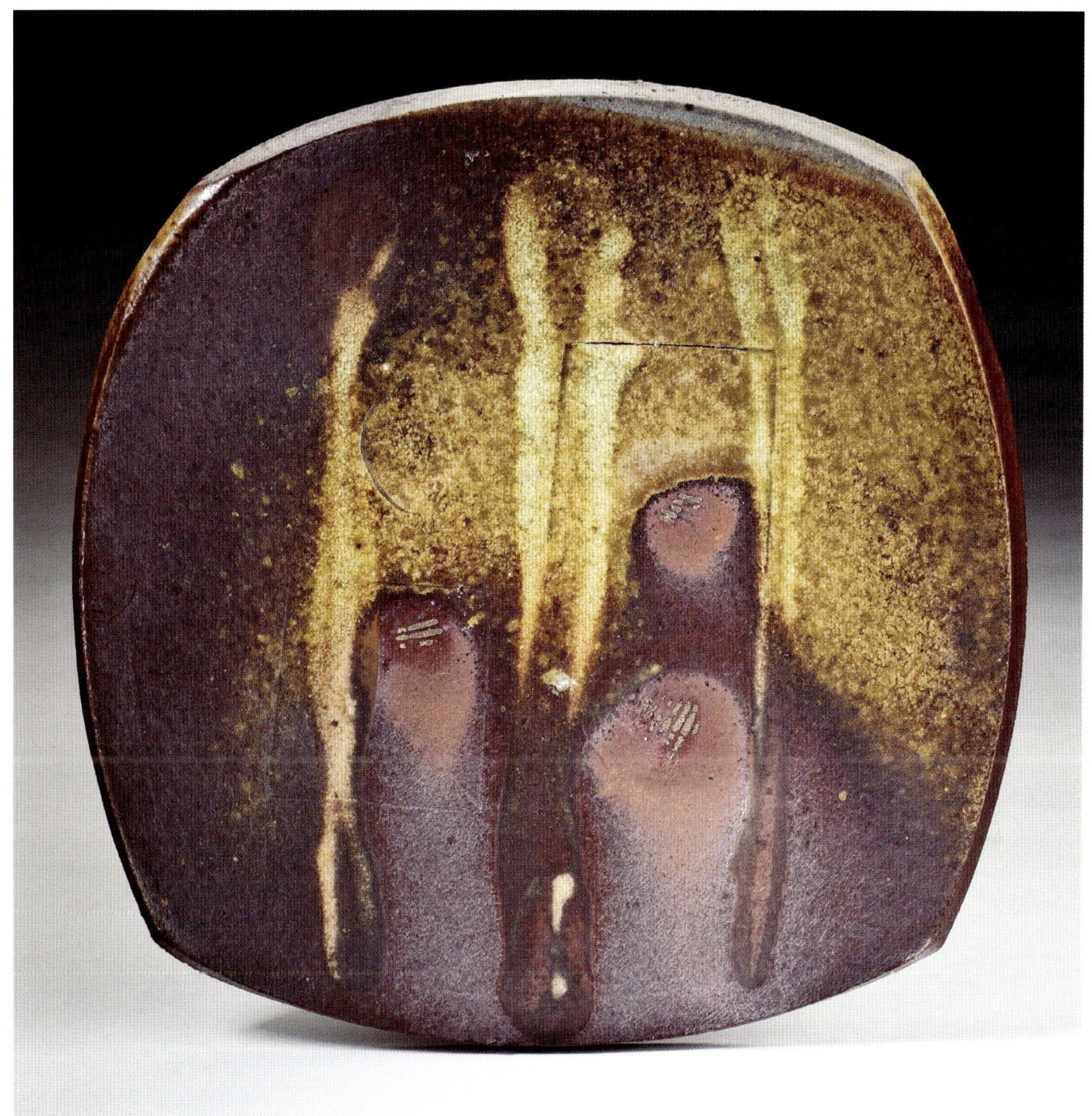

Roger E. Tolzman

Dinner Plate | 2007

1 X 9 1/2 X 9 1/2 INCHES (2.5 X 24.1 X 24.1 CM)

Drape-molded and slab-built stoneware; slips; wood fired, cone 11; seashell inclusions

PHOTO BY JUDITH KIMBRELL

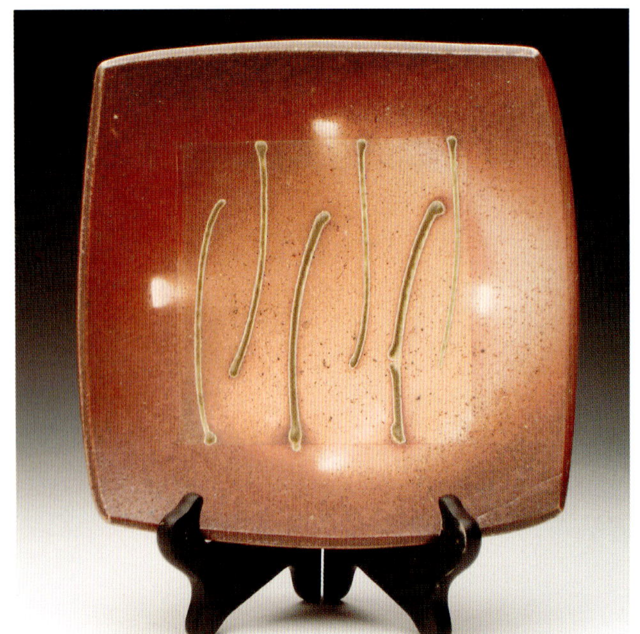

Bradley C. Birkhimer

Green Ash Series | 2007

2 X 9½ X 9½ INCHES (5.1 X 24.1 X 24.1 CM)

Slab-built white stoneware with thrown and altered foot; ash glazes, wood and soda fired, cone 10

PHOTO BY ARTIST

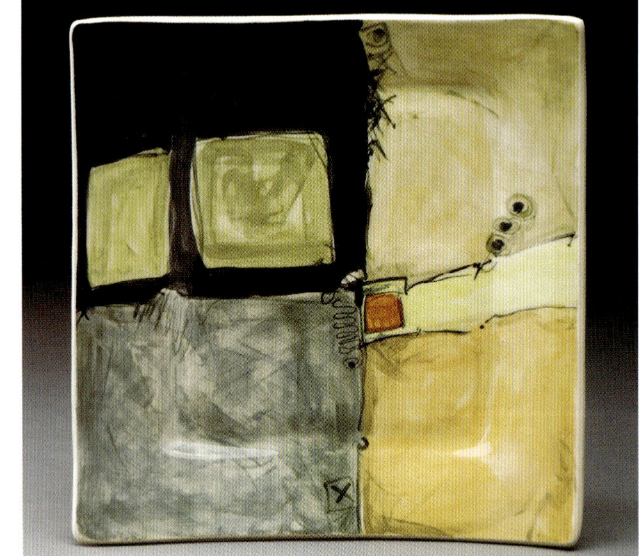

Susan Vey

Google Earth Plate | 2007

1½ X 8 X 8 INCHES (3.8 X 20.3 X 20.3 CM)

Hand-built white stoneware; underglaze painting, clear glaze; electric fired, cone 6

PHOTO BY RANDY SMITH

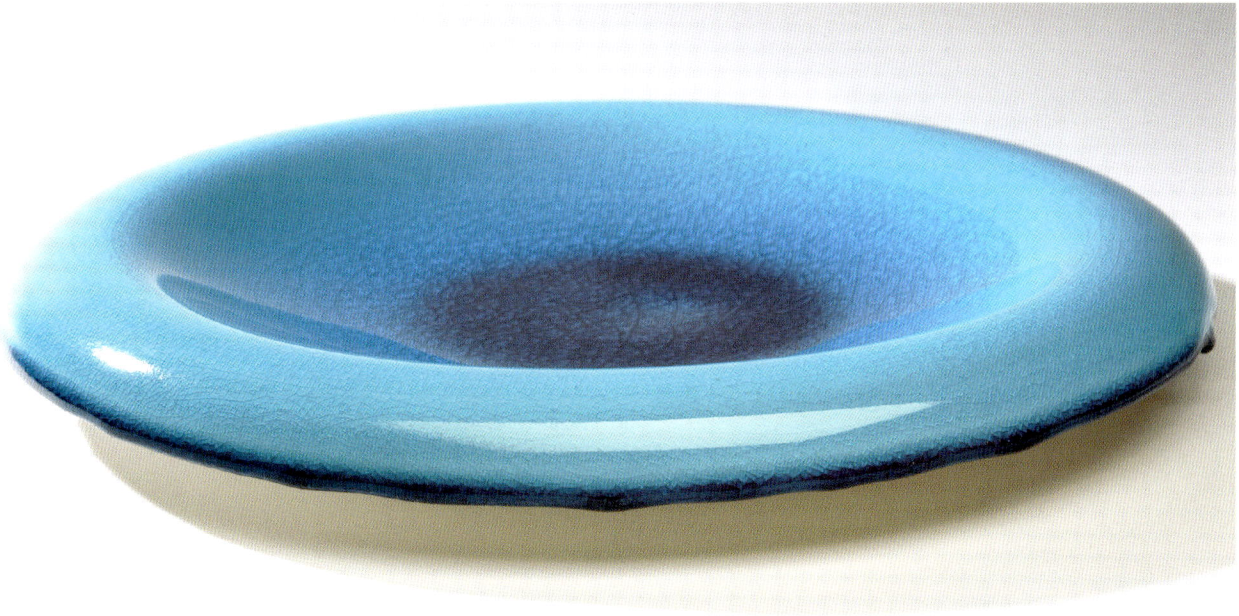

Peter Collis

Rolled Edged Platter | 2007

$17^{3}/_{4}$ INCHES (45 CM) IN DIAMETER

Wheel-thrown mid-fired stoneware; electric fired, bisque, cone 4; glaze, cone 03

PHOTOS BY SEAN MCCABE

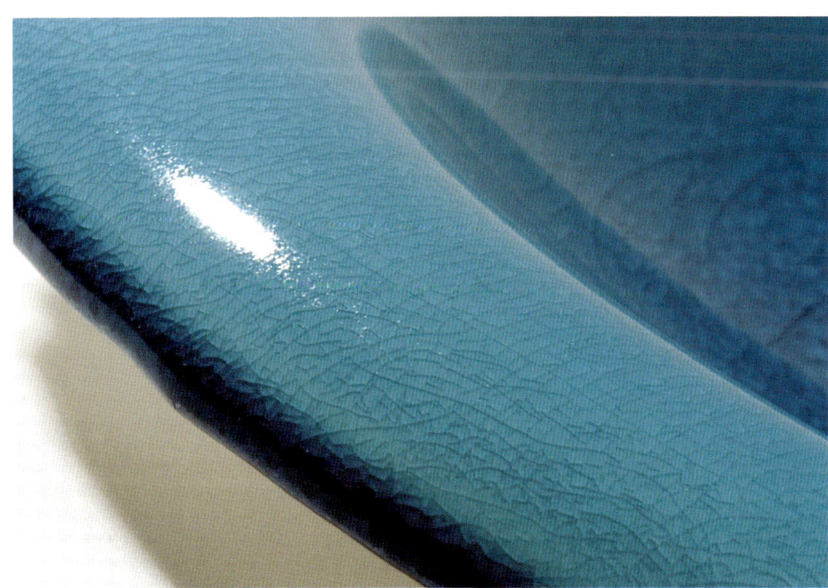

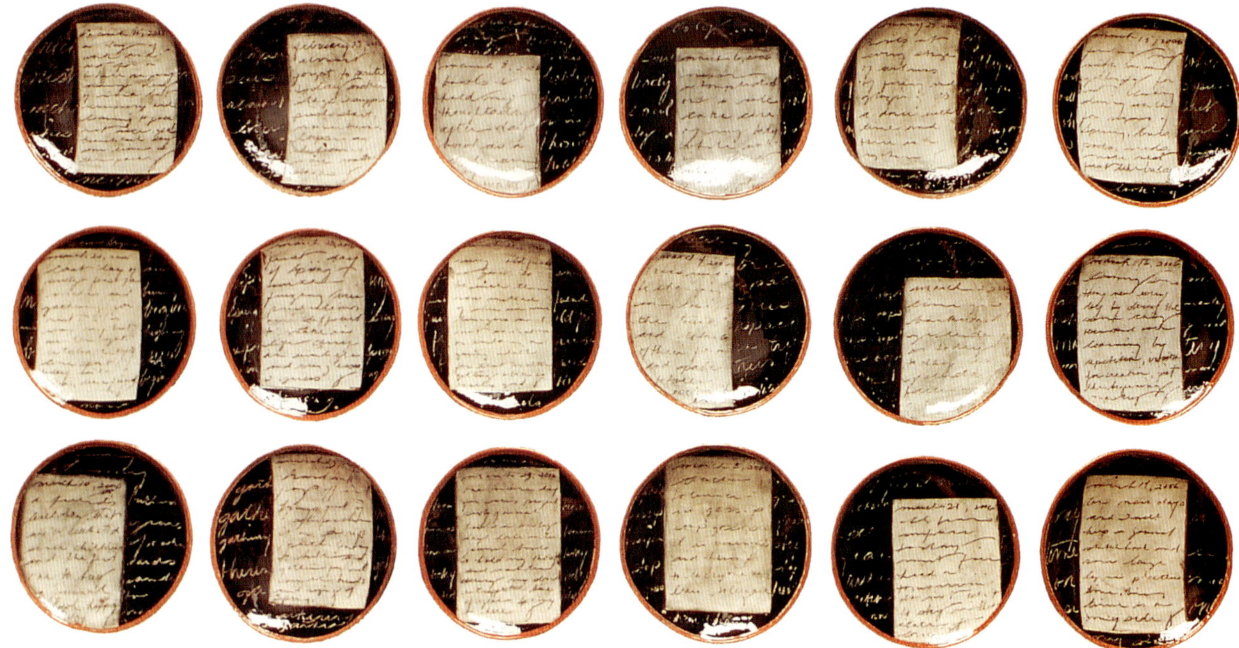

Jennifer Kincaid

Journal Bowls | 2006

EACH: 2 1/2 X 12 INCHES (6.4 X 30.5 CM)

Slab and extruded earthenware; sgraffito; electric fired, cone 06; wash and glaze, cone 04

PHOTO BY DAVID RAMSEY

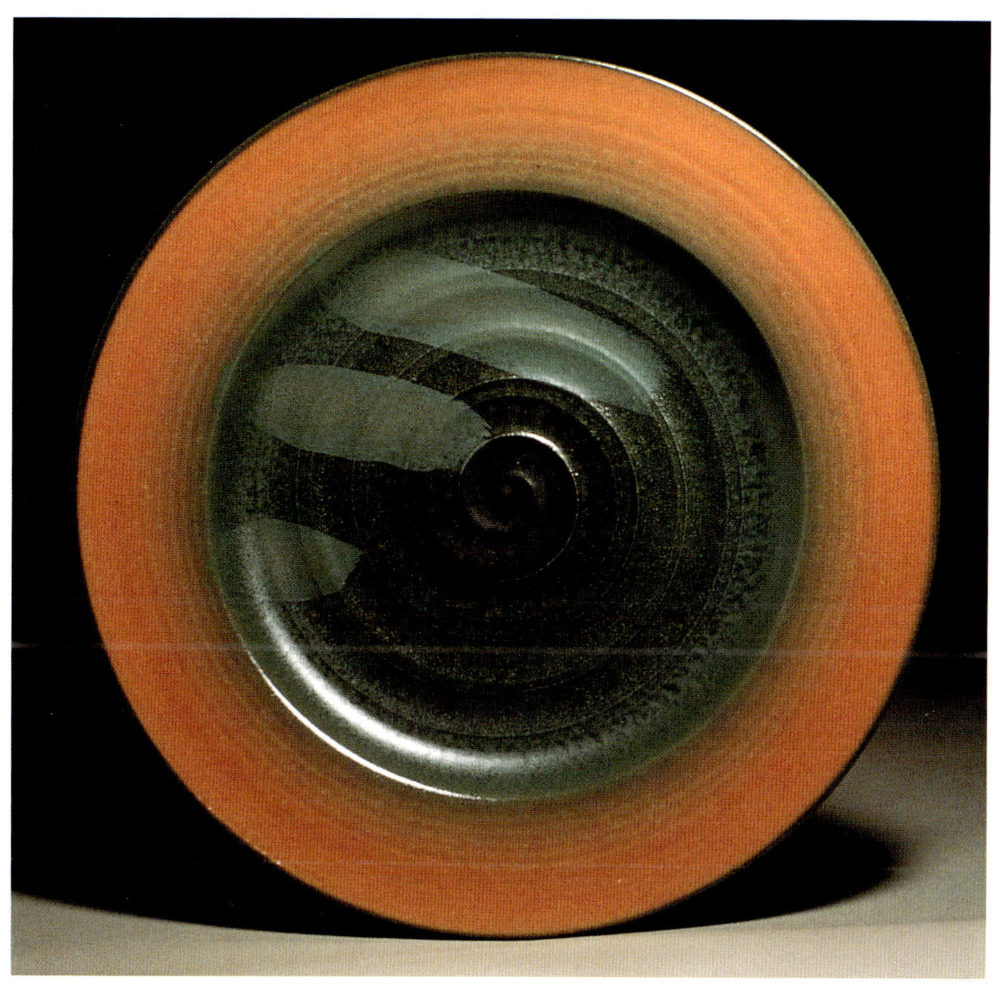

Cathryn Schroeder Hammond

Untitled | 1999

2 X 15 INCHES (5.1 X 38.1 CM)

Wheel-thrown stoneware; sprayed and brushed glazes, electric fired, cone 5

PHOTO BY ARTIST

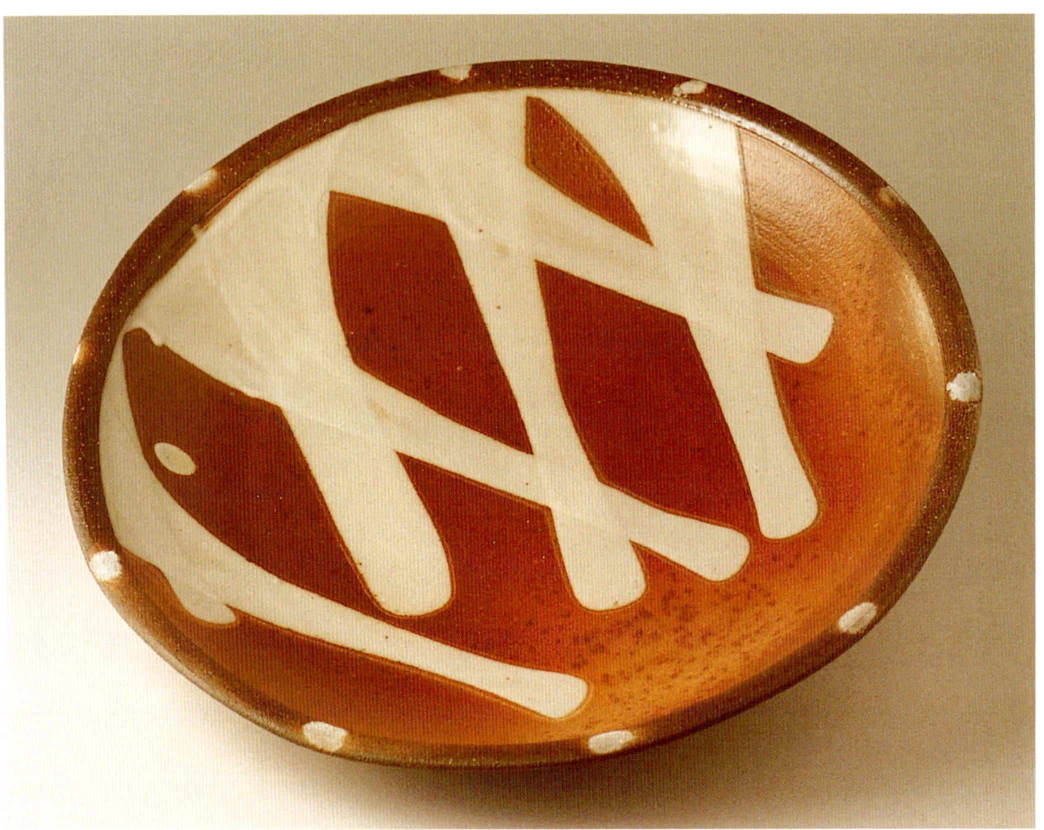

Alex Johnson

Spotlight Series: Serving Plate | 2006

5 X 18 X 18 INCHES (12.7 X 45.7 X 45.7 CM)

Thrown stoneware; kaolin slip and shino glaze; fired upside down over salt pack; wood fired, cone 10

PHOTO BY JEFF SAXMAN

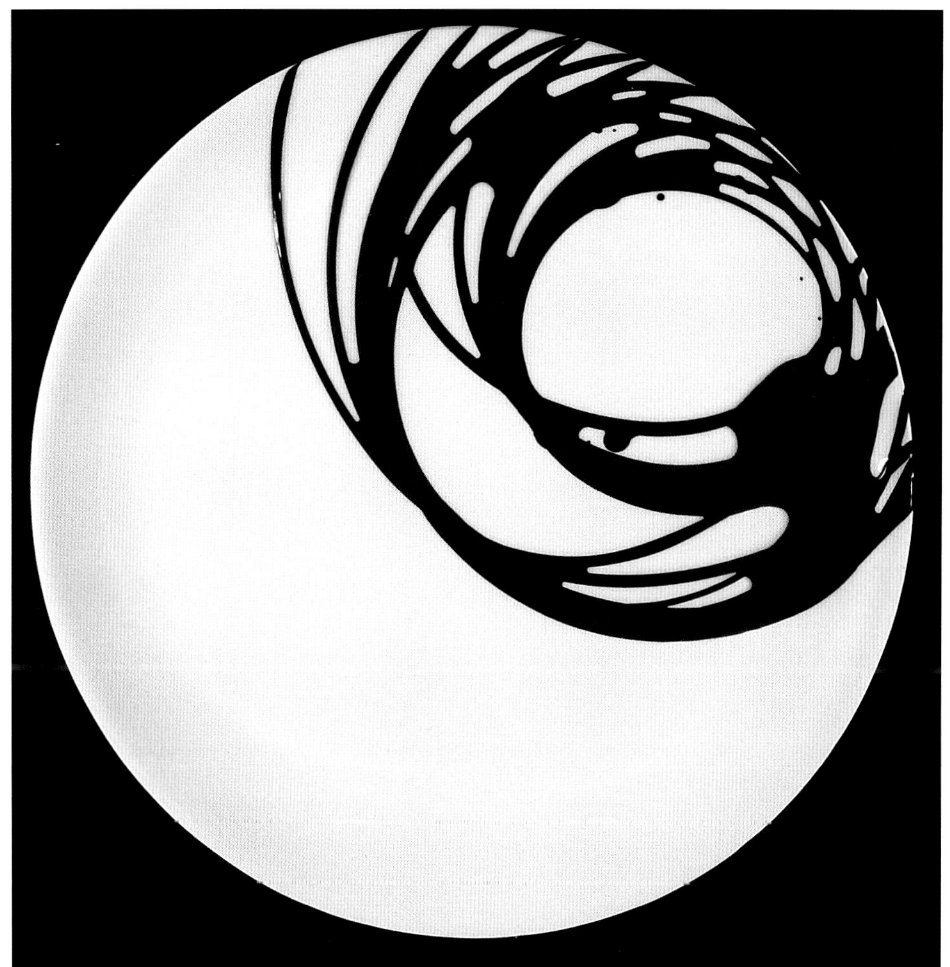

Suzanne Masterson

Taken from the Universal Tem-plate Series | 2007

1 X 11 INCHES (2.5 X 27.9 CM)

Porcelain-slipped earthenware; machine-Jolleyed plate, free-form slip-trailed; electric fired, cone 5; transparent glaze, cone 03

PHOTO BY ARTIST

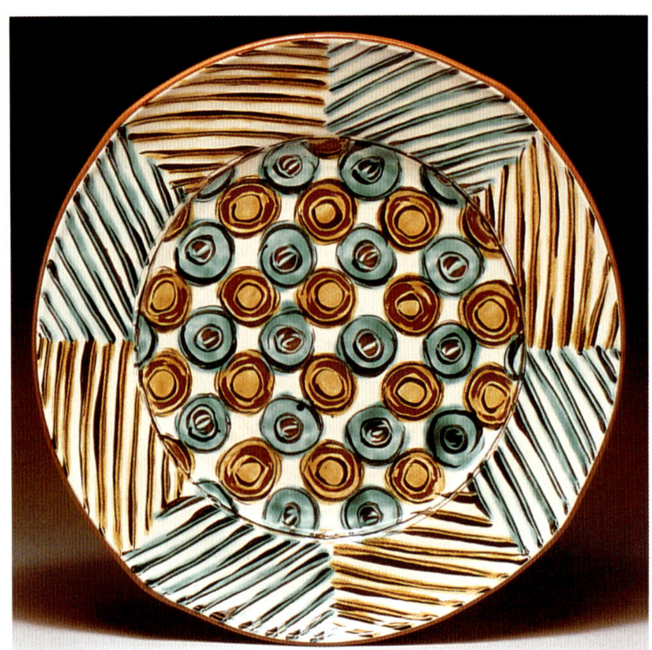

Laura MacLean

Untitled | 2004

3 X 16 INCHES (7.6 X 40.6 CM)

Wheel-thrown earthenware; slips and glazes; electric fired, cone 04

PHOTO BY ARTIST

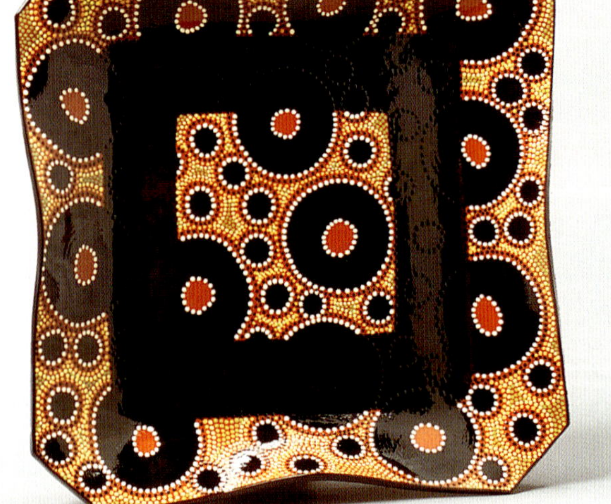

Michael Baines
Jeani Holder

Wavy inside-out floating donut square | 2006

4 X 17 X 17 INCHES (10.2 X 43.2 X 43.2 CM)

Slab-formed red earthenware; underglaze decoration; clear glaze, electric multi-fired, cone 04

PHOTO BY STEVE SMITH

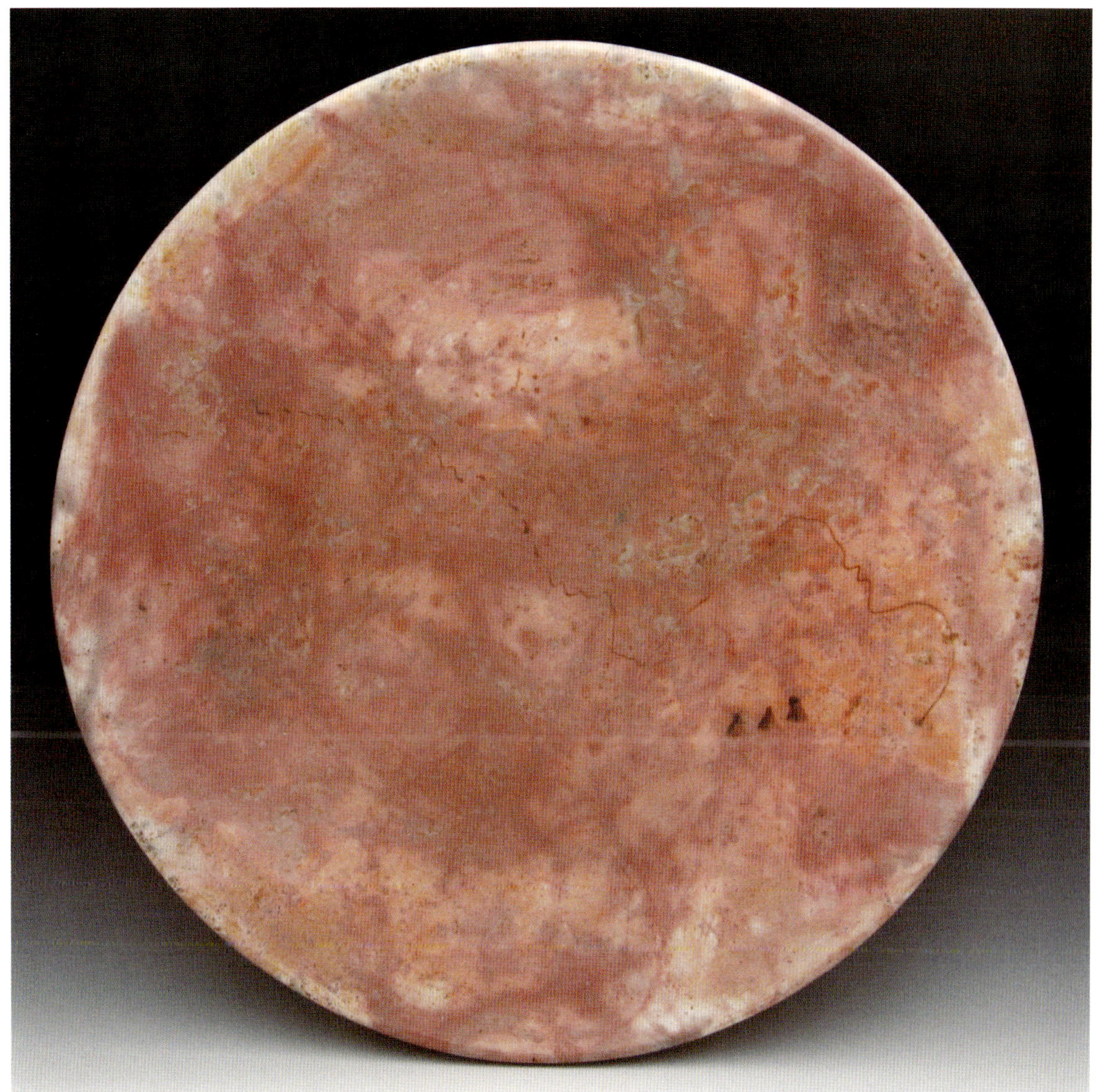

George Tomkins

Yuma Sunset #3 | 2006

3 X 22 INCHES (7.6 X 55.9 CM)

Slab built with thrown foot; bisque fired, cone 04; gas fired in heavy reduction with copper, iron, and salt, cone 010

PHOTO BY ARTIST

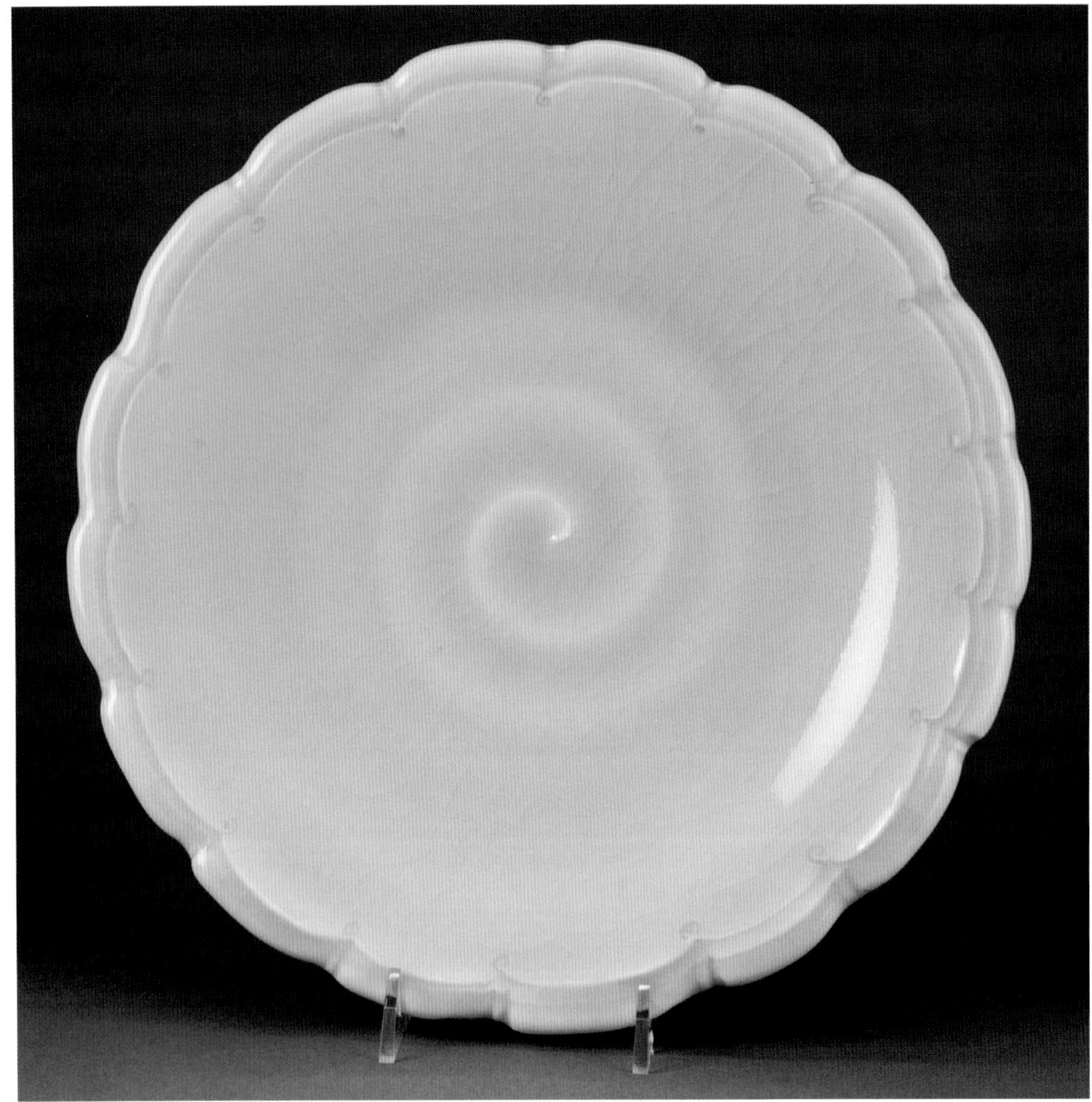

Catherine Boswell

Untitled | 2007

1 1/4 X 10 INCHES (3.2 X 25.4 CM)

Wheel-thrown porcelain; altered; celadon glaze, gas fired, cone 11

PHOTO BY JEFF WILLIAMS

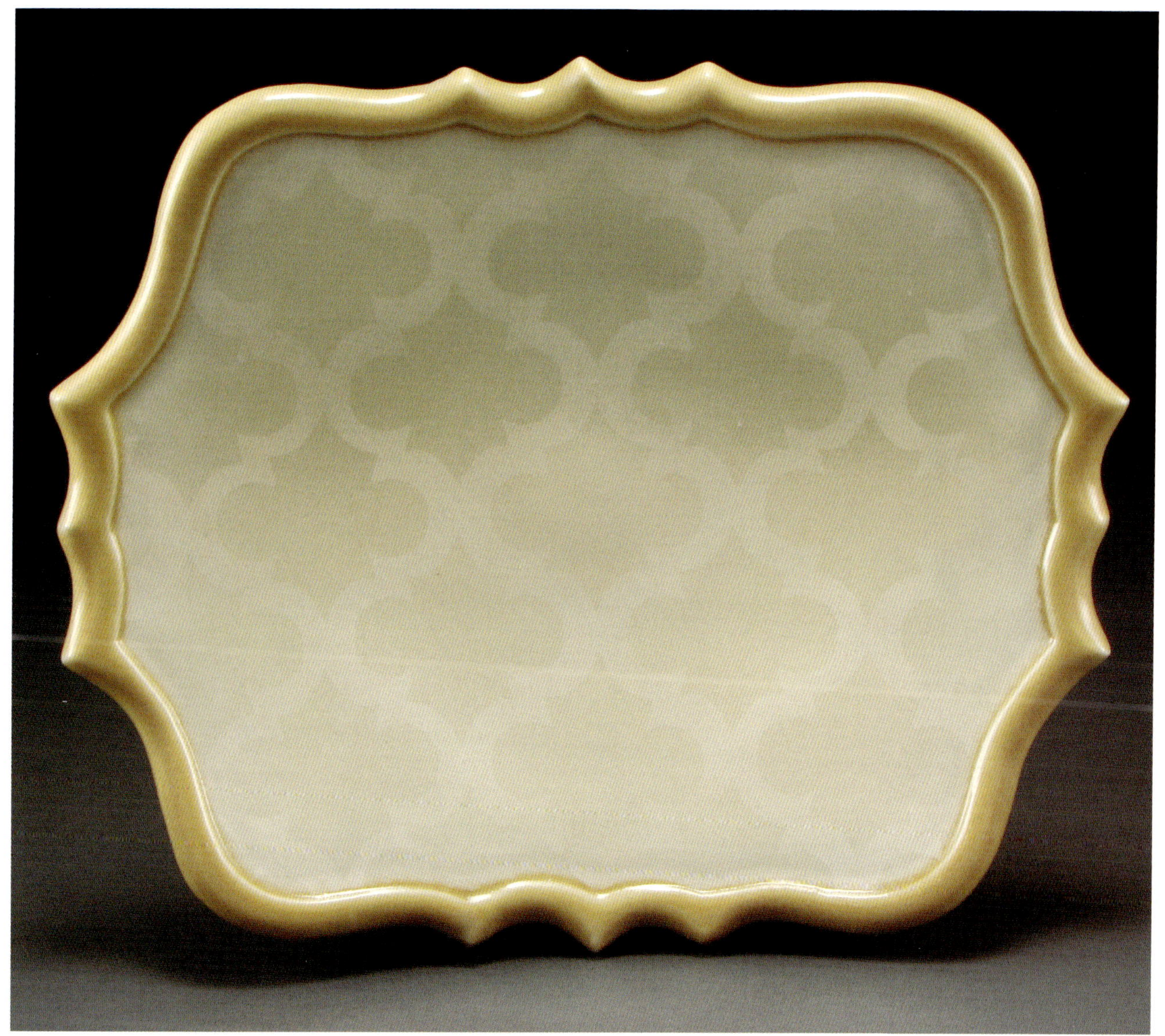

Alyssa Welch

Pattern Plate | 2007

2 X 10 X 12 INCHES (5 X 25.4 X 30.5 CM)

Wheel-thrown and altered porcelain; electric fired, cone 9

PHOTO BY ARTIST

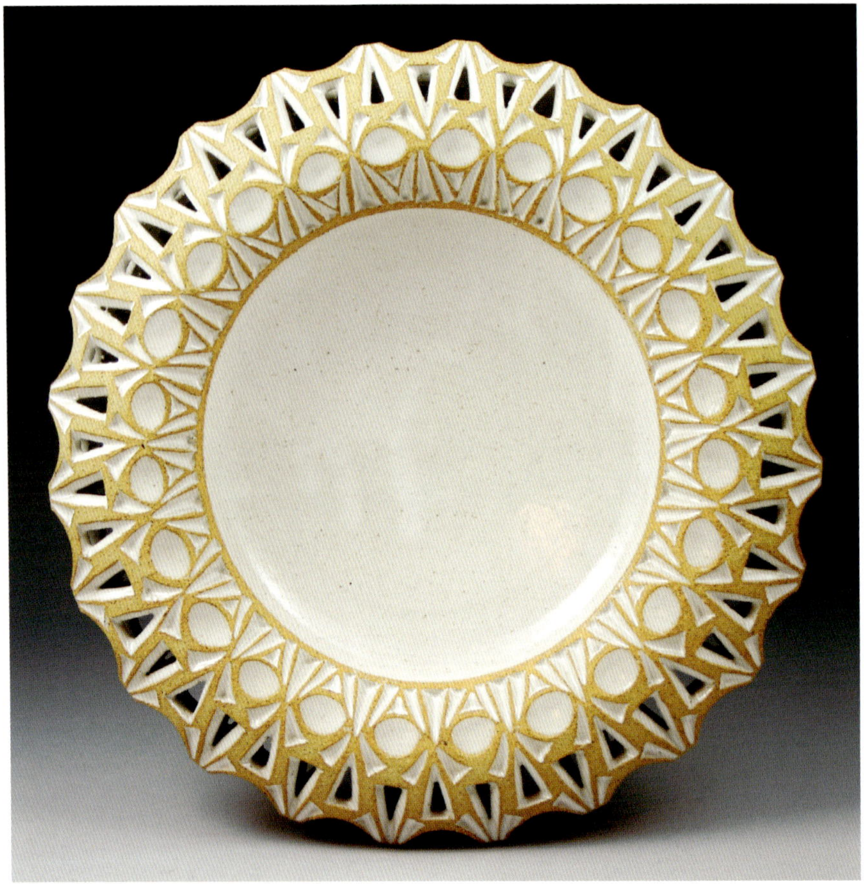

Itsuko Ishiguro

Double Wall Plate I | 2007

2 X 10 INCHES (5.1 X 25.4 CM)

Wheel-thrown stoneware; cut; electric fired, cone 6

PHOTOS BY ARTIST

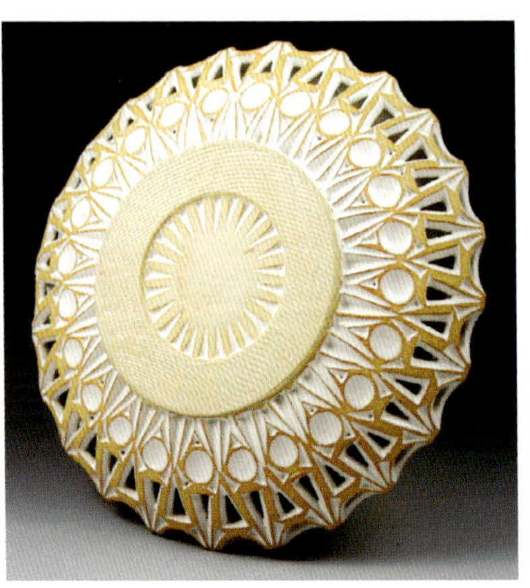

Kathryn Bowling

Petal Plate | 2007

$1\frac{1}{2}$ X 9 X 9 INCHES (3.8 X 22.9 X 22.9 CM)

Wheel-thrown and altered porcelain; engobes and clear glaze; reduction fired, cone 10

PHOTO BY WALKER MONTGOMERY

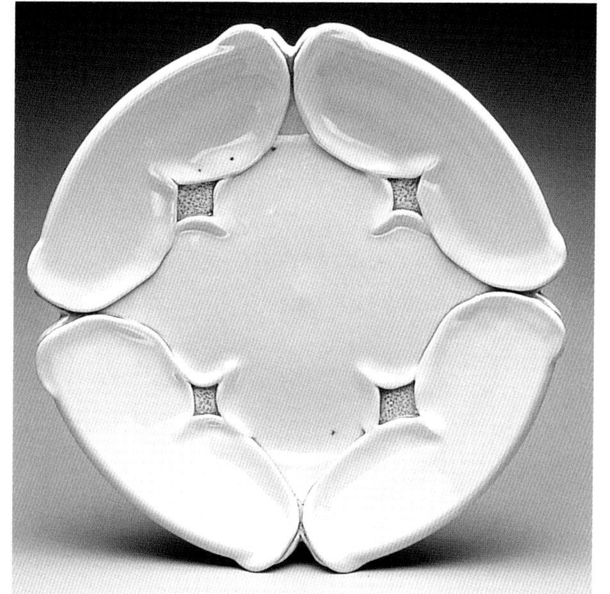

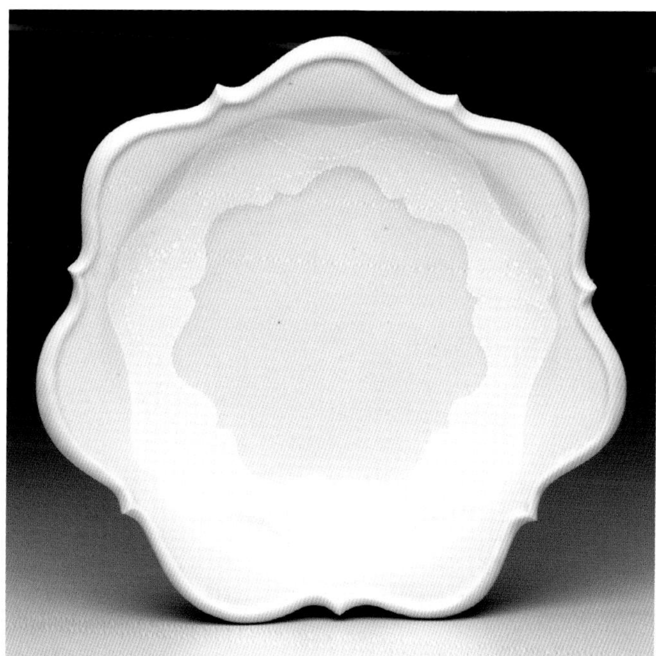

Blair Clemo

Plate | 2007

$1\frac{1}{2}$ X 10 INCHES (3.8 X 25.4 CM)

Wheel-thrown and altered porcelain; gas fired in reduction, cone 10

PHOTO BY PETER LEE

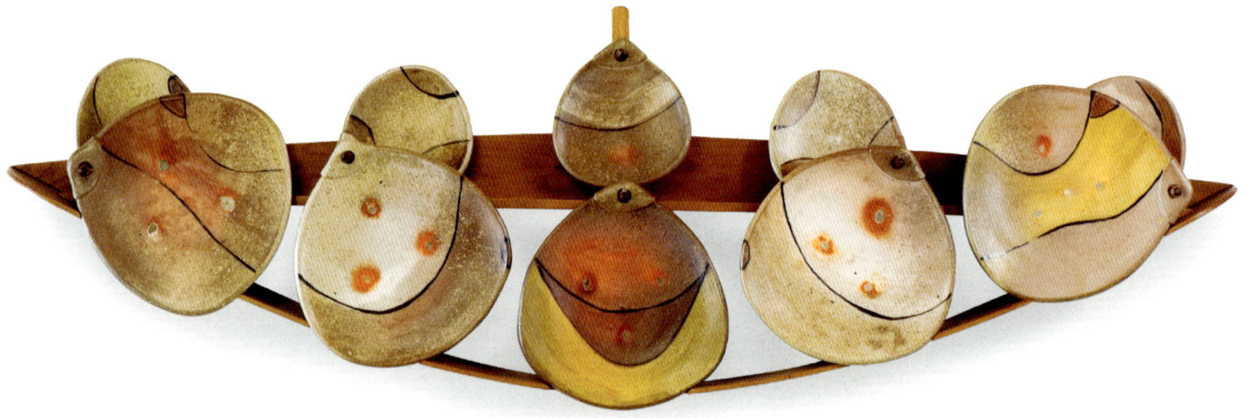

Seth Payne

Plate Set | 2006

OVERALL: 5 X 68 X 22 INCHES (12.7 X 172.7 X 55.9 CM)

Wheel-thrown stoneware; wood fired, cone 9; steam-bent cherry rack

PHOTO BY ARTIST

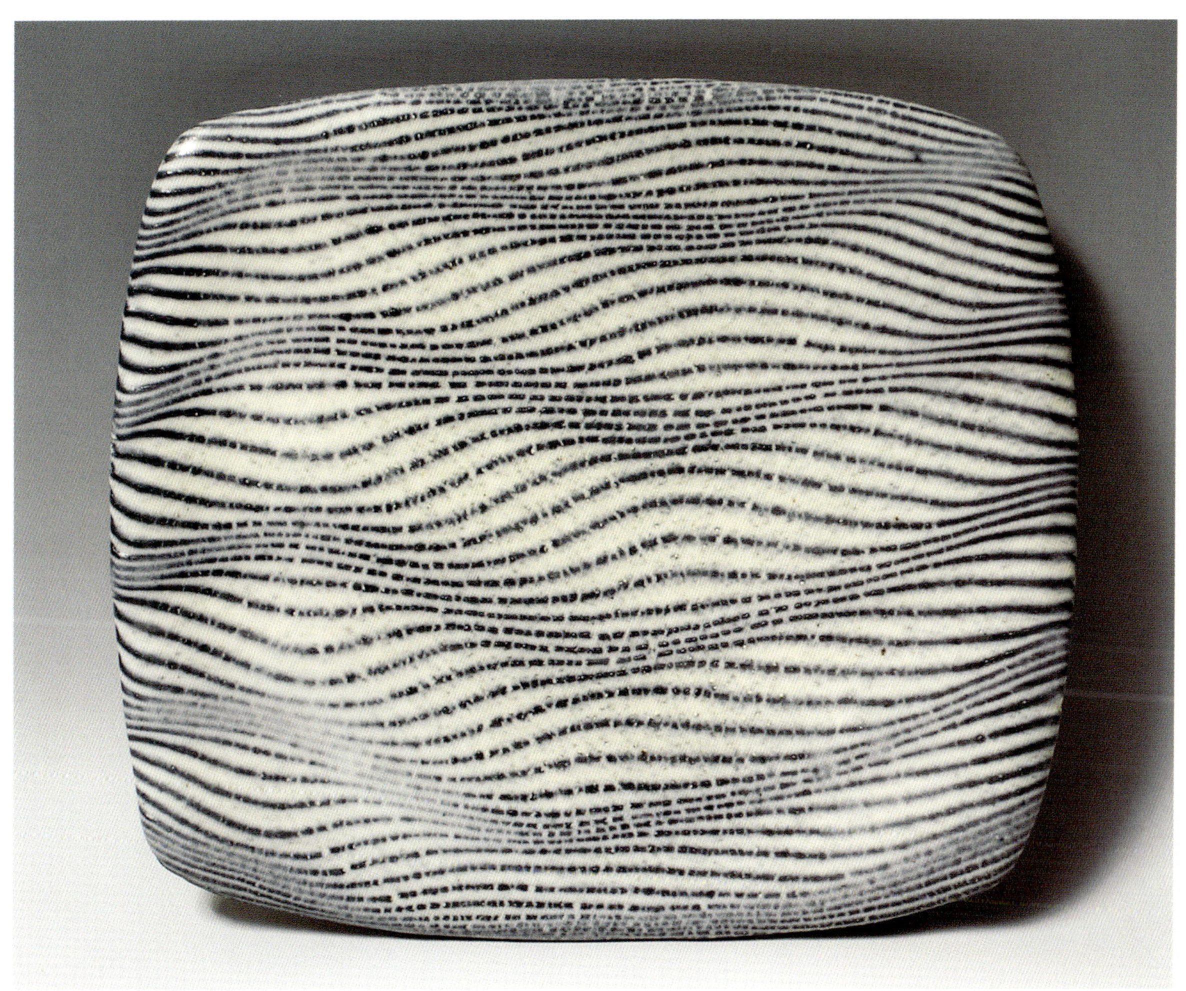

Enno Jaekel

Wave | 2007

1 1/2 X 14 X 10 INCHES (3.8 X 35.6 X 25.4 CM)

Hand-built stoneware; incised and stained; glaze, electric fired, cone 6

PHOTO BY ARTIST

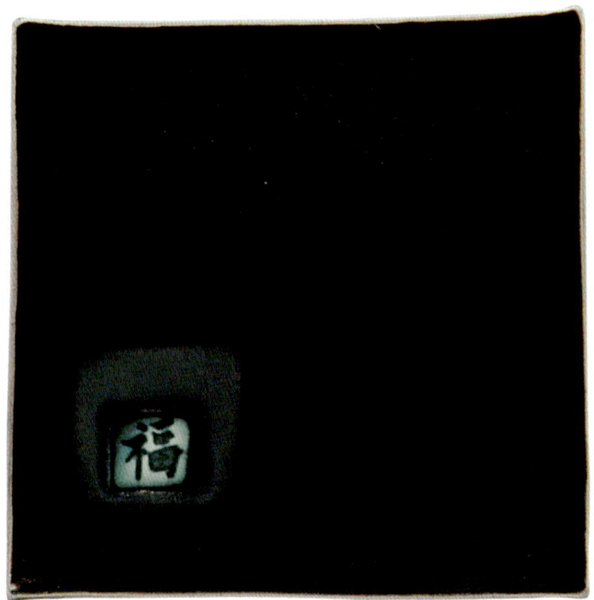

Christine Shadic

Happiness | 2006

1/4 X 7 3/4 X 7 3/4 INCHES (0.6 X 19.7 X 19.7 CM)

Slab-built and stamped stoneware; glossy black glaze; sprayed detail; electric fired, cone 8

PHOTO BY JENNIFER FRANKEL

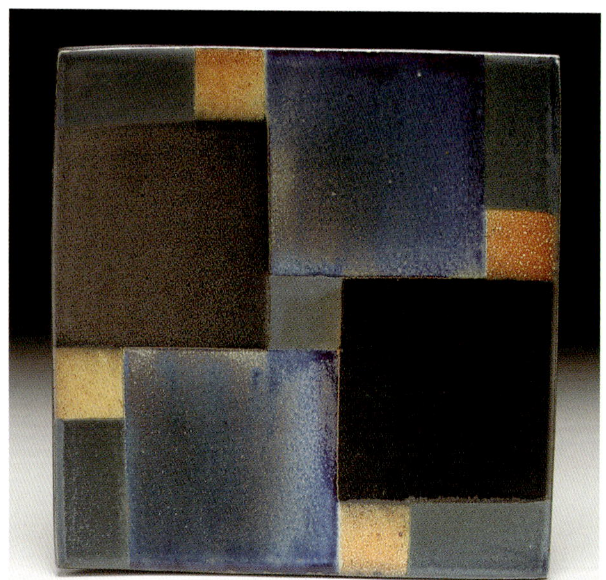

David Crane

Color Block Platter | 2005

14 X 14 INCHES (35.6 X 35.6 CM)

Slab-built stoneware; salt fired

PHOTO BY TIM BARNWELL

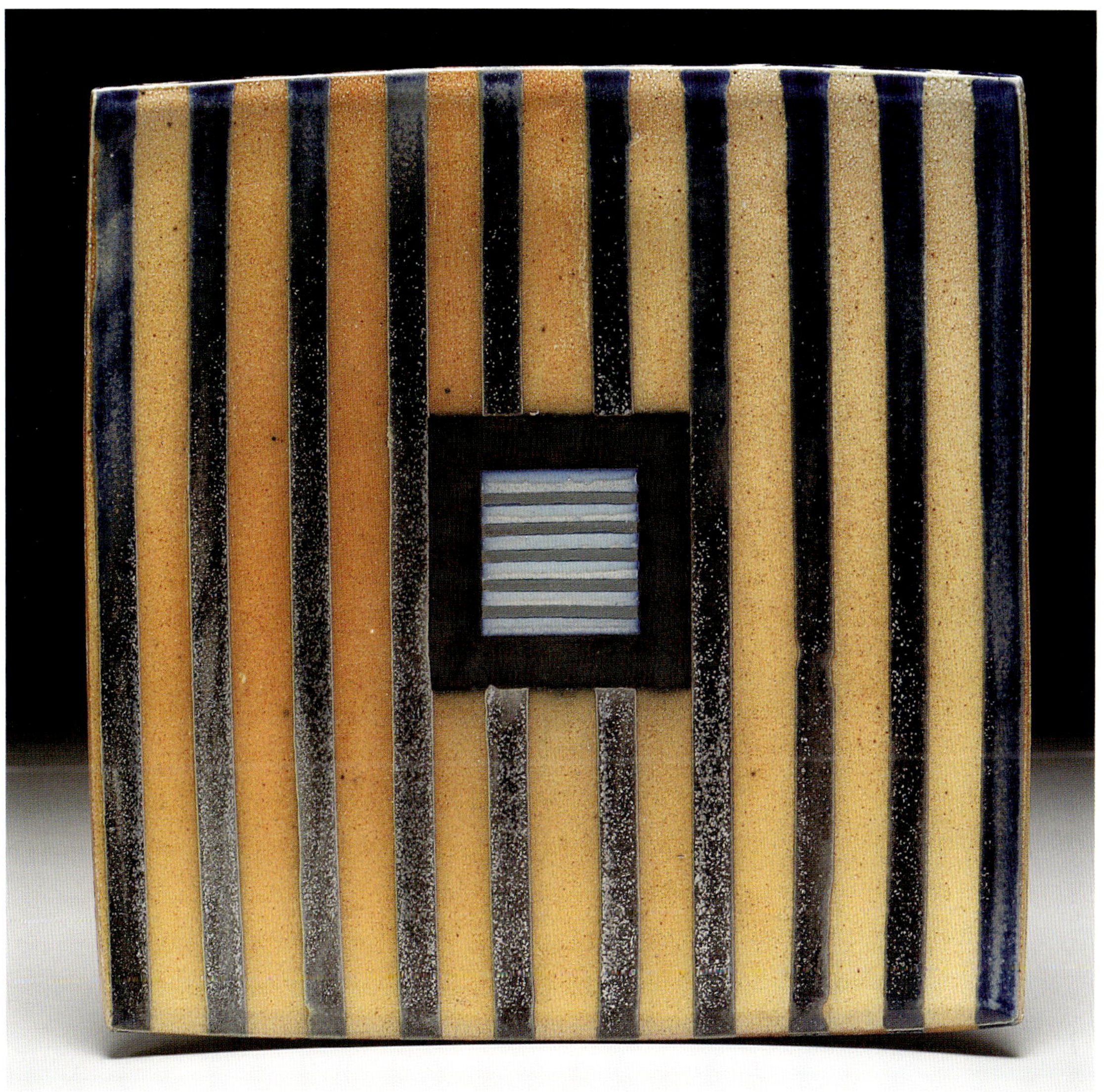

David Crane

Chief Platter—Blue & Black | 2006

2 X 16 X 16 INCHES (5.1 X 40.6 X 40.6 CM)

Slab-built stoneware; high-temp salt fired

PHOTO BY TIM BARNWELL

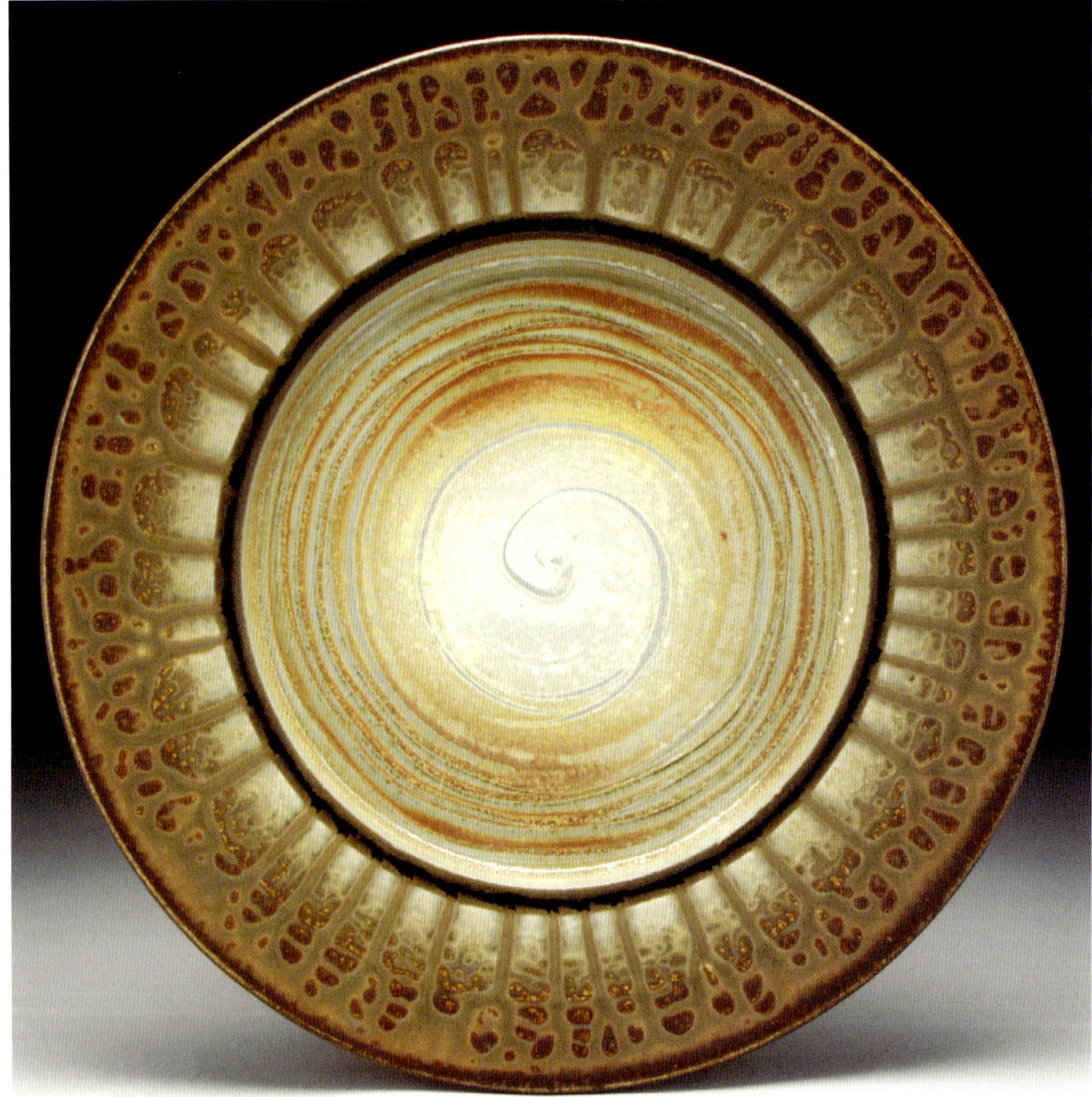

Jed Schlegel

Platter | 2007

1 1/2 X 14 INCHES (3.8 X 35.6 CM)

Wheel-thrown porcelain; ash glaze, matte crystalline glaze with oxide; gas fired in reduction, cone 10

PHOTO BY ARTIST

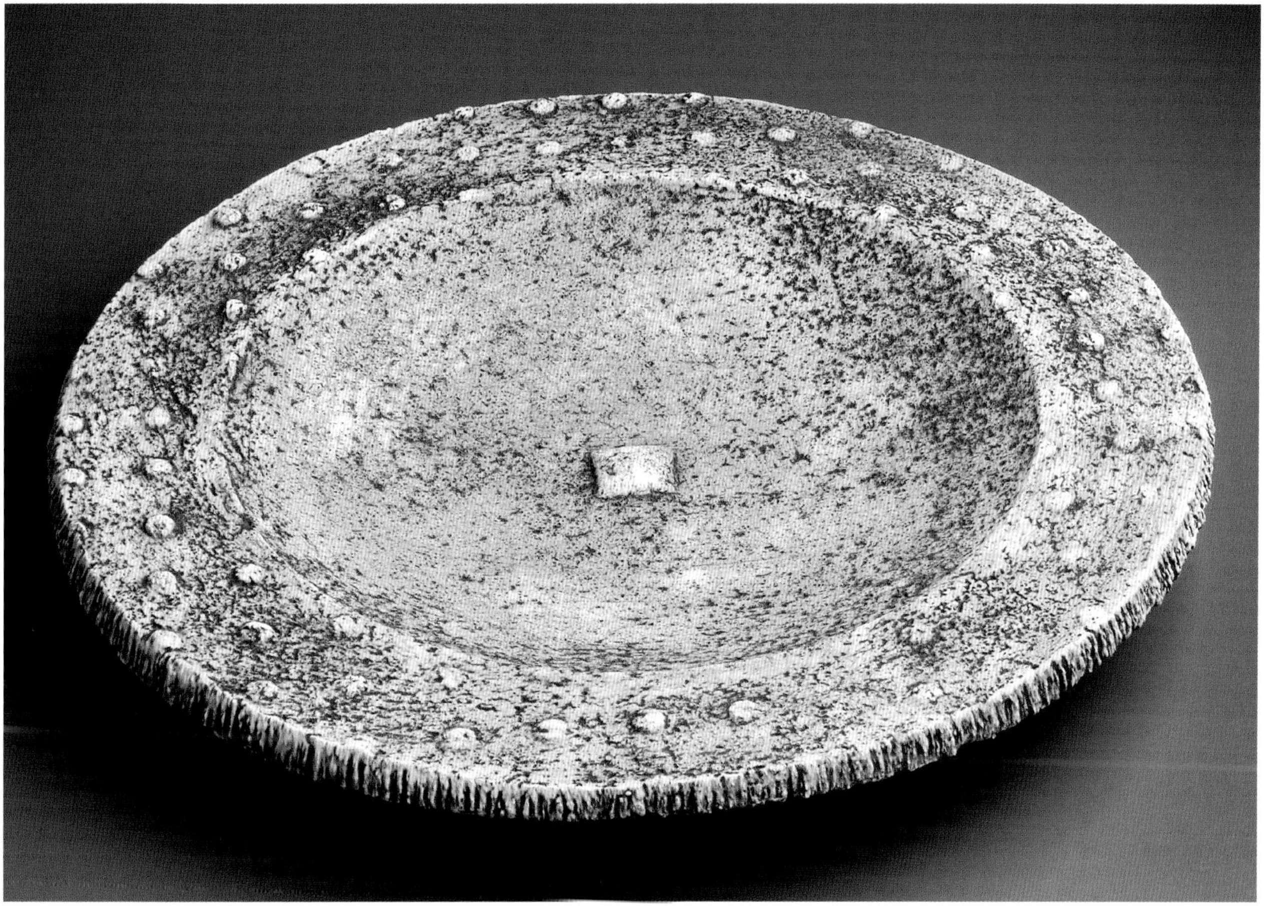

John Stewart

Plough Platter | 2003

4 X 24 INCHES (10.2 X 61 CM)

Cast and modeled white earthenware and perlite; slip and oxide; unglazed; electric fired, cone 1

PHOTOS BY DAVID YOUNG

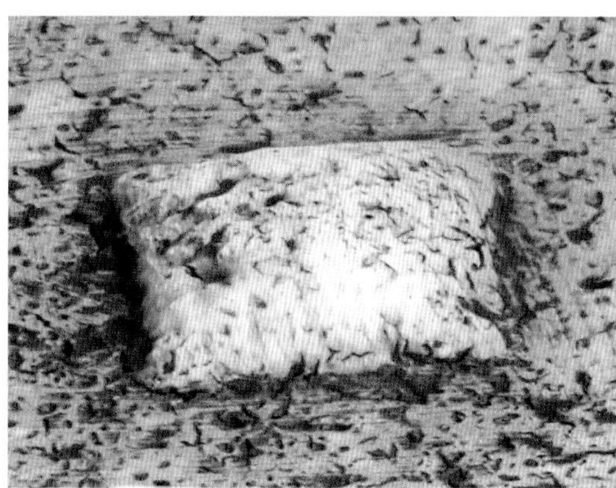

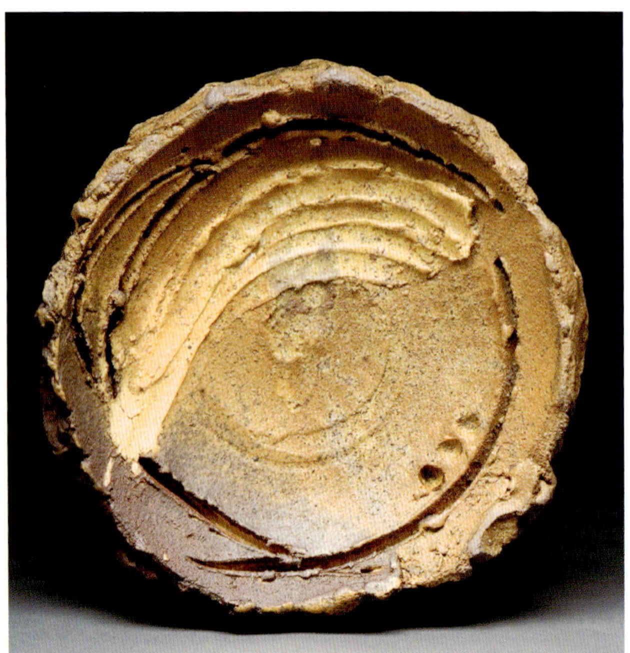

Broc Allen

Koka | 2007

3 X 14 X 13 1/2 INCHES (7.6 X 35.6 X 34.3 CM)

Wheel-thrown high-fire stoneware; anagama fired, cone 10

PHOTO BY DAN SWANSON

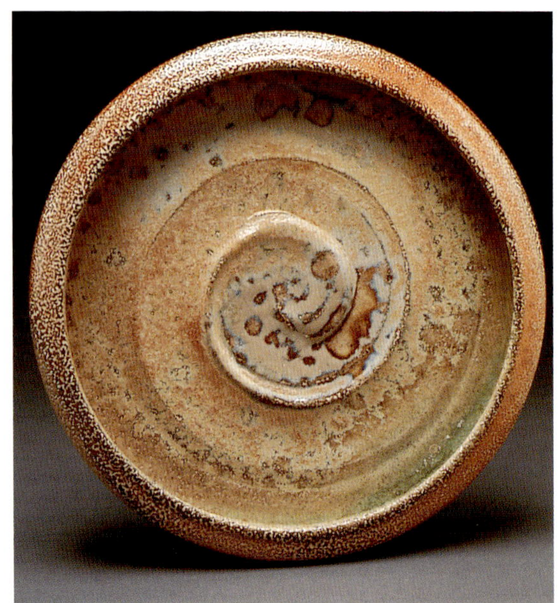

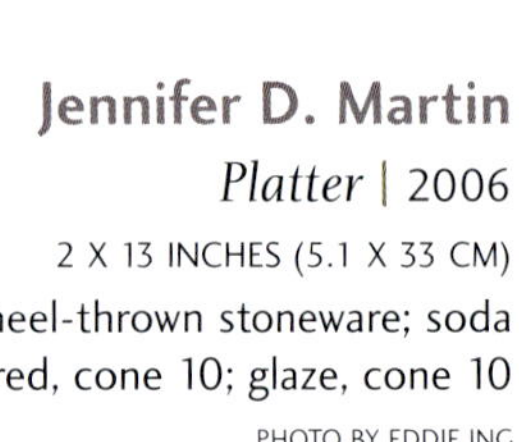

Jennifer D. Martin

Platter | 2006

2 X 13 INCHES (5.1 X 33 CM)

Wheel-thrown stoneware; soda fired, cone 10; glaze, cone 10

PHOTO BY EDDIE ING

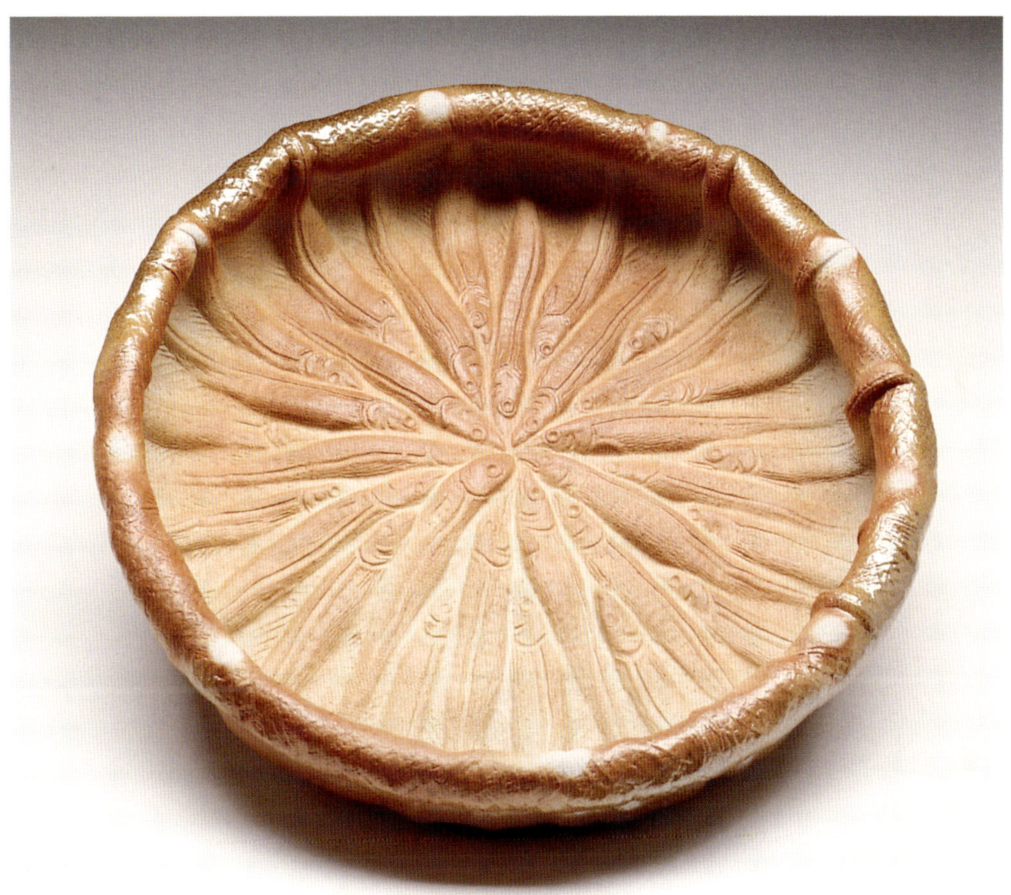

David Hayashida
Linda Yates
Nicky's Nose Cove Caplien Platter | 2007
3 X 13 X 13 INCHES (7.6 X 33 X 33 CM)
Hand-built white stoneware; slabs pressed into bisque mold; salt and soda fired, cone 10, crash cooled
PHOTO BY NED PRATT

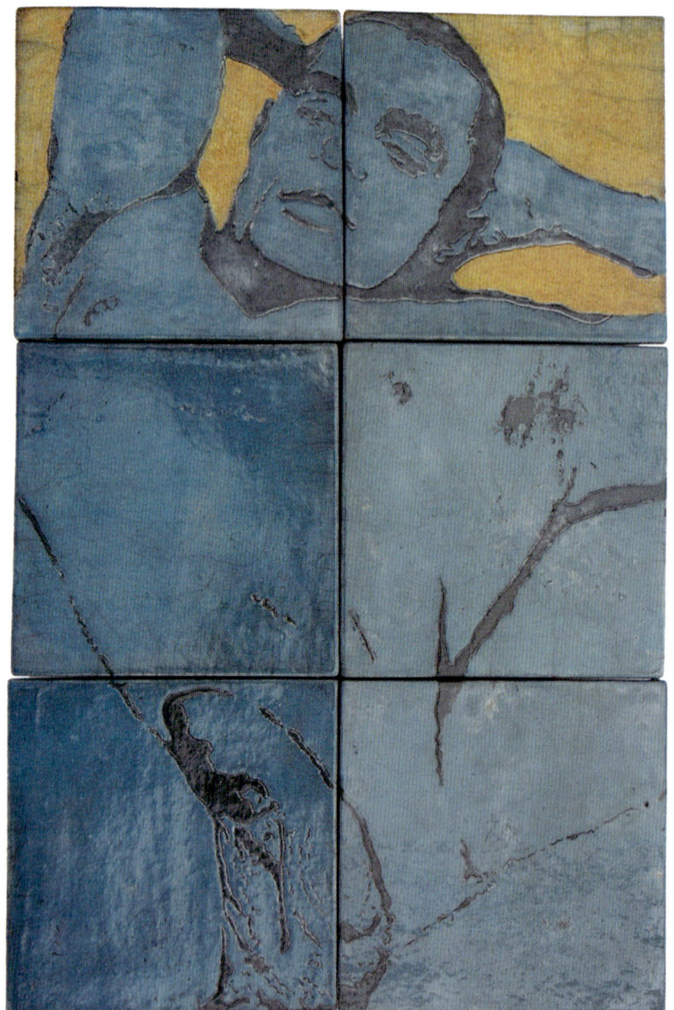

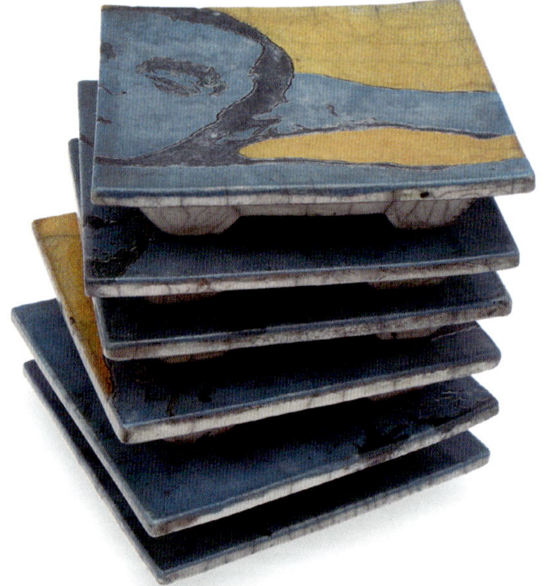

Douglas E. Gray

Blue and Yellow Beef Cake Plate Set | 2007

EACH: 1 X 6 X 6 INCHES (2.5 X 15.2 X 15.2 CM)

Stoneware; water-based image transfer; sgraffito; underglaze; raku fired

PHOTOS BY ARTIST

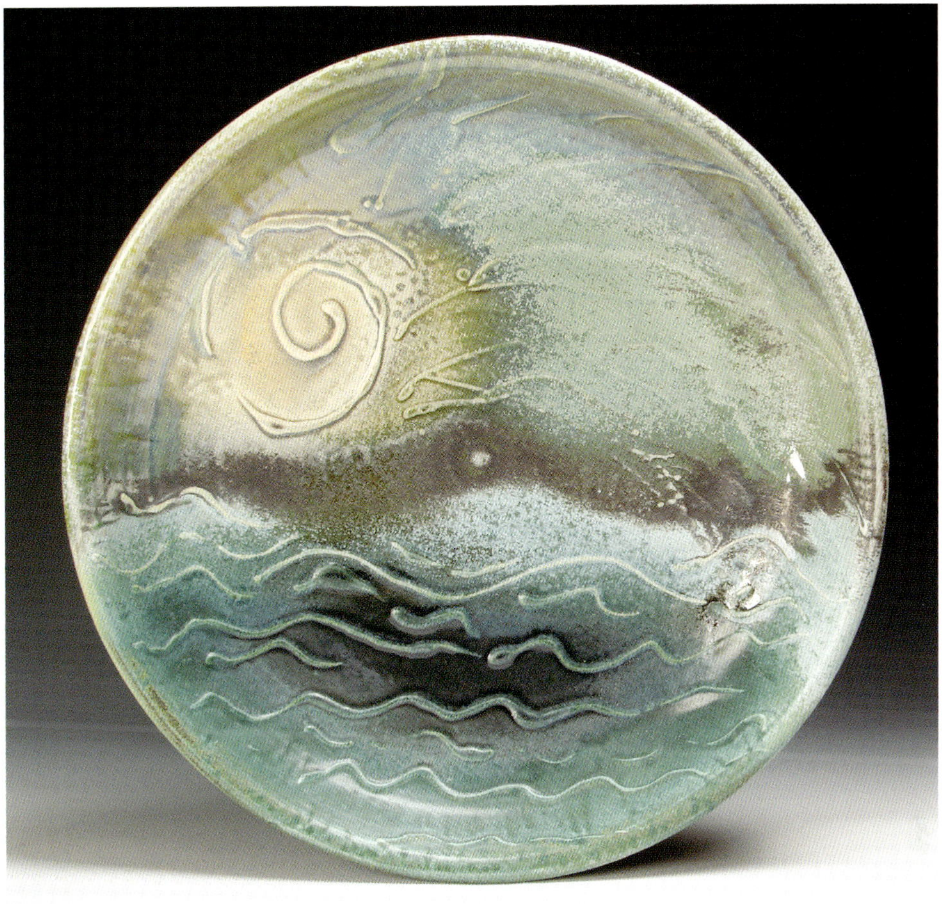

Yasmine Redding

Ocean Sunset Platter | 2006

3 X 16½ INCHES (7.6 X 41.9 CM)

Wheel-thrown stoneware; slip, sprayed glazes; gas fired in reduction, cone 10

PHOTOS BY ARTIST

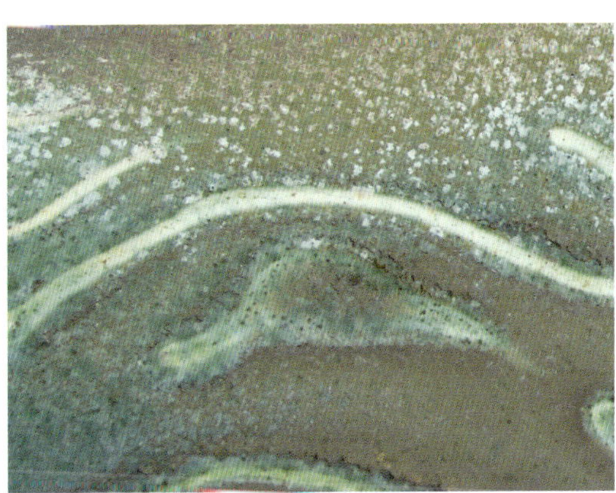

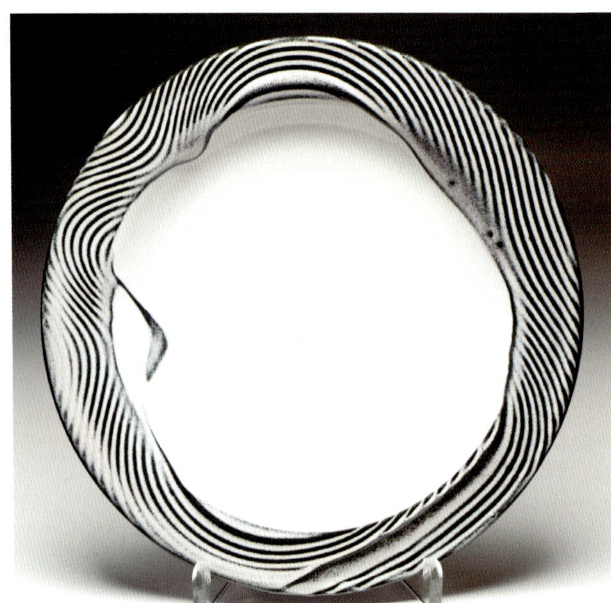

David Beumée

Untitled | 2005

$1\frac{1}{2}$ X 11 INCHES (3.8 X 27.9 CM)

Wheel-thrown porcelain; reduction fired, cone 10

PHOTO BY CHARLIE ROY

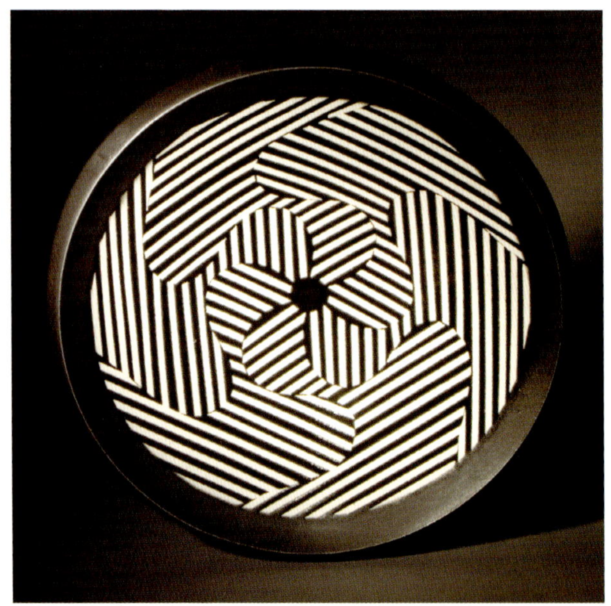

Frank Gaydos

Terra-Cotta Platter | 2007

4 X 20 INCHES (10.2 X 50.8 CM)

Hump-molded terra cotta with thrown rim and foot; electric fired, cone 04, with tape-resist design; black glaze over white slip

PHOTO BY ART DANEK

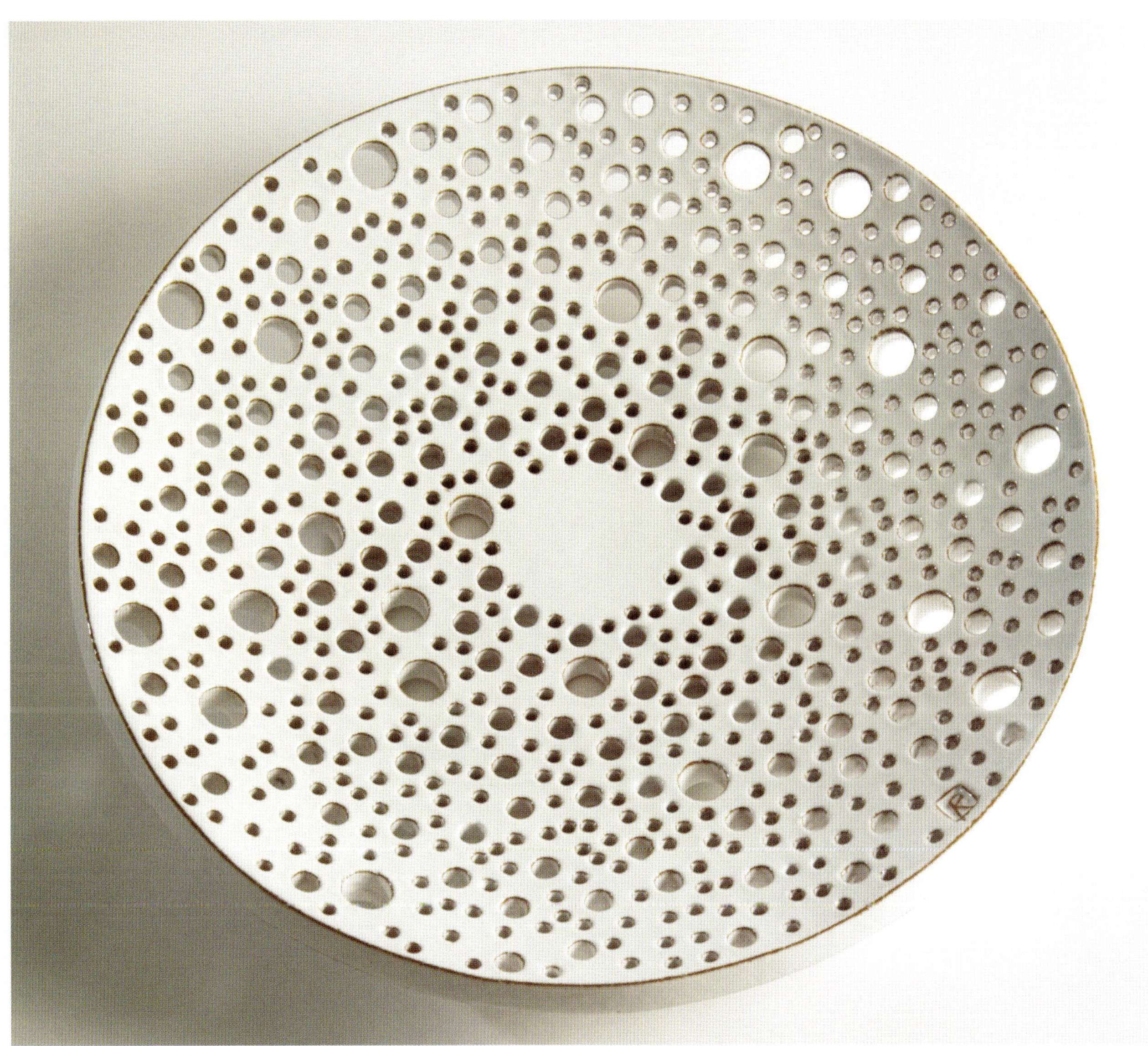

Rūta Šipalytė

Snowing II | 2004

4 X 20 INCHES (10.2 X 50.8 CM)

Hand-built brown clay; electric fired; glazes, cone 05

PHOTO BY SAULIUS PAUKSTYS

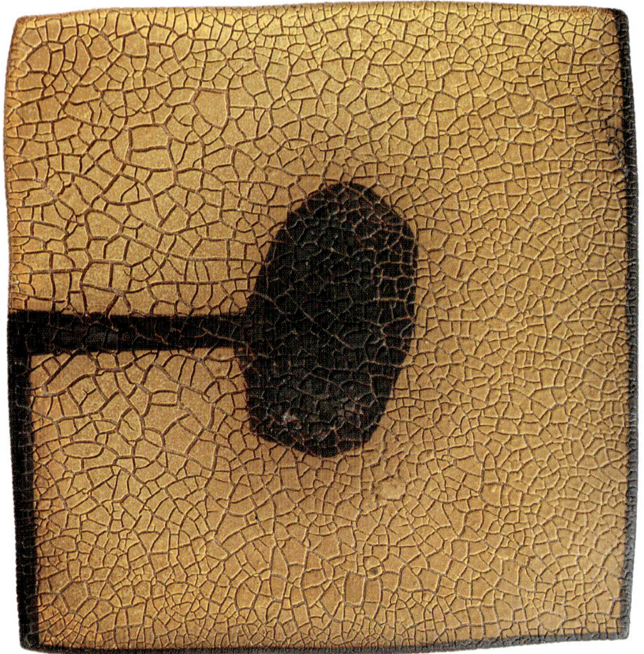

Ruth Krauskopf

Untitled | 2007

13 X 13 INCHES (33 X 33 CM)

Wheel-thrown stoneware; gas fired in reduction, cone 10

PHOTO BY ALVARO MARDONES

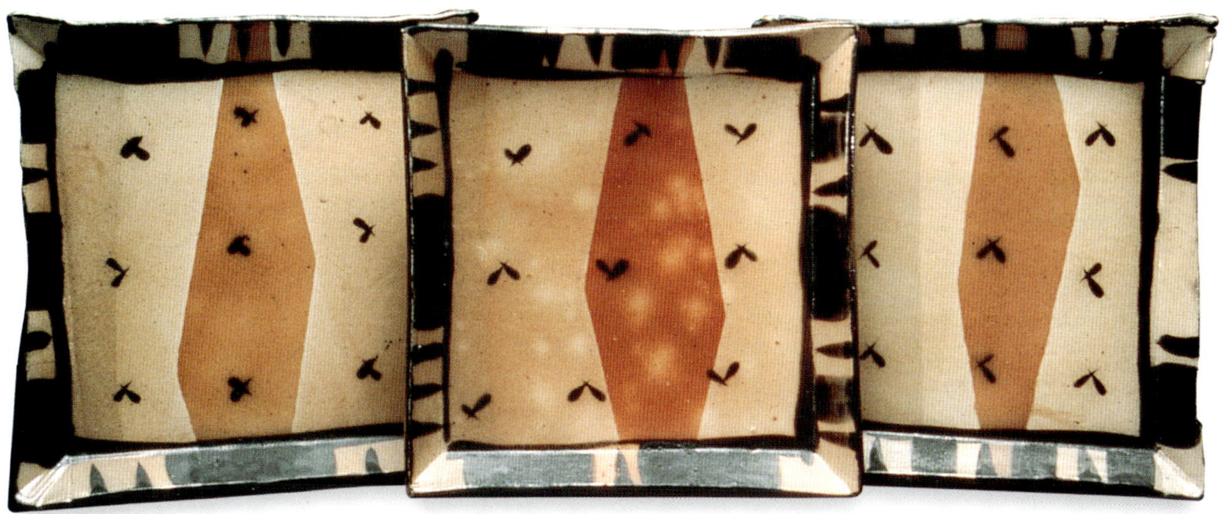

Terry Gess

Three Square Plates | 2000

EACH: 1 X 9 X 9 INCHES (2.5 X 22.9 X 22.9 CM)

Hand-built white stoneware; reduction fired, cone 10; multiple porcelain slips and glaze, salted

PHOTO BY ARTIST

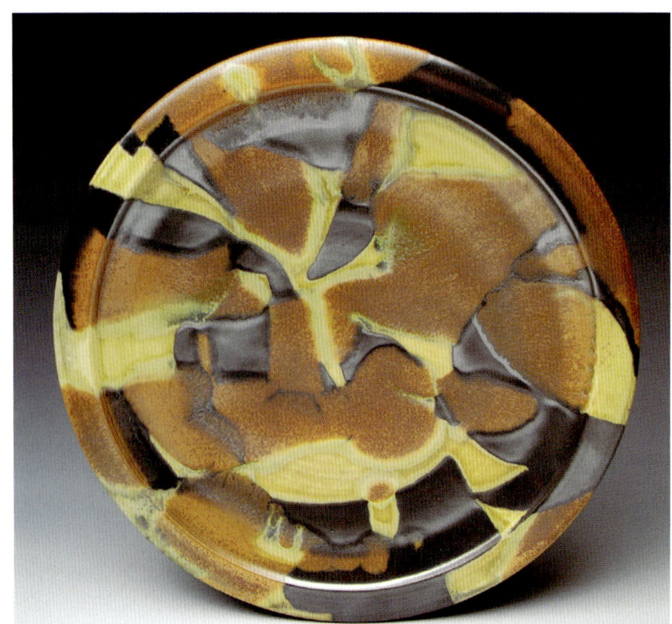

Jake Johnson

Untitled | 2007

2 X 16 INCHES (5.1 X 40.6 CM)

Wheel-thrown stoneware; tape and wax resist; multiple glazes, salt fired, cone 10

PHOTO BY ARTIST

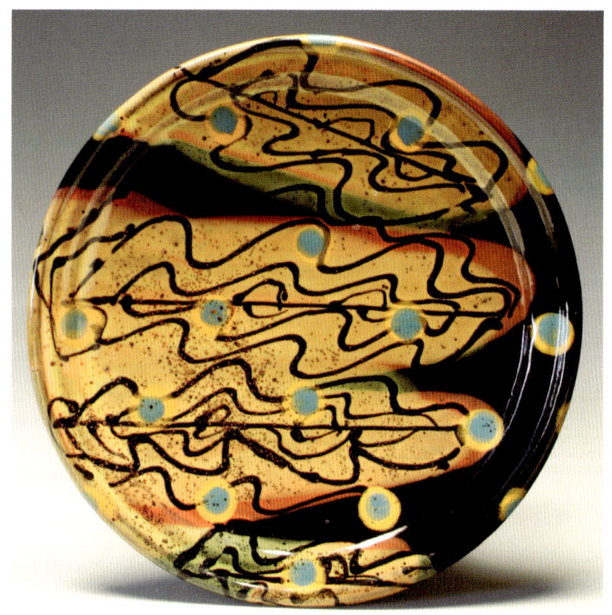

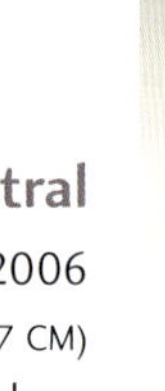

James D. Watral

Untitled | 2006

$1\frac{1}{2}$ X $10\frac{1}{2}$ INCHES (3.8 X 26.7 CM)

Hand-built earthenware; glaze, electric fired, cone 03

PHOTO BY JOHN O. LEWIS

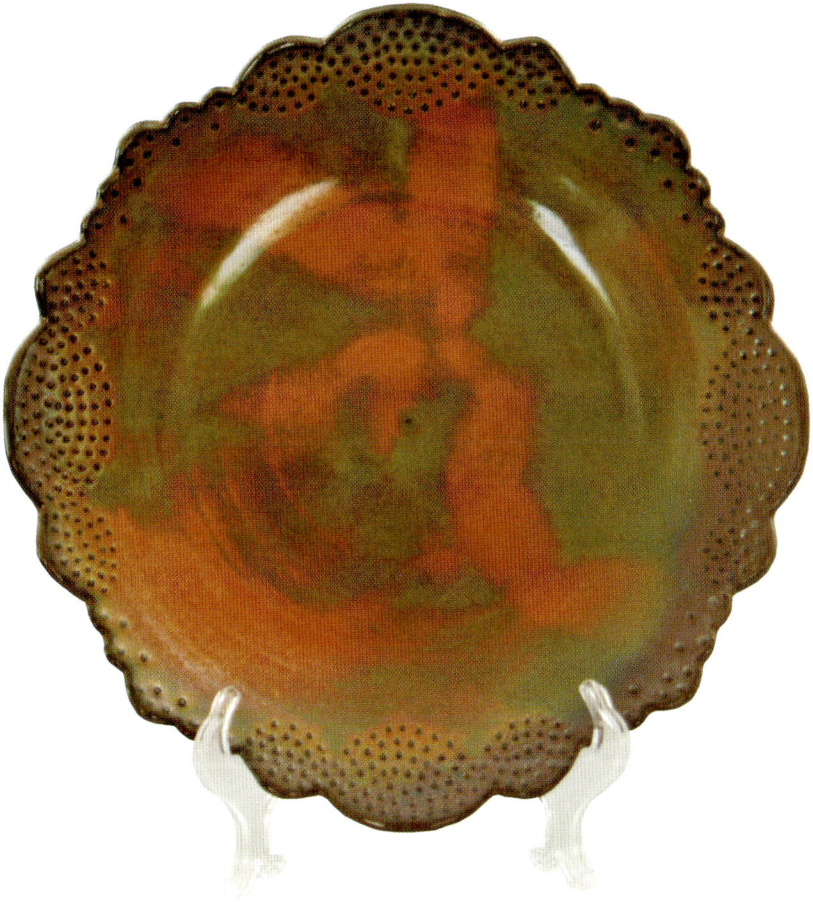

Althea Vail

Scallop-Edged Serving Dish | 2007

$1\frac{1}{2}$ X $12\frac{1}{2}$ INCHES (3.8 X 31.8 CM)

Wheel-thrown and altered stoneware; slip accents; iron red glaze; electric fired, cone 6

PHOTOS BY ALTHEA VAIL

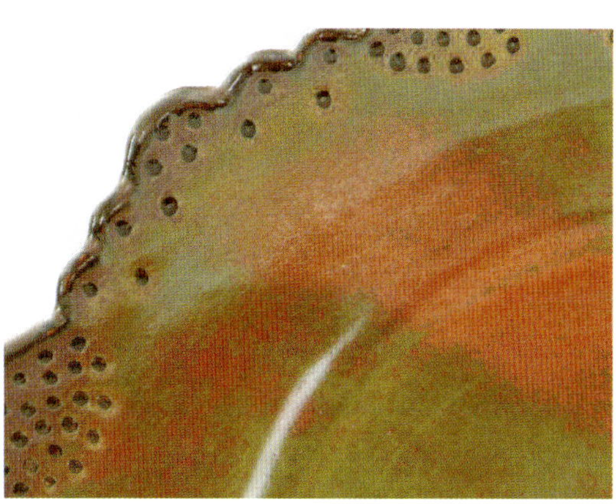

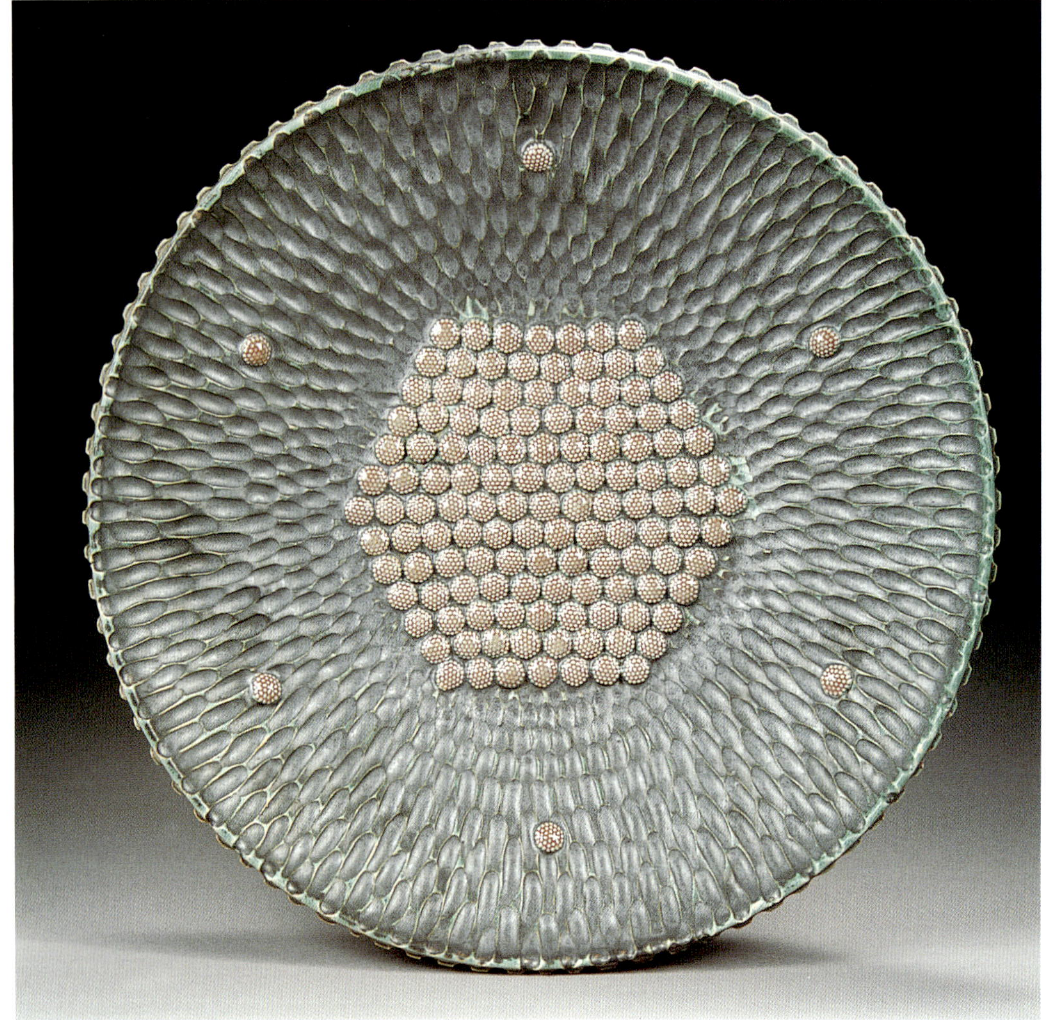

Amy Higgason

Green Sprigged Platter | 2003

$2^1/_2$ X 14 INCHES (6.4 X 35.6 CM)

Wheel-thrown white stoneware; sprigs and carvings; glazes, gas fired in reduction, cone 10

PHOTO BY GUY NICOL

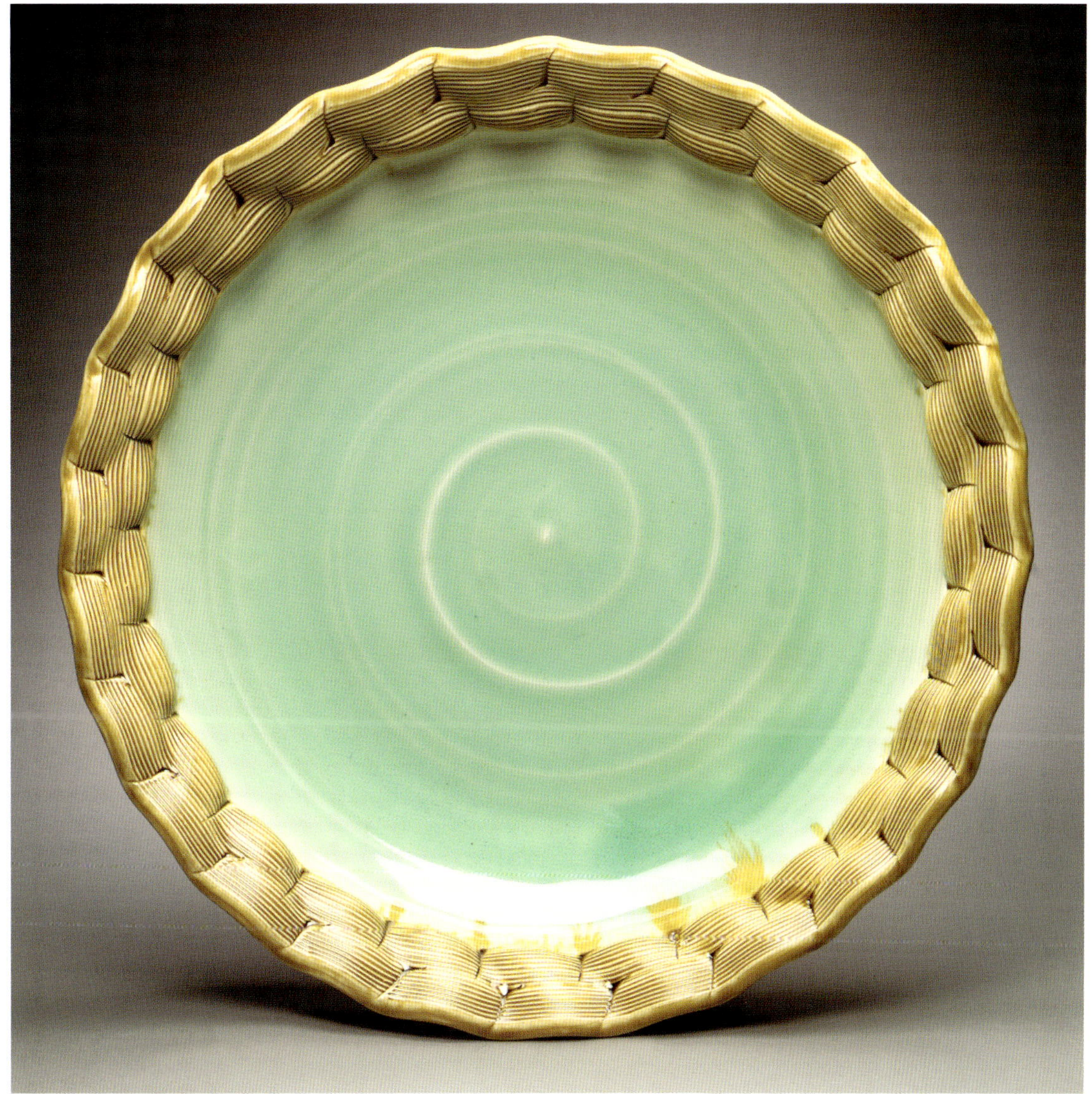

Amelia Stamps

Woven Platter in Celadon | 2007

3 X 15 INCHES (7.6 X 38.1 CM)

Wheel-thrown white stoneware; celadon and fake ash glaze; electric fired, cone 6

PHOTO BY ARTIST

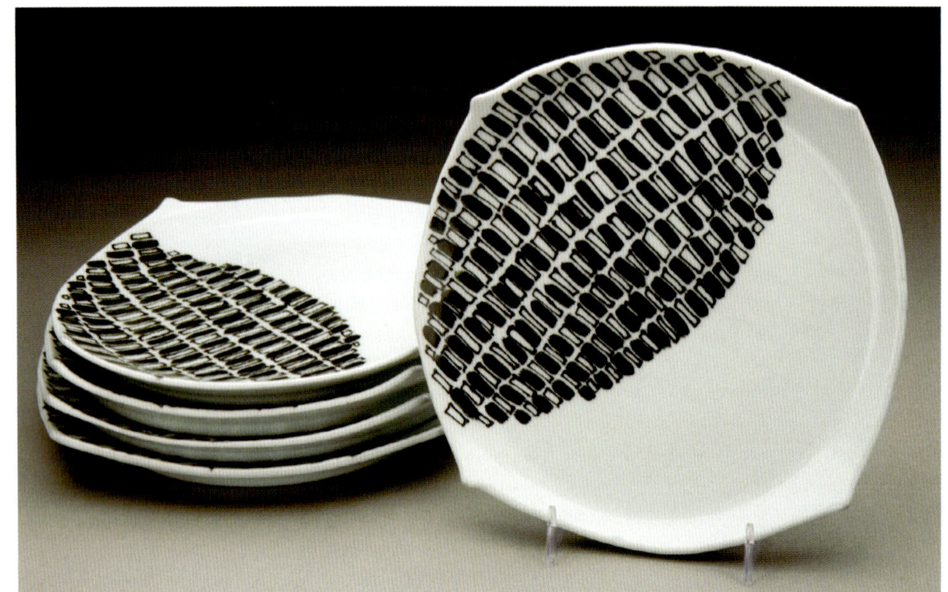

Loren Maron

Metropolis | 2007

EACH: $\frac{1}{2}$ X 8 X 8 INCHES (1.3 X 20.3 X 20.3 CM)

Wheel-thrown and altered porcelain; underglaze decoration, clear overglaze; reduction fired, cone 10

PHOTO BY ARTIST

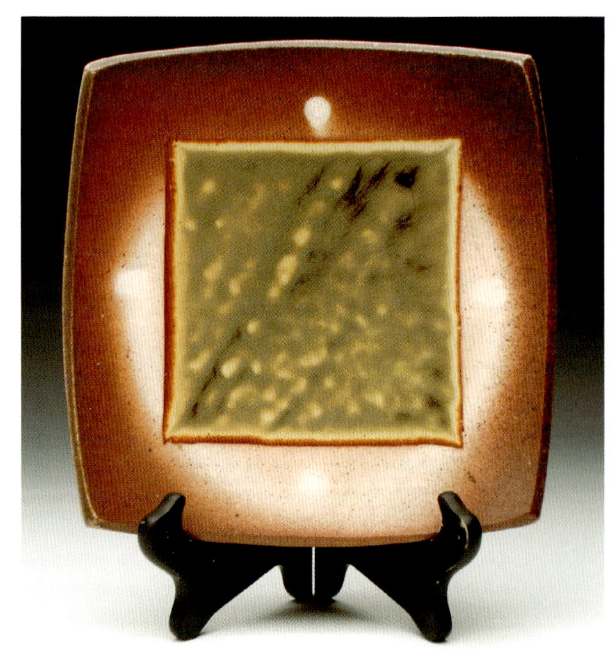

Bradley C. Birkhimer

Chinese Red | 2007

2 X $9\frac{1}{2}$ X $9\frac{1}{2}$ INCHES (5 X 24.1 X 24.1 CM)

Slab-built white stoneware with thrown and altered foot; wood and soda fired, cone 10; ash glazes

PHOTO BY ARTIST

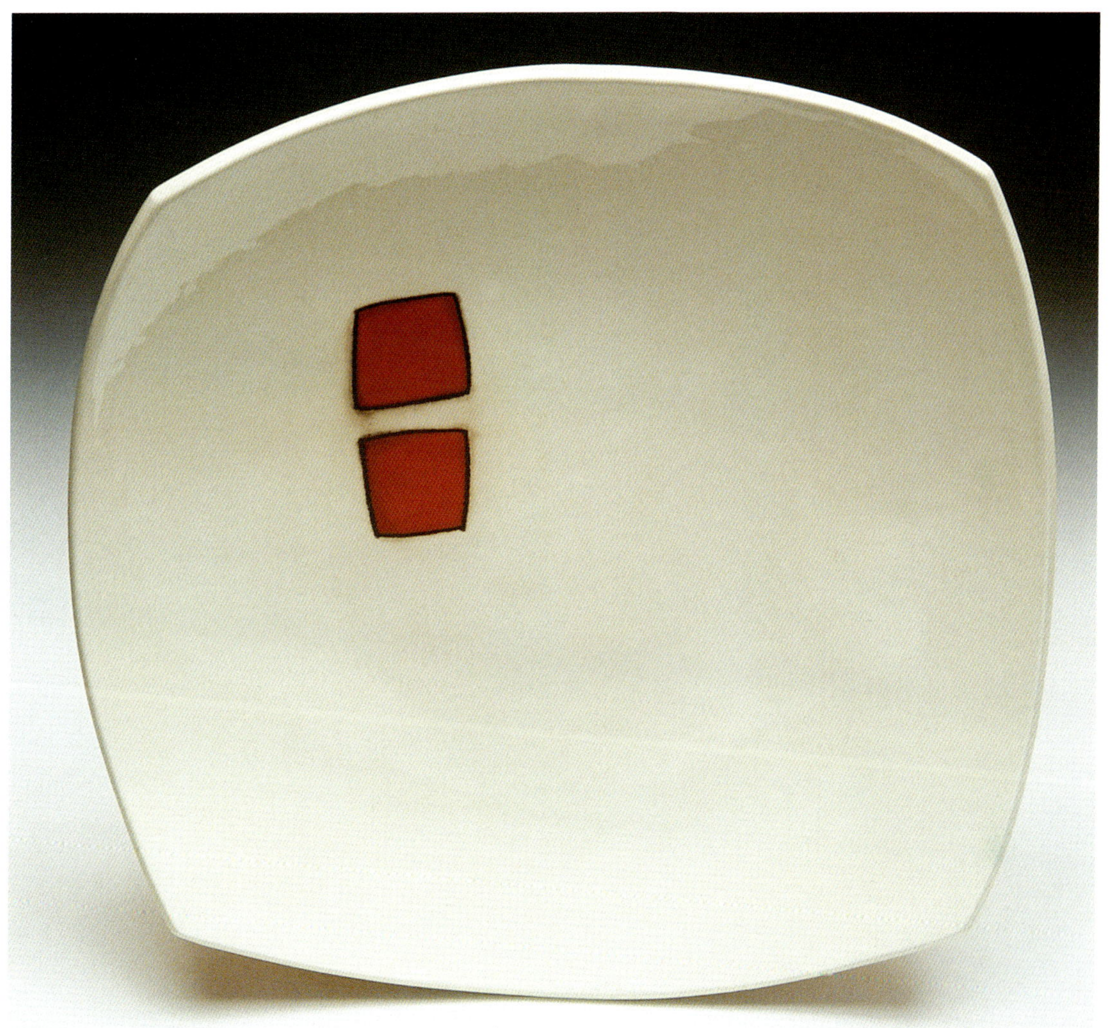

Lori Ehrlich Katz

Untitled | 2007

3 X 14 INCHES (7.6 X 35.6 CM)

Slab-built white earthenware; underglazed; clear glaze, electric fired, cone 04; glaze, cone 06

PHOTO BY GREG STALEY

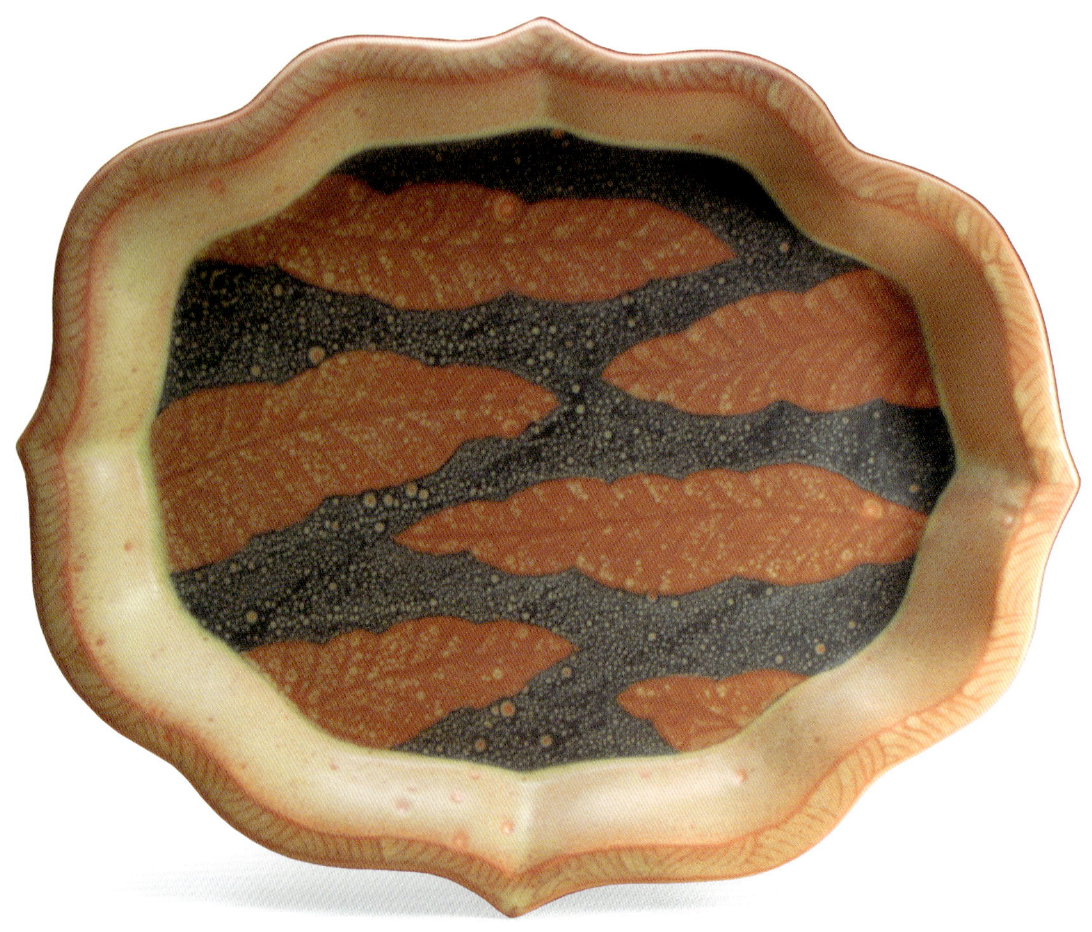

Donna Polseno

Untitled | 2006

2 X 16 X 13 INCHES (5.1 X 40.6 X 33 CM)

Slip-cast mid-range porcelain;
electric fired, cone 5

PHOTO BY ARTIST

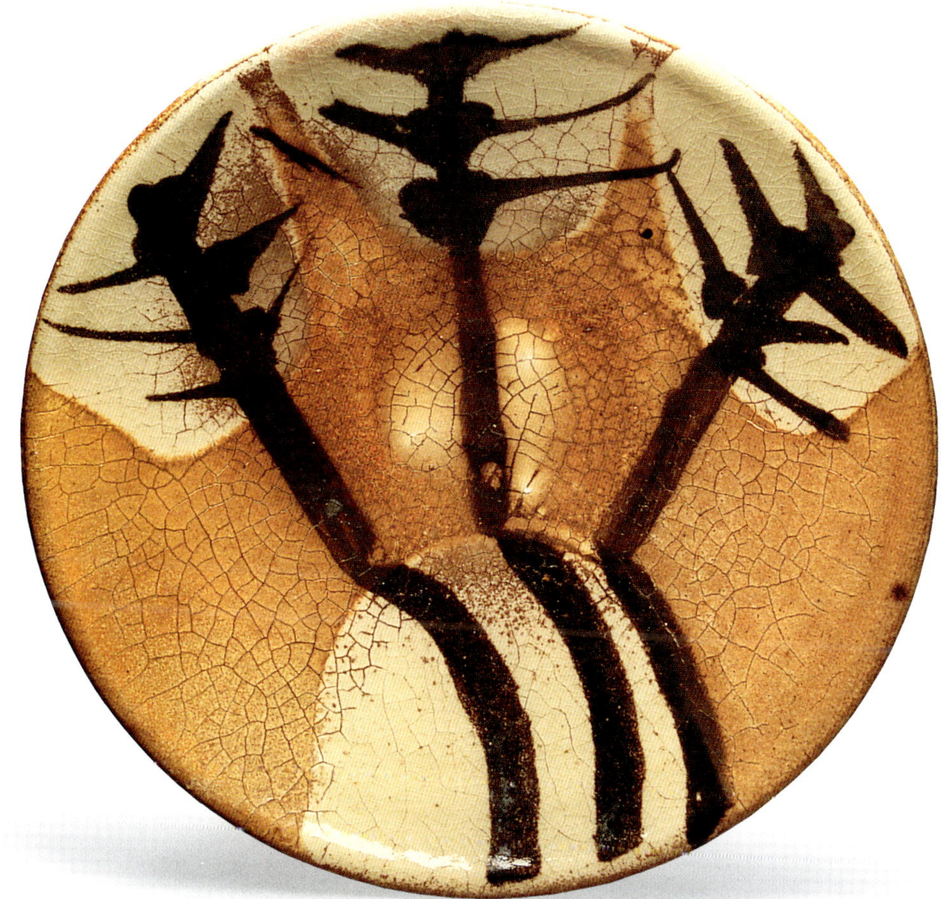

Lowell T. Hoisington II

Trees on a Hill | 2006

1 1/2 X 8 INCHES (3.8 X 20.3 CM)

Wheel-thrown stoneware; flashing slip, shino glaze, overglaze brushwork; wood fired with salt and soda, cone 10

PHOTO BY ARTIST

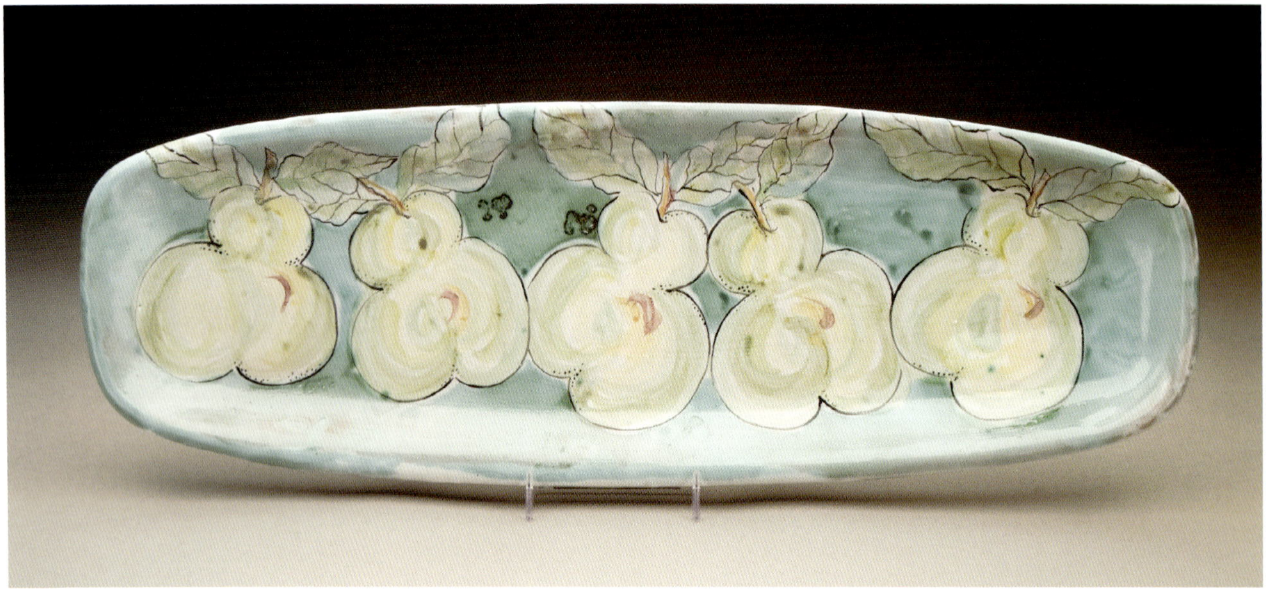

Roberta Shapiro

Pear Platter | 2006

21 1/2 X 7 1/2 (54.6 X 19.1 CM)

Hand-built terra cotta; majolica, underglazes; electric fired, cone 04

PHOTO BY LOREN MARON

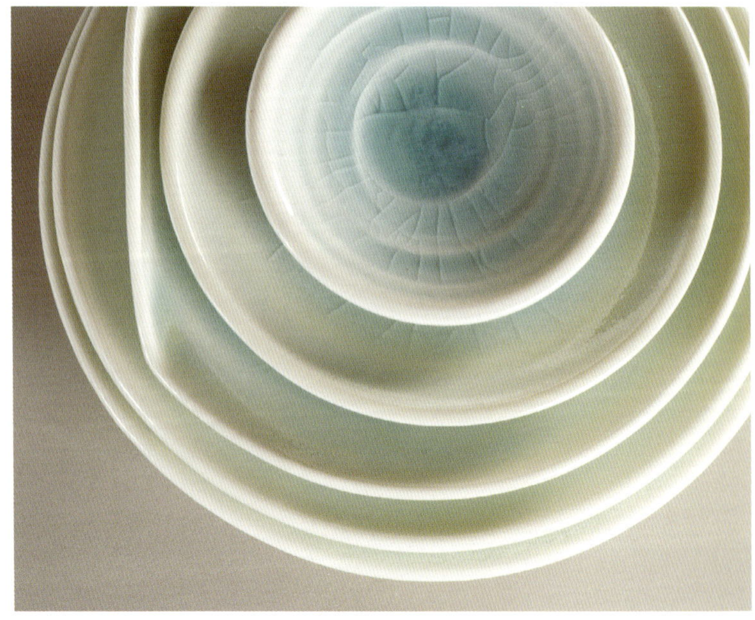

Carole Epp

Snow Series: Set of Plates | 2007

LARGEST: 9 1/2 INCHES (24.1 CM) IN DIAMETER

Wheel-thrown Southern Ice porcelain; blue copper glaze and clear glaze; electric fired, cone 10

PHOTO BY GRANT KERNAN

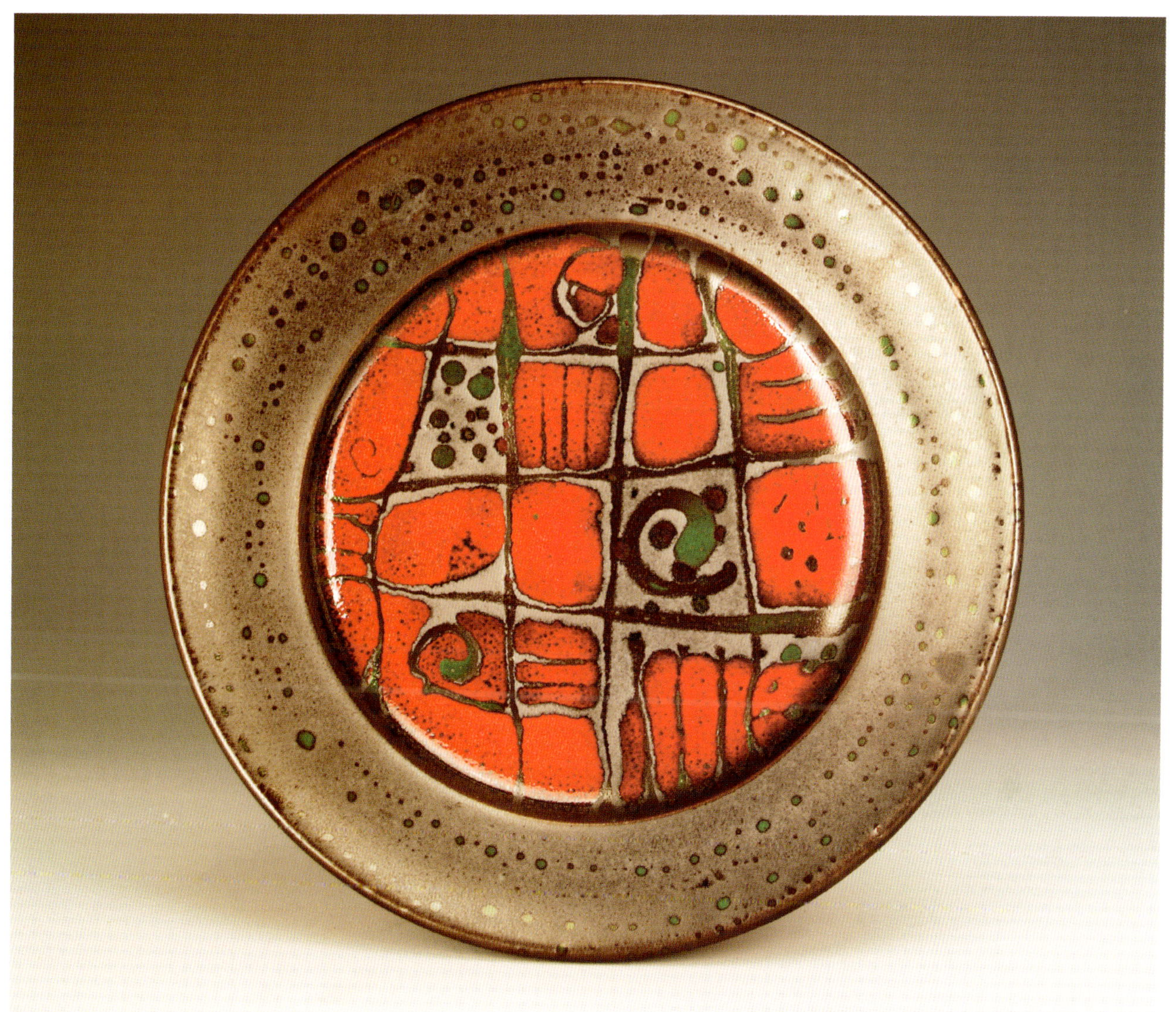

Donna Cole

Red Geometric | 2006

1 X 8 INCHES (2.5 X 20.3 CM)

Wheel-thrown stoneware; glaze trailed, wax resist; copper chrome and black glazes; reduction fired, cone 10

PHOTO BY ARTIST

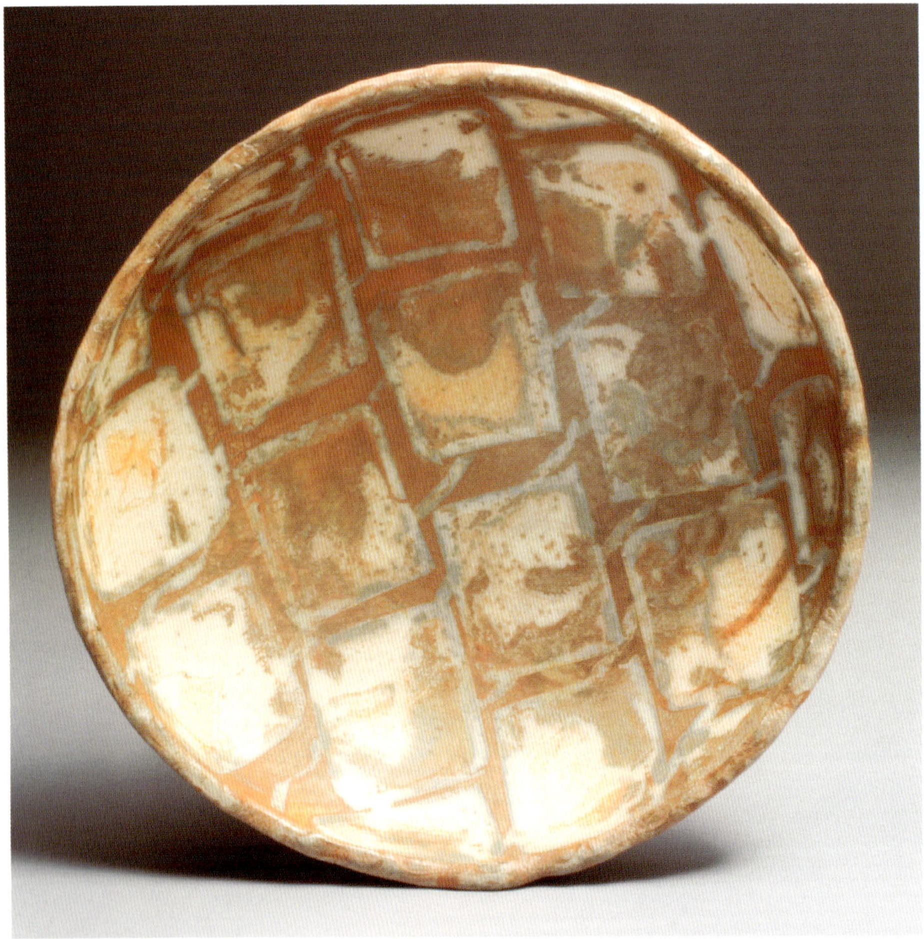

Russel Fouts

By This Sign All Smokes Know Each Other | 2007

12 INCHES (30.5 CM) IN DIAMETER

Hand-built terra cotta; terra sigillata, tape, paper, and soda resist; smoke fired in electric kiln

PHOTOS BY ARTIST

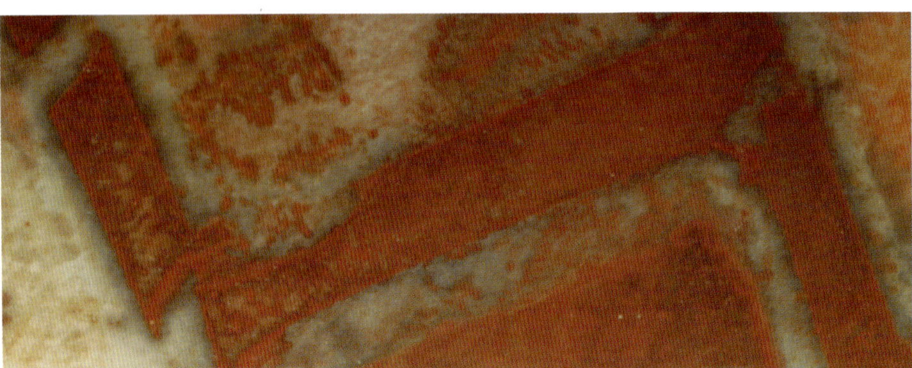

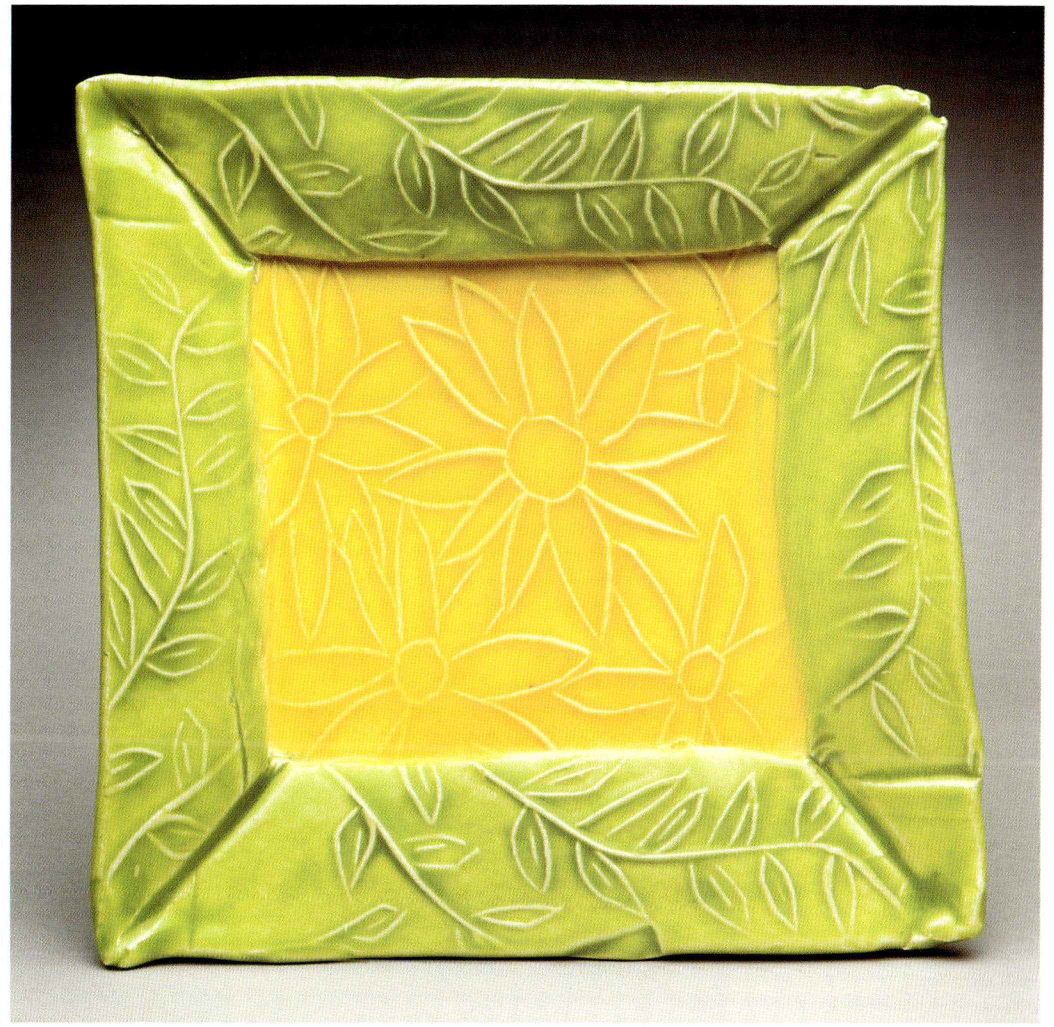

Vanessa Grubbs

Flower Plate | 2006

4 X 7 X 7 INCHES (10.2 X 17.8 X 17.8 CM)

Slab-built white earthenware; impressed texture; bisque fired, cone 04; glaze, cone 06

PHOTO BY WALKER MONTGOMERY

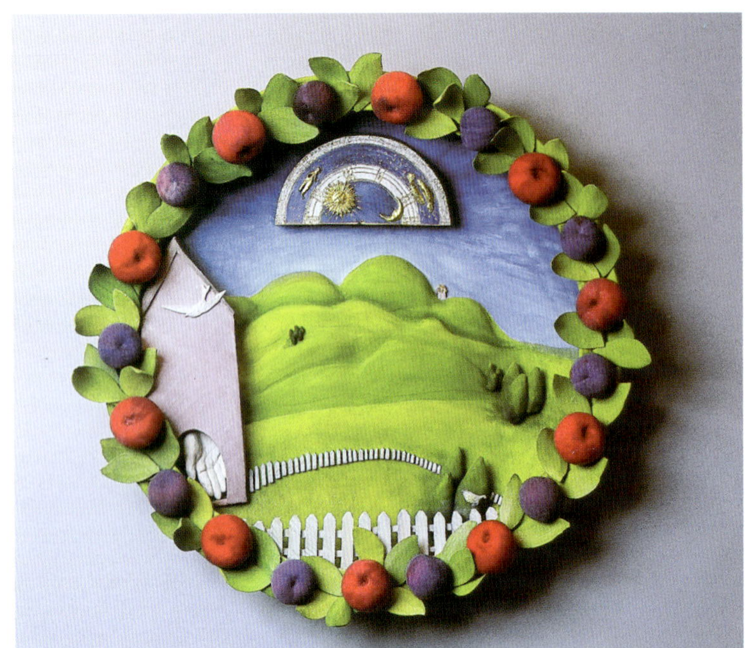

Paula Smith

Giving | 2004

6 X 25 INCHES (15.2 X 63.5 CM)

Slip-cast, press-molded, and slab-built stoneware; electric fired, cone 01; oil paint, gold leaf, epoxy

PHOTO BY ARTIST

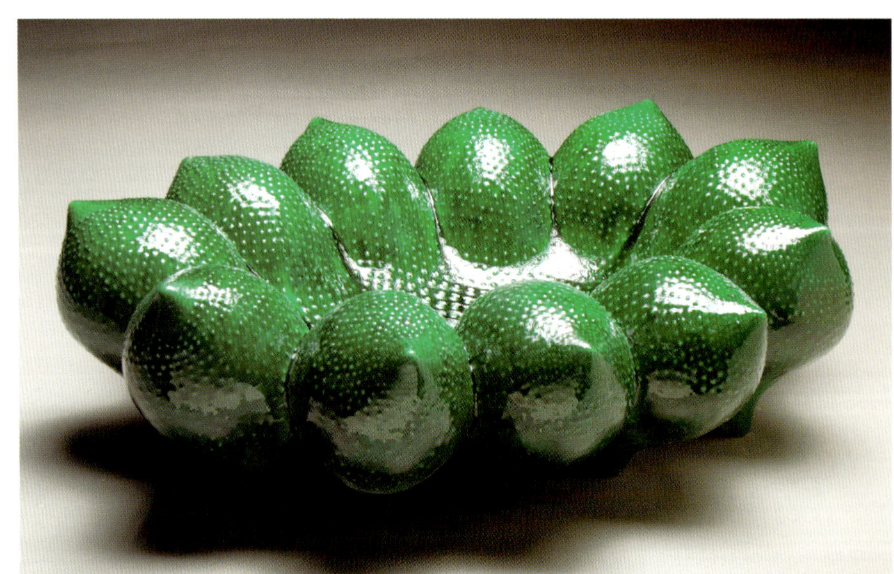

Tina Reuterberg

Pascal | 2007

7 X 16 X 12 INCHES (17.8 X 40.6 X 30.5 CM)

Hand-built earthenware, electric fired, cone 05

PHOTO BY ARTIST

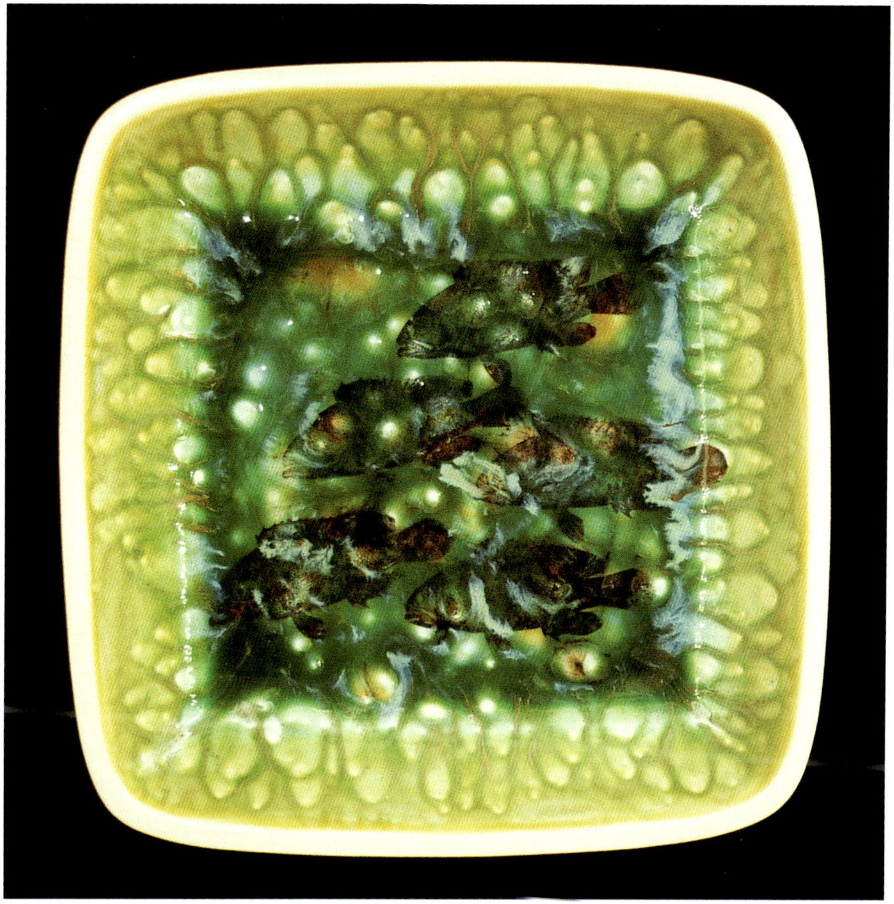

John McCuistion

Rock Fish Platter | 2006

3 X 16 X 16 INCHES (7.6 X 40.6 X 40.6 CM)

Slip cast; low-fire white slip; electric fired; low-fire underglaze and glaze, cone 5

PHOTOS BY ARTIST

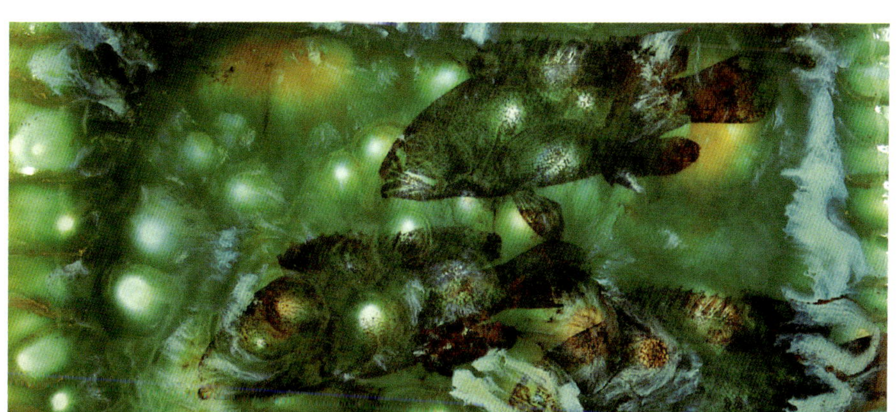

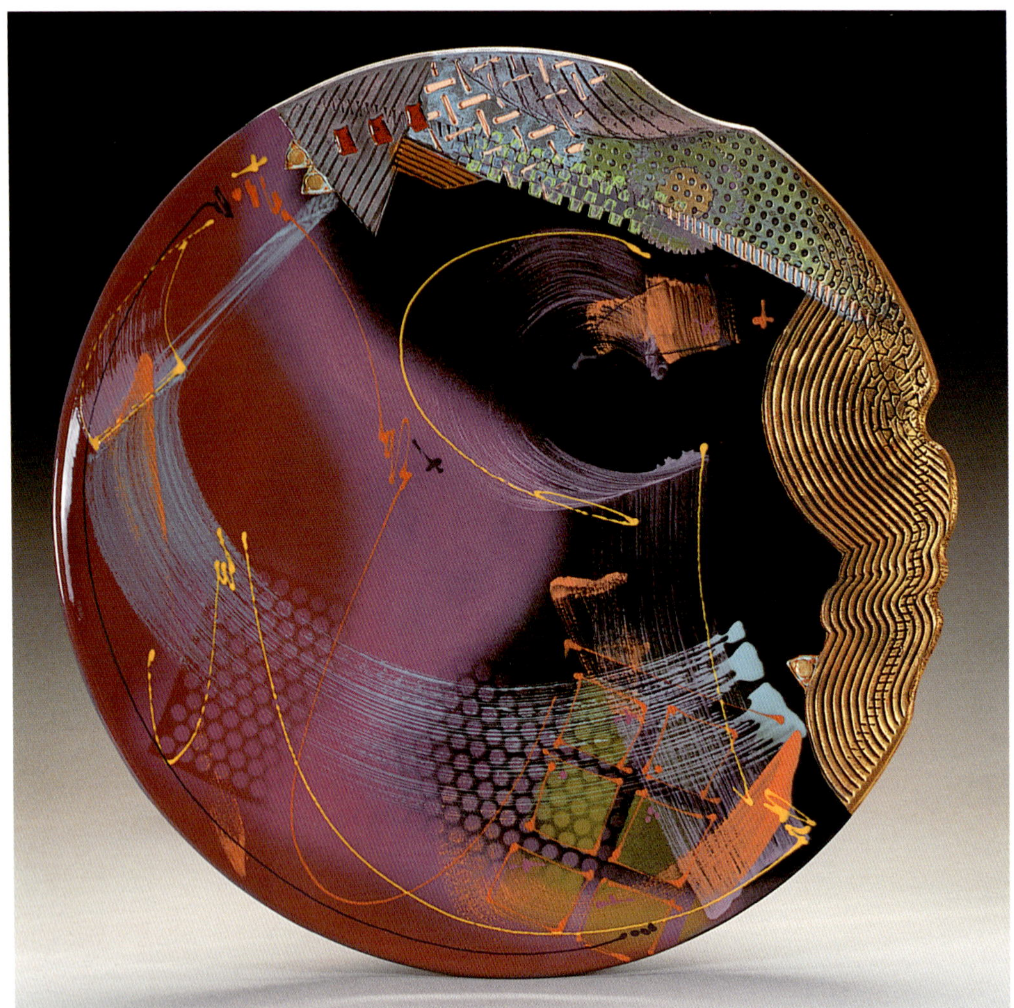

Michael Kifer

Textured Platter | 2005

3 X 20 INCHES (7.6 X 50.8 CM)

Slab-built and wheel-thrown white earthenware; textured; electric fired, cone 02; glaze, cone 05; stain, patina

PHOTO BY LARRY SANDERS

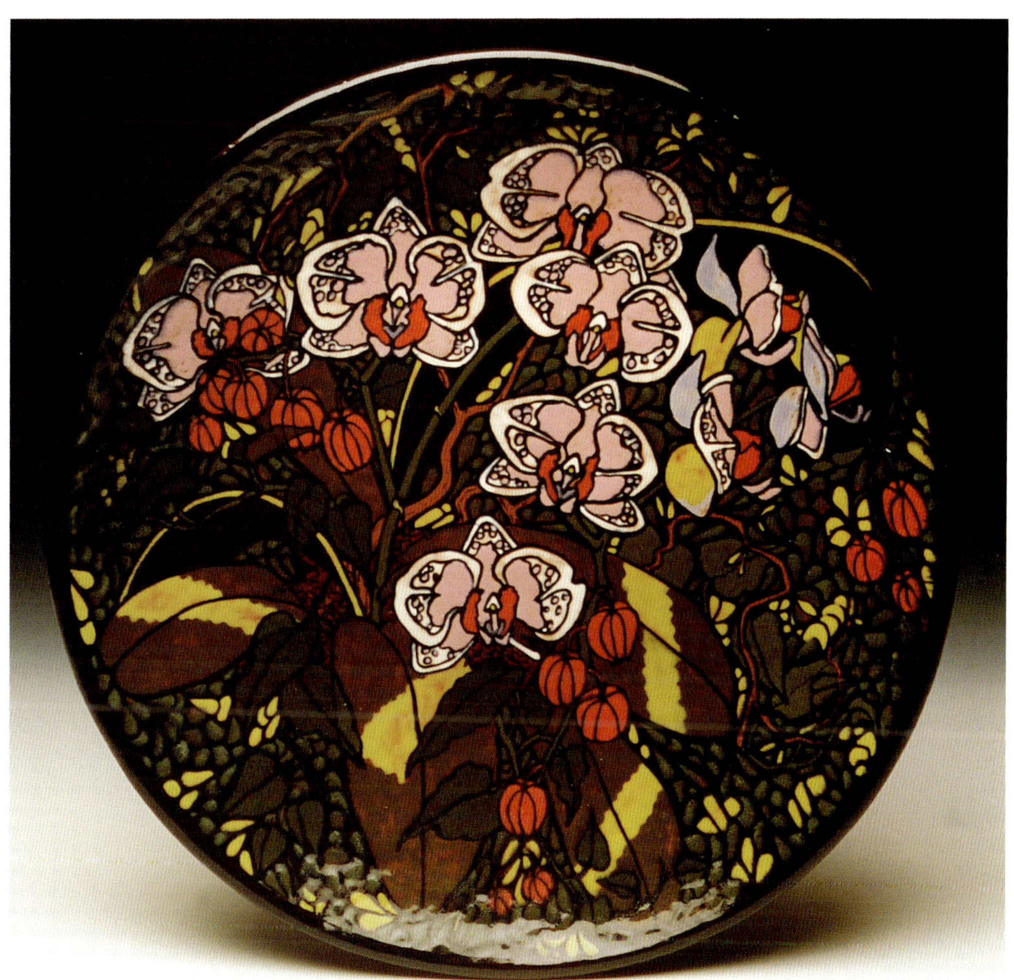

Mary Paul

Orchid Platter | 2006

16 INCHES (40.6 CM) IN DIAMETER

Hand-built earthenware; underglaze and clear glaze; electric fired, cone 04

PHOTO BY SETH TICE-LEWIS

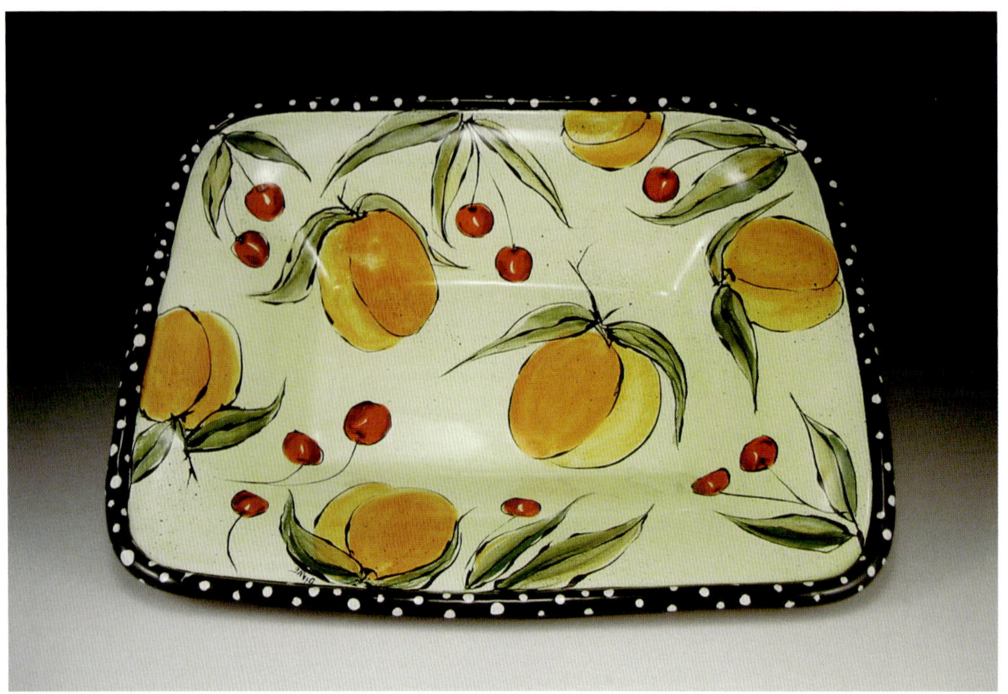

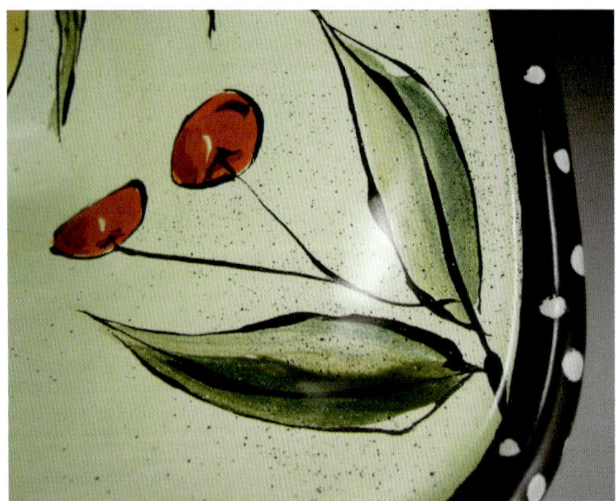

Diane Demers-Smith

Fruit Platter | 2006

$2^1/_2$ X 16 X $12^1/_2$ INCHES (6.4 X 40.6 X 31.8 CM)

Hand-built earthenware; majolica; electric fired, cone 04

PHOTOS BY ARTIST

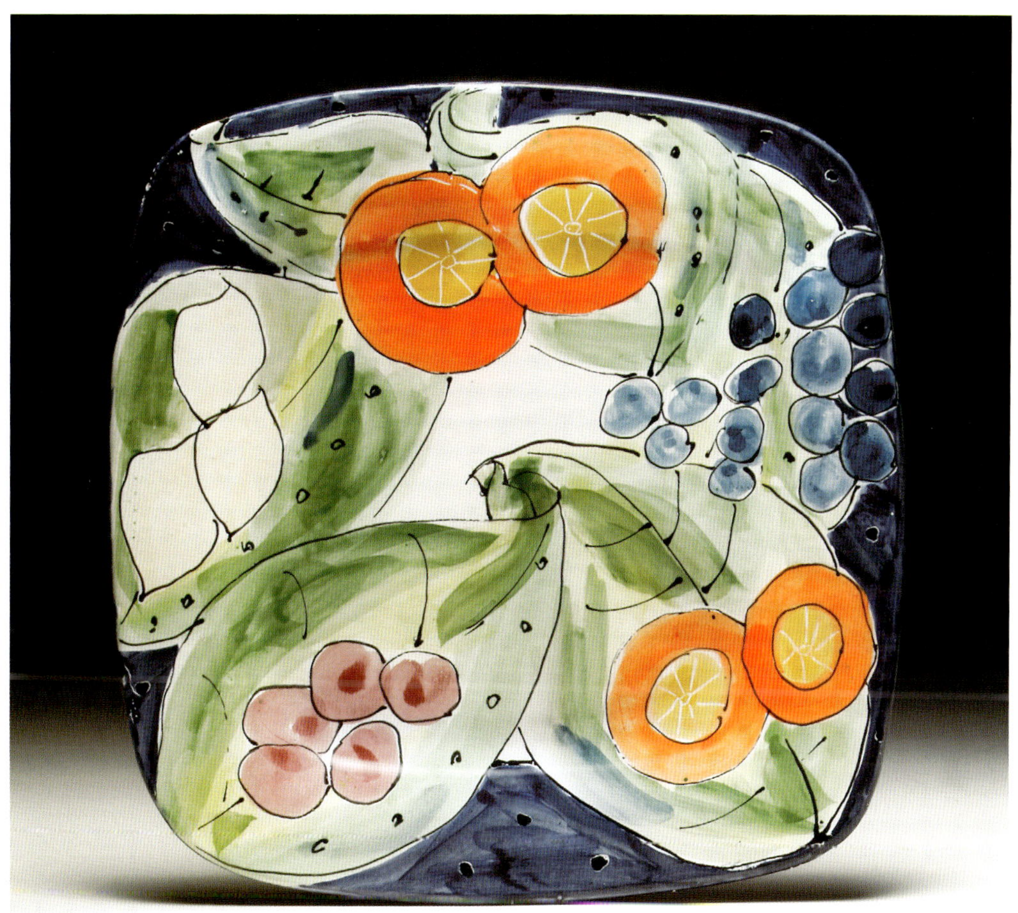

Margery K. Pozefsky

Fruit Platter | 2007

1 X 12 X 12 INCHES (2.5 X 30.5 X 30.5 CM)

Slab-built terra cotta; majolica; electric fired, cone 05

PHOTO BY JESSICA BROAD

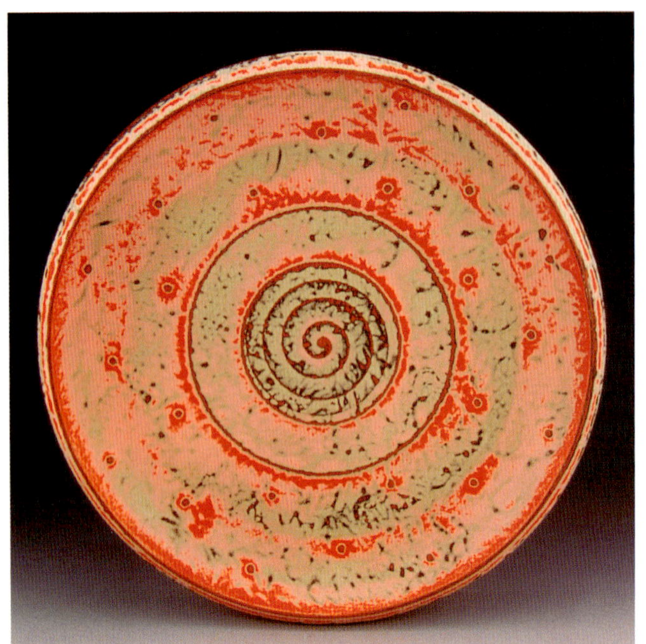

Jeffrey Nichols

Pink/Red Wall Plate | 2006

1 1/2 X 15 INCHES (3.8 X 38.1 CM)

Wheel-thrown earthenware; engobes; electric fired, cone 02

PHOTO BY ARTIST

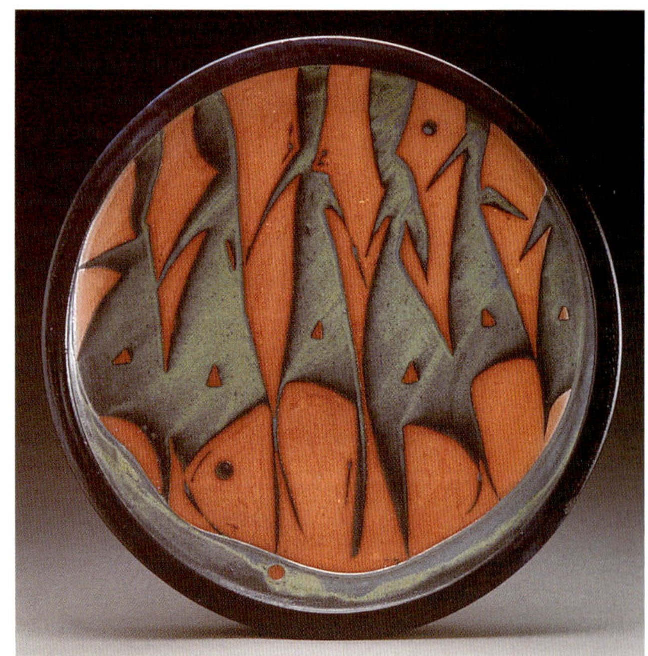

Nicholas Joerling

Untitled | 2007

19 INCHES (48.3 CM) IN DIAMETER

Wheel-thrown, high-temp stoneware; wax resist; reduction glaze, gas-fired downdraft, cone 10

PHOTO BY TOM MILLS

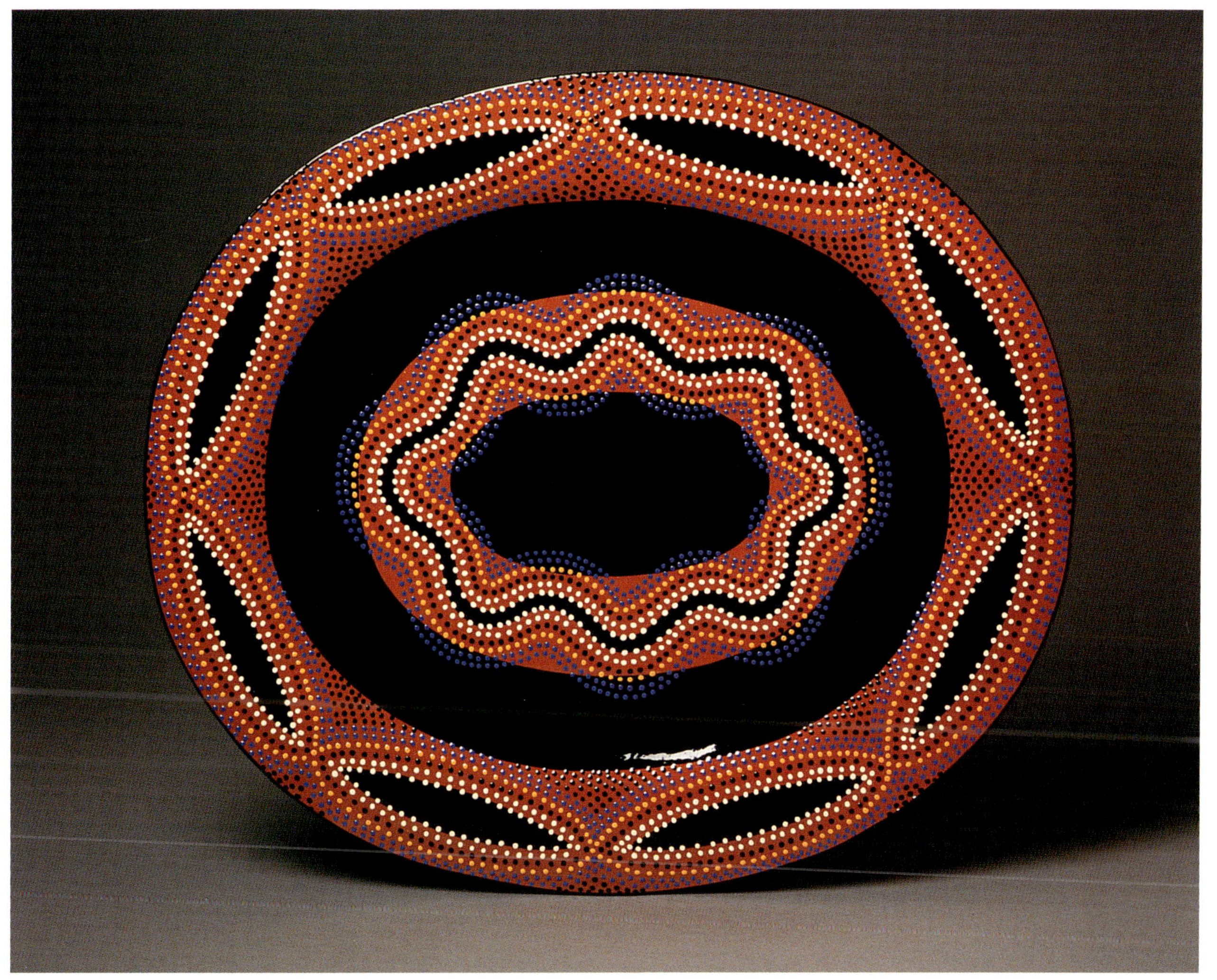

Jeani Holder
Michael Baines

benjammin' oval platter | 2005

3 X 23 X 19 INCHES (7.6 X 58.4 X 48.3 CM)

Slab-formed red earthenware; brushed and dotted underglaze decoration; multi-fired, clear glaze, electric fired, cone 04

PHOTO BY STEVE SMITH

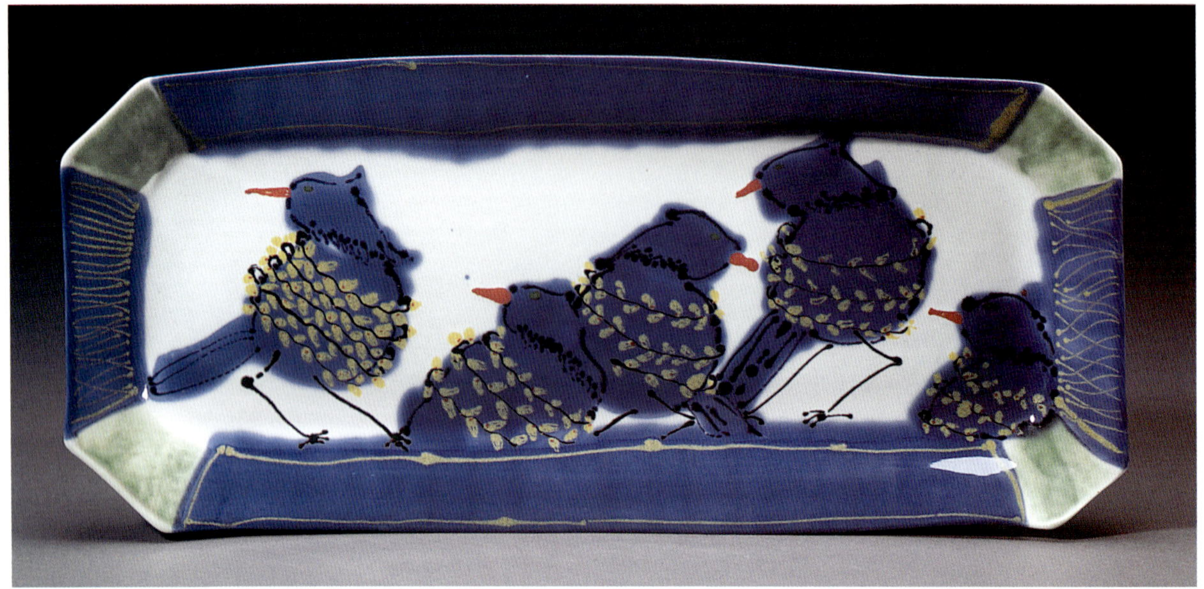

Marie Deborah Wald

Bluebirds Wrapped in Forsythia Branches | 2006

1 X 16 X 7 INCHES (2.5 X 40.6 X 17.8 CM)

Slab-built porcelain; overglaze brushwork; gas fired, reduction, cone 11

PHOTO BY JEFF BRUCE

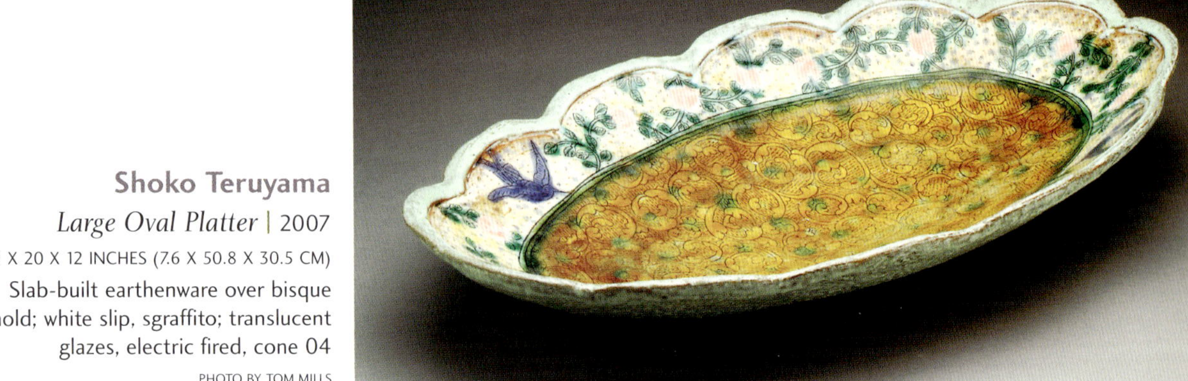

Shoko Teruyama

Large Oval Platter | 2007

3 X 20 X 12 INCHES (7.6 X 50.8 X 30.5 CM)

Slab-built earthenware over bisque mold; white slip, sgraffito; translucent glazes, electric fired, cone 04

PHOTO BY TOM MILLS

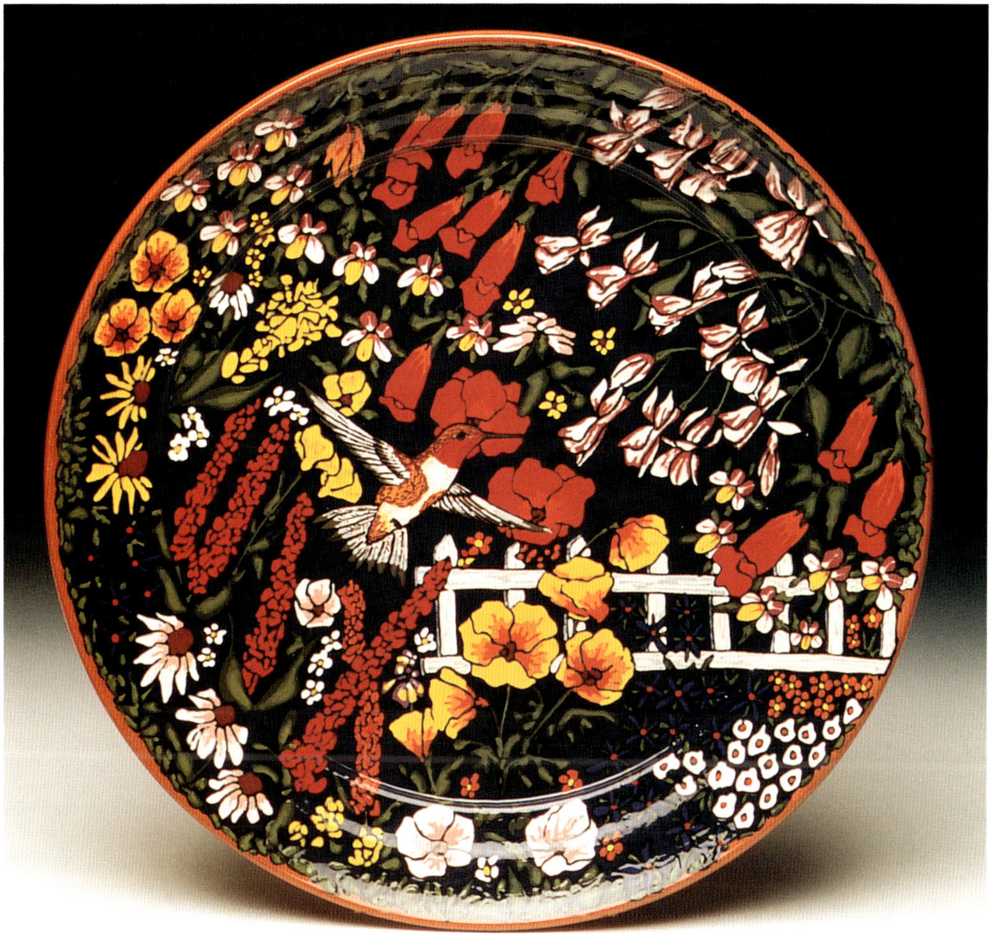

John Garland

Hummingbird Platter | 2007

16 INCHES (40.6 CM) IN DIAMETER

Wheel-thrown earthenware; underglaze, clear glaze; electric fired, cone 04

PHOTOS BY SETH TICE-LEWIS

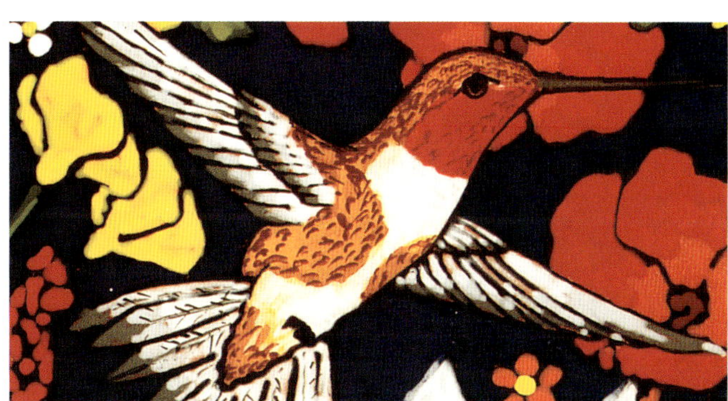

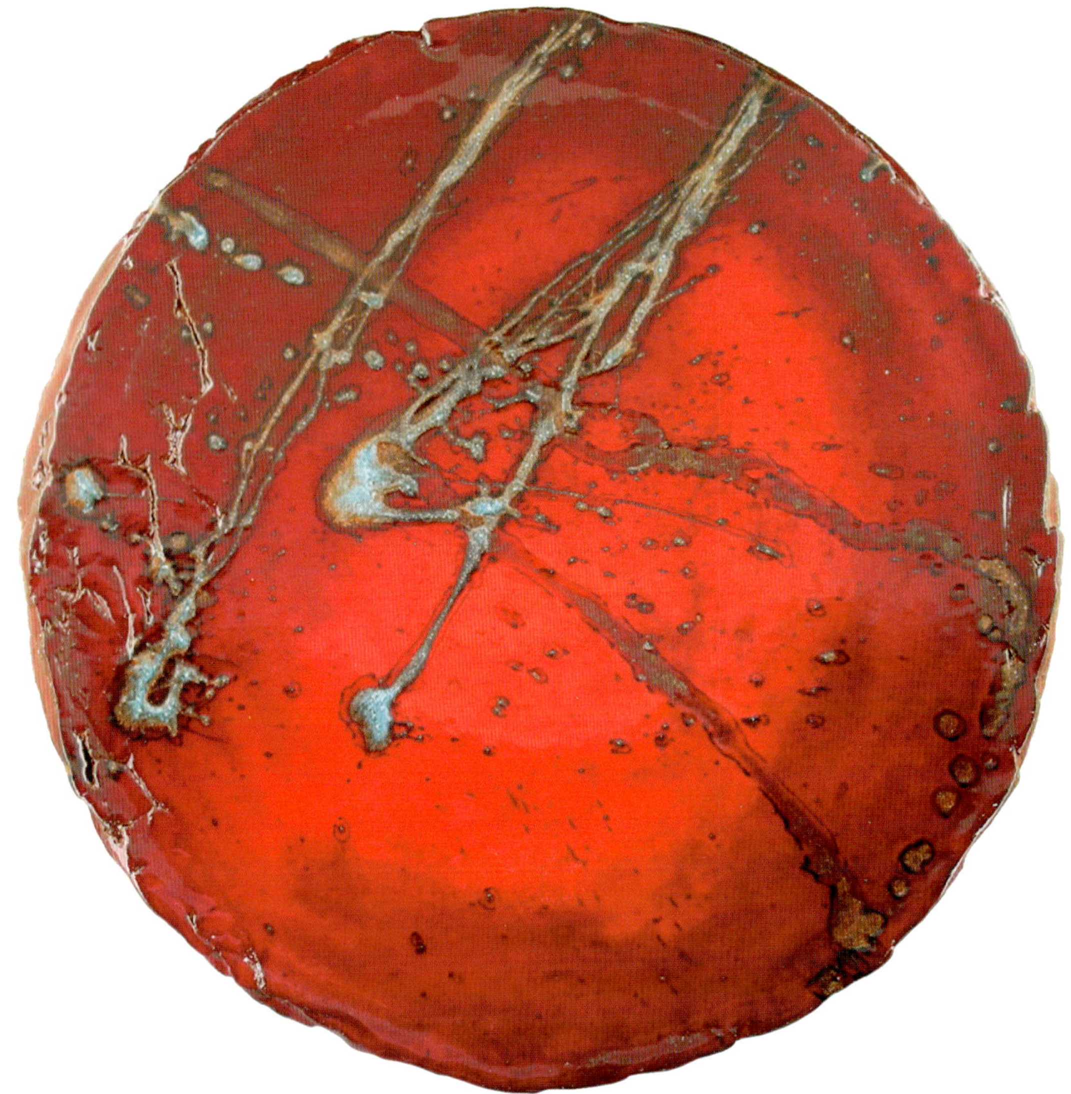

David L. Gamble

Rojo con Lagrima | 2006

2½ X 22 INCHES (6.4 X 55.9 CM)

Hand-built and wheel-thrown low-fire terra cotta; bisque fired in electric kiln, cone 03; glaze, cone 06

PHOTO BY ARTIST

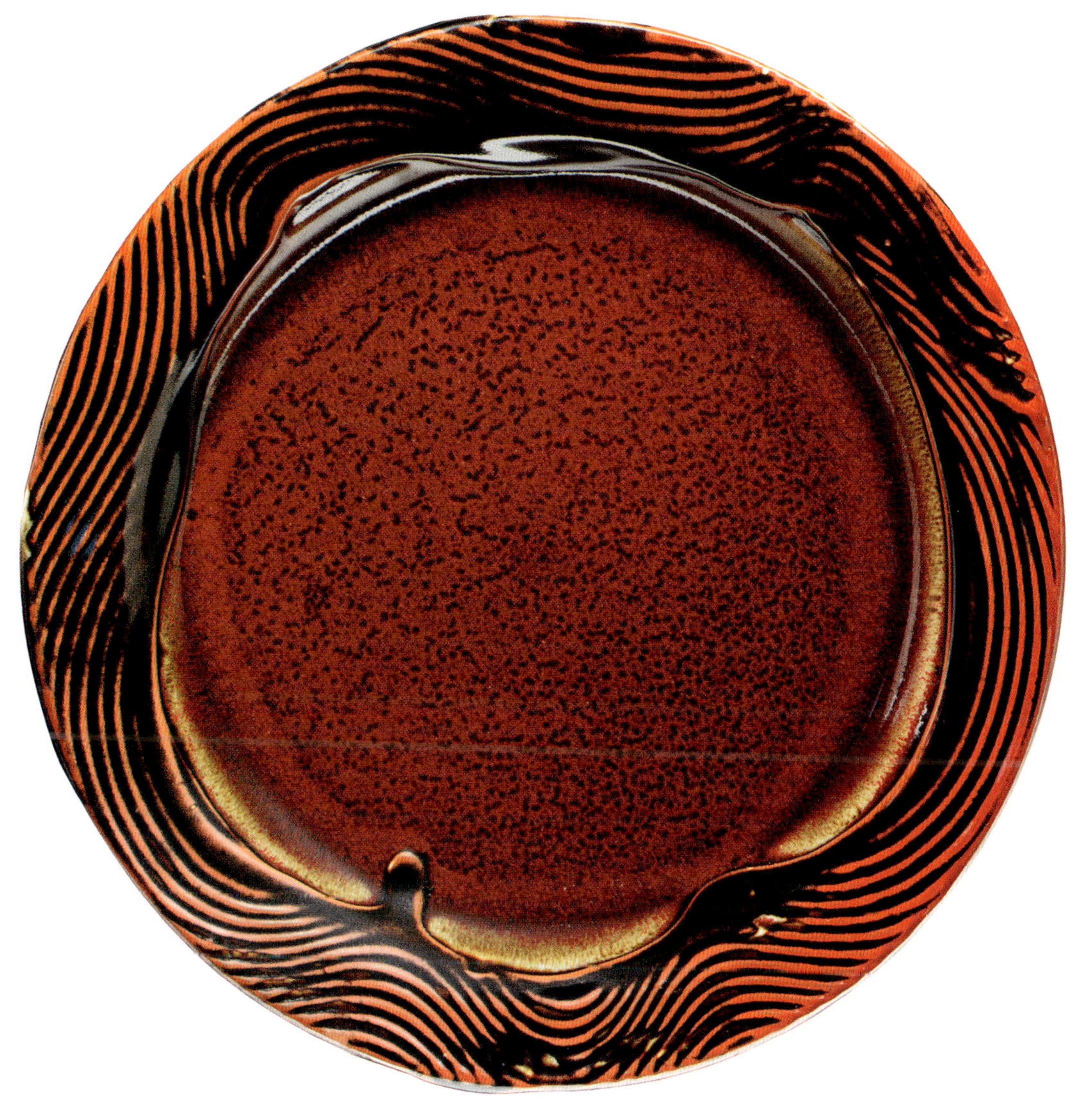

David Beumée

Untitled | 2005

1 1/2 X 11 INCHES (3.8 X 27.9 CM)

Porcelain; reduction fired, cone 10

PHOTO BY CHARLIE ROY

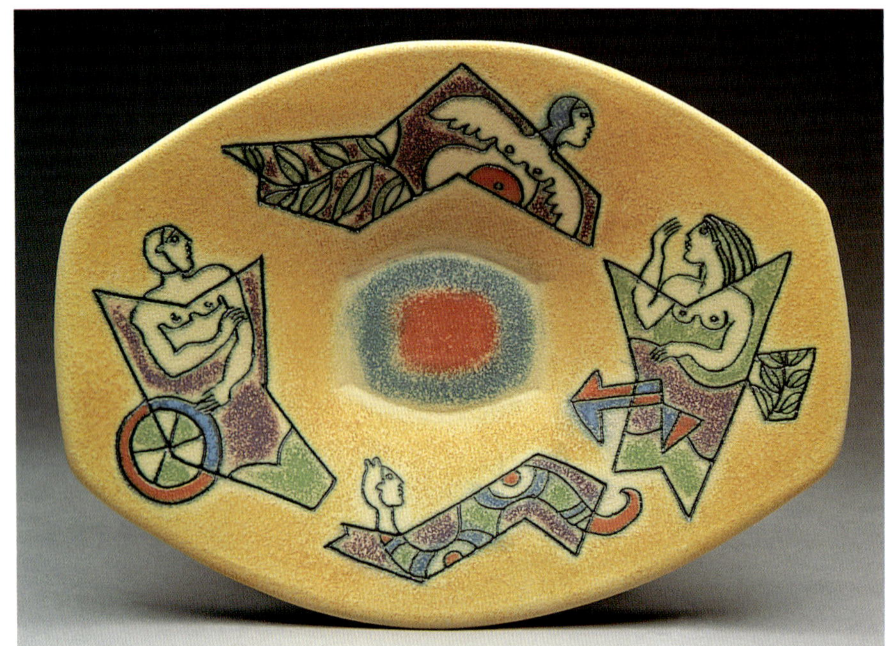

Matthias Ostermann

Untitled | 2005

4 X 11 X 7 INCHES (10.2 X 27.9 X 17.8 CM)

Slab and drape-molded earthenware; vitreous engobes, sgraffito, copper inlay; on-surface stains; electric multi-fired, cone 06

PHOTO BY JAN THIJS

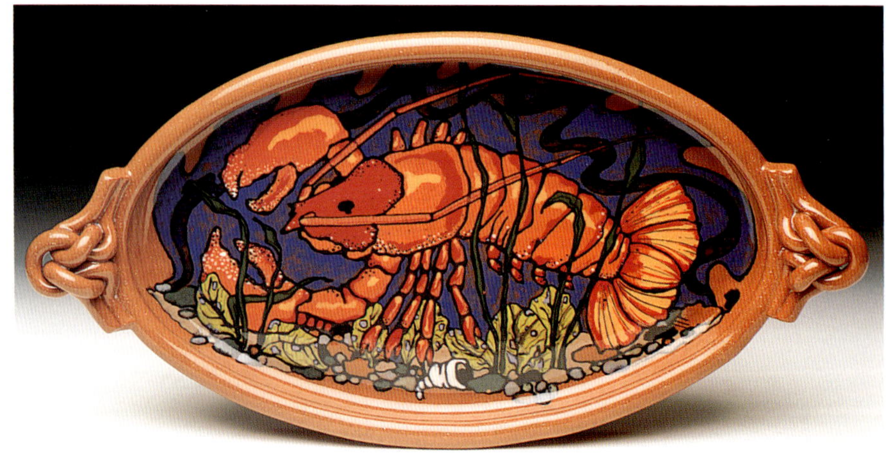

Mary Paul

Lobster Platter | 2007

15 X 10 INCHES (38.1 X 25.4 CM)

Hand-built earthenware; underglaze, clear glaze; electric fired, cone 04

PHOTO BY SETH TICE-LEWIS

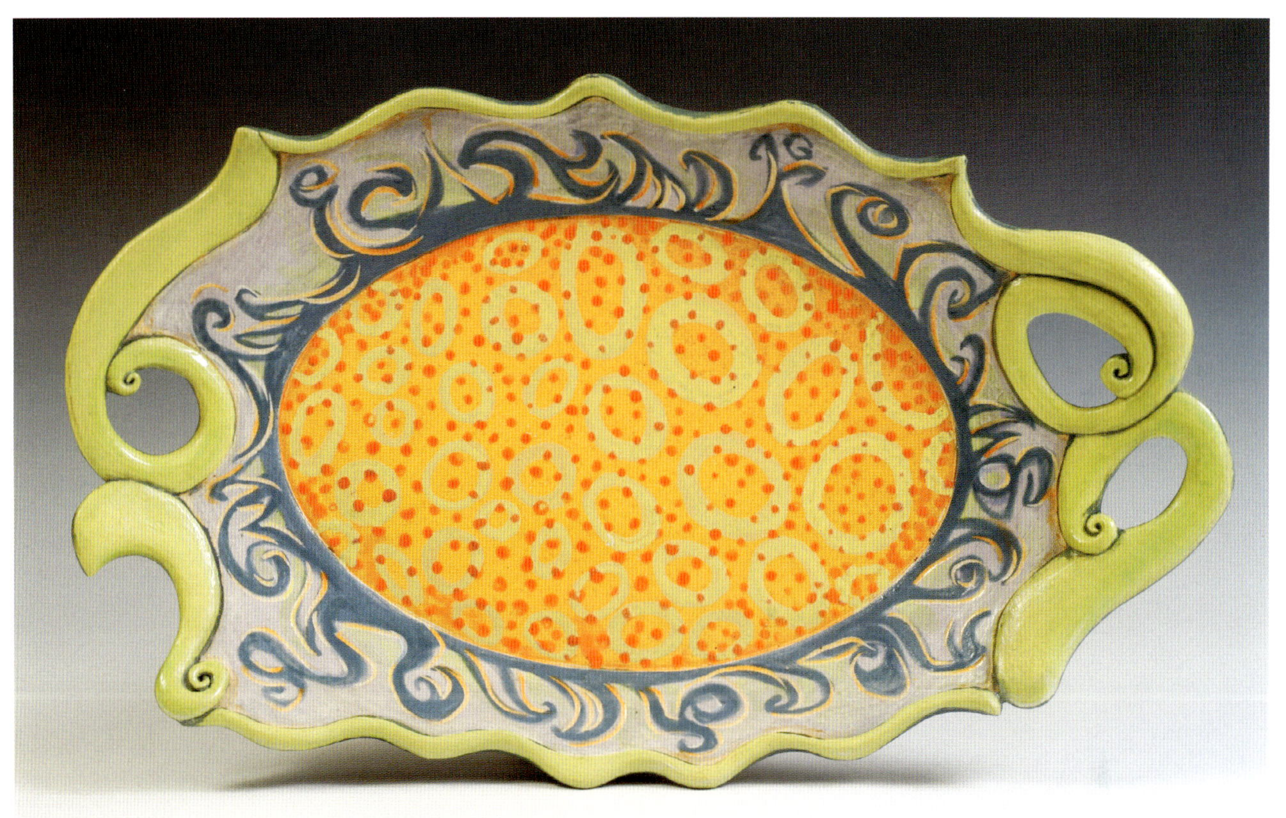

Carol Ann Wedemeyer
Smoke Rings Party Tray | 2004
4 X 27 X 18 INCHES (10.2 X 68.6 X 45.7 CM)
Hand-built Arctic white clay;
Mason stains and glazes
PHOTO BY WILFRED J. JONES

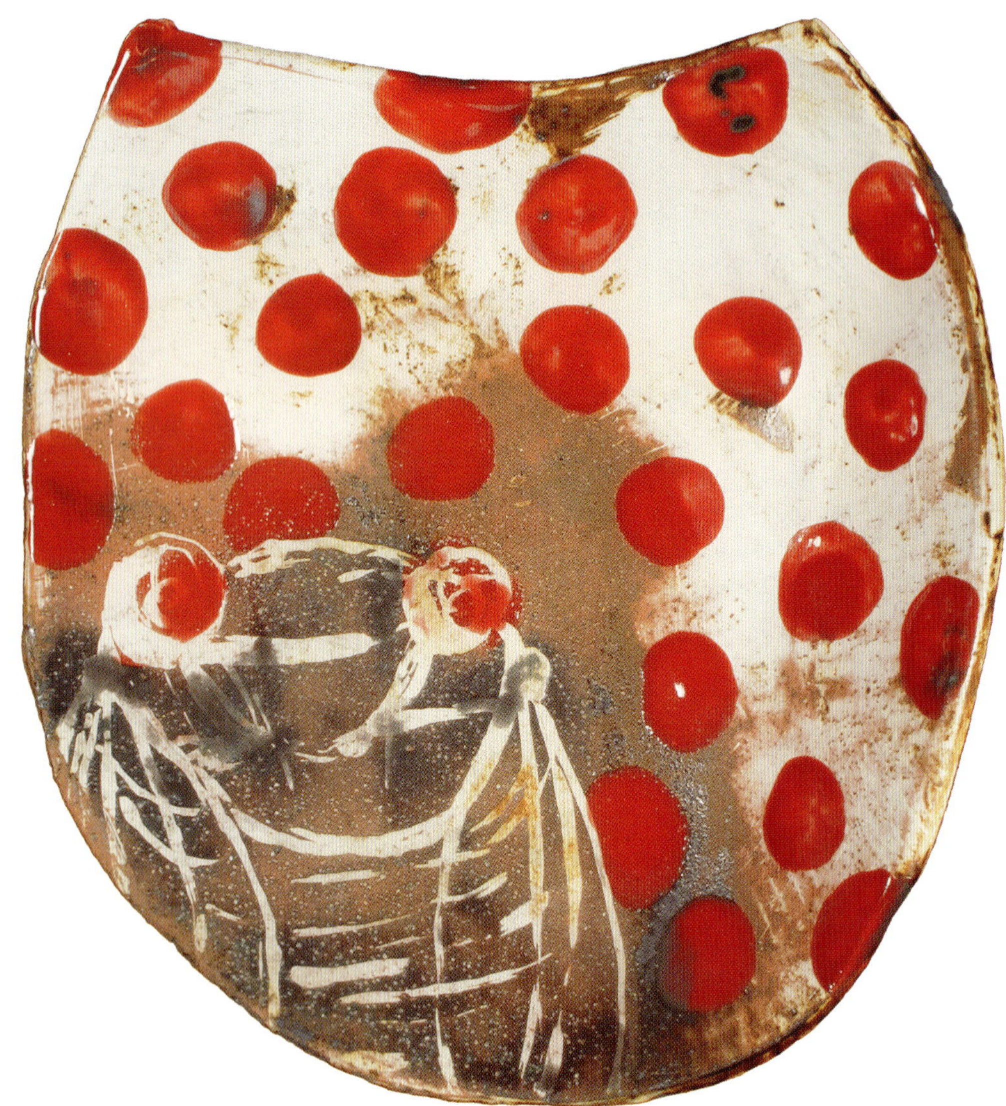

Jill Foote-Hutton

Awake (Cicada) | 2006

1 X 5½ X 6 INCHES (2.5 X 14 X 15.2 CM)

Slump-molded earthenware slab; wax resist; cone 05; terra sigillata, copper carbonate wash; electric fired, cone 04

PHOTO BY DAN HERMAN

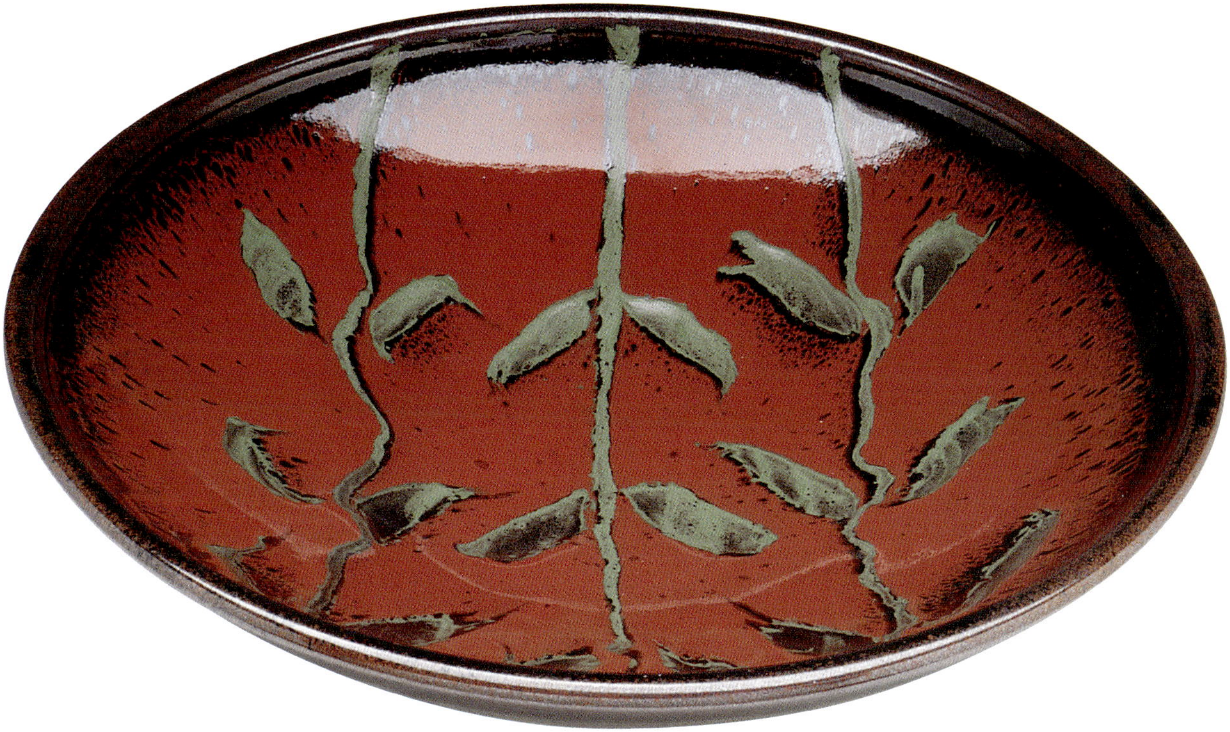

Chris Harford

Vine | 2005

2 X 14 X 14 INCHES (5.1 X 35.6 X 35.6 CM)

Wheel-thrown stoneware; glaze-on-glaze, latex resist; gas fired, cone 10

PHOTOS BY ANU PHOTOGRAPHY

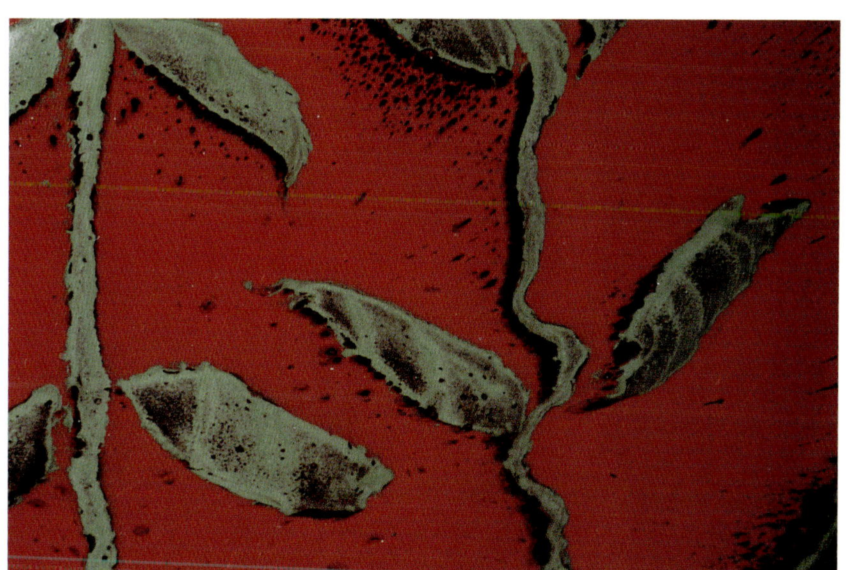

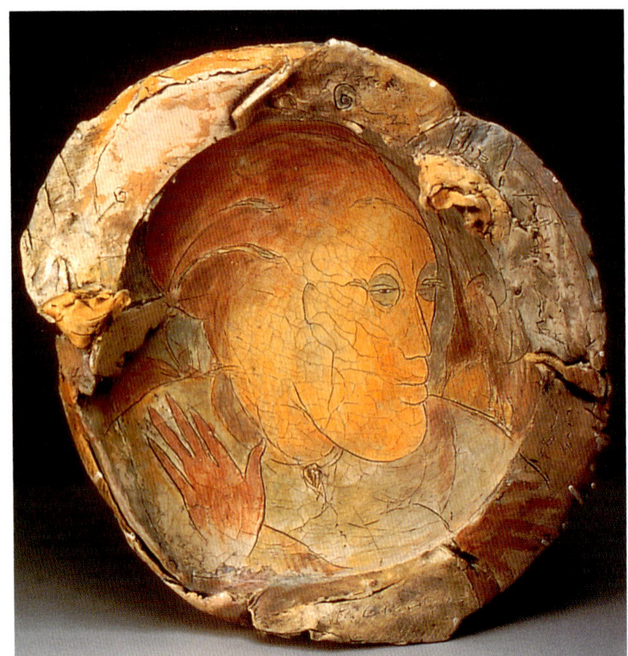

Bede Clark

A Window Opens There | 1999

5 X 28 X 26 INCHES (12.7 X 71.1 X 66 CM)

Wheel-thrown and hand-built earthenware; polychrome engobes; glaze, electric fired, cone 03

PHOTO BY ARTIST

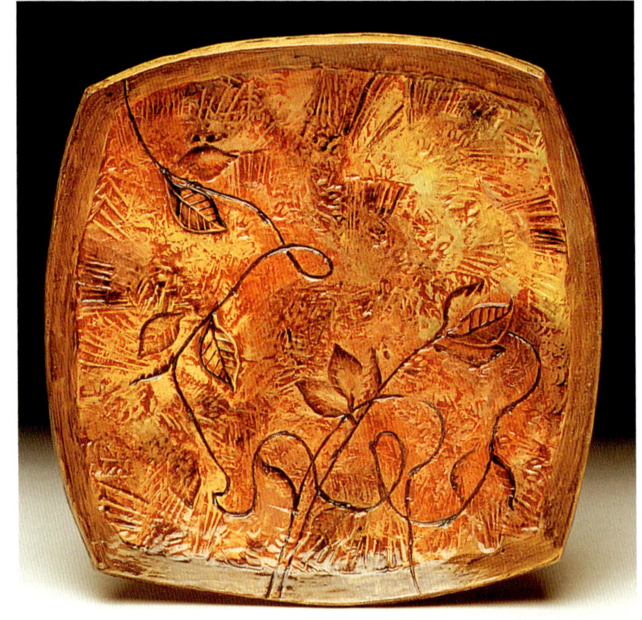

Susan Farrar Parrish

Leaf Lines | 2006

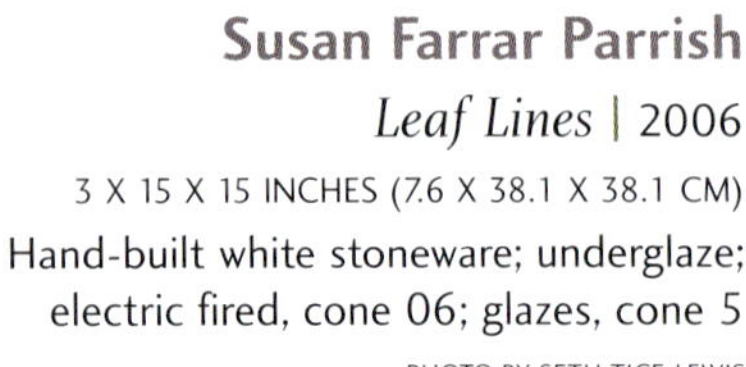

3 X 15 X 15 INCHES (7.6 X 38.1 X 38.1 CM)

Hand-built white stoneware; underglaze; electric fired, cone 06; glazes, cone 5

PHOTO BY SETH TICE-LEWIS

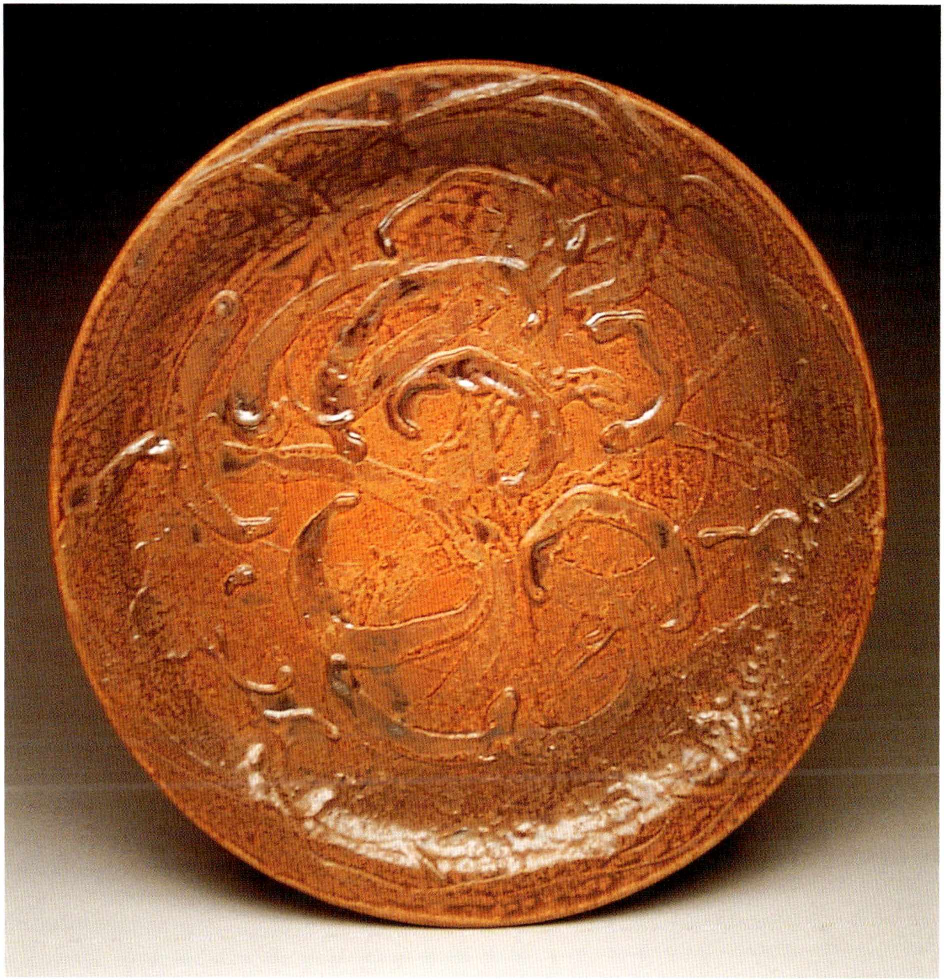

Debbie Little

Slip Textured Platter | 2007

2 X $14^{1}/_{4}$ INCHES (5.1 X 36.2 CM)

Wheel-thrown stoneware; slip textured; electric fired, cone 06; layered glazes, electric fired, cone 6

PHOTOS BY ARTIST

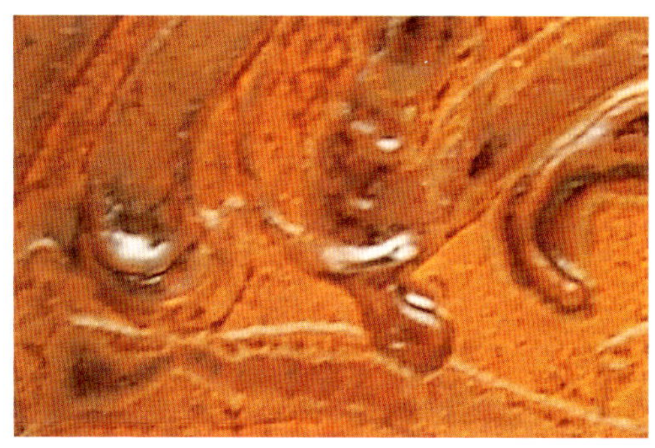

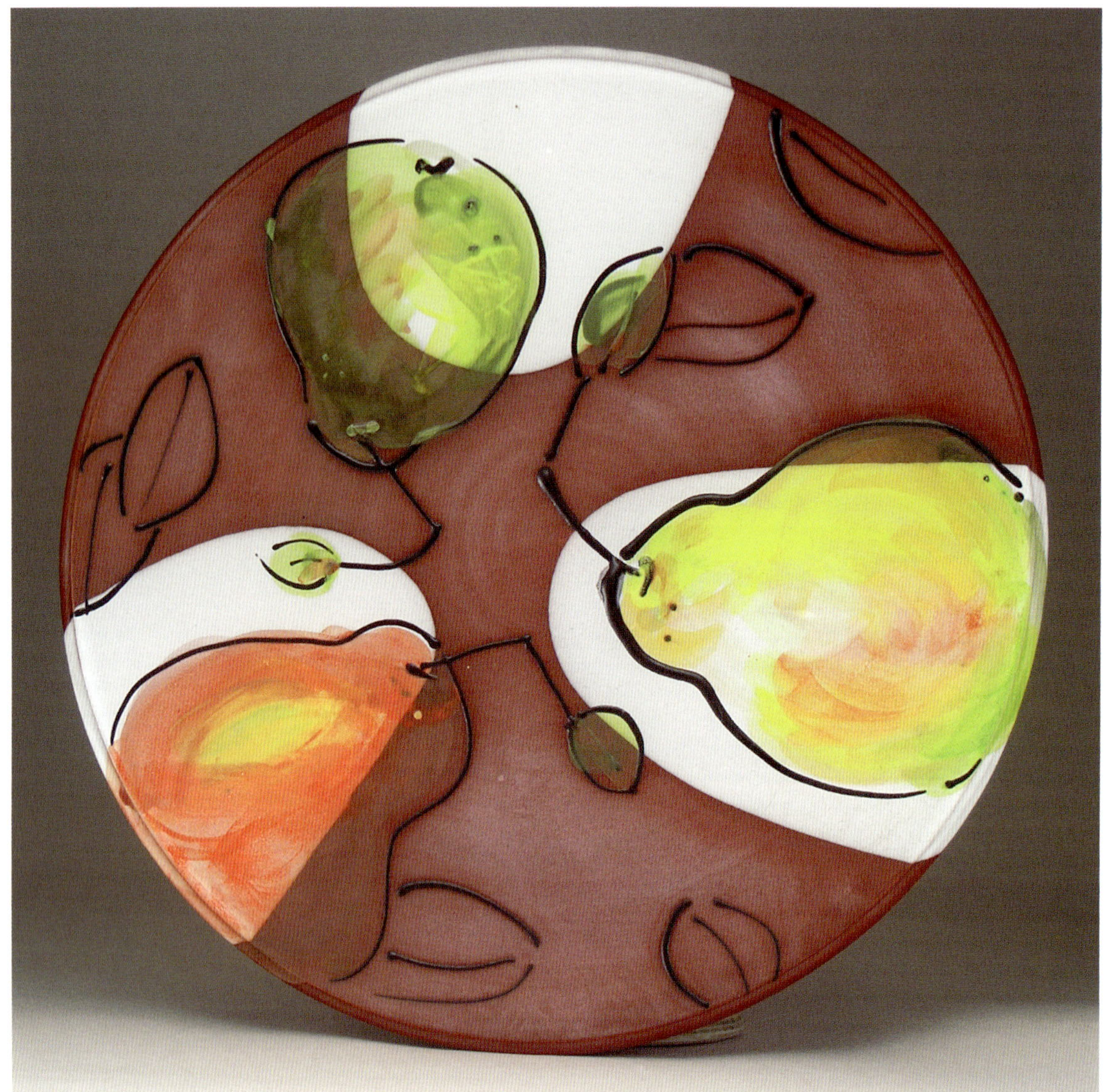

Wynne Wilbur

Pears Platter | 2004

1 X 16 INCHES (2.5 X 40.6 CM)

Slab and wheel-thrown terra cotta; terra sigillata; majolica; electric fired, cone 03

PHOTO BY ARTIST

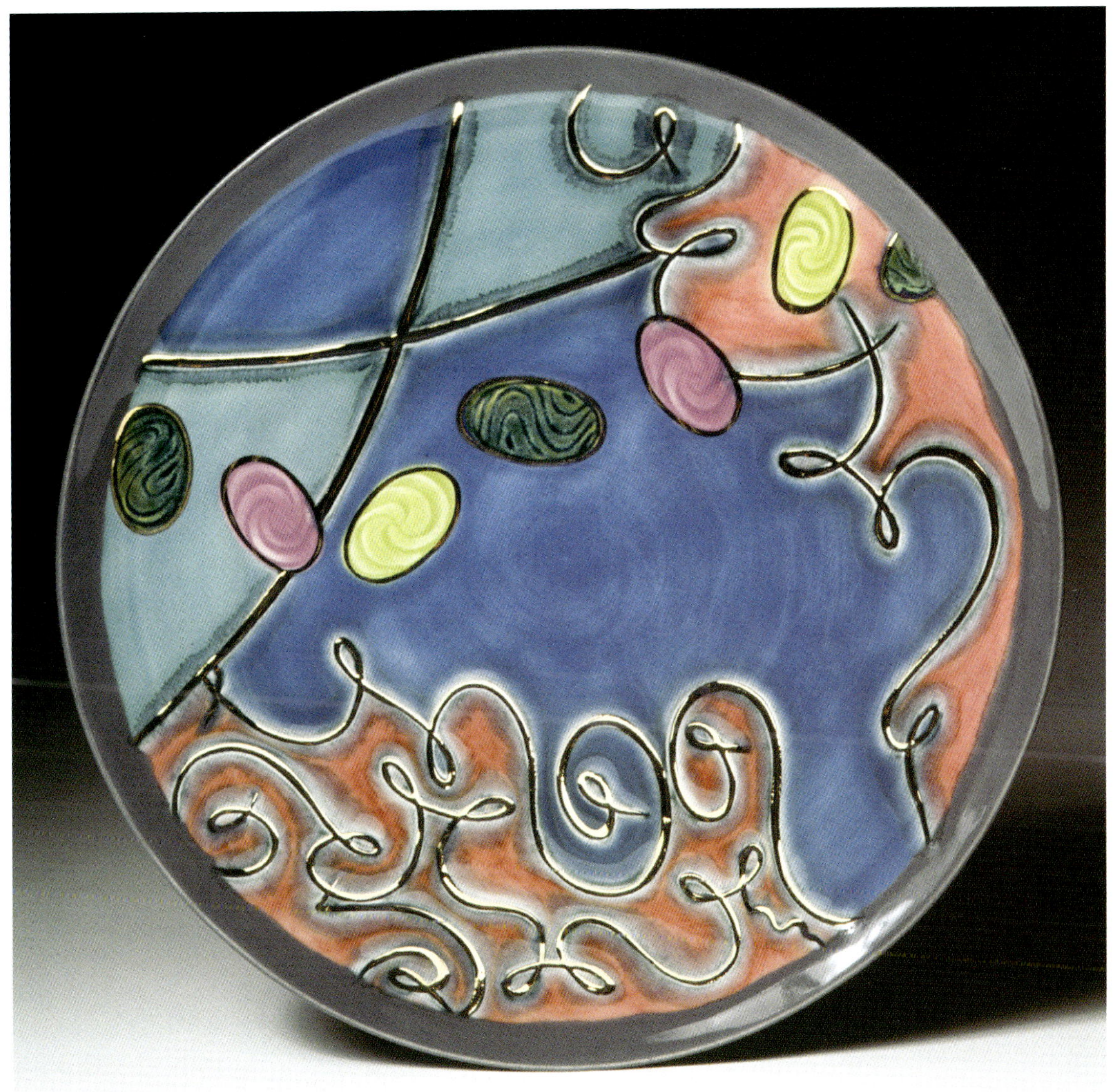

Lynn Goodman

Big X Platter | 2006

1 X 13 INCHES (2.5 X 33 CM)

Thrown and carved porcelain; glaze inlays; electric fired, cone 6; gold luster, cone 018

PHOTO BY D. JAMES DEE

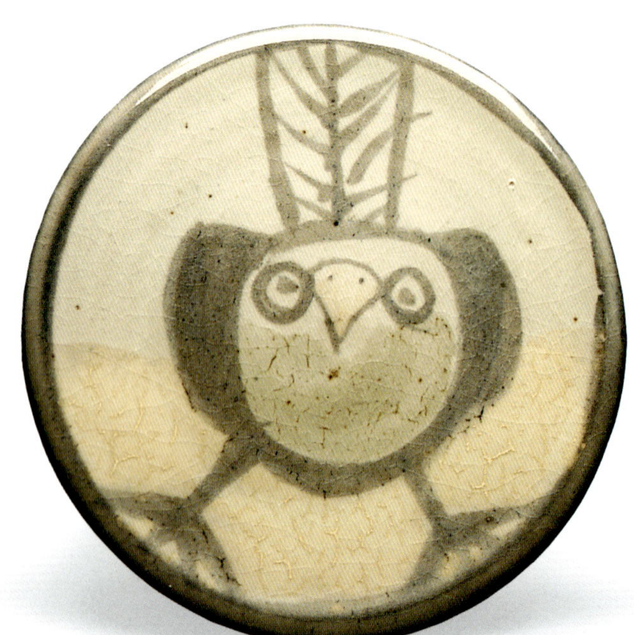

Lowell T. Hoisington II

Bird Plate | 2006

1 X 6½ INCHES (2.5 X 16.5 CM)

Wheel-thrown stoneware; celadon glaze, overglaze brushwork; gas fired in reduction, cone 10

PHOTO BY ARTIST

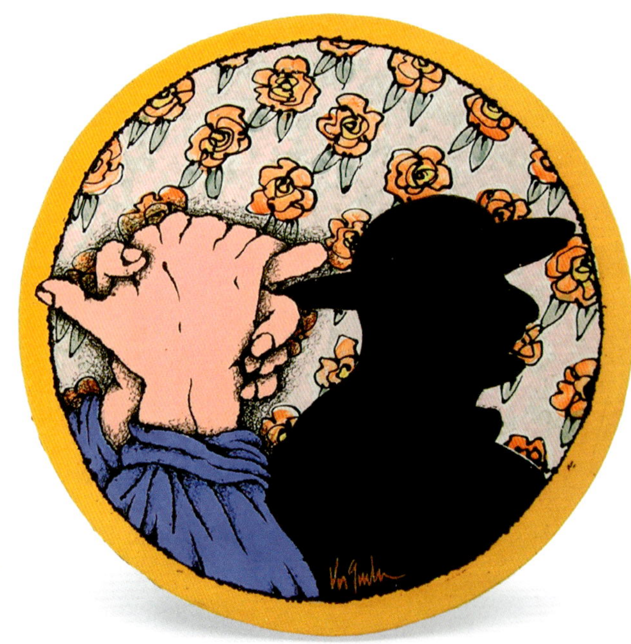

Rimas VisGirda

The Spanish Guy | 2000

1 X 14½ INCHES (2.5 X 36.8 CM)

Hand-built terra cotta; underglazes, wax inlay, slip trail, underglaze pencil; electric fired, cone 3

PHOTO BY ARTIST

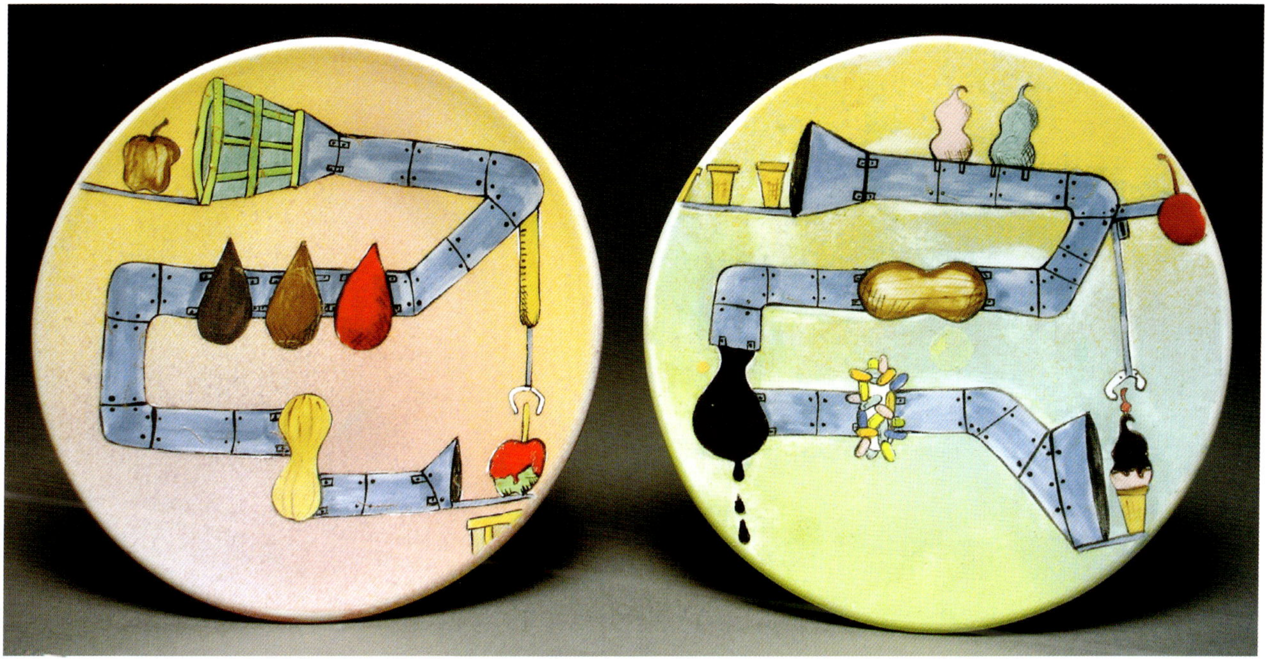

Melissa Lee

Happy Factories | 2007

EACH: 1 X 6 1/2 INCHES (2.5 X 16.5 CM)

Slip-cast porcelain; hand-painted underglazes; oxidation fired, cone 10

PHOTOS BY ARTIST

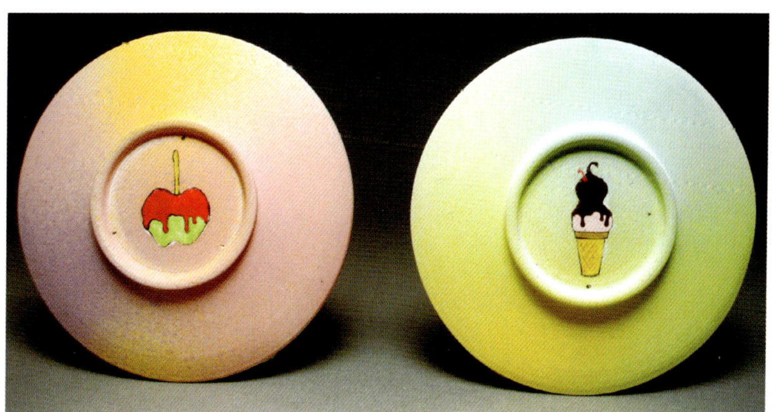

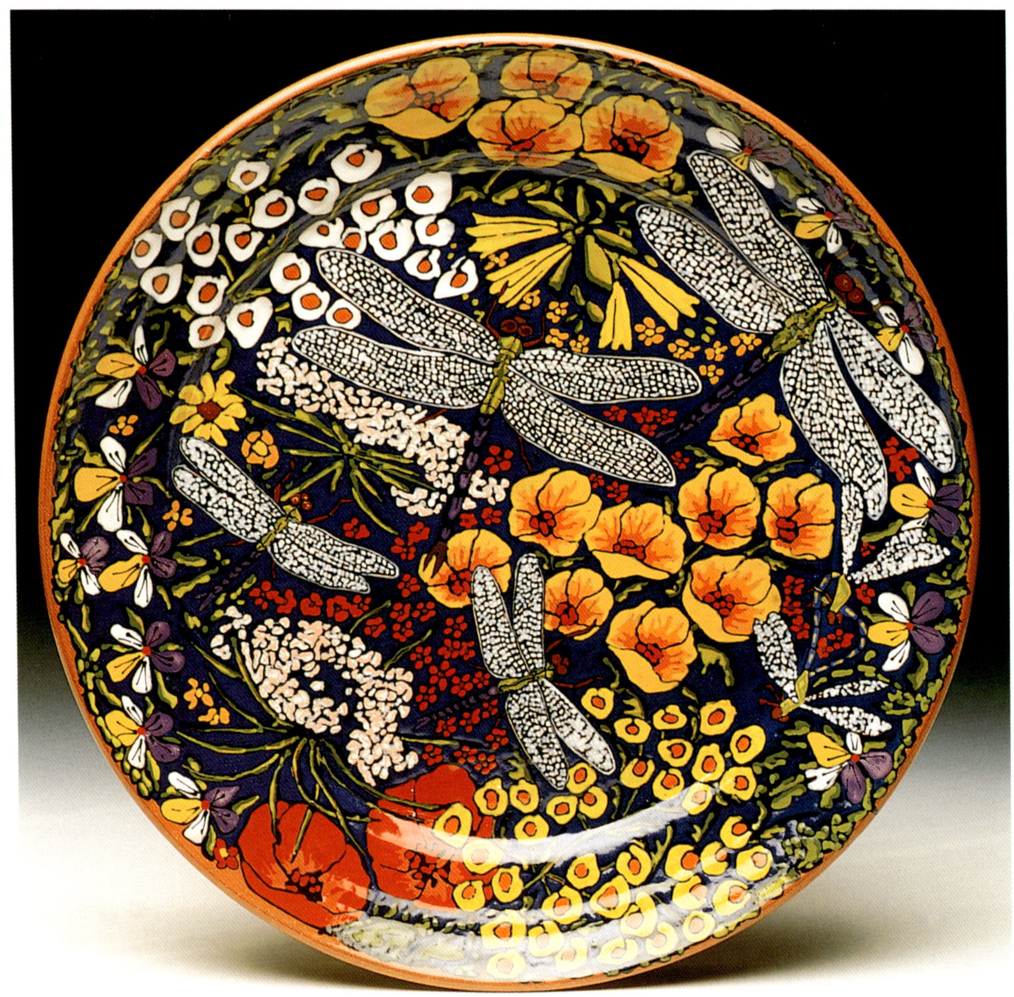

John Garland

Dragonfly Platter | 2007

16 INCHES (40.6 CM) IN DIAMETER

Wheel-thrown earthenware; underglaze and clear glaze; electric fired, cone 04

PHOTO BY SETH TICE-LEWIS

Lea M. Cundy

Wildflower Oval Rim Platter | 2007

1 X 17 X 13 INCHES (2.5 X 43.2 X 33 CM)

Hand-built earthenware; underglaze, clear dipped glaze; electric fired, cone 02; glazes, cone 04

PHOTO BY ED ALONSO

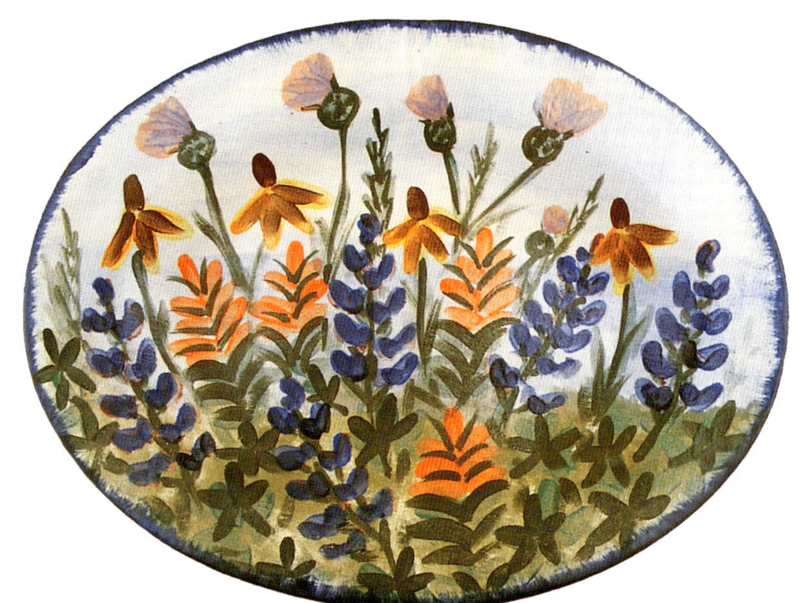

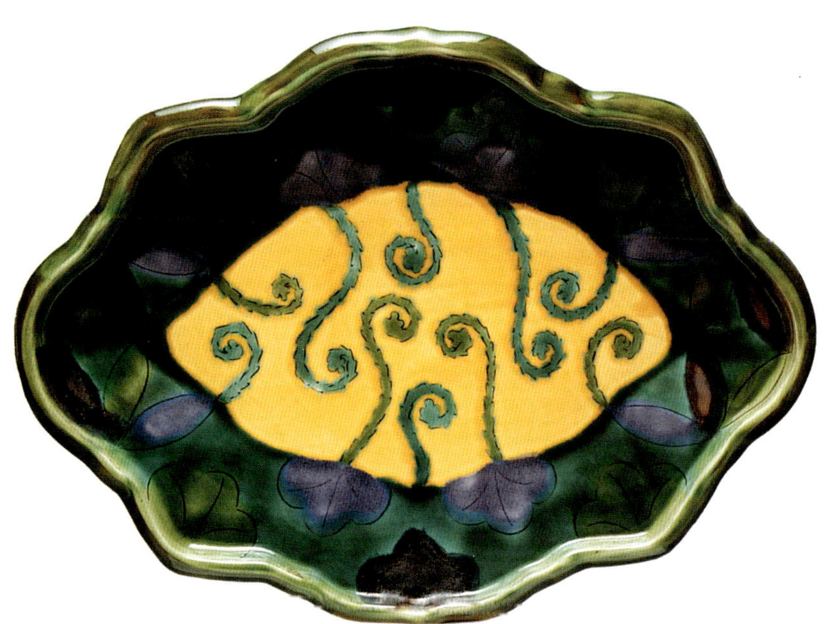

Joan Bruneau

Spring Platter with Fiddleheads | 2004

3 X 20 X 15 INCHES (7.6 X 50.8 X 38.1 CM)

Wheel-thrown and hand-built earthenware; slip, sgraffito; polychrome glazes

PHOTO BY ARTIST

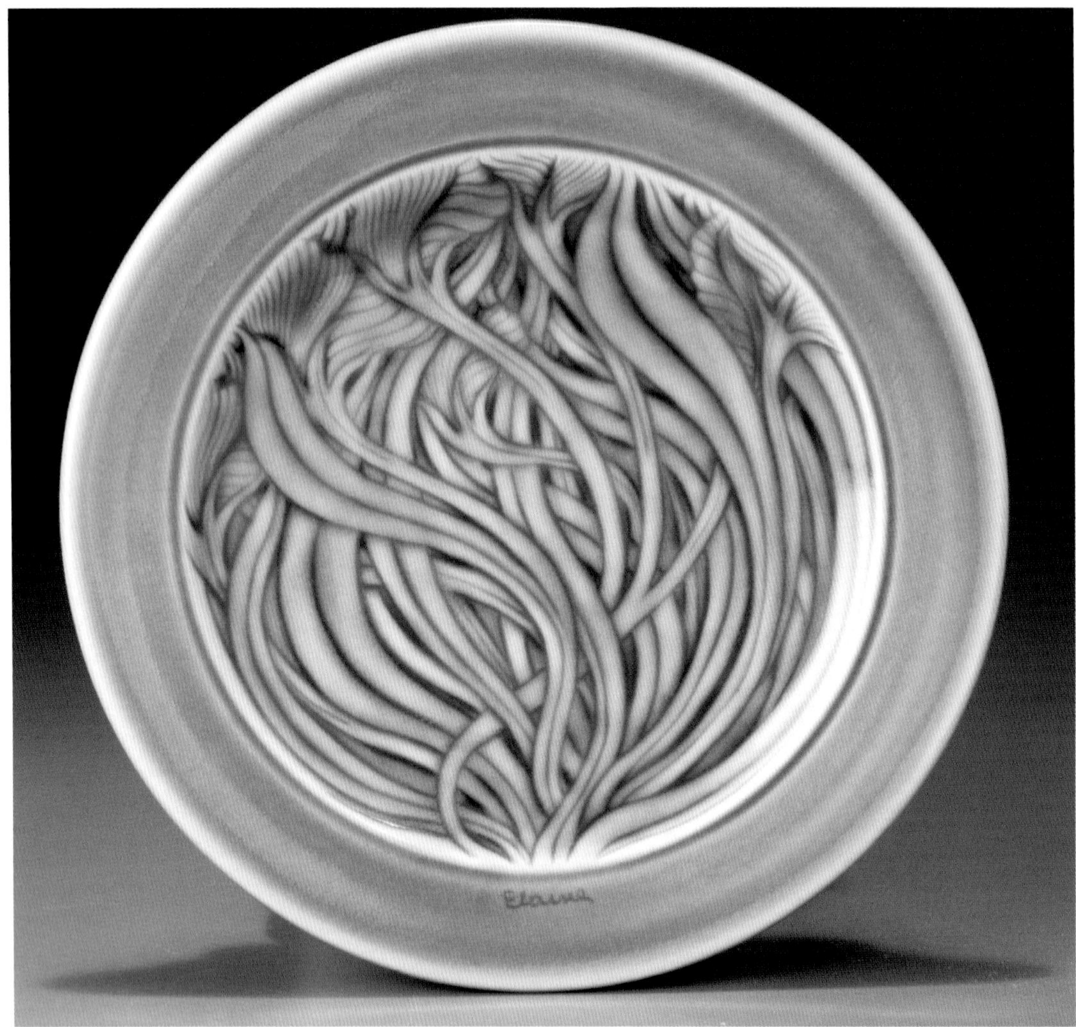

Elaine Coleman
Tom Coleman

Untitled | 2007

1 1/8 X 9 1/2 INCHES (2.9 X 24.1 CM)

Thrown Coleman porcelain; incised; steel blue celadon glaze, cone 10 reduction

PHOTO BY TOM C OLEMAN

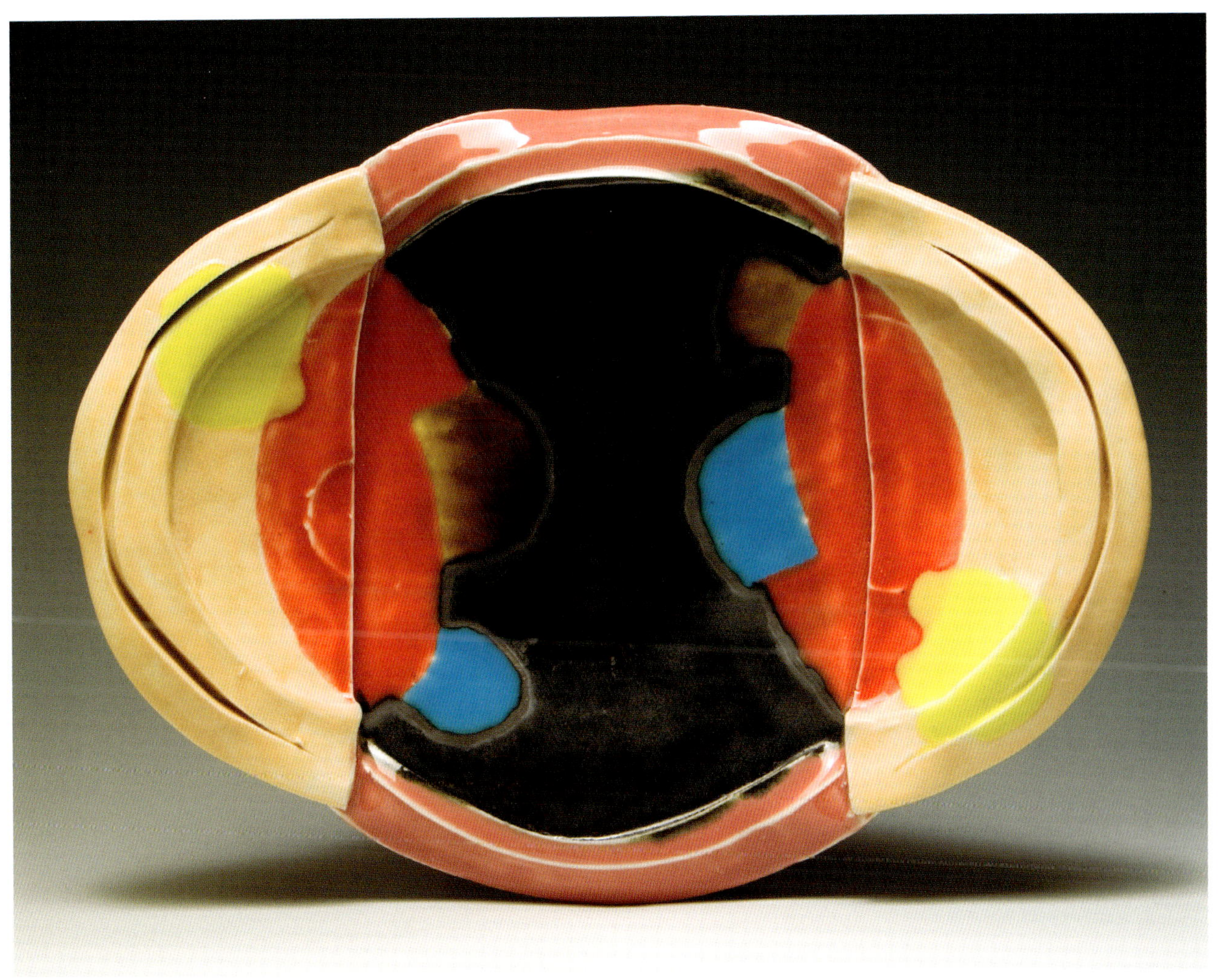

Frank Martin

Untitled | 2005

$2^1/_2$ X $12^1/_2$ X $9^1/_2$ INCHES (6.4 X 31.8 X 24.1 CM)

Wheel-thrown vitreous china with wheel-thrown and hand-formed additions; electric fired, cone 4

PHOTO BY ARTIST

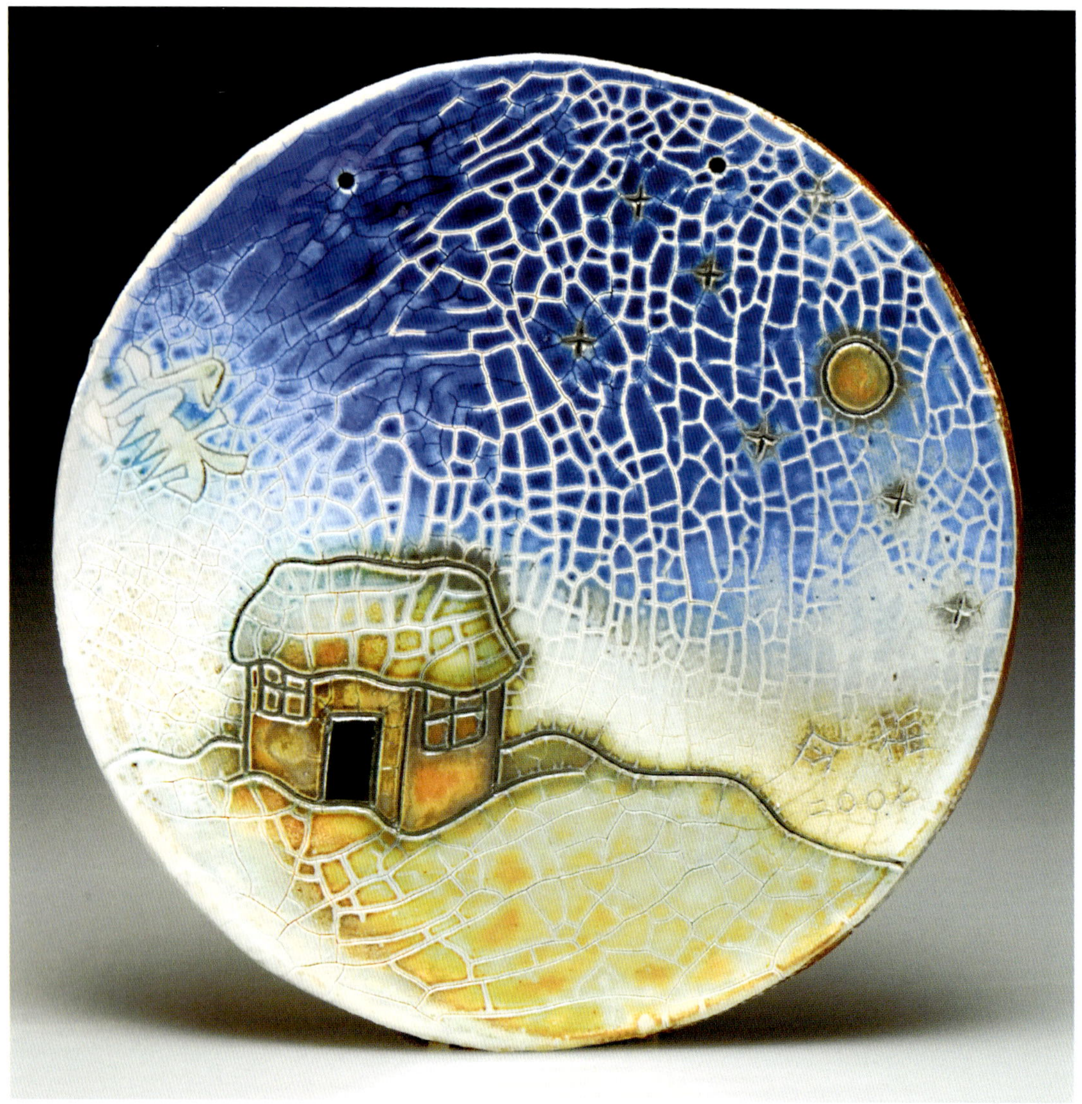

Mei Wu

Untitled | 2007

½ X 11 INCHES (1.3 X 27.9 CM)

Hand-built slab stoneware; carved, painted with slips; electric fired, cone 06; sprayed glazes, soda fired, cone 10

PHOTO BY GUY NICOL

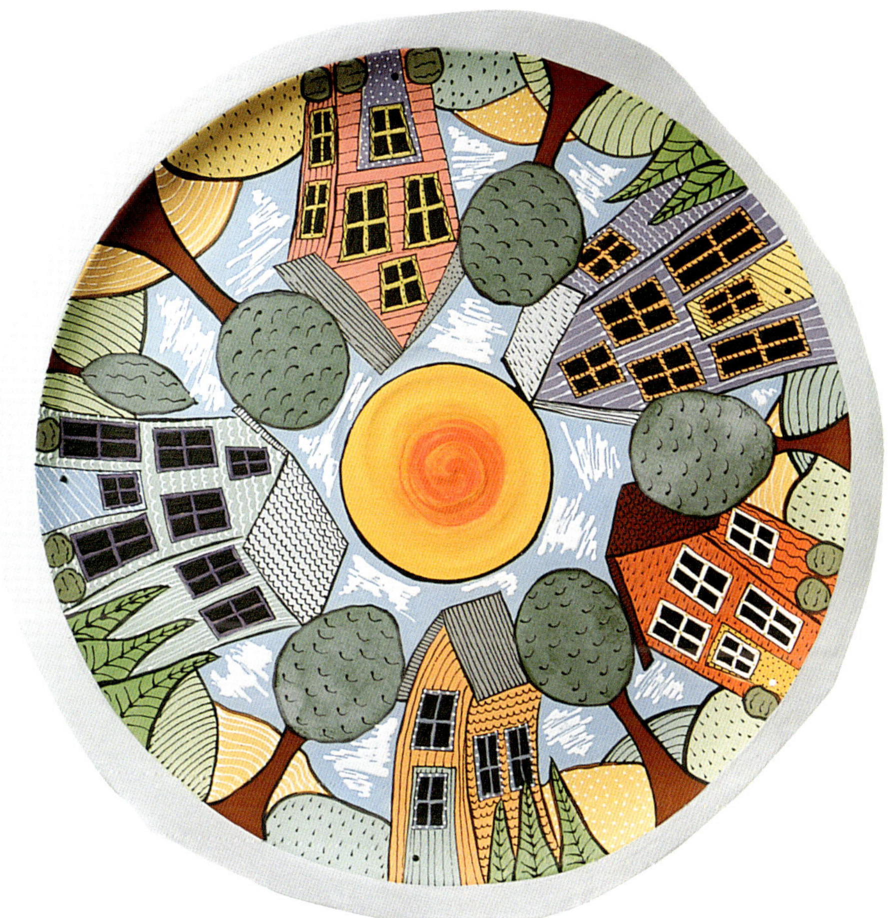

Kimberly Rorick

Painting the Town | 2006

20 INCHES (50.8 CM) IN DIAMETER

Press molded from rolled slab porcelain; underglaze, sprayed acrylic finish; electric fired, cone 5

PHOTO BY JOHN ESCOSA

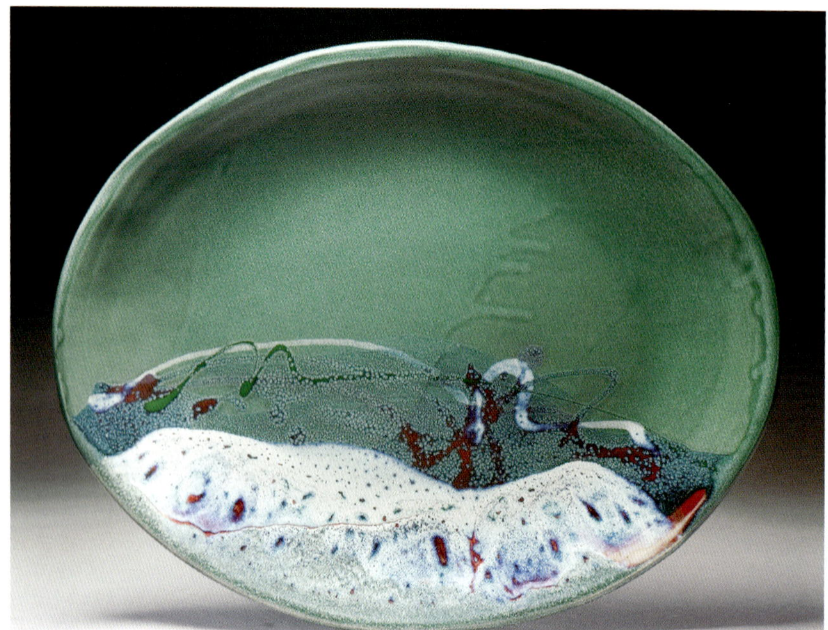

Macy Dorf
Oval Serving Tray | 2007
1 X 20 X 16 INCHES (2.5 X 50.8 X 40.6 CM)
Slump-molded white stoneware; copper red glaze, overglazes, glaze
PHOTO BY CHARLIE ROY

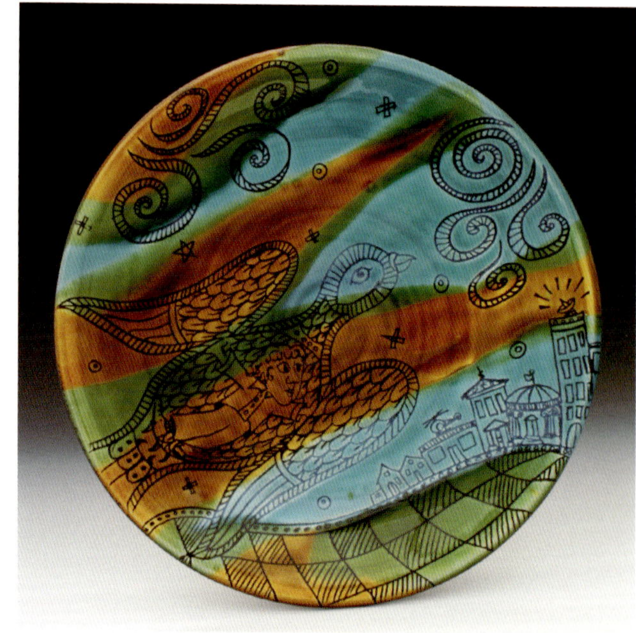

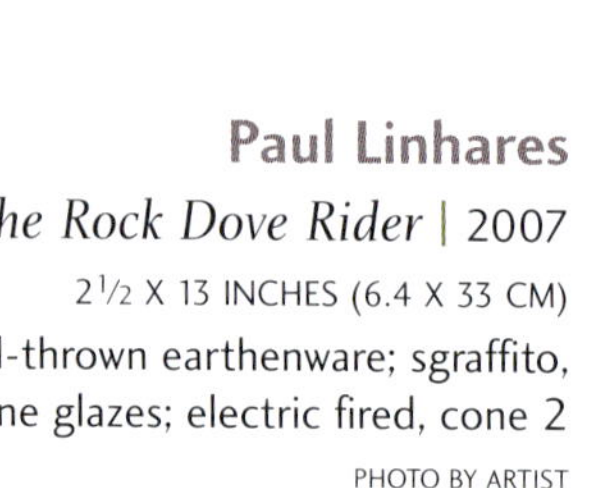

Paul Linhares
Approach of the Rock Dove Rider | 2007
2 1/2 X 13 INCHES (6.4 X 33 CM)
Wheel-thrown earthenware; sgraffito, alkaline glazes; electric fired, cone 2
PHOTO BY ARTIST

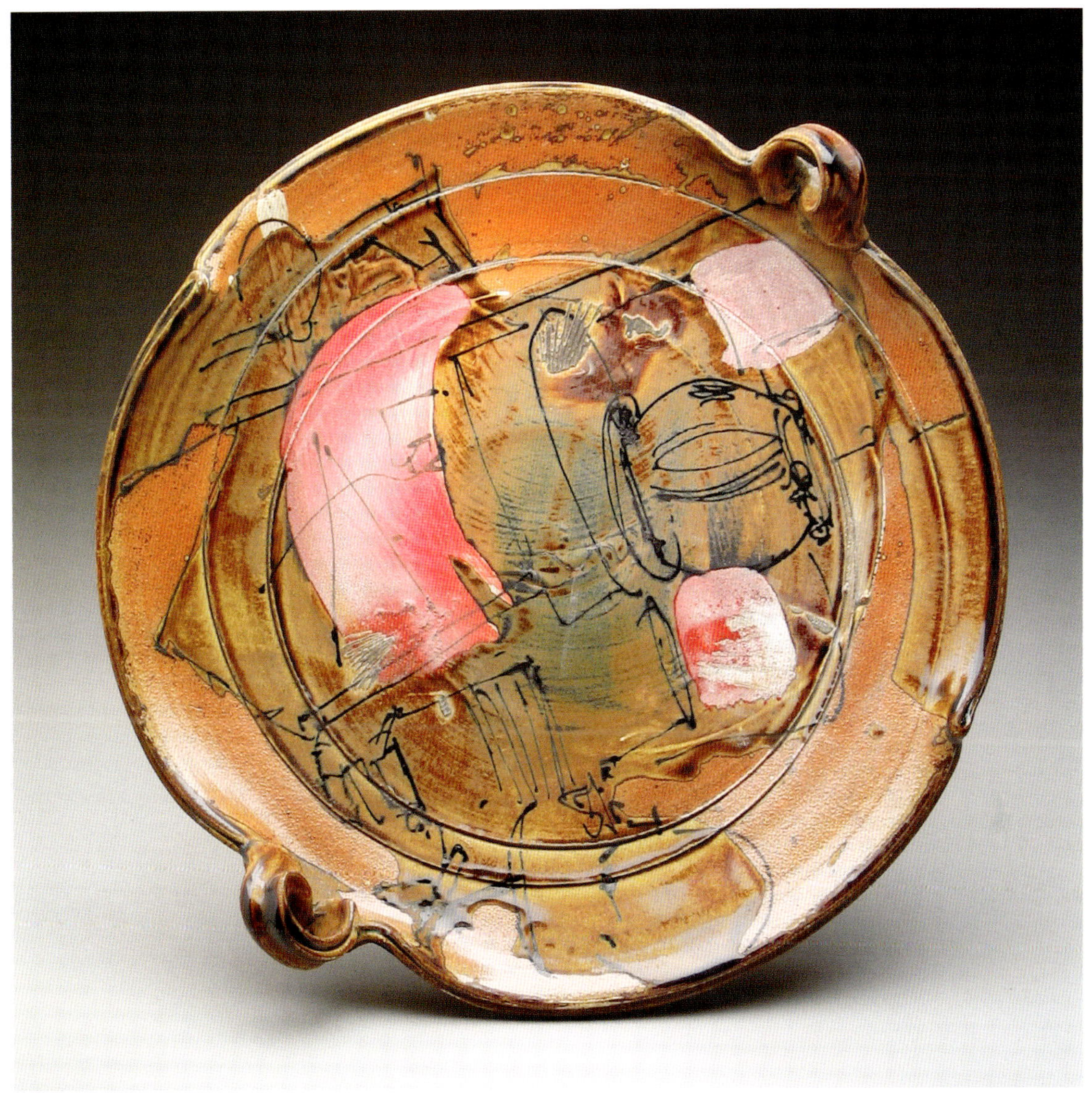

Josh DeWeese

Platter | 2007

4 X 17 INCHES (10.2 X 43.2 CM)

Wheel-thrown stoneware; underglaze and glaze; salt and soda fired, cone 10

PHOTO BY ARTIST

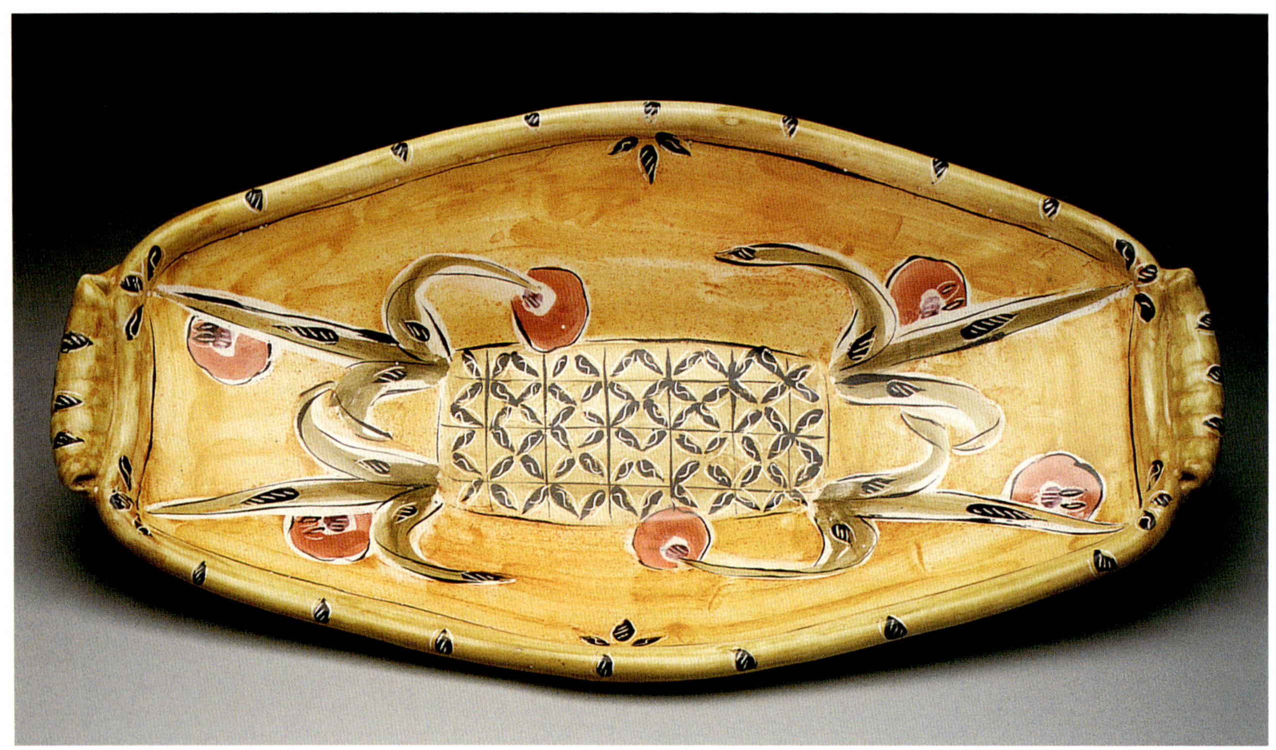

Posey Bacopoulos

Oval Platter | 2007

3 1/2 X 19 X 10 INCHES (8.9 X 48.3 X 25.4 CM)

Slab-built terra cotta; majolica, electric fired, cone 04

PHOTO BY KEVIN NOBEL

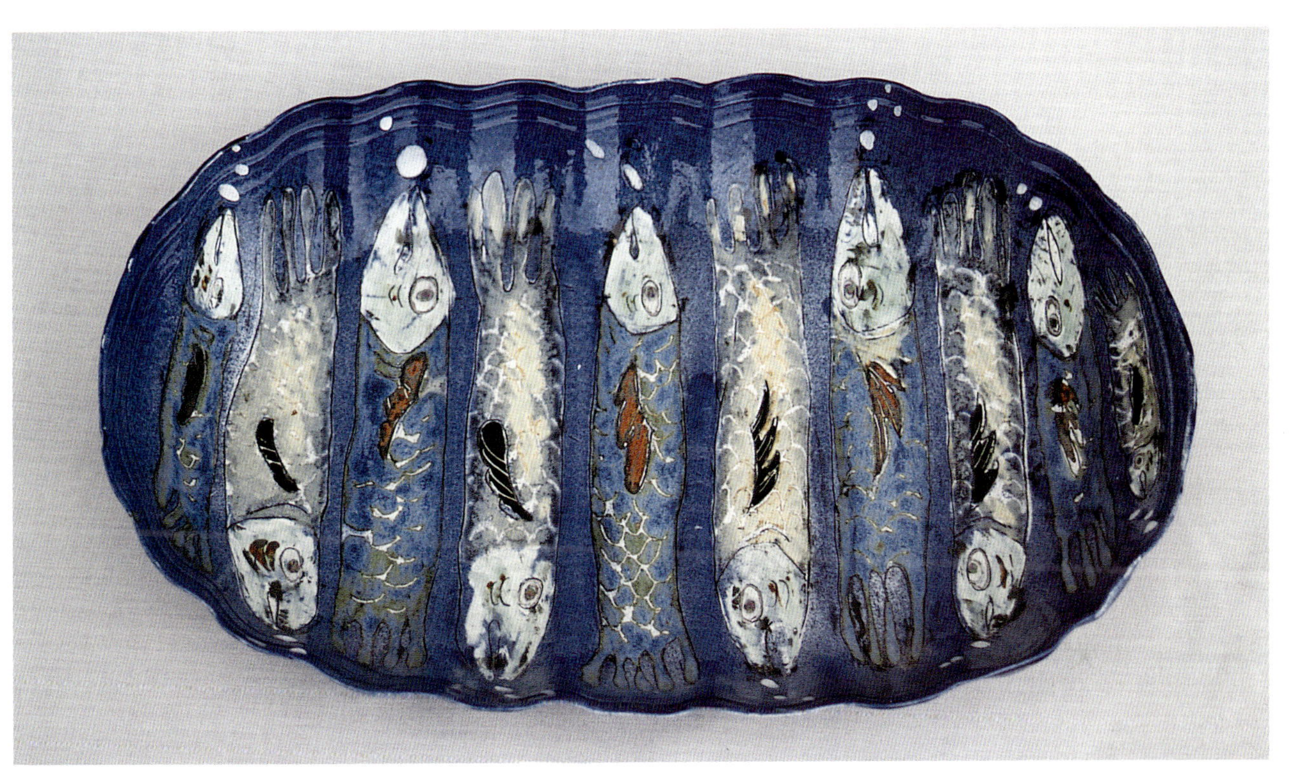

Skuja Braden

Fish Platter | 2001

1 3/4 X 14 X 9 INCHES (4.4 X 35.6 X 22.9 CM)

Hand-built, slip-cast porcelain; inscribed; glazes, stains; electric fired, cone 10; lusters

PHOTO BY MELISSA BRADEN

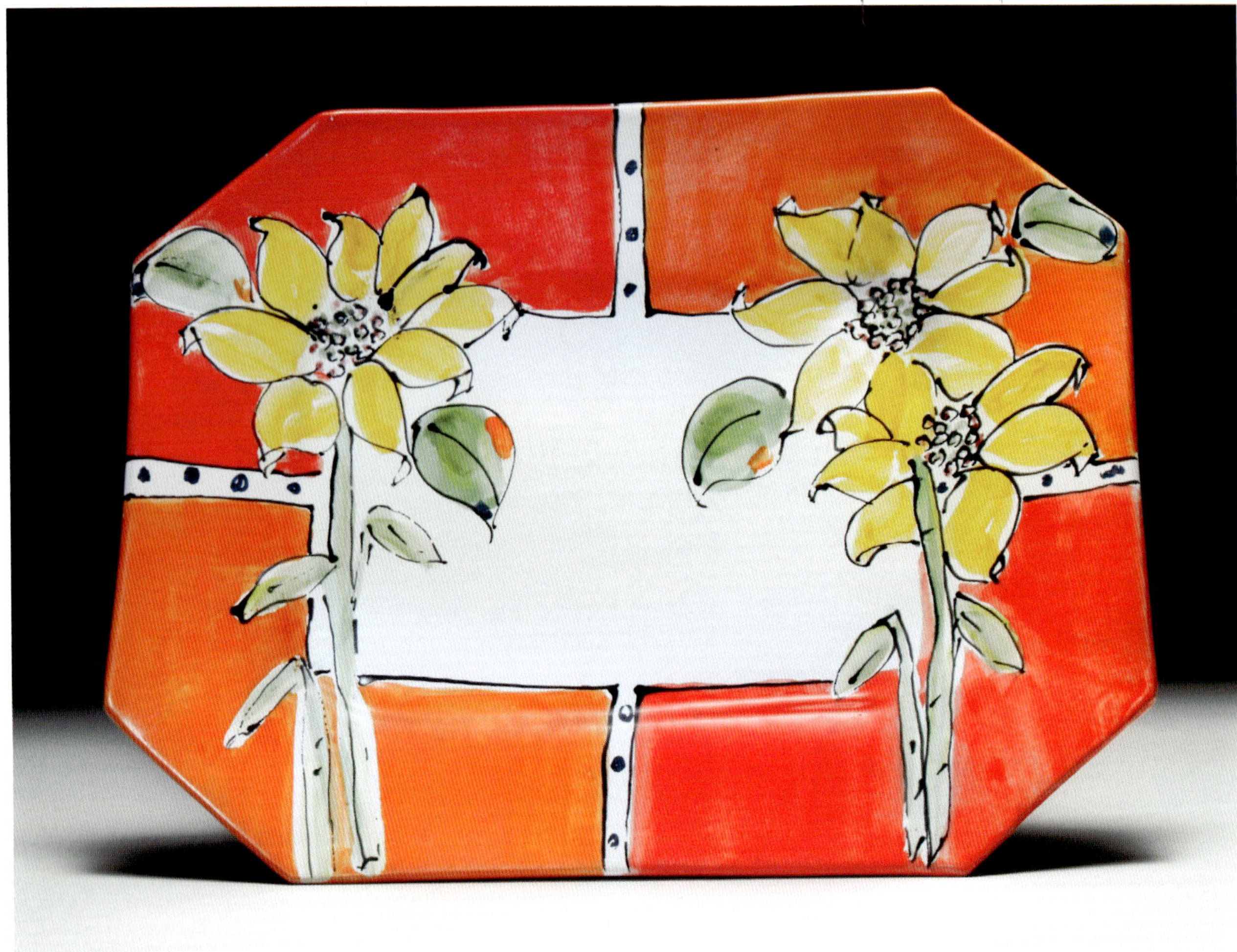

Margery K. Pozefsky

Yellow Flowers | 2007

1 X 14 X 9 INCHES (2.5 X 35.6 X 22.9 CM)

Slab-built terra cotta; majolica, electric fired, cone 05

PHOTO BY JESSICA BROAD

Cindy Teyro

Sunny Bloom | 2007

2 X 13 X 11 INCHES (5.1 X 33 X 27.9 CM)

Hand-formed and slab-built stoneware; electric fired, cone 04; cone 5

PHOTO BY LINDA LITTERAL

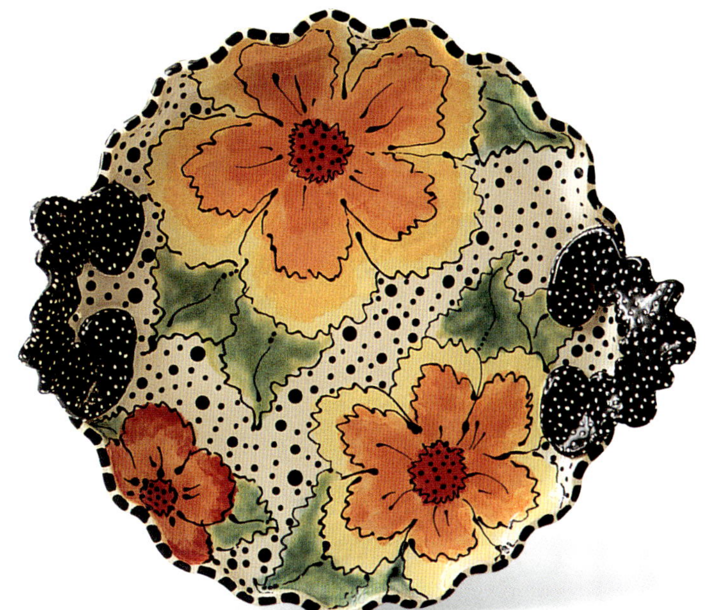

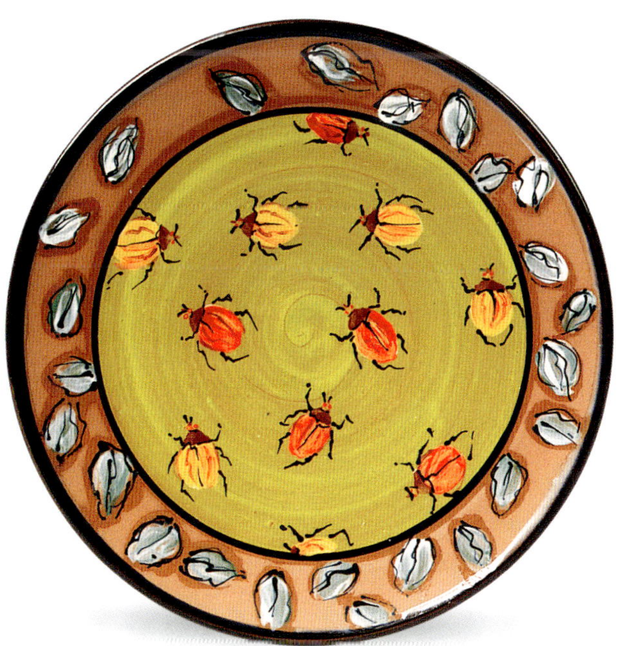

Mark Strom

Bugs and Leaves | 2007

1 1/2 X 11 1/2 INCHES (3.8 X 29.2 CM)

Wheel-thrown terra cotta; low-fire underglazes; electric fired, cone 05

PHOTO BY RICHARD NICOL

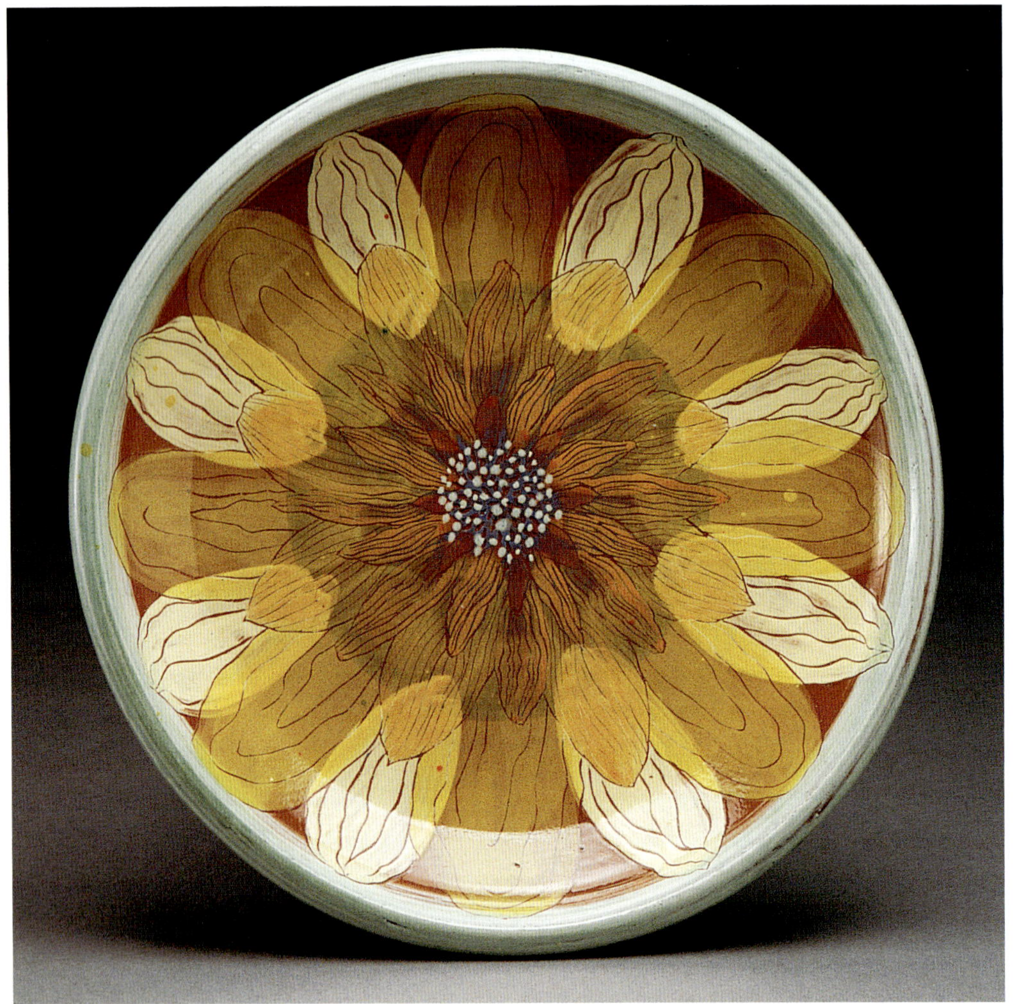

Molly Lithgo

Floral Platter | 2007

$1\,{}^{1}/_{2}$ X 12 INCHES (3.8 X 30.5 CM)

Wheel-thrown earthenware; hand-painted slips and underglazes, incised, sgraffito; electric fired, cone 04; glazes, cone 04

PHOTO BY TOM MILLS

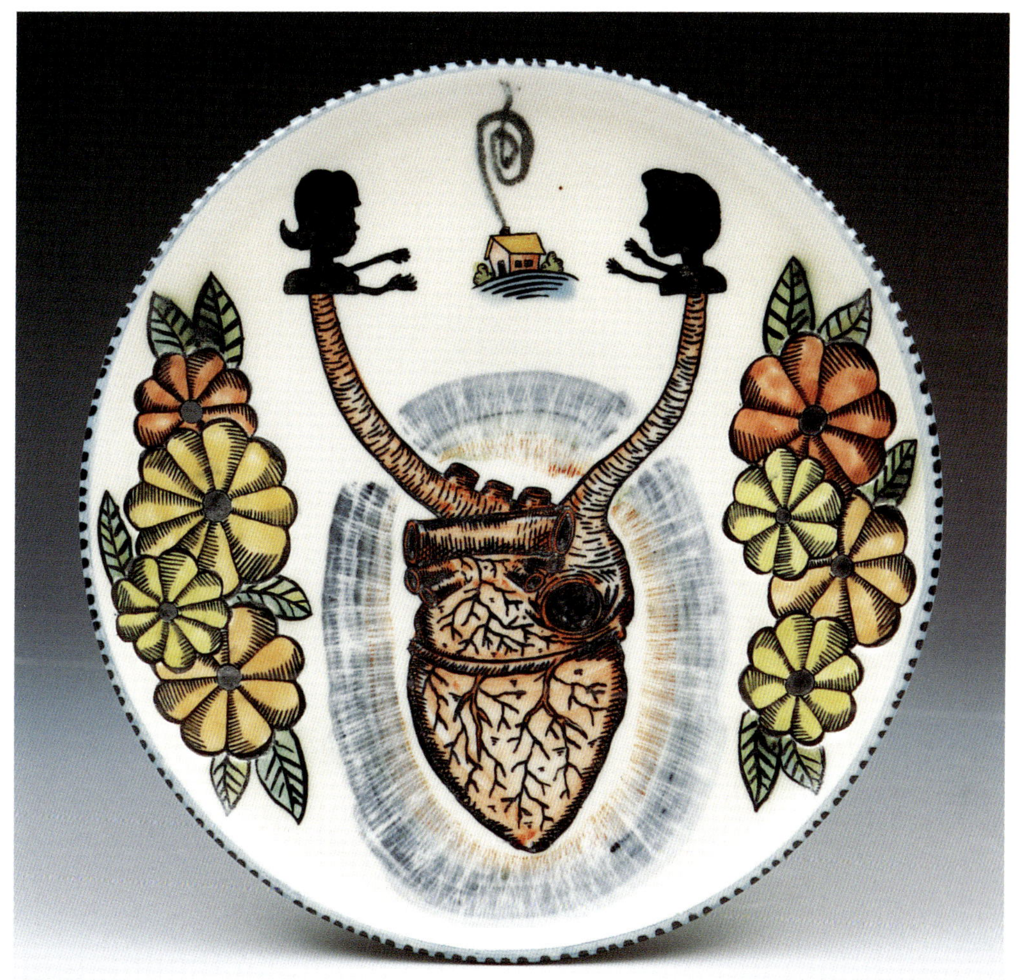

Michael Corney

Wedding Plate | 2006

1 1/2 X 11 INCHES (3.8 X 27.9 CM)

Wheel-thrown porcelain; brush painted; electric fired, cone 10

PHOTO BY MARGO GEIST

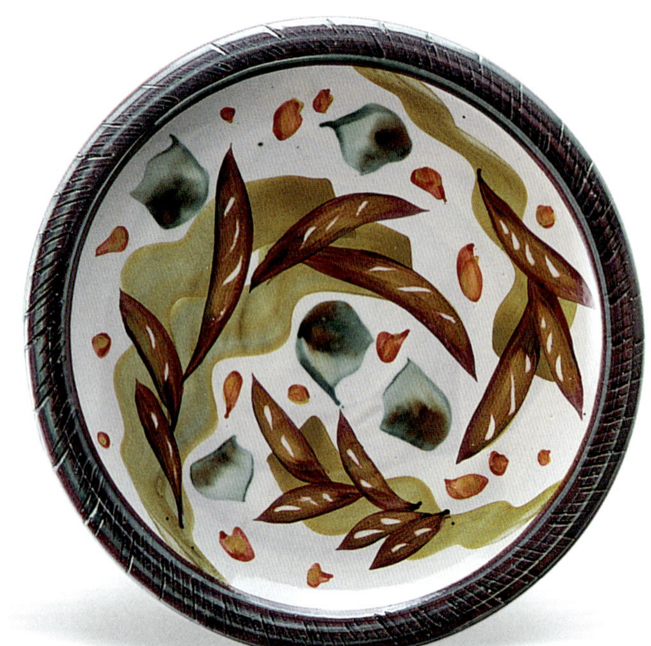

Stanley Mace Andersen

Platter | 2007

1 1/2 X 15 INCHES (3.8 X 38.1 CM)

Wheel-thrown earthenware; majolica; fritted glaze, commercial stains; electric fired, cone 03

PHOTO BY TOM MILLS

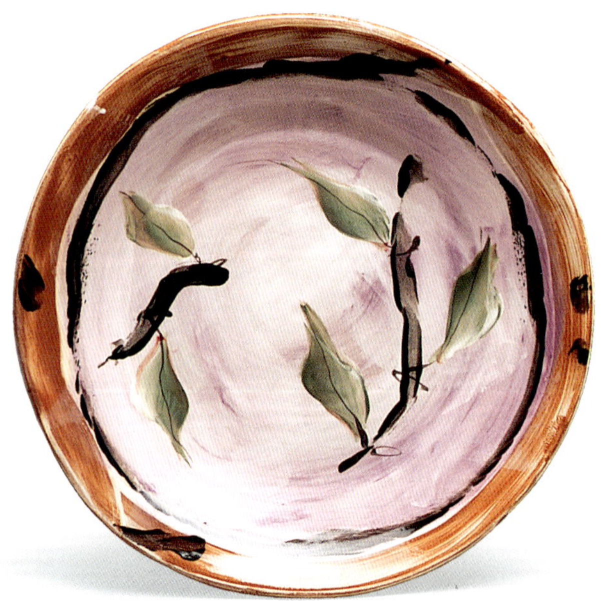

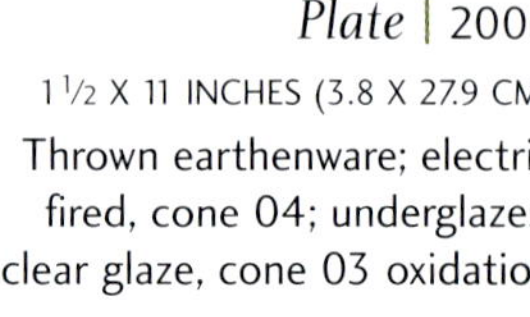

George McCauley

Plate | 2006

1 1/2 X 11 INCHES (3.8 X 27.9 CM)

Thrown earthenware; electric fired, cone 04; underglazes; clear glaze, cone 03 oxidation

PHOTO BY ARTIST

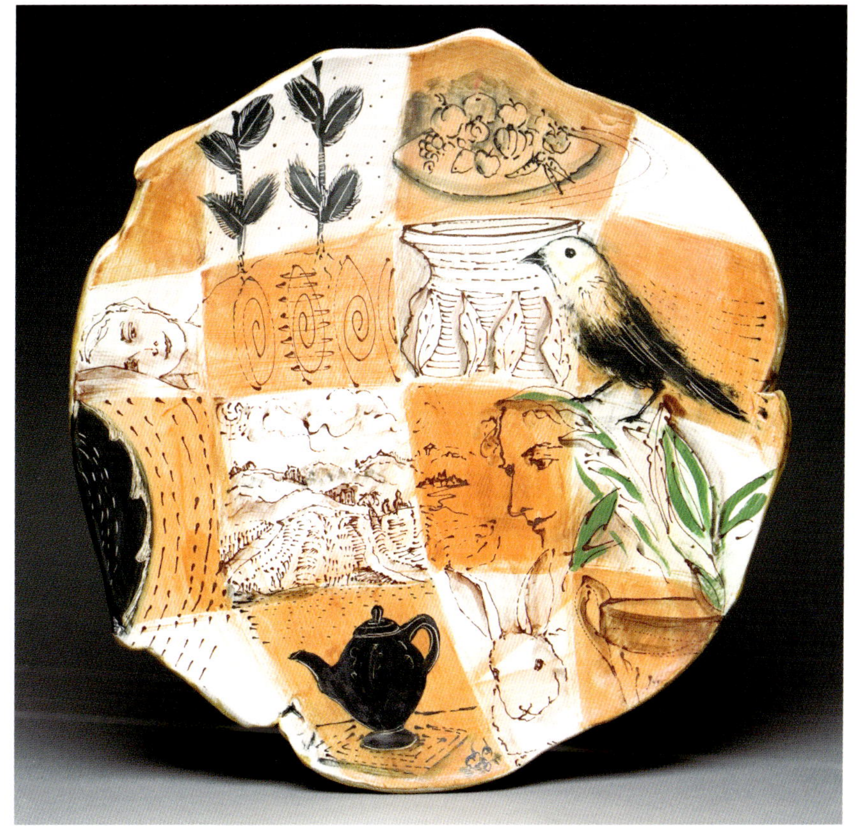

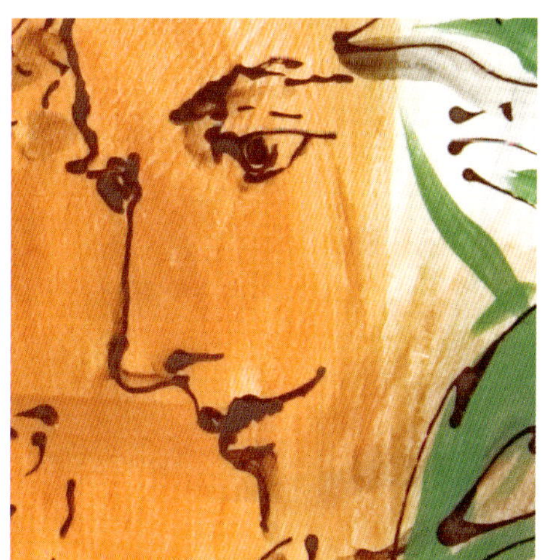

Laurie Shaman

Untitled | 2006

3 X 12 X 12 INCHES (7.6 X 30.5 X 30.5 CM)

Hand-built earthenware; slip trail and brushwork with underglazes; electric fired, cone 04; glazes, cone 06

PHOTOS BY PETER KIAR

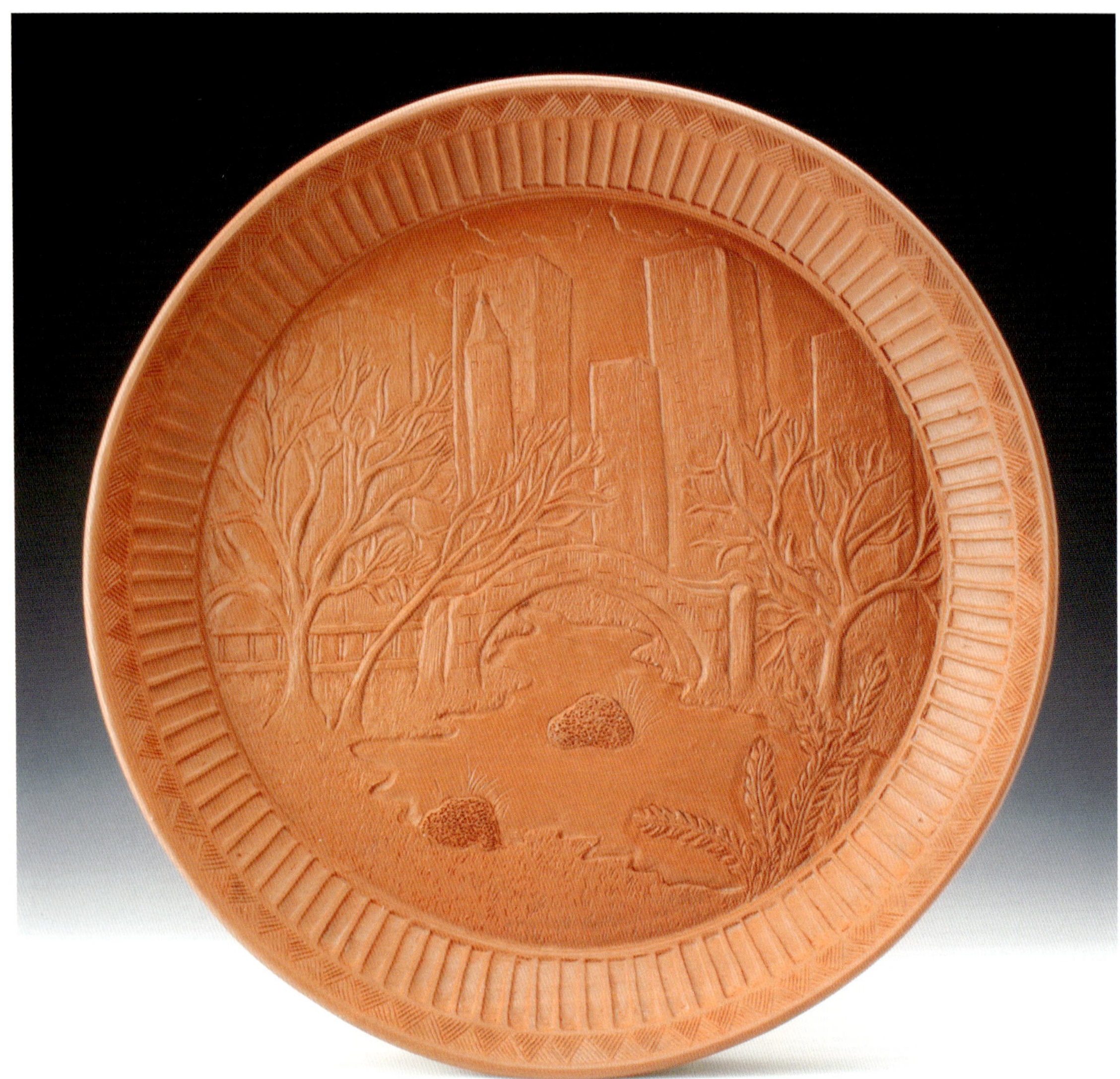

Shikha Joshi

Coexistence | 2007

2 X 16 INCHES (5.1 X 40.6 CM)

Wheel-thrown and hand-carved red clay; electric fired, cone 4

PHOTO BY ANAND JOSHI

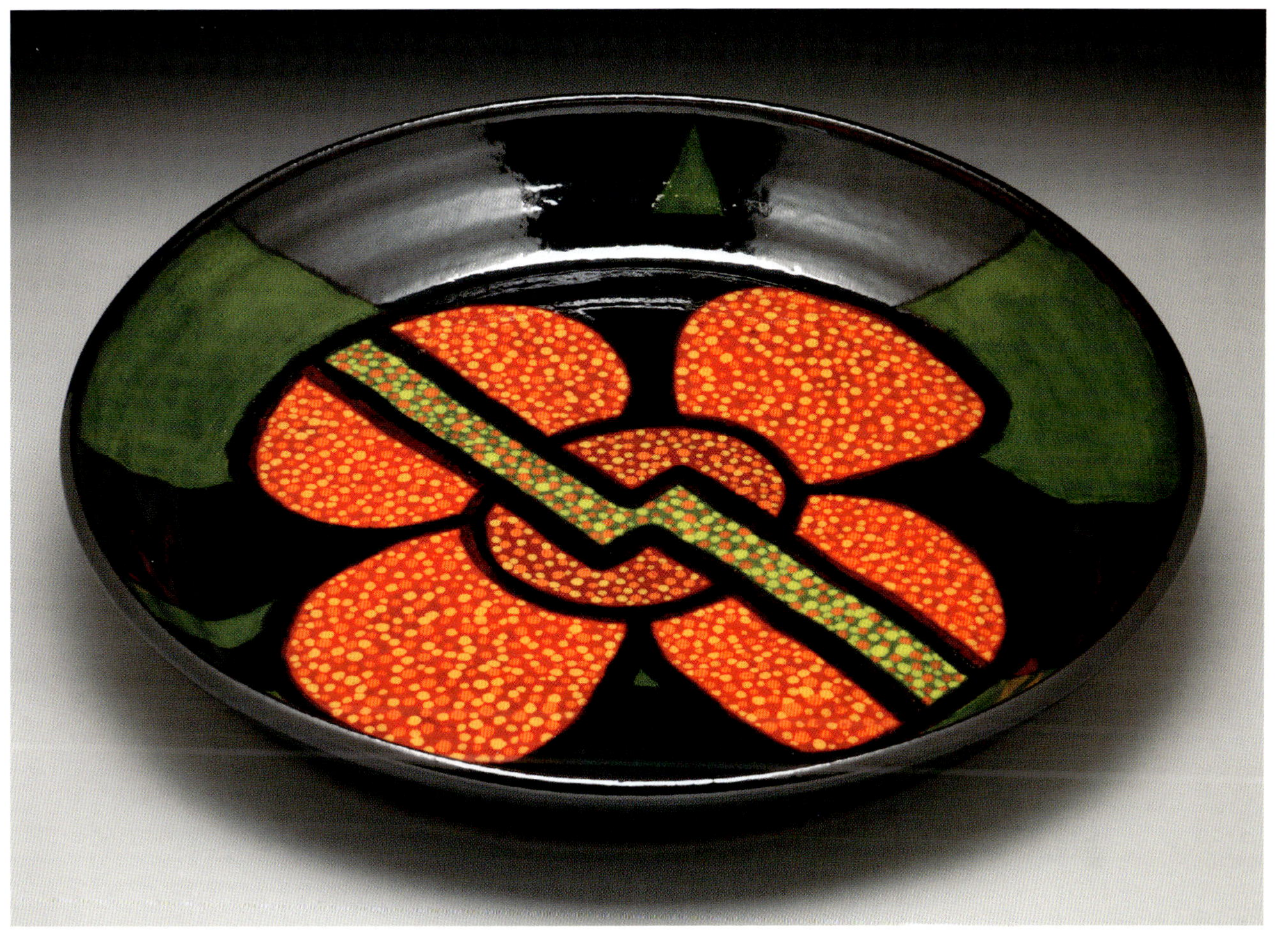

Debbie Bowden

Large Polka Platter | 2007

2 3/4 X 20 INCHES (7 X 50.8 CM)

Wheel-thrown orange earthenware; underglaze, metallic and clear glazes; electric fired, cone 05

PHOTO BY PETER GORMAN

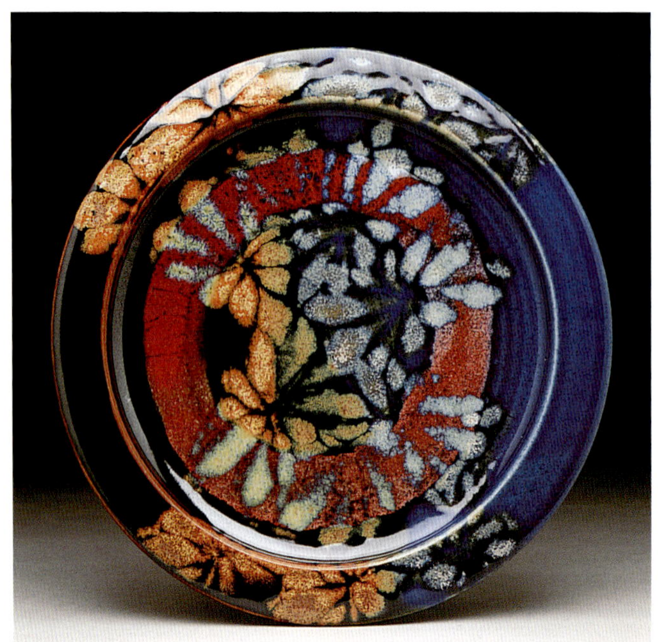

Rikki Gill

Dinner Plate | 2005

$\frac{1}{2}$ X 11 INCHES (1.3 X 27.9 CM)

Wheel-thrown porcelain; stamped; multi-glazed, gas fired in reduction, cone 11

PHOTO BY ARTIST

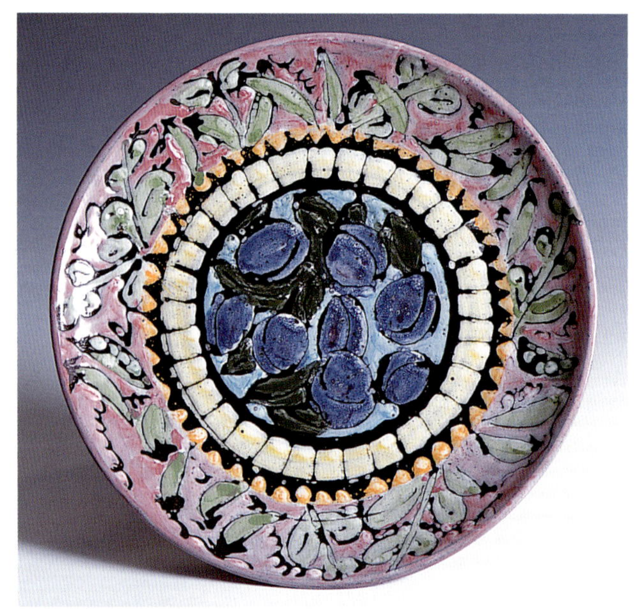

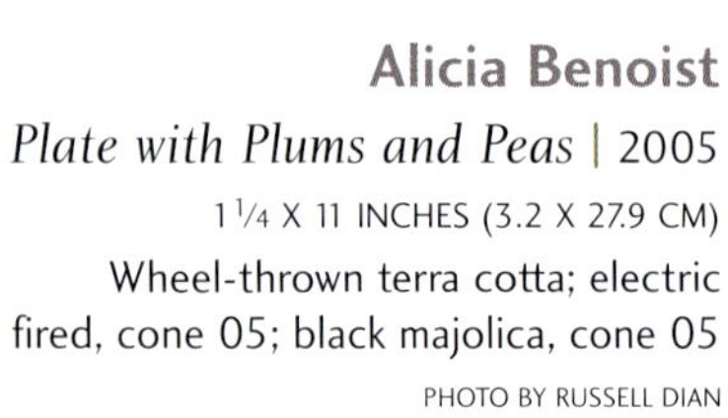

Alicia Benoist

Plate with Plums and Peas | 2005

1 $\frac{1}{4}$ X 11 INCHES (3.2 X 27.9 CM)

Wheel-thrown terra cotta; electric fired, cone 05; black majolica, cone 05

PHOTO BY RUSSELL DIAN

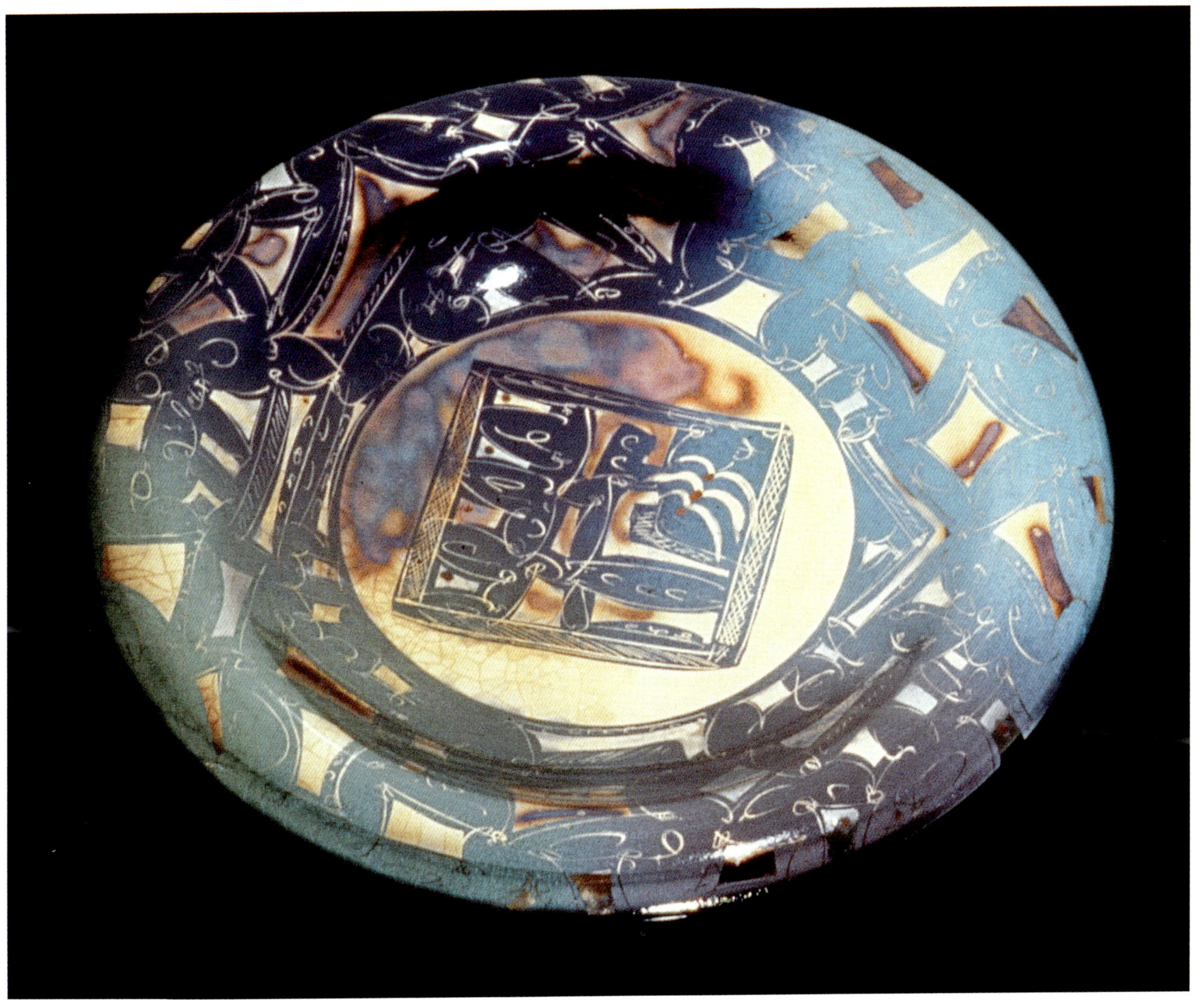

Greg Daly

Luster-Decorated Platter with Glaze-Over-Glaze | 2000

4 X 22 INCHES (10.2 X 55.9 CM)

Wheel-thrown stoneware; gas fired in oxidation, cone 9; resin luster, cone 017

PHOTO BY RUSSELL BAADER

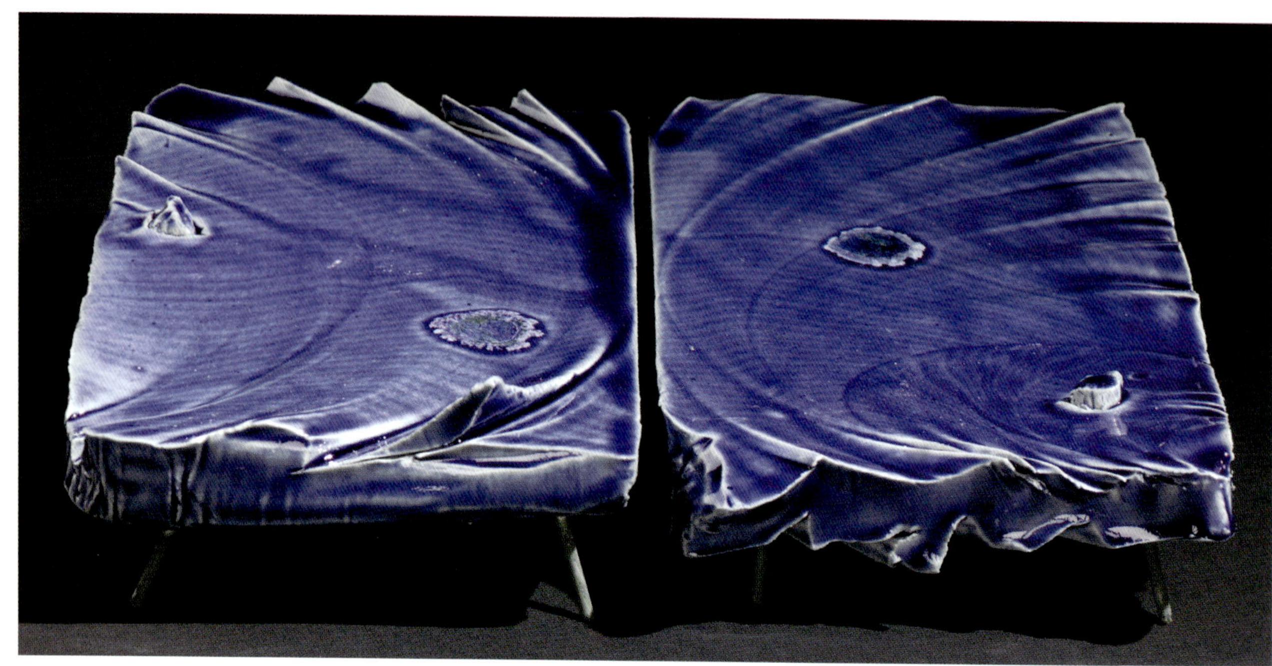

Ray Chen

Wave | 2007

3 X 13 X 10 INCHES (7.6 X 33 X 25.4 CM)

Slab-wired stoneware; electric fired, cone 6; glaze, cone 6

PHOTO BY ARTIST

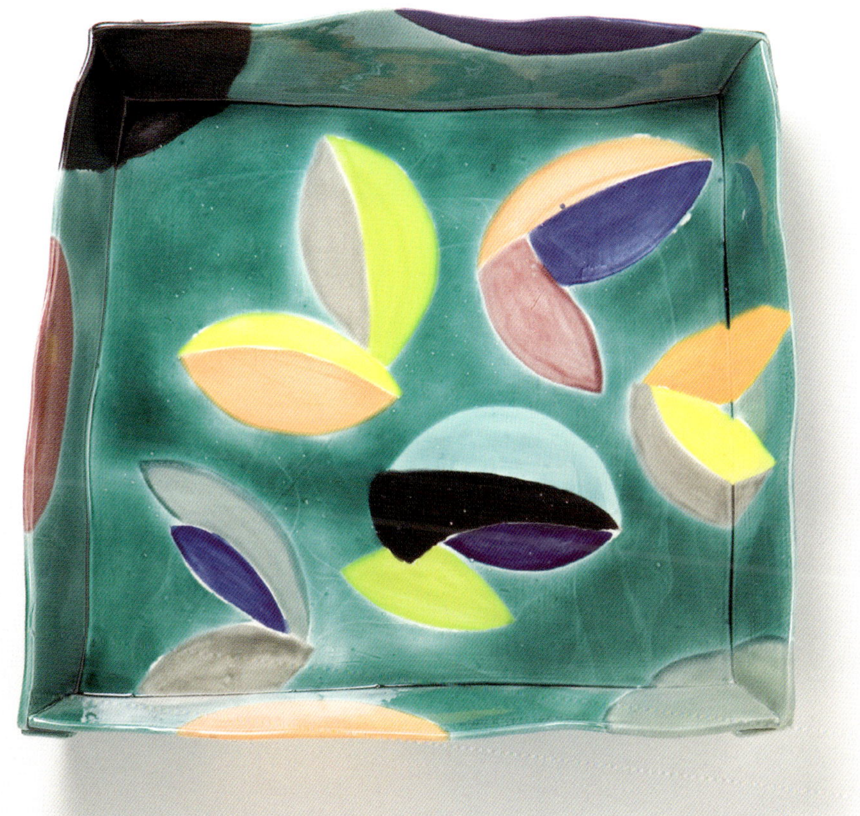

Judith Salomon

Green Square Platter | 2006

3 X 17 X 17 INCHES (7.6 X 43.2 X 43.2 CM)

Hand-built with slip-cast slabs of white terra cotta; electric fired, cone 03 bisque; glazes, cone 05

PHOTO BY ANTHONY GRAY

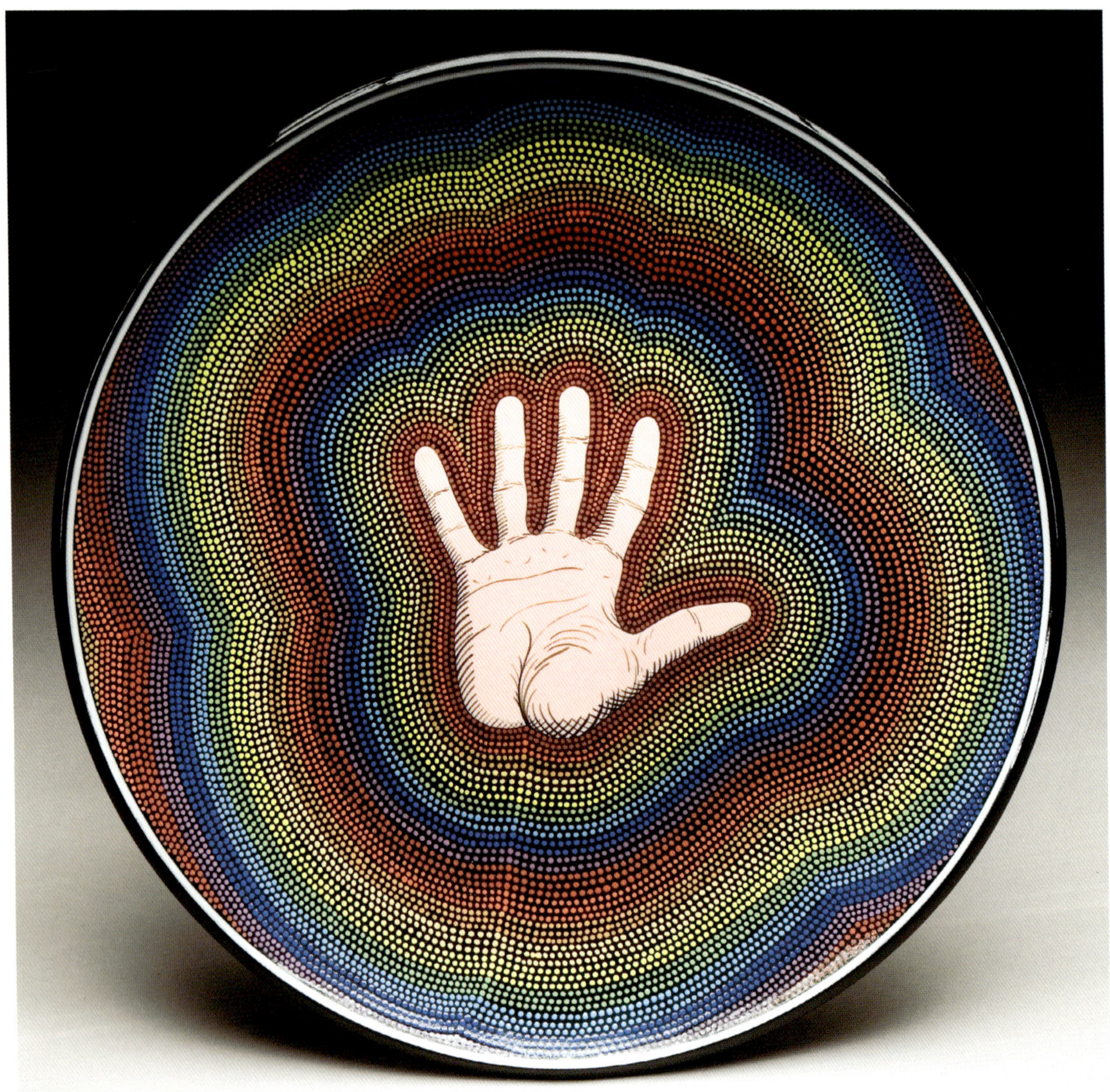

Patrick L. Dougherty
Right Hand Man | 2006
$4\frac{1}{2}$ X 24 INCHES (11.4 X 61 CM)
Wheel-thrown earthenware; underglazes, clear glaze; oxidation fired, cone 04
PHOTO BY JAY BACHEMIN

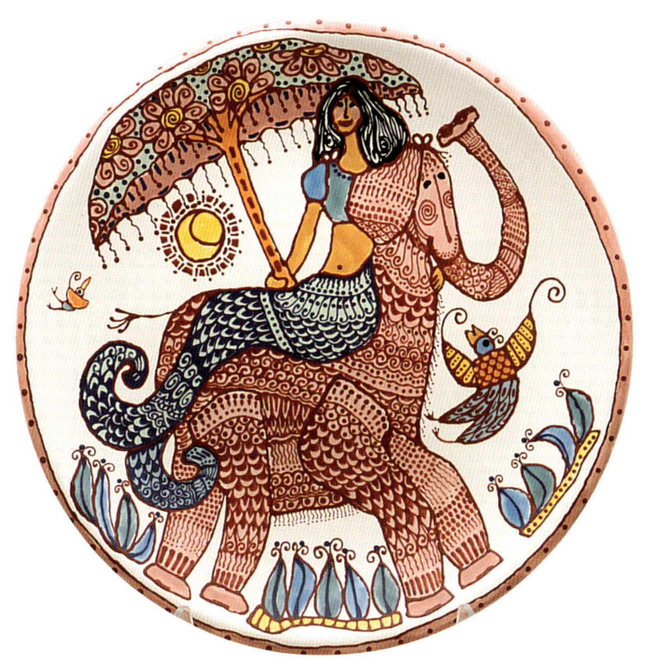

Julie Szerina Stein

Untitled | 2002

2 X 17 INCHES (5.1 X 43.2 CM)

Slip-cast low-fire whiteware; commercial glazes, electric fired, cone 06

PHOTO BY JACK R. KULAWIK

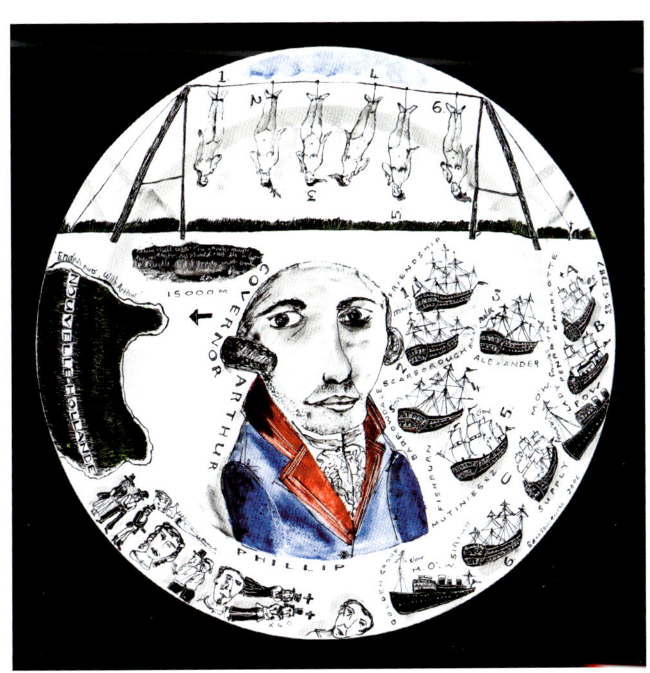

Bern Emmerichs

Endeavours with Arthur | 2006

1 X $16^{1/2}$ INCHES (2.5 X 41.9 CM)

Earthenware; electric multi-fired, 850°F (454°C); glazes

PHOTO BY GRAHAM BARING

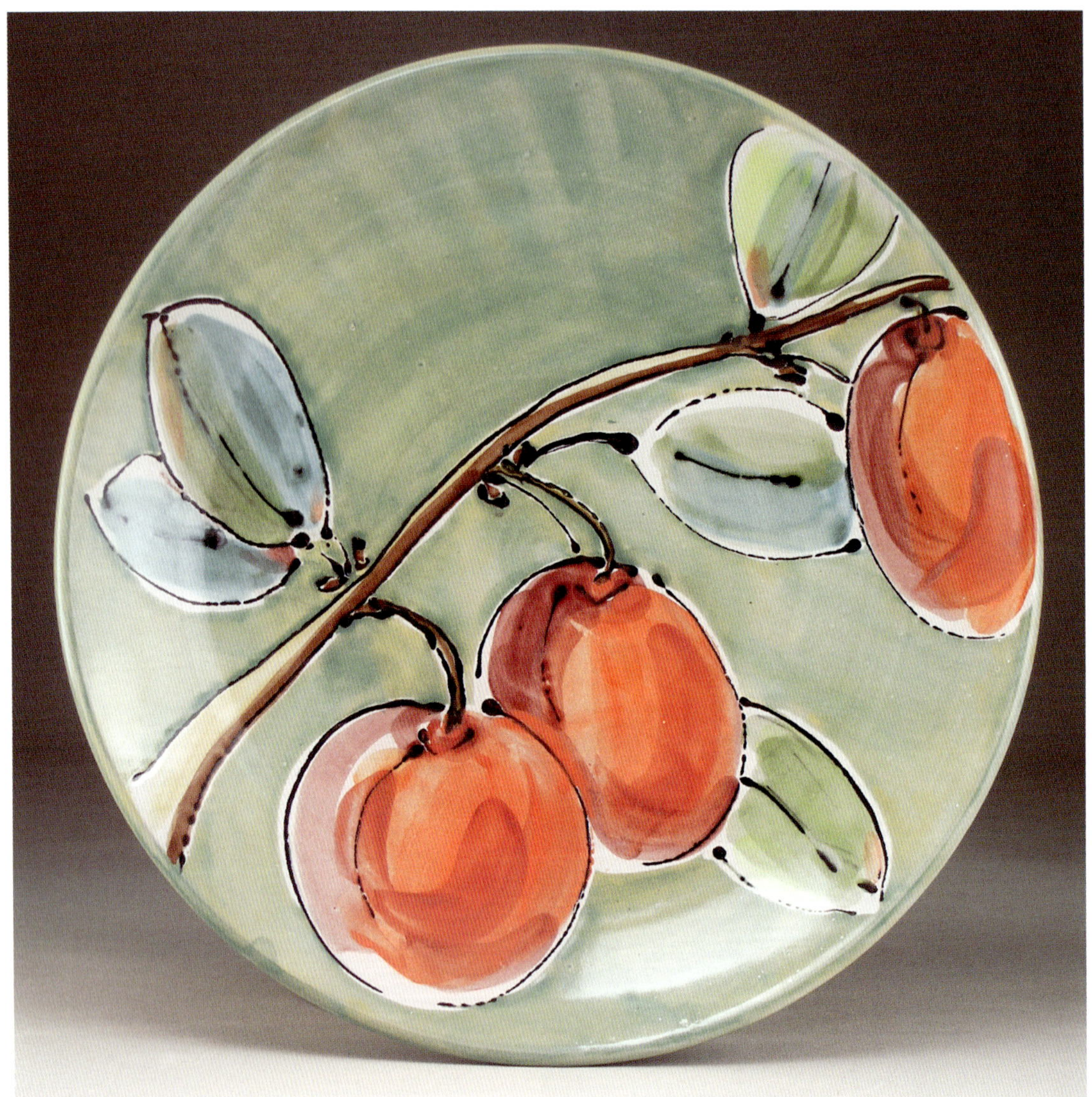

Wynne Wilbur

Cherries Plate | 2007

$1\frac{1}{2}$ X $10\frac{1}{2}$ INCHES (3.8 X 26.7 CM)

Wheel-thrown terra cotta; majolica; electric fired, cone 03

PHOTO BY ARTIST

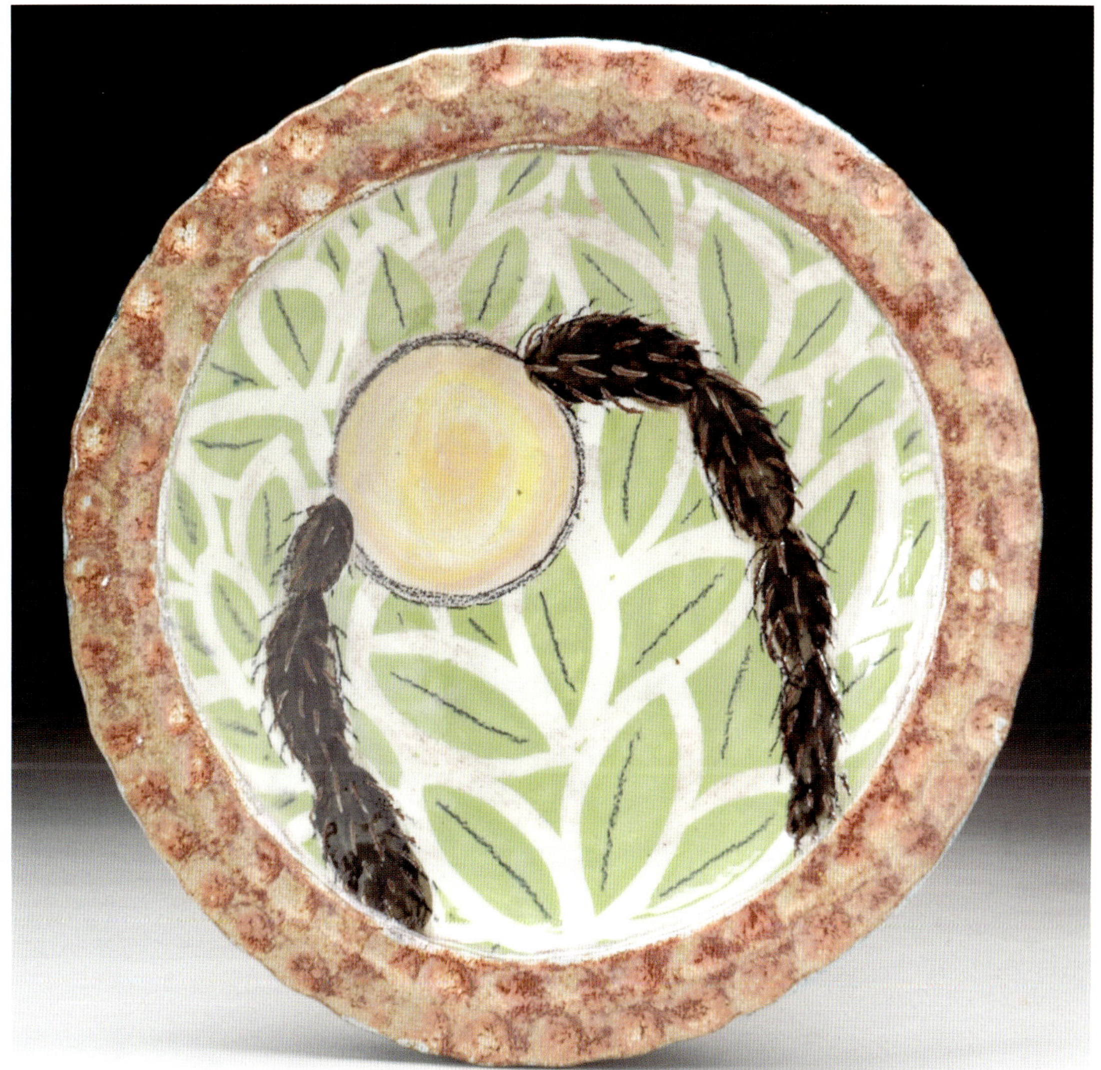

Ronan Kyle Peterson

Bug Sandwich Plate | 2006

2 X 9 INCHES (5.1 X 22.9 CM)

Hand-built and press-molded earthenware; slips, underglazes, sgraffito; electric fired, cone 04; glazes, cone 03

PHOTO BY NIEL HORA

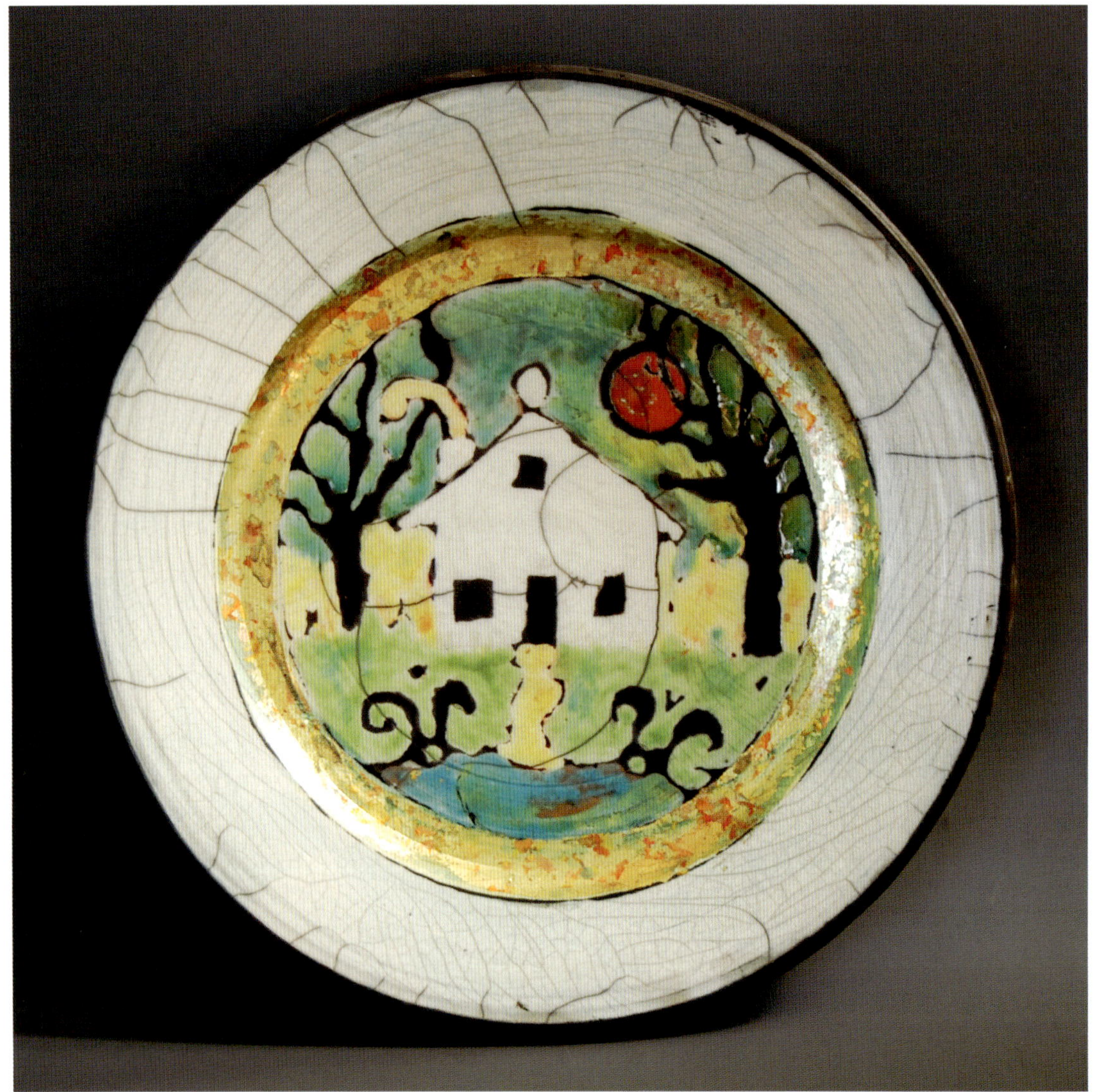

Peggy Peak

Red Moon Rising | 2007

3 X 15 INCHES (7.6 X 38.1 CM)

Wheel-thrown porcelain; raku fired, cone 06; glazes and gold leaf

PHOTO BY ARTIST

Susan M. Kolbe

Double Majolica: "Catbit" | 2006

2 X 6 X 9 INCHES (5.1 X 15.2 X 22.9 CM)

Hand-built terra cotta with thrown foot; terra sigillata details; electric bisque, cone 06; majolica, double-glazed white over black, cone 04

PHOTO BY JULIAN BEVERIDGE

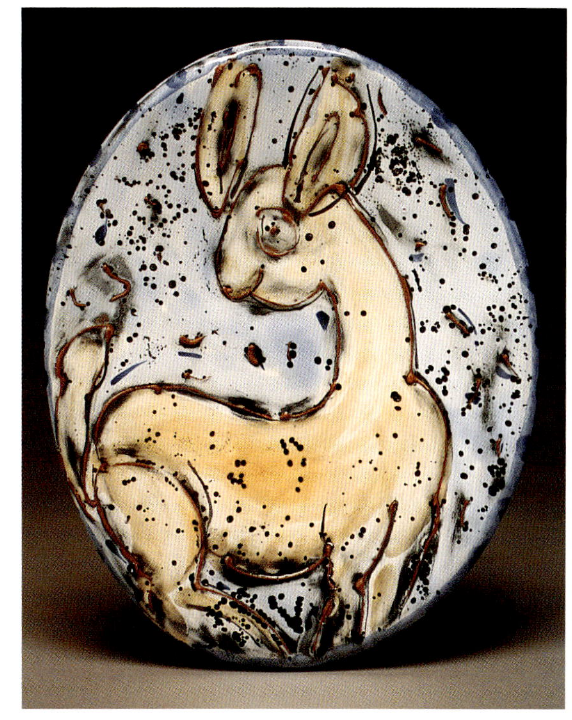

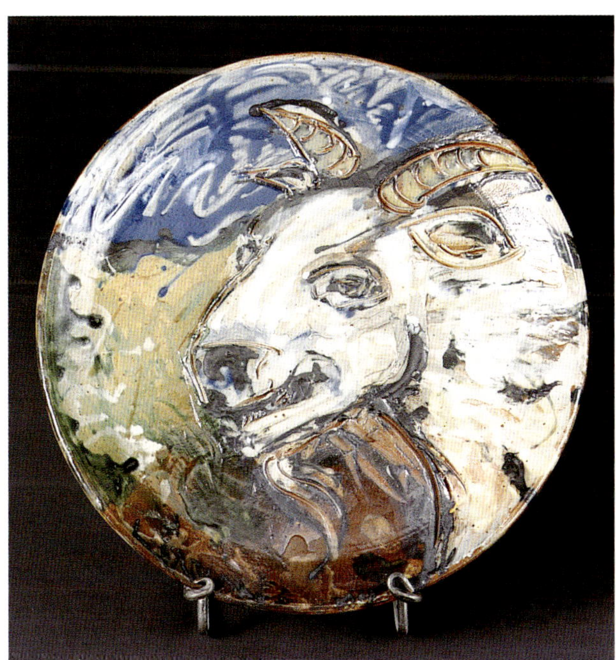

Andrew P. Linton

Goat Plate | 2006

1 5/8 X 13 INCHES (4.1 X 33 CM)

Wheel-thrown stoneware; impasto slip decoration; Pete's Clear glaze, cone 10 reduction

PHOTO BY SHANE BASKIN

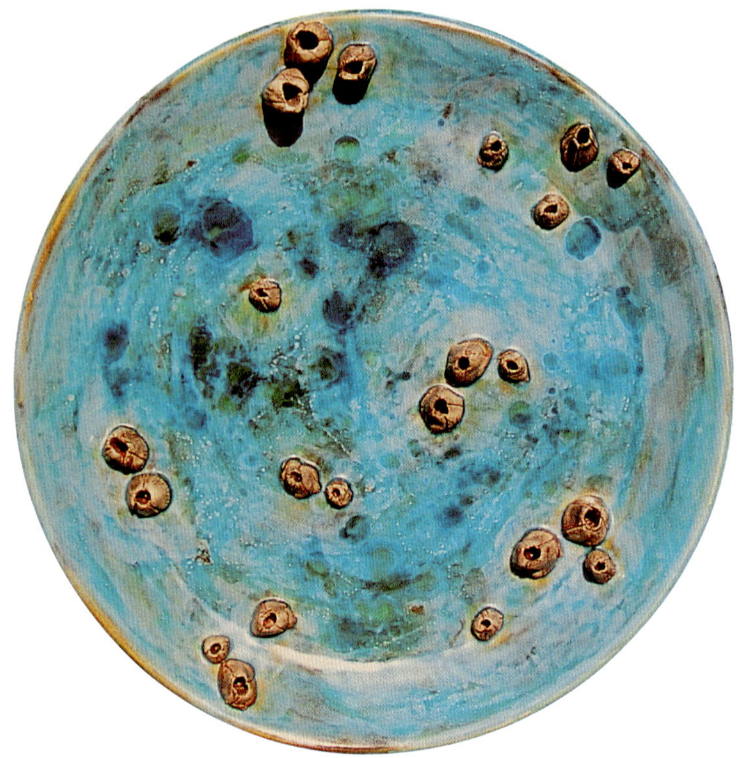

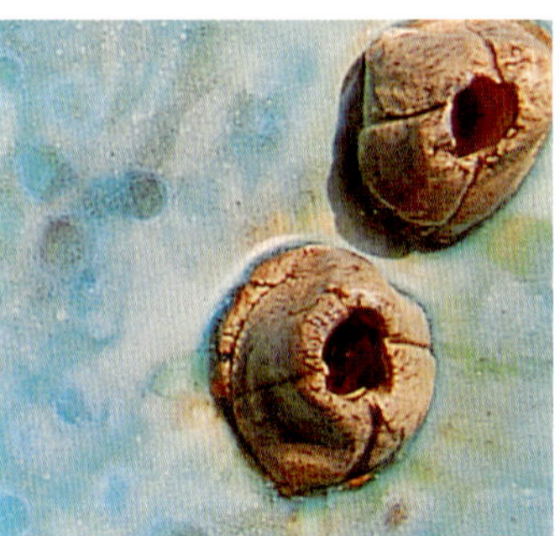

Christine Lush-Rodriguez

Barnacle Plate #2 | 2006

2¾ X 11¼ INCHES (7 X 28.6 CM)

Wheel-thrown earthenware with hand-built barnacles; electric fired, cone 4; layered glazes and loose crystals, cone 06

PHOTOS BY ARTIST

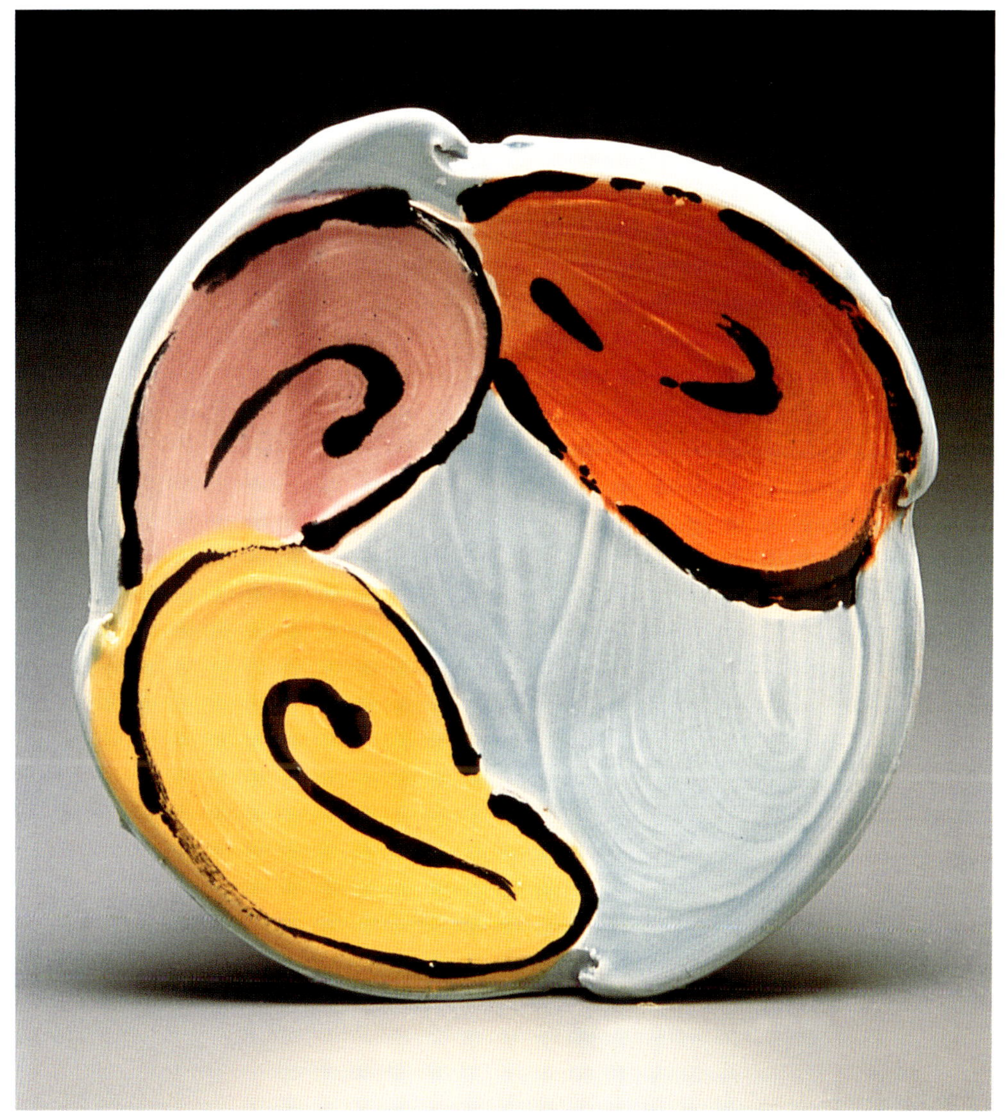

Kate Fisher

Dessert Plate | 2006

1 1/2 X 6 1/2 X 6 1/2 INCHES (3.8 X 16.5 X 16.5 CM)

Wheel-thrown and altered porcelain; cone 6

PHOTO BY MARK BUTLER

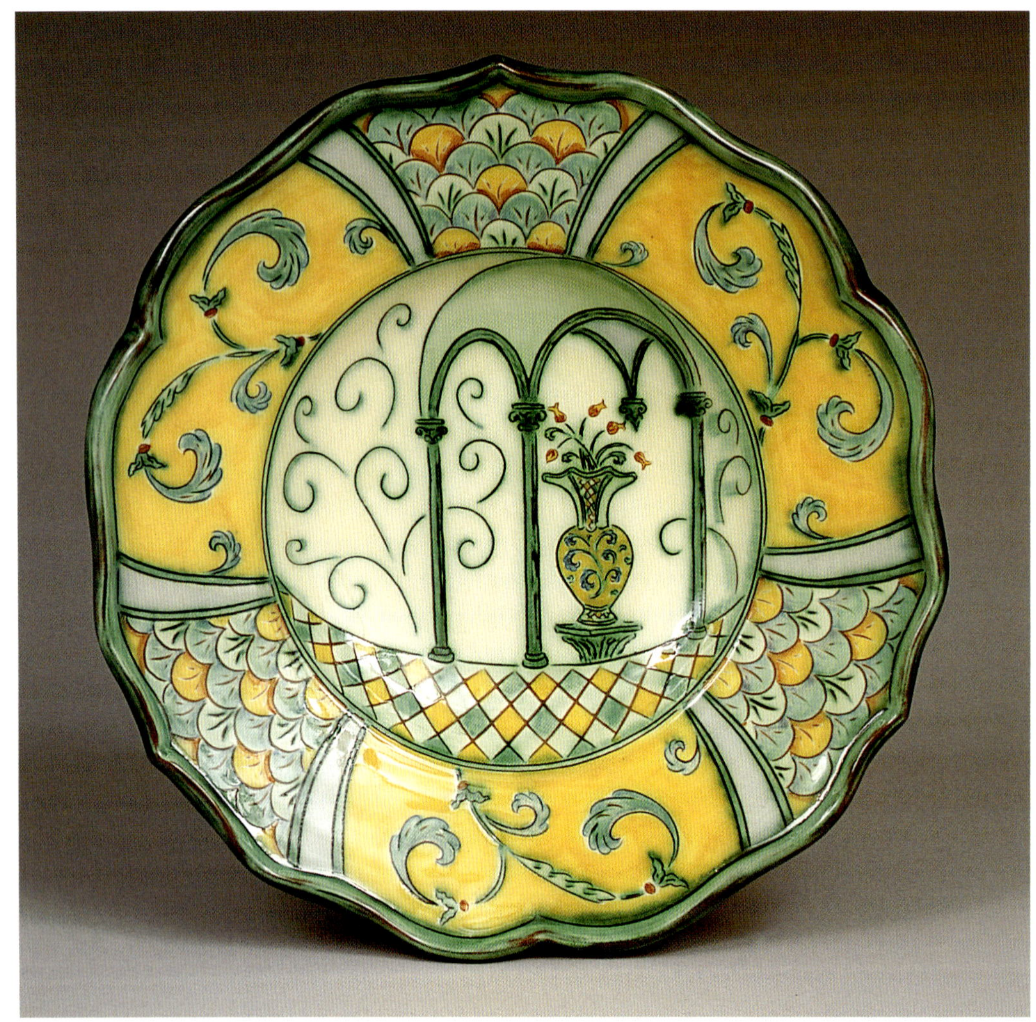

Jim Smith

Charger with Vase and Cupola | 2006

3 1/2 X 16 INCHES (8.9 X 40.6 CM)

Wheel-thrown Nova Scotia earthenware; slip and sgraffito; clear glaze, electric fired, cone 04

PHOTO BY JULIAN BEVERIDGE

Shoko Teruyama

Flower Plate with Bird | 2007

1 X 8 X 8 INCHES (2.5 X 20.3 X 20.3 CM)

Slab-built earthenware over bisque mold; white slip, sgraffito; translucent glazes, electric fired, cone 04

PHOTO BY TOM MILLS

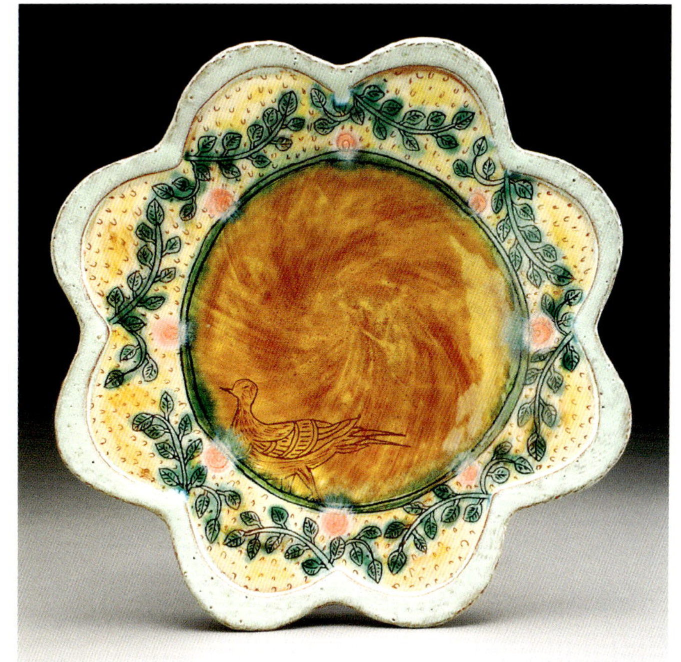

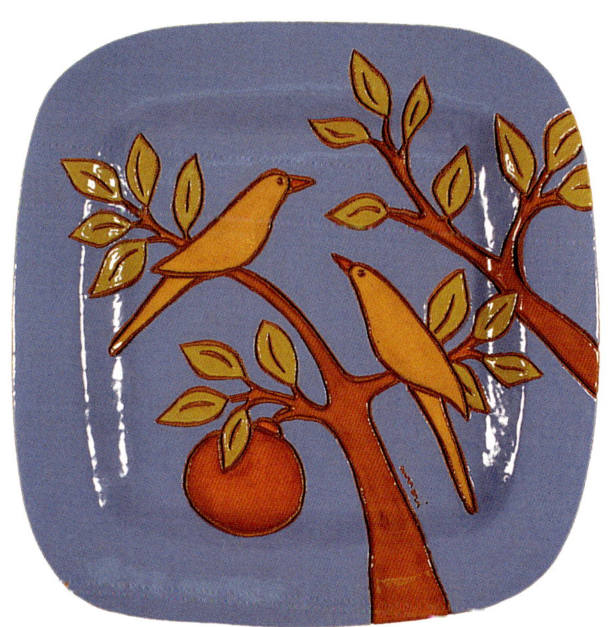

Angi Curreri

Square Platter with Birds and Fruit | 2007

2 X 14 X 14 INCHES (5.1 X 35.6 X 35.6 CM)

Slab-built and carved mid-range red clay; electric fired, cone 6; commercial glazes, electric fired, cone 05 and 07

PHOTO BY ARTIST

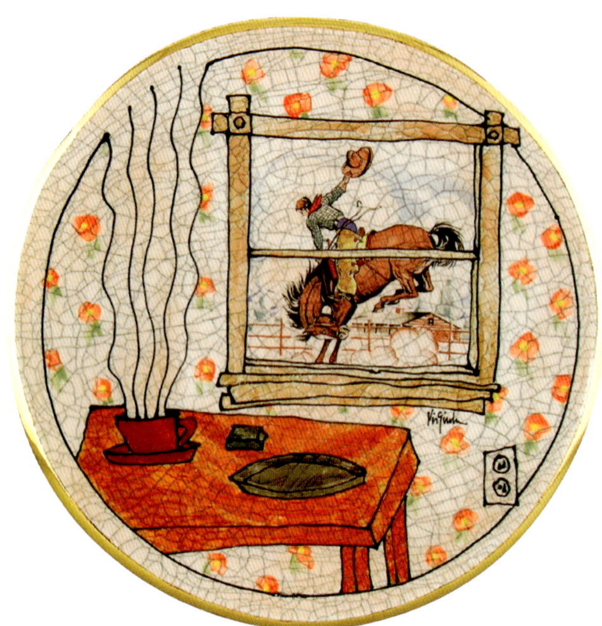

Rimas VisGirda

Angela's Window | 2007

1½ X 11 1/2 INCHES (3.8 X 29.2 CM)

Wheel-thrown stoneware; underglaze, slip trail, glaze, decal, lusters; electric fired, cones 04, 05, 017, 018

PHOTO BY ARTIST

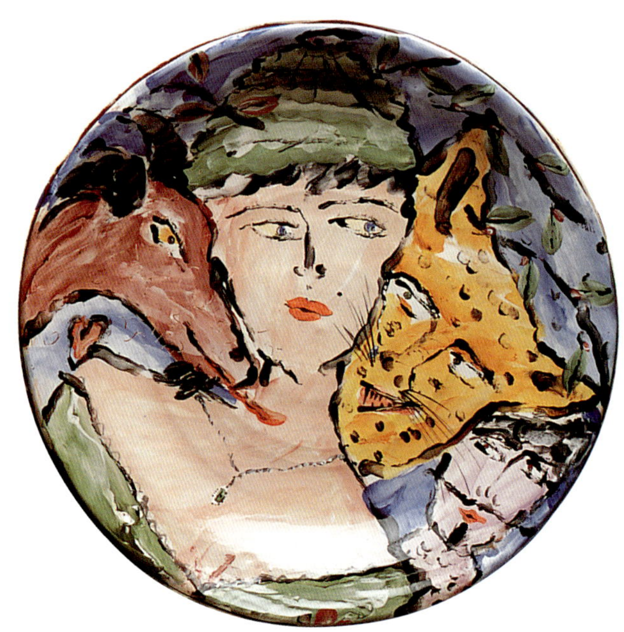

George McCauley

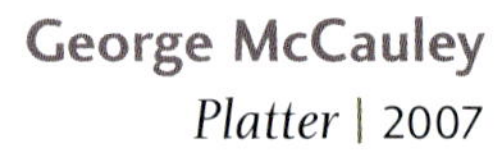

Platter | 2007

2½ X 19 INCHES (6.4 X 48.3 CM)

Thrown earthenware; electric fired, cone 04; underglazes; clear glaze, cone 03 oxidation

PHOTO BY DEAN ADAMS

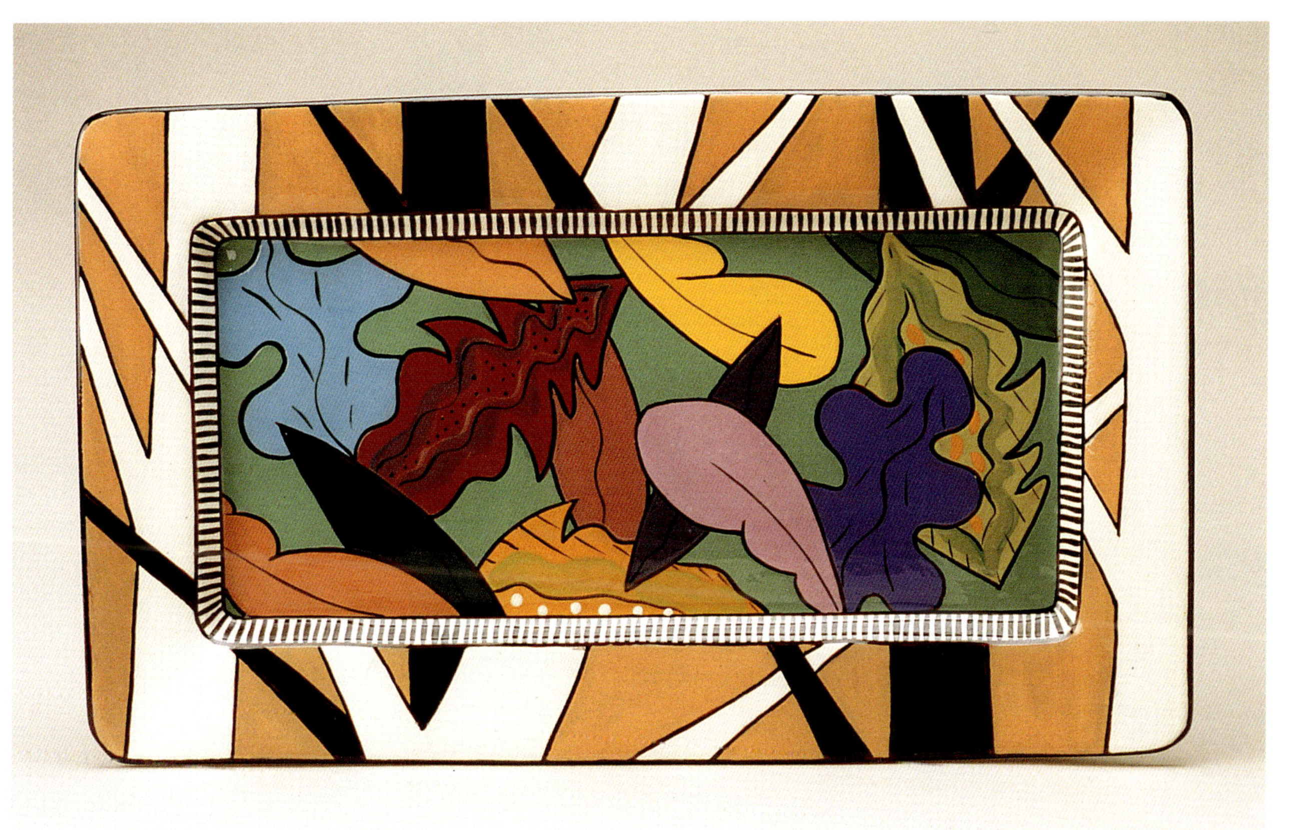

Carol Gouthro

Slab-Built Platter | 2005

1 X 15 X 8½ INCHES (2.5 X 38.1 X 21.6 CM)

Slab-built terra cotta; electric fired, cone 04; underglazes, clear glaze, cone 05

PHOTO BY ROGER SCHREIBER

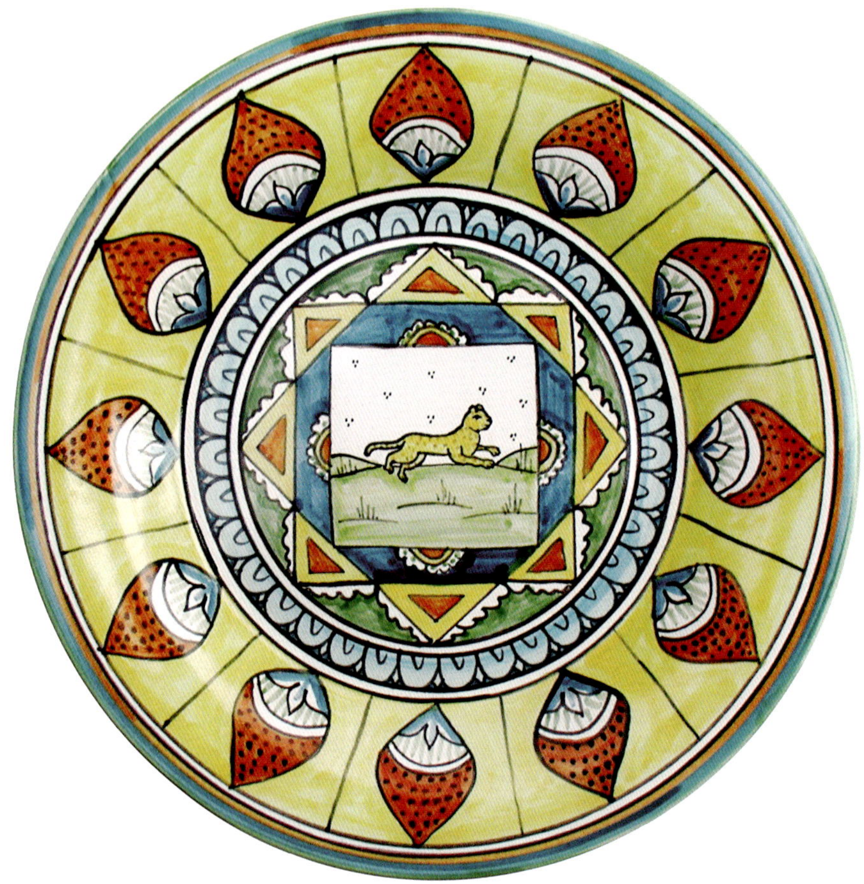

Susan Snyder

Leopard Plate from the Exotica Series | 2005

12 INCHES (30.5 CM) IN DIAMETER

Pressed earthenware; hand painted; majolica; electric fired, cone 04; glazes, cone 05

PHOTO BY ARTIST

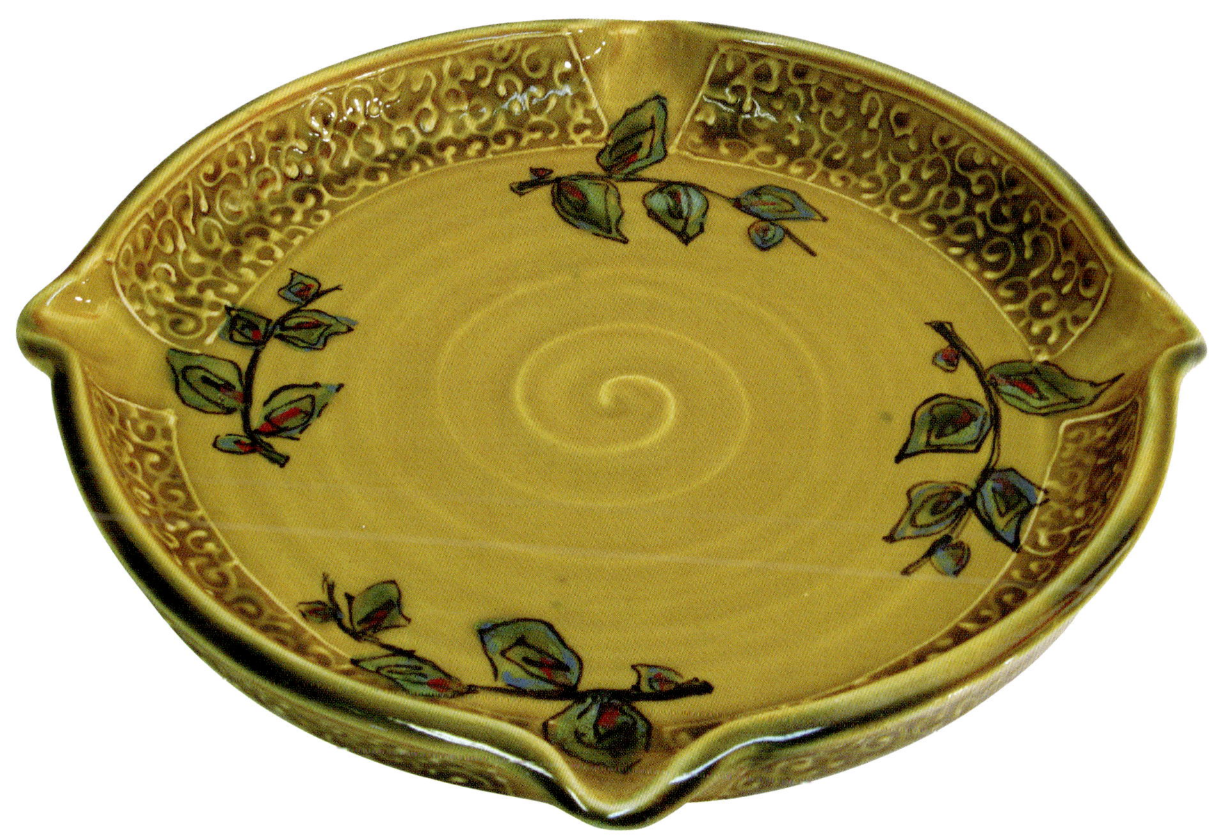

Stephen Hawes

Leaf Plate | 2007

2 X 13 3/8 INCHES (5 X 34 CM)

Wheel-thrown and altered stoneware; slips and colored glazes; electric fire, cone 6

PHOTO BY ARTIST

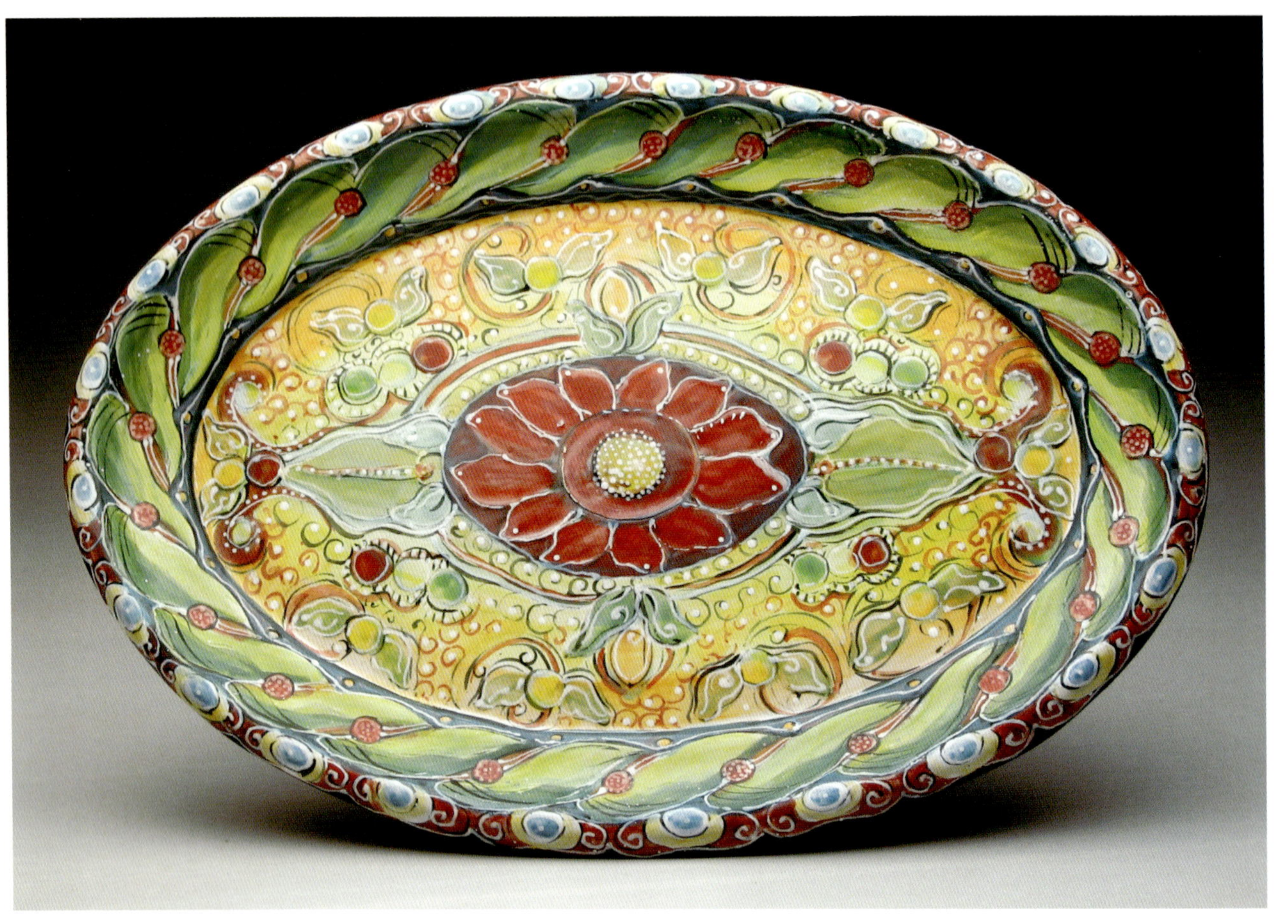

Rosalie Wynkoop

Majolica Platter | 2006

$1\frac{1}{2}$ X 16 X $10\frac{1}{2}$ INCHES (3.8 X 40.6 X 26.7 CM)

Slab-built earthenware; tin glaze and overglaze; electric fired, cone 02

PHOTO BY JOSH DEWEESE

Trent Berning

Lego Platter | 2005

7 X 22 INCHES (17.8 X 55.9 CM)

Wheel-thrown and hand-built stoneware; stains and glazes; electric fired, cone 04

PHOTO BY ARTIST

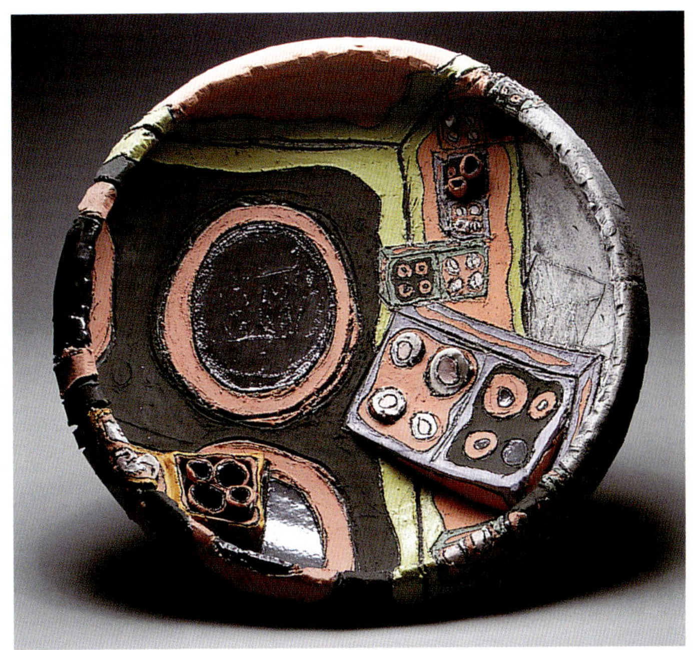

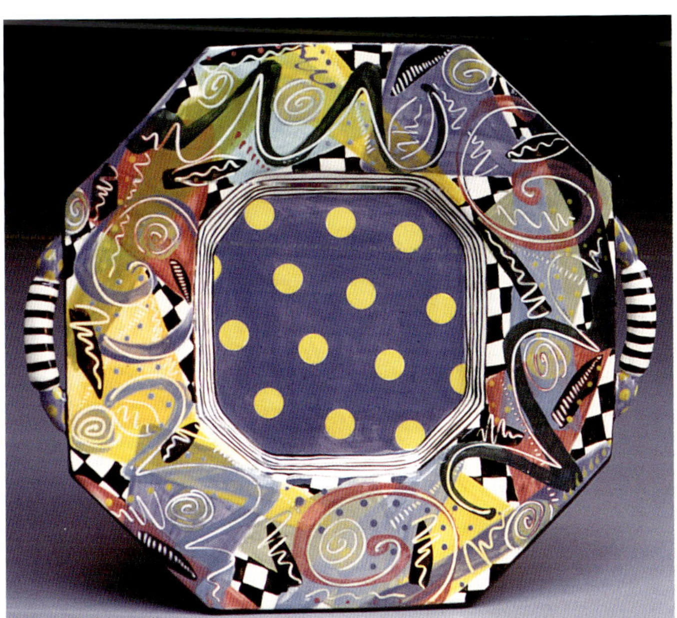

Trista Depp Chapman

Abstract Platter | 1999

10 X 10 INCHES (25.4 X 25.4 CM)

Slab-built earthenware with coil handles; underglazes and sgraffito; electric fired, cone 05; bisque, cone 04

PHOTO BY ARTIST

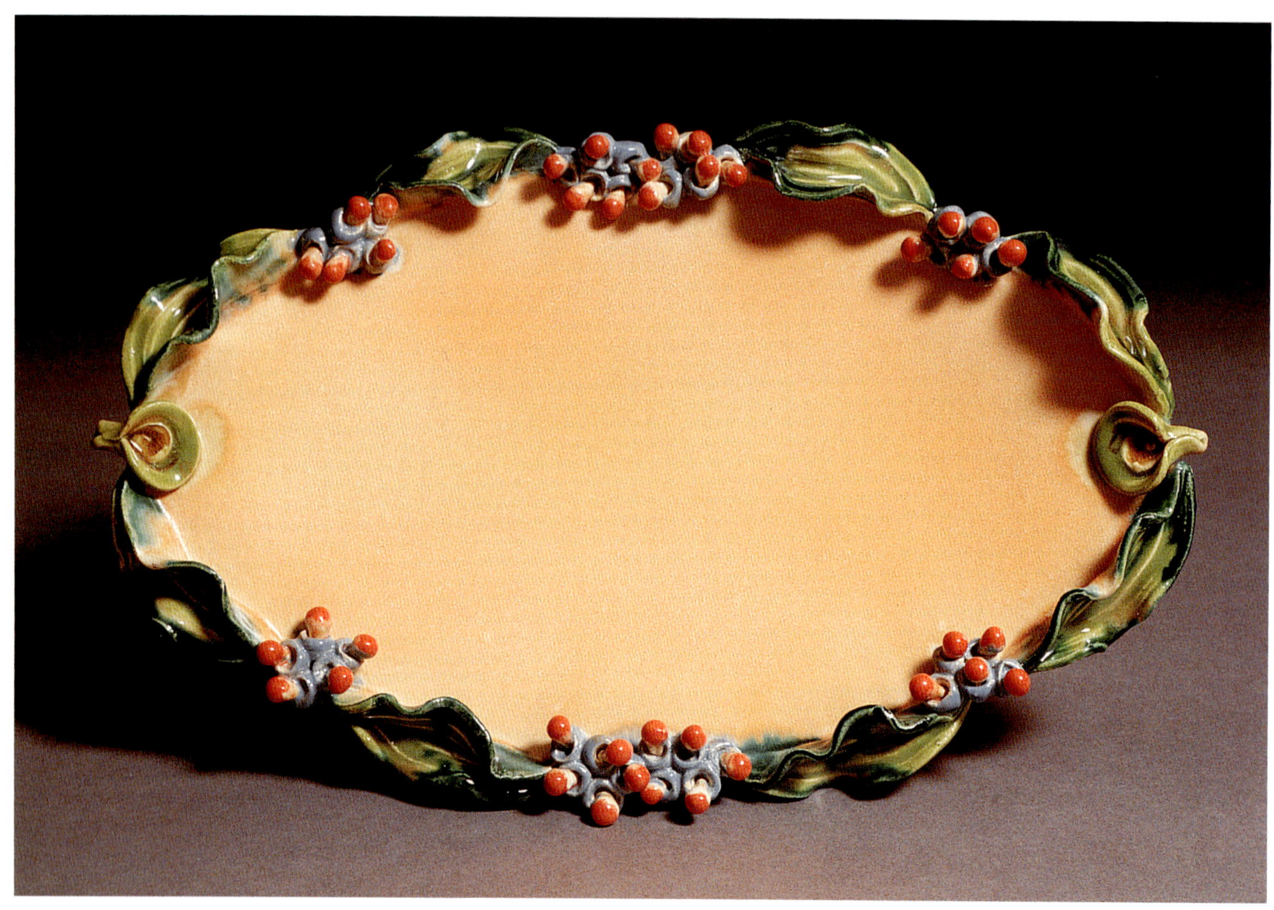

Lucy Breslin

View of My Garden #3 | 2006

3 X 15 X 10 INCHES (7.6 X 38.1 X 25.4 CM)

Hand-built white earthenware;
glaze, electric fired, cone 04

PHOTO BY MARK JOHNSON

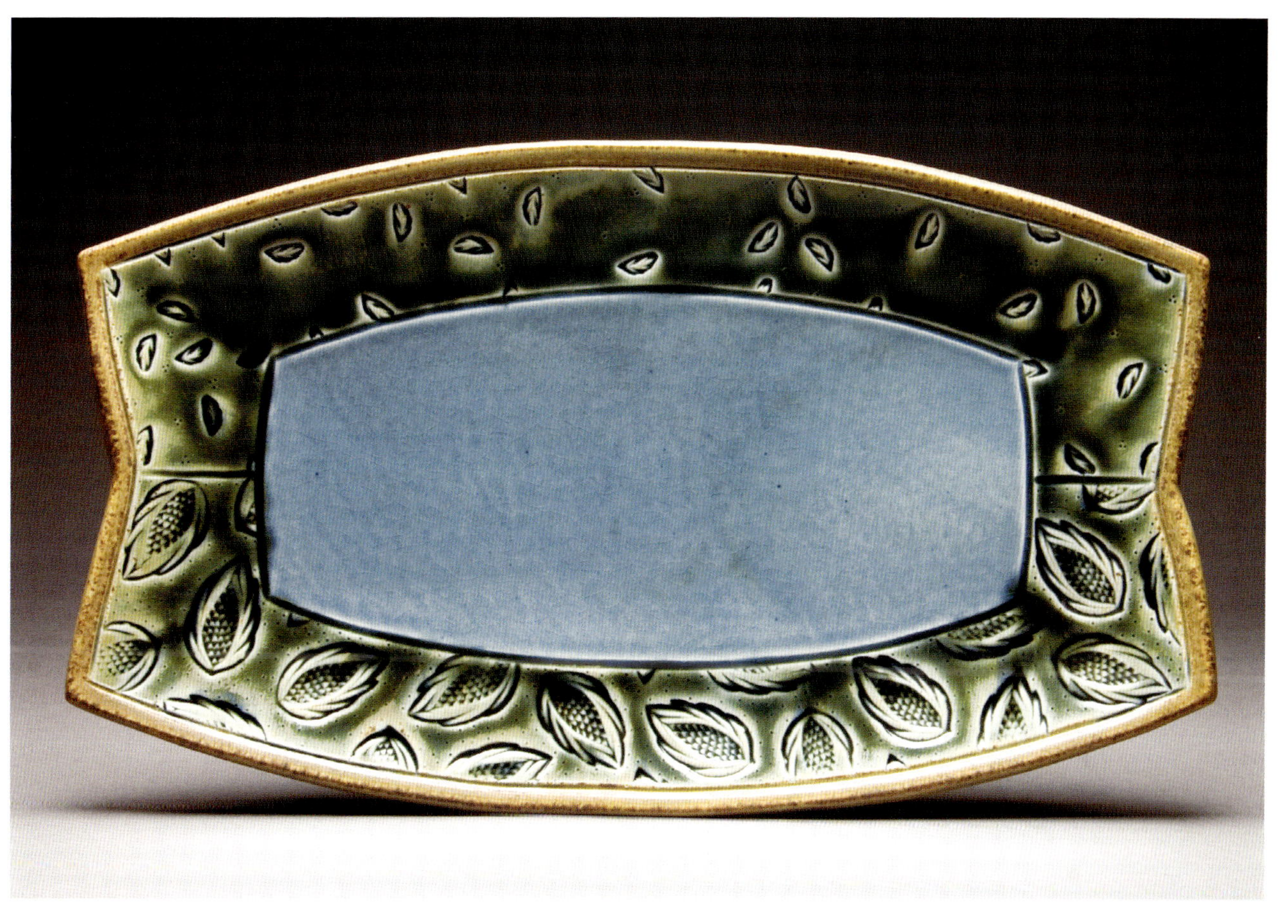

Jennifer Everett

Rectangular Platter | 2007

2 X 16 X 9 INCHES (5.1 X 40.6 X 22.9 CM)

Hand-built stoneware; stamped; multiple glazes; gas fired in reduction, cone 10

PHOTO BY ARTIST

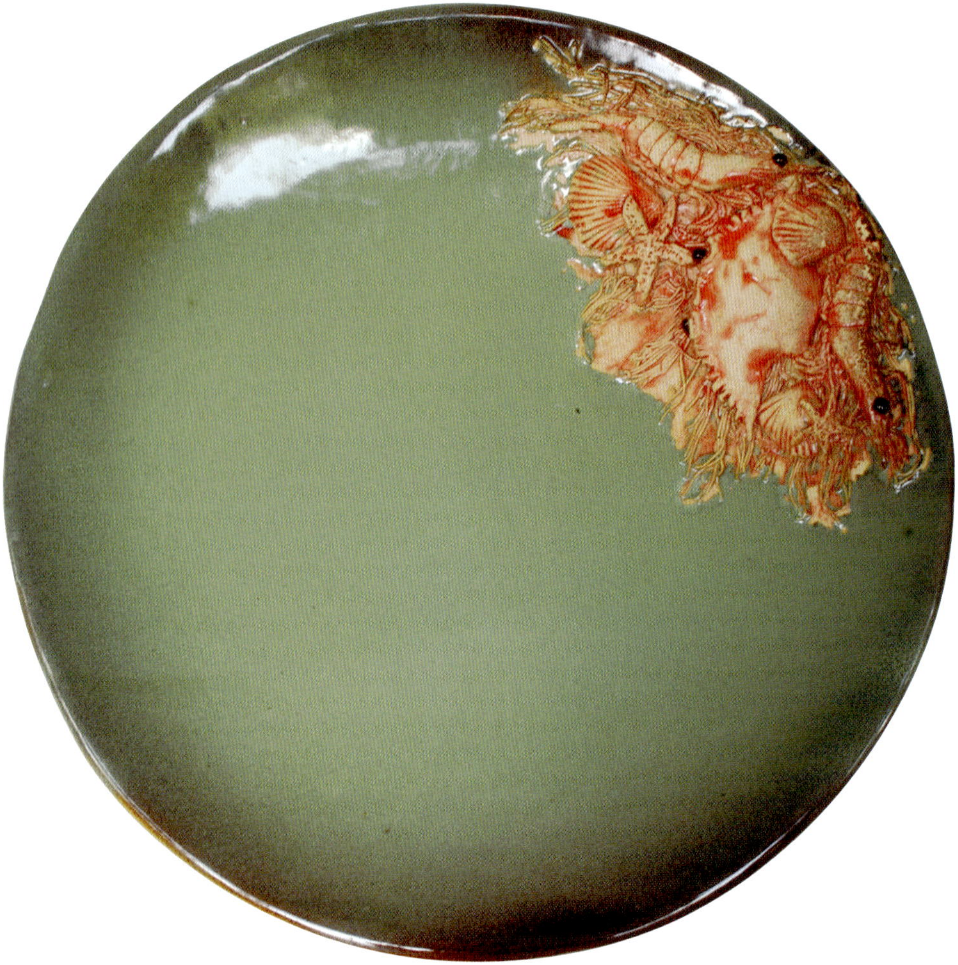

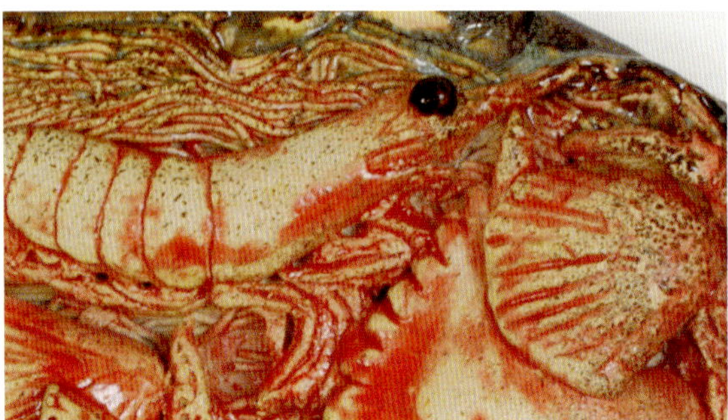

Betty Crouch

Seafood Platter | 2007

2 X 18 INCHES (5.1 X 45.7 CM)

Slab-built stoneware; red iron-oxide stain, glaze; gas fired in reduction, cone 10

PHOTOS BY ERIN HORTON

Inga Svendsen

Breeze | 2006

$1\frac{1}{16}$ X $14\frac{9}{16}$ INCHES (2.7 X 37 CM)

Wheel-thrown terra cotta; layered slips, sgraffito; glaze, cone 03

PHOTO BY ARTIST

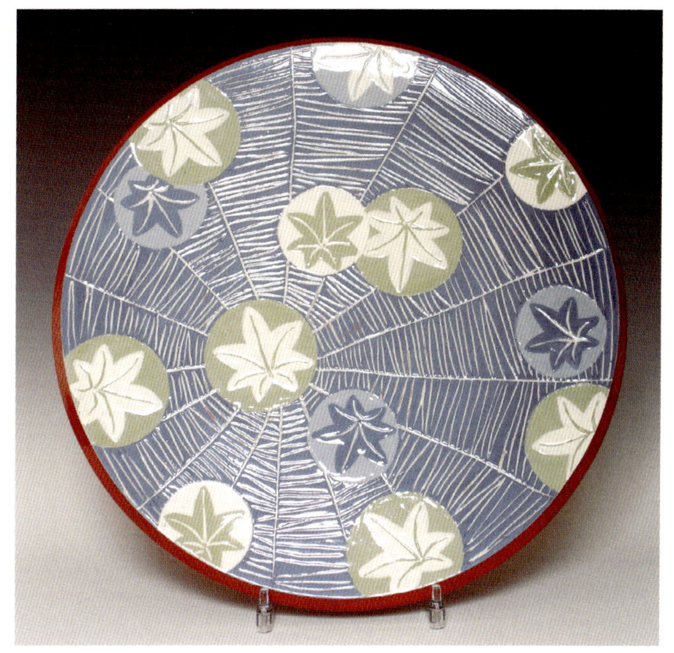

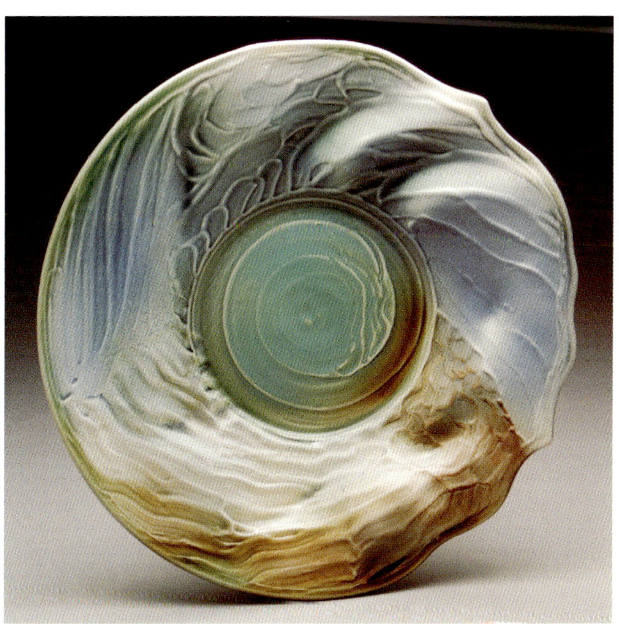

Bradley Keys

Breeze | 2007

$2\frac{1}{2}$ X 16 INCHES (6.4 X 40.6 CM)

Thrown and altered stoneware; slip; sprayed glazes; electric fired, cone 6

PHOTO BY ARTIST

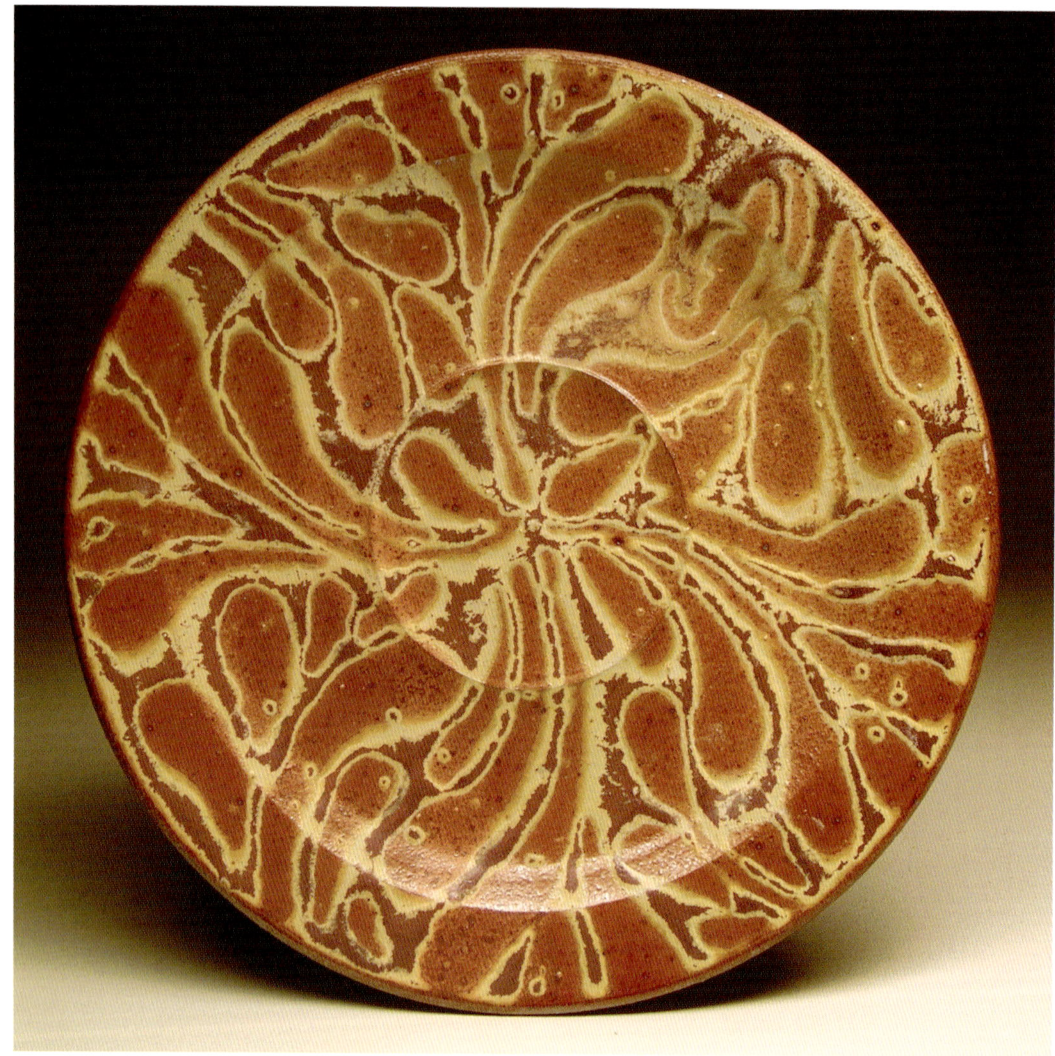

Loretta Languet

Untitled | 2007

$2\frac{1}{2}$ X 12 INCHES (6.4 X 30.5 CM)

Wheel-thrown stoneware; wax resist; salt fired, cone 6

PHOTO BY ARTIST

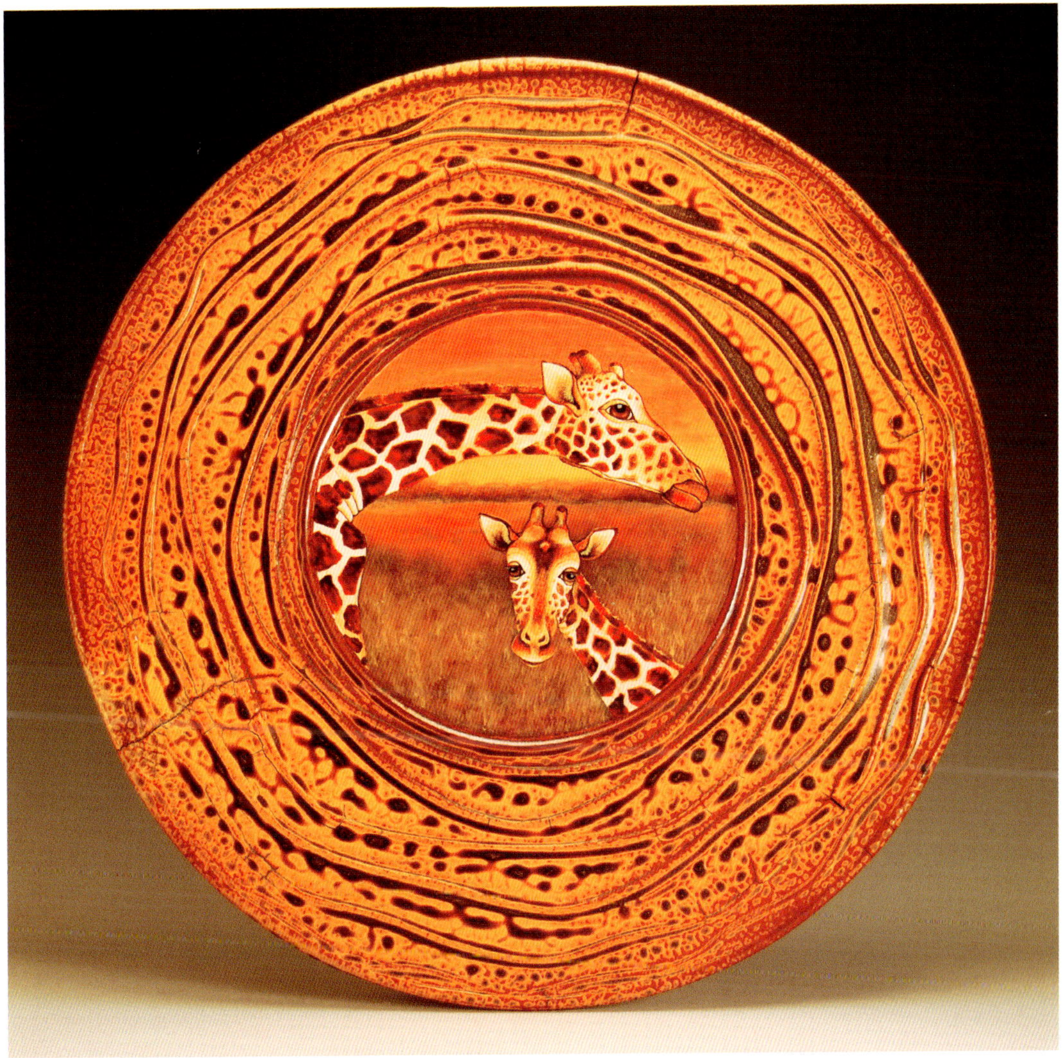

Annette Kirma

African Landscape | 2007

2½ X 20 INCHES (6.4 X 50.8 CM)

Wheel-thrown porcelain; cone 10; glaze and acrylic

PHOTOS BY ARTIST

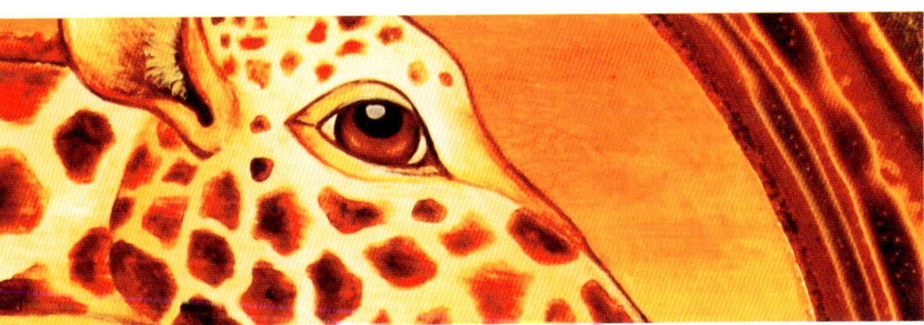

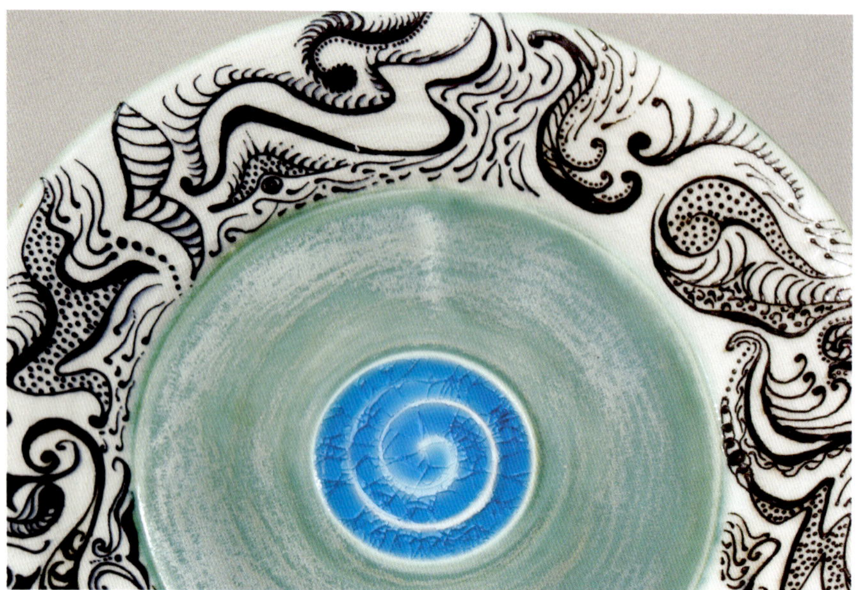

Cathy Avram

World Dance | 2007

2 X 15 INCHES (5.1 X 38.1 CM)

Wheel-thrown porcelain; slip trailed; glazes, electric fired, cone 6

PHOTO BY ARTIST

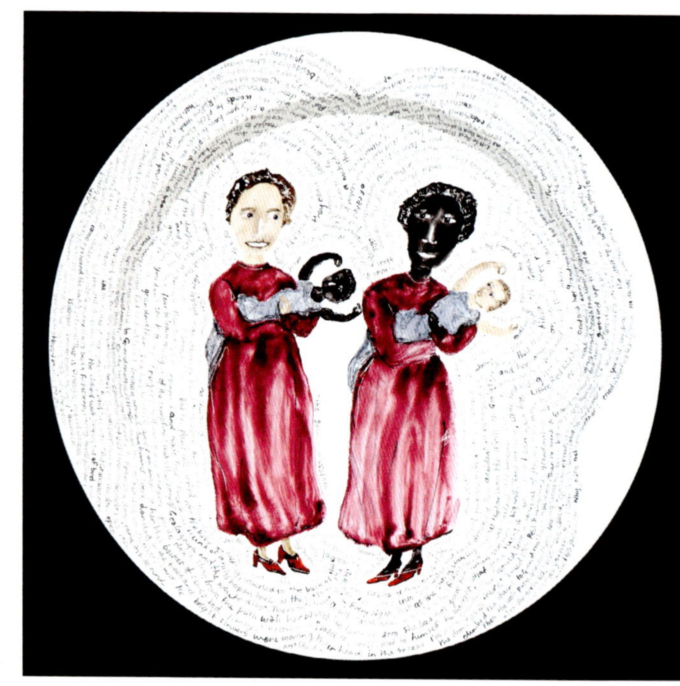

Bern Emmerichs

The Getting of Wisdom | 2006

1 X 16½ INCHES (2.5 X 41.9 CM)

Earthenware; electric multi-fired, 850°F (454°C); glazes

PHOTO BY GRAHAM BARING

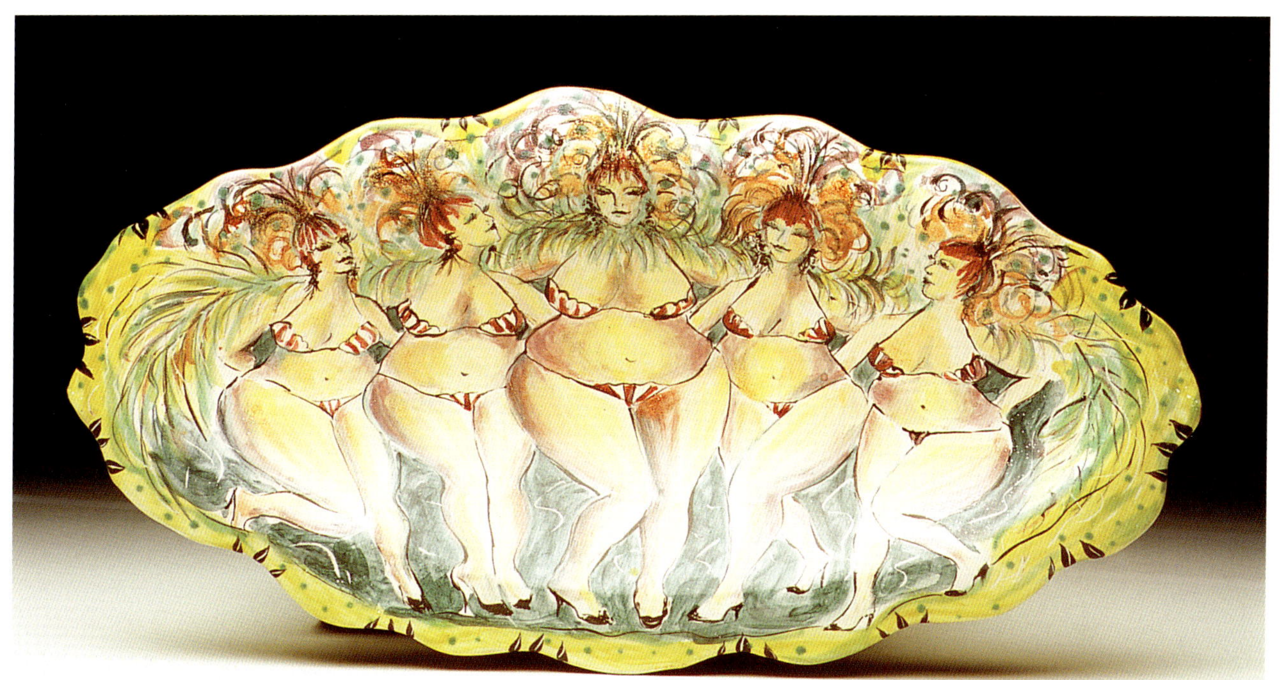

Marilyn Dennis Palsha

Dancing Girls Platter | 2007

2 X 18 X 9 INCHES (5.1 X 45.7 X 22.9 CM)

Red earthenware slab with thrown foot; electric fired, cone 03; majolica with painted stains, cone 02

PHOTO BY SETH TICE-LEWIS

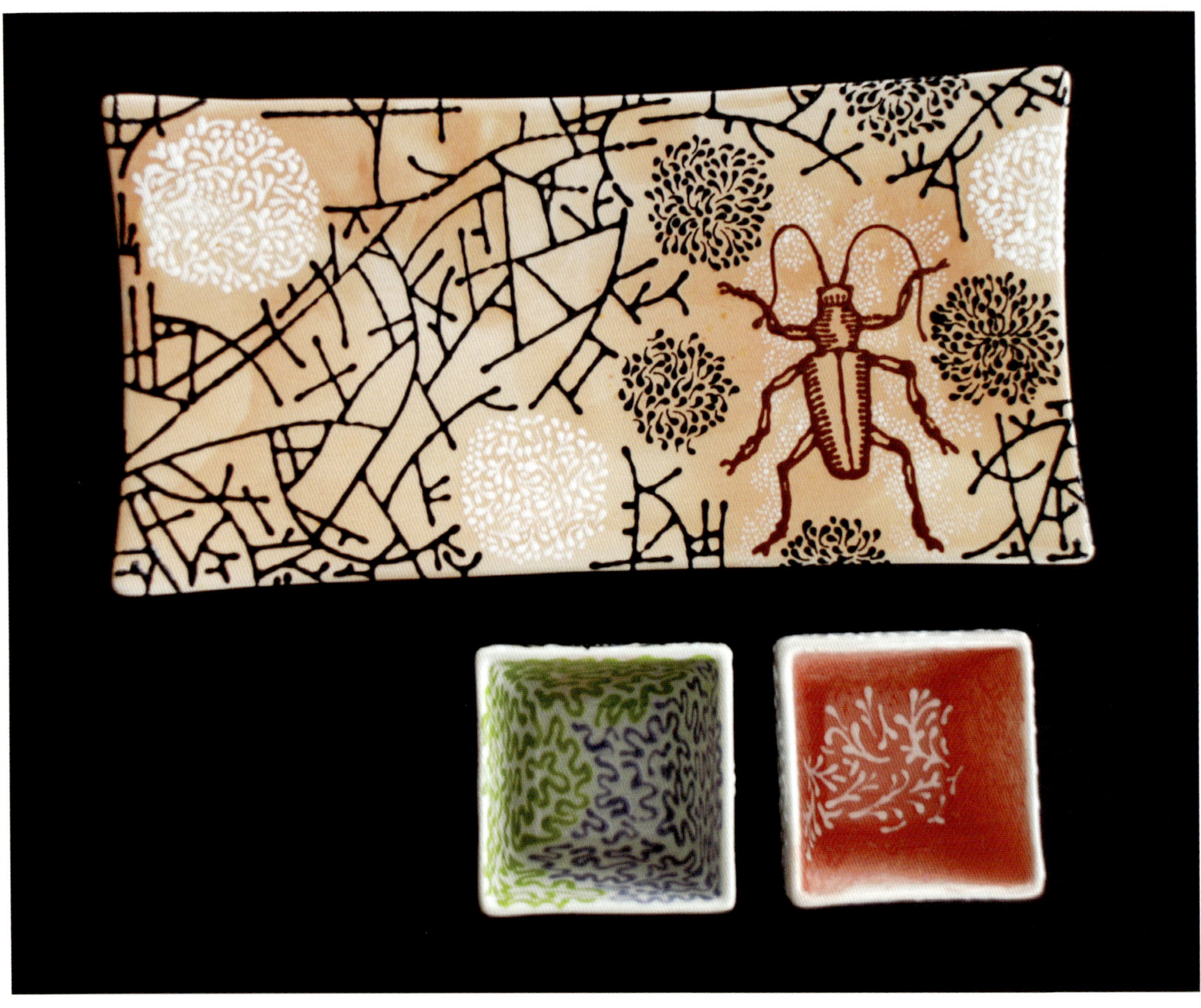

Jody Guralnick

Sushi Platter | 2007

PLATTER: 1 1/2 X 15 X 7 1/2 INCHES (3.8 X 38.1 X 19 CM)

Slip-cast low-fire white clay; electric fired, cone 06; underglazes, cone 06

PHOTO BY ARTIST

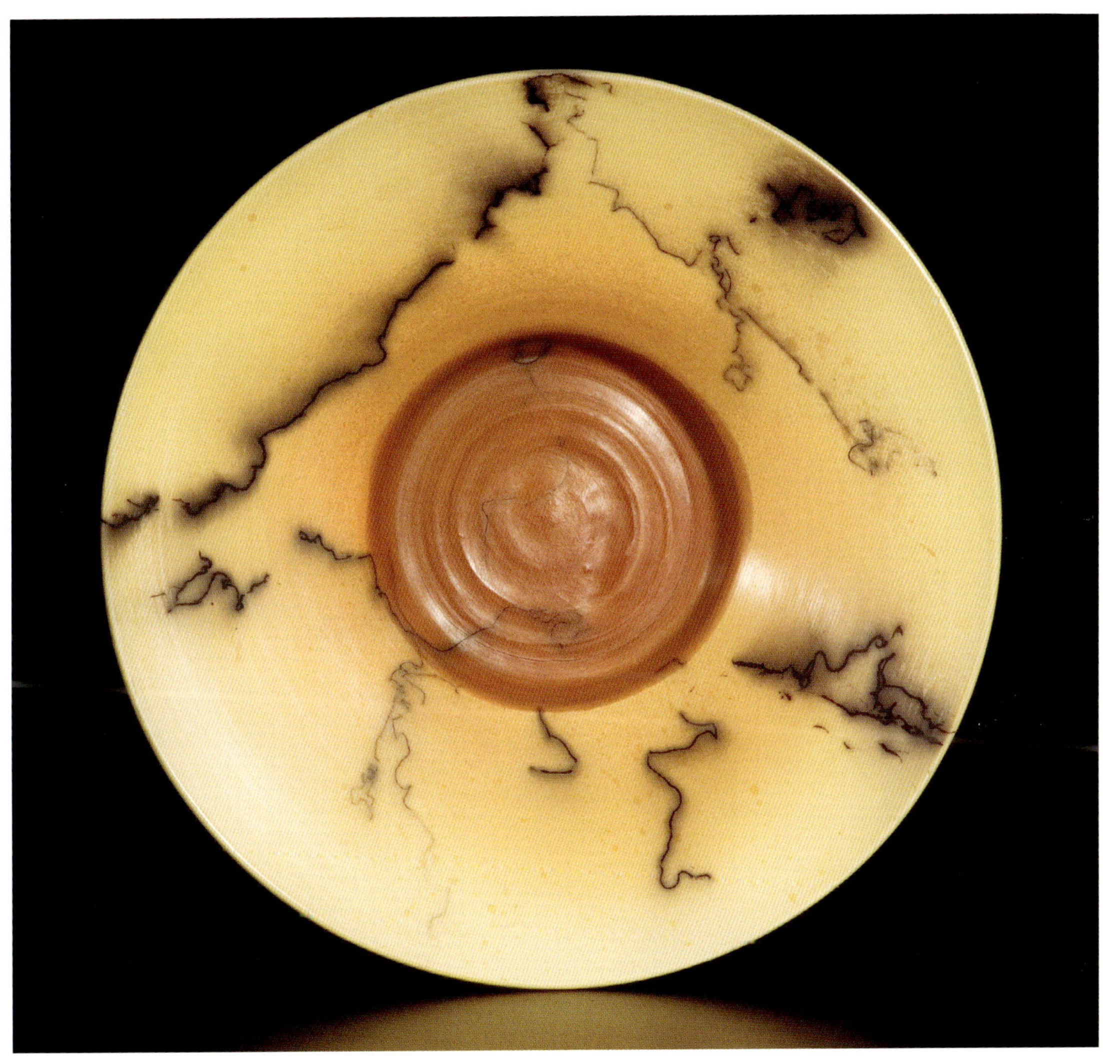

Linda Dalton

Golden Horsehair Plate | 2006

3 X 10 INCHES (7.6 X 25.4 CM)

Wheel-thrown stoneware; bisque fired, cone 6; raku fired; fumed with ferric chloride

PHOTO BY JASON DOWDLE

Tanya Gomez

Platters | 1999

LARGEST: 4 1/4 X 14 3/4 INCHES (10.8 X 37.5 CM);
SMALLEST: 4 X 4 3/4 INCHES (10.2 X 12.1 CM)

Slab-built porcelain stoneware; electric fired, cone 06; spray glazed, cone 9

PHOTO BY ARTIST

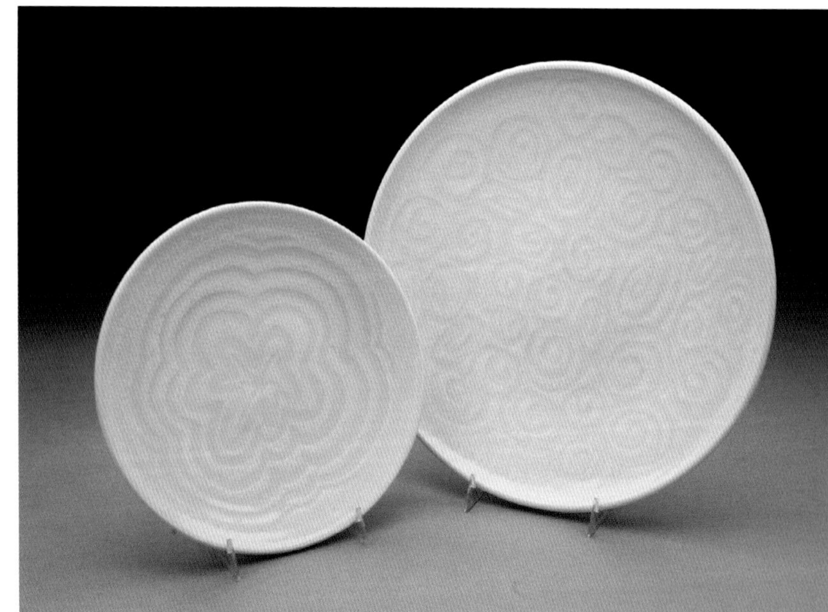

Debra Holiber

White on White Plates | 2007

LEFT: 3/4 X 8 INCHES (1.9 X 20.3 CM);
RIGHT: 3/4 X 10 1/2 INCHES (1.9 X 26.7 CM)

Wheel-thrown porcelain; wax resist, glazes; reduction fired, cone 10

PHOTO BY LOREN MARON

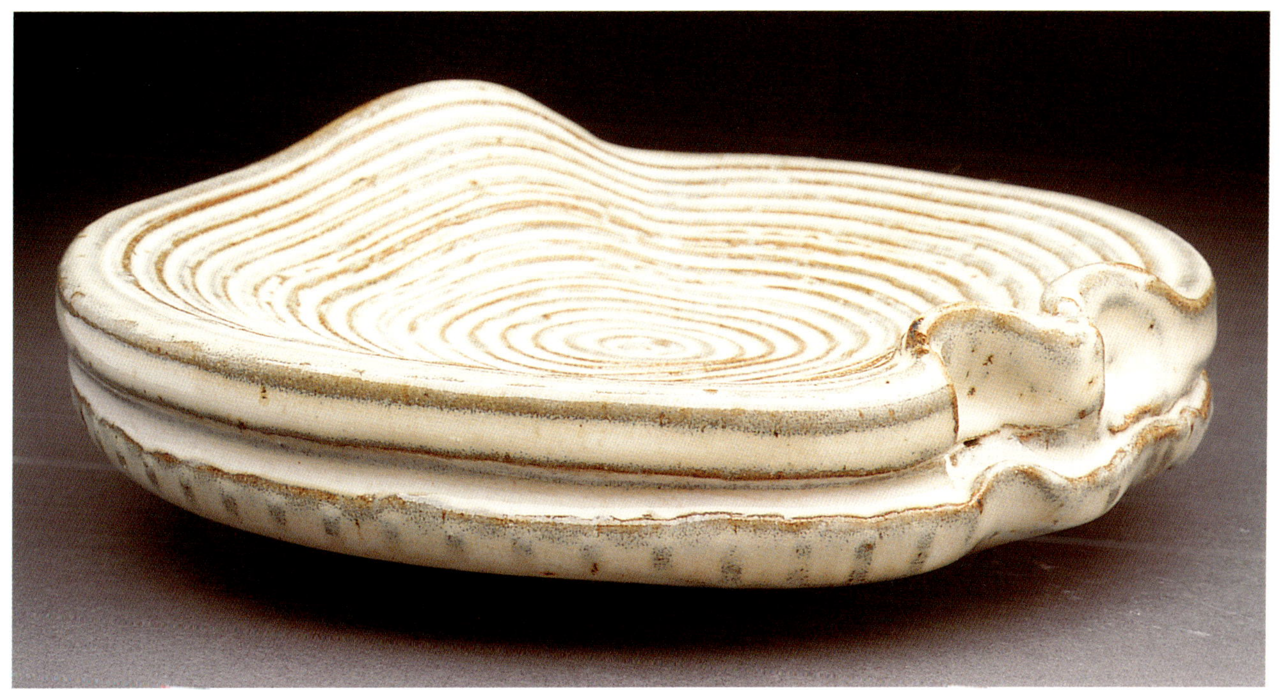

Chris Archer

Pillowed Hors d'Oeuvres Dish | 2005

2¾ X 10 X 10 INCHES (7 X 25.4 X 25.4 CM)

Thrown and altered stoneware; encased, collapsed; reduction glaze, cone 10

PHOTO BY CHARLEY FREIBERG

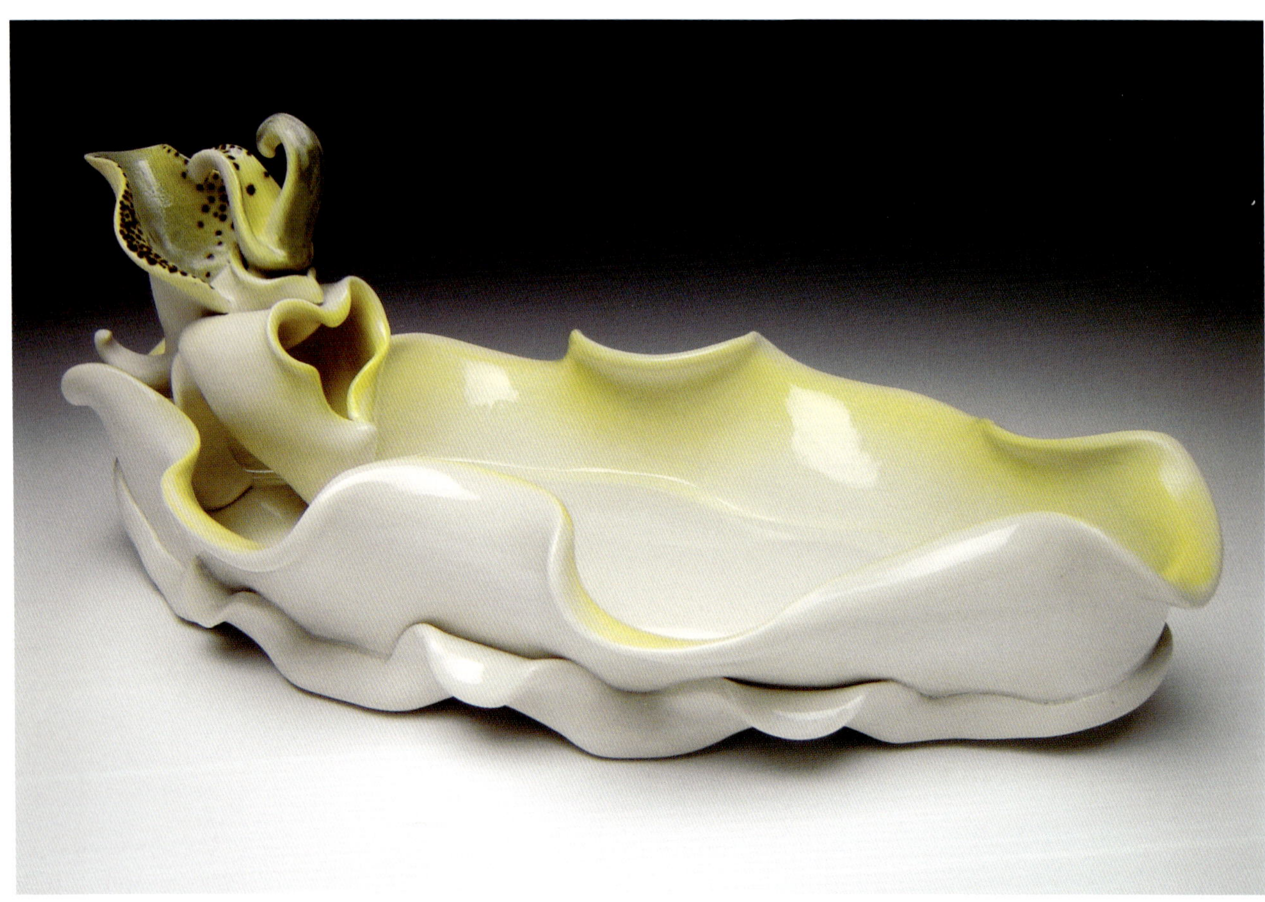

Martha H. Grover

Perfume Bottle & Tray | 2007

6 X 11 X 9 INCHES (15.2 X 27.9 X 22.9 CM)

Thrown and altered porcelain; sprayed and trailed engobes, glaze; cone 11 neutral

PHOTO BY ARTIST

Tina Reuterberg

Untitled | 2007

8 X 16 X 18 INCHES (20.3 X 40.6 X 45.7 CM)

Hand-built earthenware; electric fired, cone 05

PHOTO BY ARTIST

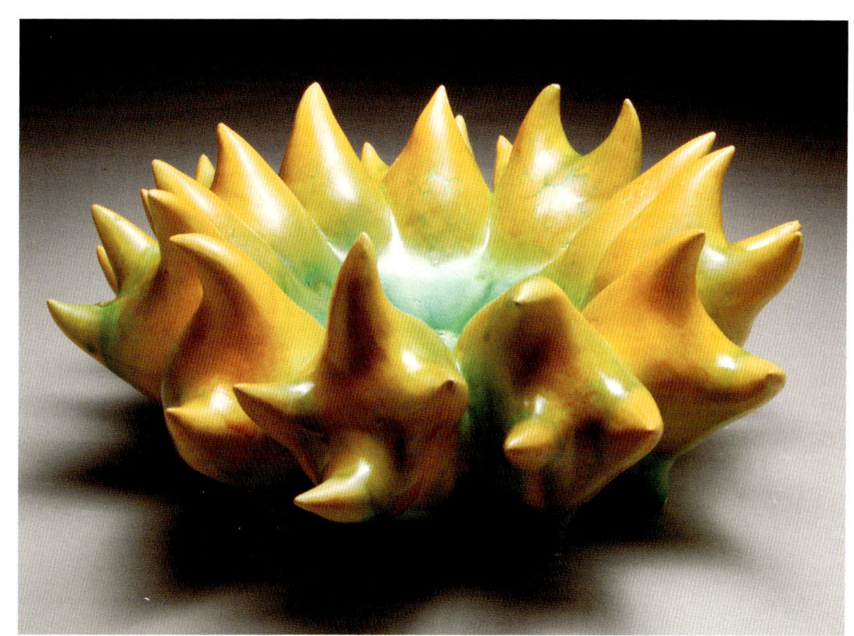

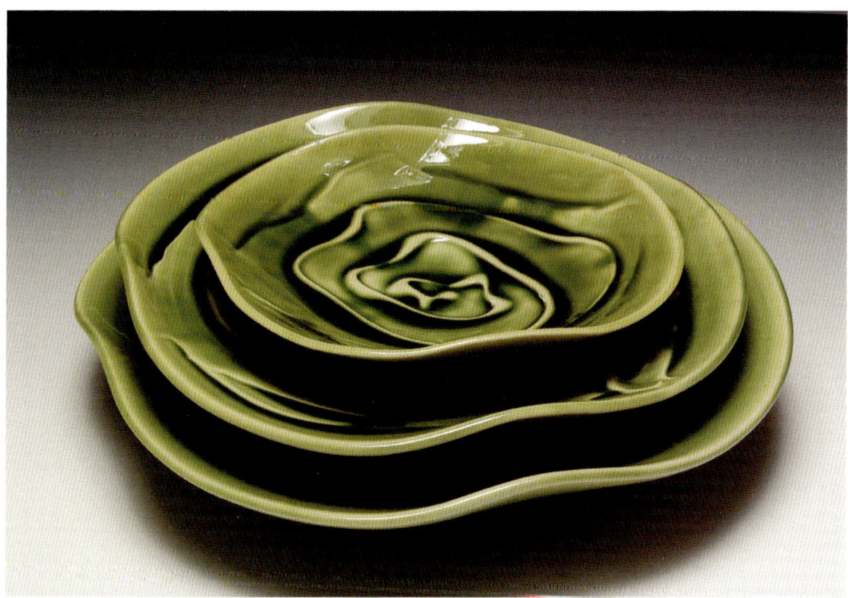

Clay Leonard

Rippled Plate Set | 2007

OVERALL: 3 1/2 X 12 X 12 INCHES (8.9 X 30.5 X 30.5 CM)

Wheel-thrown and altered porcelain; electric fired, cone 10

PHOTO BY CHARLIE CUMMINGS

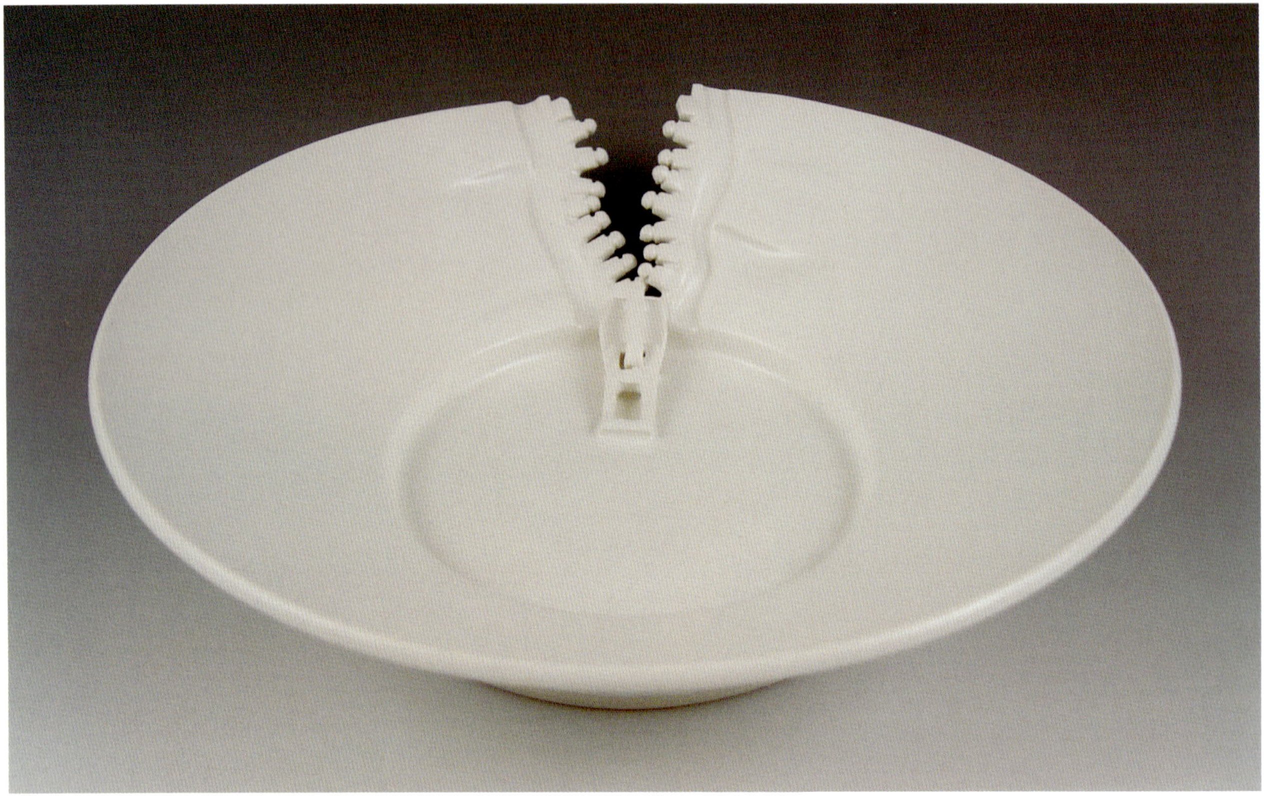

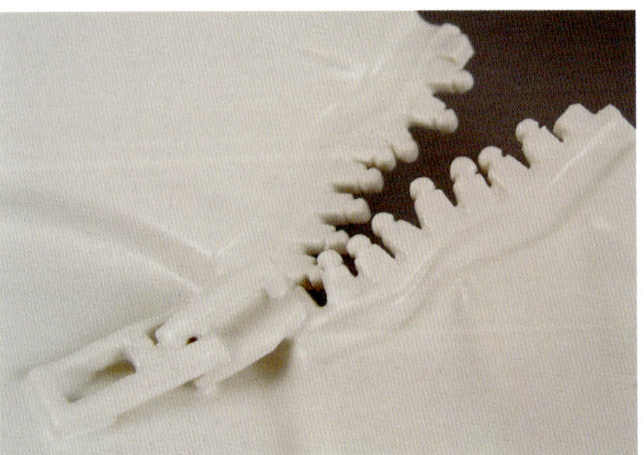

Lilach Lotan

Zipper Platter | 2007

3 X 14 X 14 INCHES (7.6 X 35.6 X 35.6 CM)

Wheel-thrown and altered porcelain; silky white glaze; electric fired, cone 6

PHOTOS BY RON LOTAN

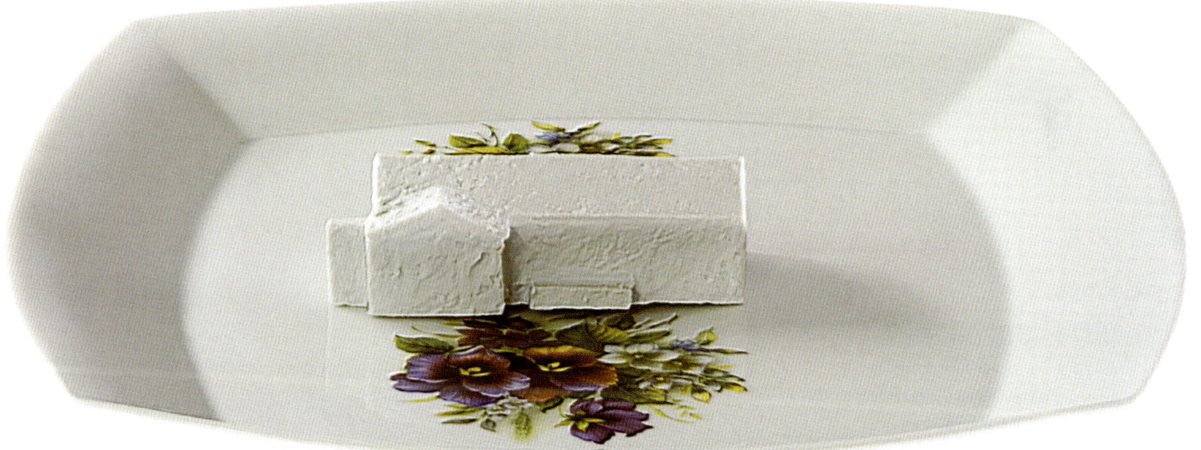

Brooke Marks-Swanson
30415 Lantern Lane | 2006
2 X 13 X 13 INCHES (5.1 X 33 X 33 CM)
Slip-cast and hand-built porcelain; clear glaze; decals
PHOTO BY DAVE HUGUS

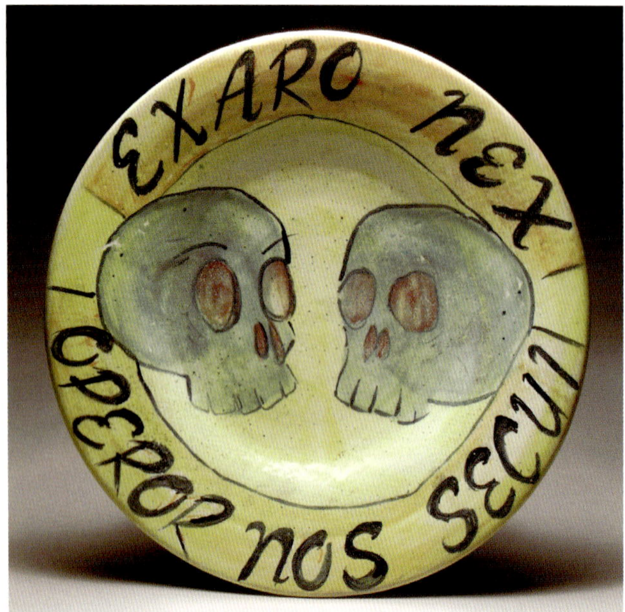

Scott Lykens

Till Death Do Us Part | 2007

3 X 14 X 14 INCHES (7.6 X 35.6 X 35.6 CM)

Wheel-thrown red earthenware; painted majolica; electric fired, cone 3

PHOTO BY ARTIST

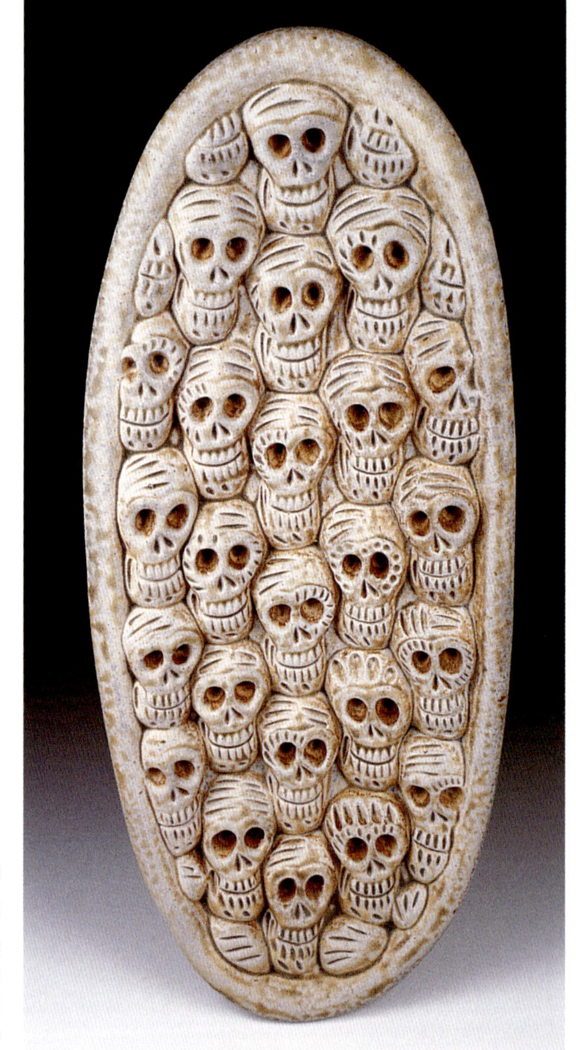

Kurt Brian Webb

The Hour Is Late | 2006

$2\frac{1}{2}$ X 10 X $23\frac{1}{2}$ INCHES (6.4 X 25.4 X 59.7 CM)

Hand-built earthenware; carved and press molded; wood fired

PHOTO BY KURT BRIAN WEBB

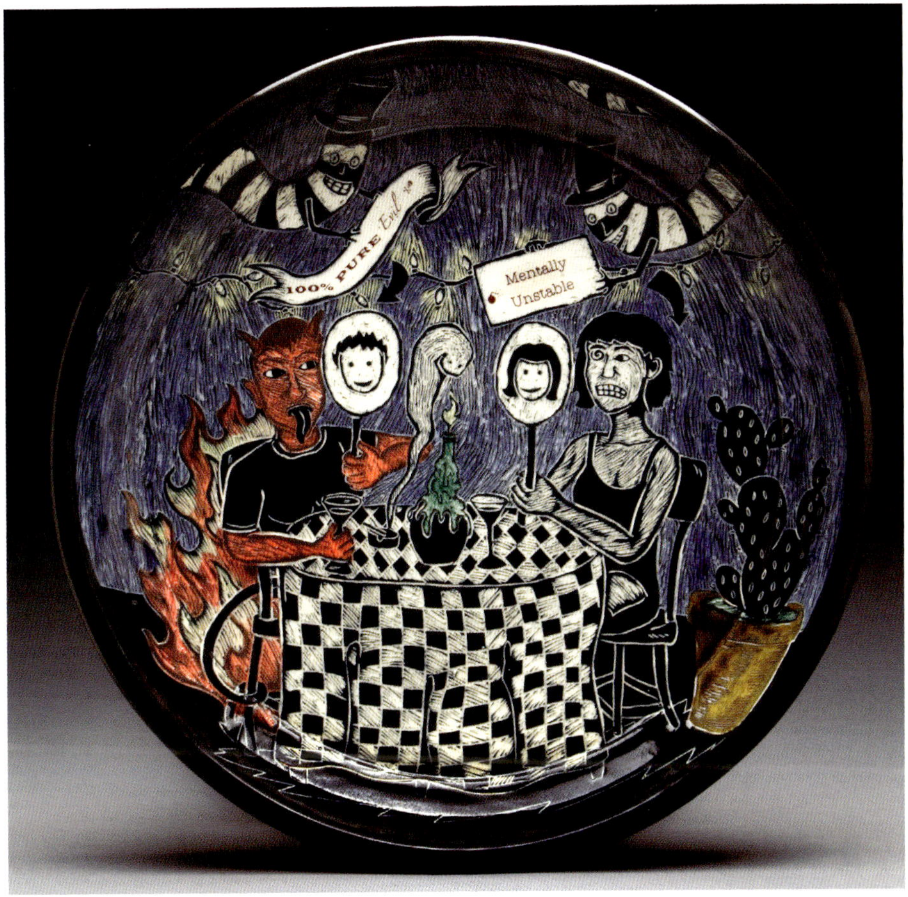

Kathy King

Blind Date | 2007

3 X 13 INCHES (7.6 X 33 CM)

Wheel-thrown mid-range porcelain; sgraffito; clear glaze, cone 06; china paint, laser decals

PHOTOS BY EDDIE ING PHOTOGRAPHY

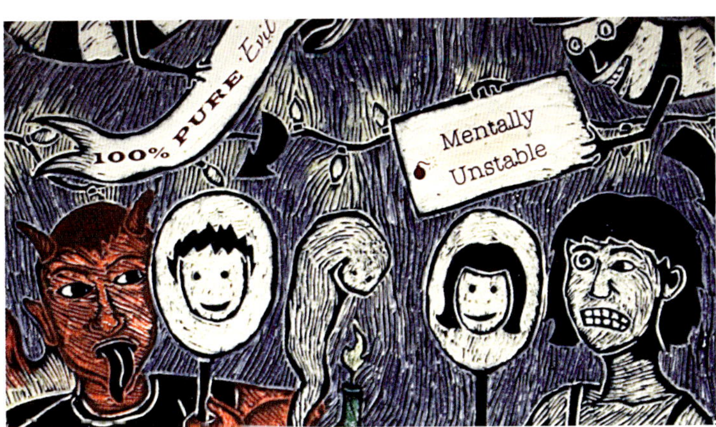

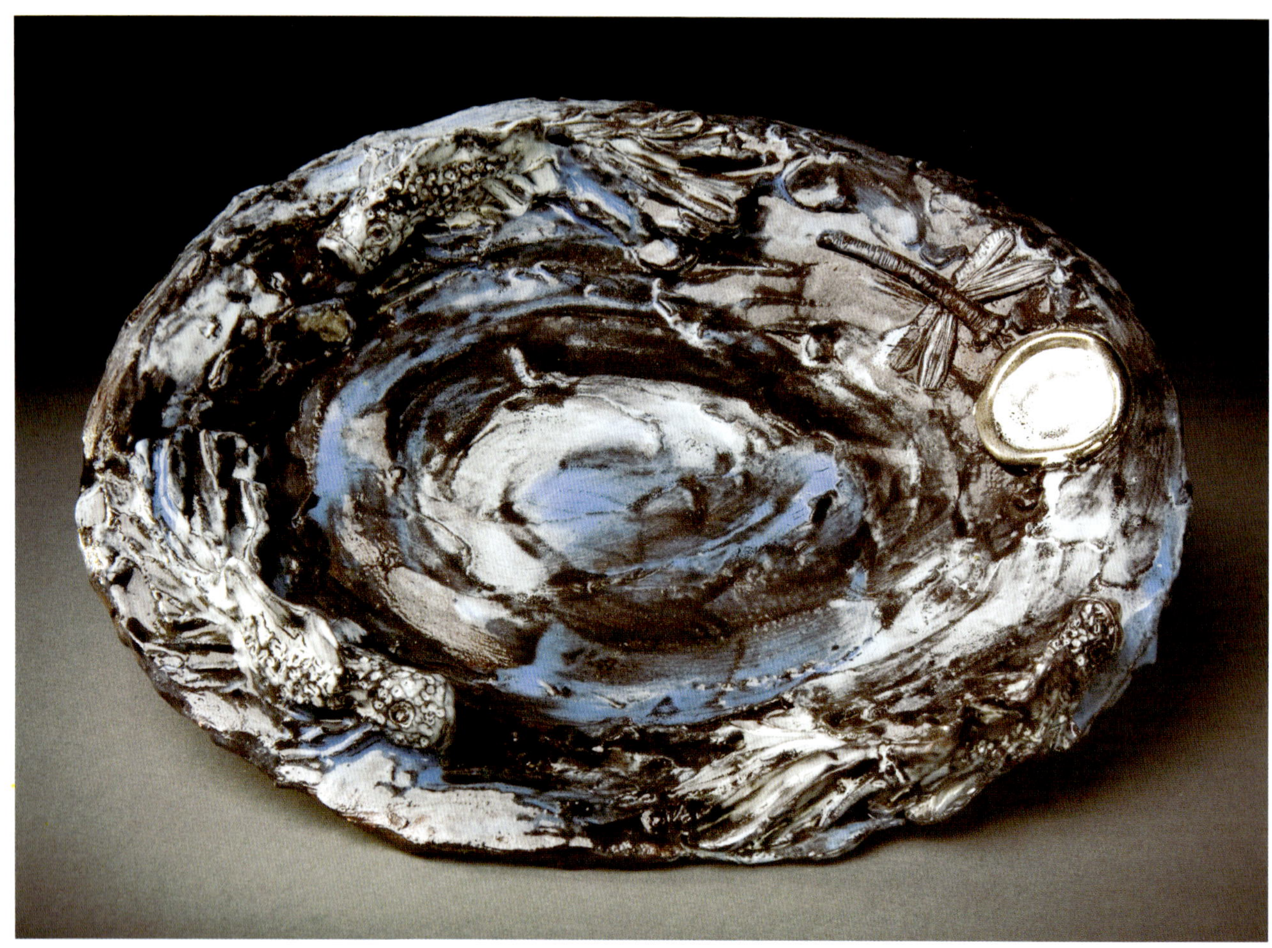

Harriet Ann Thompson

Fish Pond Platter | 2007

2 X 12 X 10 INCHES (5.1 X 30.5 X 25.4 CM)

Hand-built terra cotta; rolled, pinched, and pressed; glaze and overglaze; electric fired, cone 04; luster, cone 019

PHOTO BY SHANE BASKIN/BLACK BOX STUDIOS

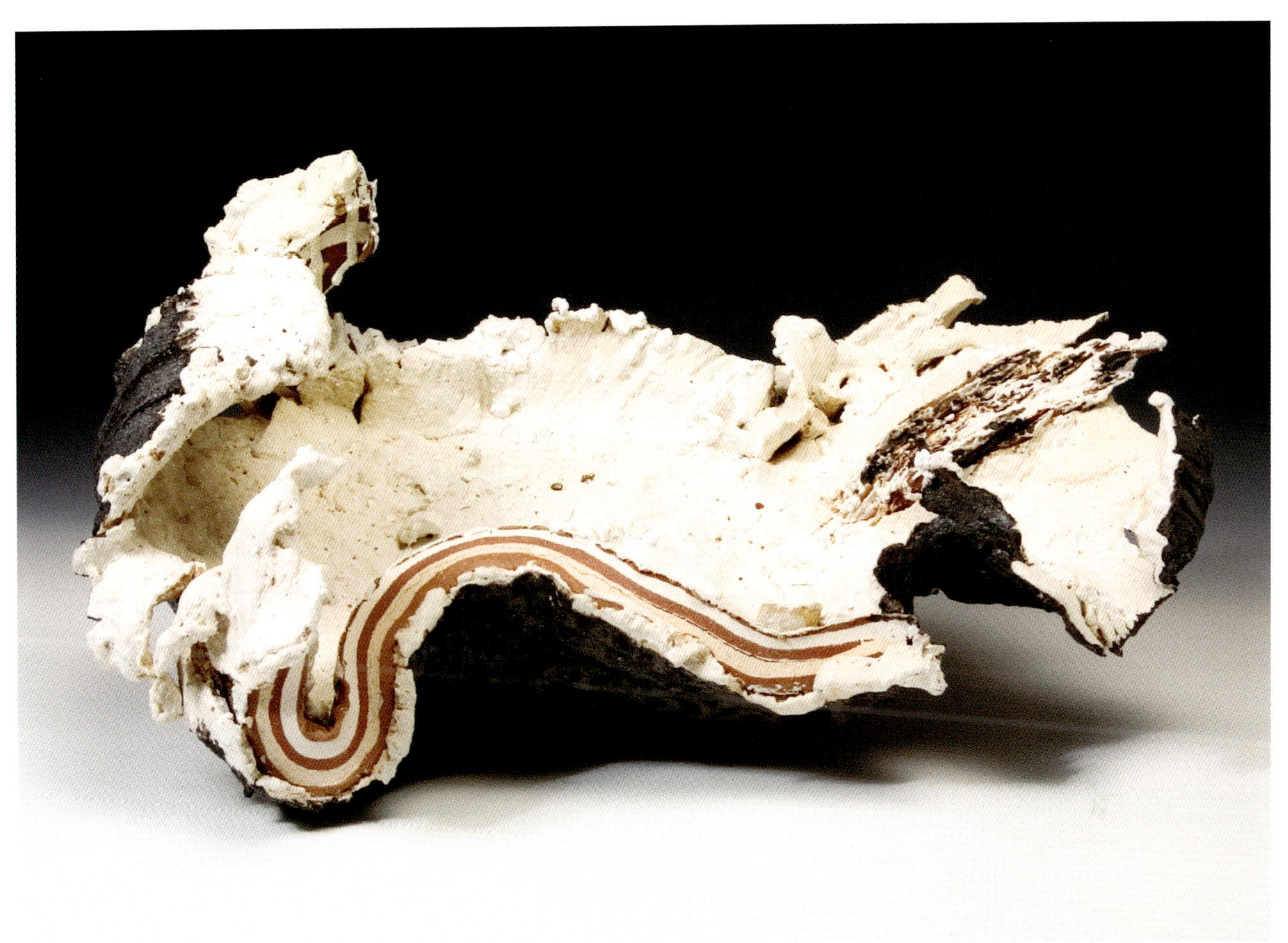

Gloria Searles

Flitch | 2007

16 X 12 INCHES (40.6 X 30.5 CM)

Hand-built crank clay with porcelain and terra-cotta laminations; manganese/volcanic glaze; electric fired, 2120°F (1160°C)

PHOTO BY ARTIST

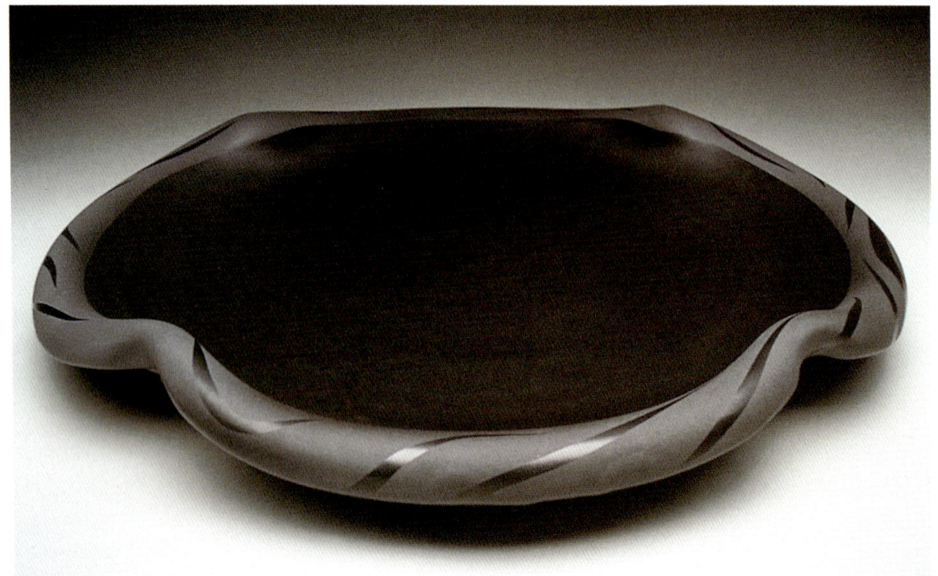

Eric Rempe

Untitled | 2007

2 X 15 X 15 INCHES (5.1 X 38.1 X 38.1 CM)

Wheel-thrown stoneware; gas reduction, cone 10; sandblasted

PHOTO BY ARTIST

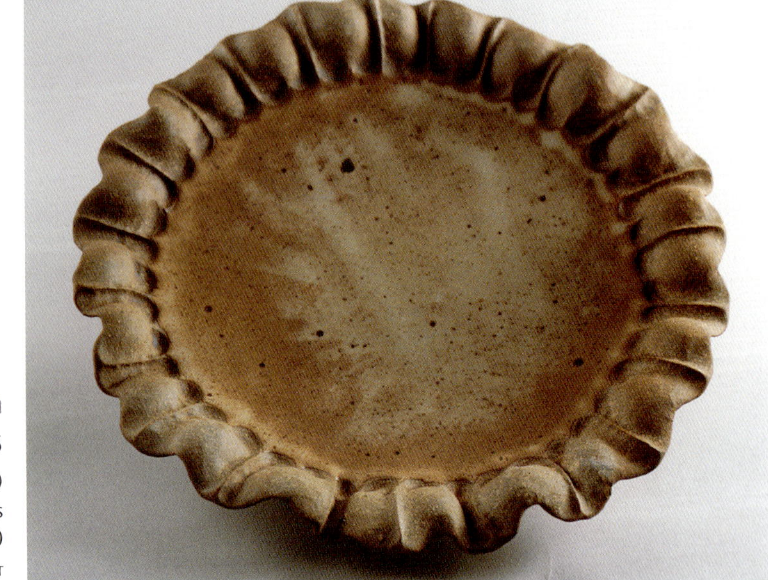

Barbara Walch

Dinner Plate | 1996

1 X 10 INCHES (2.5 X 25.4 CM)

Hand-built stoneware; gas fired in reduction, cone 10

PHOTO BY ARTIST

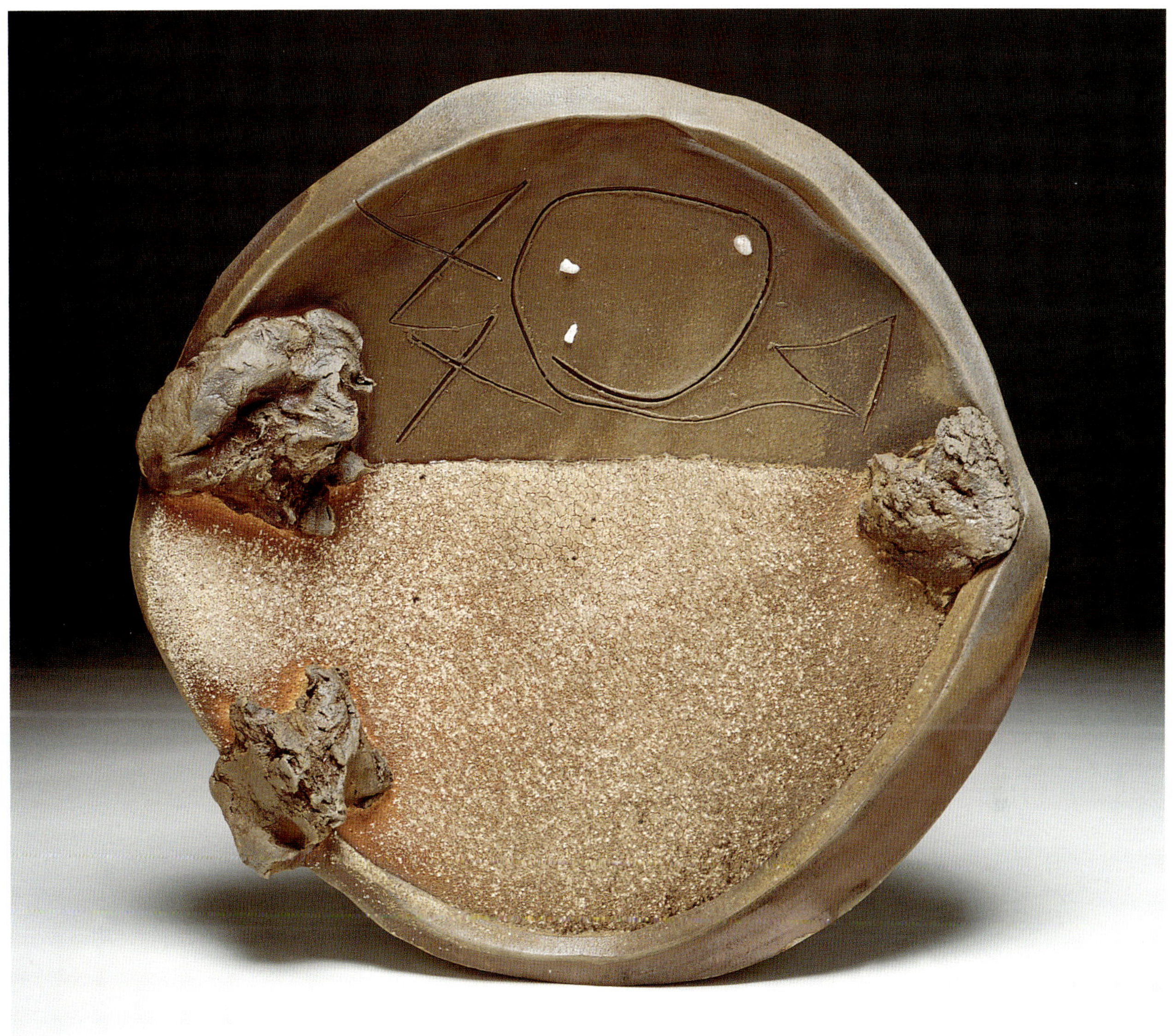

Randy Edmonson

Untitled | 1995

3 X 10 INCHES (7.6 X 25.4 CM)

Hand-built stoneware; slip, incised, feldspar inclusions; wood fired in Noborigama kiln

PHOTO BY TAYLOR DABNEY

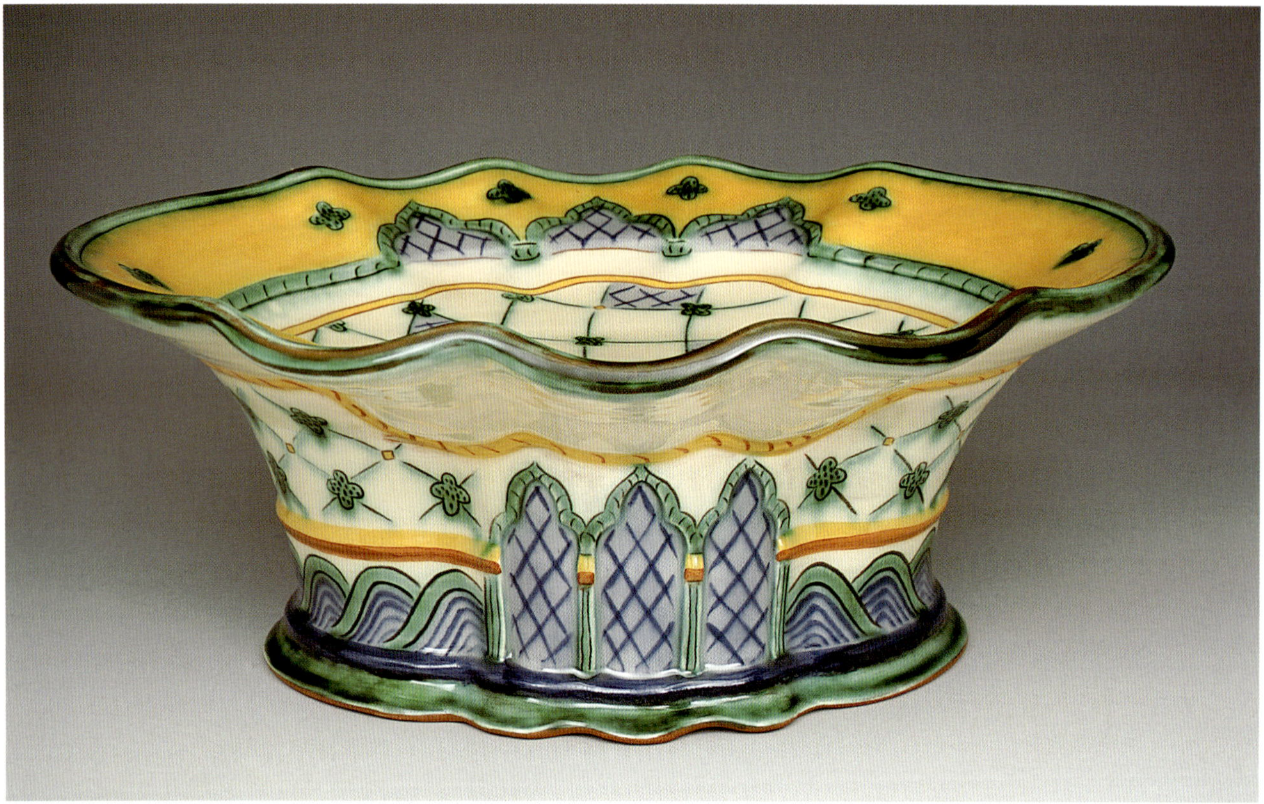

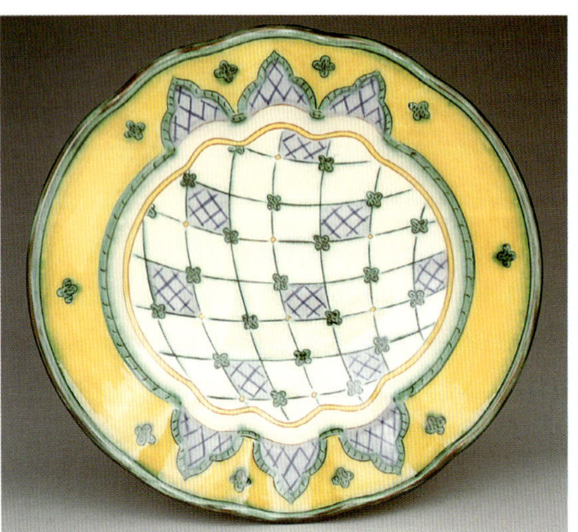

Jim Smith

Platter for a Venetian Flood | 2005

6 X 15 X $13\frac{1}{2}$ INCHES (15.2 X 38.1 X 34.3 CM)

Wheel-thrown and altered Nova Scotia earthenware; slip and sgraffito; clear glaze, electric fired, cone 04

PHOTOS BY JULIAN BEVERIDGE

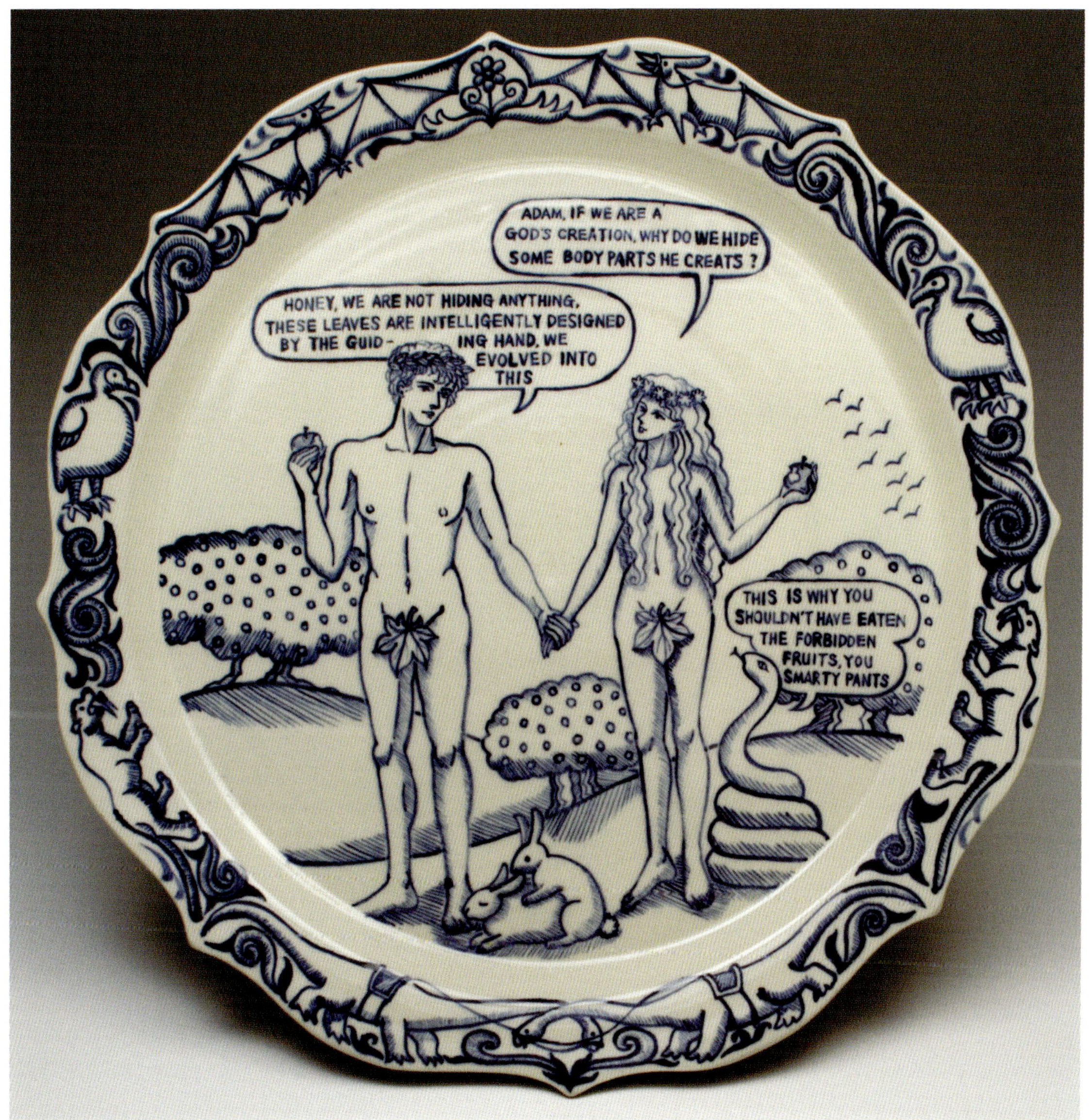

Yoko Sekino-Bové

Human Evolution (Working Title) | 2007

3 X 15 INCHES (7.6 X 38.1 CM)

Wheel-thrown porcelain; cone 6

PHOTO BY JIM BOVÉ

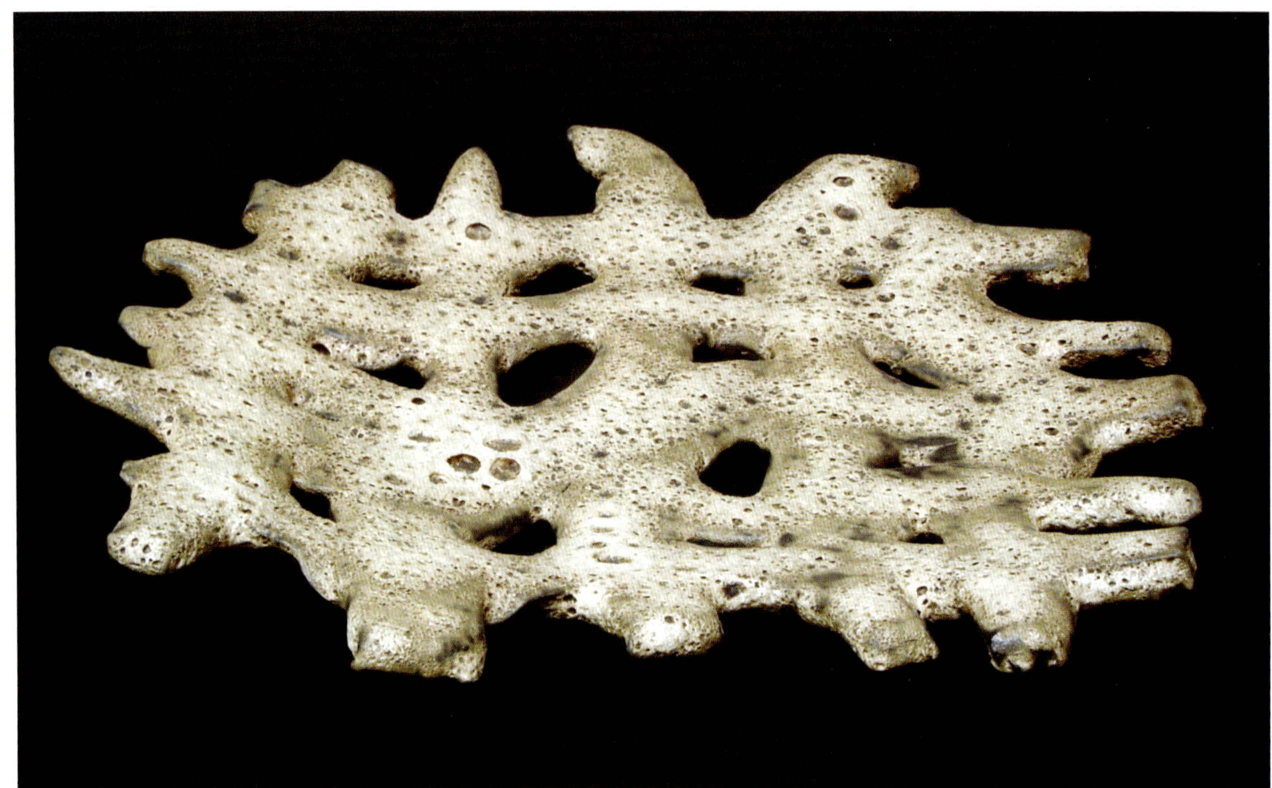

Anna Choi

Square Platter | 2007

1 X 11 X 11 INCHES (2.5 X 27.9 X 27.9 CM)

Hand-built raku; black slip; volcanic glaze, oxidation fired, cone 8

PHOTO BY ARTIST

Renée Brown

Oval Platter | 2007

4 X 15 X 11 INCHES (10.2 X 38.1 X 27.9 CM)

Wheel-thrown and altered mid-range earthenware; colored slips, underglazes, sgraffito; clear glaze, electric fired, cone 5

PHOTO BY ARTIST

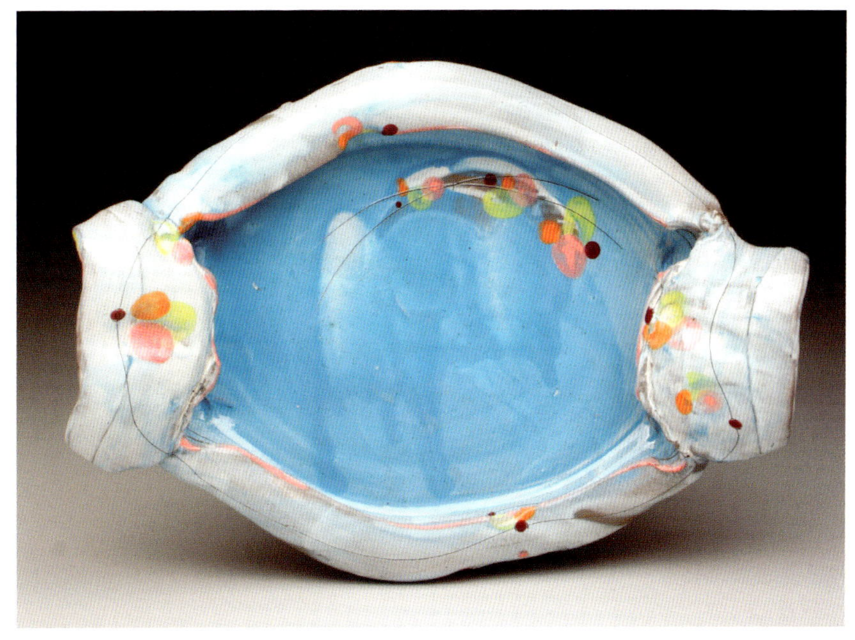

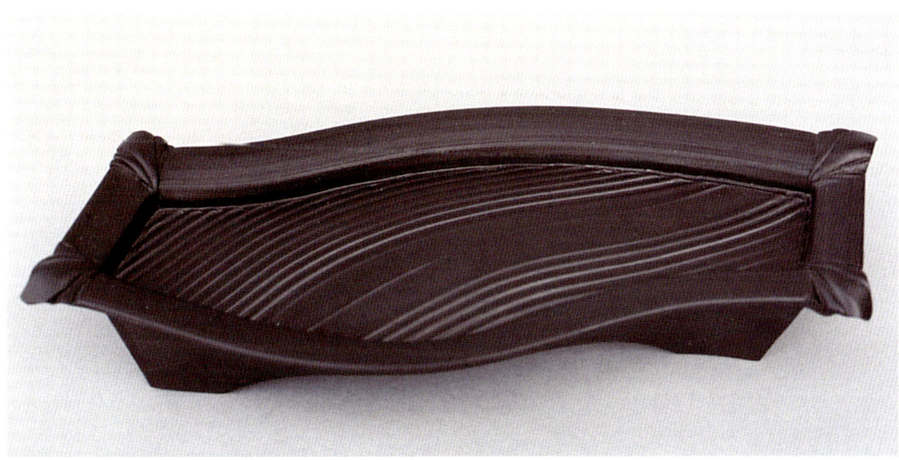

Todd Turek

Tray | 1990

3 X 17 X 7 INCHES (7.6 X 43.2 X 17.8 CM)

Hand-built black clay; electric fired, cone 5

PHOTO BY ARTIST

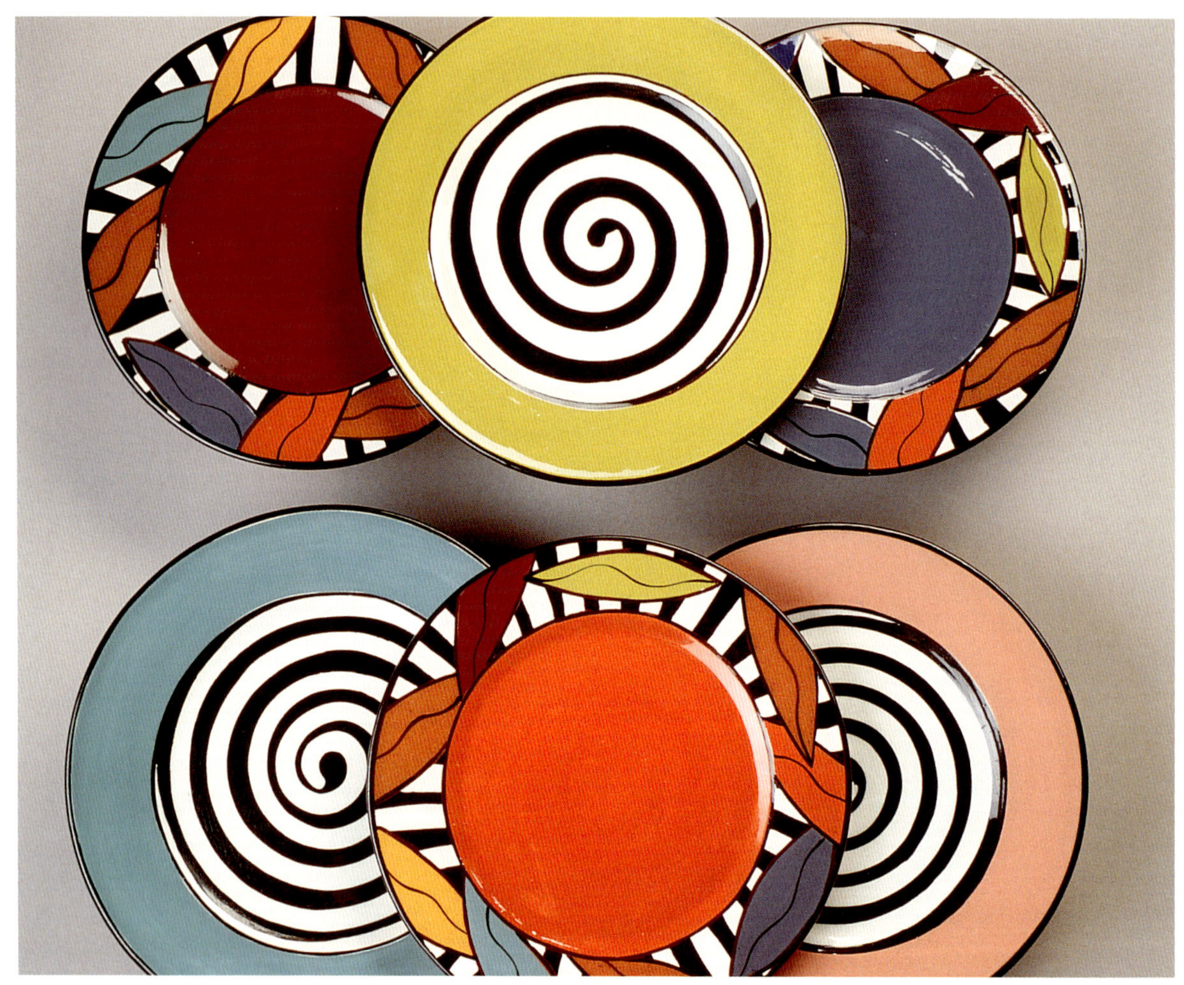

Carol Gouthro

Spiral & Leaves Salad/Dessert Plates | 2006

EACH: 8 INCHES (20.3 CM) IN DIAMETER

Slip cast from wheel-thrown original terra cotta; electric fired, cone 04; underglazes, clear glaze, cone 05

PHOTO BY ROGER SCHREIBER

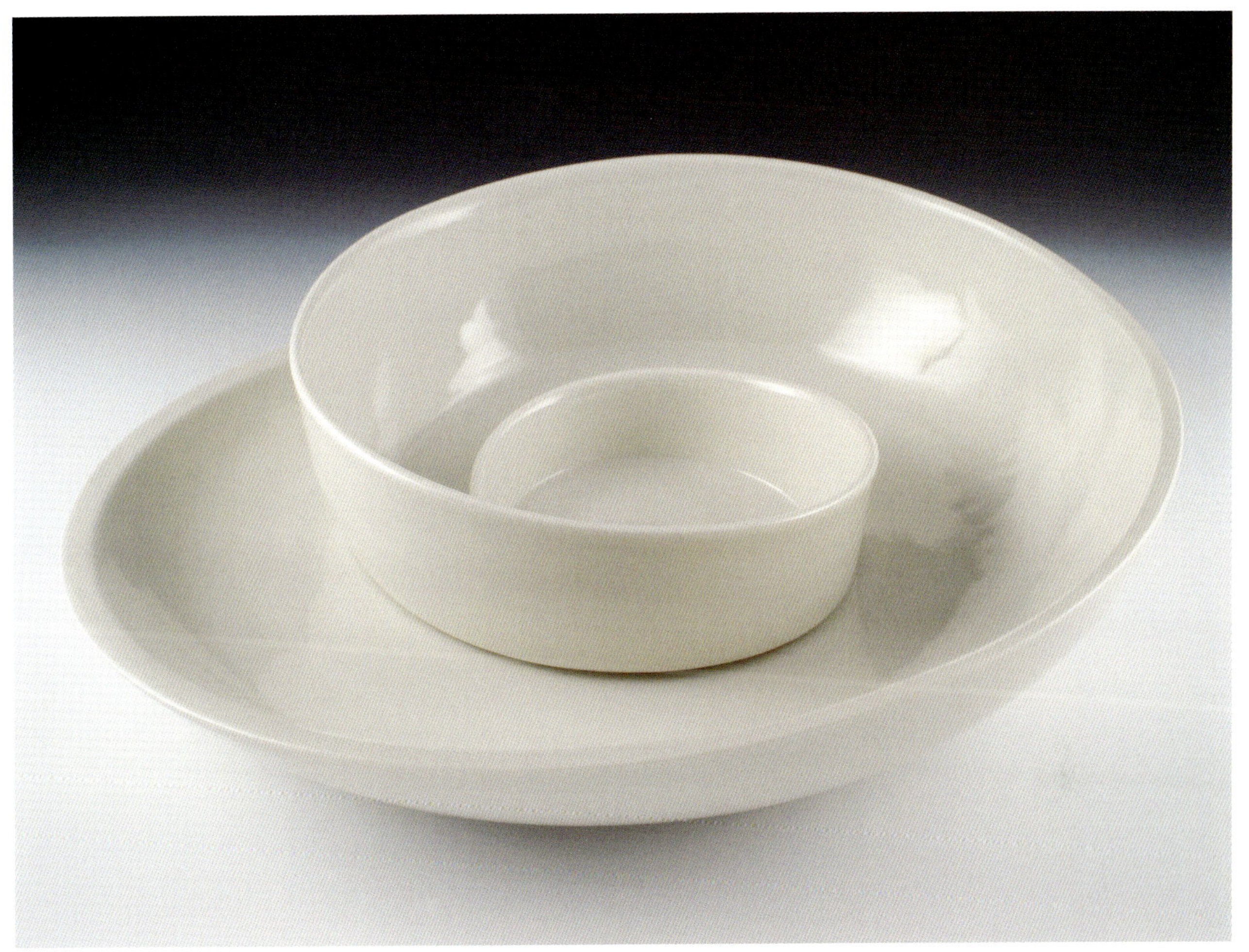

Kim Westad

Whirl Serving Platter | 2007

2 1/2 X 10 1/4 X 10 1/4 INCHES (6.4 X 26 X 26 CM)

Wheel-thrown and altered porcelain; clear glaze, electric fired, cone 6

PHOTO BY ARTIST

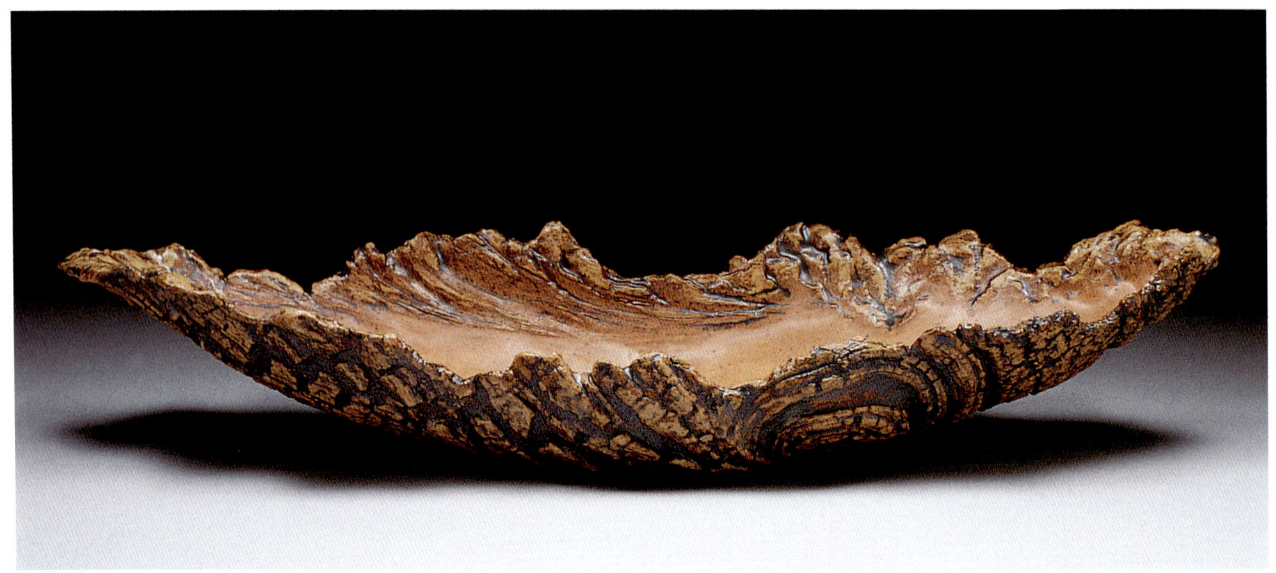

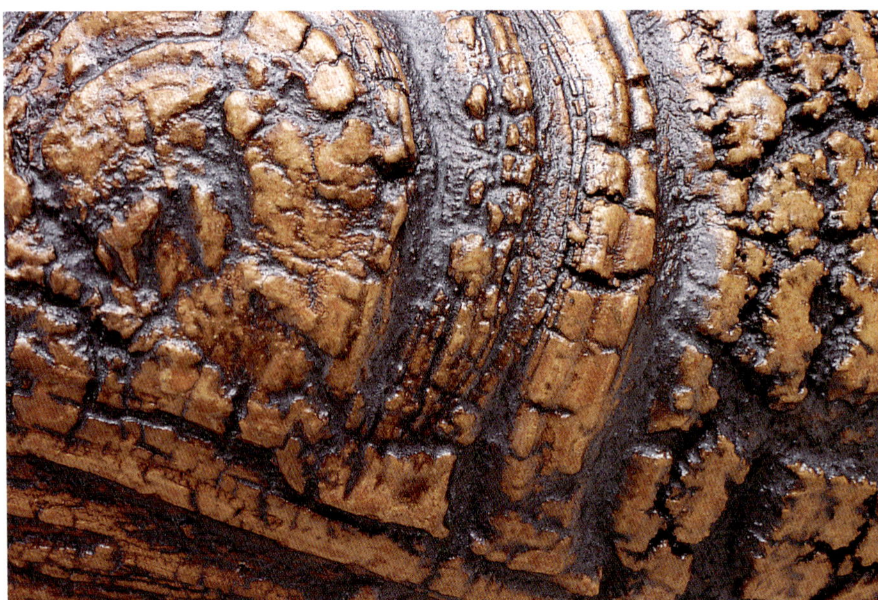

Sarah Rossiter

Colorado | 2003

4 X 23 X 7 INCHES (10.2 X 58.4 X 17.8 CM)

Hand-built stoneware; gas fired in reduction, cone 10

PHOTOS BY ARTIST

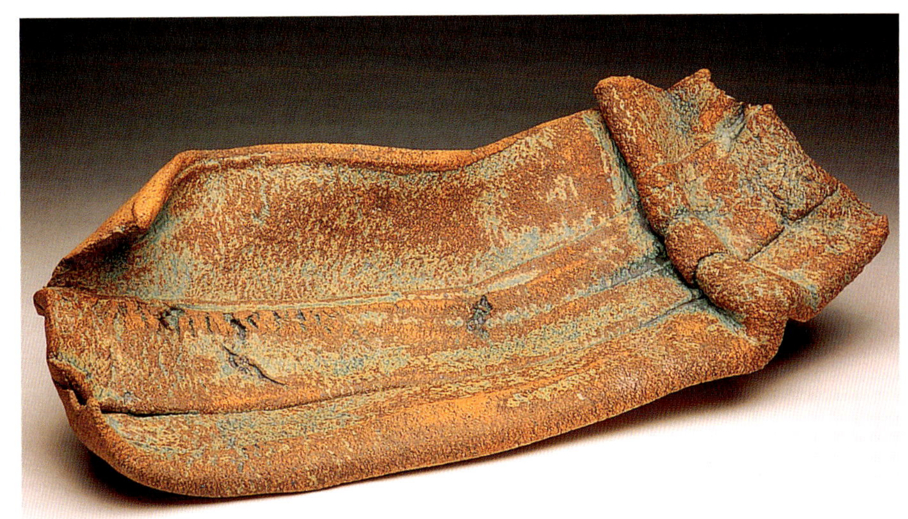

Natalie R. Kase

Platter | 2006

3½ X 15 X 7 INCHES (8.9 X 38.1 X 17.8 CM)

Hand-built stoneware; slab, stretched, stained; glaze, gas reduction, cone 10

PHOTO BY JOSEPH GIUNTA

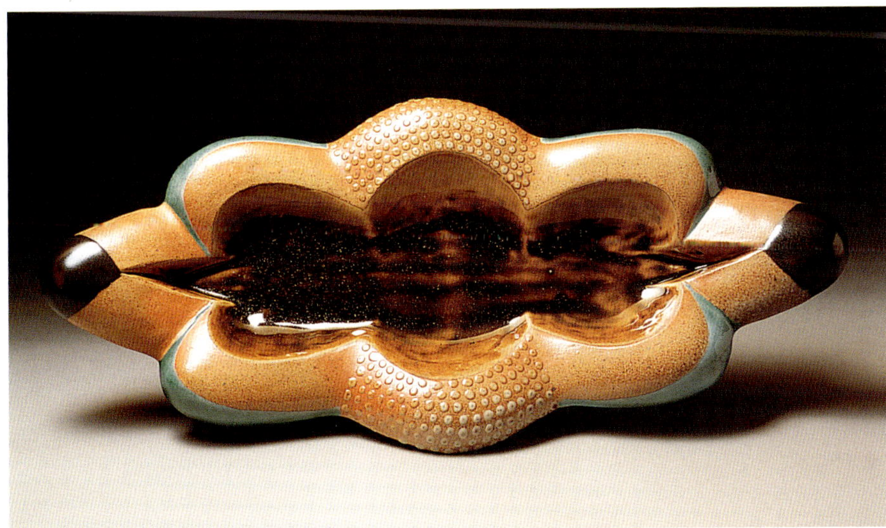

Mark Johnson

Platter | 2006

3 X 18 X 12 INCHES (7.6 X 45.7 X 30.5 CM)

Press-molded white stoneware; wax resist, layered glazes; soda fired, cone 10

PHOTO BY ARTIST

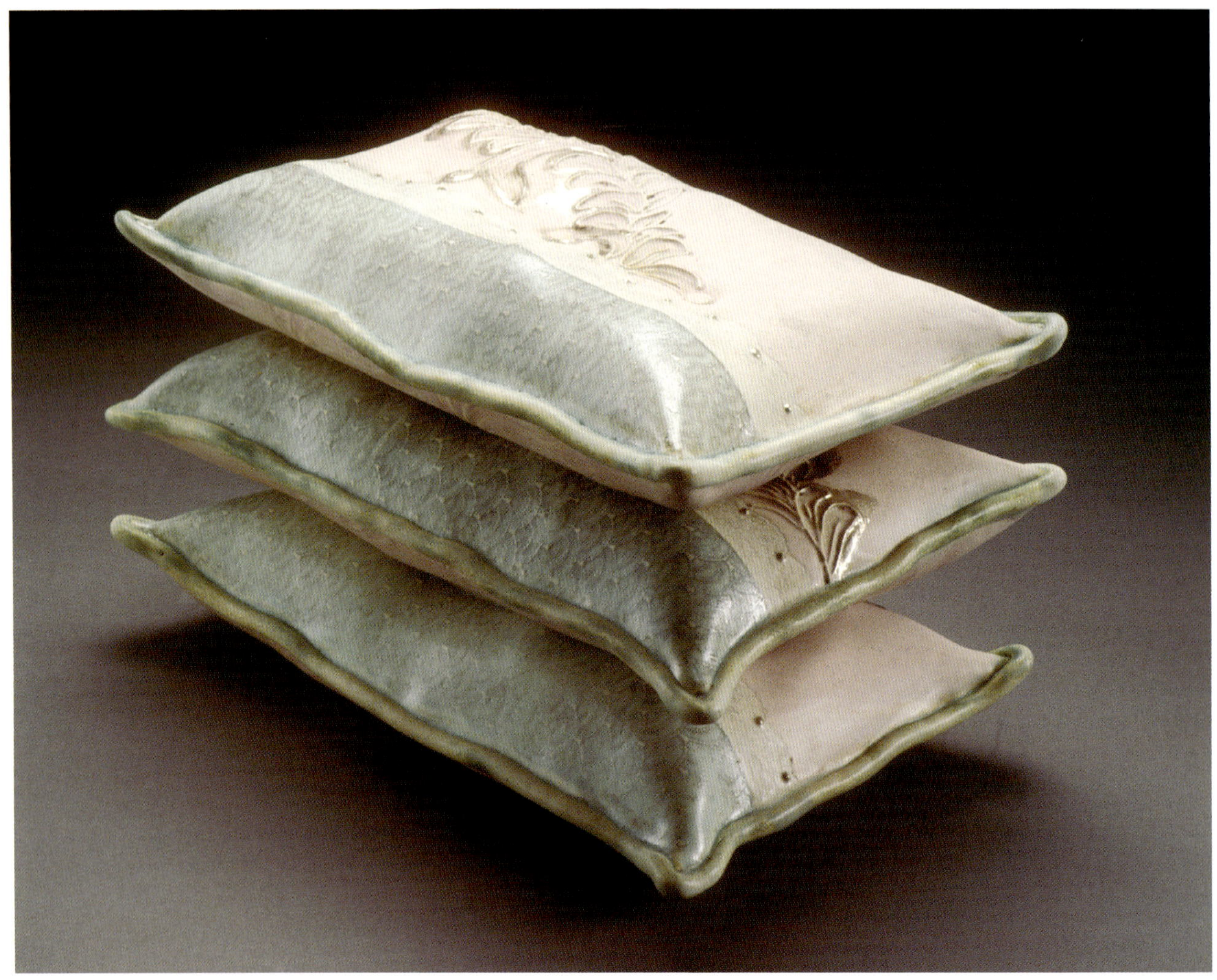

Joanna Stecker

Set of Three Serving Pillows | 2006

EACH: 3 X 13 X 7 INCHES (7.6 X 33 X 17.8 CM)

Hand-built porcelain stoneware blend; electric fired, cone 6; gold leaf

PHOTO BY BART KASTEN

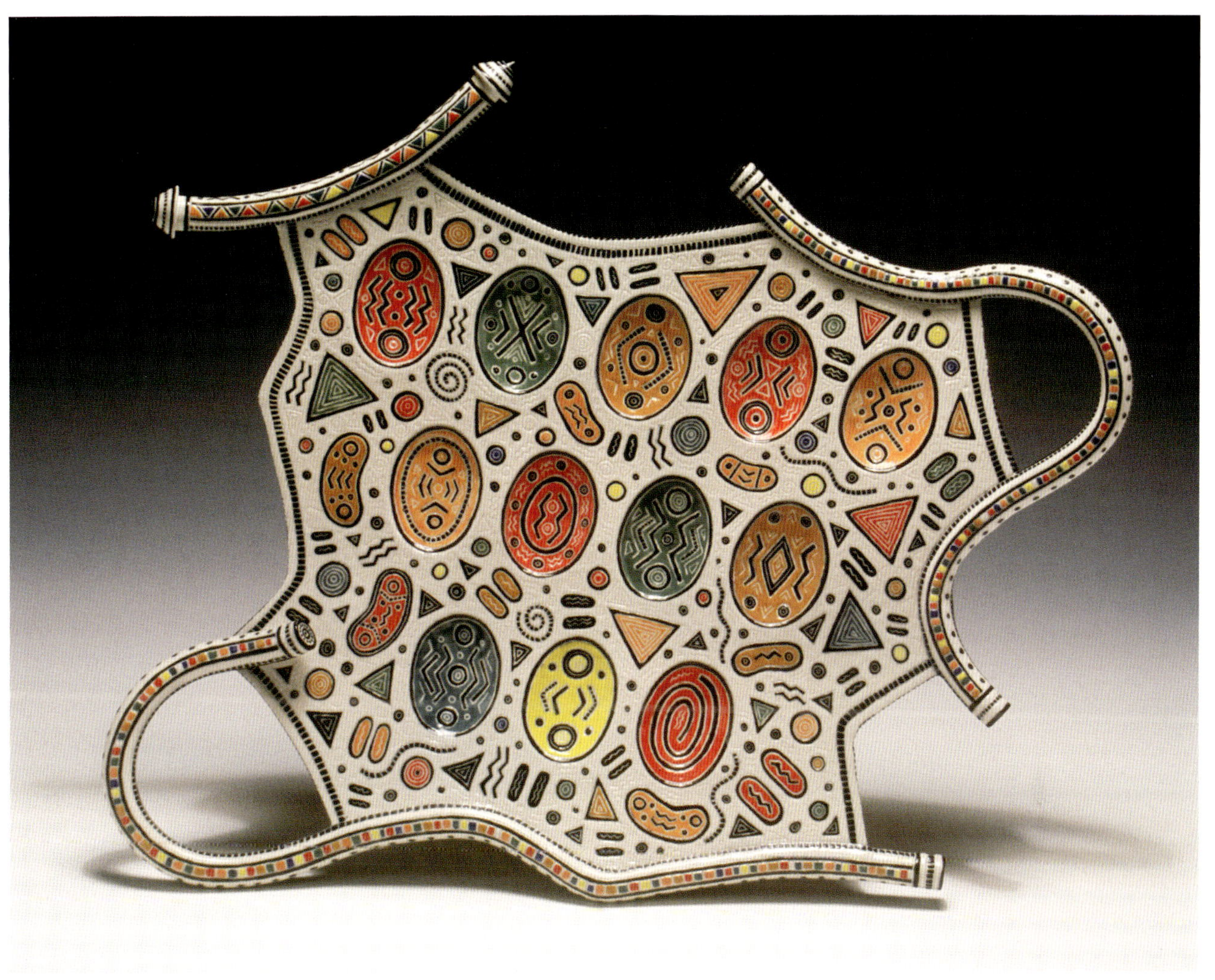

Marko Fields

Dang Deviled Egg Tray Thinks It's Alive; Wants to Go to Las Vegas and Serve Wayne Newton | 2004

1½ X 17 X 12 INCHES (3.8 X 43.2 X 30.5 CM)

Hand-built stoneware; incised, sgraffito; oxidation fired, cone 6; underglazed

PHOTO BY ARTIST

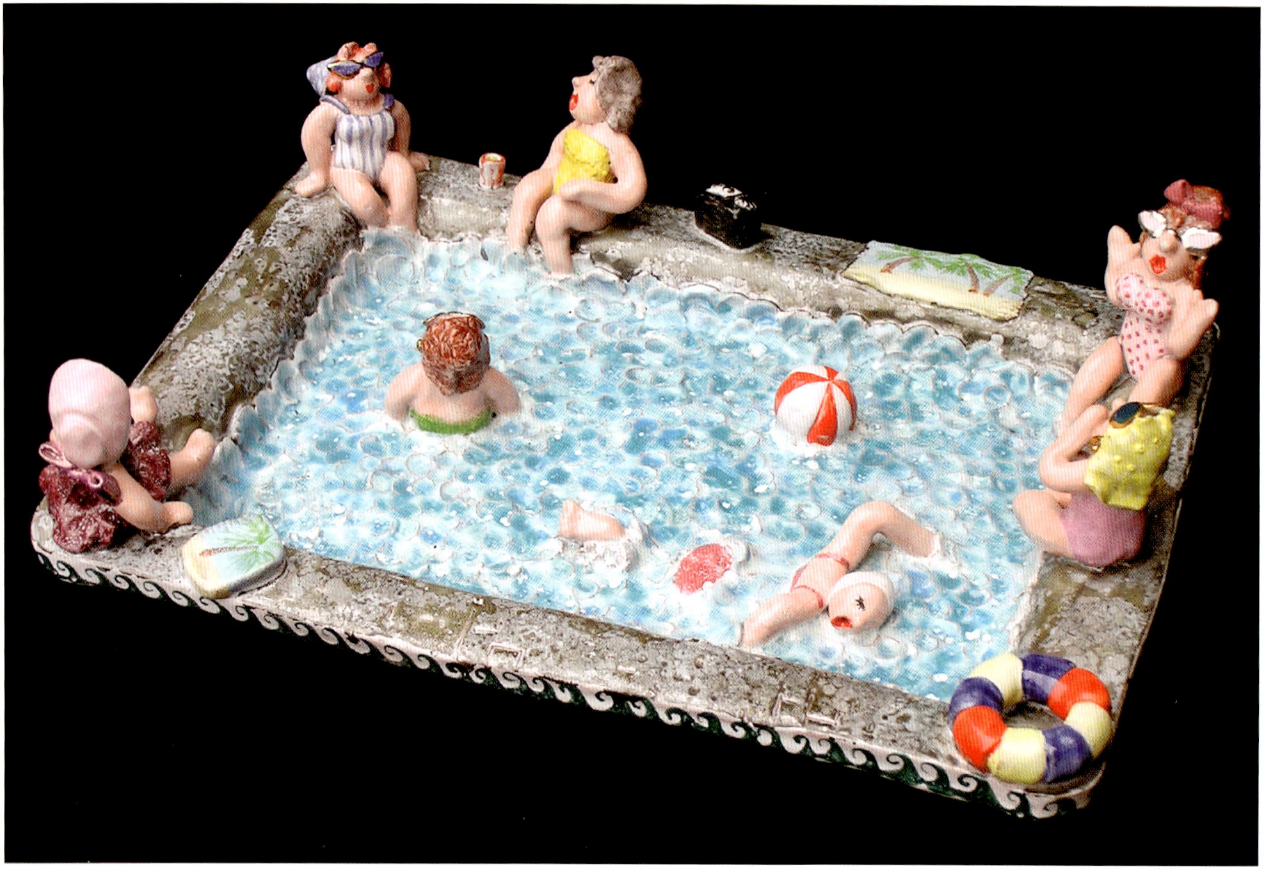

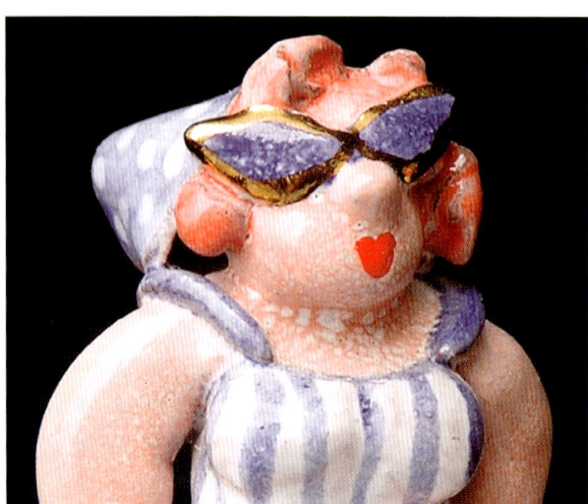

Janice Farley

Poolside Platter | 2005

1 1/2 X 14 X 9 1/2 INCHES (3.8 X 35.6 X 24.1 CM)

Hand-built earthenware; majolica;
oxidation fired, cone 04;
lusters, china paint

PHOTOS BY ARTIST

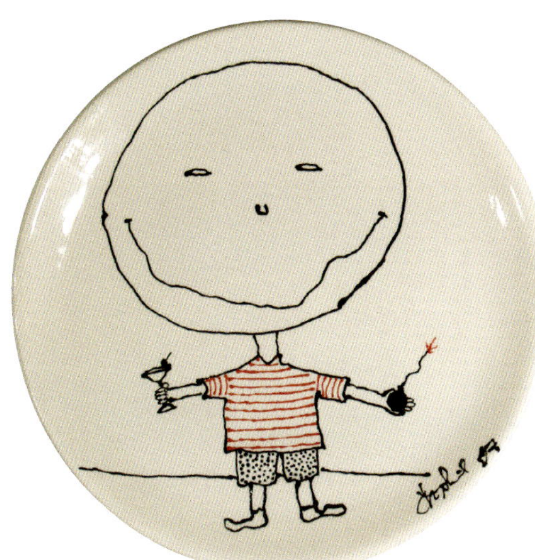

Lenny Dowhie

Cocktail Man | 2007

1 X 16 INCHES (2.5 X 40.6 CM)

Slip-cast whiteware; slip drawing; glaze, cones 04 and 06

PHOTO BY ARTIST

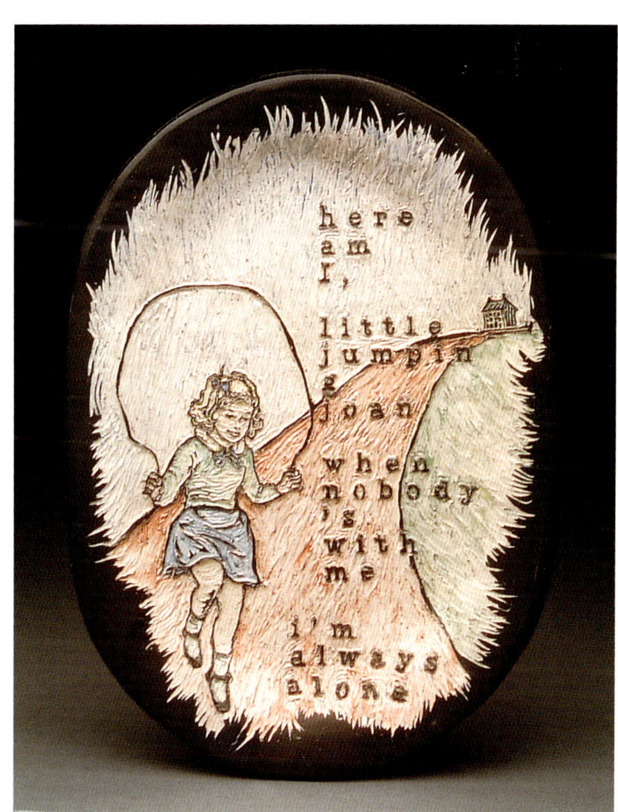

Barbara E. Wolf

Jumping Joan | 2007

10 1/2 X 14 1/2 INCHES (26.7 X 36.8 CM)

Hand-built and slab-constructed earthenware; sgraffito; electric fired, cone 04; china paints, cone 018

PHOTO BY DAVID GULISANO

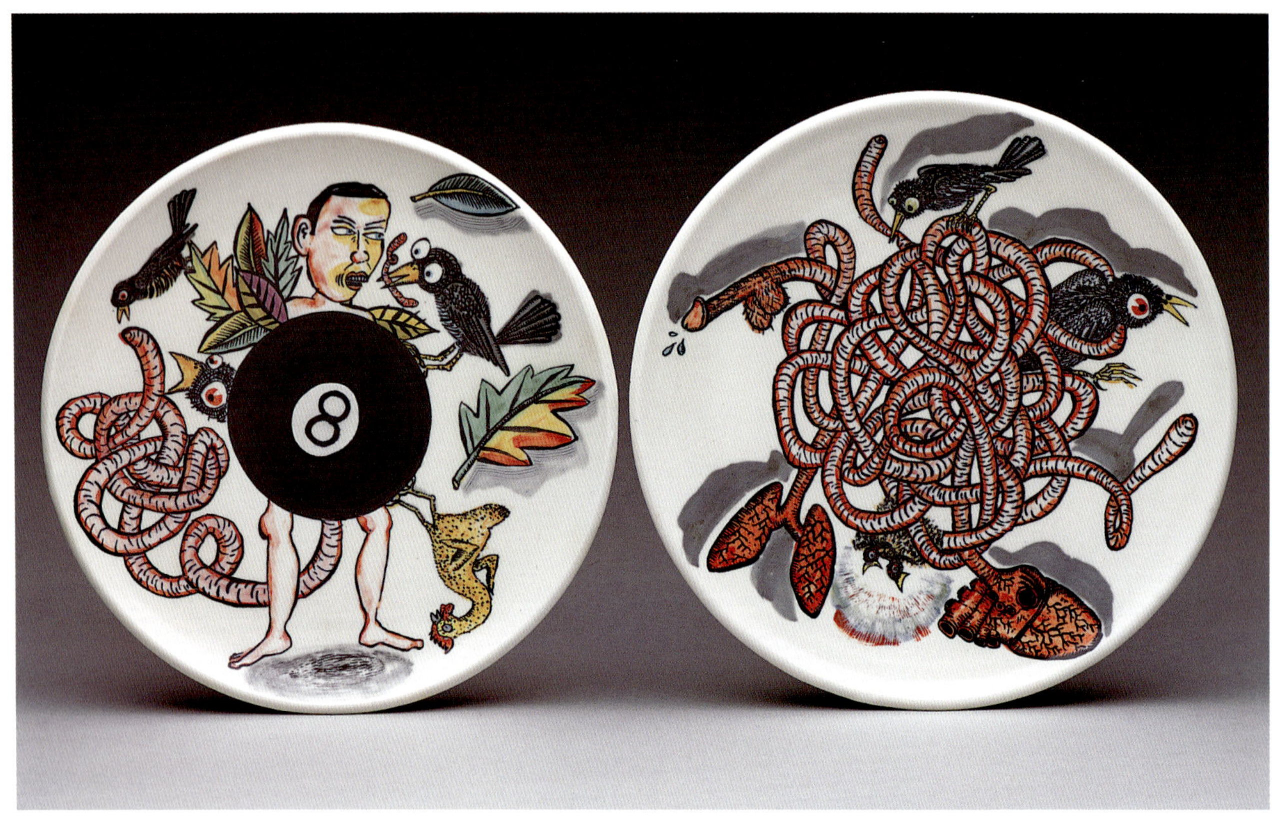

Michael Corney

Baby Bird Series . . . | 2006

EACH: APPROXIMATELY 11 INCHES (27.9 CM) IN DIAMETER

Wheel-thrown porcelain; brush painted; electric fired, cone 10

PHOTO BY MARGO GEIST

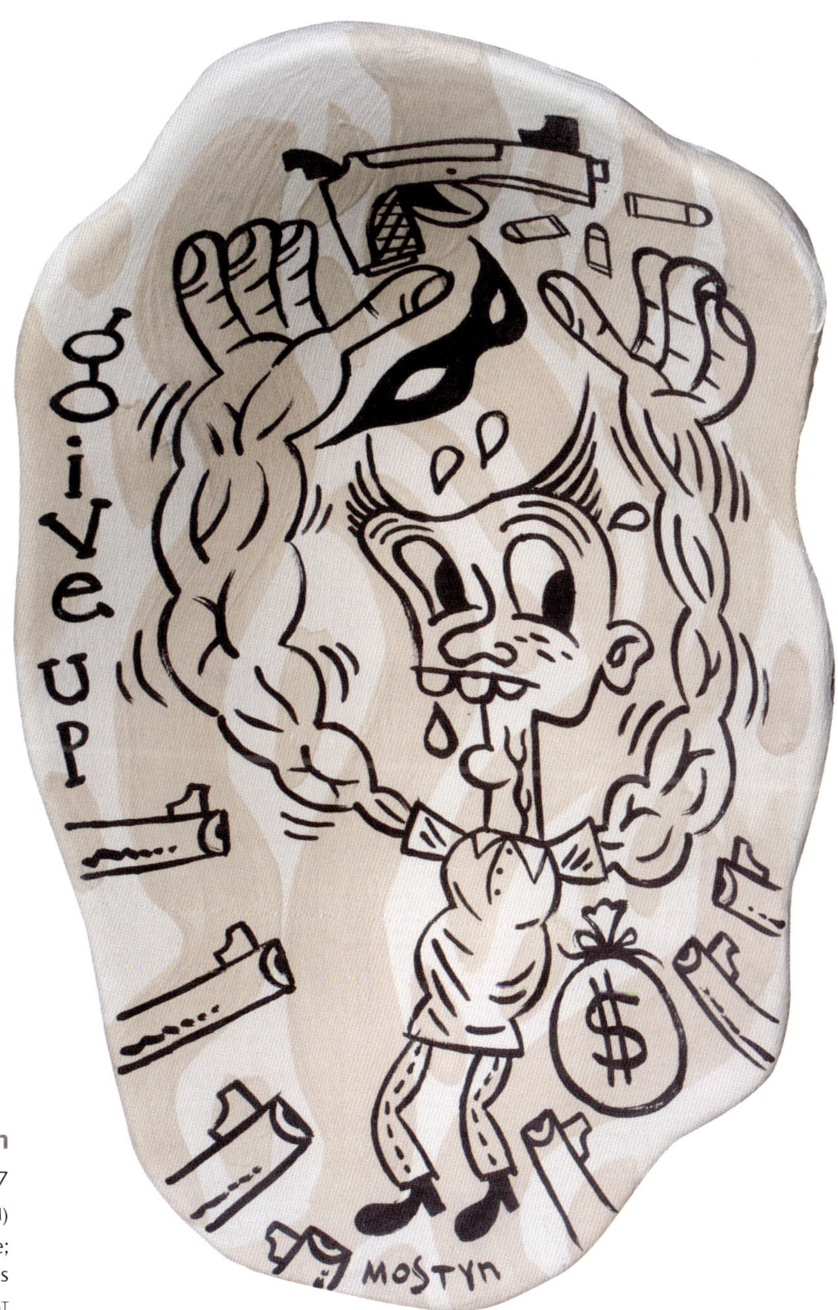

Chris Mostyn
Give Up | 2007
$2^{1}/_{2}$ X $12^{1}/_{2}$ X $7^{1}/_{4}$ INCHES (6.4 X 31.8 X 18.4 CM)
Hand-built low-fire earthenware; electric fired, cone 04, engobes
PHOTO BY ARTIST

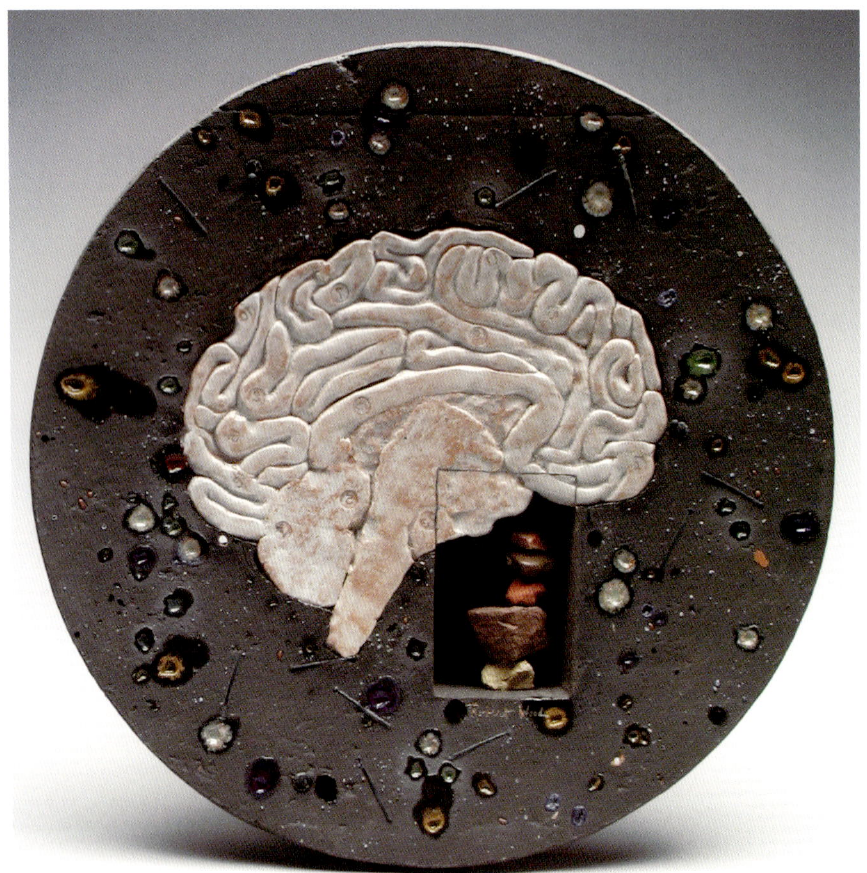

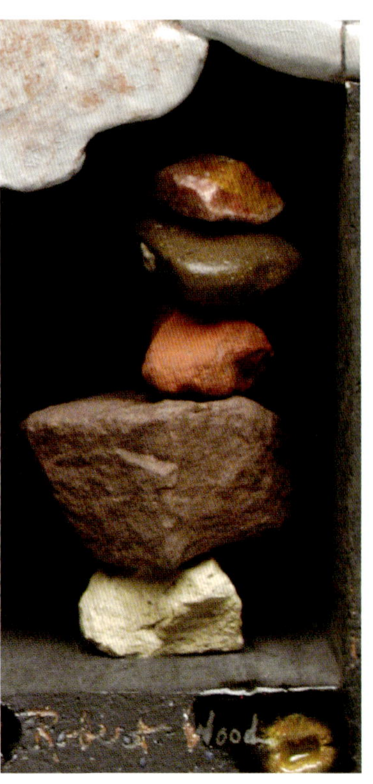

Robert Wood

Braindead | 2003

$19\frac{1}{2}$ INCHES (49.5 CM) IN DIAMETER

Slump-molded, hand-built, and wheel-thrown earthenware; slip, terra sigillata; electric fired, cone 1; clear glaze, cone 04

PHOTOS BY ARTIST

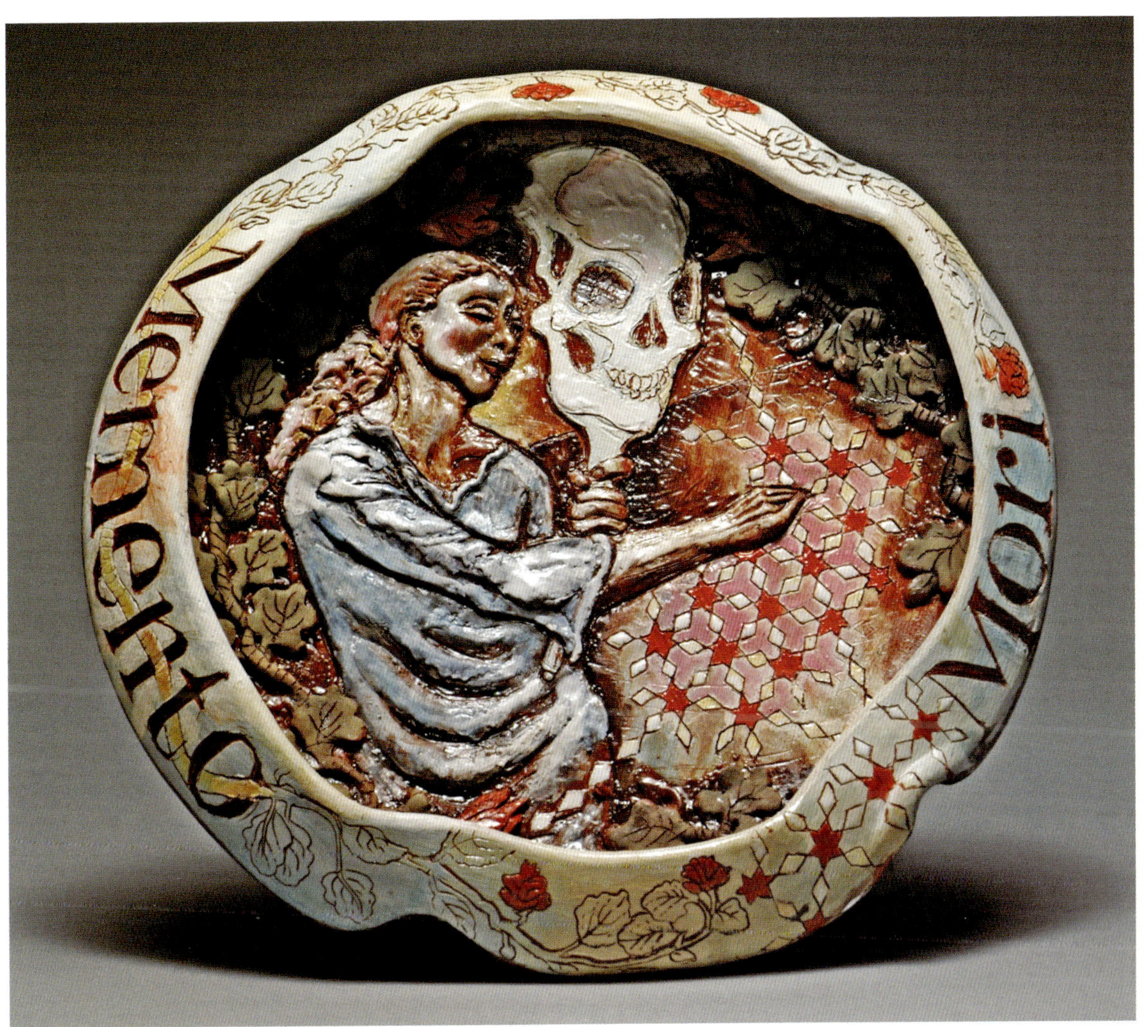

Ruth Ann Reese

Memento Mori | 2007

4 X 17 X 17 INCHES (10.2 X 43.2 X 43.2 CM)

Wheel-thrown and hand-built earthenware; engobes, stains, majolicas; electric fired, cone 05

PHOTO BY ARTIST

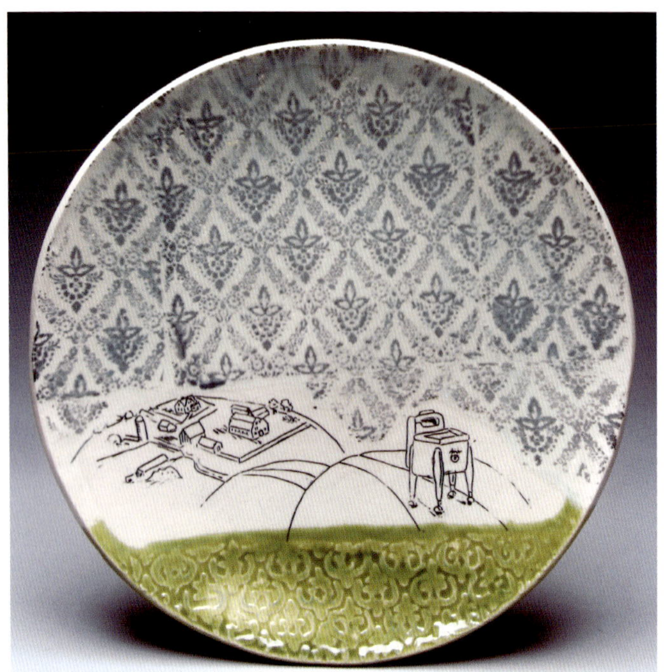

Kelly McKibben

Leaving the Farm | 2007

4 X 17 INCHES (10.2 X 43.2 CM)

Hand-built white stoneware; inlay, silkscreen slip transfer, shellac resist; cone 10 oxidation

PHOTO BY ARTIST

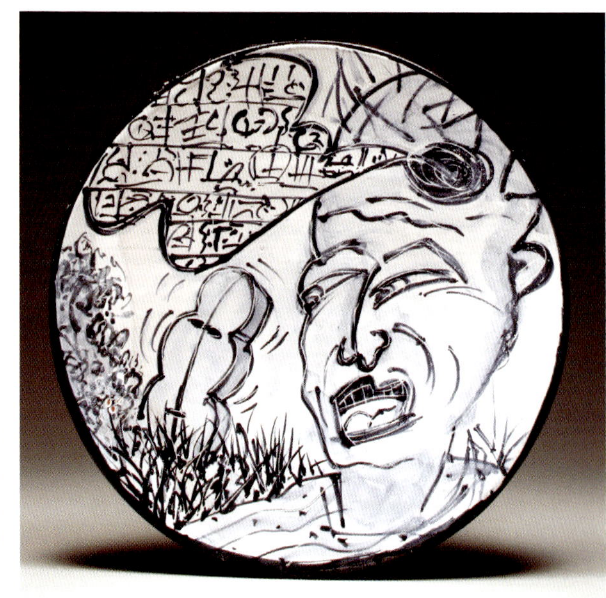

James D. Watral

What Is That! | 2006

2 1/4 X 11 3/4 INCHES (5.7 X 29.8 CM)

Hand-built earthenware; tin glaze and cobalt stain; electric fired, cone 03

PHOTO BY JOHN O. LEWIS

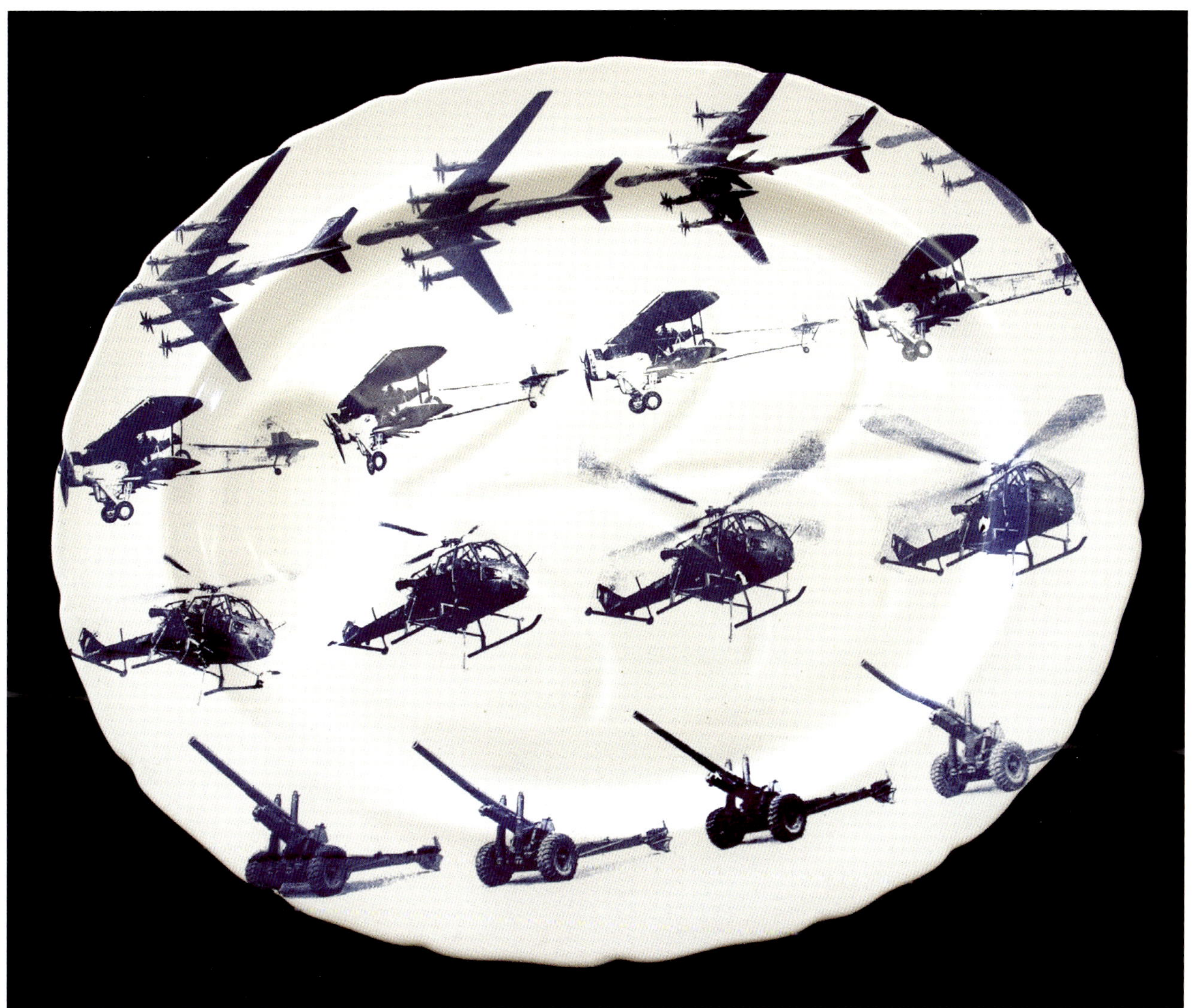

Beth Brown

Code Name Bear (Tupolev TU-20, Four-Turboprop Long-Range Strategic Bomber, Russia) | 2007

15 3/4 INCHES (40 CM) ACROSS

Slip-cast white earthenware; silkscreen print; cobalt oxide; electric fired, cone 04; glaze, cone 06

PHOTO BY STEVE RUTTER

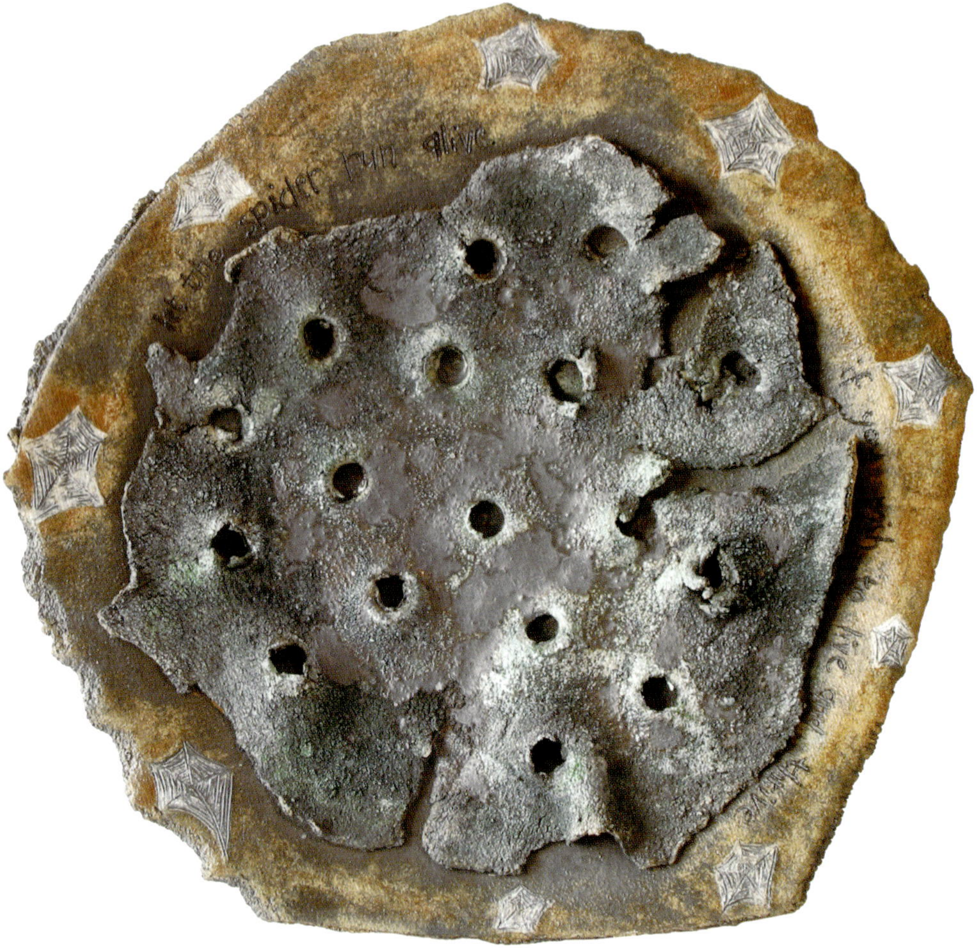

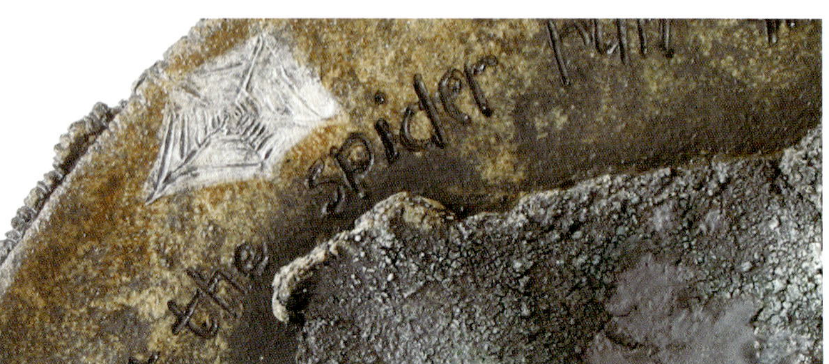

Alice Shepherd

If You Wish to Live and Thrive, Let the Spider Run Alive | 2006

$11\frac{1}{2}$ X $11\frac{1}{2}$ INCHES (29.2 X 29.2 CM)

Press-molded and hand-built stoneware; slip and oxides; electric fired, cone 6; overglaze, cone 017

PHOTOS BY KATE BARRY

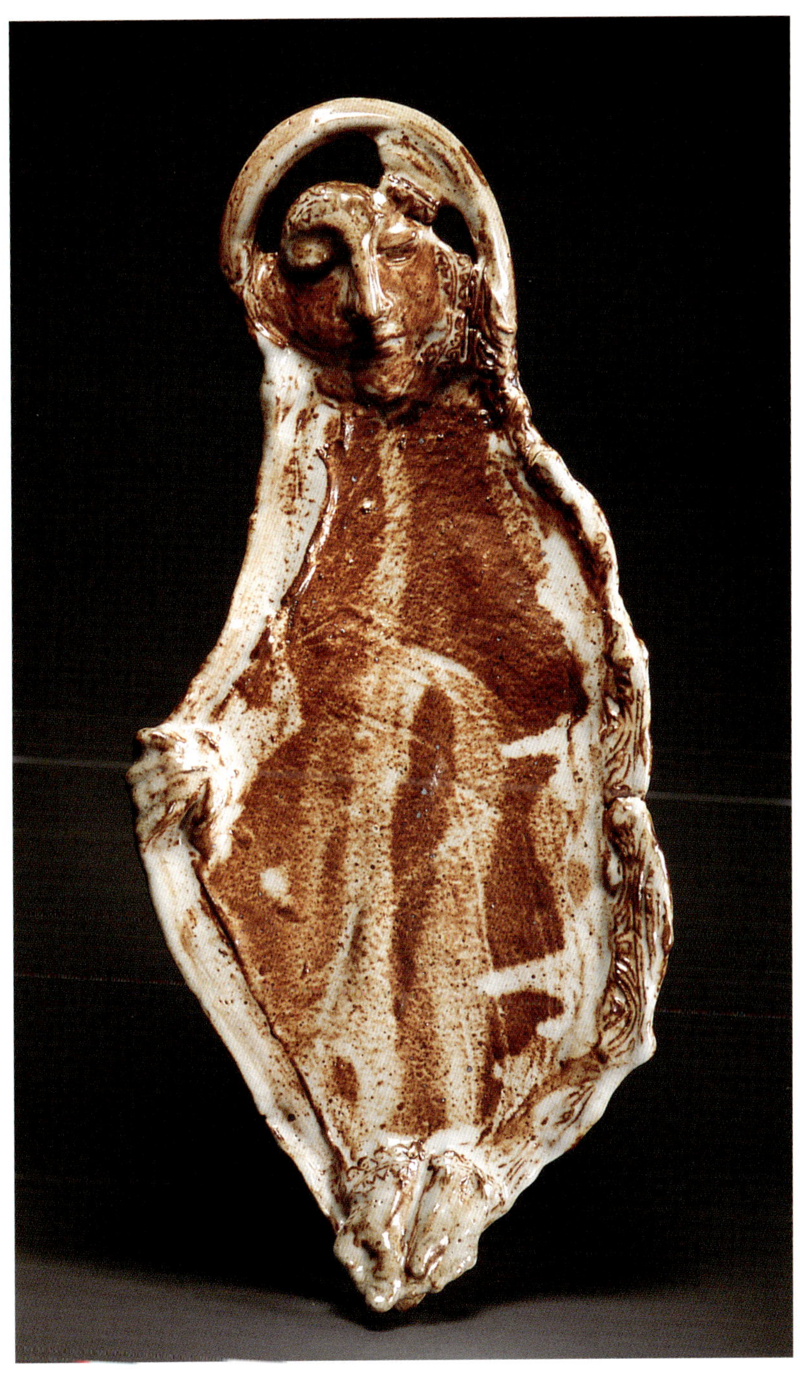

Rita Victoria Lewis

Virgin Tray | 2007

3 X 11 X 24 INCHES (7.6 X 27.9 X 61 CM)

Hand-built and wheel-thrown stoneware; slab with sprig molds and slip; shino glaze; gas fired in reduction, cone 10

PHOTO BY RICHARD SARGENT

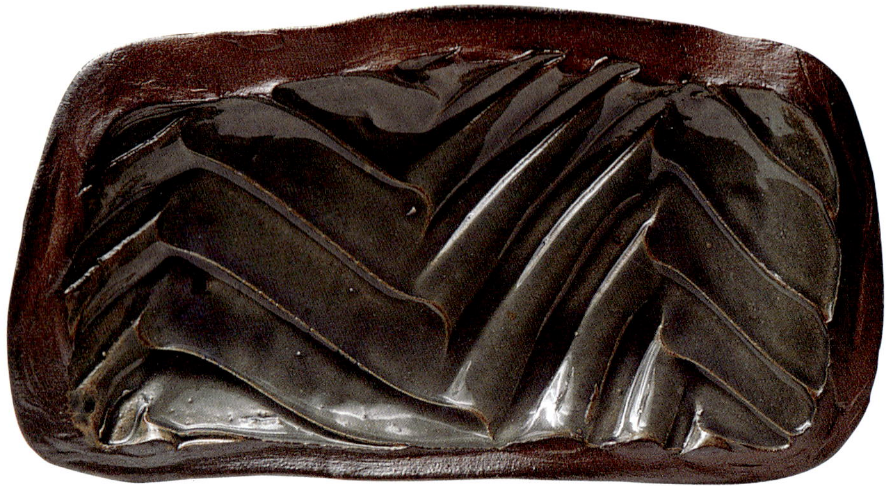

Sara Lee Patterson

Zig Zag Platter | 2003

1 X 13 X 7 INCHES (2.5 X 33 X 17.8 CM)

Stoneware slab; wood fired, cone 10

PHOTO BY D. JAMES DEE

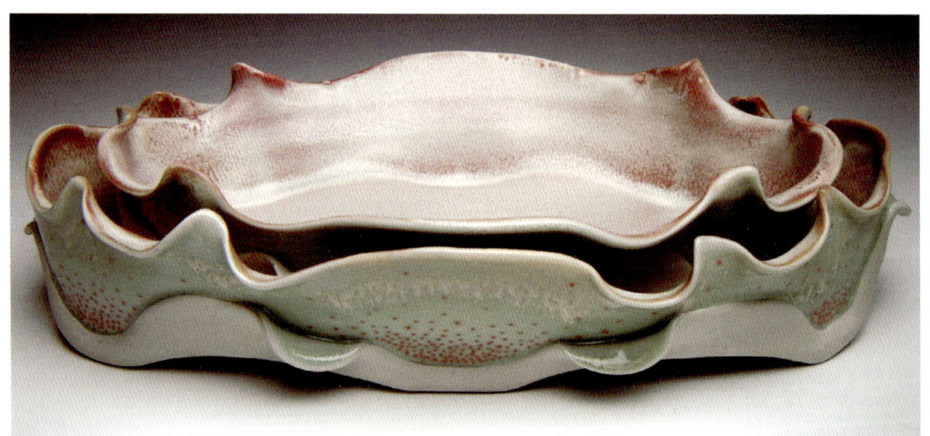

Martha H. Grover

Two Serving Trays | 2007

OVERALL: 4 X 15 X 8 INCHES (10.2 X 38.1 X 20.3 CM)

Thrown and altered porcelain; sprayed and trailed engobes and glazes; cone 11 neutral

PHOTO BY ARTIST

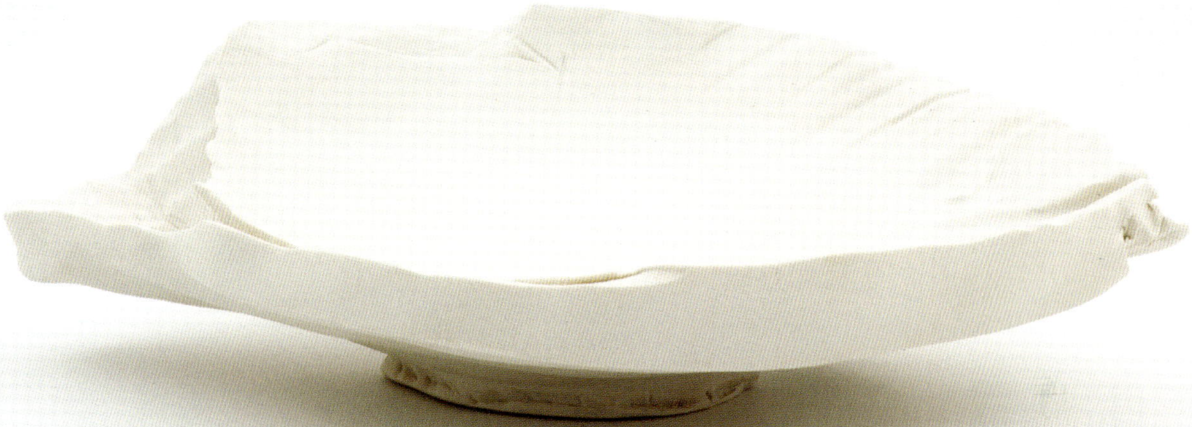

Rebecca Harvey

Offering | 2007

3 X 13 X 8 INCHES (7.6 X 33 X 20.3 CM)

Thrown and sliced porcelain; glaze poured; electric oxidized, cone 7

PHOTOS BY ADRIAN NEWMAN

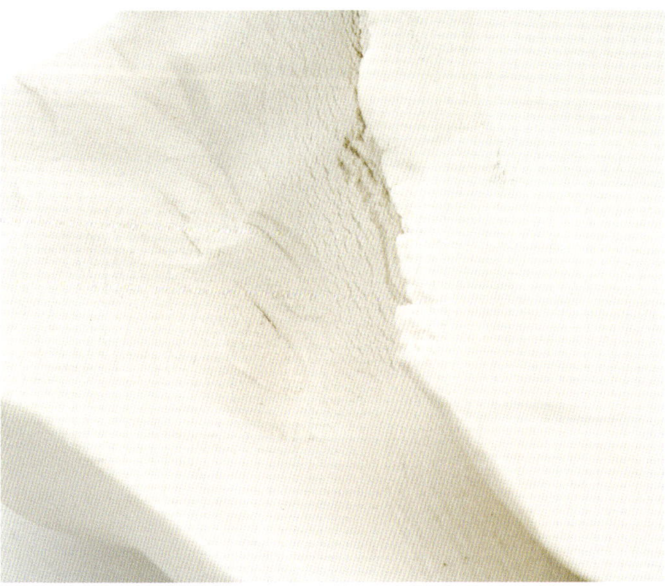

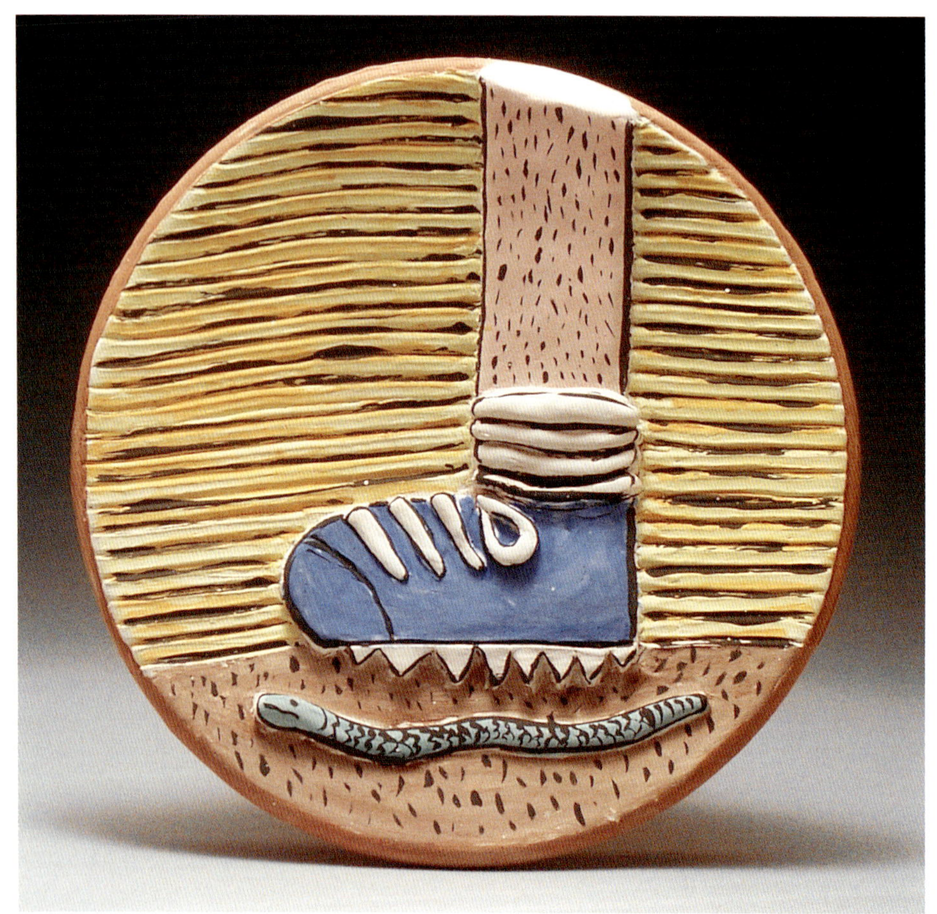

Bo Bedilion

Untitled | 2006

2 X 10 INCHES (5.1 X 25.4 CM)

Wheel-thrown and altered stoneware; slips, underglaze; electric fired, cone 04

PHOTO BY ARTIST

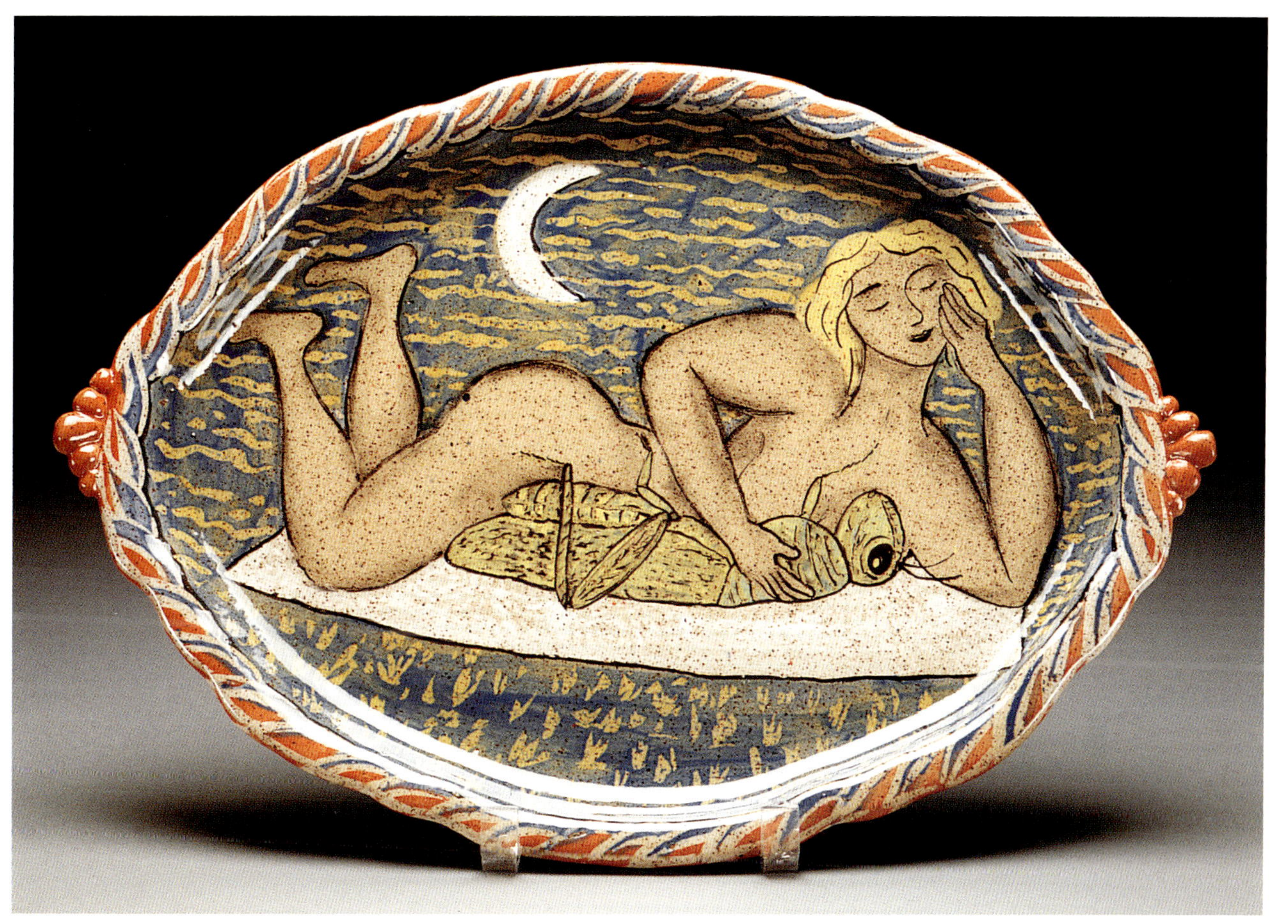

Ana Varela

The Grasshopper and the Ant | 2007

1 X 17 X 11 1/2 INCHES (2.5 X 43.2 X 29.2 CM)

Slump-molded stoneware; slips, engobes, wax resist; clear glaze, cone 8 oxidation

PHOTO BY JOHN KNAUB

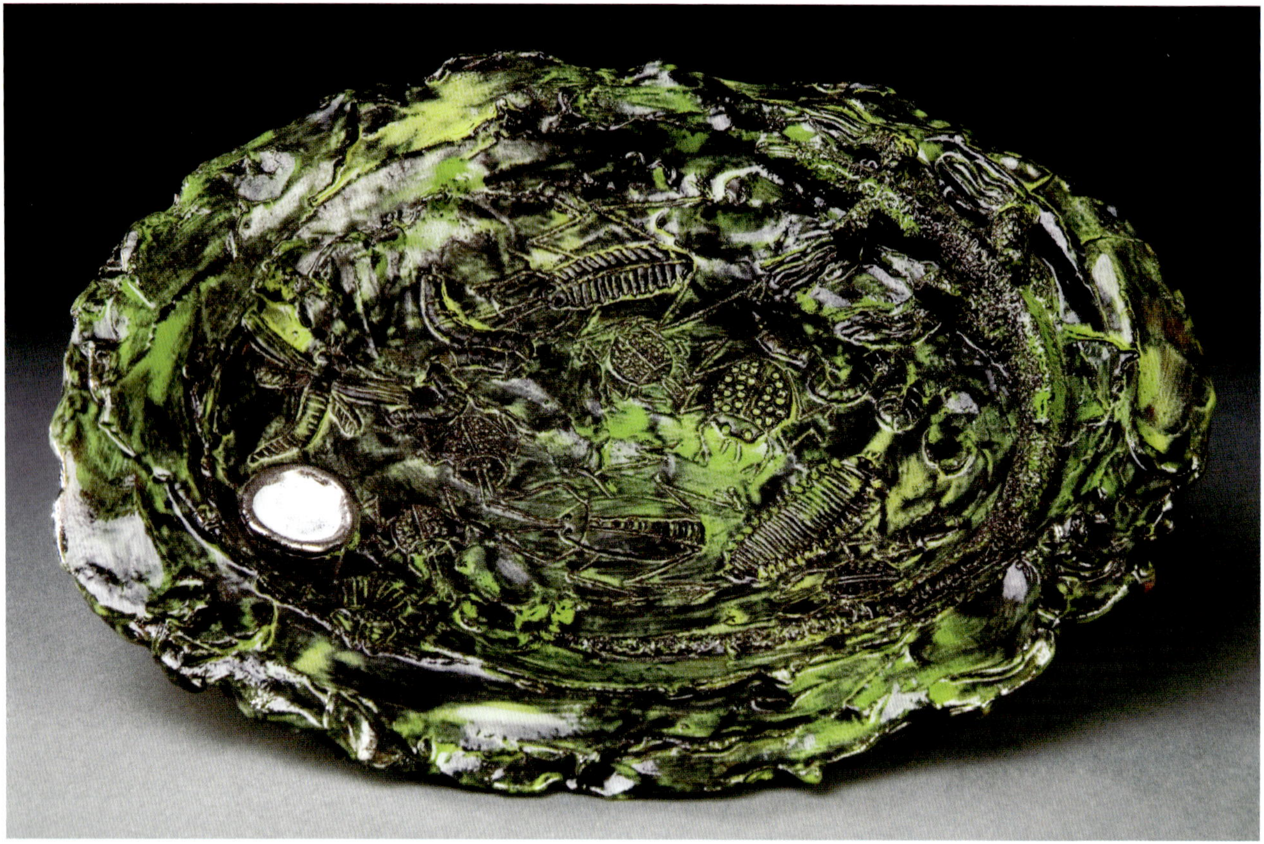

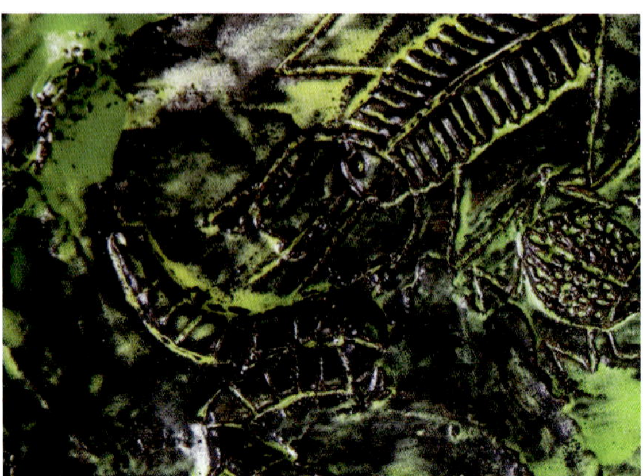

Harriet Ann Thompson

Insect Invasion Platter | 2005

1 1/2 X 11 1/2 X 9 INCHES (3.8 X 29.2 X 22.9 CM)

Hand-built terra cotta; rolled, pinched, and pressed; glaze and overglaze; electric fired, cone 04; luster, cone 019

PHOTOS BY SHANE BASKIN/BLACK BOX STUDIOS

Jenny Kljucaric

Flow of Courage | 2007

2 X 11 X 9 INCHES (5.1 X 27.9 X 22.9 CM)

Hand-built stoneware; reduction fired, cone 10

PHOTO BY ARTIST

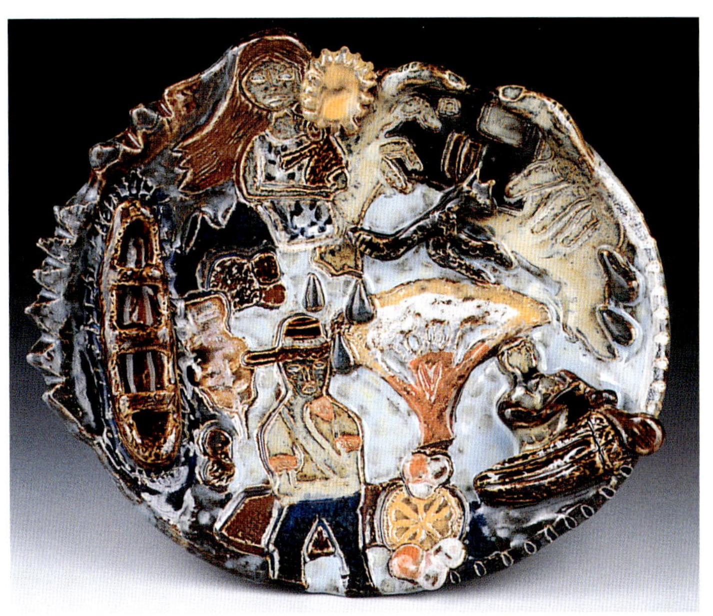

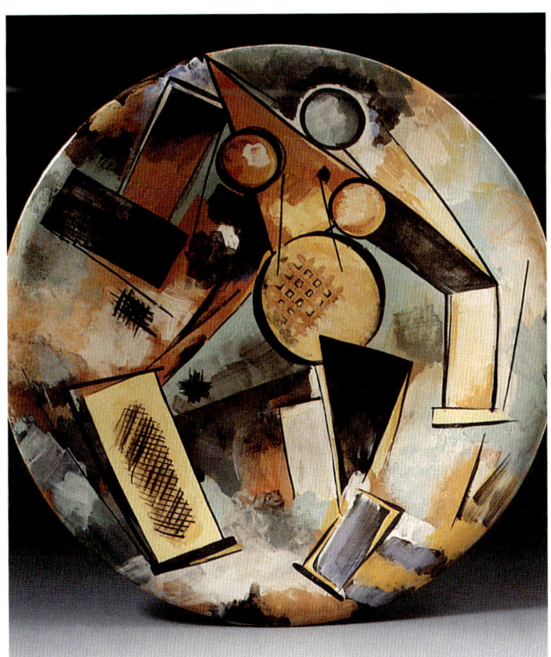

Jacqueline Thompson

Stephanova | 2006

18 INCHES (45.7 CM) IN DIAMETER

Wheel-thrown, low-fire whiteware; cone 03; underglaze decoration, clear glaze

PHOTO BY ARTIST

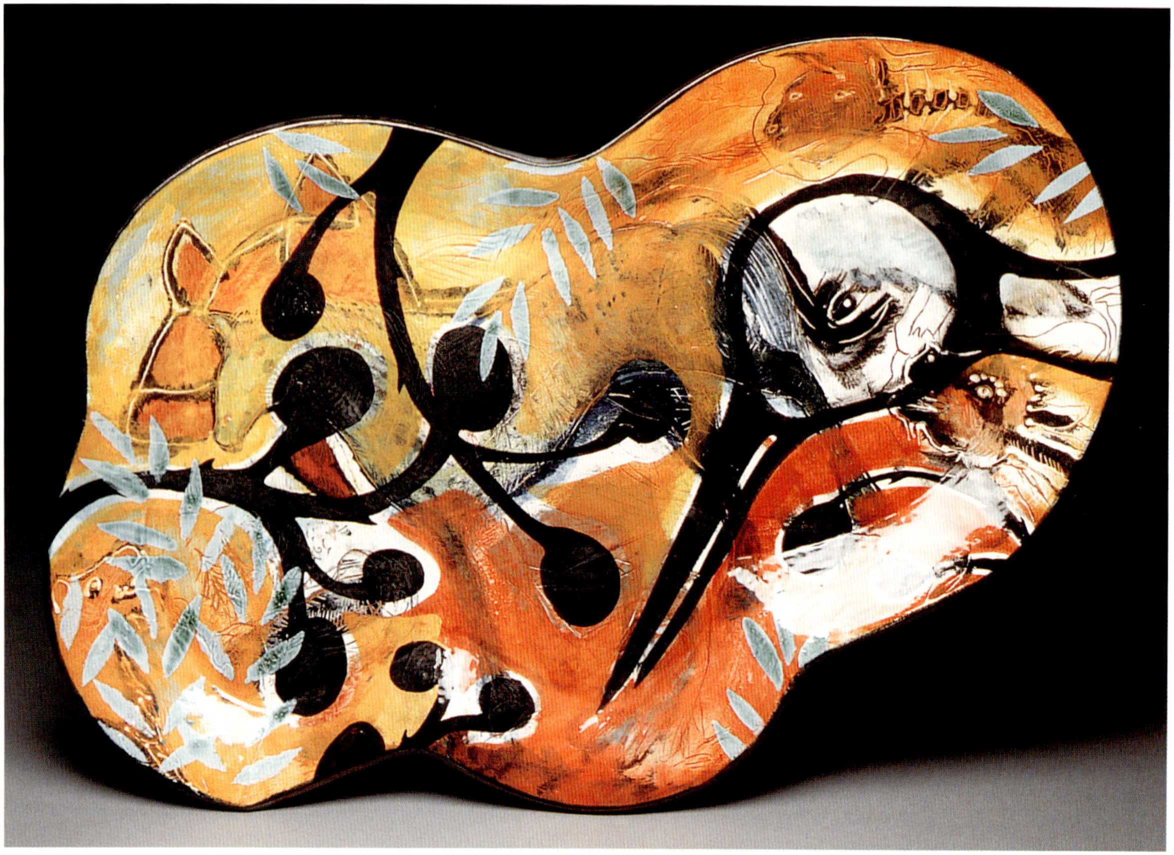

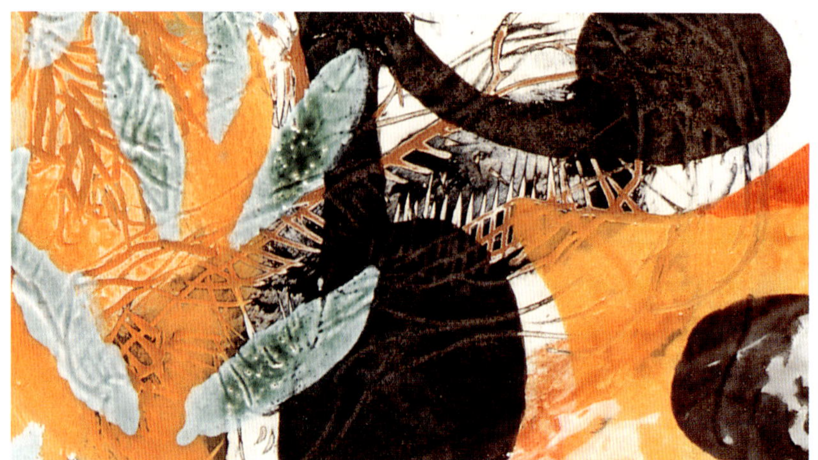

Sally Campbell

Plenty | 2006

4½ X 30 X 19 INCHES (11.4 X 76.2 X 48.3 CM)

Slab-built earthenware; underglaze, slips, glaze; electric fired, cone 03

PHOTOS BY JOHN KNAUB

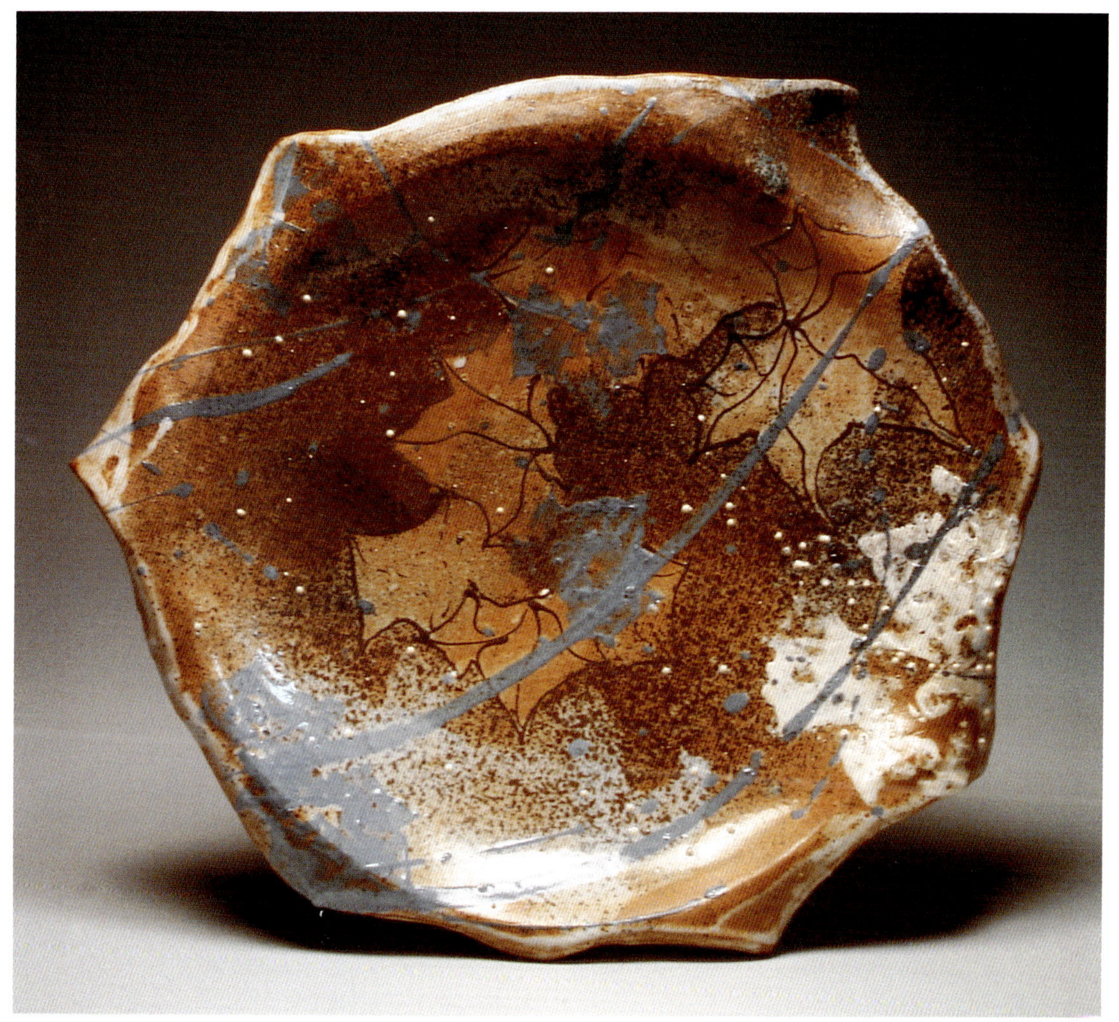

Billie Heath

Little Blue Leaf | 2007

3 X 16 X 16 INCHES (7.6 X 40.6 X 40.6 CM)

Hand-built and slump-molded stoneware; oxides, slips; glazes with ash; gas fired in reduction, cone 10

PHOTO BY JOHN OLIVER LEWIS

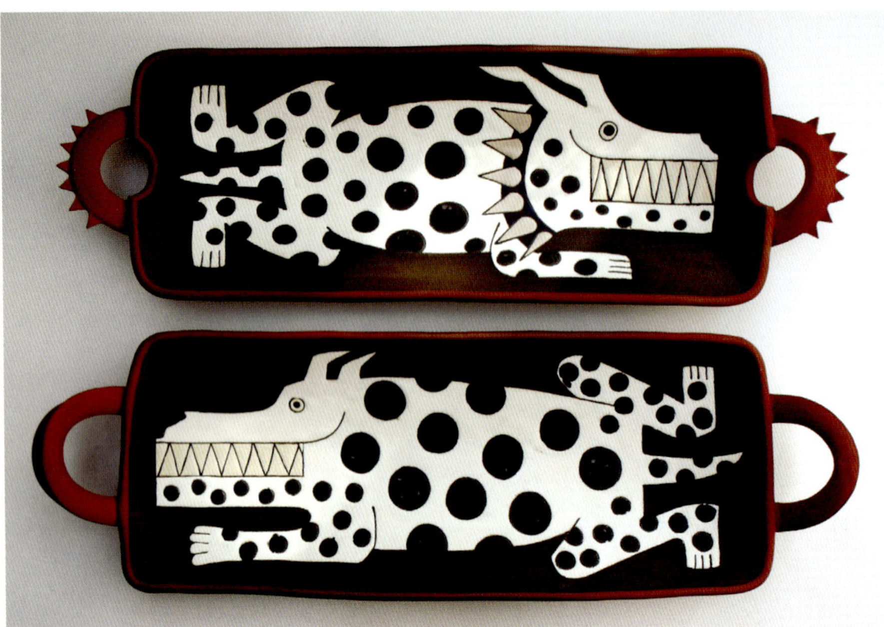

Christine Hester Smith

"Fierce Dog" and "Even Fiercer Dog" Chargers | 2007

EACH: 1 1/2 X 10 X 32 INCHES (3.8 X 25.4 X 81.3 CM)

Hump-molded red earthenware; black slip; matte glazes; electric fired, cone 1

PHOTO BY ROGER SMITH

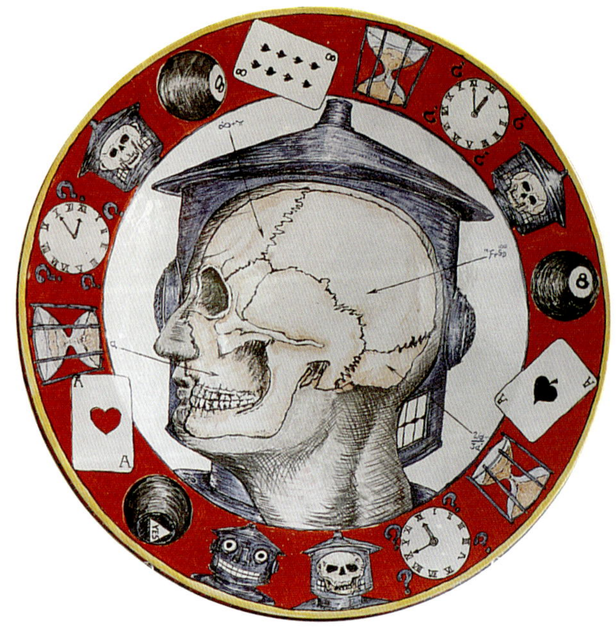

William Brouillard

Technology Haunted by Phrenology | 2005

5 X 26 INCHES (12.7 X 66 CM)

Wheel-thrown red earthenware; majolica; electric fired, cone 04 oxidation

PHOTO BY ARTIST

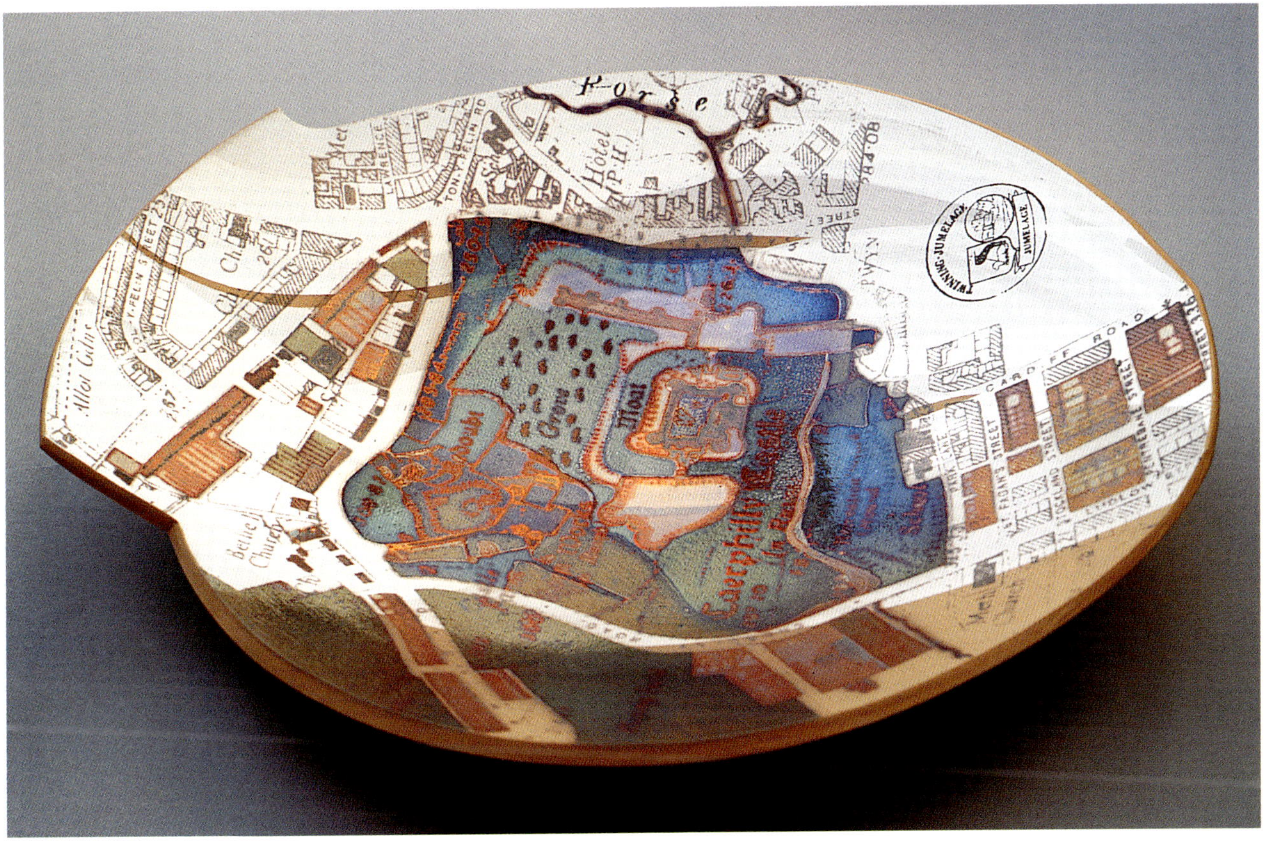

Pauline Monkcom

Untitled | 2006

2 X 12 X 10 INCHES (5.1 X 30.5 X 25.4 CM)

Thrown and cut red earthenware; terra sigillata slip, reduced luster glazes with screenprinted oxides; electric fired in gas reduction, cone 04

PHOTOS BY ARTIST

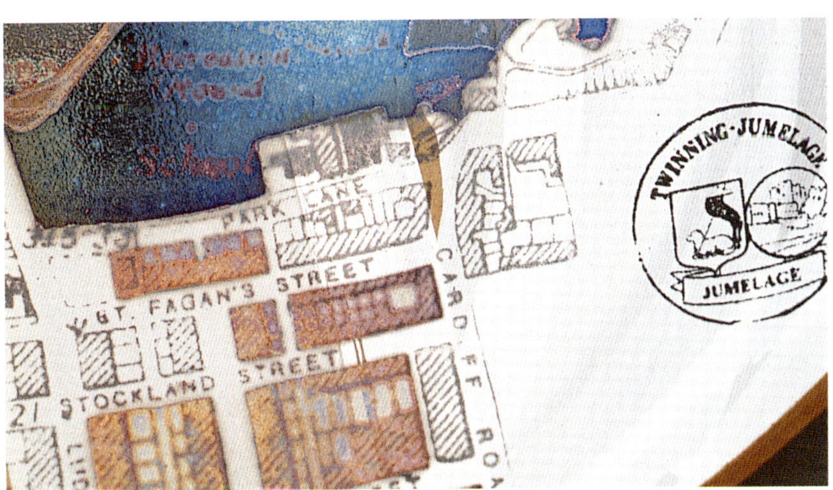

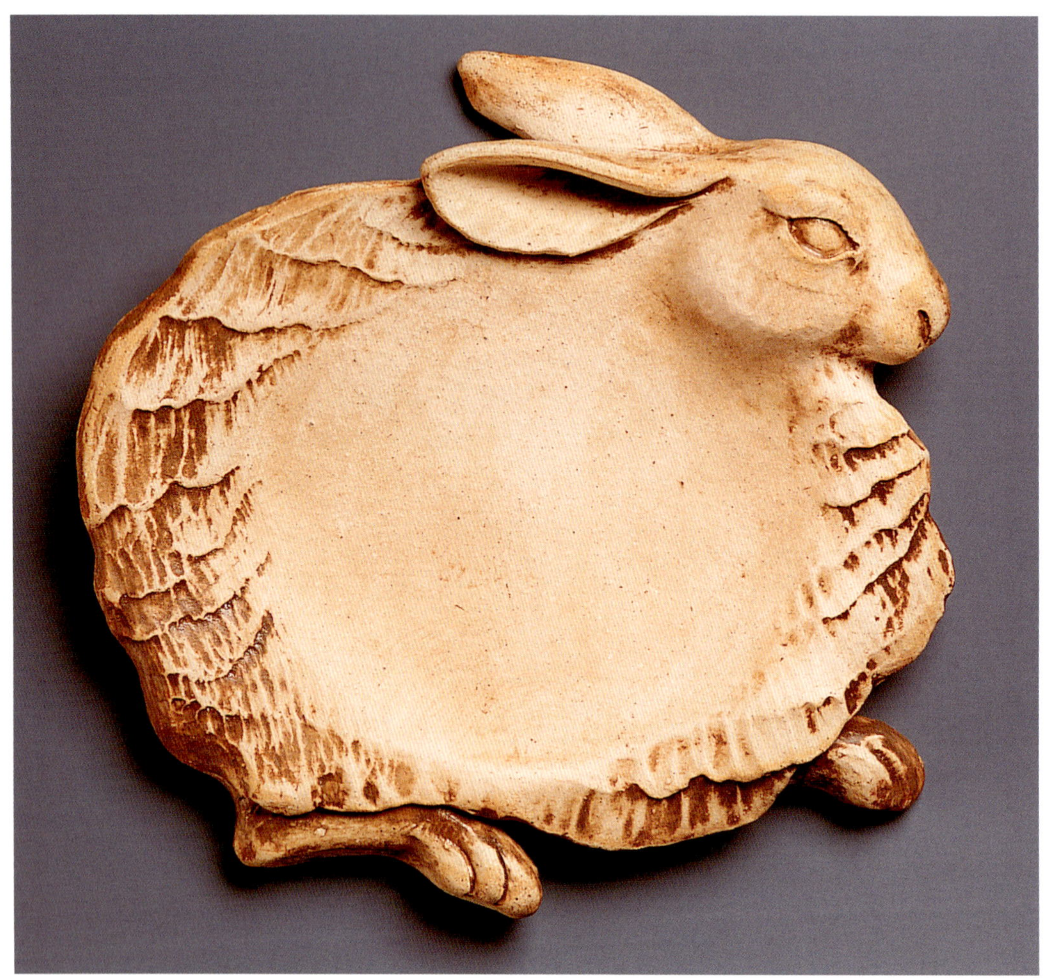

Carolyn Ann Kleiner

Rabbit Platter | 2007

3 X 10 X 9 INCHES (7.6 X 25.4 X 22.9 CM)

Wheel-thrown, altered, and hand-sculpted stoneware; oxides; electric fired, cone 6

PHOTO BY MARK LOZIER

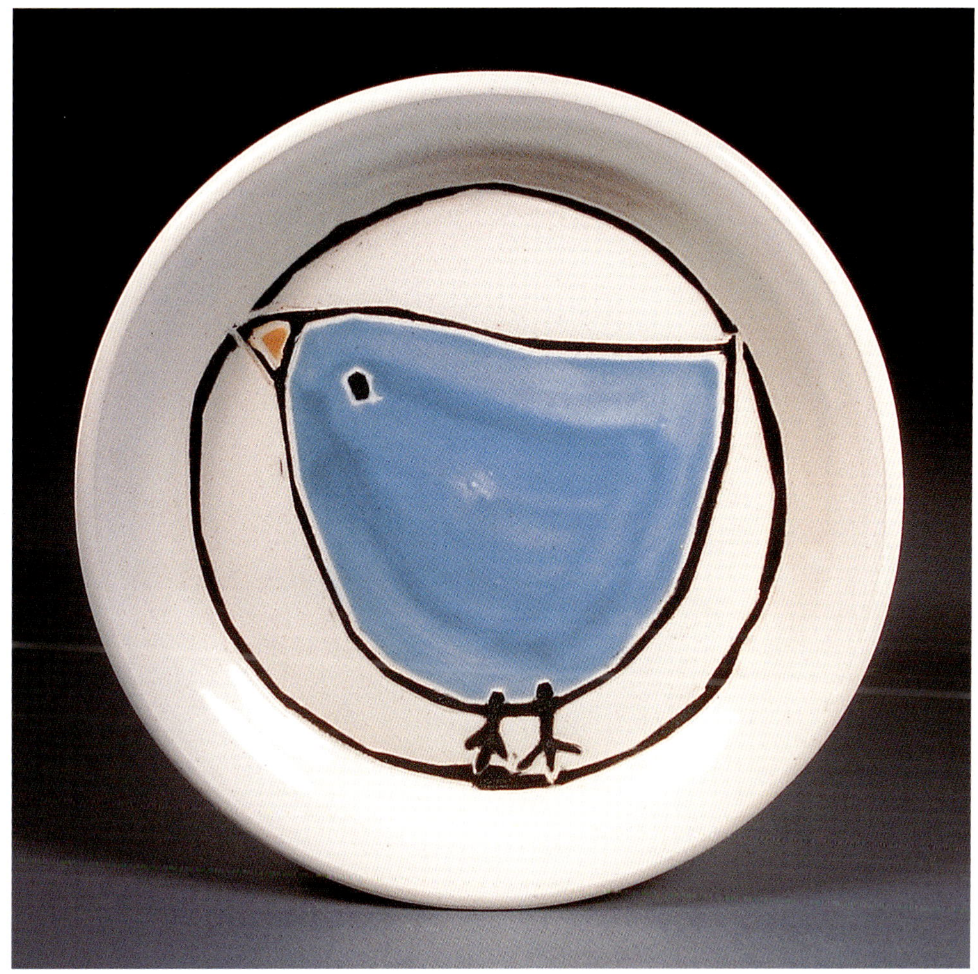

Susan P. Smith

Blue Bird Butter Plate | 2007

1 X 7¼ INCHES (2.5 X 18.4 CM)

Wheel-thrown white stoneware; sgraffito, overglaze design; electric fired, cone 8

PHOTO BY ARTIST

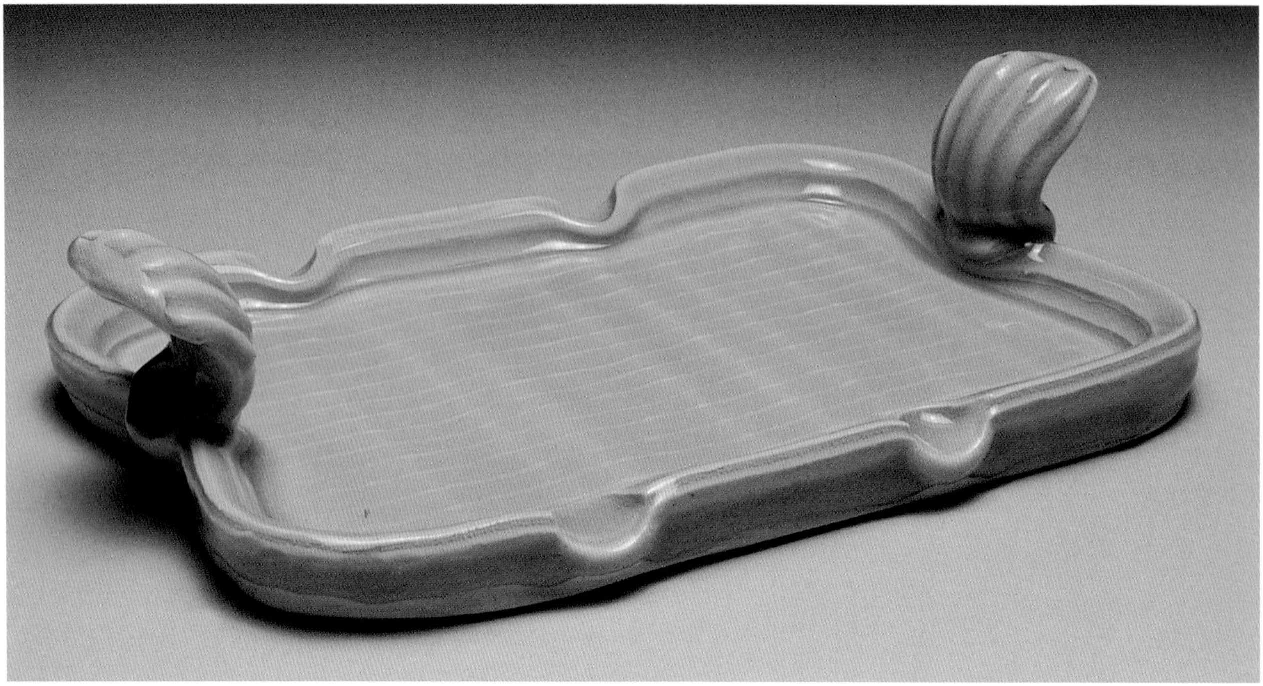

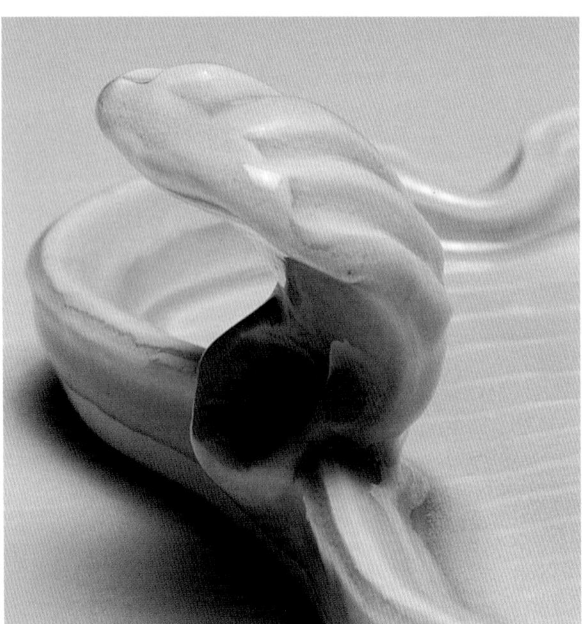

Zane Wilcox

Platter | 2005

3 X 10 X 6 INCHES (7.6 X 25.4 X 15.2 CM)

Wheel-thrown, altered, and hand-built porcelain; celadon glaze; reduction fired, cone 10

PHOTOS BY ARTIST

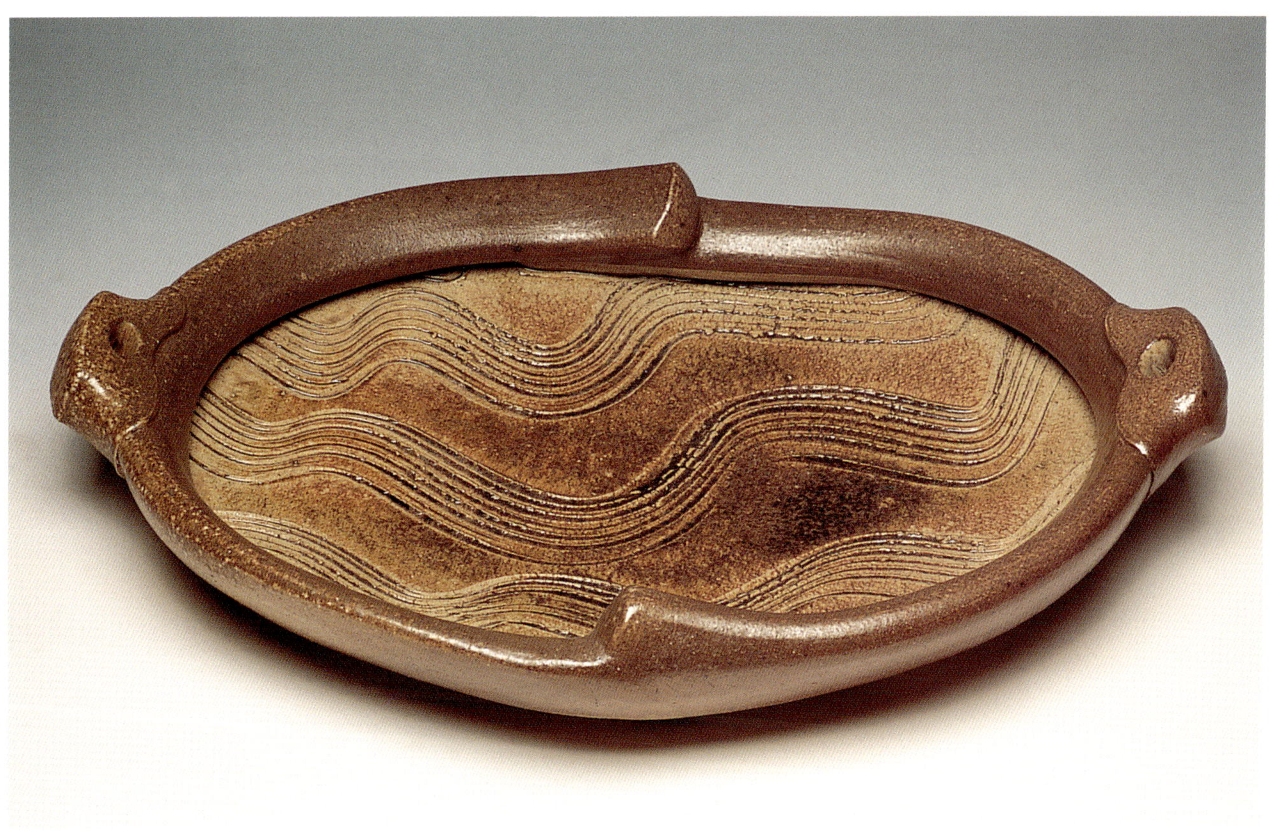

Louise Harter

Wishbone Platter | 2005

4 X 21 X 13 INCHES (10.2 X 53.3 X 33 CM)

Wheel-formed slab and hand-built stoneware; textured with nail-gun cartridge; amber glaze; wood and salt fired, cone 10

PHOTO BY IMAGE CONSTRUCTION

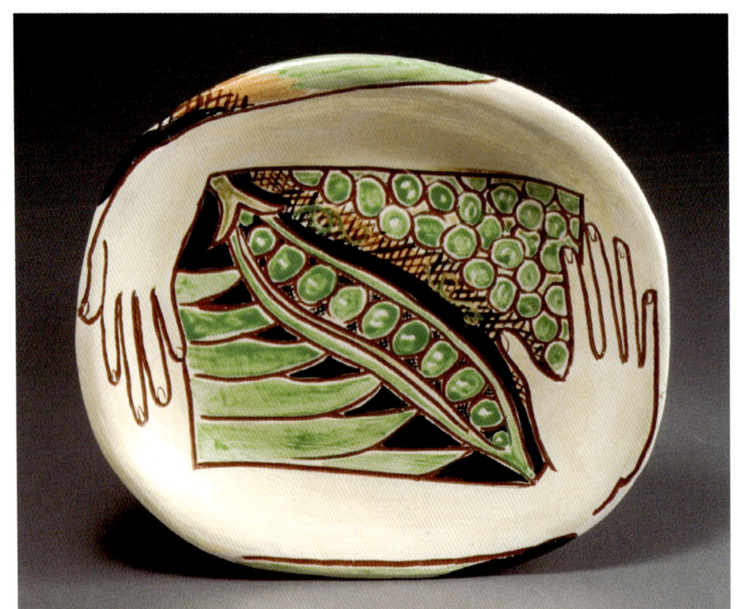

Laura O'Donnell

Harvest Series: Peas and Fish | 2007

1 X 9½ X 8 INCHES (2.5 X 24.1 X 20.3 CM)

Press-molded earthenware; white slip, sgraffito, underglaze; bisque fired, cone 08; clear glaze, Mason stains; oxidation fired, cone 04

PHOTO BY BRYAN HEATON

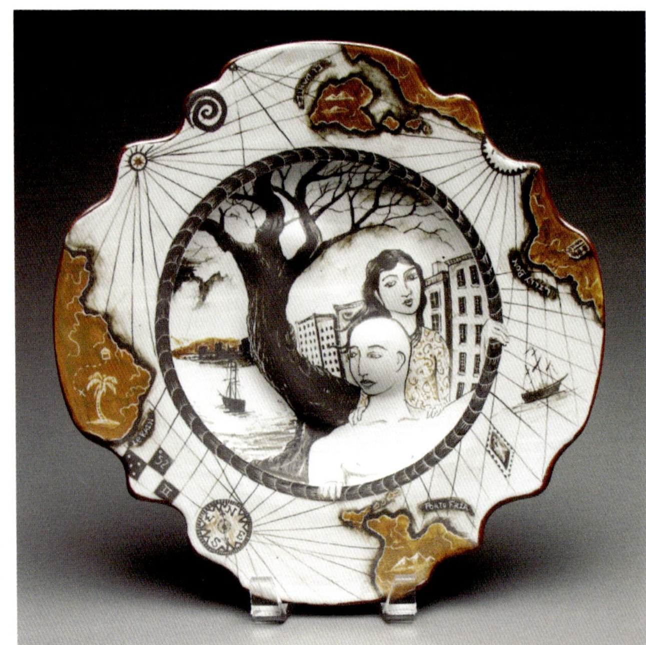

Seth Rainville

New Way Home | 2007

2 X 12 X 12 INCHES (5.1 X 30.5 X 30.5 CM)

Thrown, altered, and assembled porcelain; slip imagery, O'Hara Khaki glaze; gas fired, cone 10

PHOTO BY ARTIST

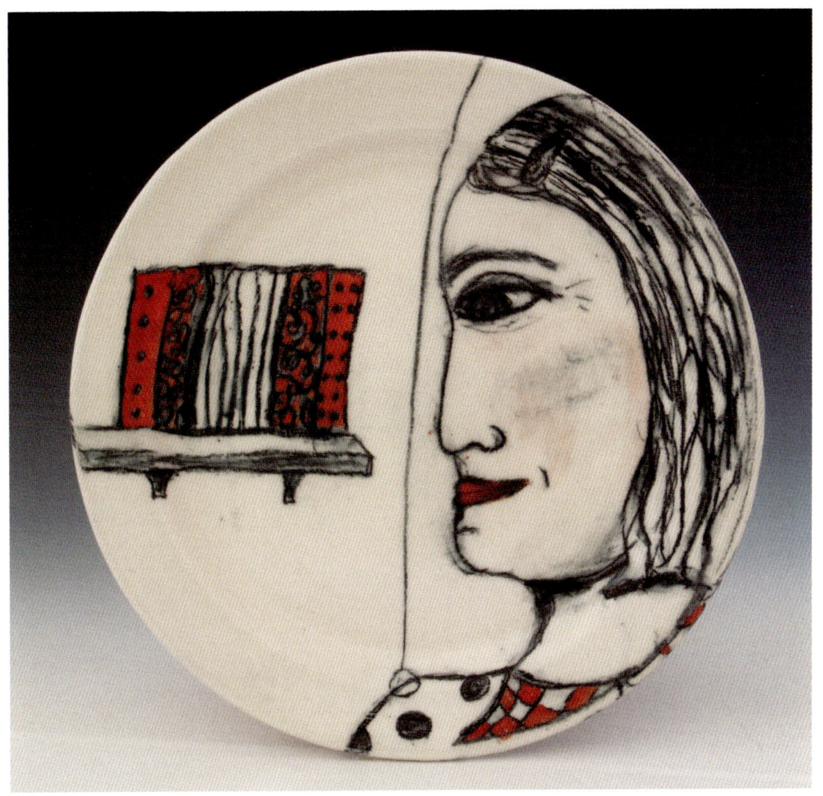

Wendy Olson

Me, Marionette | 2007

1 1/2 X 10 INCHES (3.8 X 25.4 CM)

Wheel-thrown porcelain; underglaze pencil, underglaze, glaze; electric fired, cone 6

PHOTOS BY JAY JENSEN

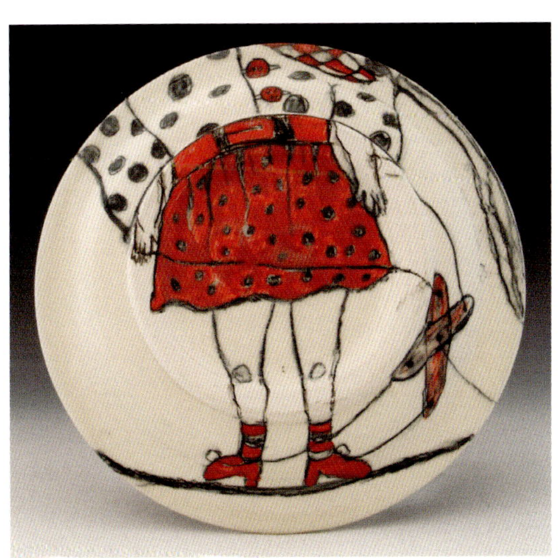

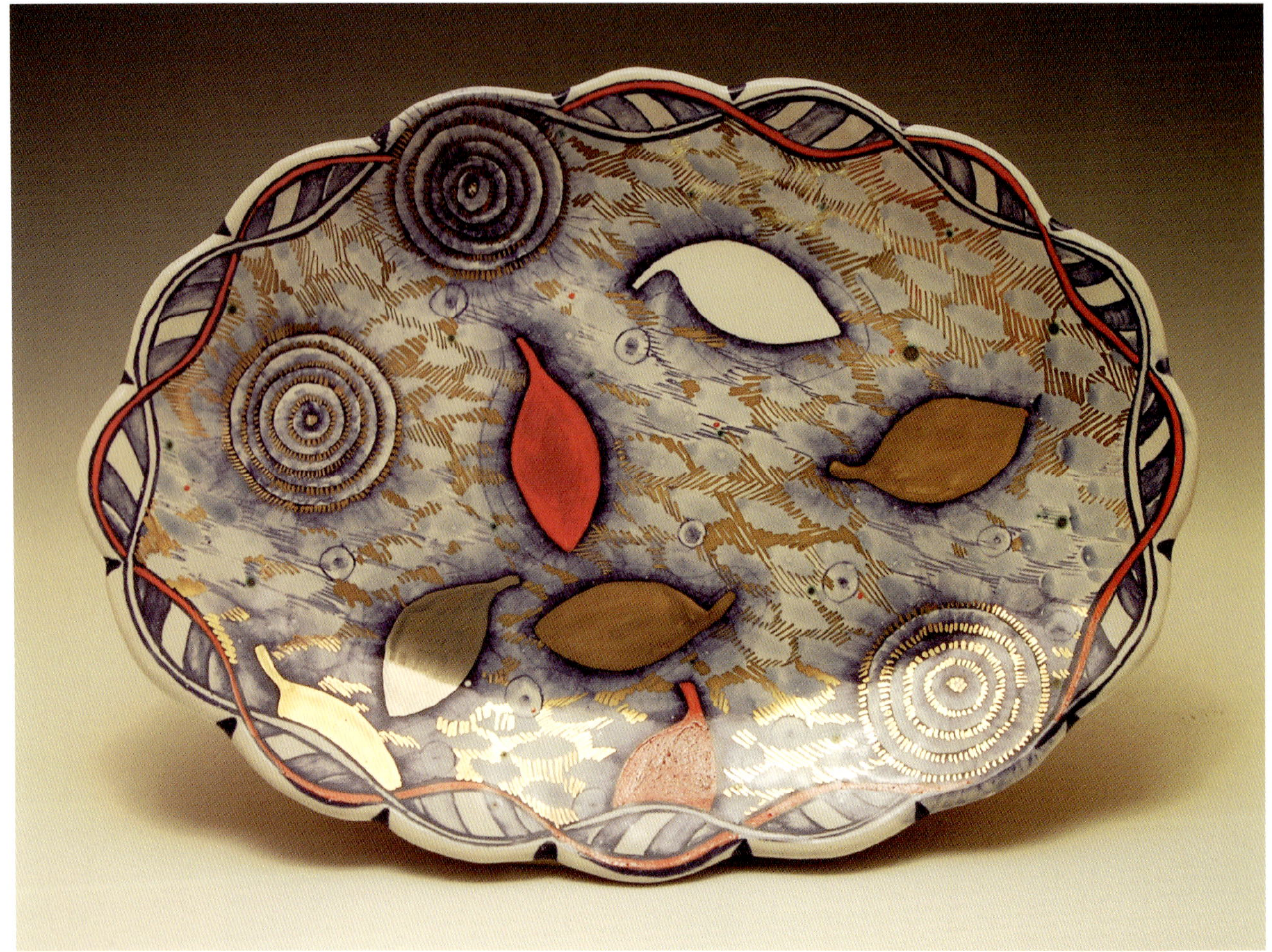

Liz Quackenbush

Untitled | 2007

1 1/2 X 11 X 8 INCHES (3.8 X 27.9 X 20.3 CM)

Hand-built terra cotta; glaze, electric fired, cone 04; luster, cone 017; glass enamels, cone 022

PHOTO BY ARTIST

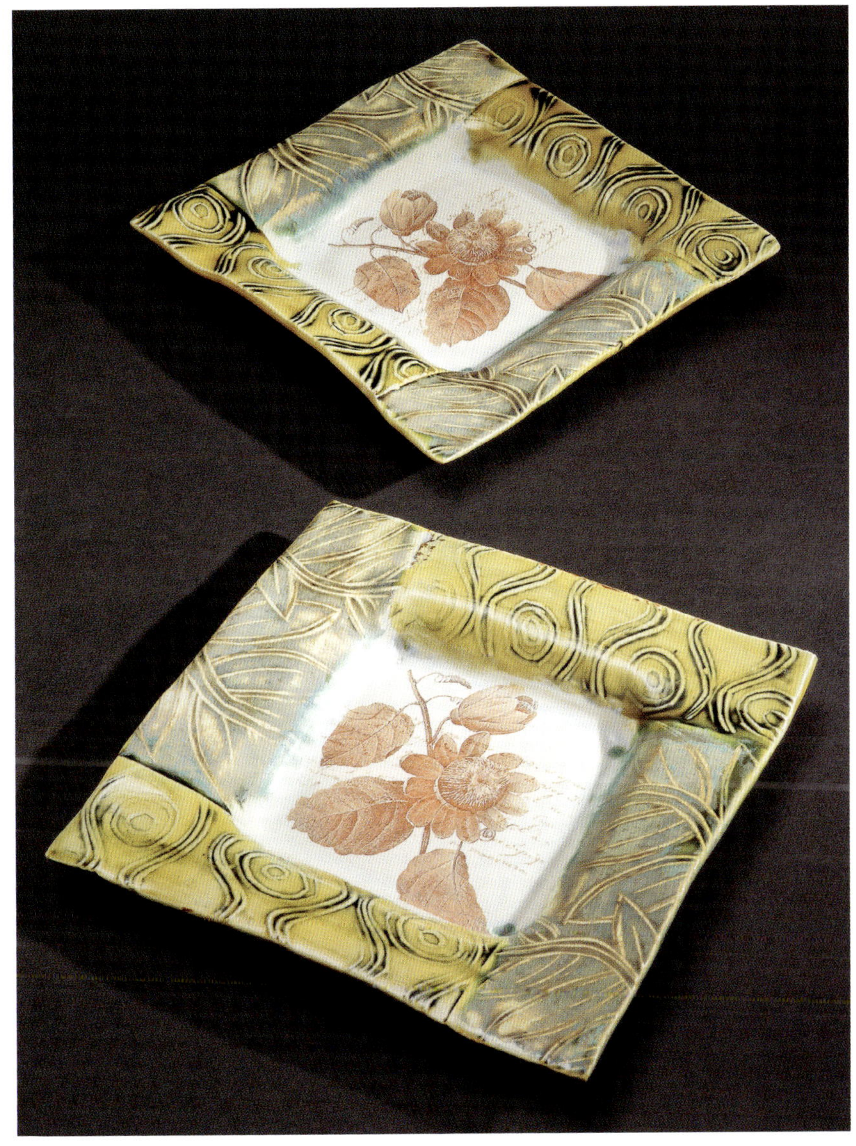

Maggie Mae Beyeler

Passion Flower Dessert Plates | 2007

EACH: 1/2 X 8 X 8 INCHES (1.3 X 20.3 X 20.3 CM)

Slab-built mid-range stoneware; embossed, image transfer; electric fired, cone 6

PHOTO BY CHAS MCGRATH

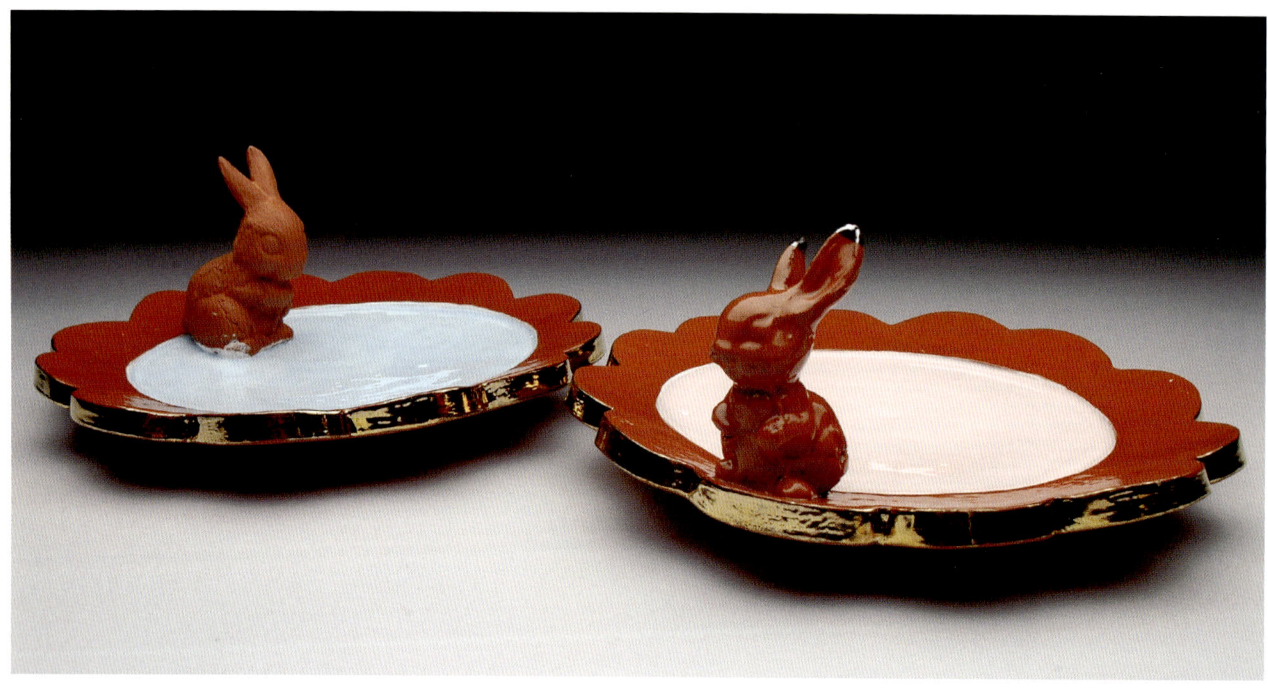

Wesley Harvey

bunny plates | 2007

EACH: 4 1/2 X 9 X 18 INCHES (11.4 X 22.9 X 45.7 CM)

Hand-built and press-molded earthenware; electric fired, cones 01 and 06; luster, cone 017

PHOTO BY ARTIST

Anna Calluori Holcombe

White Tondo III | 2007

12 INCHES (30.5 CM) IN DIAMETER

Wheel-thrown and slip-cast porcelain; electric fired; glaze, cone 10; decals and luster, cone 018

PHOTO BY GLEN BROWN

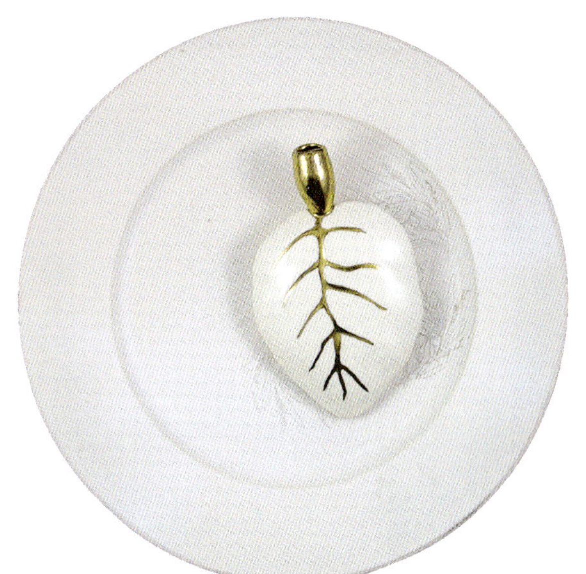

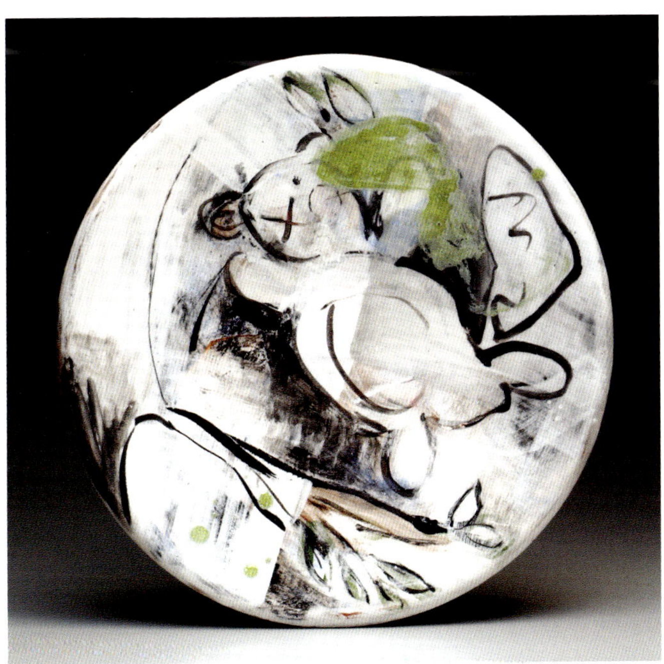

Donna Flanery

Flying Squirrel Platter | 2007

2 X 13 INCHES (5.1 X 33 CM)

Wheel-thrown earthenware; electric fired, cone 03

PHOTO BY PETER LEE

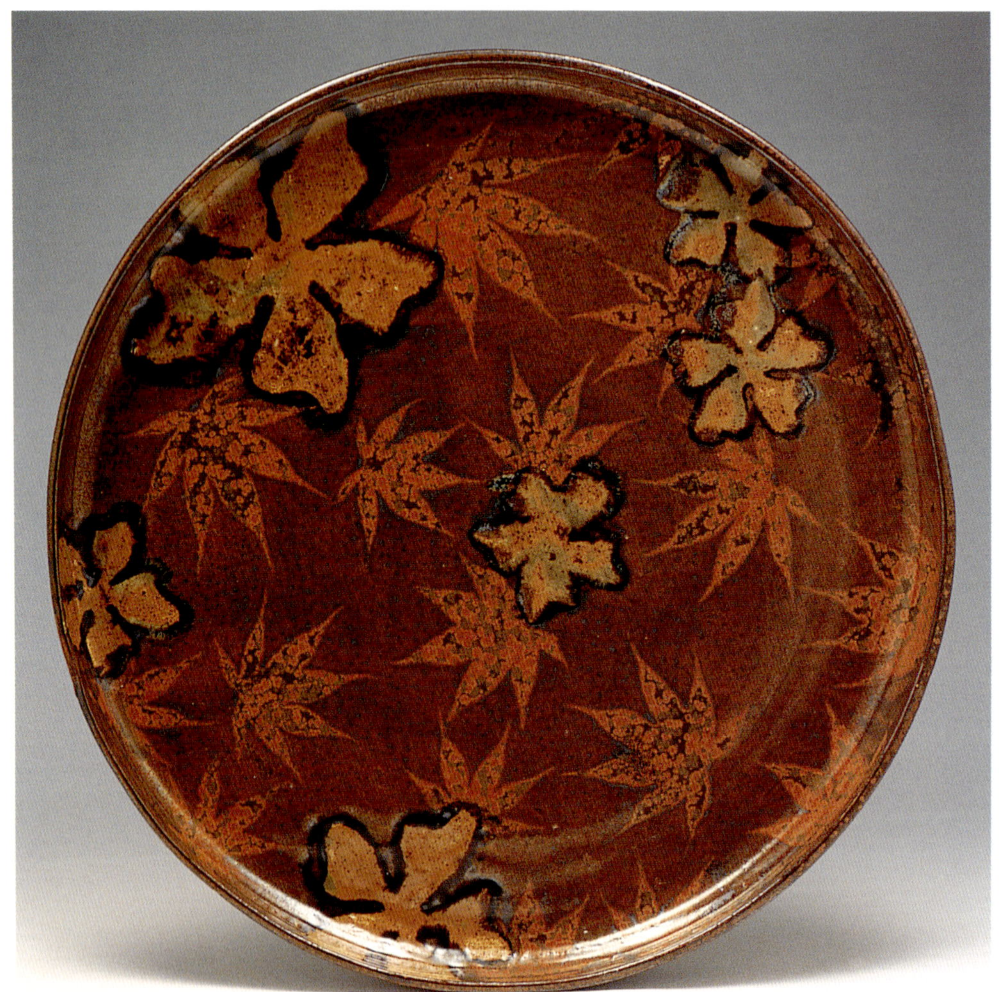

Margaret Tatton-Brown

Leaves and Flowers | 2005

17 INCHES (43.2 CM) IN DIAMETER

Wheel-thrown stoneware; resist, black slip; electric fired, cone 02; latex resist, red glaze; electric fired, cone 08

PHOTO BY STEPHEN BRAYNE

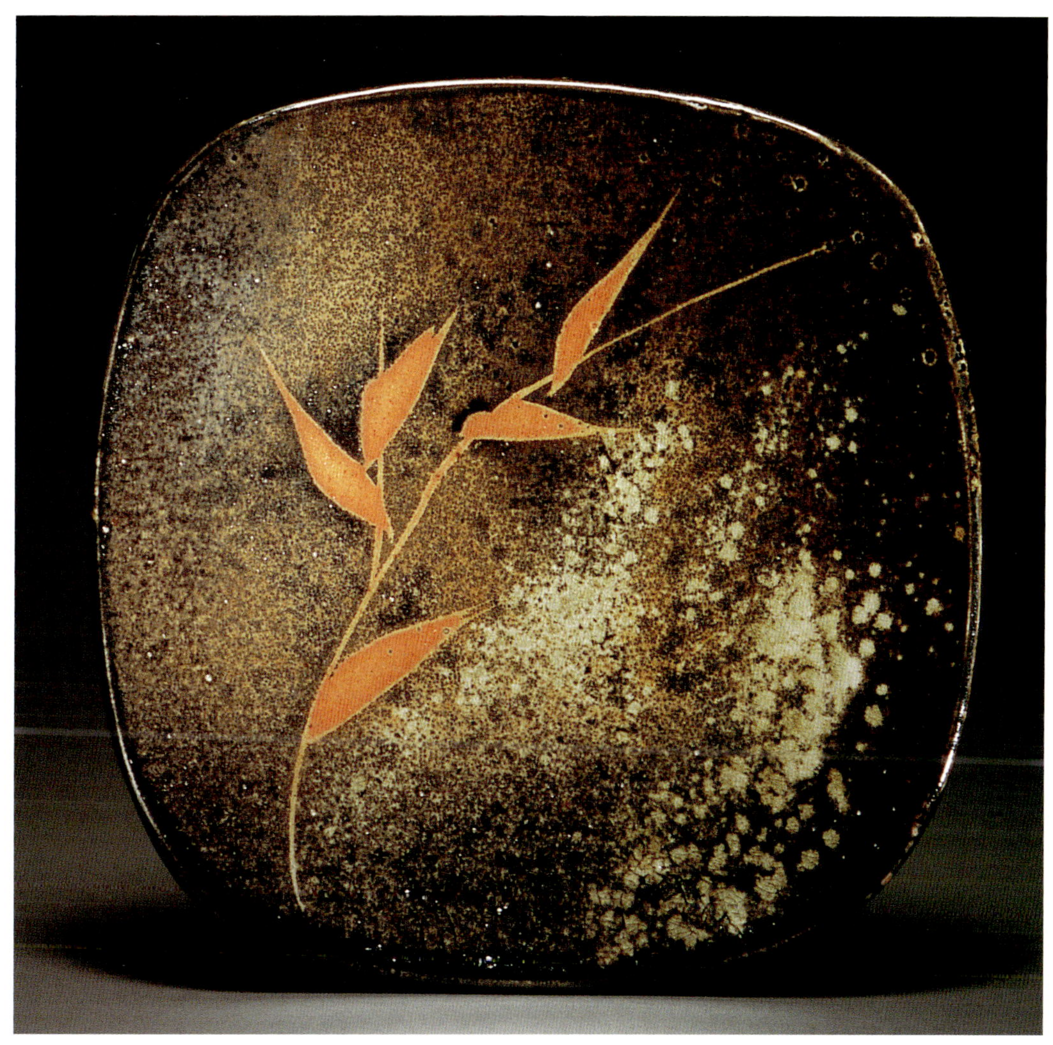

Jiri Minarik

Square Plate | 2007

2 X 9 X 9 INCHES (5.1 X 22.9 X 22.9 CM)

Slab-built porcelain;
brushwork; shino, cone 10

PHOTO BY RICHARD SARGEANT

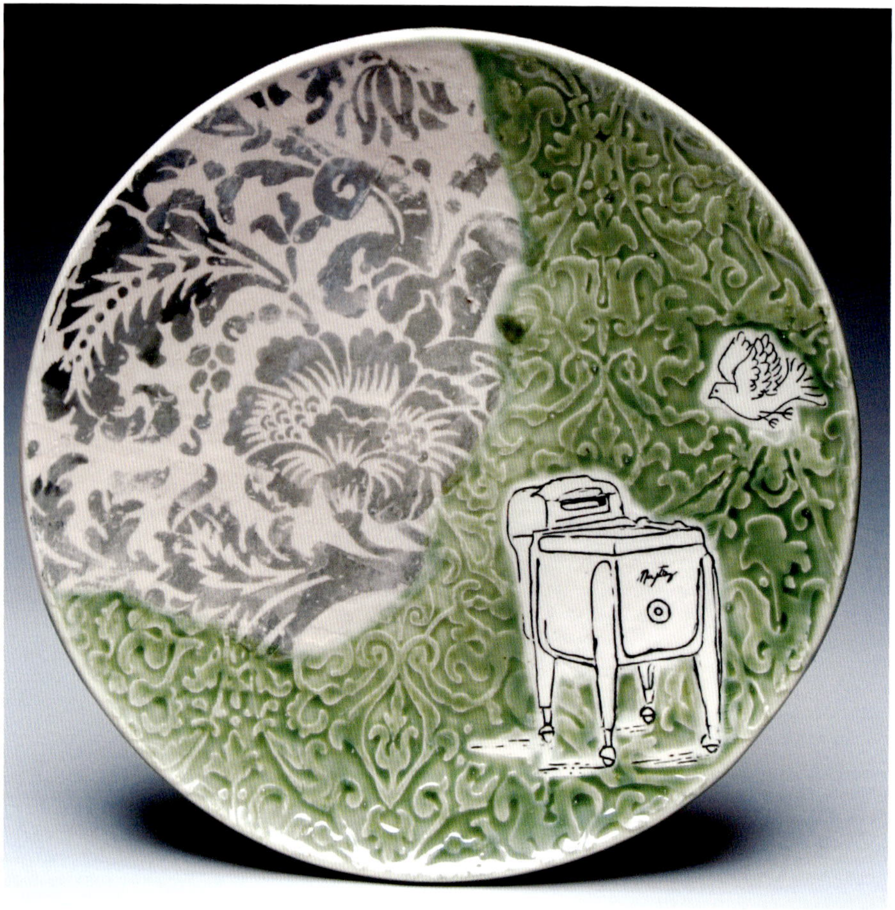

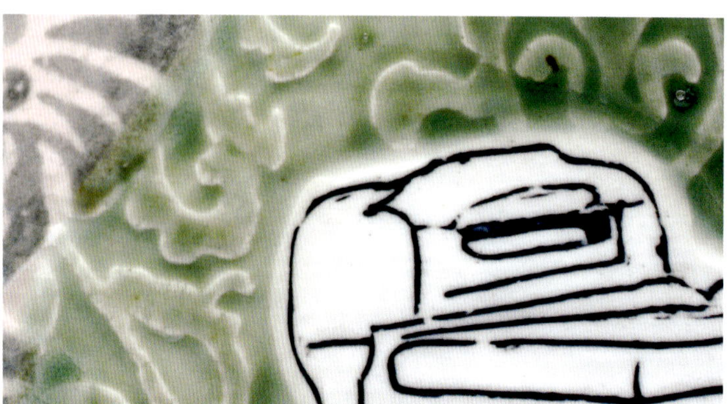

Kelly McKibben

Going for a Stroll | 2007

4 X 17 INCHES (10.2 X 43.2 CM)

Hand-built white stoneware; inlay, silkscreen slip transfer, shellac resist; cone 10 oxidation

PHOTOS BY ARTIST

Kelly O'Briant

Early Garden Platter | 2007

1 1/2 X 11 1/2 INCHES (3.8 X 29.2 CM)

Wheel-thrown porcelain; underglaze, stain, carved; clear glaze, electric fired, cone 6

PHOTO BY TOM MILLS

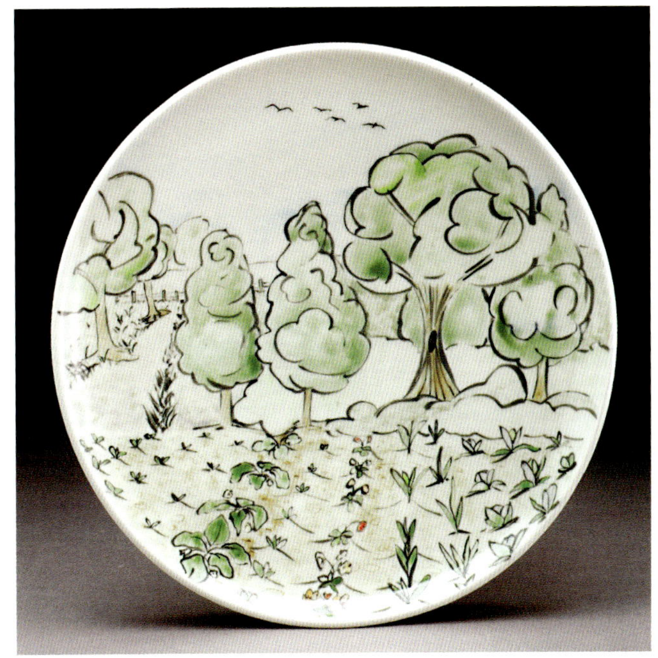

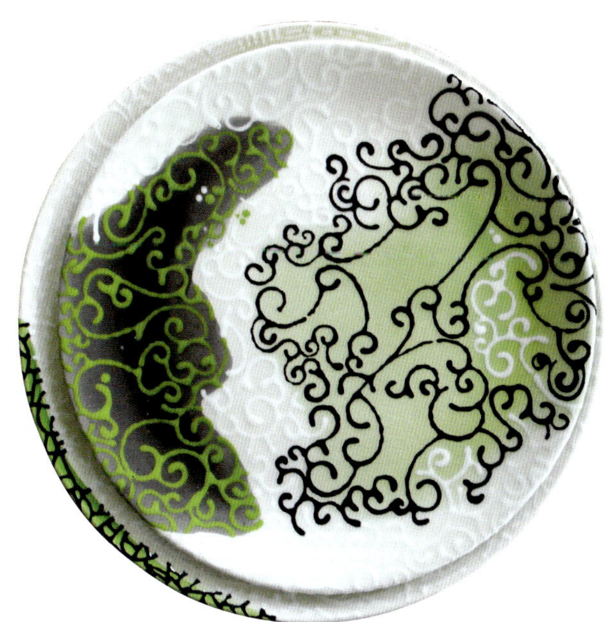

Jody Guralnick

1 plate, 1 charger | 2006

LARGEST: 1 X 13 INCHES (2.5 X 33 CM)

Slip-cast low-fire white clay; electric fired, cone 06; underglazes, cone 06

PHOTO BY ARTIST

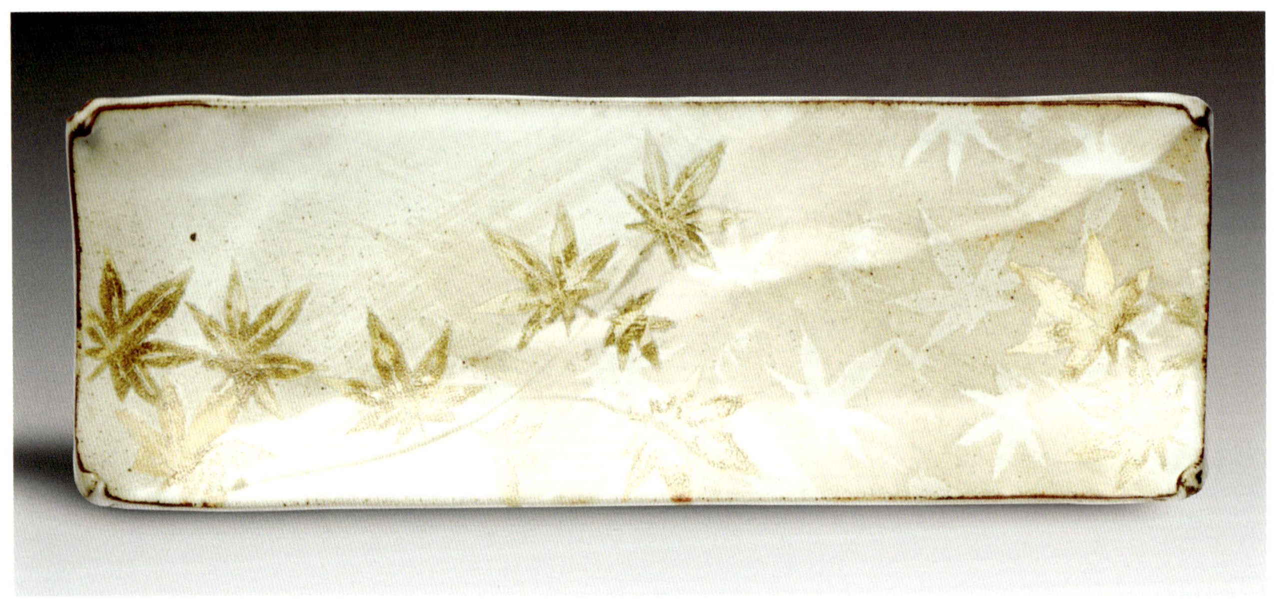

Maggie Zerafa

Maple Leaf Slab Platter | 2004–2005

$10^{5}/_{8}$ X $19^{11}/_{16}$ X 2 INCHES (27 X 50 X 5 CM)

Hand-built stoneware; glaze, gas fired, cone 11

PHOTO BY ANDREW HASLAM

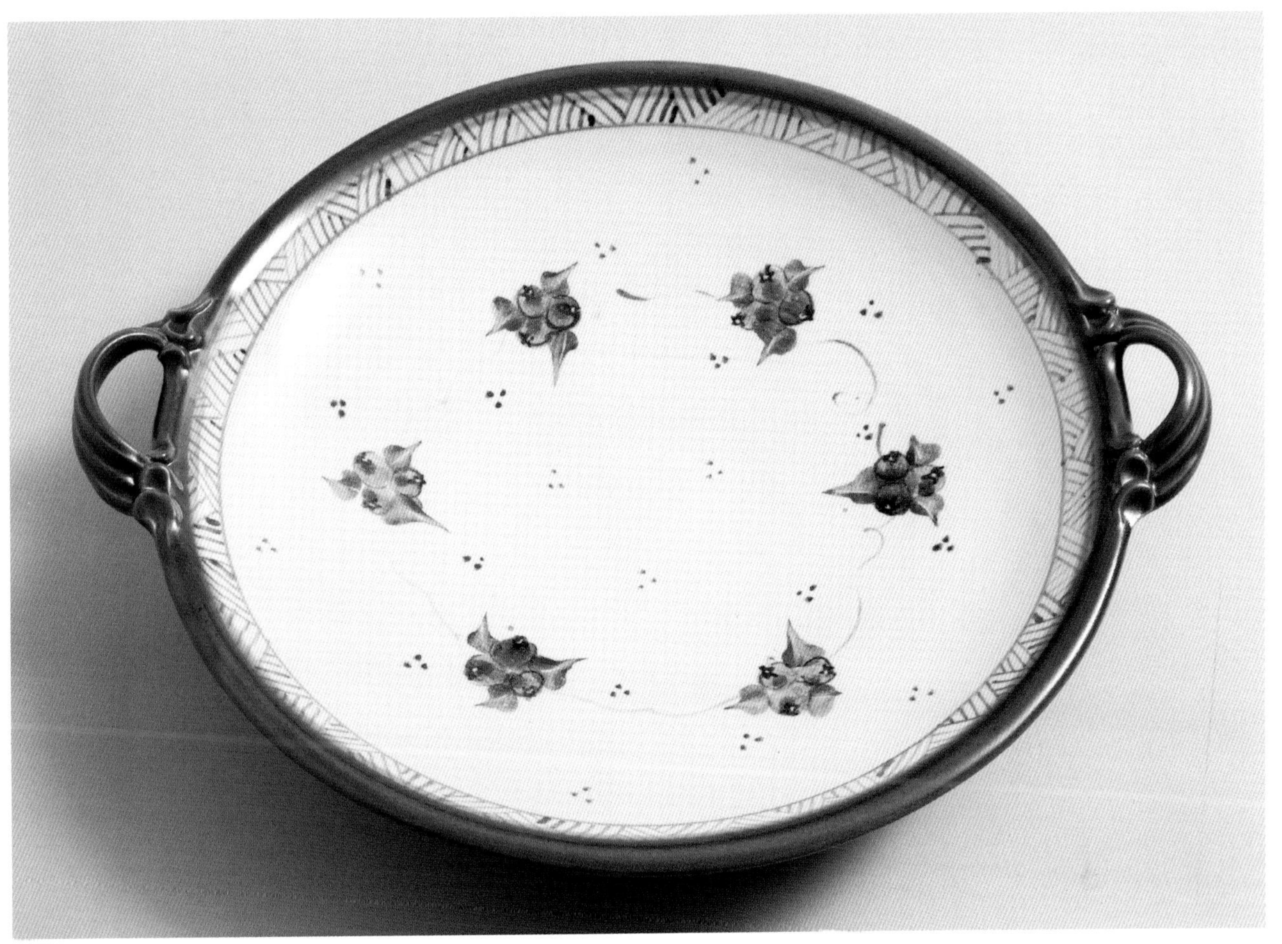

Susan Weaver

Plate with Handles: Blueberry Brunch | 2006

$2^1/_2$ X $13^1/_2$ INCHES (6.4 X 34.3 CM)

Wheel-thrown earthenware; electric fired, cone 3; hand-painted decoration

PHOTO BY GUY L'HEUREUX

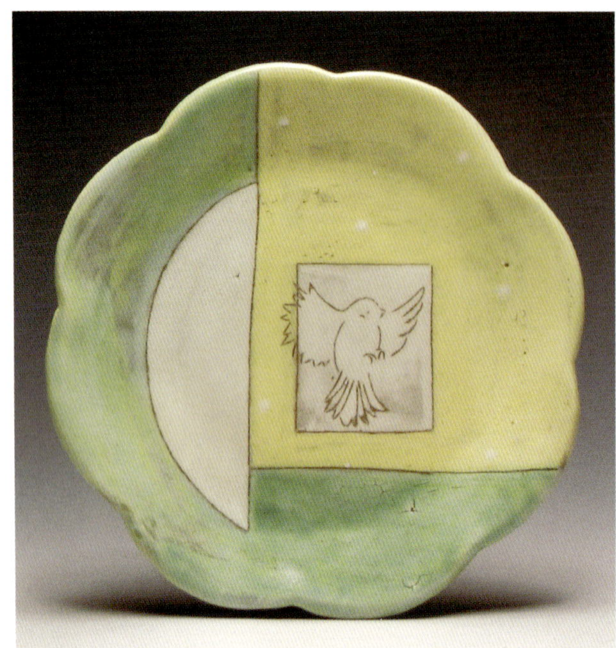

Rachel Berg

Suspended | 2007

1 X 8 X 8 INCHES (2.5 X 20.3 X 20.3 CM)

Slab-built stoneware; brushed slips, sgraffito; electric fired, cone 6

PHOTO BY ARTIST

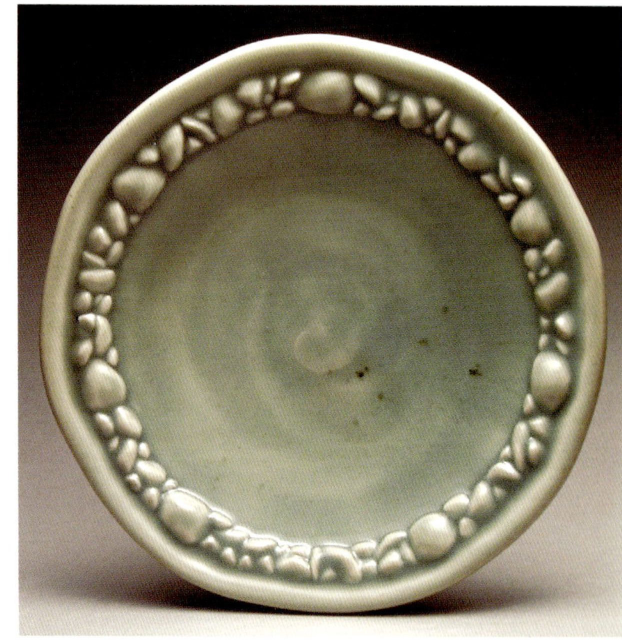

Becca Van Fleet

Stone Plate | 2007

2 X 11 INCHES (5.1 X 27.9 CM)

Wheel-thrown and hand-built stoneware; celadon glaze; reduction fired, cone 10

PHOTO BY ARTIST

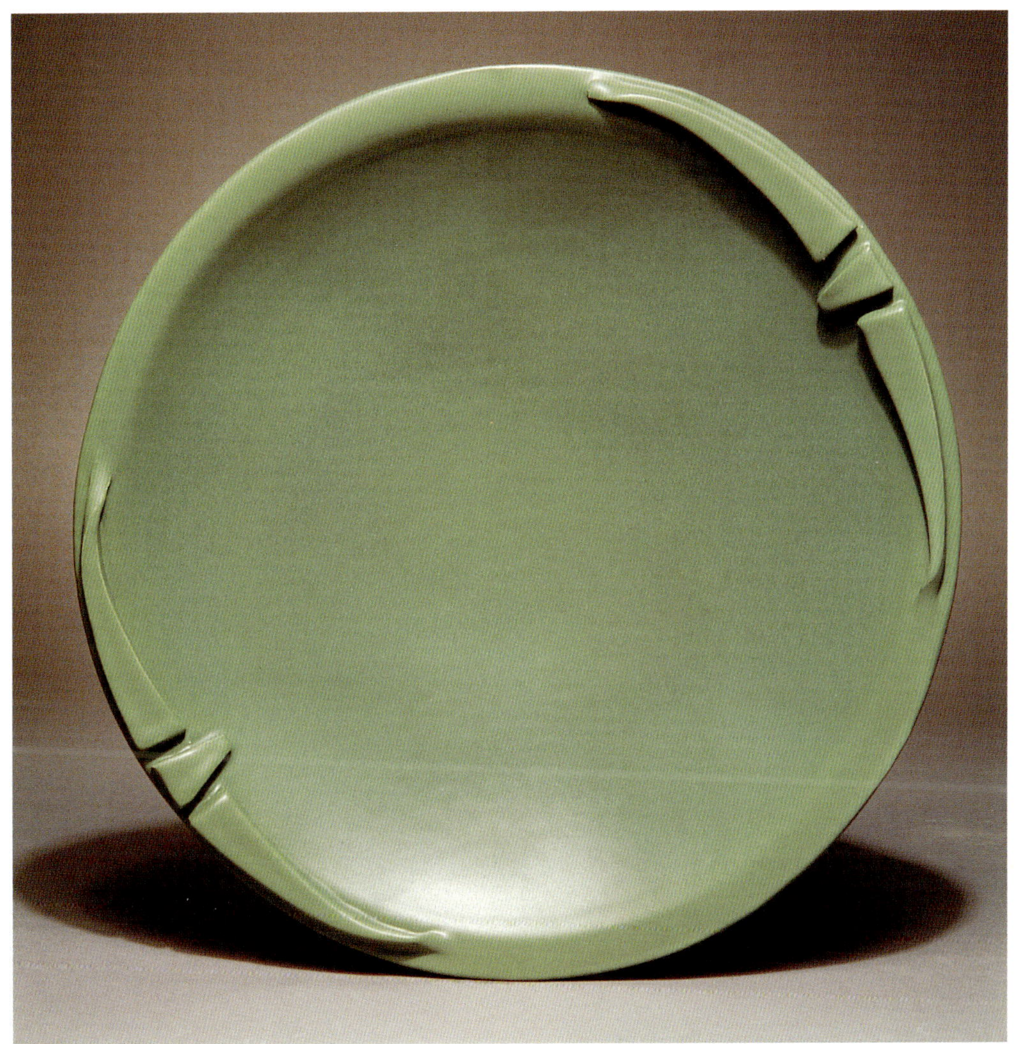

Linda Fox

Platter with Deco Motif | 2006

4 X 17 INCHES (10.2 X 43.2 CM)

Hand-built and wheel-thrown porcelain; sprayed matte green glaze, electric fired, cone 7

PHOTO BY JOHN BEDESSEM

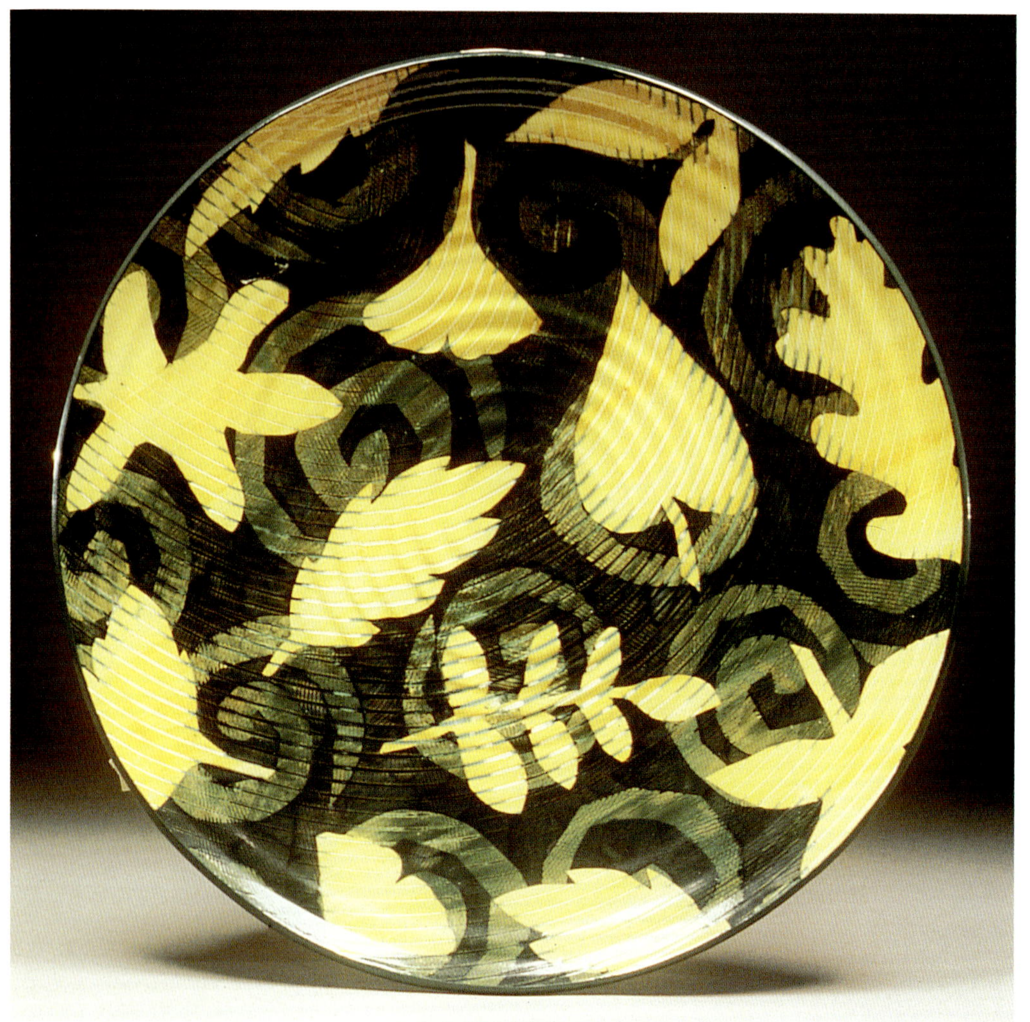

Leslie Eckmann

Yellow Leaves on Blue Water | 2005

$3\frac{1}{2}$ X 18 INCHES (8.9 X 45.7 CM)

Slab-built and wheel-formed white earthenware; stenciled, textured, hand-painted, underglaze; cone 02; clear glaze, electric fired, cone 06

PHOTO BY GREG STALEY

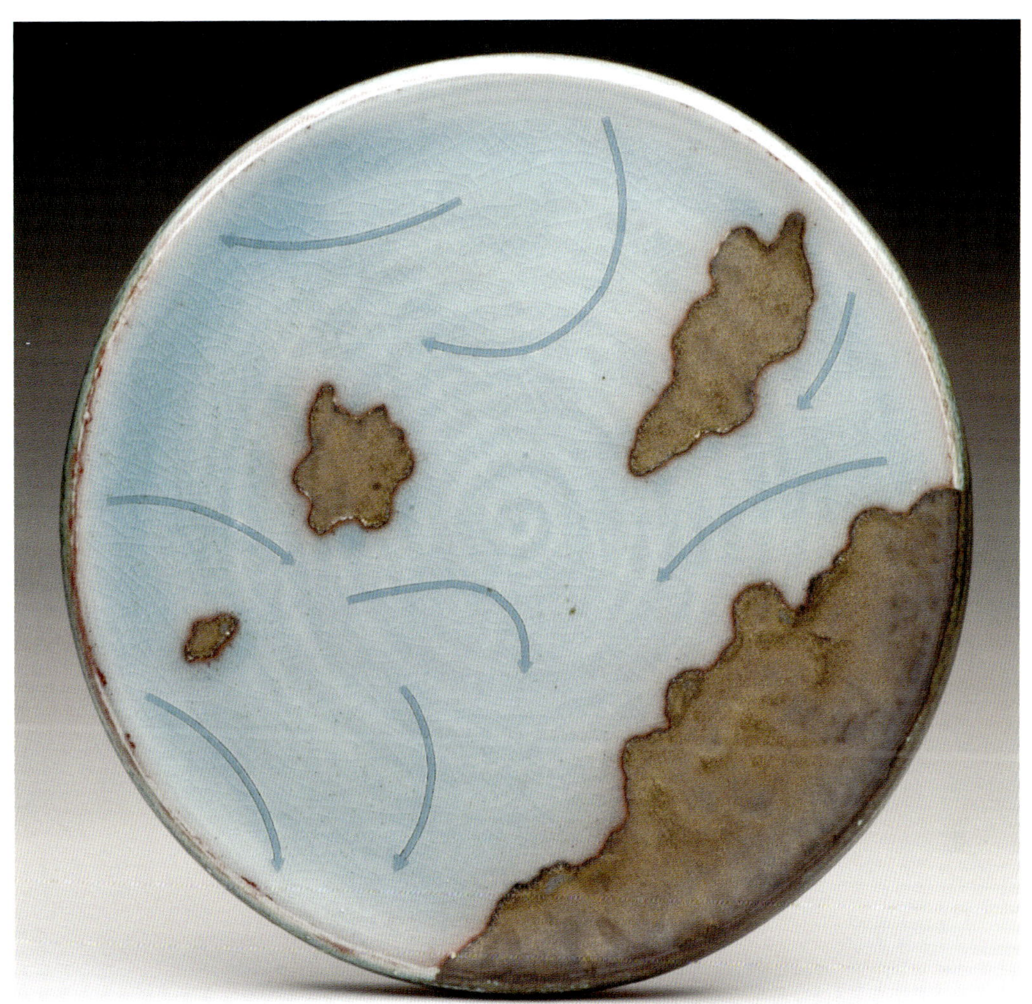

John Williams
Currento | 2006
2 X 18 INCHES (5.1 X 45.7 CM)
Stoneware
PHOTO BY ARTIST

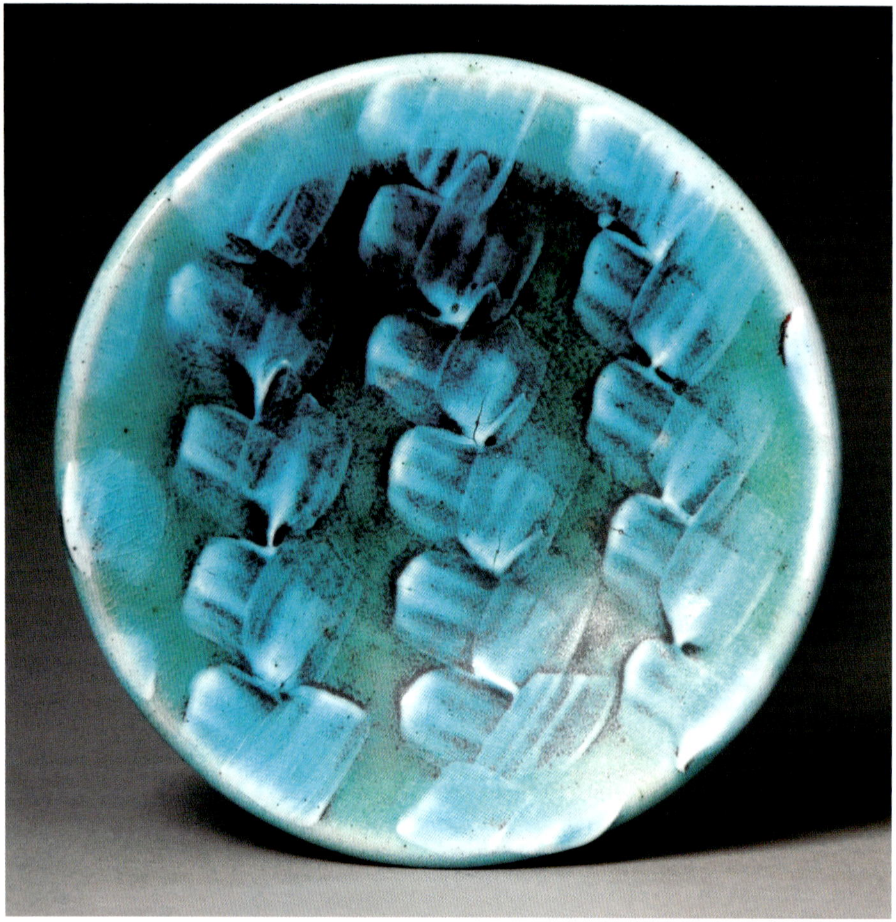

Kate Biderbost

Untitled | 2004

1 X 6 INCHES (2.5 X 15.2 CM)

Wheel-thrown stoneware; slips; soda fired, cone 10

PHOTOS BY WILLIAM BIDERBOST

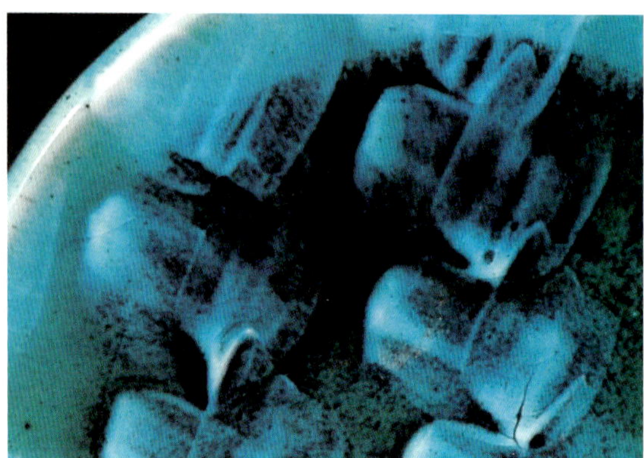

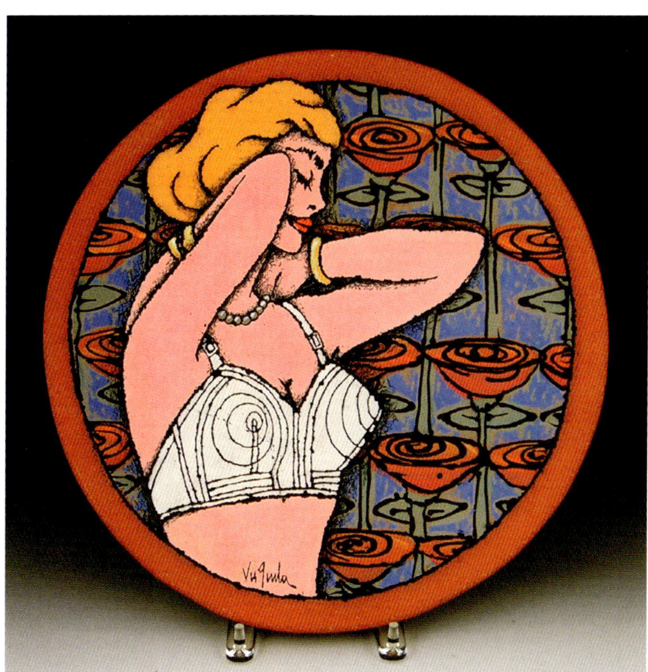

Rimas VisGirda

Roses are red | 2000

1 X 16 INCHES (2.5 X 40.6 CM)

Slab-built terra cotta; wax inlay, slip trailed; underglazes, underglaze pencil; electric fired, cone 3

PHOTO BY ARTIST

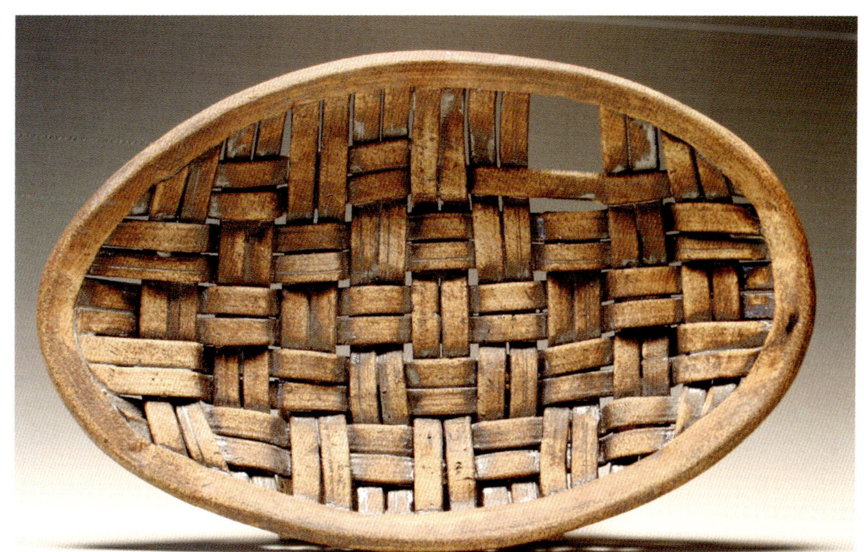

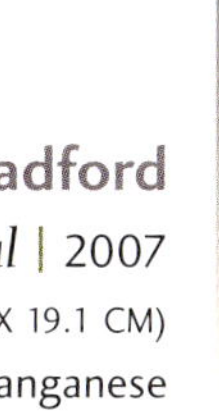

Carolyn G. Bradford

Woven Plate, Oval | 2007

1 X 11 3/4 X 7 1/2 INCHES (2.5 X 29.8 X 19.1 CM)

Hand-built stoneware; manganese dioxide; gas fired, cone 10

PHOTO BY JOHN LEWIS

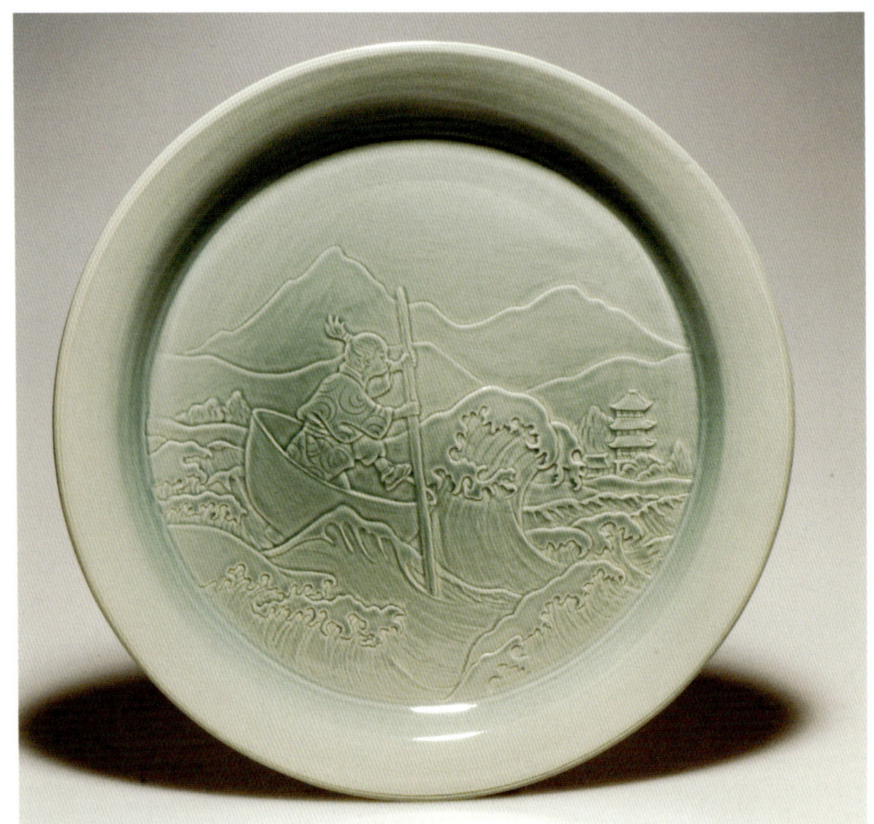

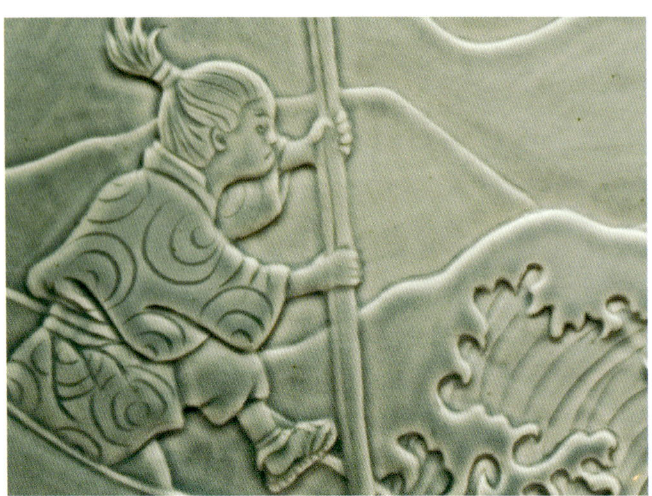

M. Kathleen Matsushita

Isunboshi (Japanese Tom Thumb) | 2003

13 5/8 INCHES (34.6 CM) IN DIAMETER

Wheel-thrown porcelain; carved, sprayed; electric fired, cone 6

PHOTOS BY DALE RODDICK

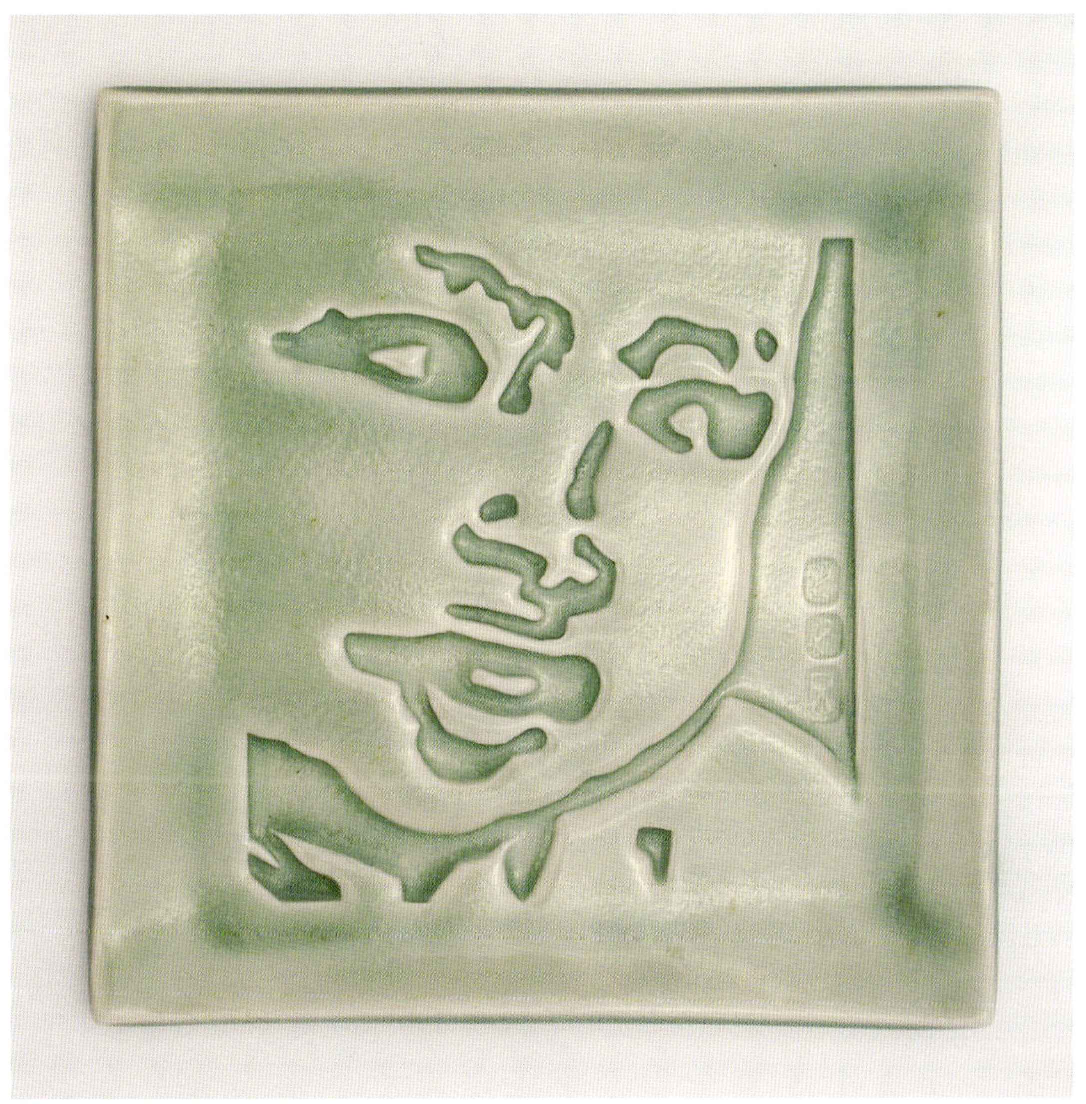

Douglas E. Gray
Celadon Son | 2006
8 X 8 INCHES (20.3 X 20.3 CM)
Slab-built porcelain; relief print image transfer; faux celadon, electric fired, cone 6
PHOTO BY ARTIST

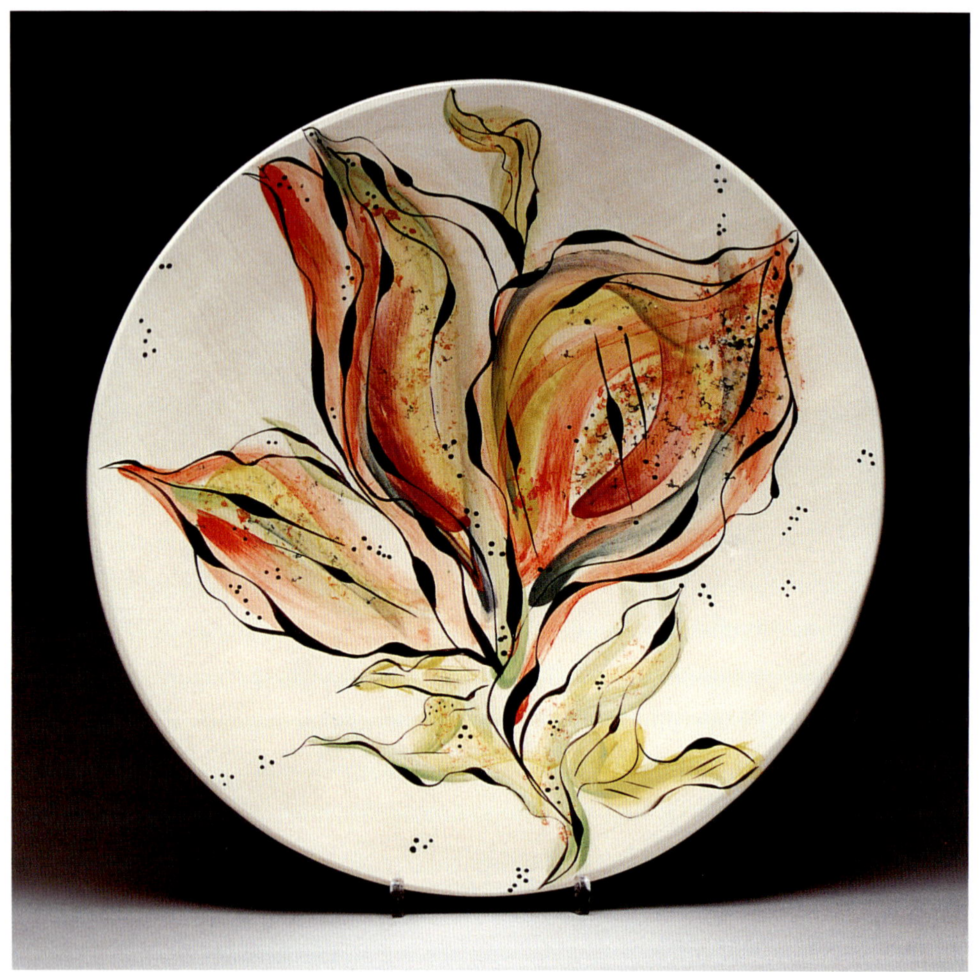

Lambeth W. Marshall

Platter with Thrown Foot | 2006

4 X 20 INCHES (10.2 X 50.8 CM)

White earthenware; sanded, dampened, slips, underglaze; bisque fired, cone 04; clear glaze, cone 06

PHOTO BY DIANE DAVIS

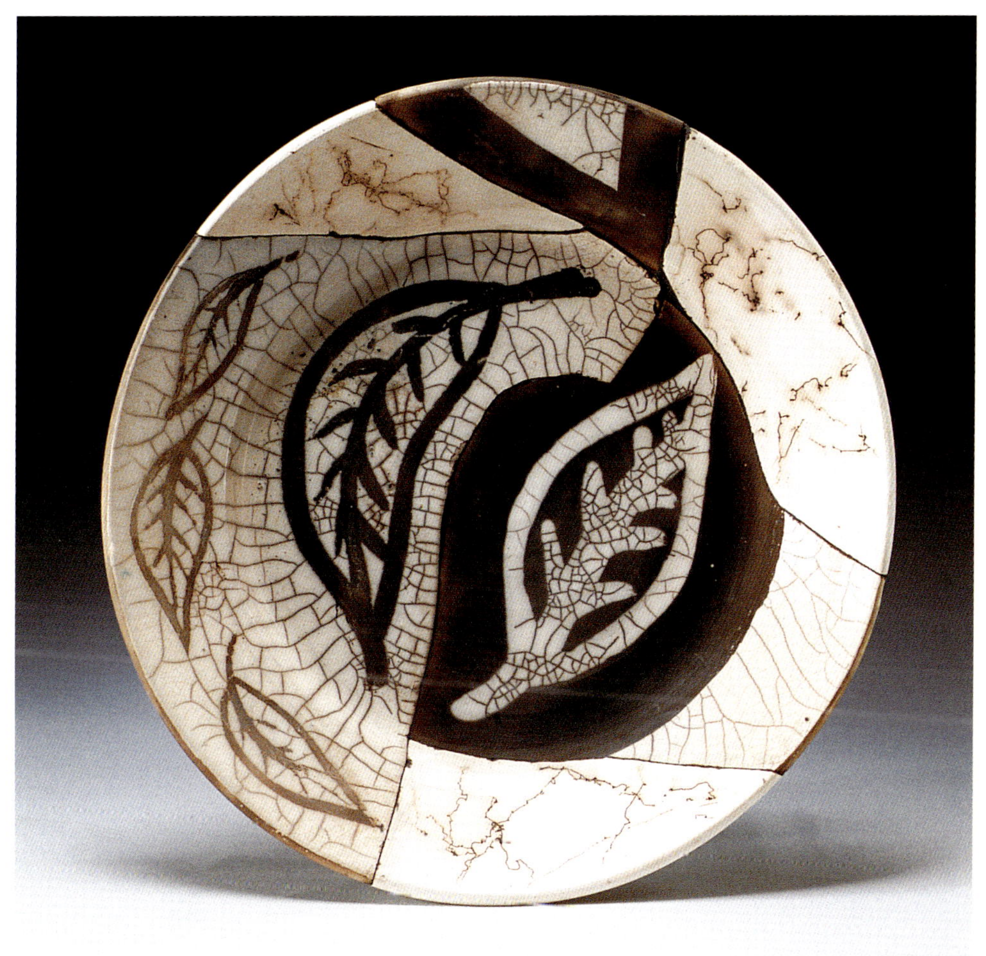

Jerri D. G. Neddermeyer

Leaves | 2006

2½ X 12 INCHES (6.4 X 30.5 CM)

Wheel-thrown porcelain; bisque fired in electric kiln, cone 06; raku fired in pieces with crackle and horsehair; reassembled with epoxy

PHOTO BY PETRONELLA J. YTSMA

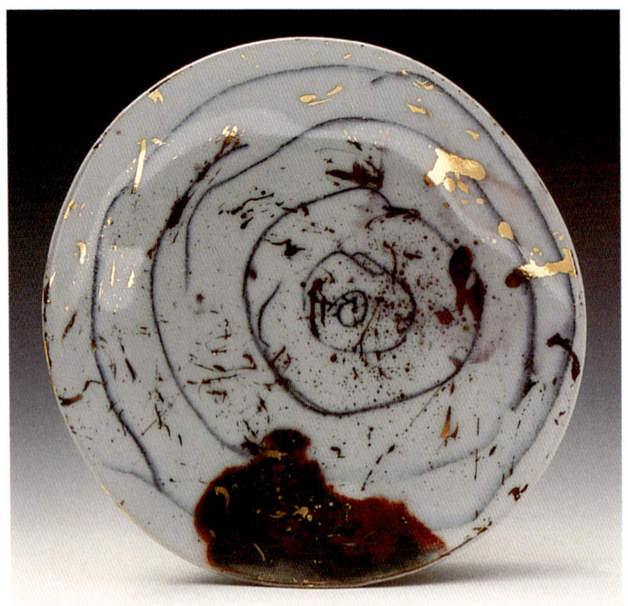

Georgette Ore

Rascal Ware Plate | 2006

11 INCHES (27.9 CM) IN DIAMETER

Porcelain

PHOTO BY MOSLEY BUNKHAM

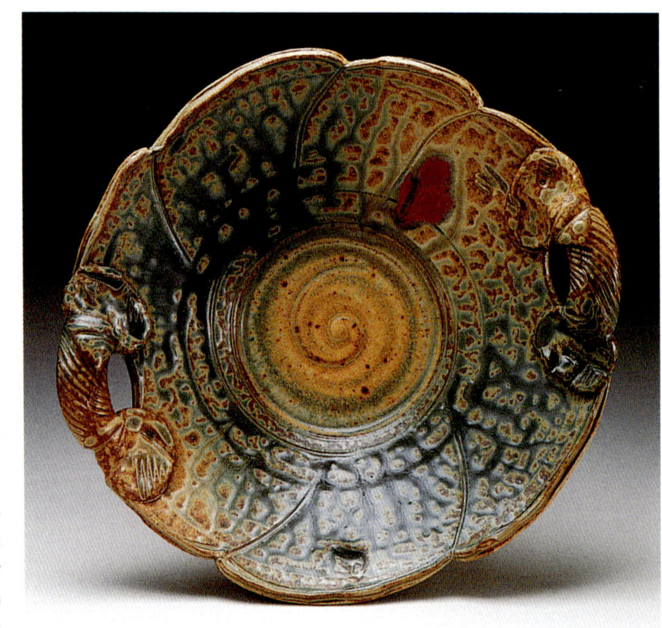

Bob Brothenton

Untitled | 2005

12 1/2 INCHES (31.8 CM) IN DIAMETER

Wheel-thrown and altered stoneware; wax resist, Albany faux glazes; cone 9 reduction

PHOTO BY TOM MILLS

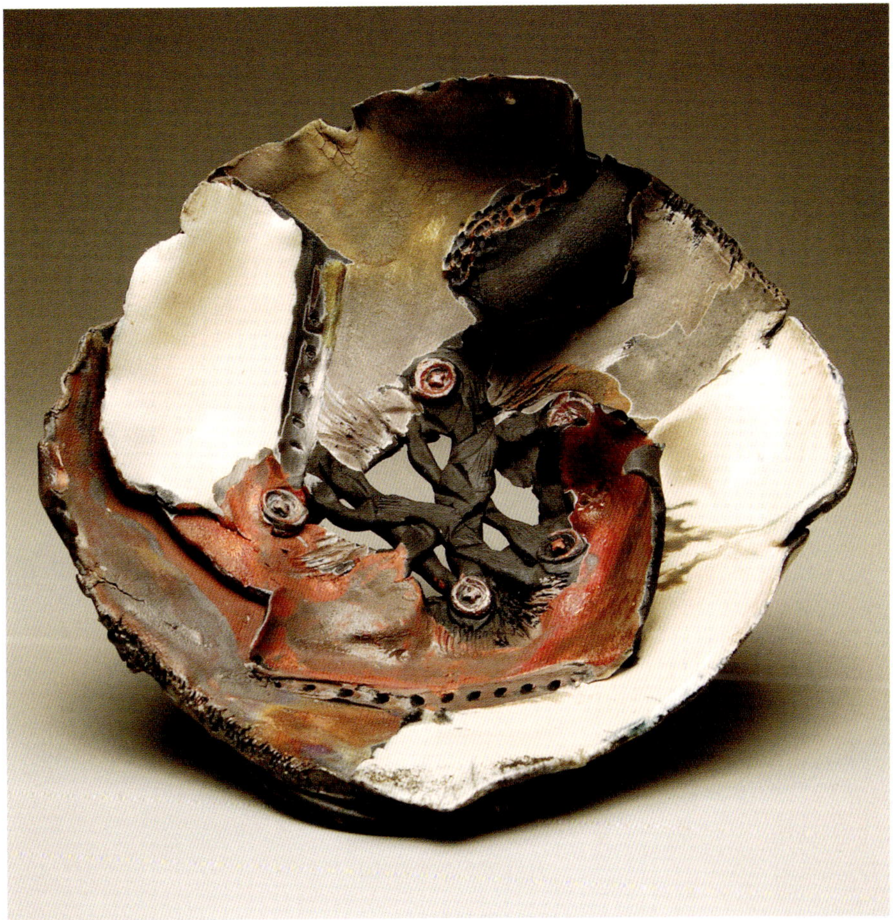

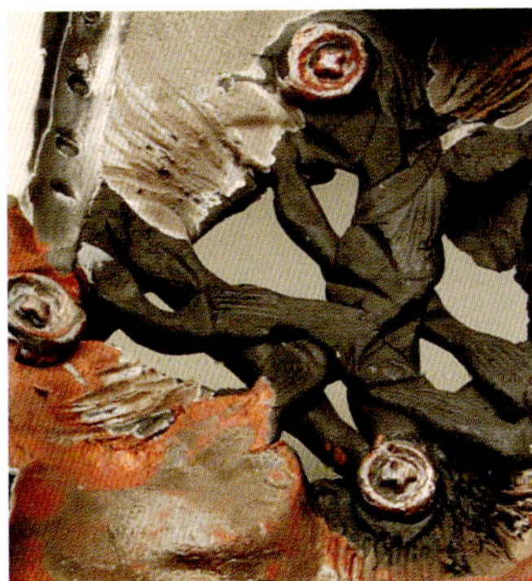

Mirtha Aertker

Receko | 2007

12 INCHES (30.5 CM) IN DIAMETER

Hand-built raku; gas fired, cone 06; glazes, cone 06

PHOTOS BY ARTIST

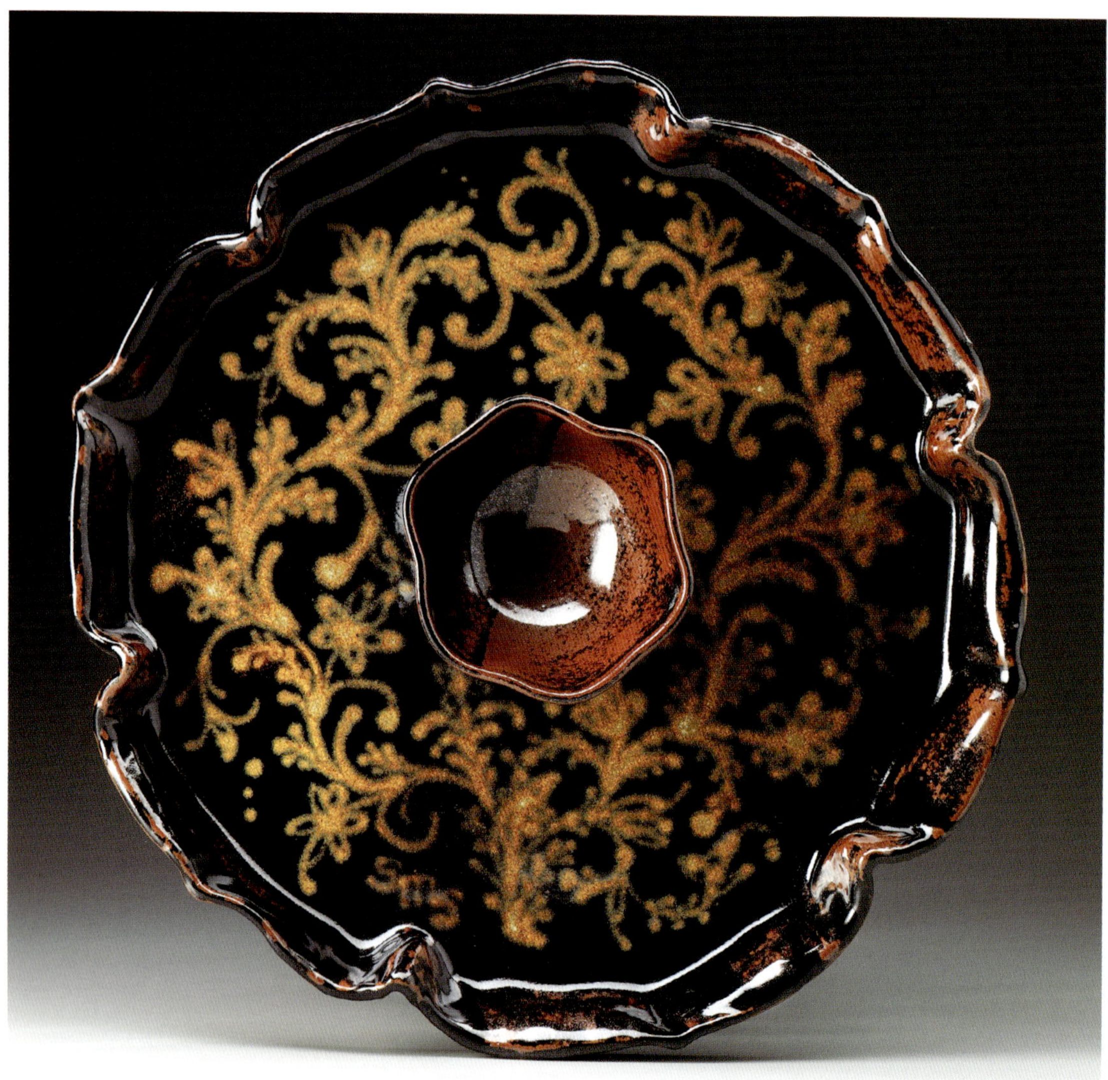

Sheila Staubus

Oro Chip and Dip Platter | 2007

2 X 15 X 15 INCHES (5.1 X 38.1 X 38.1 CM)

Hand-built and wheel-thrown stoneware; temmoku glaze and glaze trailing; gas fired in reduction, cone 10

PHOTO BY STEVEN TIGGEMANN

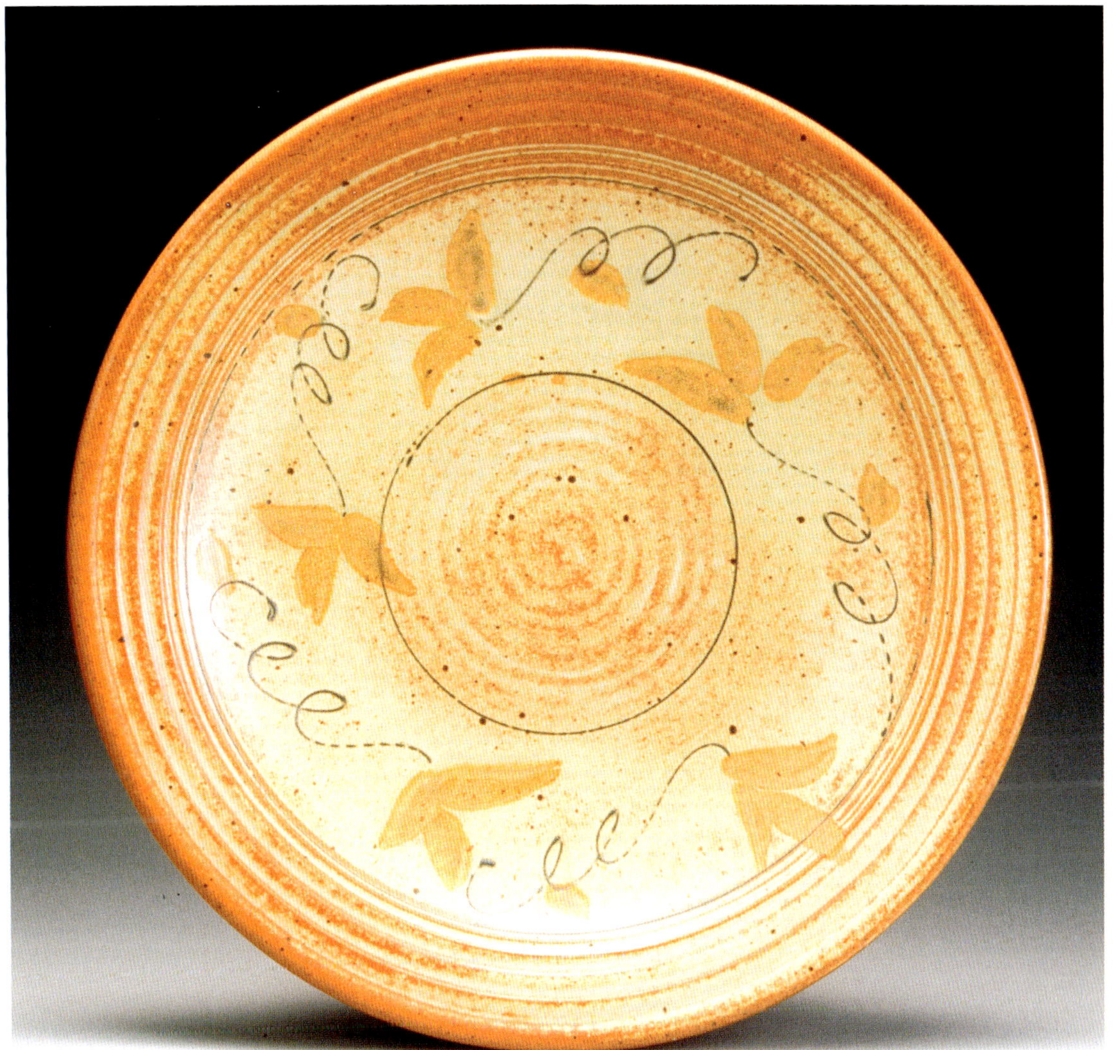

Rebecca Plummer
Jon Ellenbogen

Round Platter | 2006

18 INCHES (45.7 CM) IN DIAMETER

Wheel-thrown stoneware; underglaze decoration; reduction fired, cone 10

PHOTO BY TOM MILLS

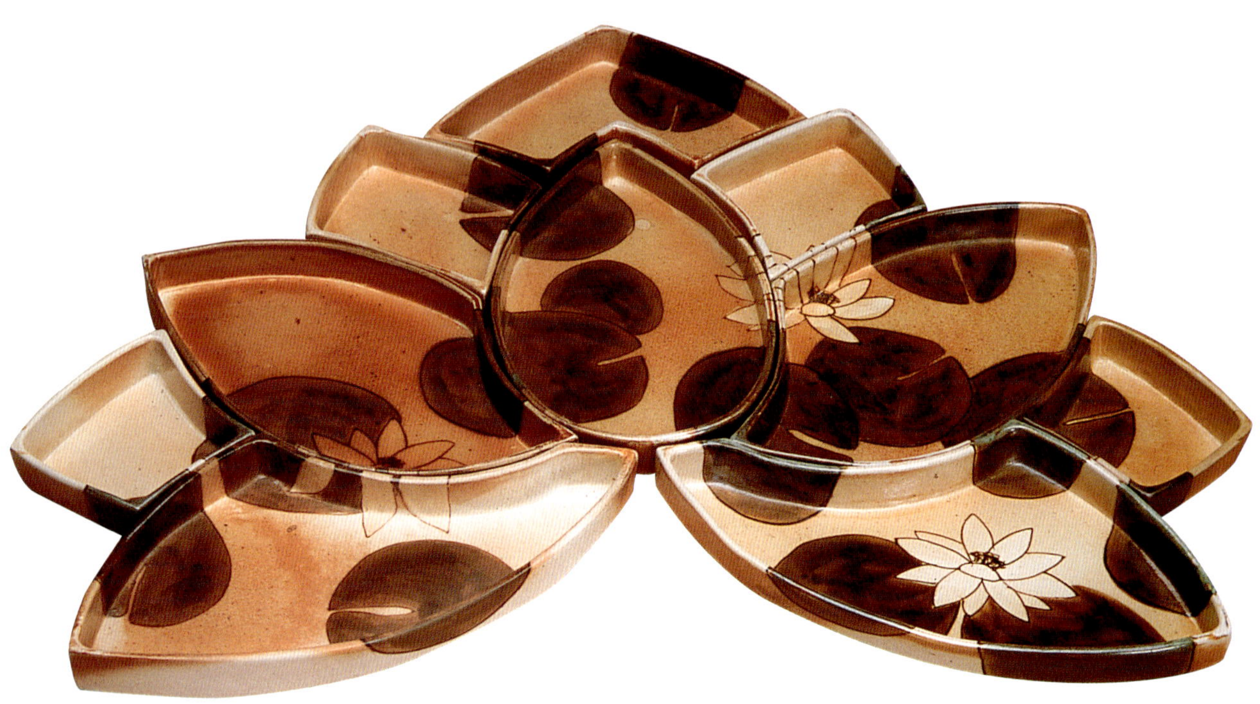

Cathi Jefferson

Lily on Lily Sushi Set | 2005

1 X 21 X 18 INCHES (2.5 X 53.3 X 45.7 CM)

Hand-built porcelaneous stoneware; salt/soda fired

PHOTO BY HANS SIPMA

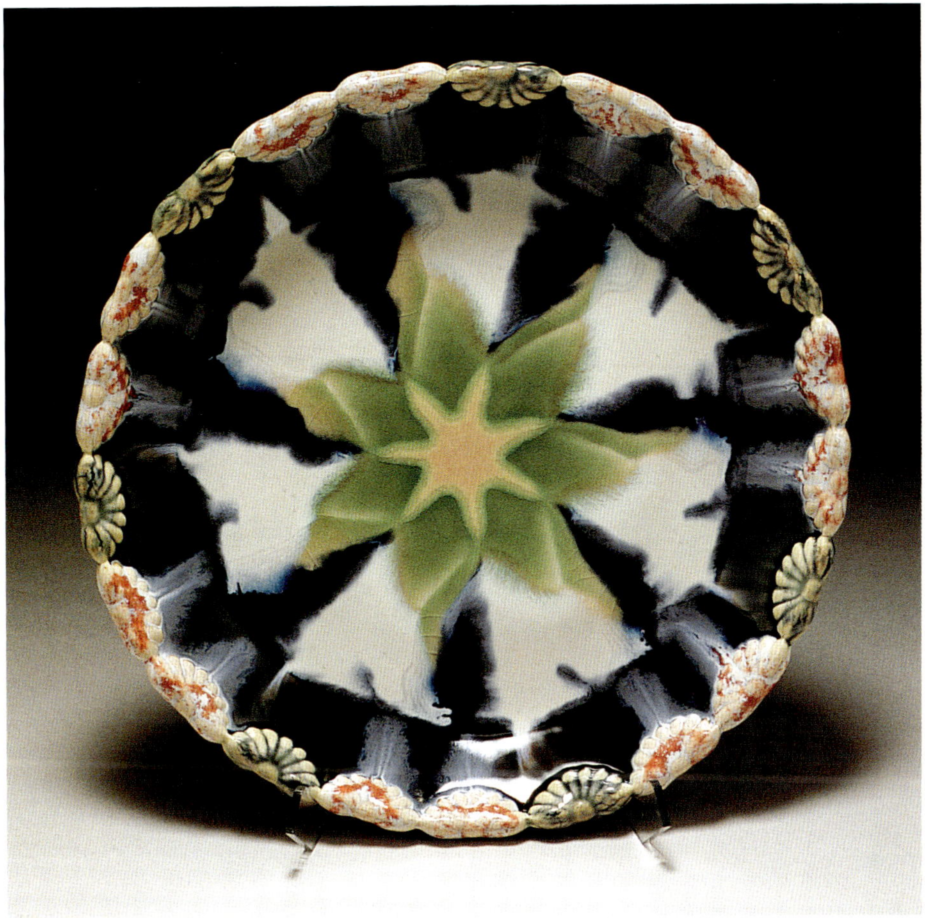

Ying-Yueh Chuang

Decorated Plate | 2003

1 1/2 X 10 INCHES (3.8 X 25.4 CM)

Slab built with mold paper clay; hand painted; glazes, electric fired, cone 6

PHOTOS BY ARTIST

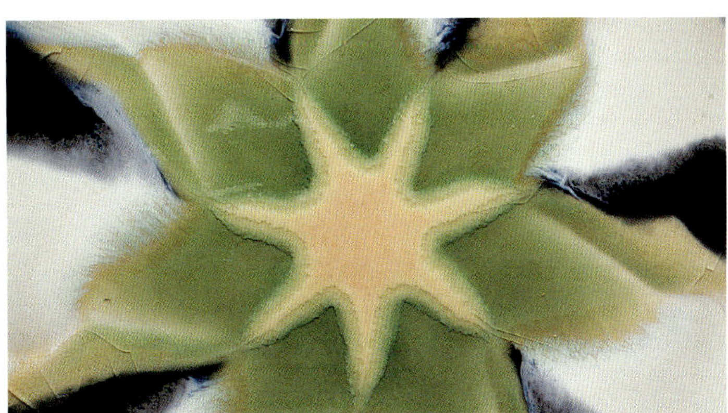

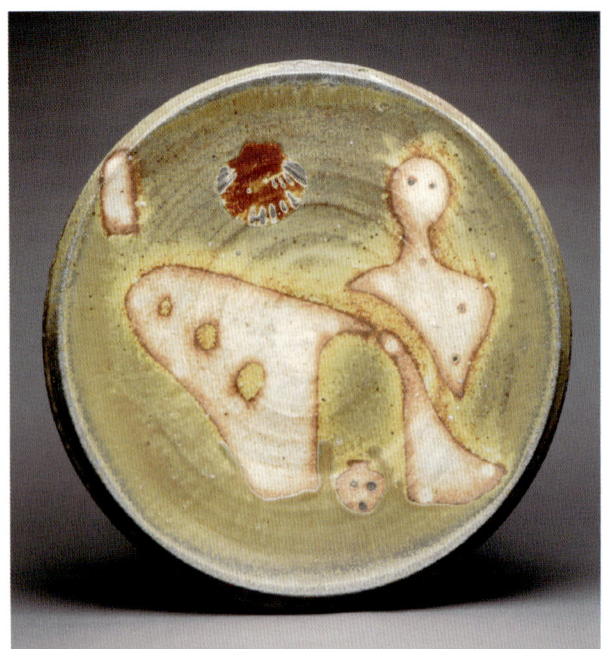

Gary Hootman

Anagama/Painting with Ash | 2007

4 1/8 X 24 1/2 INCHES (10.5 X 62.2 CM)

Wheel-thrown Hootman's stoneware; white slip; natural ash; Hootagama wood kiln, cone 11

PHOTO BY MARK TADE

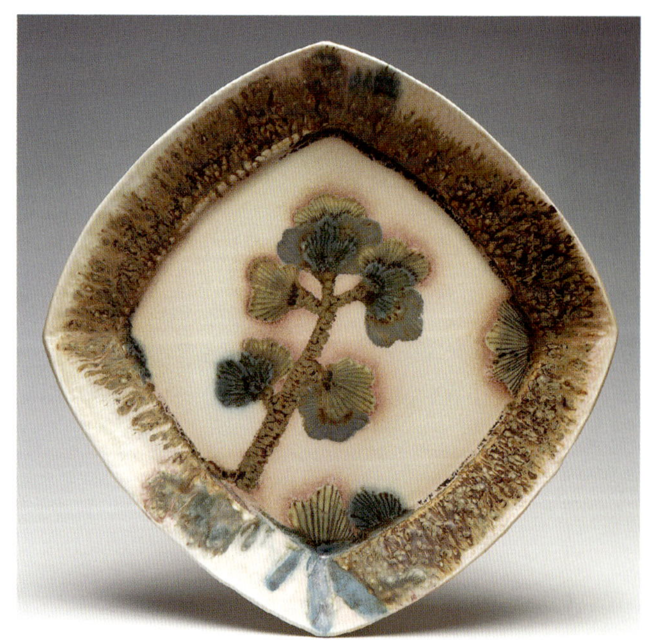

Ji Youl Choi

Untitled | 2007

1 5/8 X 19 X 19 INCHES (4.1 X 48.3 X 48.3 CM)

Hand-built porcelain; electric fired, cone 8

PHOTO BY KWANG-CHOON PARK

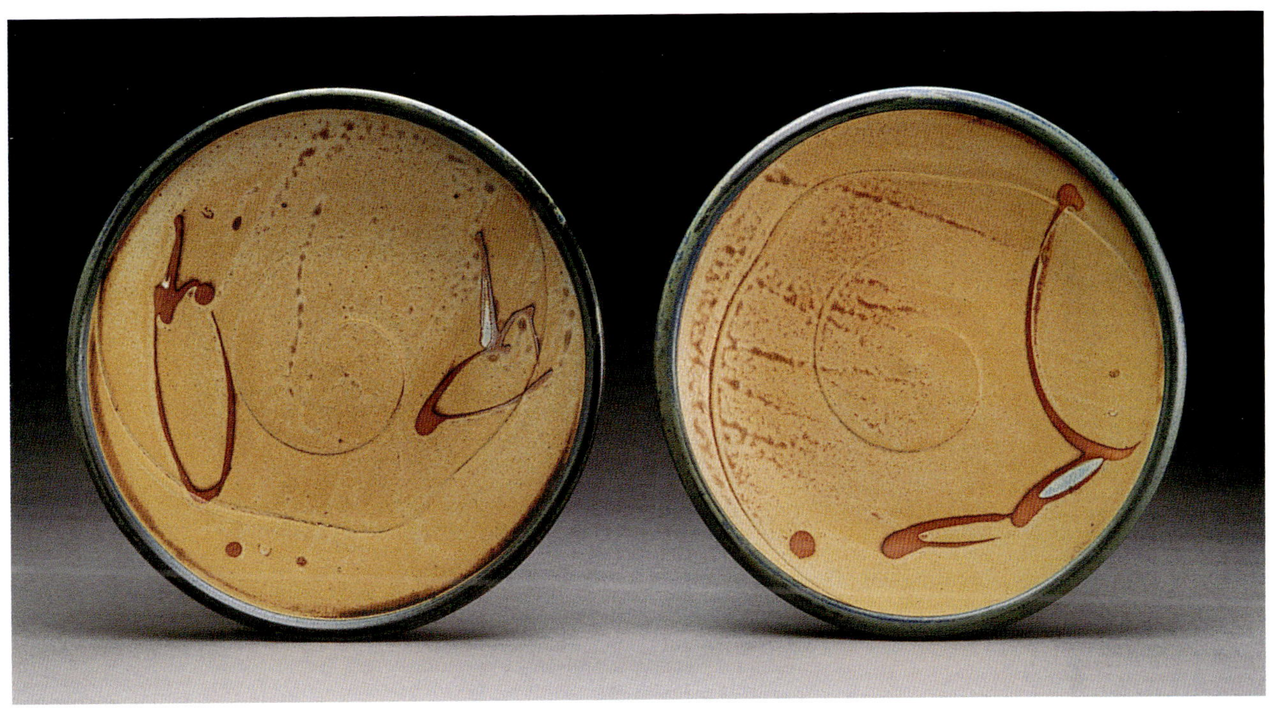

Nicholas Joerling

Dinner Plates | 2007

EACH: 11 INCHES (27.9 CM) IN DIAMETER

Wheel-thrown, high-temp stoneware; wax resist; reduction glazes, gas-fired downdraft, cone 10

PHOTO BY TOM MILLS

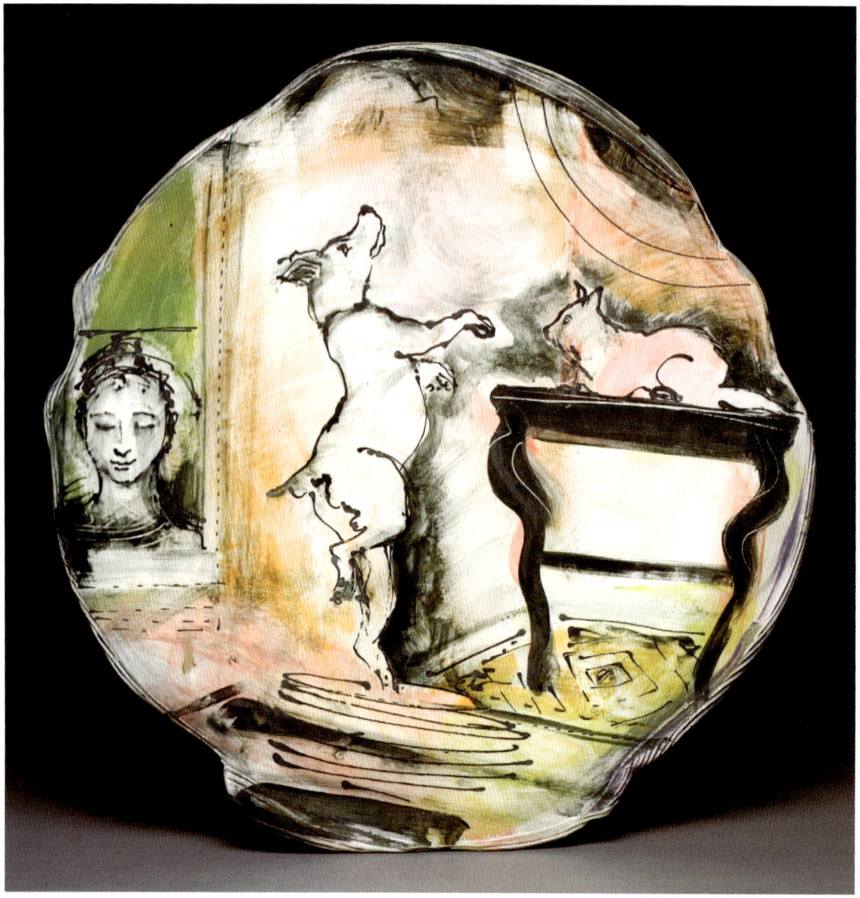

Laurie Shaman

State of Enlightenment | 2006

3 X 12 INCHES (7.6 X 30.5 CM)

Hand-built earthenware; slip trailing and brushwork with underglazes; electric fired, cone 04; glazes, cone 06

PHOTOS BY PETER KIAR

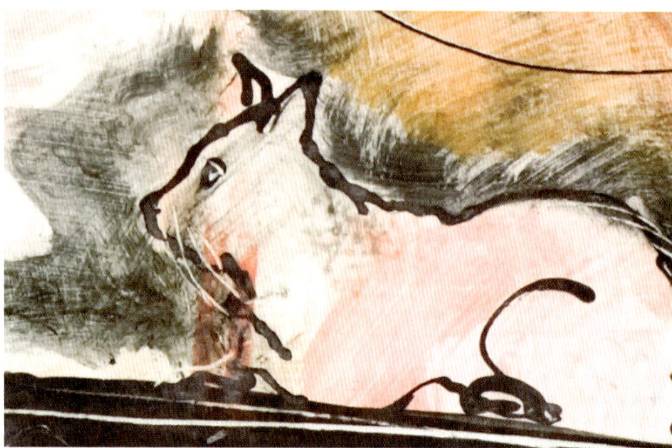

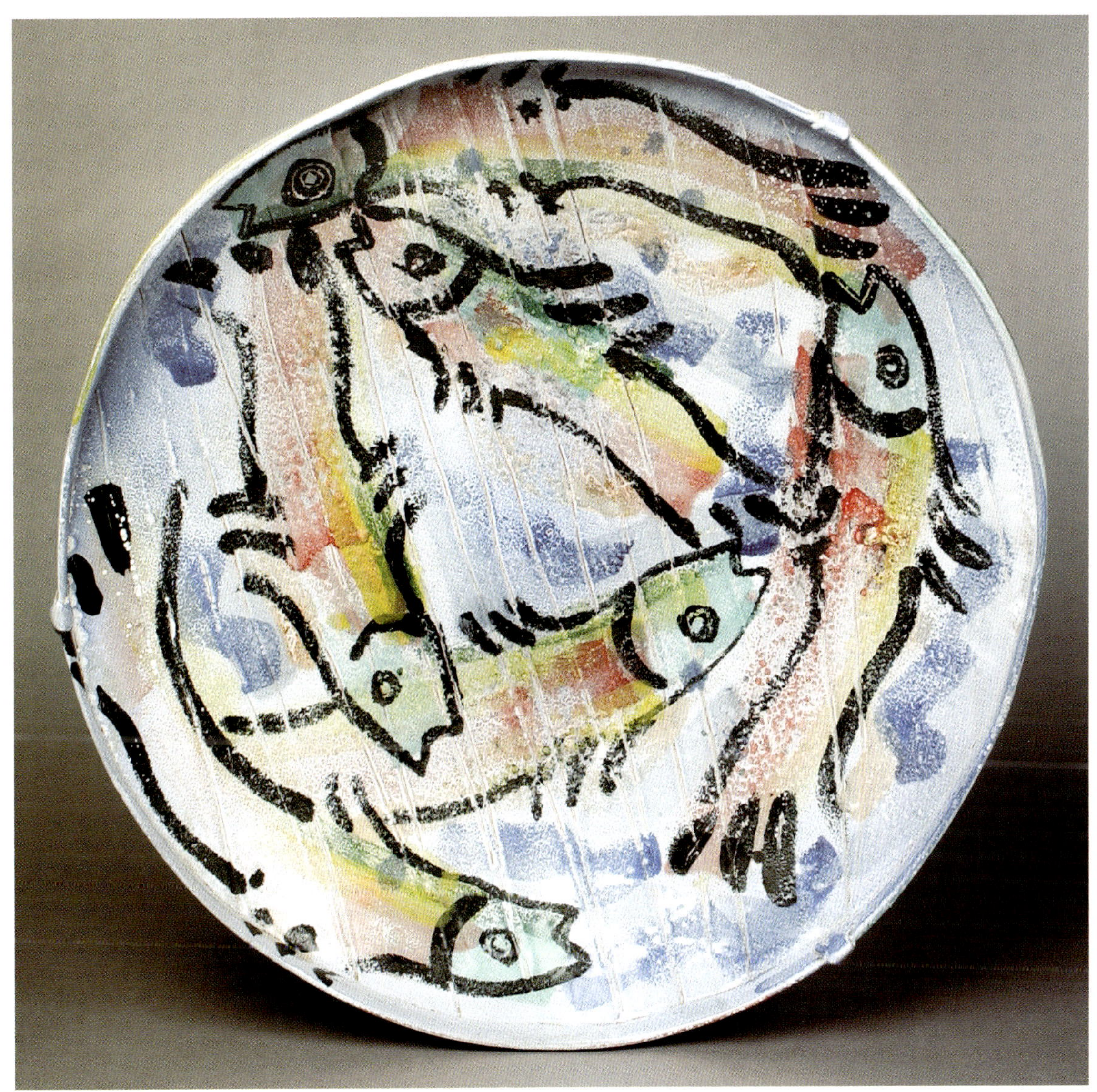

Cat Connor-Talasek
Fish Pond | 2006
4 X 22 INCHES (10.2 X 55.9 CM)
Hand-built earthenware;
electric fired, cone 04
PHOTO BY LON BRAUER

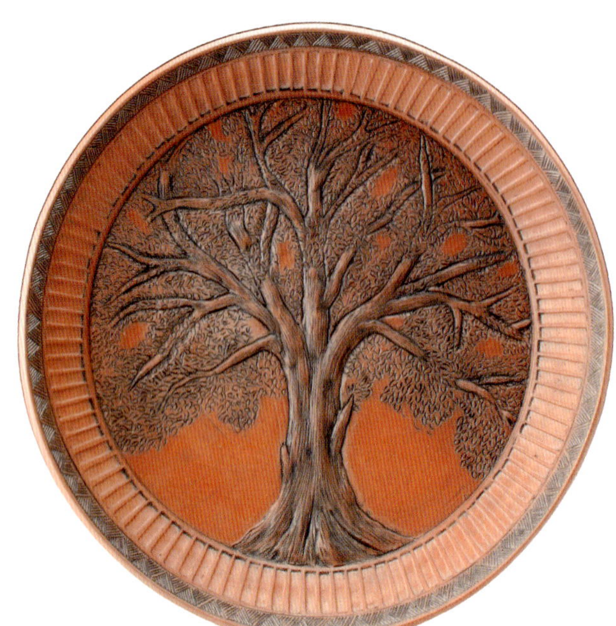

Shikha Joshi

Serenity | 2007

2 X 16 INCHES (5 X 40.6 CM)

Wheel-thrown and hand-carved red clay; electric fired, cone 6; black underglaze wipe-off, cone 41

PHOTO BY ANAND JOSHI

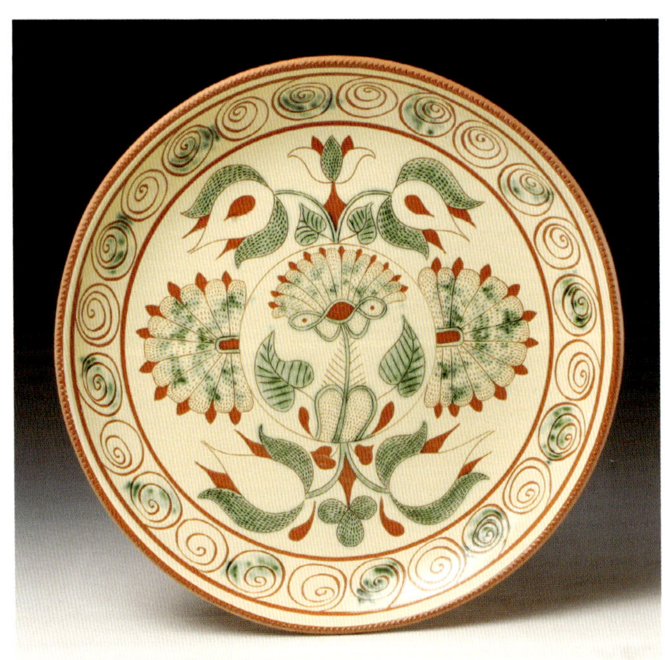

Anne Borrello

Sgraffito Platter | 2005

3 X 17 INCHES (7.6 X 43.2 CM)

Drape-molded redware; slip lined; sgraffito; copper oxide; bisque fired, cone 08; clear glaze, electric fired, cone 03

PHOTO BY RUDY RUZICSKA

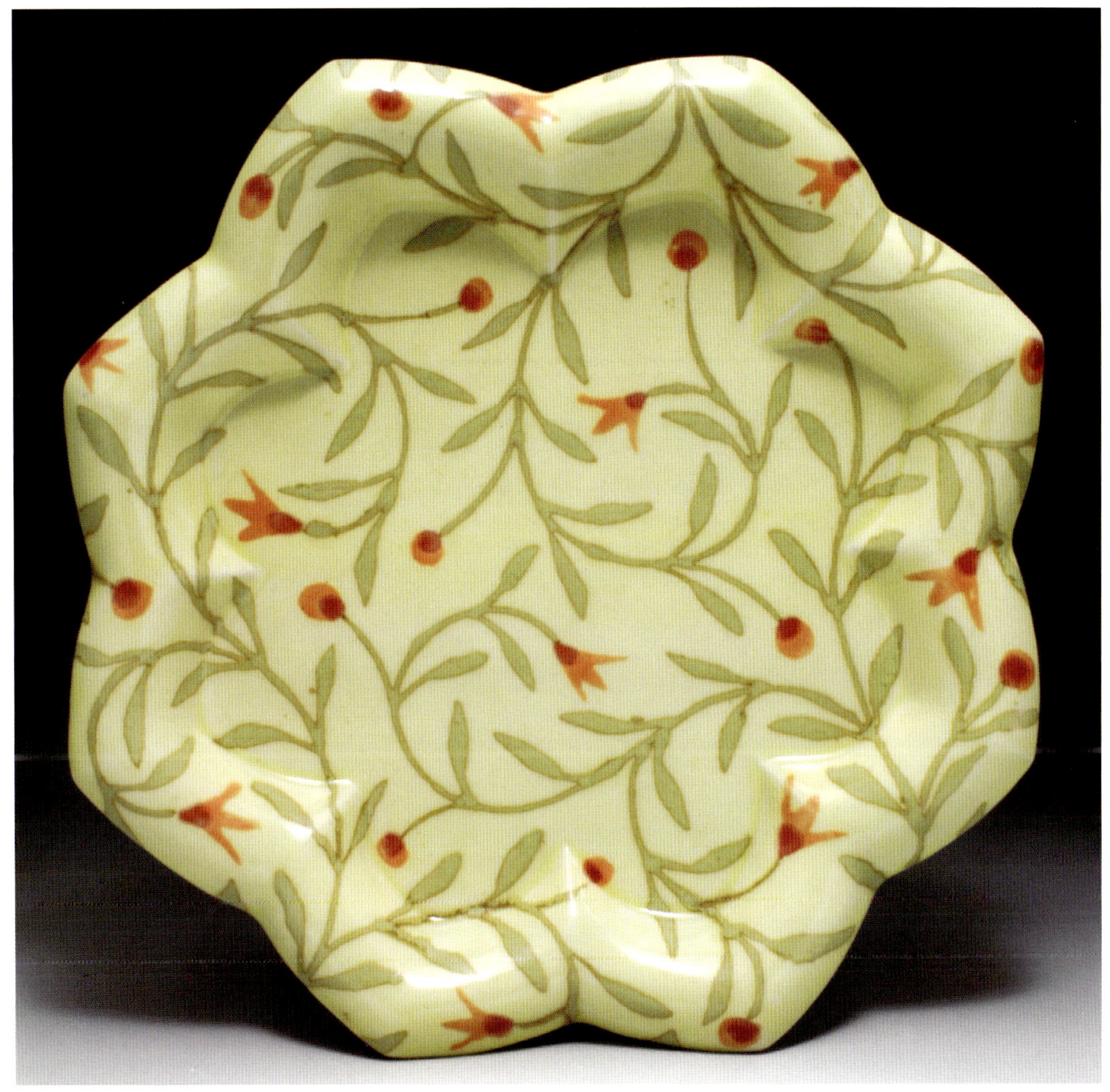

Brenda Quinn

Scalloped Platter | 2007

3 X 13 X 13 INCHES (7.6 X 33 X 33 CM)

Press-molded and extruded porcelain; wax resist, carved glaze; electric fired, cone 6

PHOTO BY KEITH RENNER

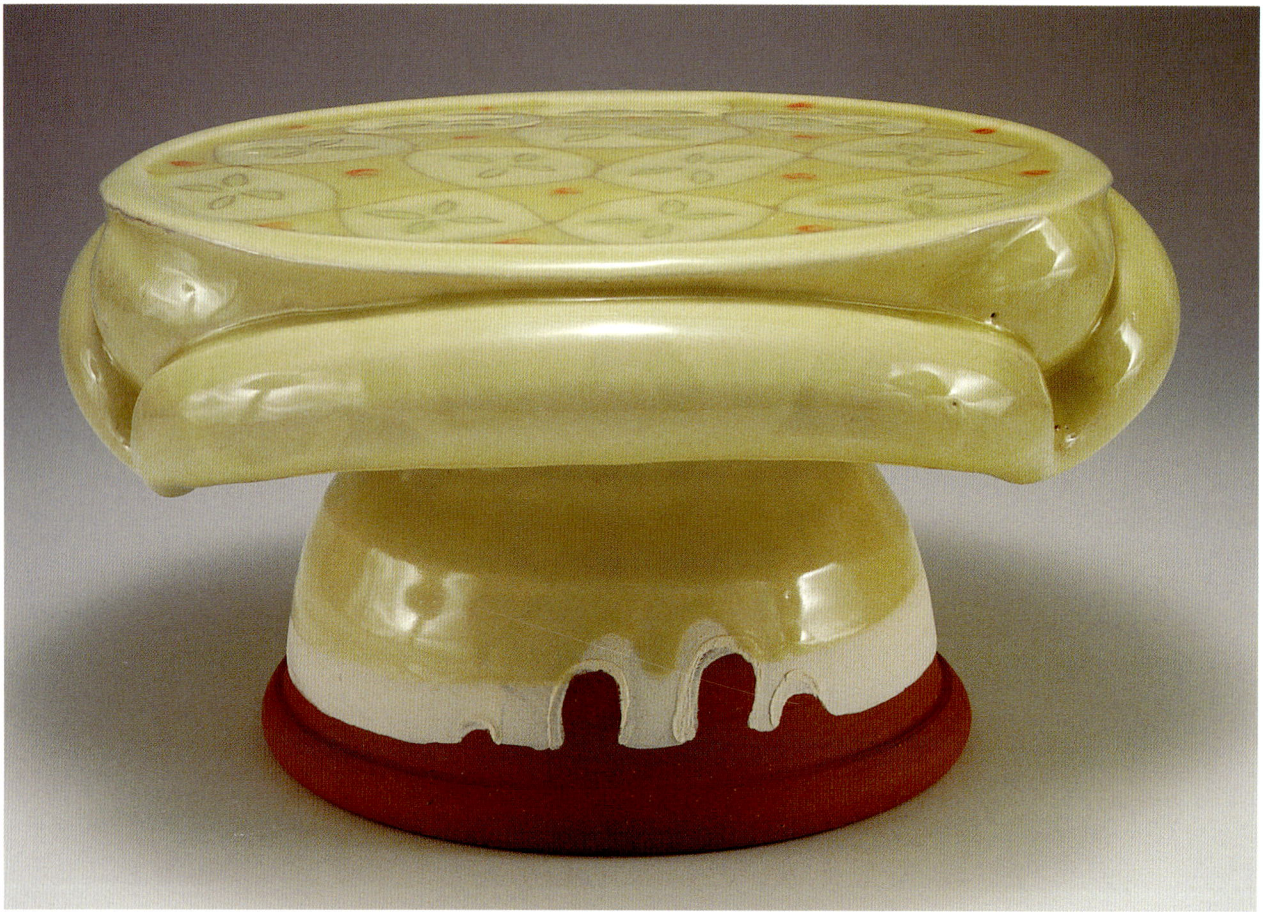

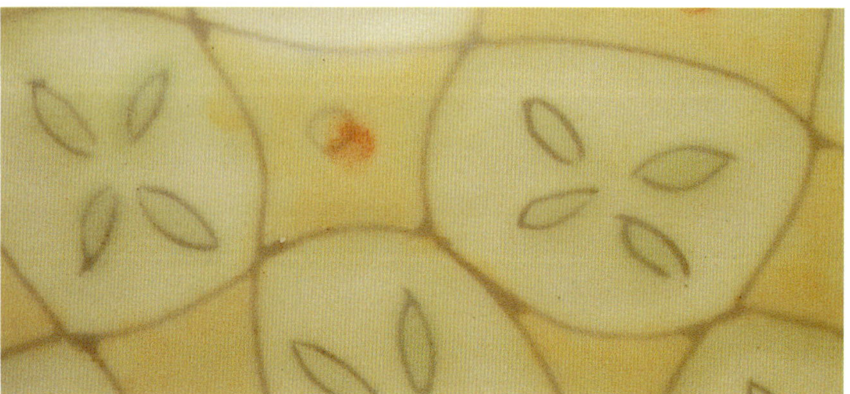

Kristin Pavelka

Cake Plate | 2006

5 X 10 X 10 INCHES (12.7 X 25.4 X 25.4 CM)

Wheel-thrown, altered, and assembled earthenware; sgraffito, slip; polychrome glazes; electric fired, cone 04

PHOTOS BY ARTIST

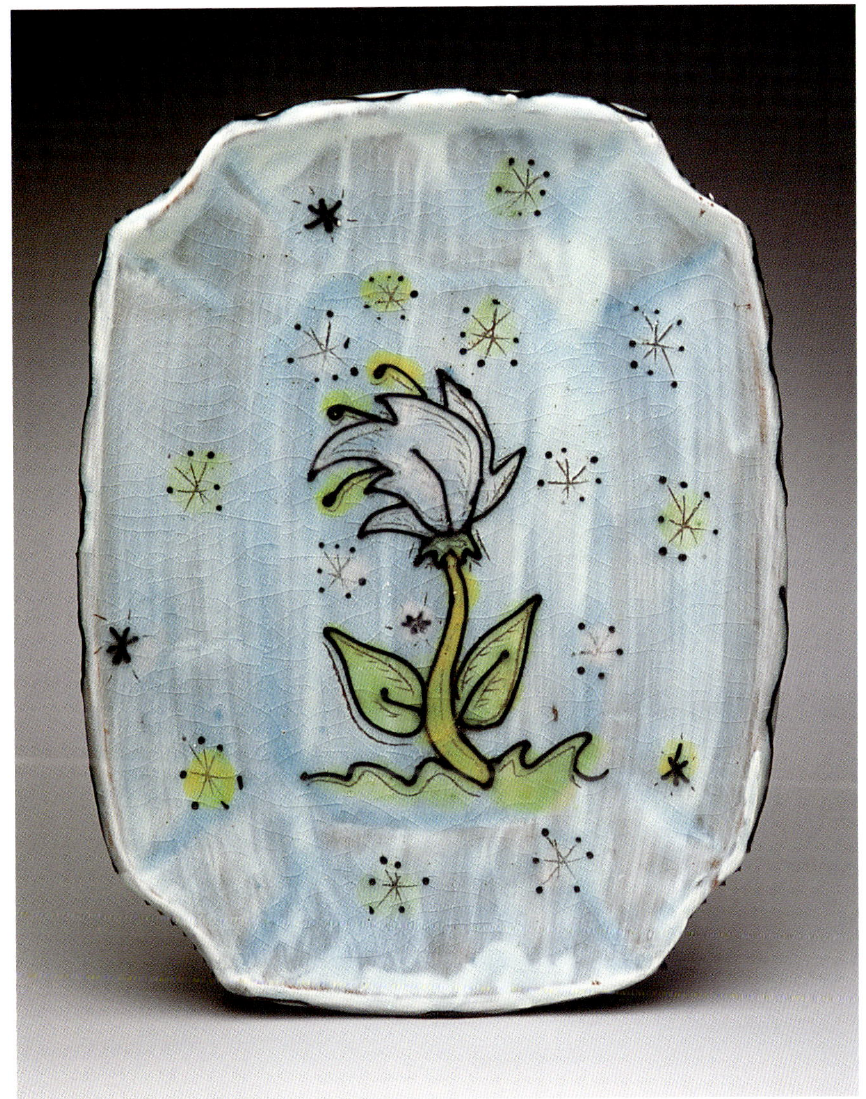

Katie McFarland

Lily | 2007

2 X 8 X 10 INCHES (5.1 X 20.3 X 25.4 CM)

Hand-built red earthenware; white and black slip, carved; colored transparent glaze; electric fired, cone 04

PHOTO BY WALKER MONTGOMERY

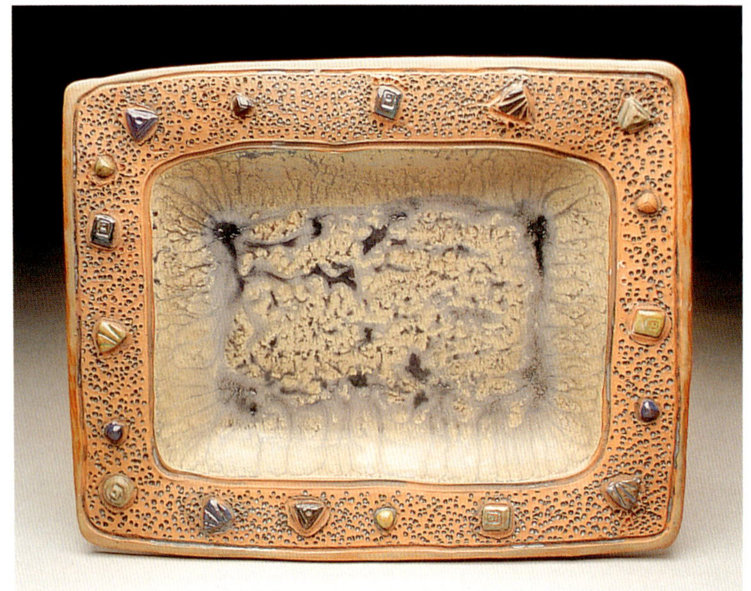

Janice Mann

Platter | 2007

3 X 17 X 13 INCHES (7.6 X 43.2 X 33 CM)

Hand-built earthenware; electric fired, cone 04; glazes, cone 05

PHOTO BY PAUL NORTHWAY

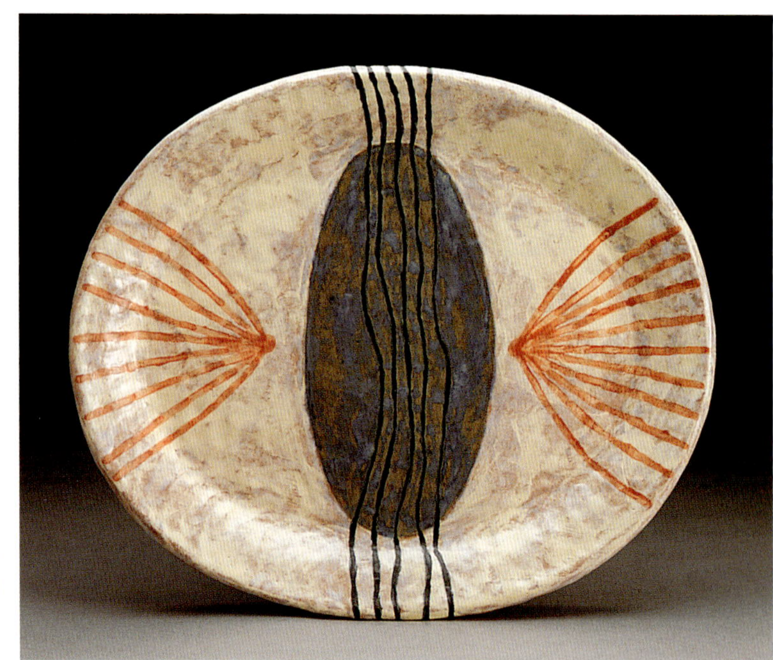

Holly Walker

Red Twig, Stream | 2005

$1\frac{1}{2}$ X $16\frac{1}{2}$ X $13\frac{3}{4}$ INCHES (3.8 X 41.9 X 34.9 CM)

Slab- and hand-built terra cotta; painted slips and glazes; electric fired, cone 05

PHOTO BY TOM MILLS

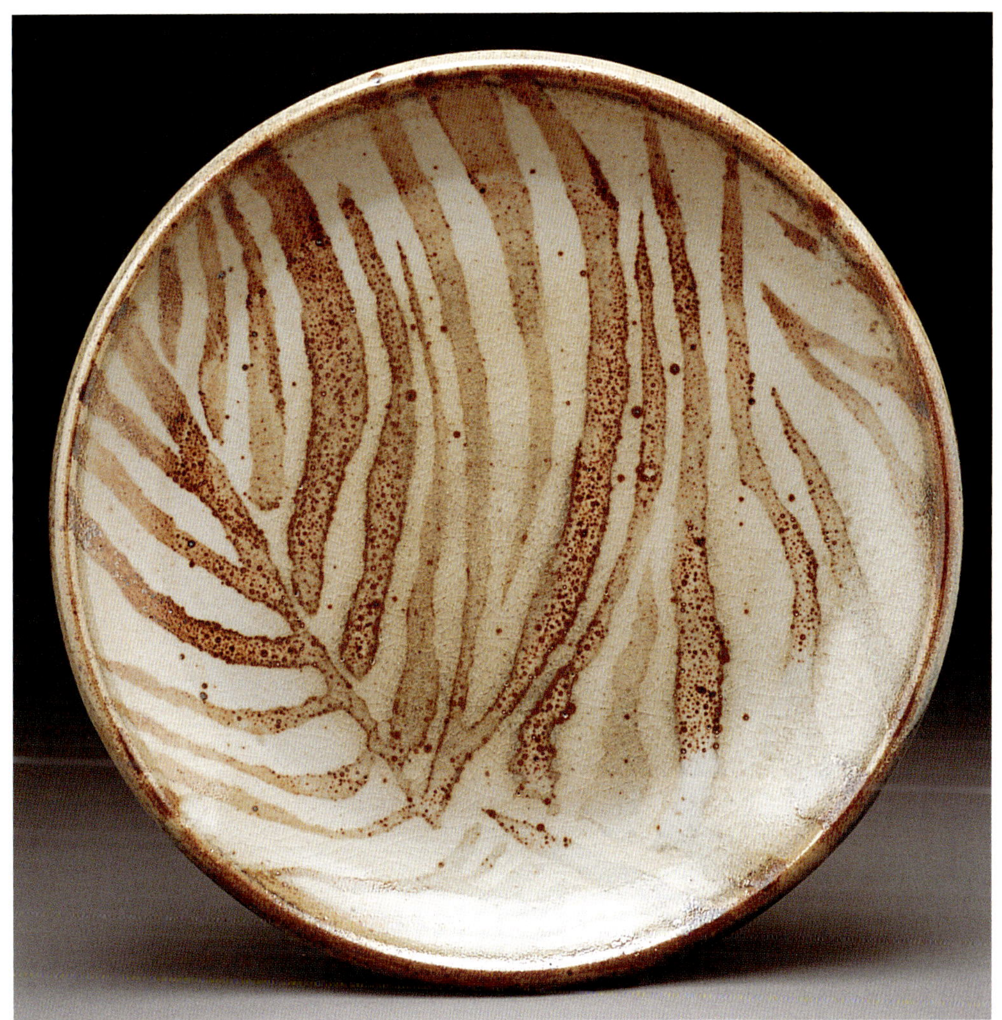

Eloise Hally

Platter with Stripes | 2003

1 X 12 INCHES (2.5 X 30.5 CM)

Wheel-thrown stoneware; oxides and shino glaze; gas fired, cone 10

PHOTO BY BART KASTEN

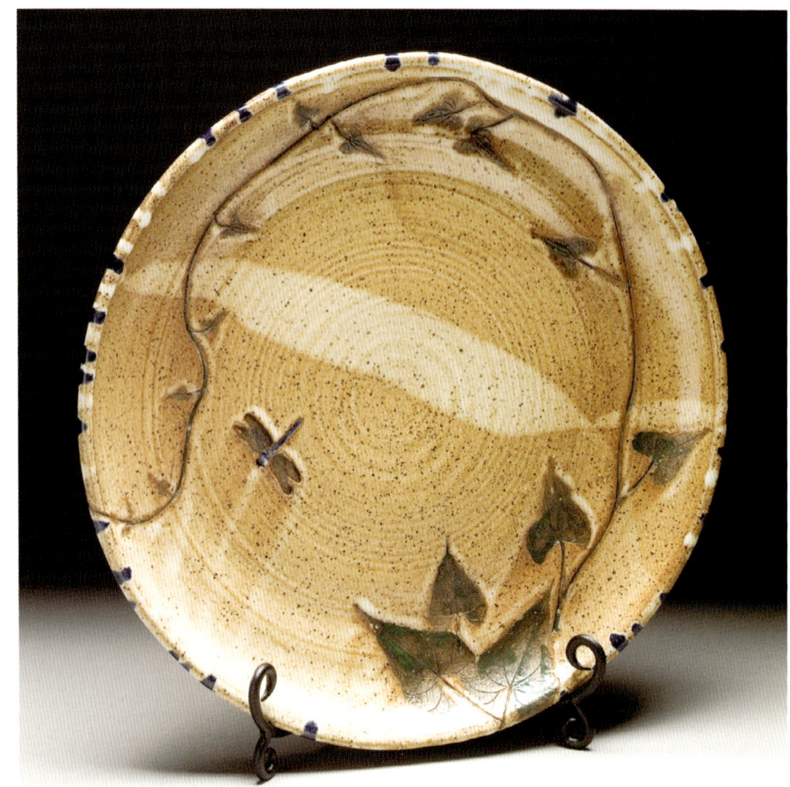

Jeff Hodges

Dragonfly among the Potato Vines | 2007

1 1/2 X 15 INCHES (3.8 X 38.1 CM)

Wheel thrown; pressed with leaves and dragonfly stamp; clay and glazes, cone 6

PHOTOS BY PIGEON PHOTOGRAPHY

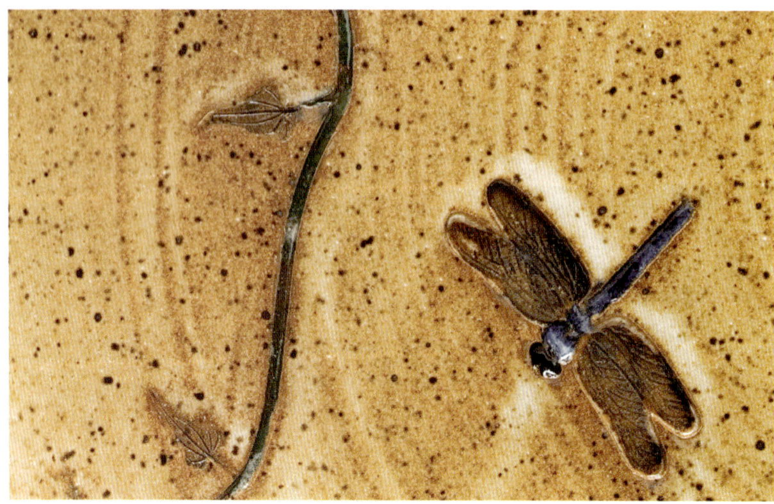

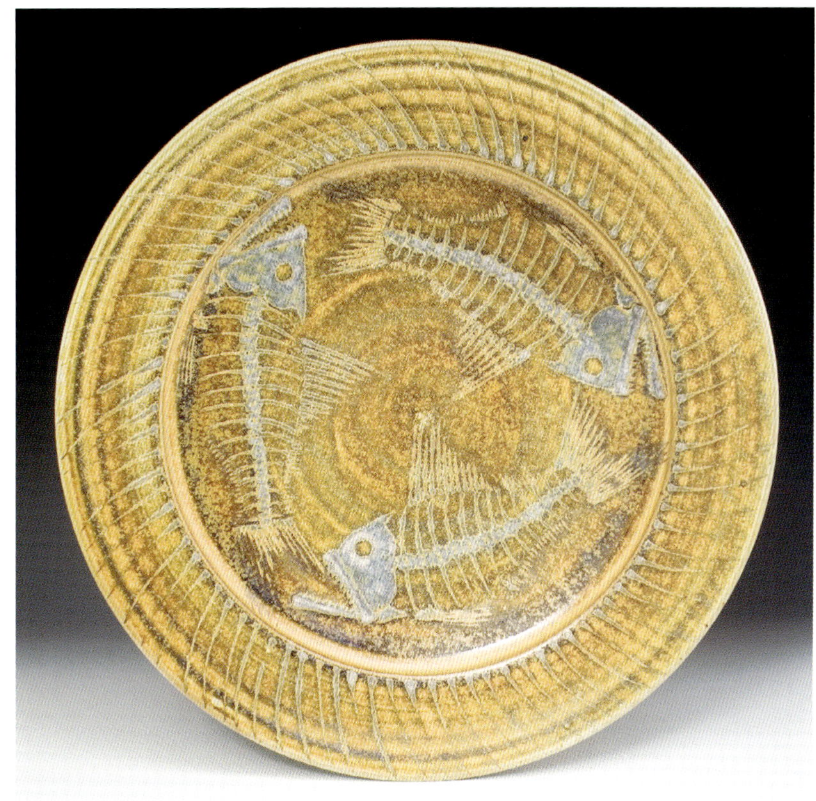

Bruce Gholson

Three Bony Fish | 2007

2 X 17 INCHES (5.1 X 43.2 CM)

Wheel-thrown stoneware; iron engobe, trailed glaze, satin matte glaze; gas fired in reduction, cone 10

PHOTOS BY BULLDOG POTTERY

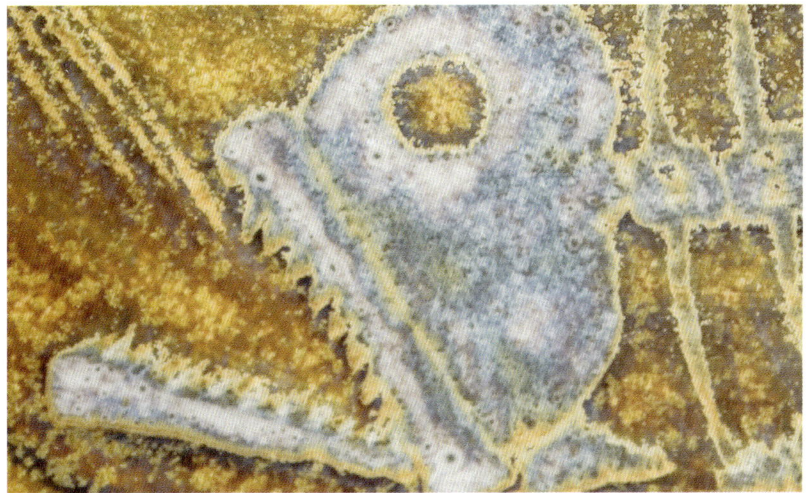

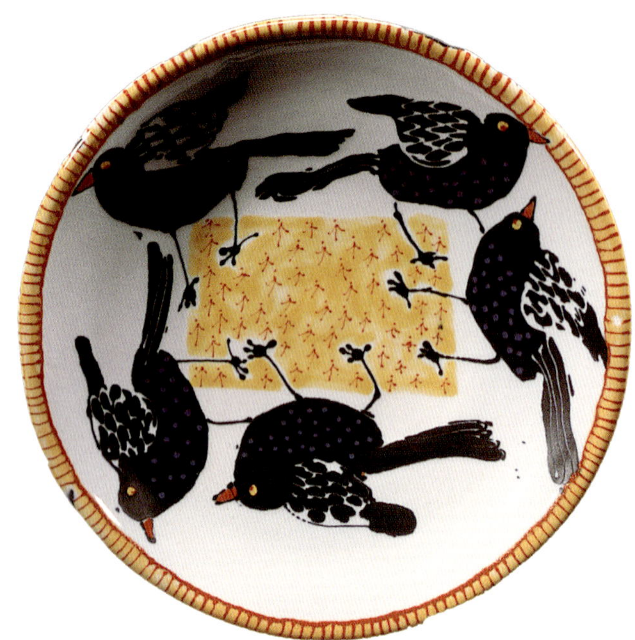

Marie Deborah Wald

Red-Winged Blackbirds | 2007

2 X 16 INCHES (5.1 X 40.6 CM)

Wheel-thrown porcelain; latex resist and trailed glaze; glaze, gas fired in reduction, cone 11

PHOTO BY JEFF BRUCE

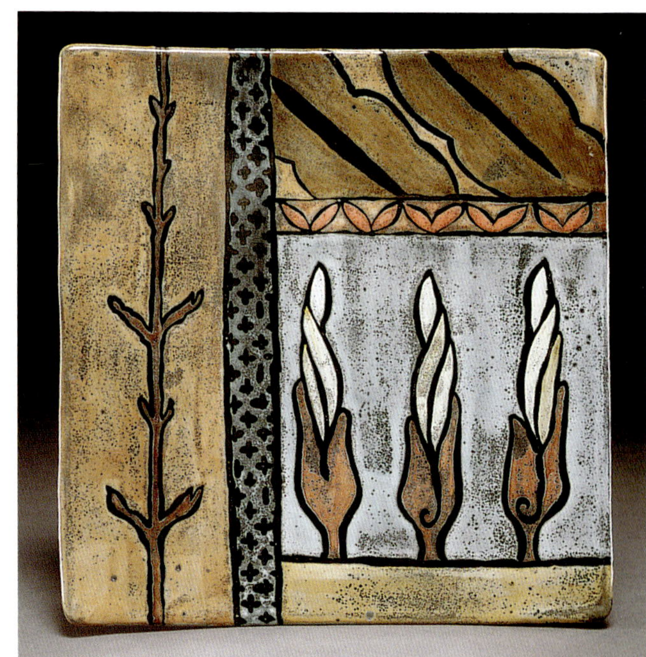

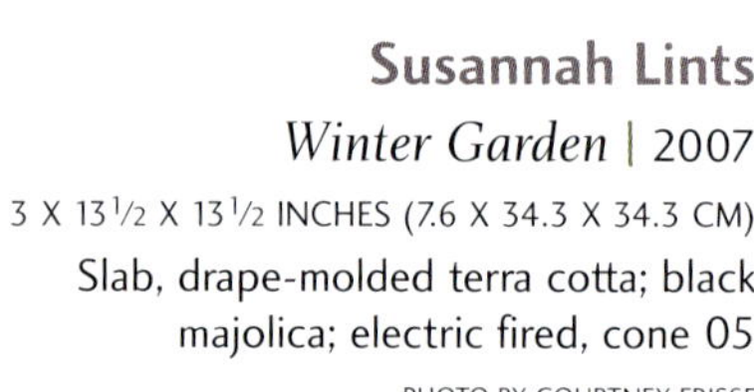

Susannah Lints

Winter Garden | 2007

3 X $13\frac{1}{2}$ X $13\frac{1}{2}$ INCHES (7.6 X 34.3 X 34.3 CM)

Slab, drape-molded terra cotta; black majolica; electric fired, cone 05

PHOTO BY COURTNEY FRISSE

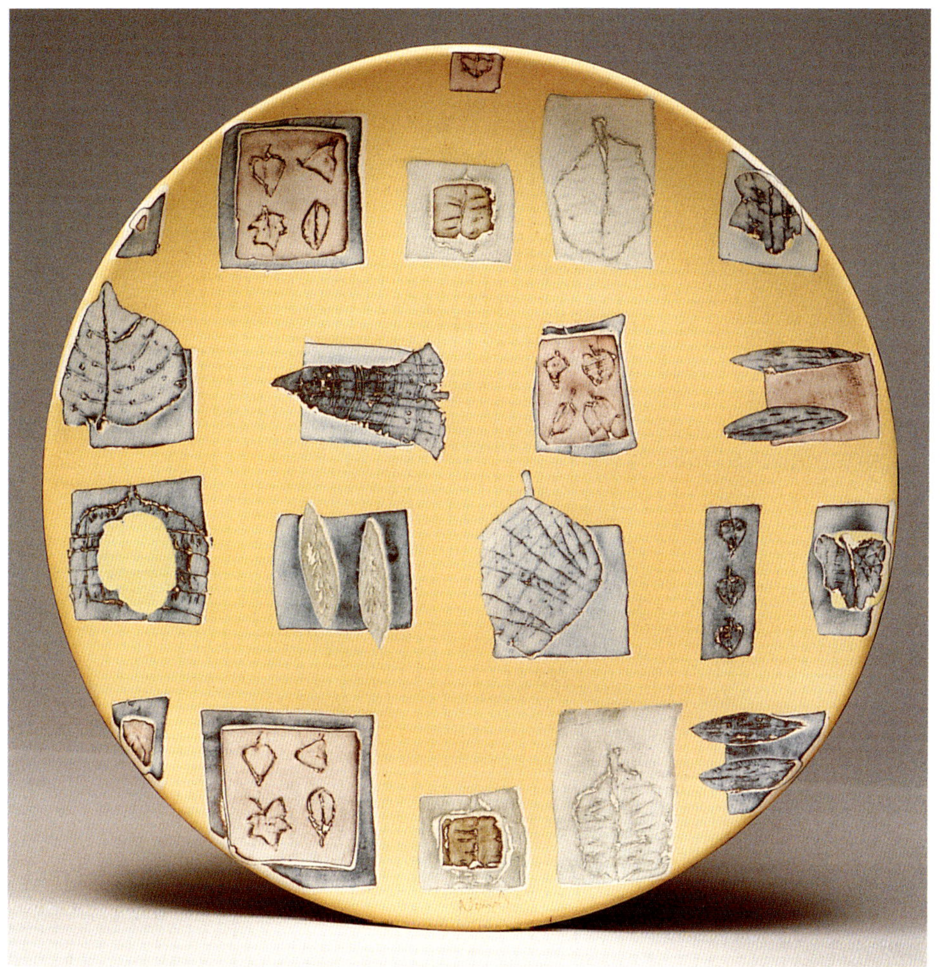

Susan Nemeth

Leaves | 2003

1 X 12 INCHES (2.5 X 30.5 CM)

Press-molded porcelain; inlaid with colored clays and slips; unglazed; electric fired, cone 9

PHOTO BY ARTIST

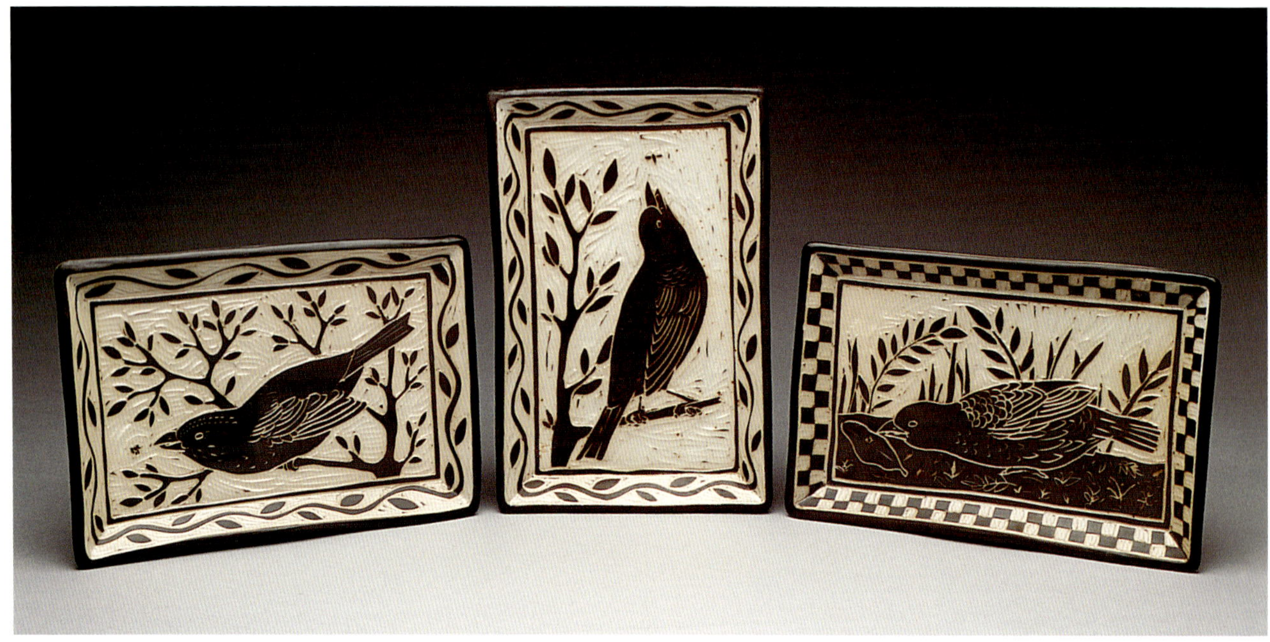

Karen Newgard

Bird Appetizer Trays | 2006

EACH: 2 X 9 X 7 INCHES (5.1 X 22.9 X 17.8 CM)

Slab-built porcelain; sgraffito, black terra sigillata; salt fired, cone 10

PHOTO BY WALKER MONTGOMERY

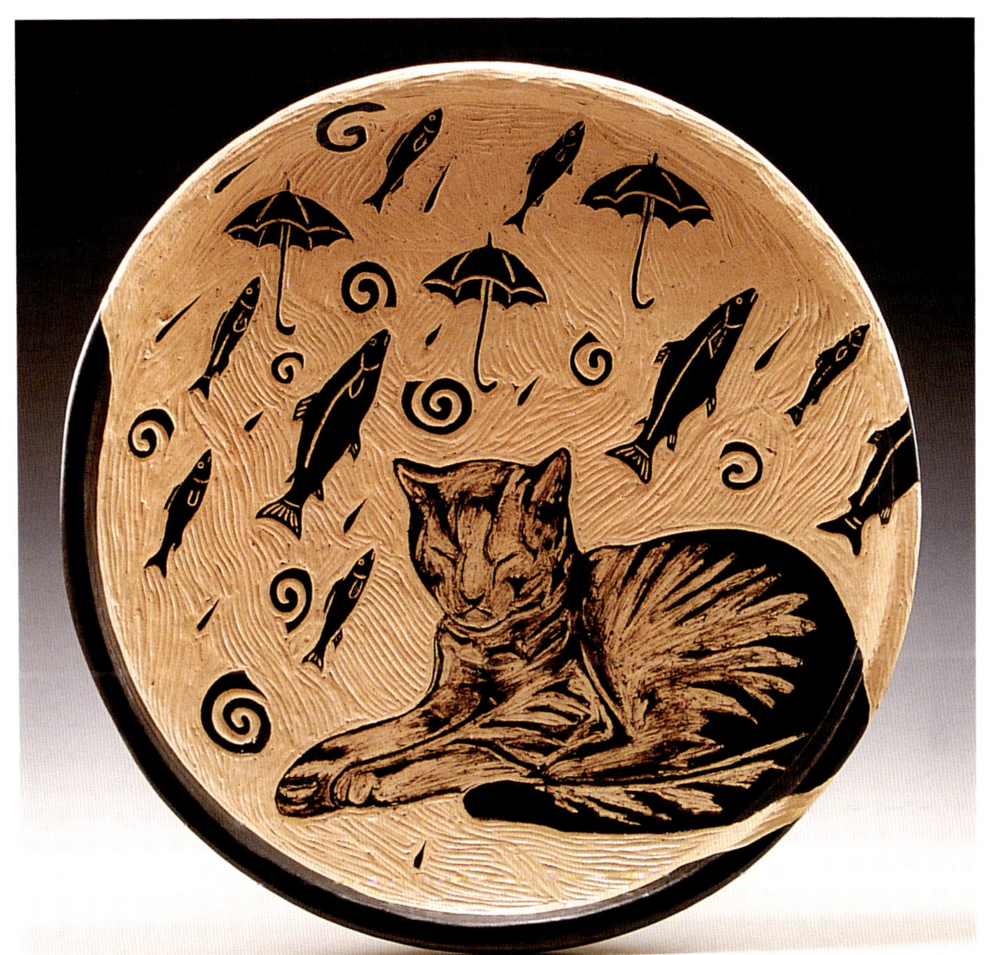

Bryan Hiveley

CAT NAP Platter | 2004

7 X 18 INCHES (17.8 X 45.7 CM)

Hand-built earthenware; sgraffito; electric fired, cone 03

PHOTO BY ARTIST

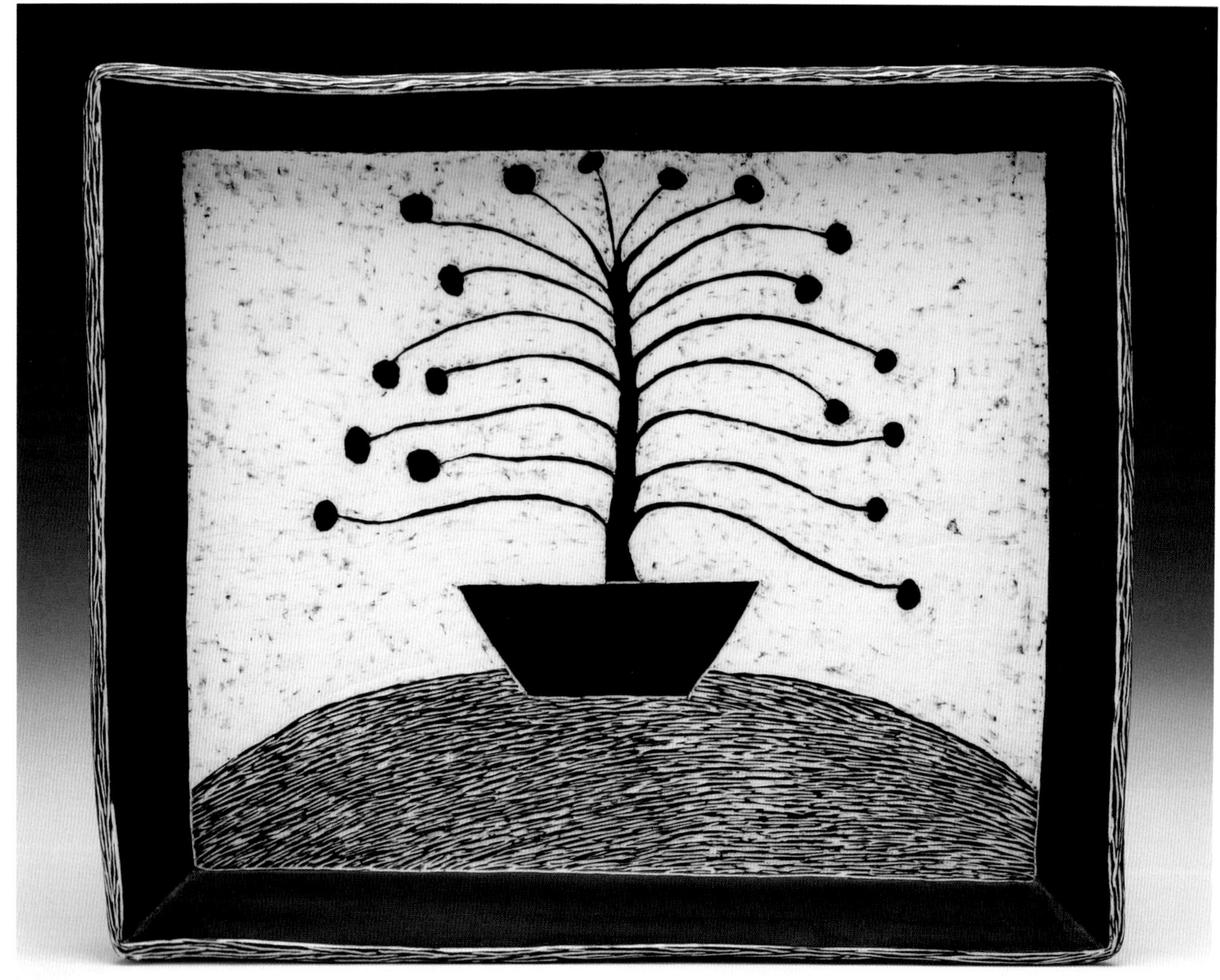

Francine Trearchis Ozereko

Aussie Tree Plate | 2004

2 X 12 X 10 INCHES (5.1 X 30.5 X 25.4 CM)

Slab-formed porcelain; black slip, sgraffito; clear glaze, electric fired, cone 7

PHOTO BY JOHN POLAK

I. Daniel Murphy

Crybaby Plate | 2006

1 1/2 X 11 INCHES (3.8 X 27.9 X 27.9 CM)

Wheel-thrown and turned iron-rich clay; white slip, ash glaze with oxides; oxidation fired, cone 8

PHOTO BY ARTIST

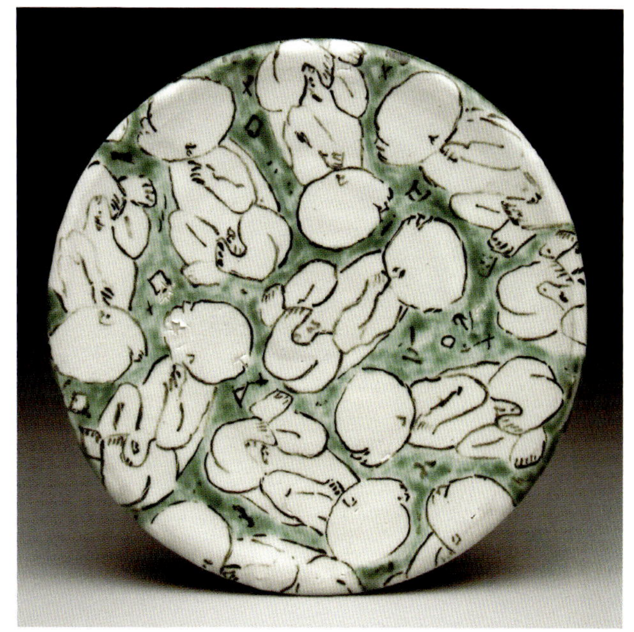

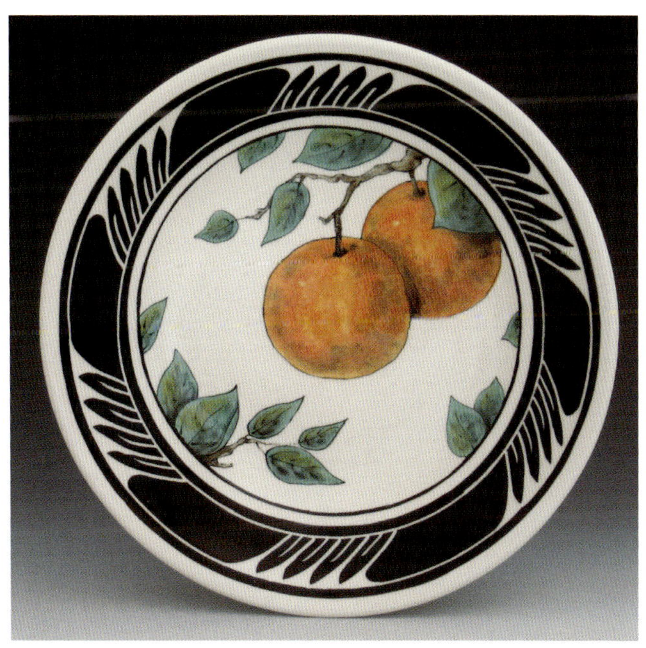

Rita McGie

Plate with Oranges | 2007

2 X 11 1/4 INCHES (5.1 X 28.6 CM)

Wheel-thrown porcelaneous stoneware; underglazes, sgraffito; clear glaze, electric fired, cone 6

PHOTO BY JOHN MCGIE

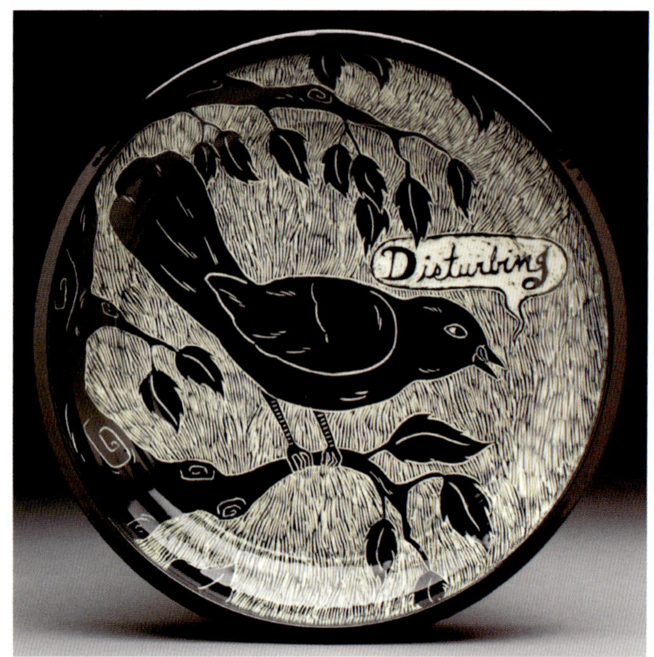

Kathy King

Disturbing Yet Delicious | 2006

EACH: 2 X 11 3/4 INCHES (5 X 30 CM)

Wheel-thrown, mid-range porcelain; sgraffito; electric fired, cone 6 oxidation

PHOTOS BY EDDIE ING PHOTOGRAPHY

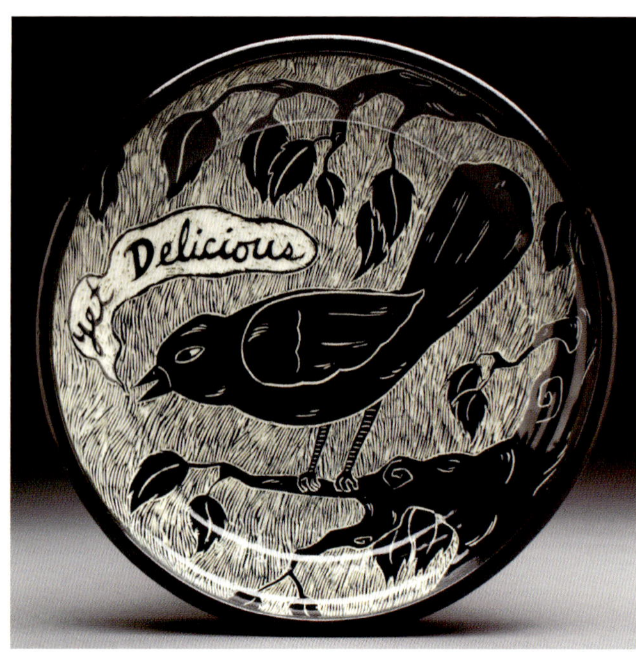

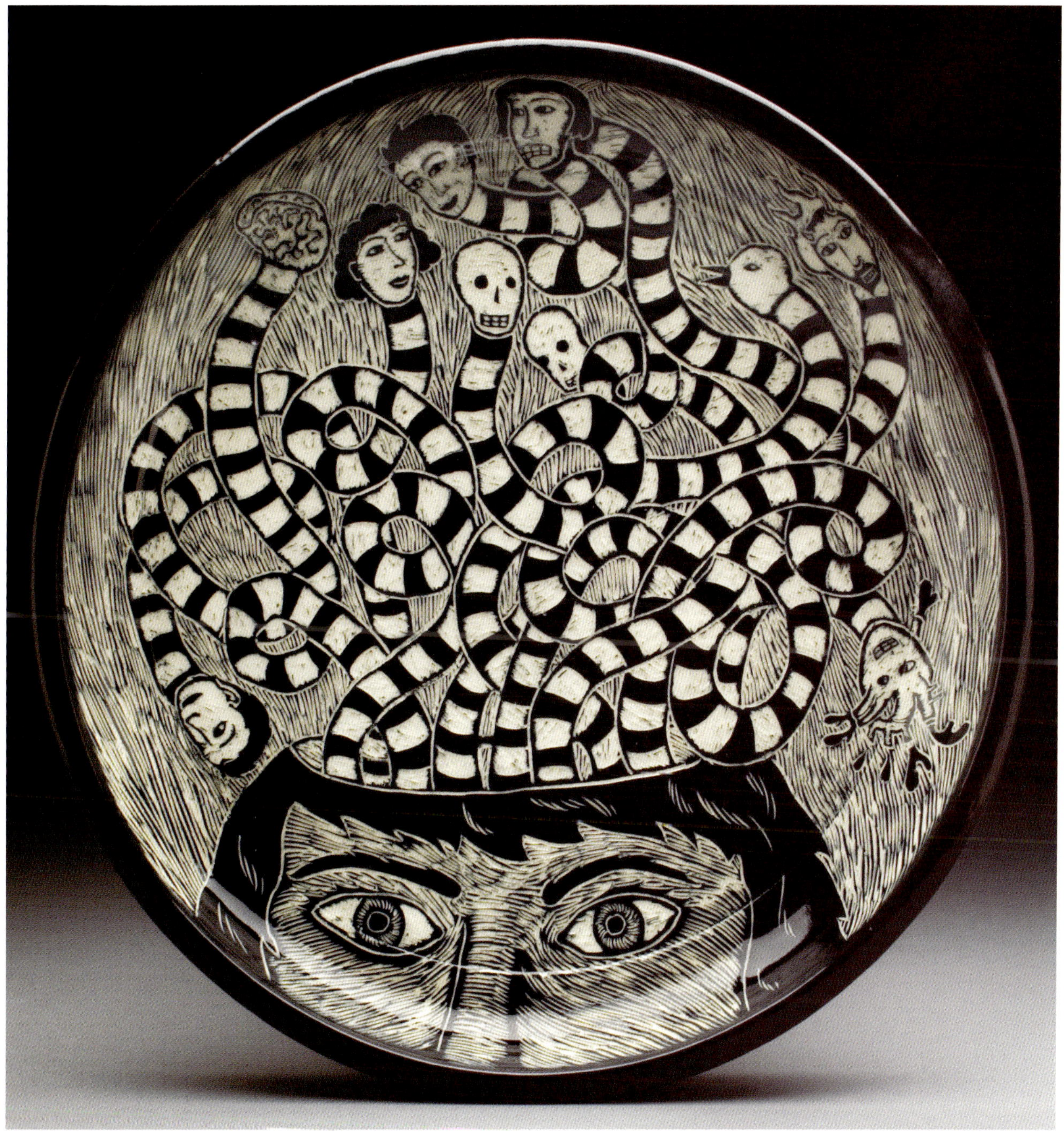

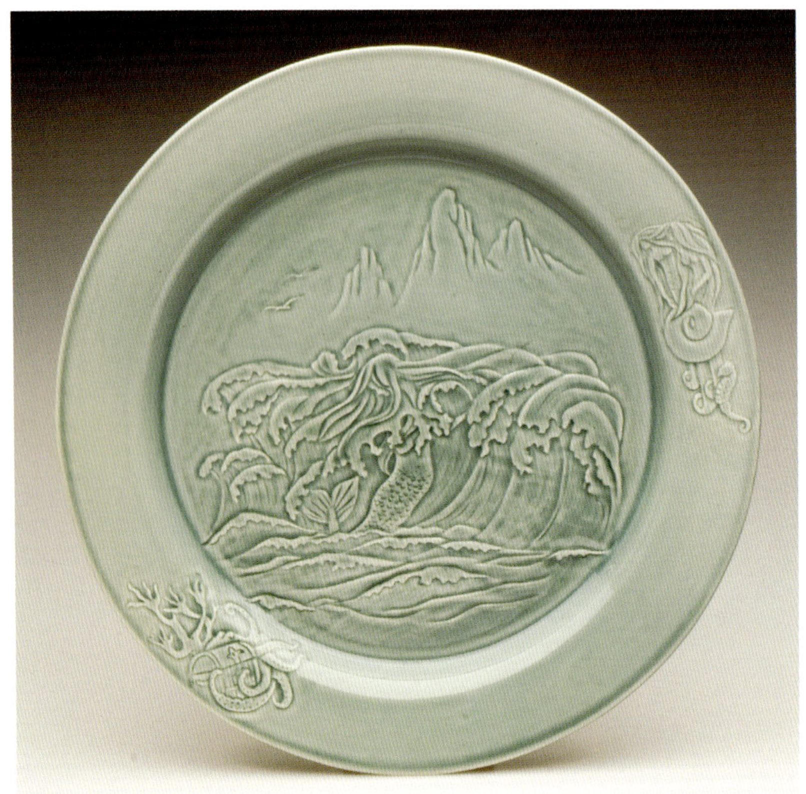

M. Kathleen Matsushita

The Little Mermaid | 2006

13 INCHES (33 CM) IN DIAMETER

Wheel-thrown porcelain; carved, sprayed; electric fired, cone 6

PHOTOS BY DALE RODDICK

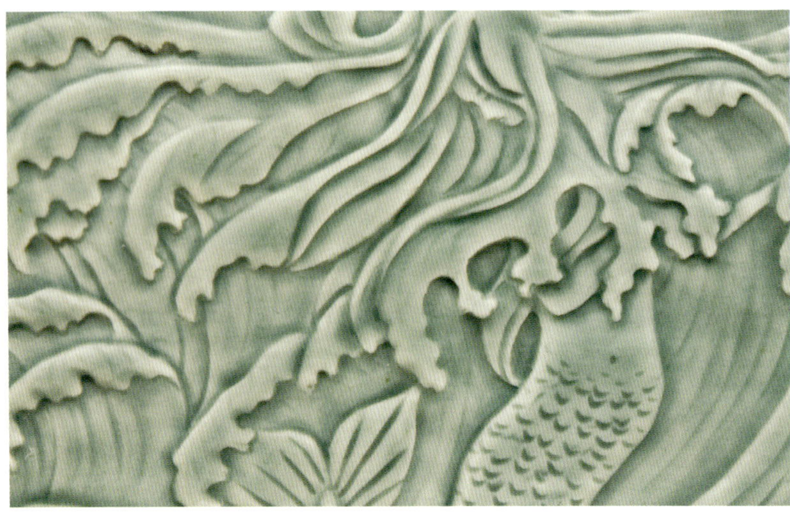

Carole M. Cascio

Untitled | 2006

3 X 11 1/2 X 11 1/2 INCHES (7.6 X 29.2 X 29.2 CM)

Slab-built, slump-molded, and hand-carved porcelain; electric fired, cone 6; glazes, cone 04 bisque

PHOTO BY ALAIN JARAMILLO

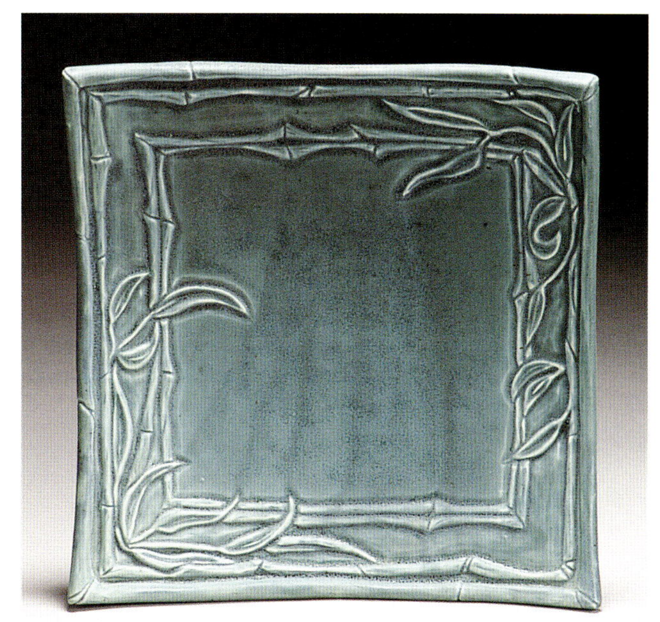

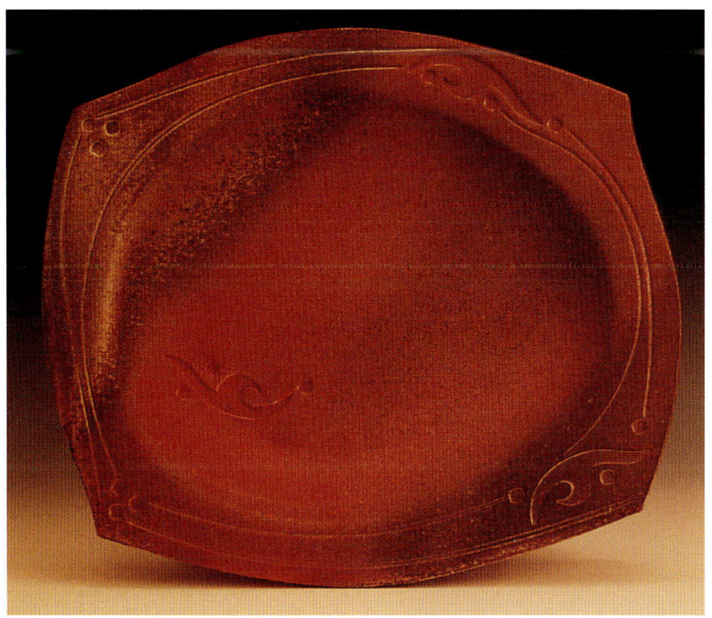

JoAnne DeKeuster

Untitled | 2007

1 X 15 X 13 INCHES (2.5 X 38.1 X 33 CM)

Hand-built white stoneware; wood fired, cone 12

PHOTO BY ARTIST

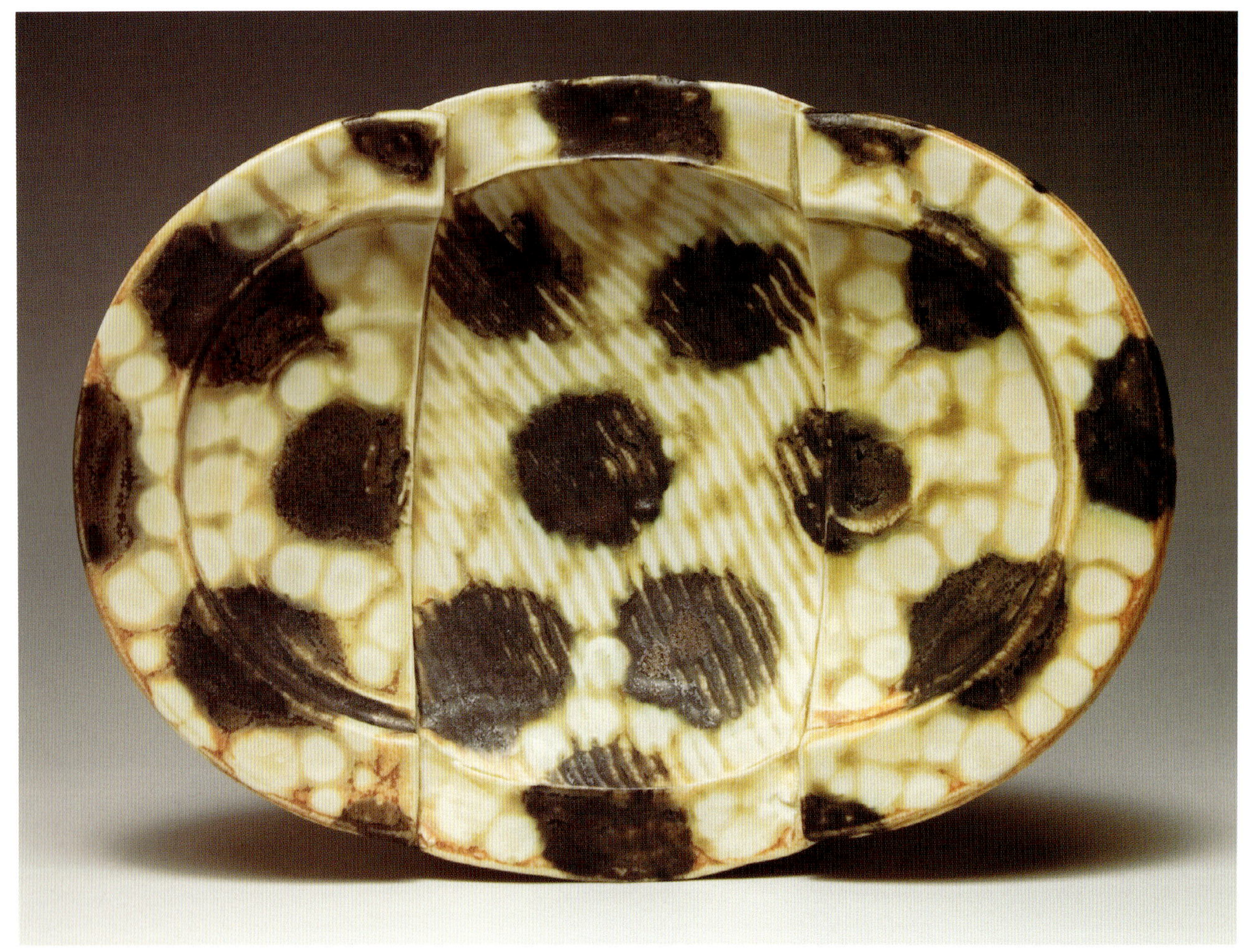

Frank Martin

Untitled | 2006

2 X 9½ X 7 INCHES (5.1 X 24.1 X 17.8 CM)

Wheel-thrown vitreous china with wheel-thrown and hand-formed additions; electric fired, cone 4

PHOTO BY ARTIST

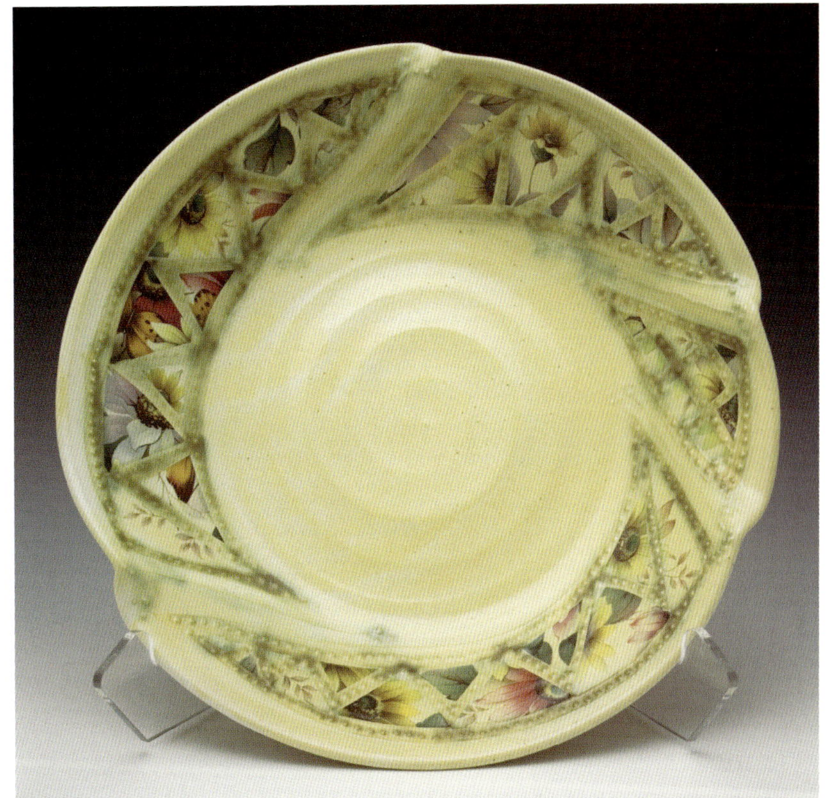

Carolynne Pynn-Trudeau

Untitled | 2007

2½ X 13 INCHES (6.4 X 33 CM)

Wheel-thrown porcelain/stoneware; electric fired, cone 9; antique ceramic decals, cone 017; overglaze enamels, cone 017

PHOTOS BY ANNE CHAMBERS

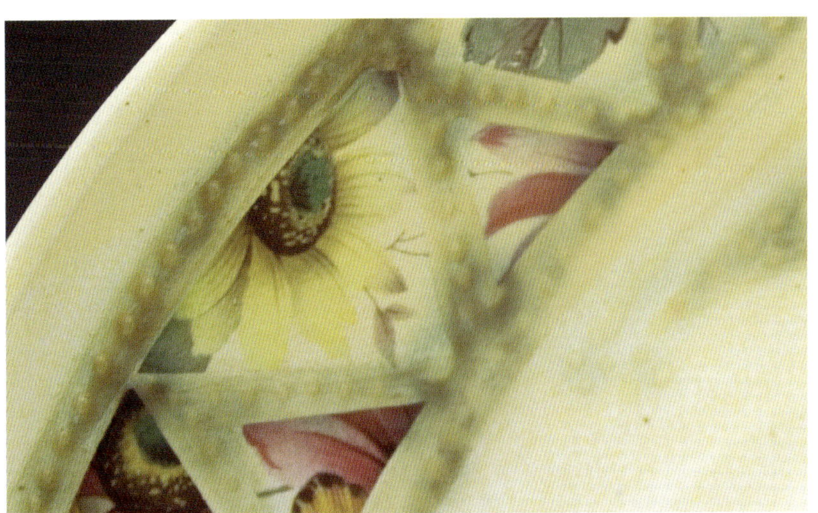

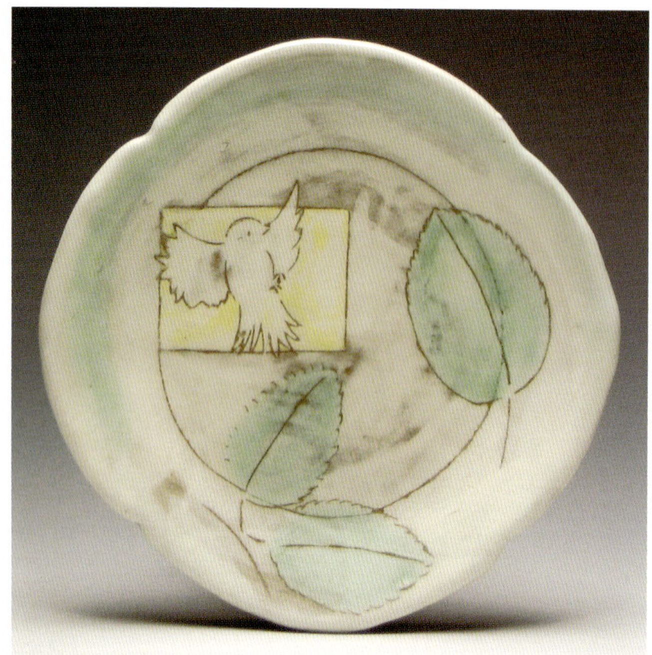

Rachel Berg

Suspended with Leaves | 2007

1 X 8 X 8 INCHES (2.5 X 20.3 X 20.3 CM)

Slab-built stoneware; brushed slips, sgraffito; electric fired, cone 6

PHOTO BY ARTIST

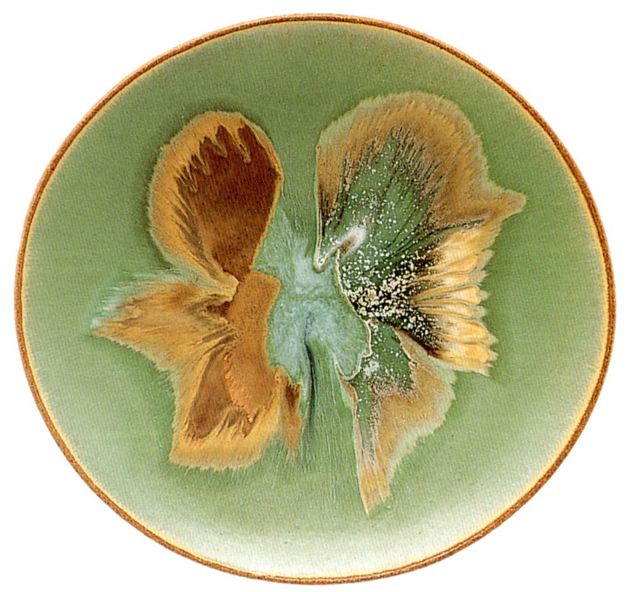

Chris Gustin

Untitled | 2002

4 X 26 X 25 INCHES (10.2 X 66 X 63.5 CM)

Wheel-thrown and altered stoneware; gas fired, cone 11; glazes, cone 11

PHOTO BY DEAN POWELL PHOTOGRAPHY

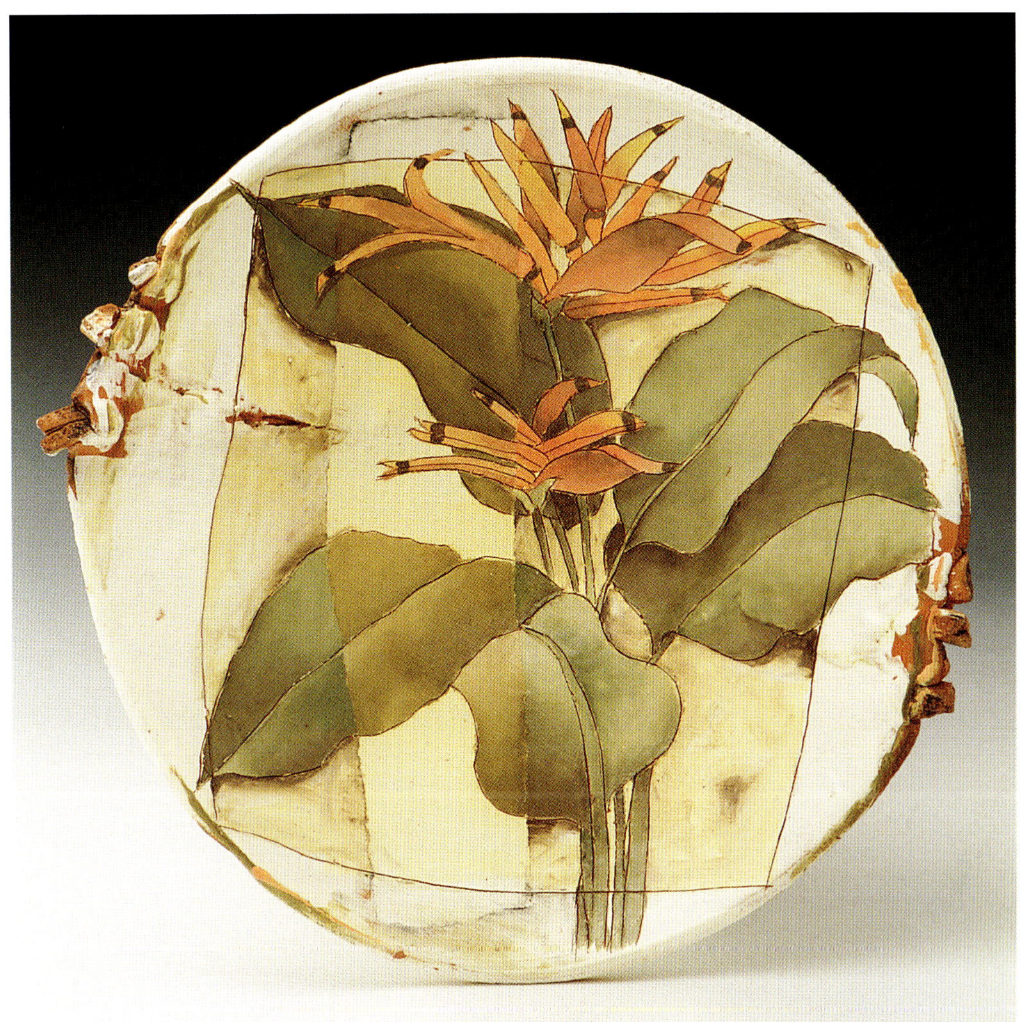

Tim Ludwig

Platter with Heliconia | 2006

4 X 20 INCHES (10.2 X 50.8 CM)

Wheel-thrown earthenware; slips and Mason stains; electric fired, cone 06

PHOTO BY RANDALL SMITH

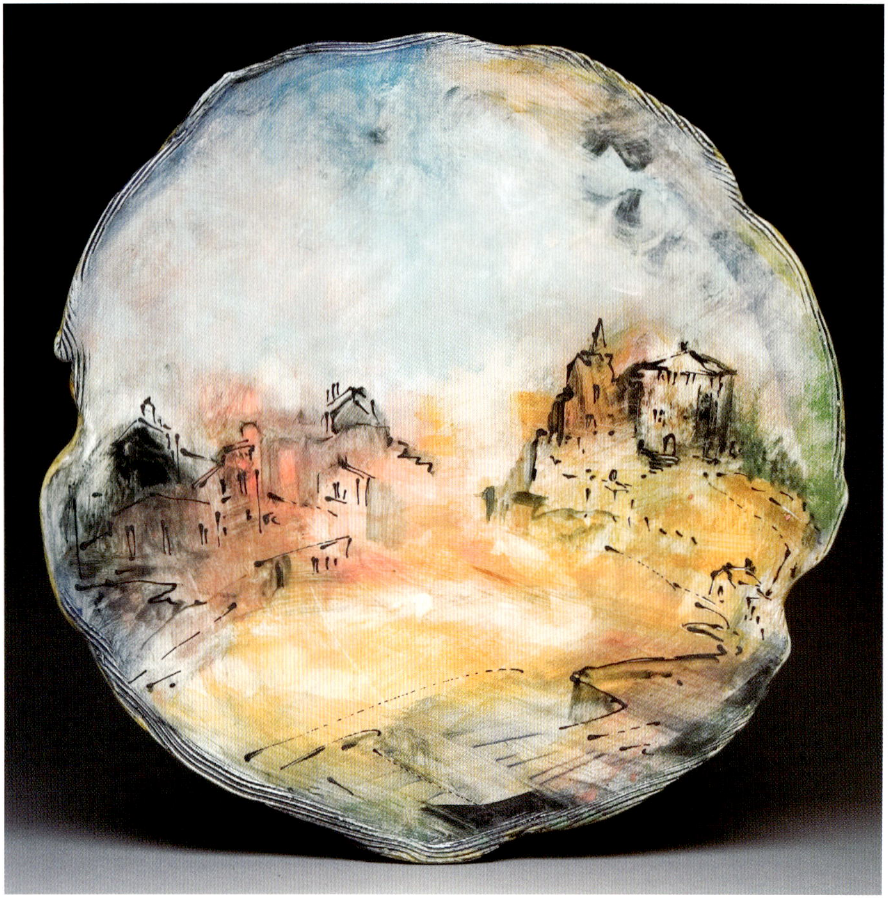

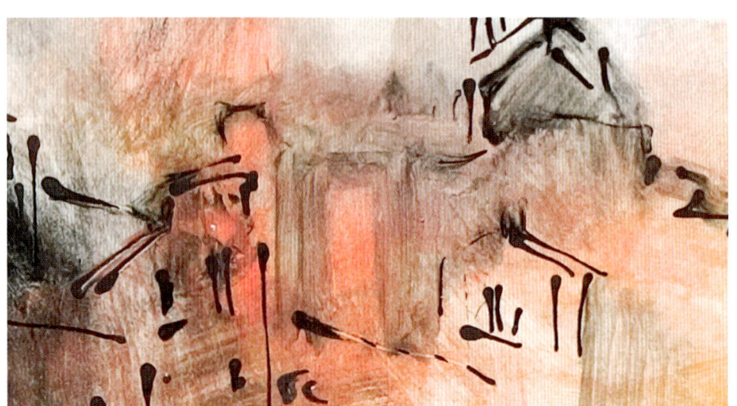

Laurie Shaman

Townscape | 2005

3 X 14 X 14 INCHES (7.6 X 35.6 X 35.6 CM)

Hand-built earthenware; slip trailed and underglazed; electric fired, cone 04; glazes, cone 06

PHOTOS BY PETER KIAR

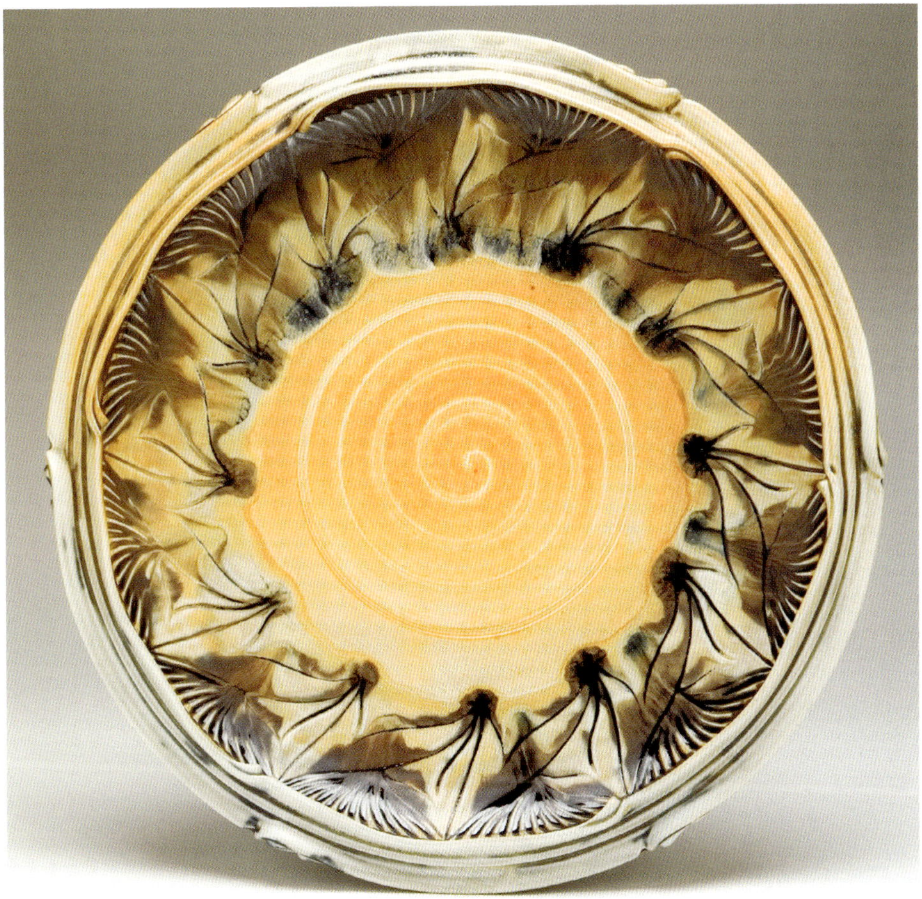

Kathryne Koop

Tan Platter | 2007

2½ X 15½ INCHES (6.4 X 39.4 CM)

Wheel-thrown, altered, and carved porcelain; multi-glazed; gas fired in reduction, cone 11

PHOTOS BY BRUCE SPIELMAN

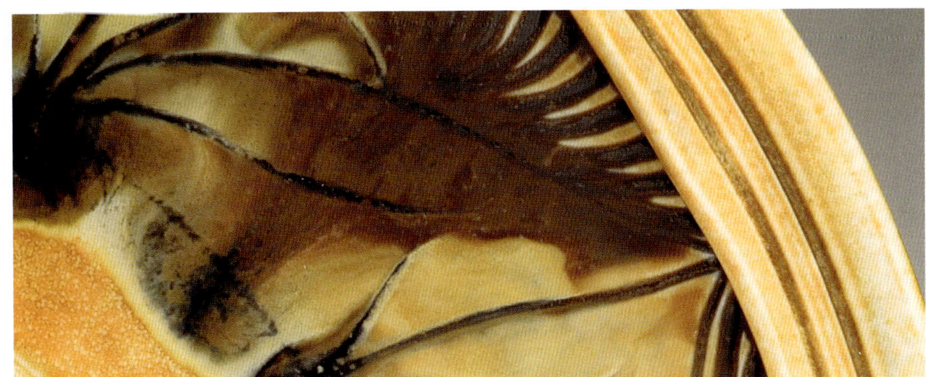

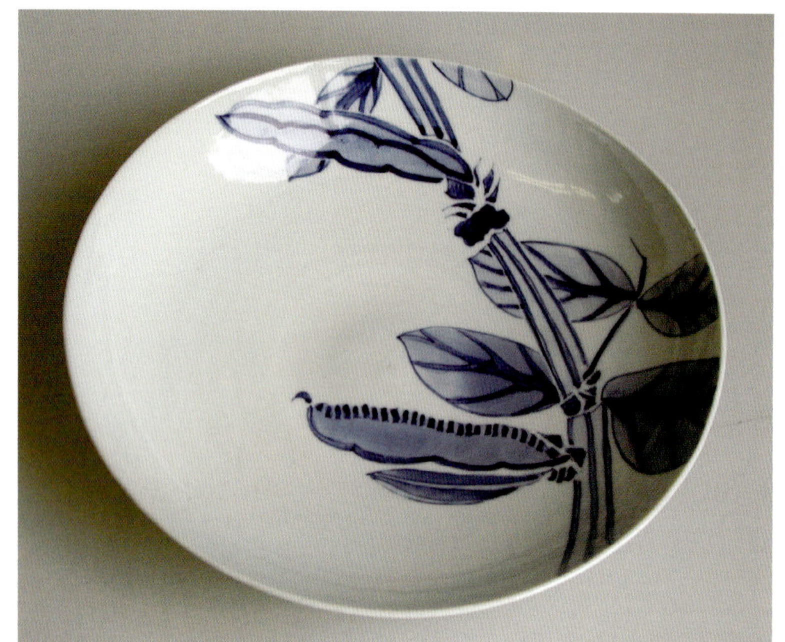

Celina Clavijo Kashu

Sora Mame | 2004

2 X 10 3/8 INCHES (5 X 26.5 CM)

Wheel-thrown porcelain; gas fired in reduction, cone 9; underglaze cobalt brushwork

PHOTO BY ARTIST

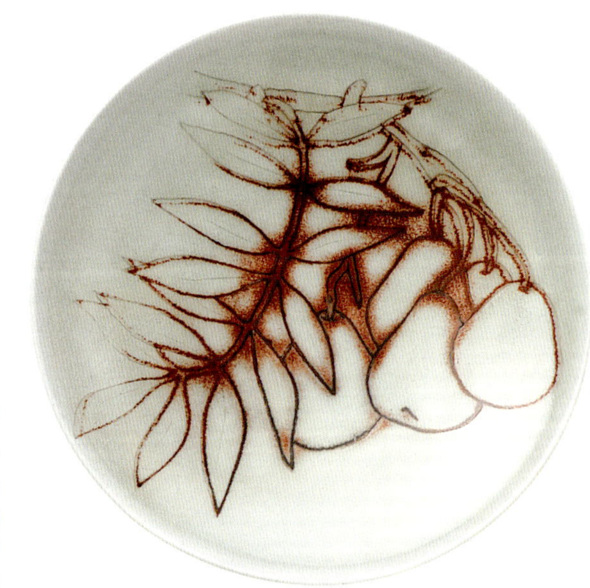

Kathryn E. Narrow

Sorb Apple Plate | 1985

1 1/2 X 9 INCHES (3.8 X 22.9 CM)

Thrown porcelain; inlay with colored slip; celadon glaze, gas fired, cone 6

PHOTO BY JOHN CARLANO

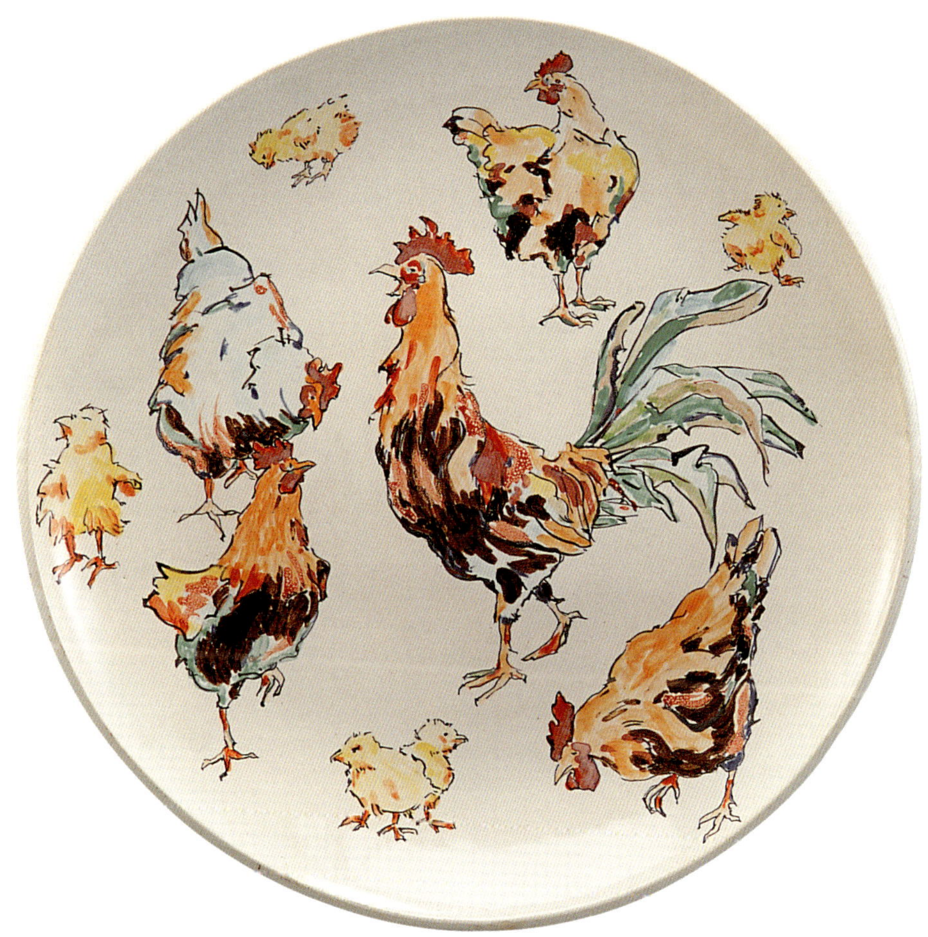

Leticia Dueñas
Petr S. Lenda

Chicken & Rooster Sampler | 2001

15 INCHES (38.1 CM) IN DIAMETER

Slab and coil hand-built earthenware;
glaze, electric fired, cone 05

PHOTO BY HAP SAKWA

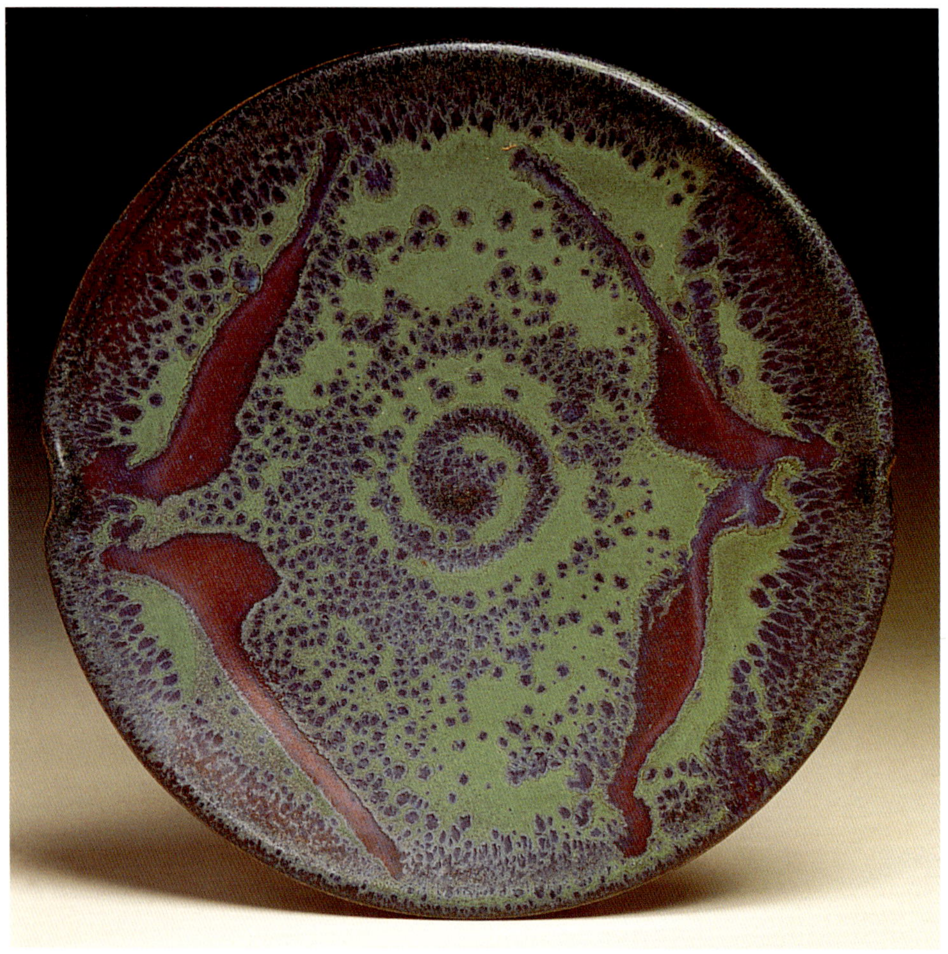

Ginny Marsh

Plate | 2007

1 1/8 X 7 1/4 INCHES (2.9 X 18.4 CM)

Wheel-thrown stoneware; matte glaze, glossy glaze, and wax; reduction fired with natural gas, cone 10

PHOTO BY ARTIST

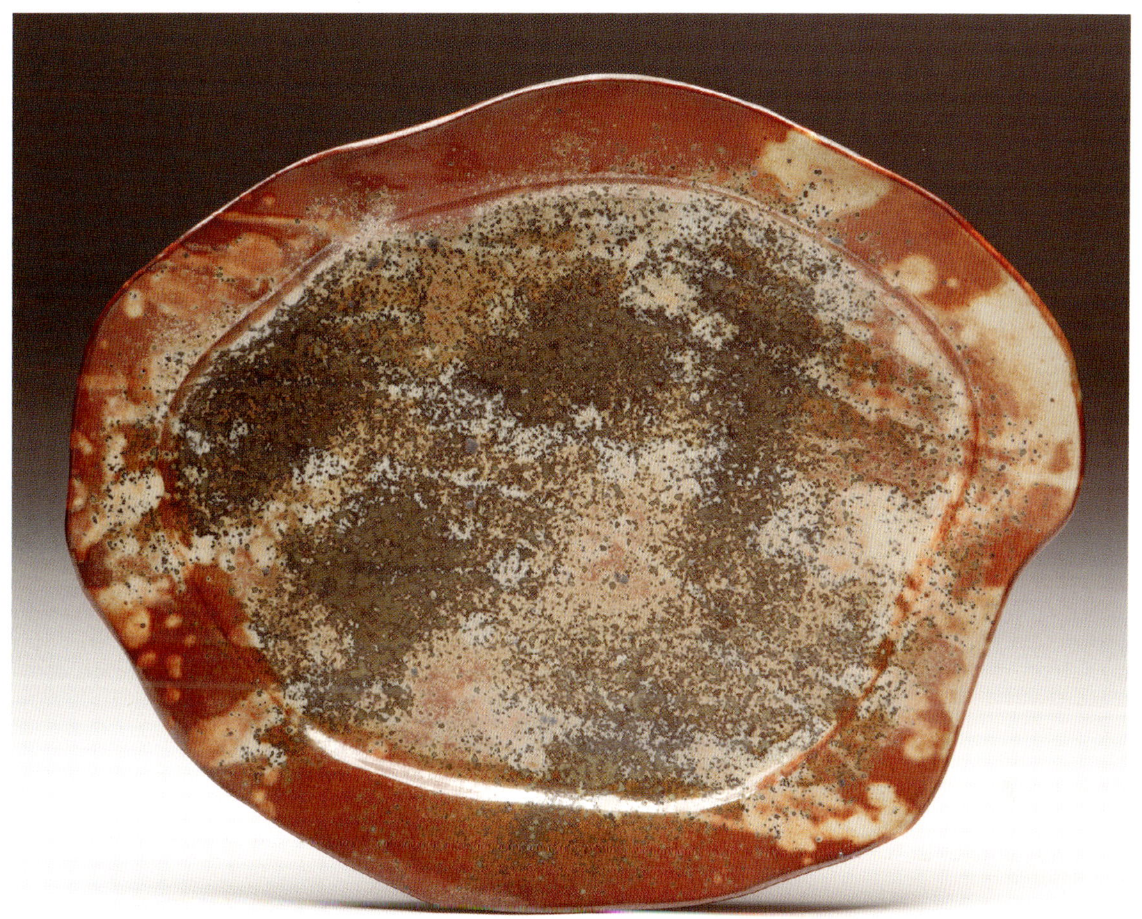

Alice Chittenden

Oval Platter | 2006

1 1/8 X 17 1/2 X 14 INCHES (2.9 X 44.5 X 35.6 CM)

Hand-built stoneware; shino glaze, wood ash; reduction fired, cone 10

PHOTO BY TOM HOPKINS

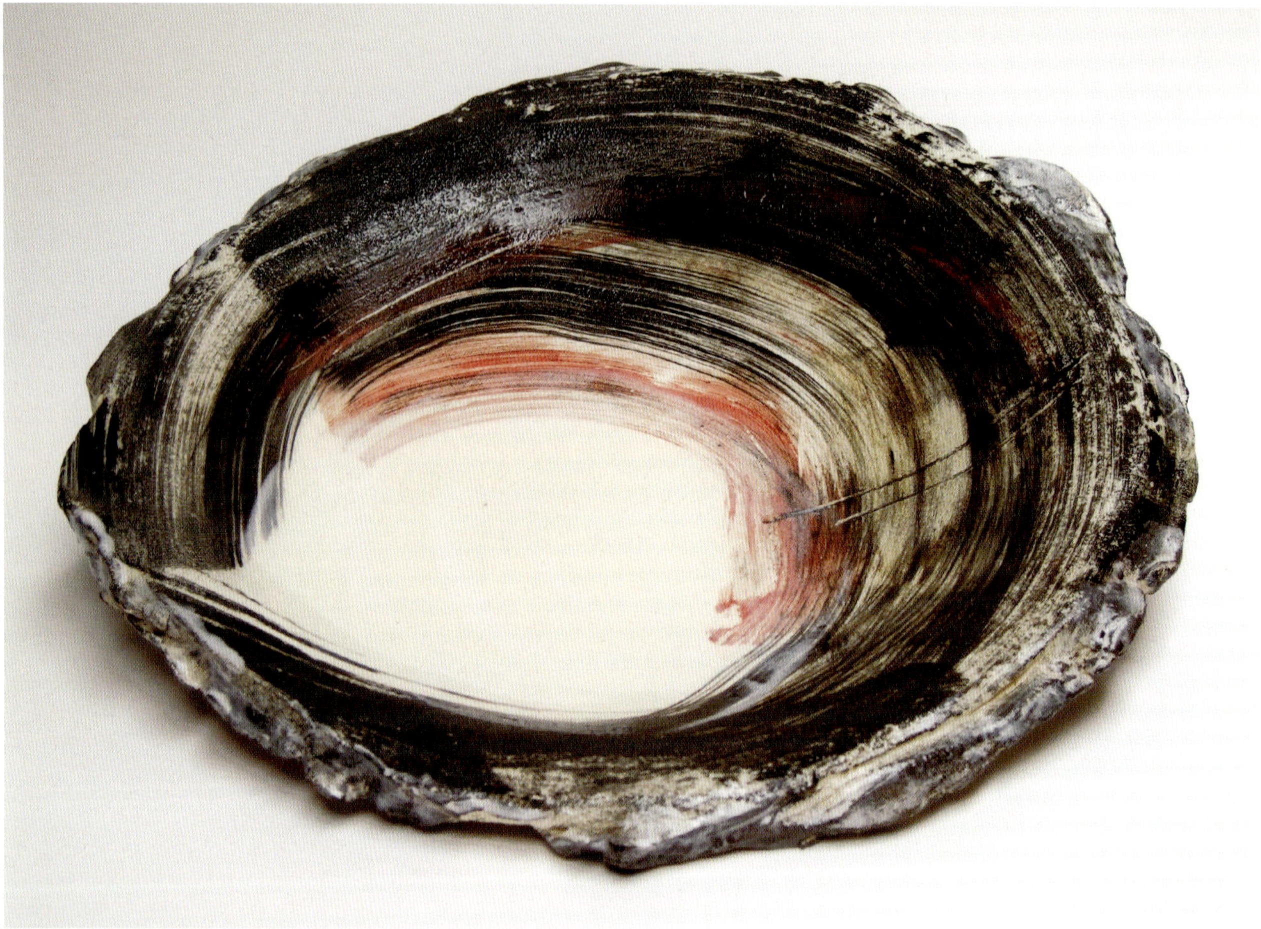

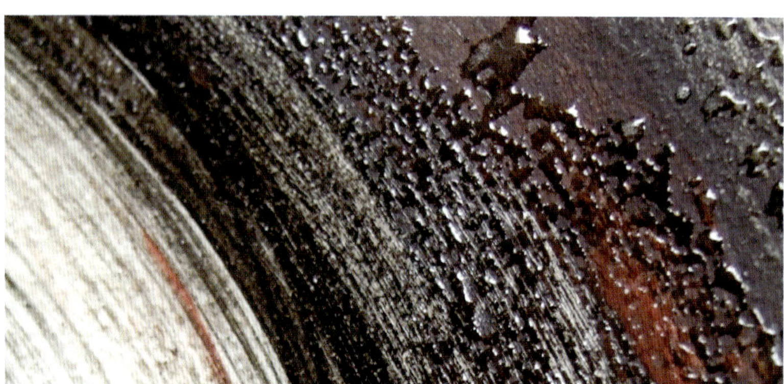

Suzanne Shelley

Abstract Retro | 2006

2 X 15 X 14 INCHES (5.1 X 38.1 X 35.6 CM)

Hand-built paper clay; gas fired, cone 9

PHOTOS BY ARTIST

Christine M. Colombarini

Red-Line Platter | 2006

5 X 20 INCHES (12.7 X 50.8 CM)

Slip cast and hand built; primitive low-fire with straw; post-fire embellishment

PHOTO BY JOHN LUCAS

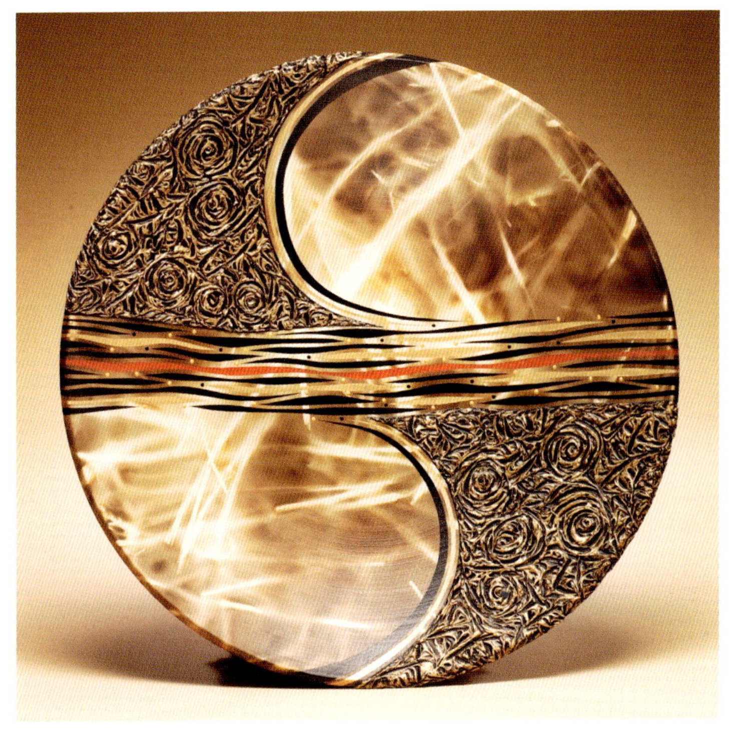

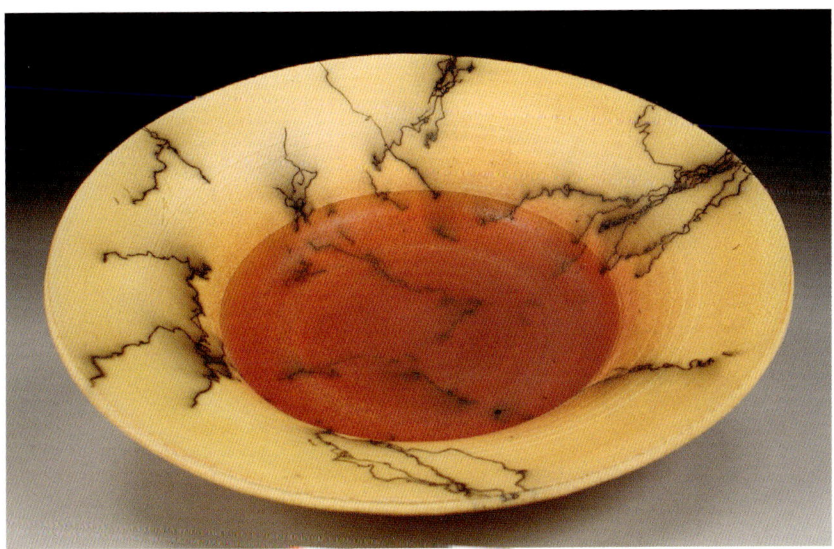

Marcy Rogge

Untitled | 2007

$2\frac{1}{2}$ X $12\frac{1}{2}$ X $12\frac{1}{2}$ INCHES (6.4 X 31.8 X 31.8 CM)

Wheel-thrown smooth raku; raku fired, 1400°F (760°C); horsehair and ferric chloride decoration

PHOTO BY TOM VICIAN

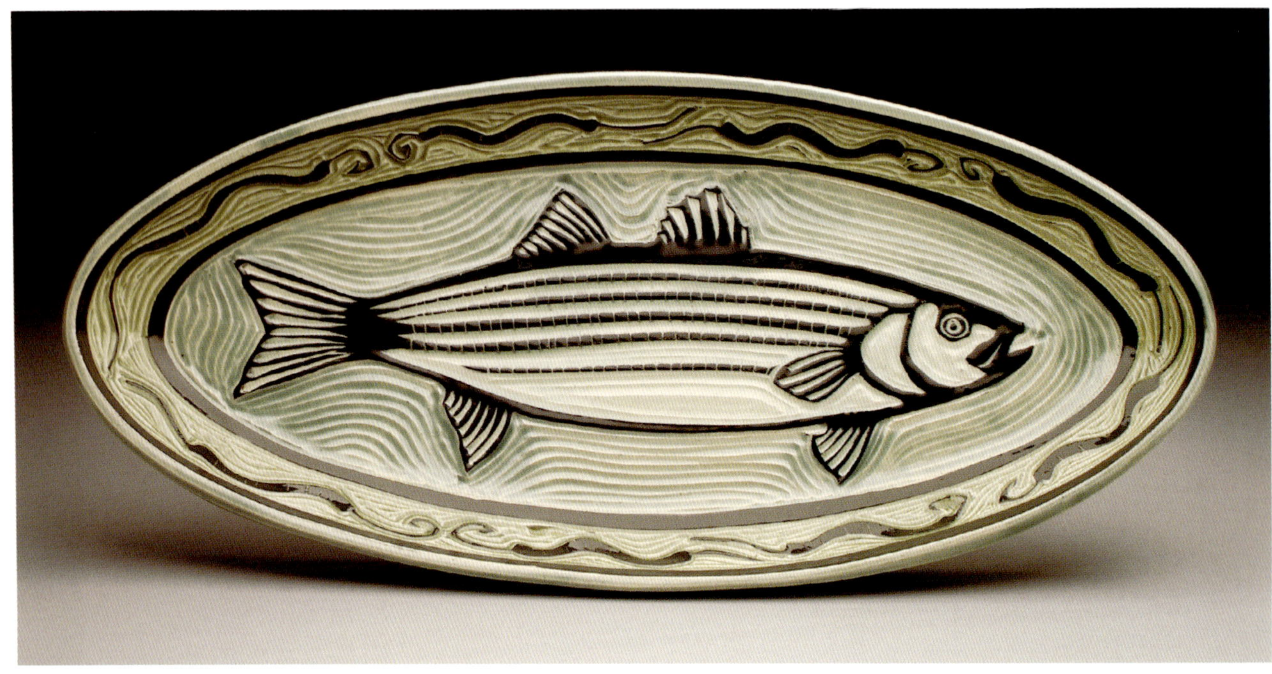

Ruchika Madan

Bass Platter | 2006

$2\frac{1}{2}$ X 19 X 10 INCHES (6.4 X 48.3 X 25.4 CM)

Hand-built white stoneware; sgraffito and carved; oxidation fired, cone 6

PHOTO BY ARTIST

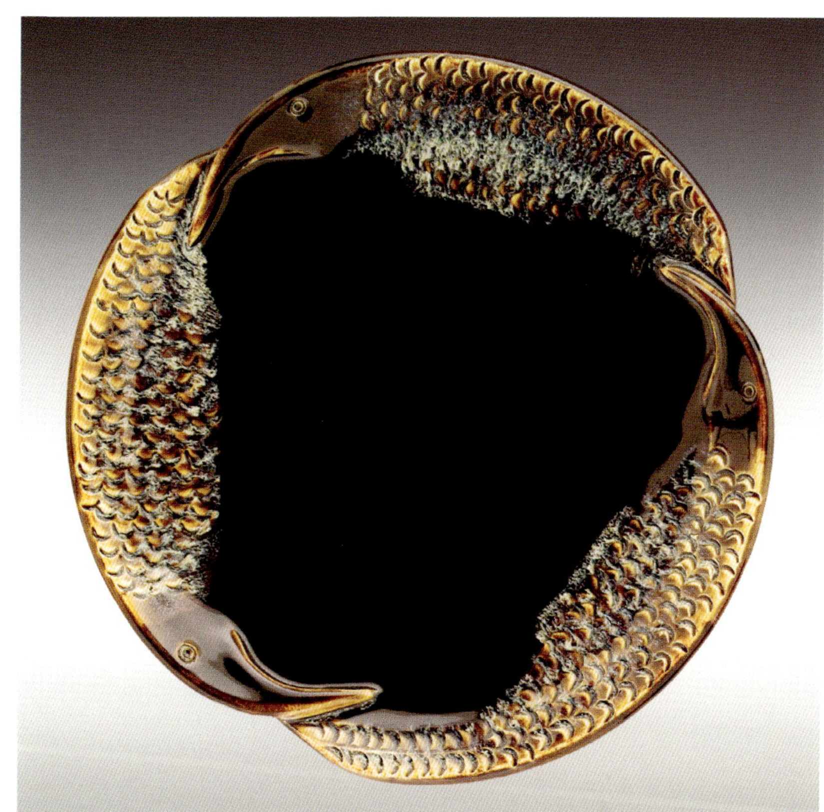

Chic Lotz

Circling | 2005

1 1/4 X 11 INCHES (3.2 X 27.9 CM)

Wheel-thrown and altered stoneware; glazes, electric fired, cone 6

PHOTOS BY STEVE BUCKLEY

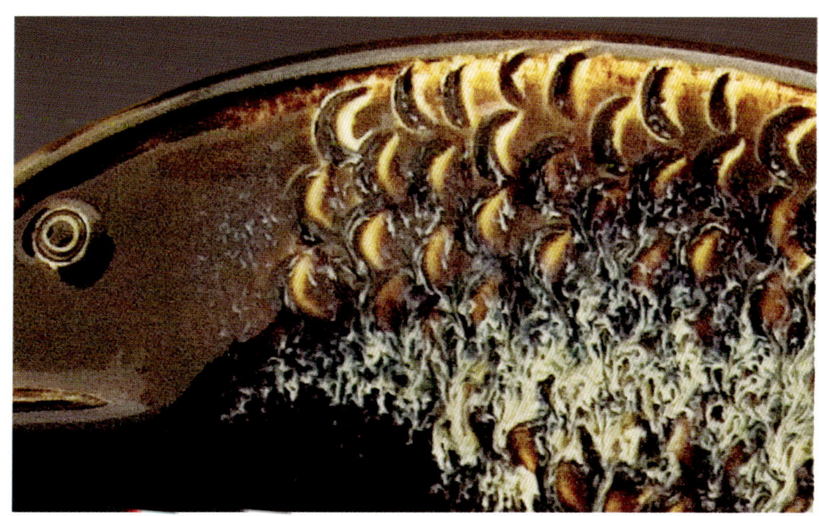

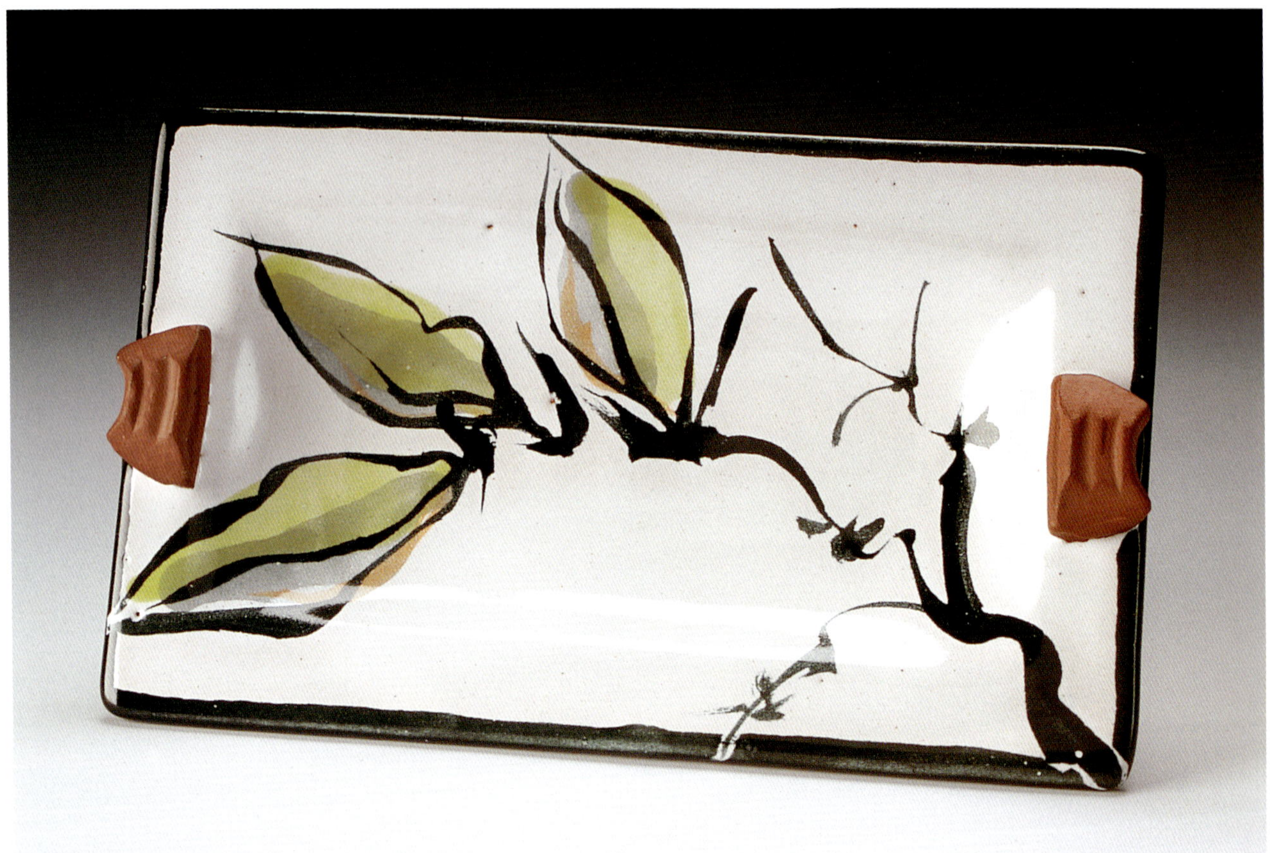

Randy Hinson

Truffle Tray | 2005

6 1/2 X 3 3/4 INCHES (16.5 X 9.5 CM)

Hand-built terra cotta; majolica; electric fired, cone 03

PHOTO BY LYNN RUCK

Jennifer Everett

Square Platter | 2006

2 X 11 X 11 INCHES (5.1 X 27.9 X 27.9 CM)

Hand-built stoneware; stamped; multiple glazes; gas fired in reduction, cone 10

PHOTO BY ARTIST

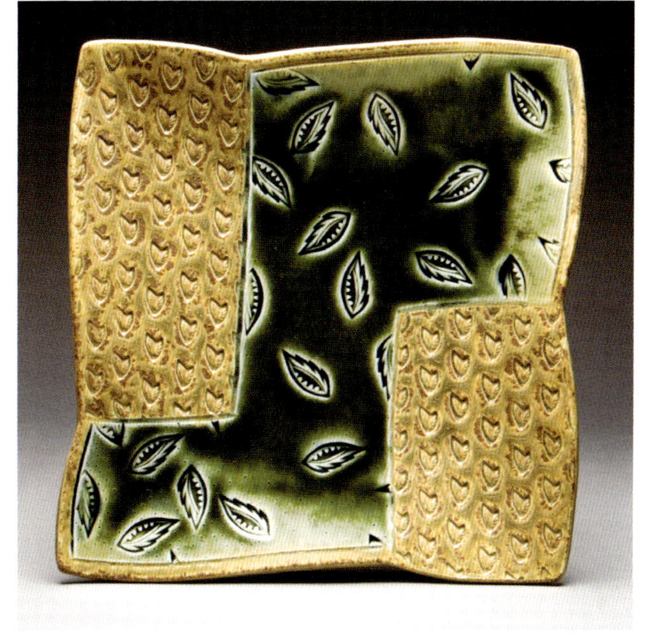

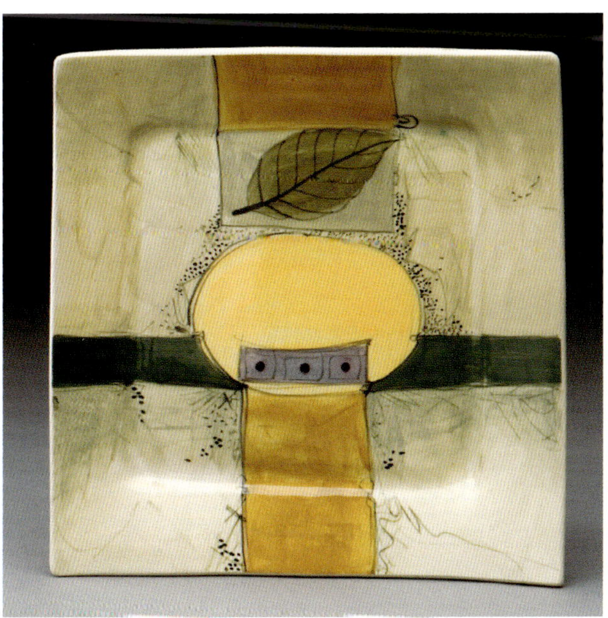

Susan Vey

Relic Plate | 2007

1 ½ X 8 X 8 INCHES (3.8 X 20.3 X 20.3 CM)

Hand-built white stoneware; underglaze painting, clear glaze; electric fired, cone 6

PHOTO BY RANDY SMITH

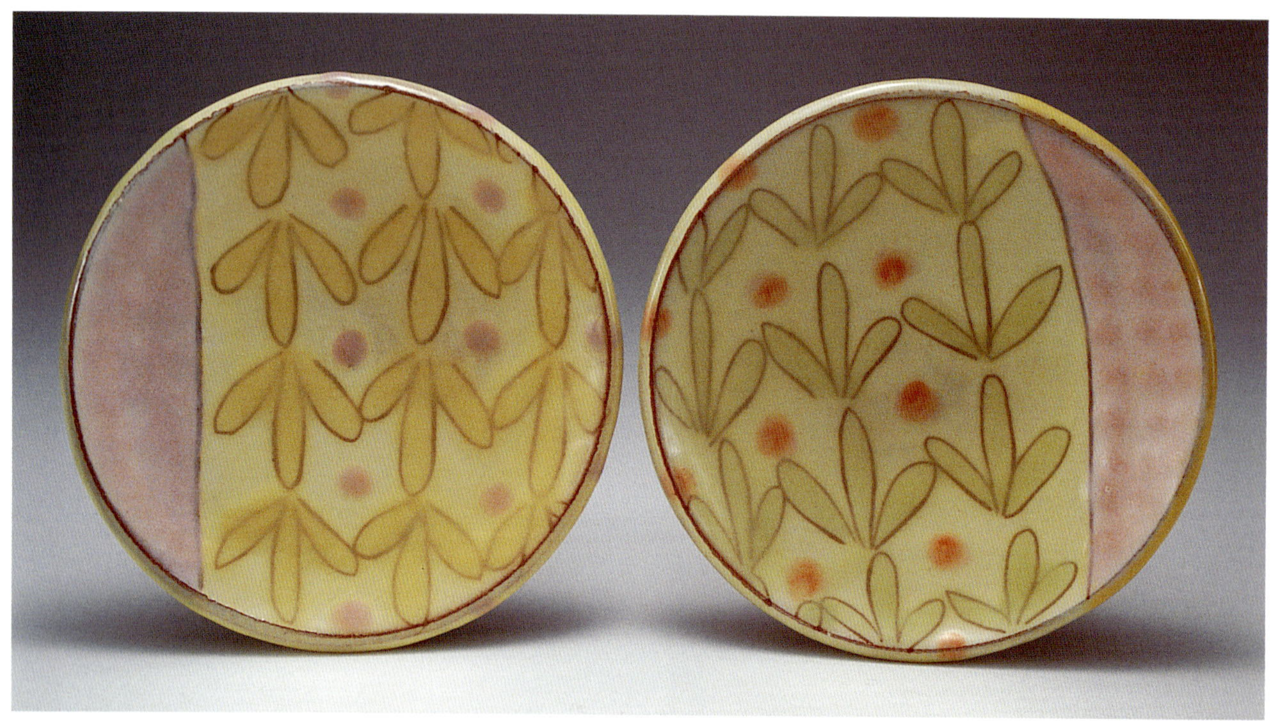

Kristin Pavelka

Tidbit Plates | 2007

EACH: 1 X 5 INCHES (2.5 X 12.7 CM)

Wheel-thrown earthenware; slip, sgraffito; polychrome glazes; electric fired, cone 04

PHOTO BY ARTIST

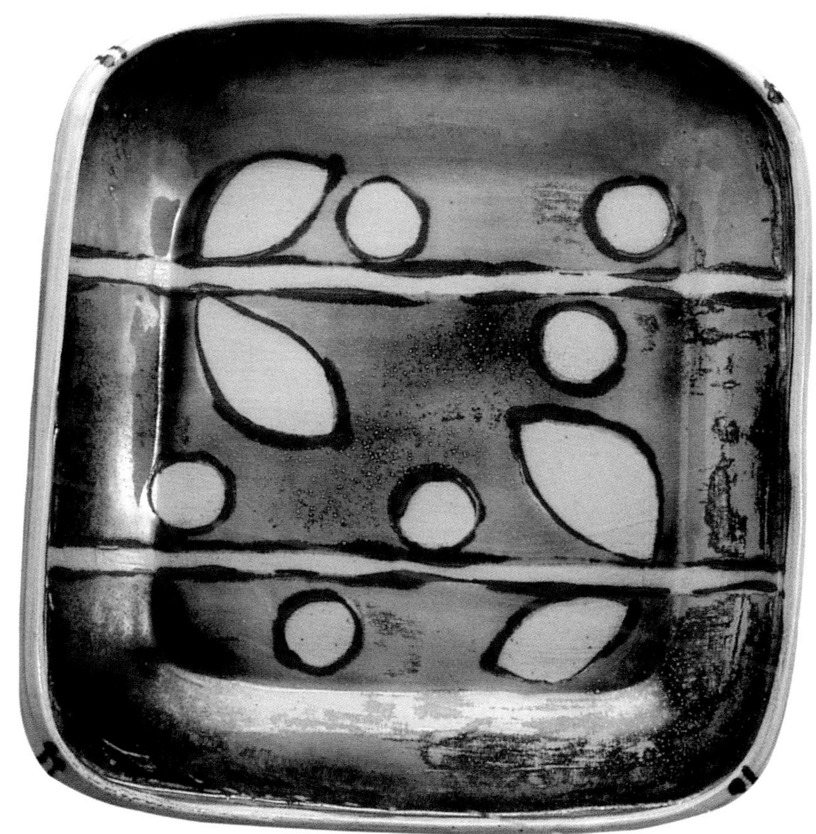

Suze Lindsay

Serving Platter | 2007

$2^1/_2$ X 14 X 14 INCHES (6.4 X 35.6 X 35.6 CM)

Slab-built stoneware; paper resist, glaze; salt fired, cone 10

PHOTO BY TOM MILLS

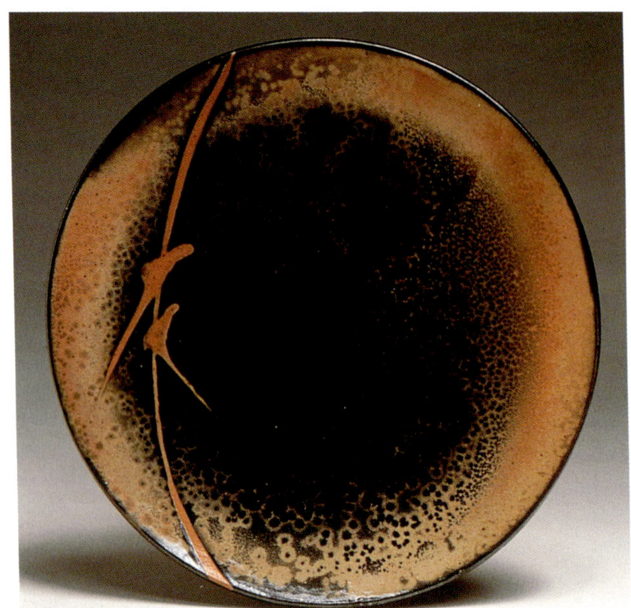

Malcolm Davis

Shino Platter | 2005

1 X 12 INCHES (2.5 X 30.5 CM)

Slab-built and thrown Grolleg porcelain; wax resist; ultra-carbonated shino-type glaze, gas fired in heavy reduction, cone 10

PHOTO BY D. JAMES DEE

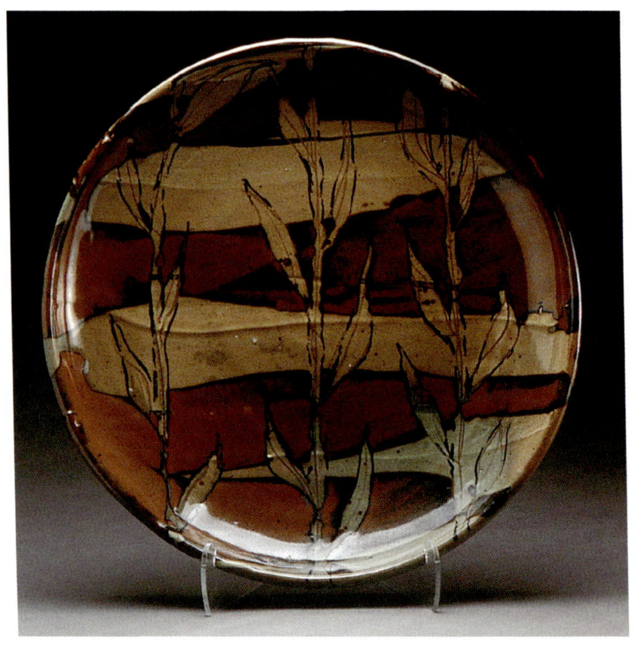

Kent McLaughlin

Platter | 2006

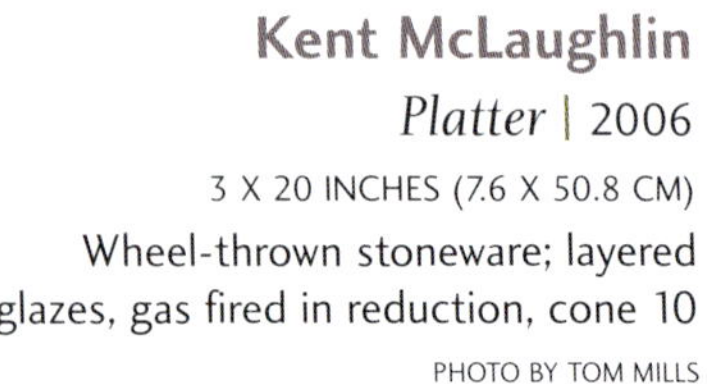

3 X 20 INCHES (7.6 X 50.8 CM)

Wheel-thrown stoneware; layered glazes, gas fired in reduction, cone 10

PHOTO BY TOM MILLS

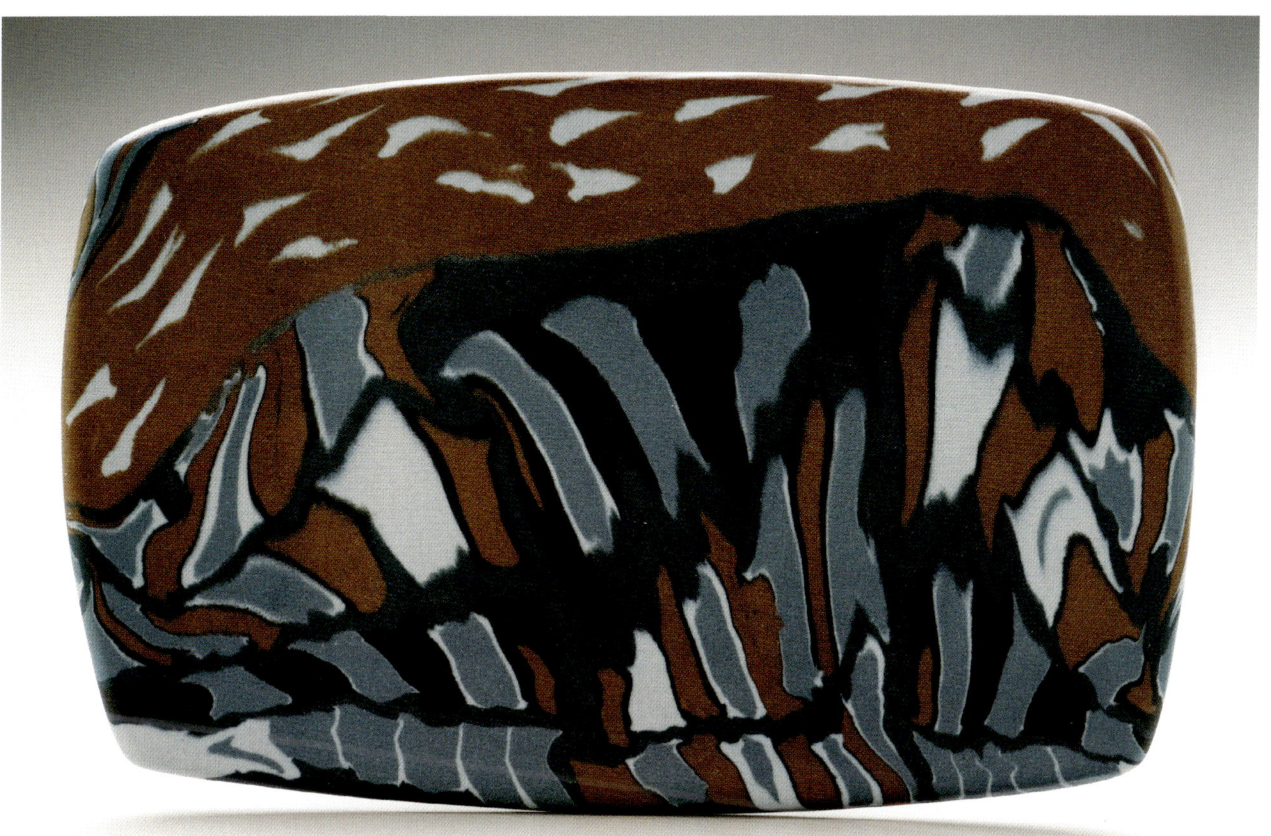

Jeanet Dreskin-Haig

Tide Pool Butter Plate | 2007

$^1/_2$ X 5$^1/_2$ X 3$^1/_2$ INCHES (1.3 X 14 X 8.9 CM)

Hand-built with laminated multi-colored porcelain; unglazed; electric fired, cone 6; polished with wet/dry sandpaper

PHOTO BY HARRISON EVANS

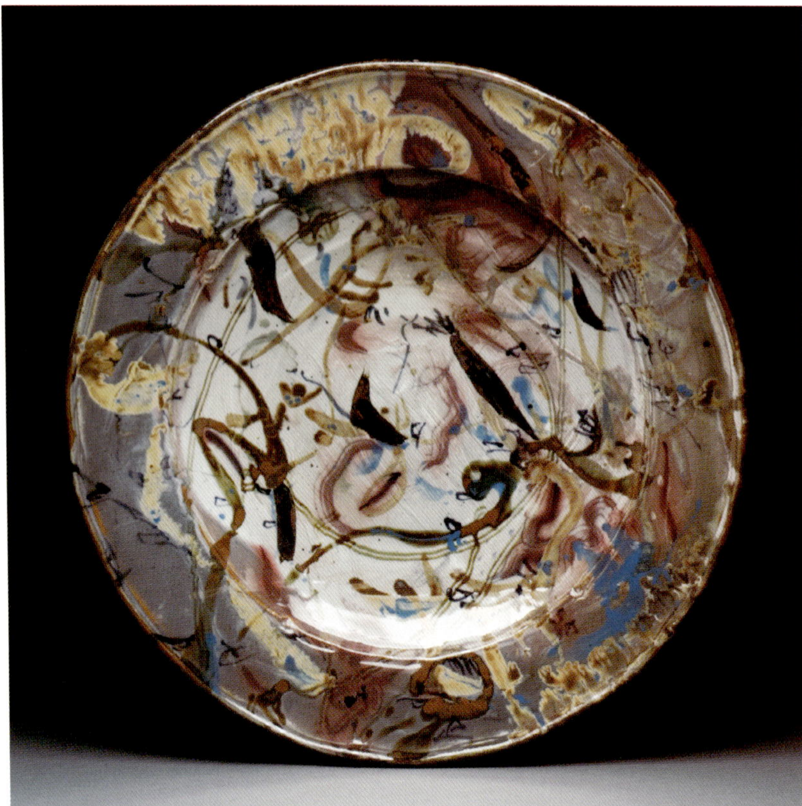

John Glick

Plate | 2007

3½ X 24 INCHES (8.9 X 61 CM)

Wheel-thrown stoneware; multiple slips and glazes; reduction fired, cone 10

PHOTOS BY ARTIST

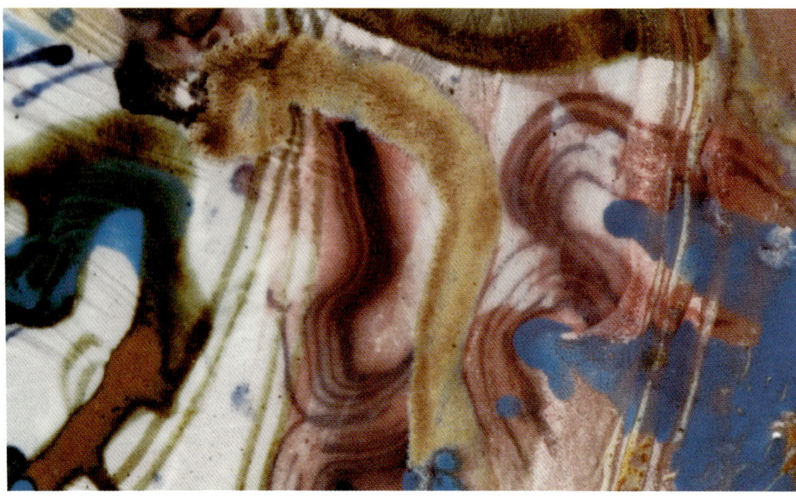

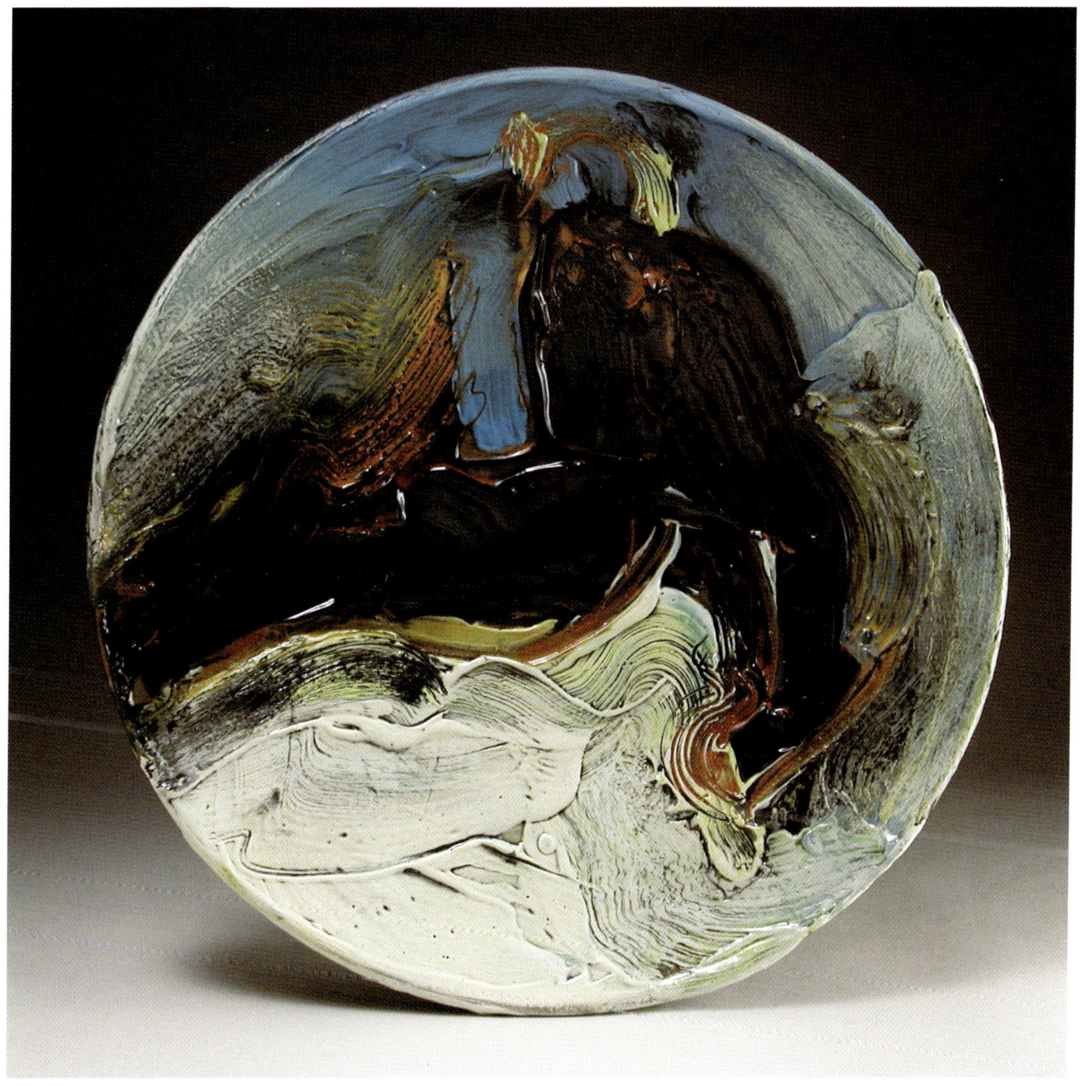

Susanne G. Stephenson

Turquoise Crevasse | 2005

2 X 18 INCHES (5.1 X 45.7 CM)

Thrown terra cotta; slips, engobes, light glaze; gas fired in reduction, cones 03 and 02

PHOTO BY ARTIST

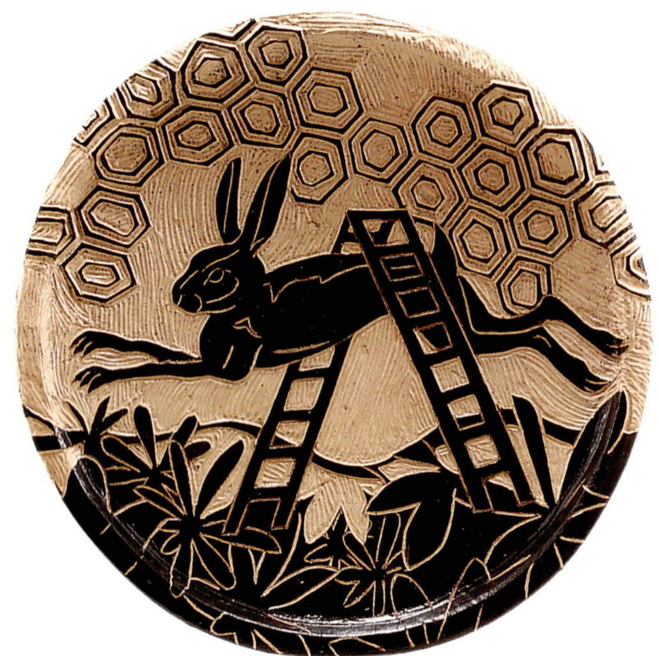

Bryan Hiveley

Rabbit Platter | 2002

7 X 18 INCHES (17.8 X 45.7 CM)

Hand-built earthenware; sgraffito; electric fired, cone 03

PHOTO BY ARTIST

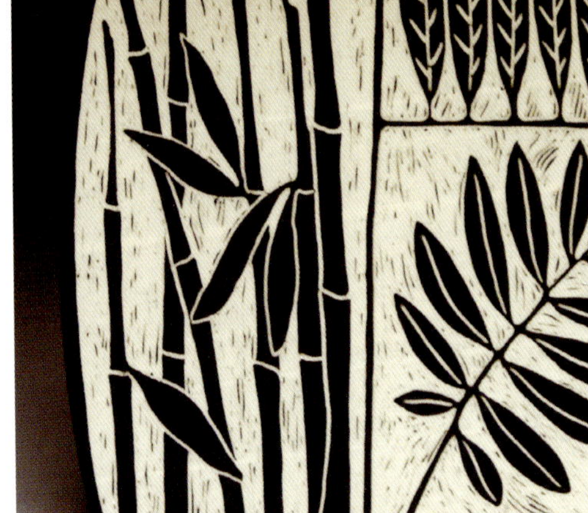

Jennifer Falter

Bamboo and Leaves | 2007

1 X 10 X 10 INCHES (2.5 X 25.4 X 25.4 CM)

Wheel-thrown porcelain; sgraffito through black slip; clear glaze, electric fired, cone 6

PHOTO BY NATHAN FALTER

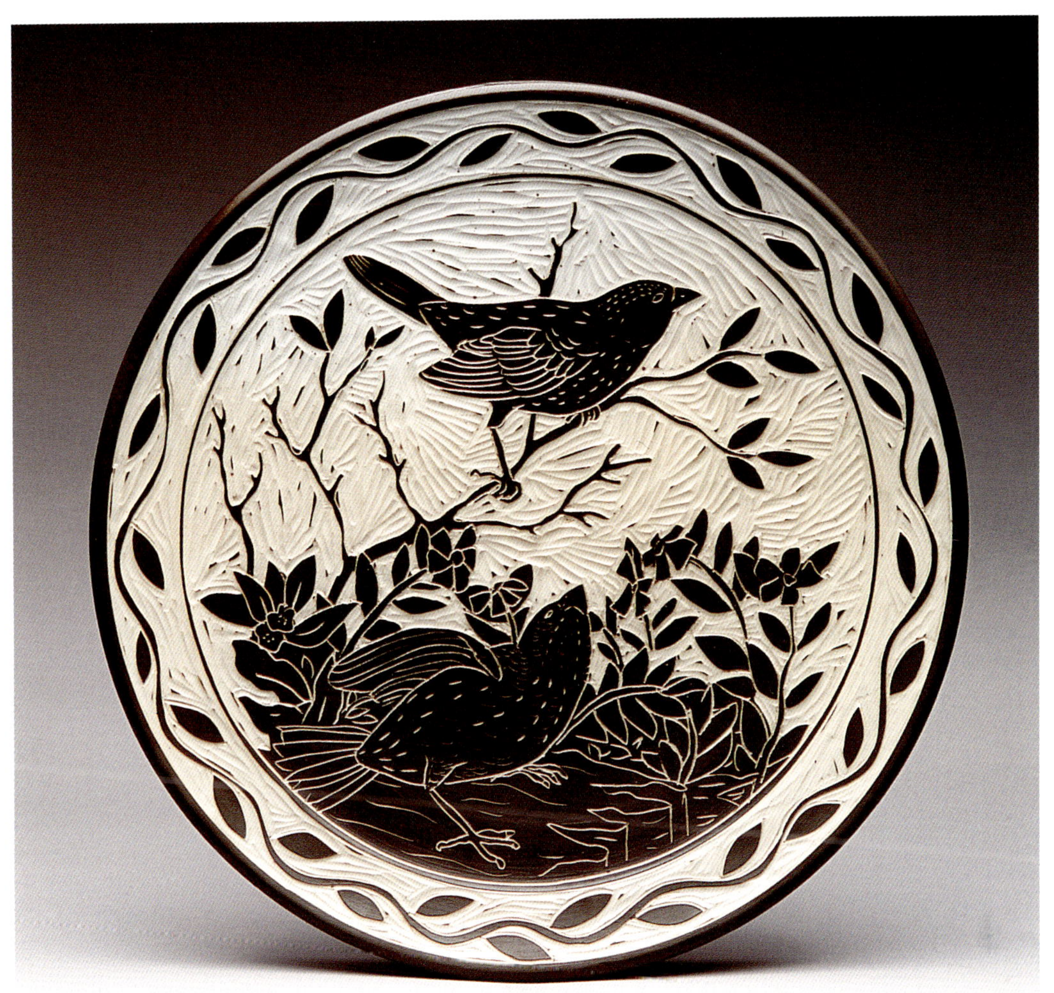

Karen Newgard

Audubon Platter | 2007

3 X 16 INCHES (7.6 X 40.6 CM)

Wheel-thrown porcelain; black terra sigillata, sgraffito; salt fired, cone 10

PHOTO BY WALKER MONTGOMERY

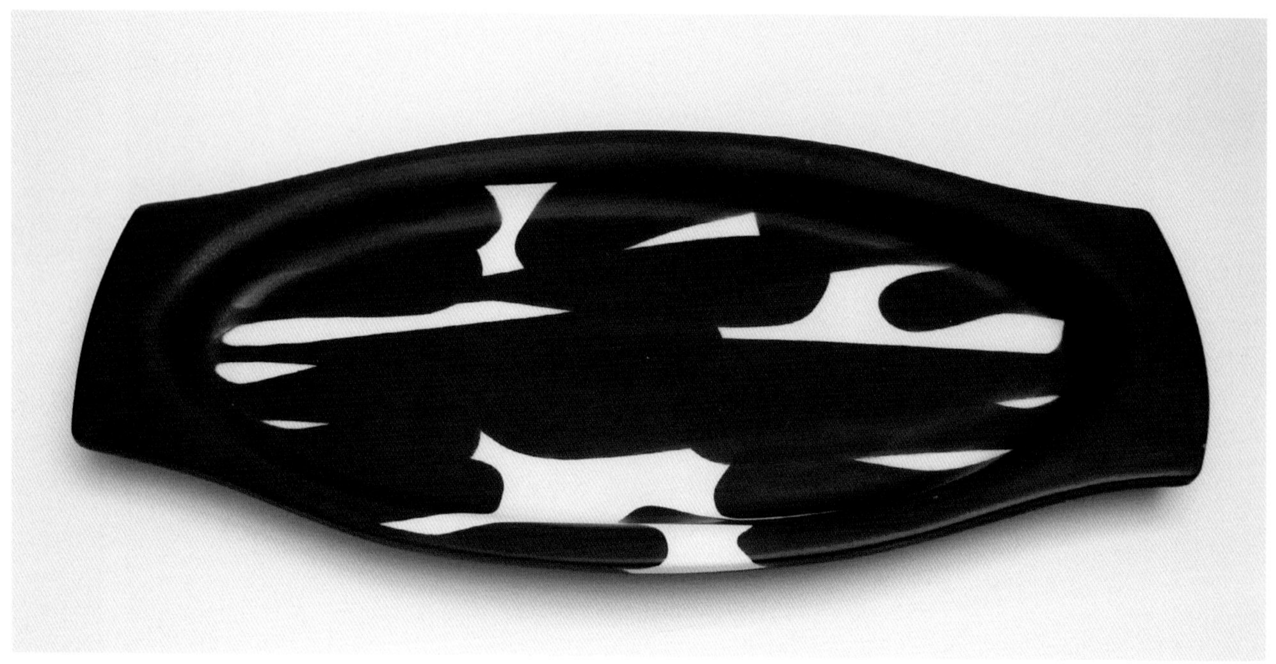

Sam Scott

Black and White Oval Platter | 2007

1 1/4 X 17 X 8 INCHES (3.2 X 43.2 X 20.3 CM)

Slump-molded, hand-built kai porcelain; black matte glaze; natural gas fired, cone 12

PHOTO BY ARTIST

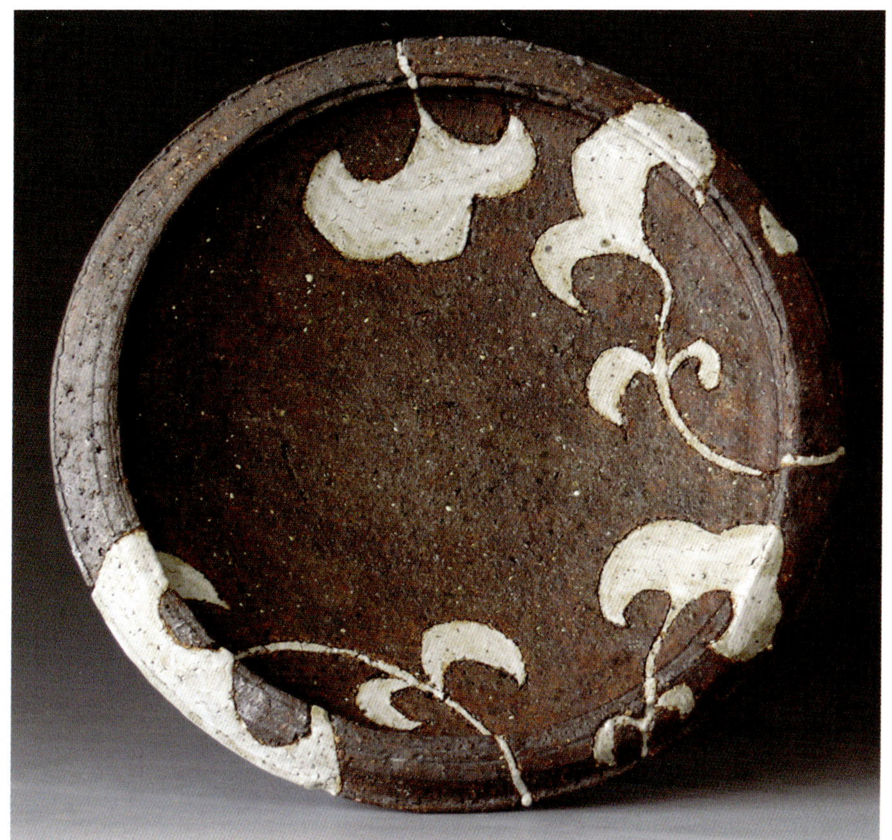

Dryden Wells

Lotus Platter | 2007

2 X 14 INCHES (5.1 X 35.6 CM)

Wheel-thrown saggar; incised, brushed, porcelain slip, iron; reduction fired, cone 11

PHOTOS BY MARIE WEICHMAN

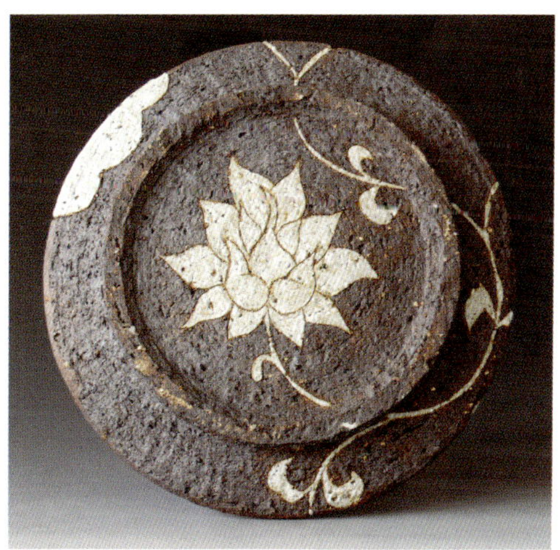

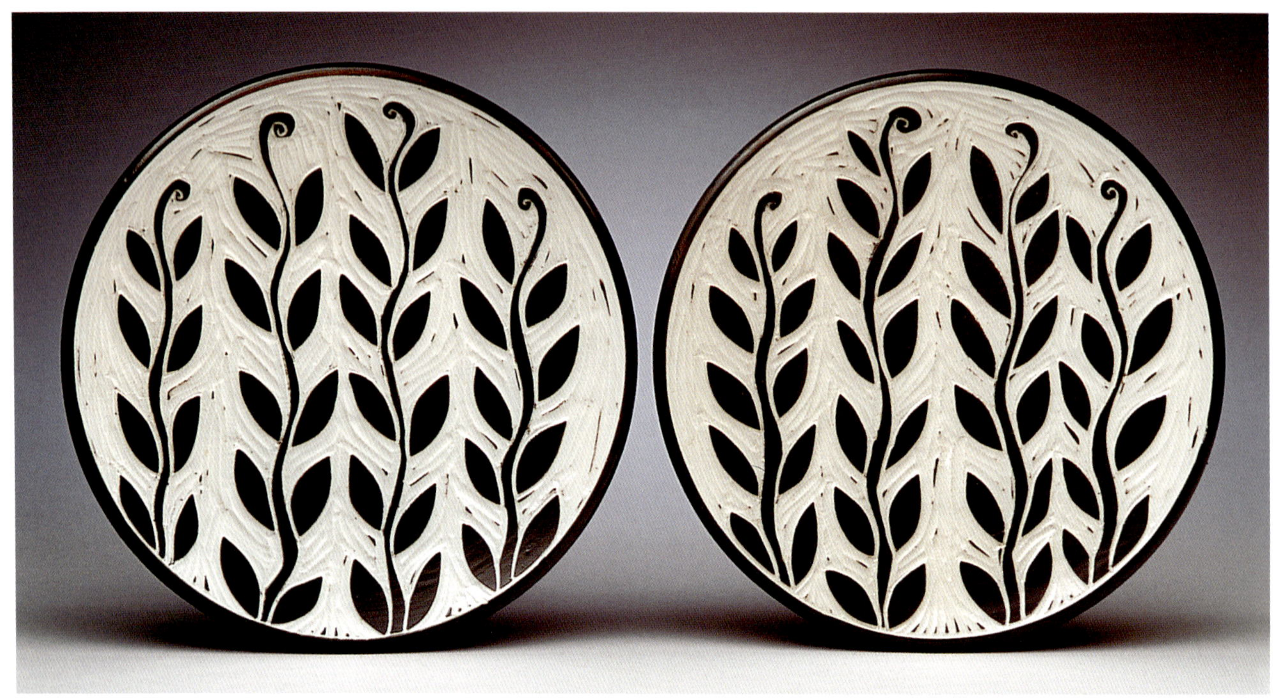

Karen Newgard

Luncheon Plates | 2007

EACH: 3 X 8 INCHES (7.6 X 20.3 CM)

Wheel-thrown porcelain; black terra sigillata, sgraffito; salt fired, cone 10

PHOTO BY WALKER MONTGOMERY

Kaitlyn Miller

Redemption | 2006

2 X 11 X 11 INCHES (5.1 X 27.9 X 27.9 CM)

Hand-built red earthenware; majolica base glaze, stains and glaze trailing; electric fired, cone 03

PHOTO BY ARTIST

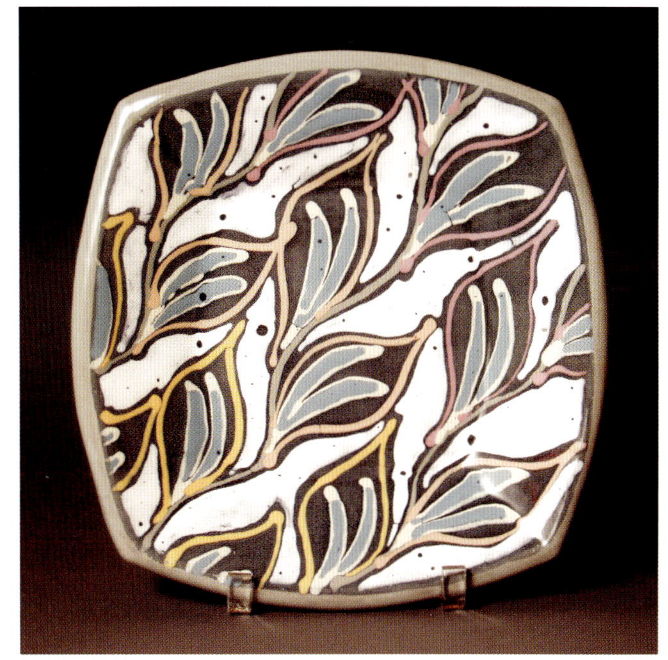

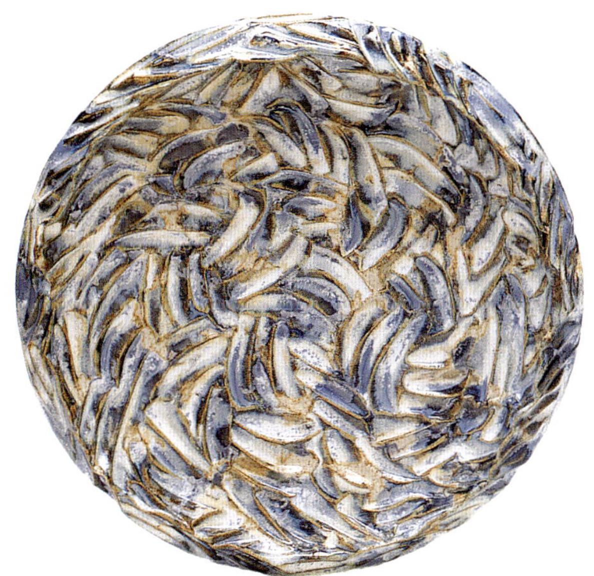

Gilles Le Corre

Textured Platter | 2006

16 INCHES (40.6 CM) IN DIAMETER

Wheel-thrown and incised stoneware; layered blue glazes; gas fired in reduction, cone 10

PHOTO BY CHRIS HONEYWELL

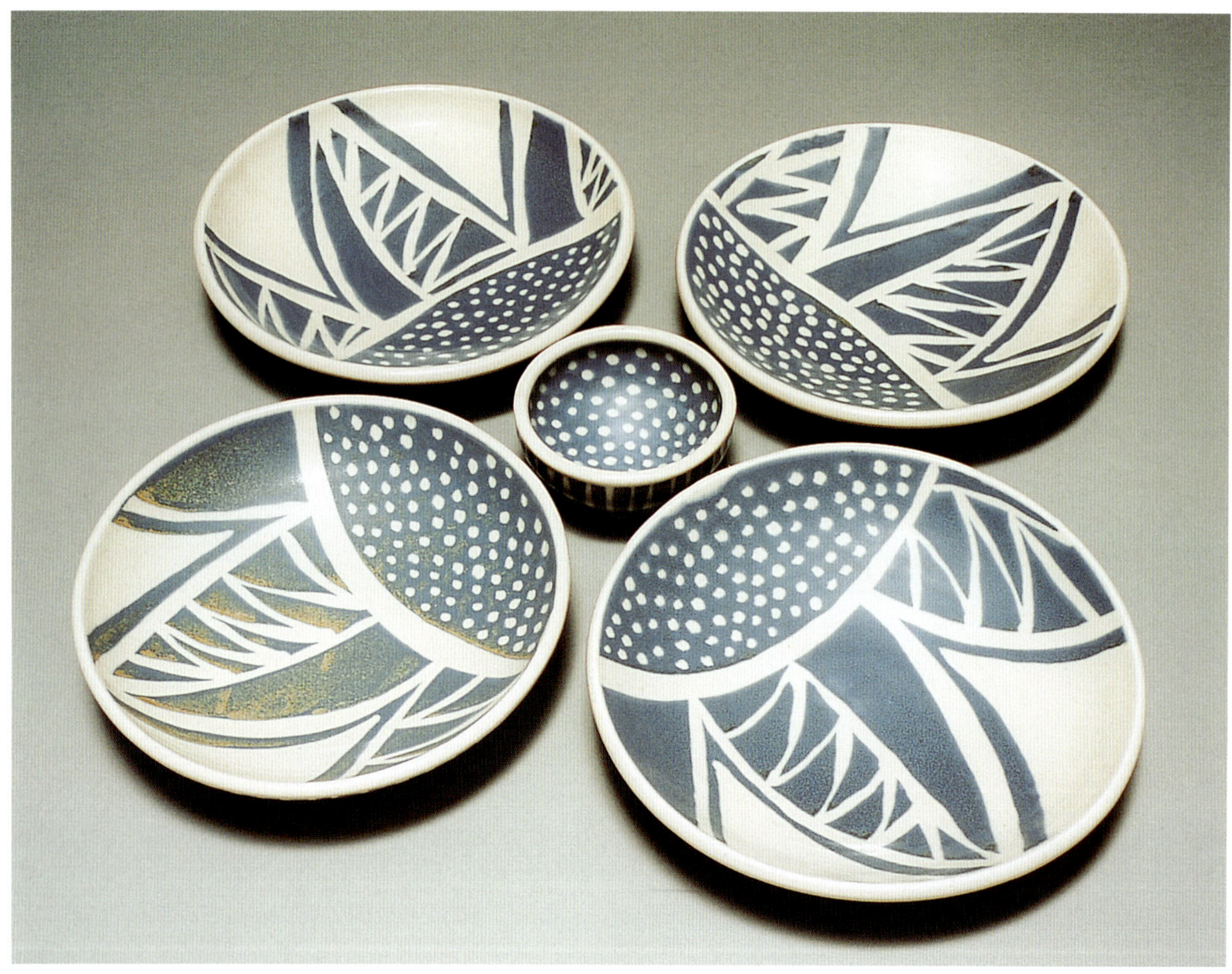

Theresa Yondo

Four Plates with Dipping Bowl | 2006

EACH PLATE: 1 1/4 X 9 INCHES (3.2 X 22.9 CM)

Wheel-thrown Grolleg porcelain;
wax resist, glaze overlap; electric fired,
bisque, cone 05; glaze, cone 10

PHOTO BY DAN MILLER

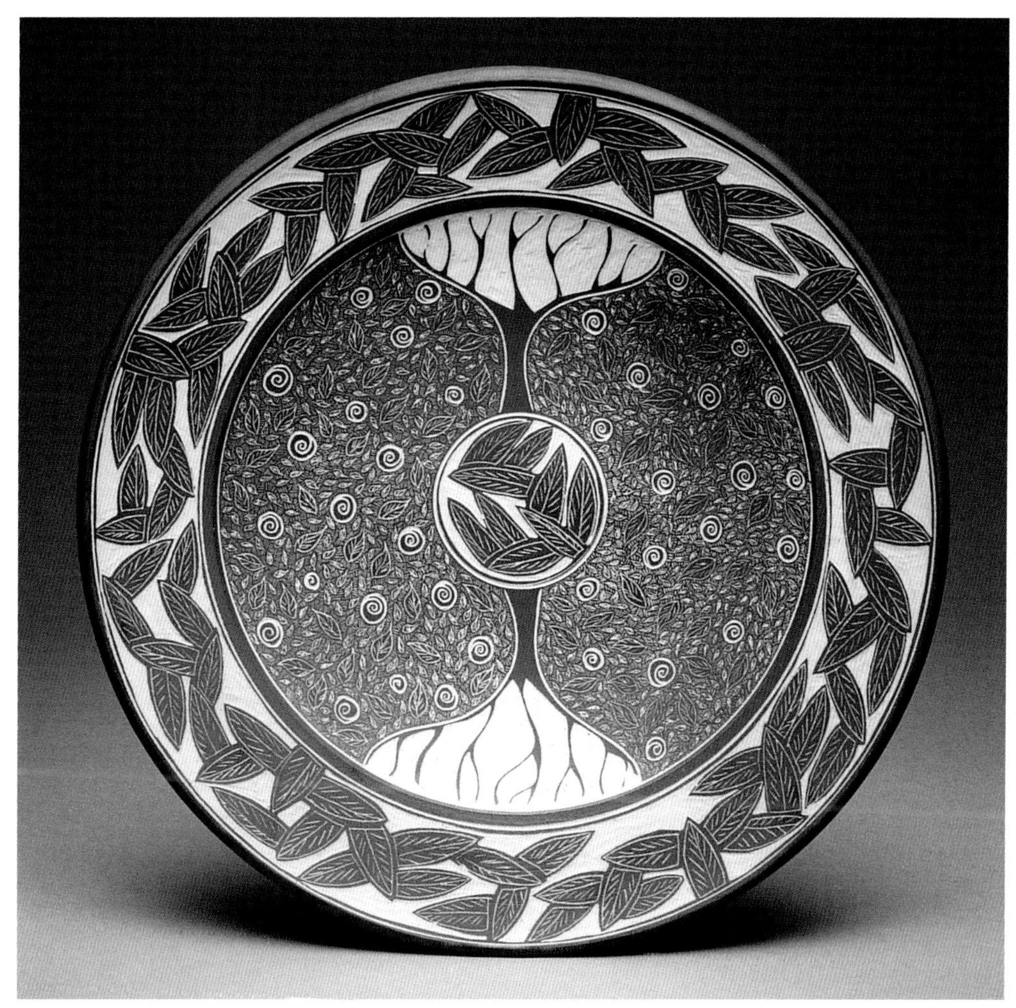

Becky Lloyd
Steve Lloyd
Platter with Trees and Leaves | 2004
$3\frac{1}{8}$ X $11\frac{7}{8}$ INCHES (8 X 30 CM)
English porcelain; terra sigillata, sgraffito
PHOTO BY PETER LEE

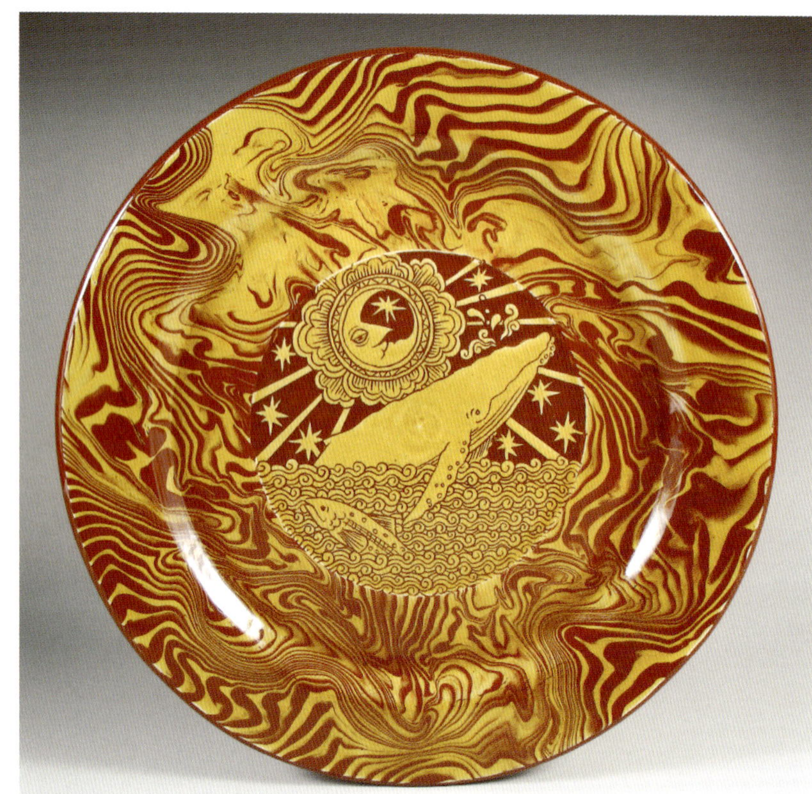

R. Geering

Untitled | 2006

1 1/4 X 11 3/8 INCHES (3.2 X 28.9 CM)

Hump-molded earthenware with wheel-thrown foot; earthenware slips, sgraffito; leadless frit glaze; electric fired, cone 04

PHOTOS BY ARTIST

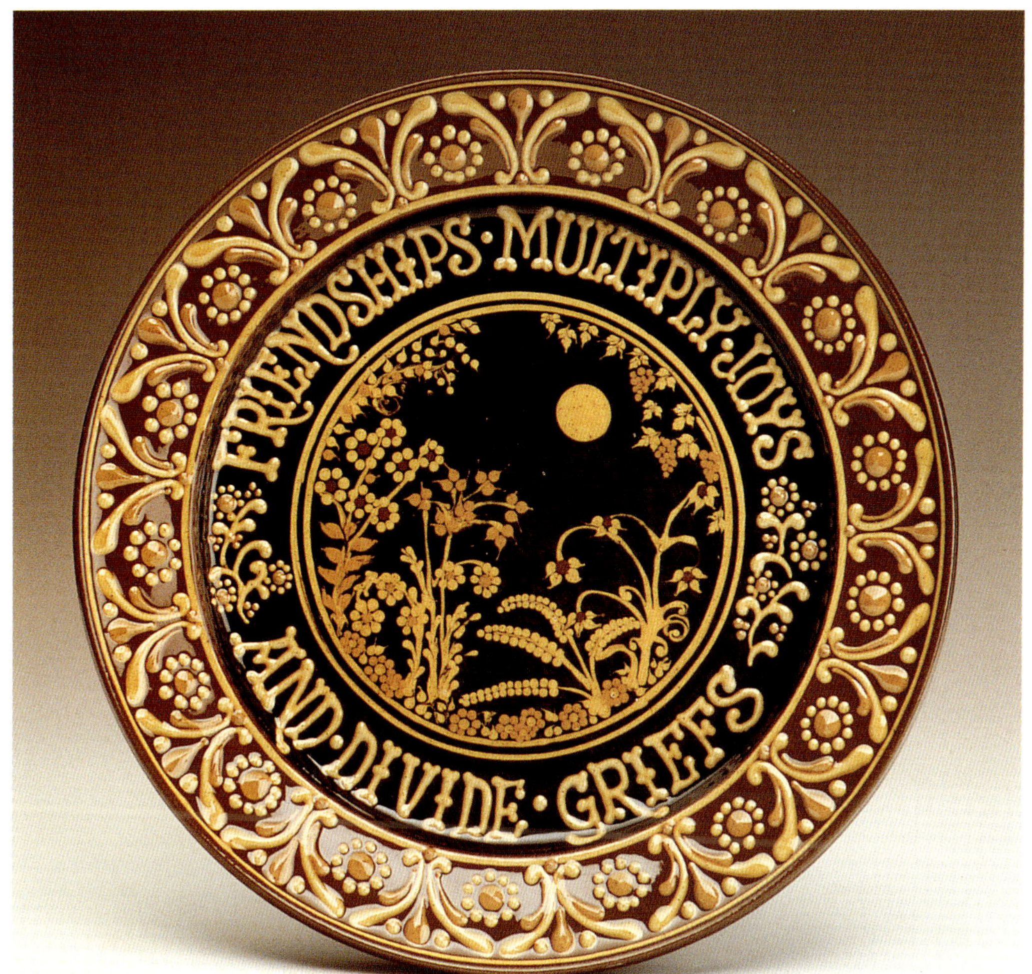

James Bassett

Friendship Plate | 2005

1 1/2 X 14 INCHES (3.8 X 35.6 CM)

Wheel-thrown red earthenware; slip trailed and lead glazed; electric fired to oxidation, bisque fired, cone 06; glaze, cone 03

PHOTO BY ARTIST

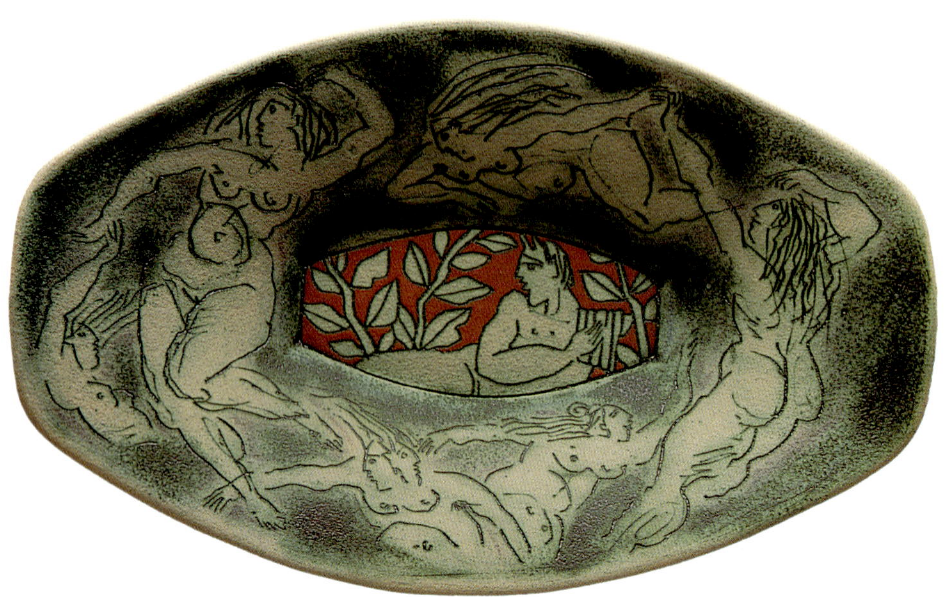

Matthias Ostermann

Bacchanale | 2005

4 X 16 X 9 INCHES
(10.2 X 40.6 X 22.9 CM)

Slab and drape-molded earthenware; vitreous engobes, sgraffito, copper inlay; on-surface stains; electric multi-fired, cone 06

PHOTO BY JAN THIJS

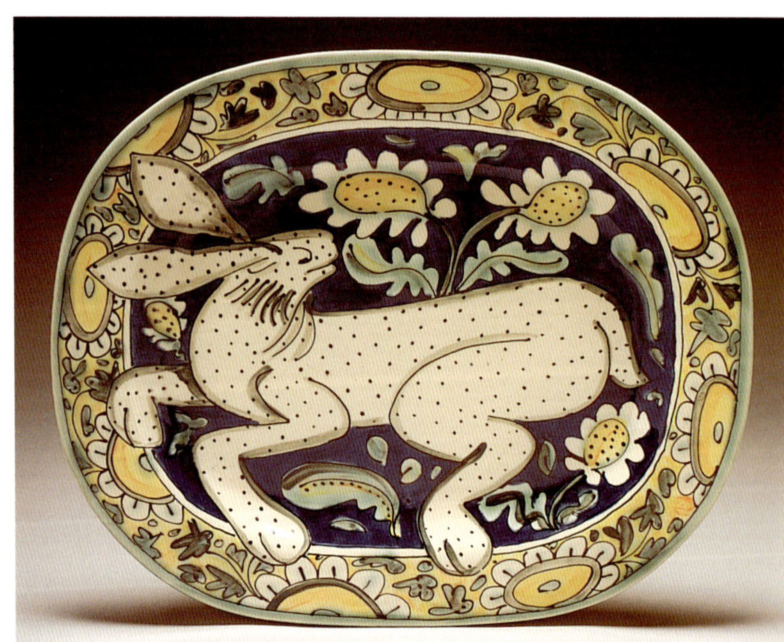

Debra Kuzyk
Ray Mackie

Rabbit Platter | 2007

1 1/4 X 16 X 12 3/4 INCHES (3.2 X 40.6 X 32.4 CM)

Hand-built and hump-molded porcelain; underglazes and clear glaze, electric fired, cone 6 oxidation

PHOTO BY JULIAN BEVERIDGE

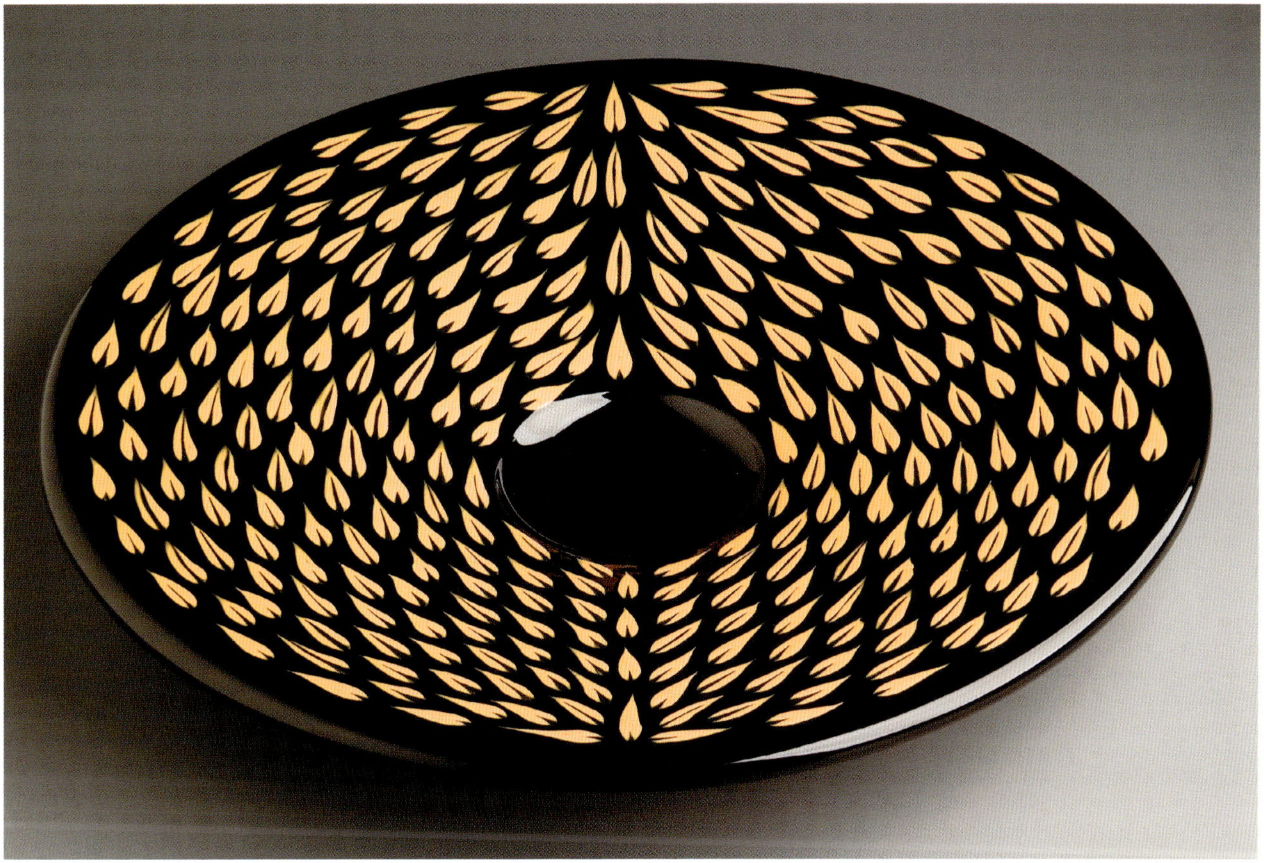

John Stewart

Echidna Platter | 2001

3 X 20 INCHES (7.6 X 50.8 CM)

Wheel-thrown white earthenware; underglaze brushwork; electric fired, cone 6; clear glaze, cone 03

PHOTOS BY DAVID YOUNG

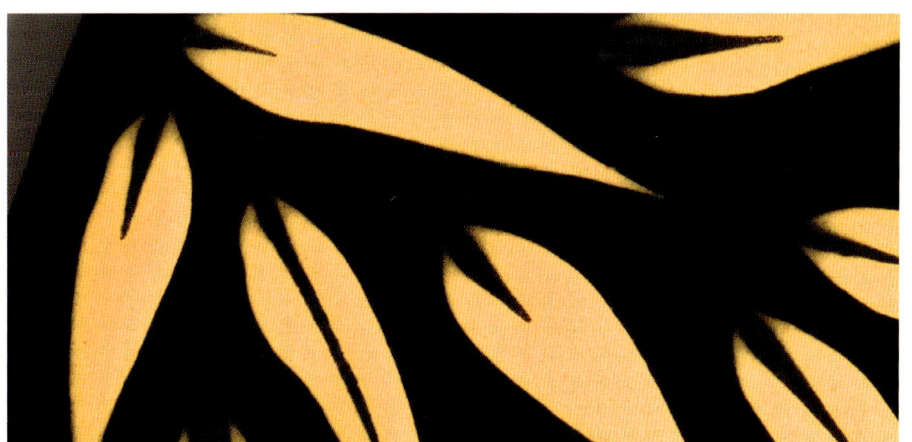

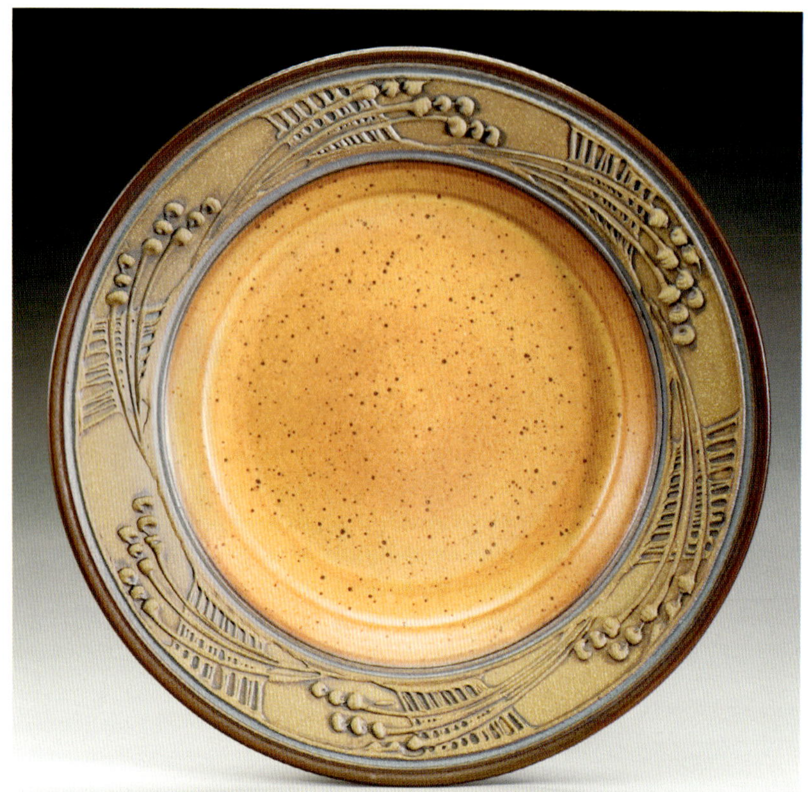

James Kachler

Platter with Wheat Pattern | 2007

3 X 23 INCHES (7.6 X 58.4 CM)

Wheel-thrown stoneware; spodumene glaze and iron wash; gas fired in reduction, cone 10

PHOTOS BY HAP SAKWA

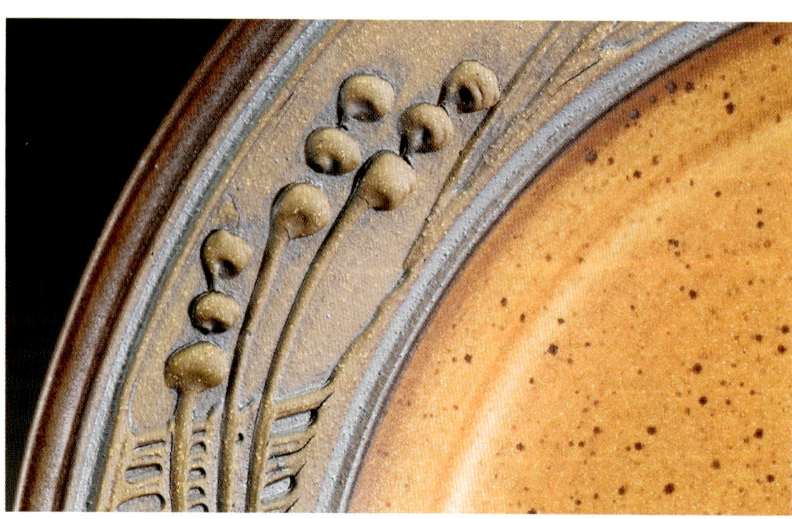

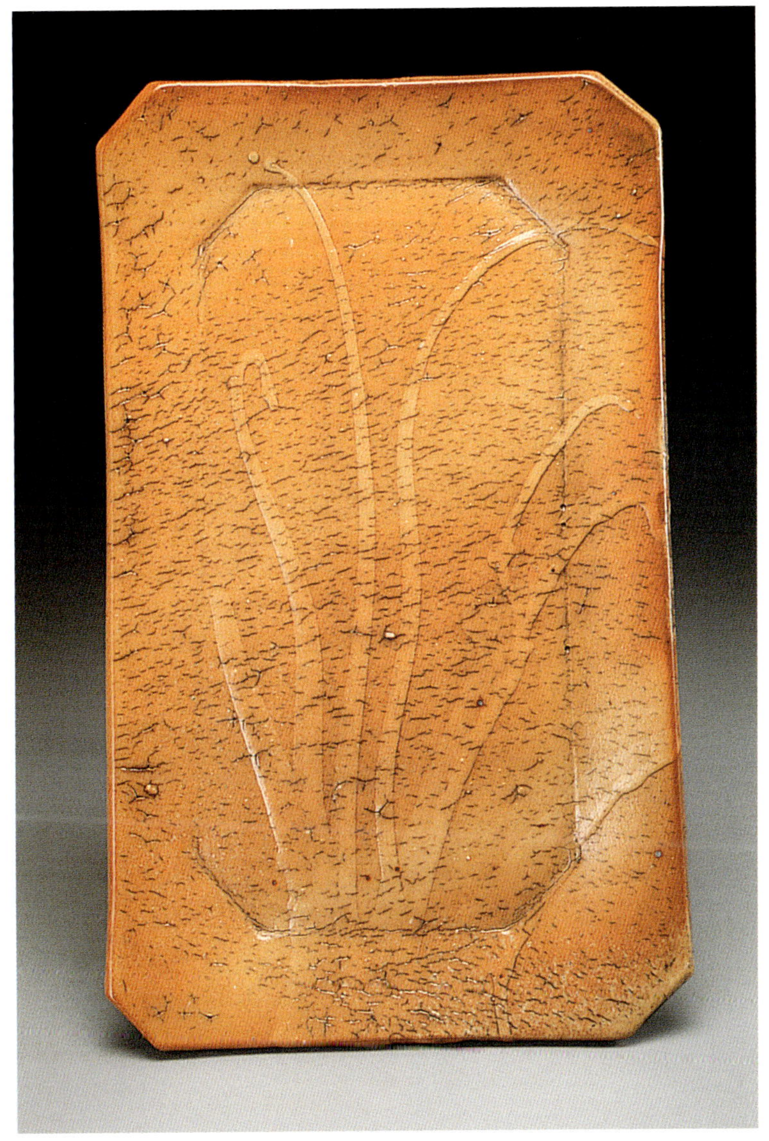

Judith Duff

Rectangular Shino Plate | 2006

$7\frac{1}{2}$ X 12 INCHES (19 X 30.5 CM)

Slab-built porcelain; poured and dripped crackle shino glaze; wood fired, cone 12

PHOTO BY JOY TANNER

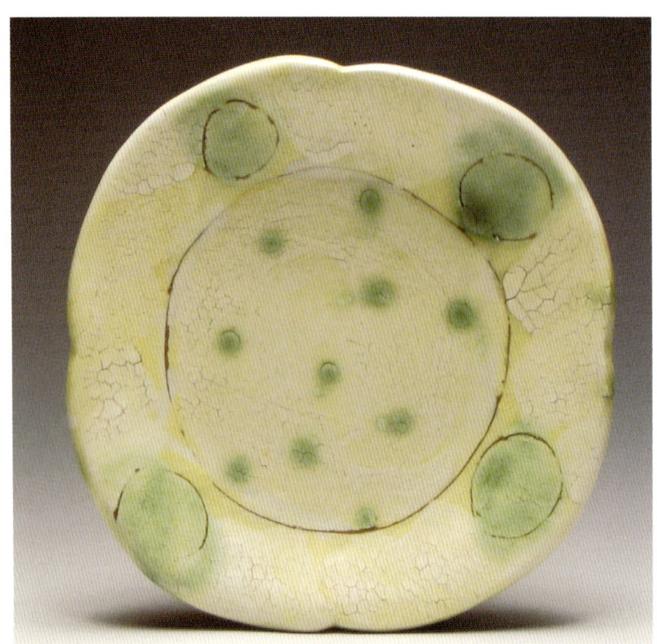

Rachel Berg

Untitled | 2007

1 X 7 X 8 INCHES (2.5 X 17.8 X 20.3 CM)

Slab-built stoneware; brushed slips, sgraffito; electric fired, cone 6

PHOTO BY ARTIST

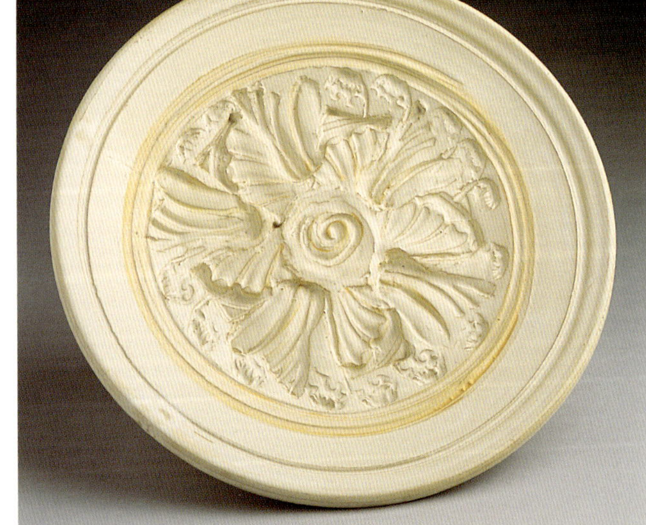

Janice Honea

Platter | 2007

3 X 13½ INCHES (7.6 X 34.3 CM)

Wheel-thrown and altered stoneware; electric fired, cone 06; glaze, cone 6

PHOTO BY ARTIST

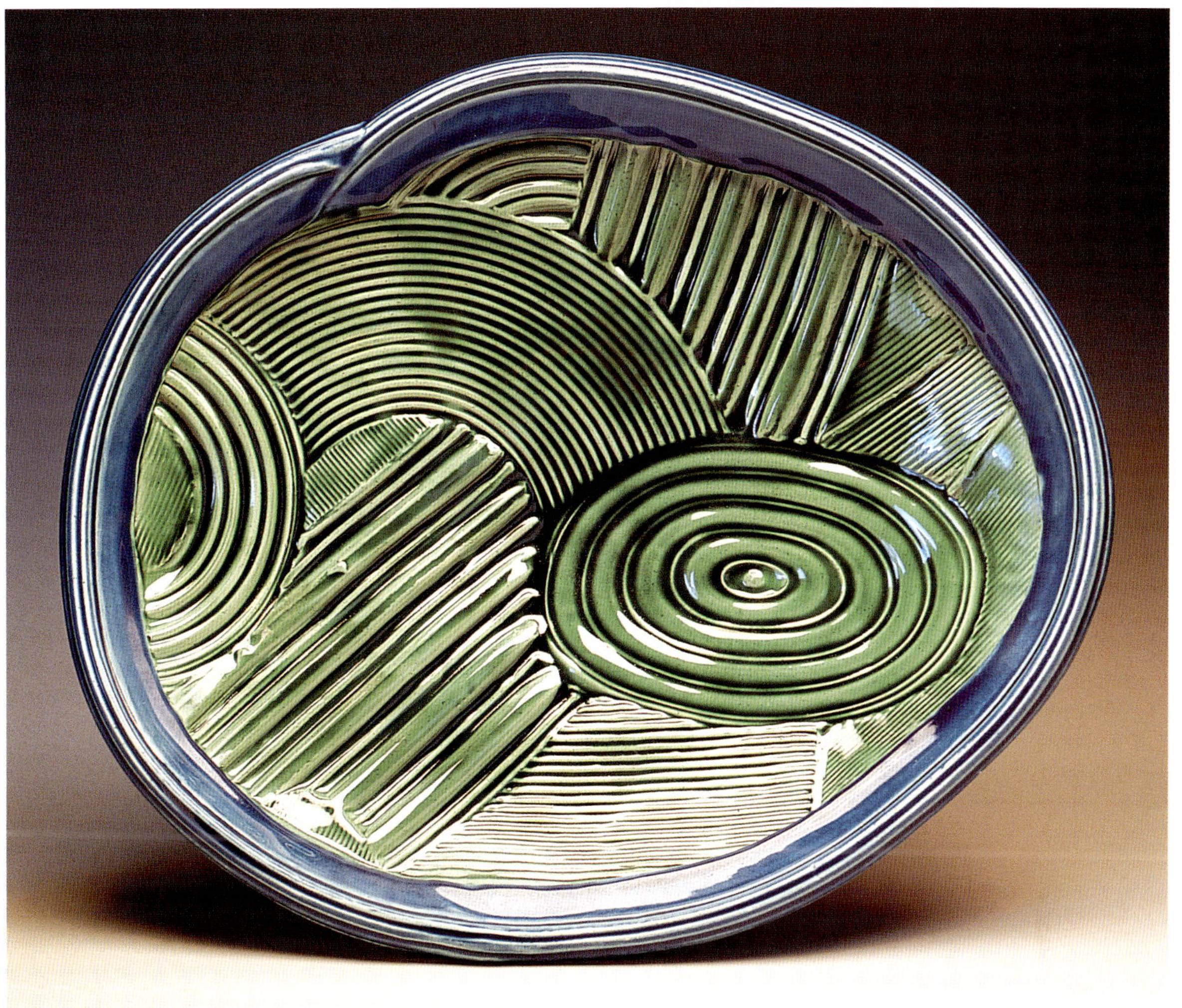

Neil Patterson

Oval Platter, Green | 2007

4 X 22 X 16 INCHES (10.2 X 55.9 X 40.6 CM)

Wheel-thrown; textured, pieced; electric fired, cone 6

PHOTO BY ARTIST

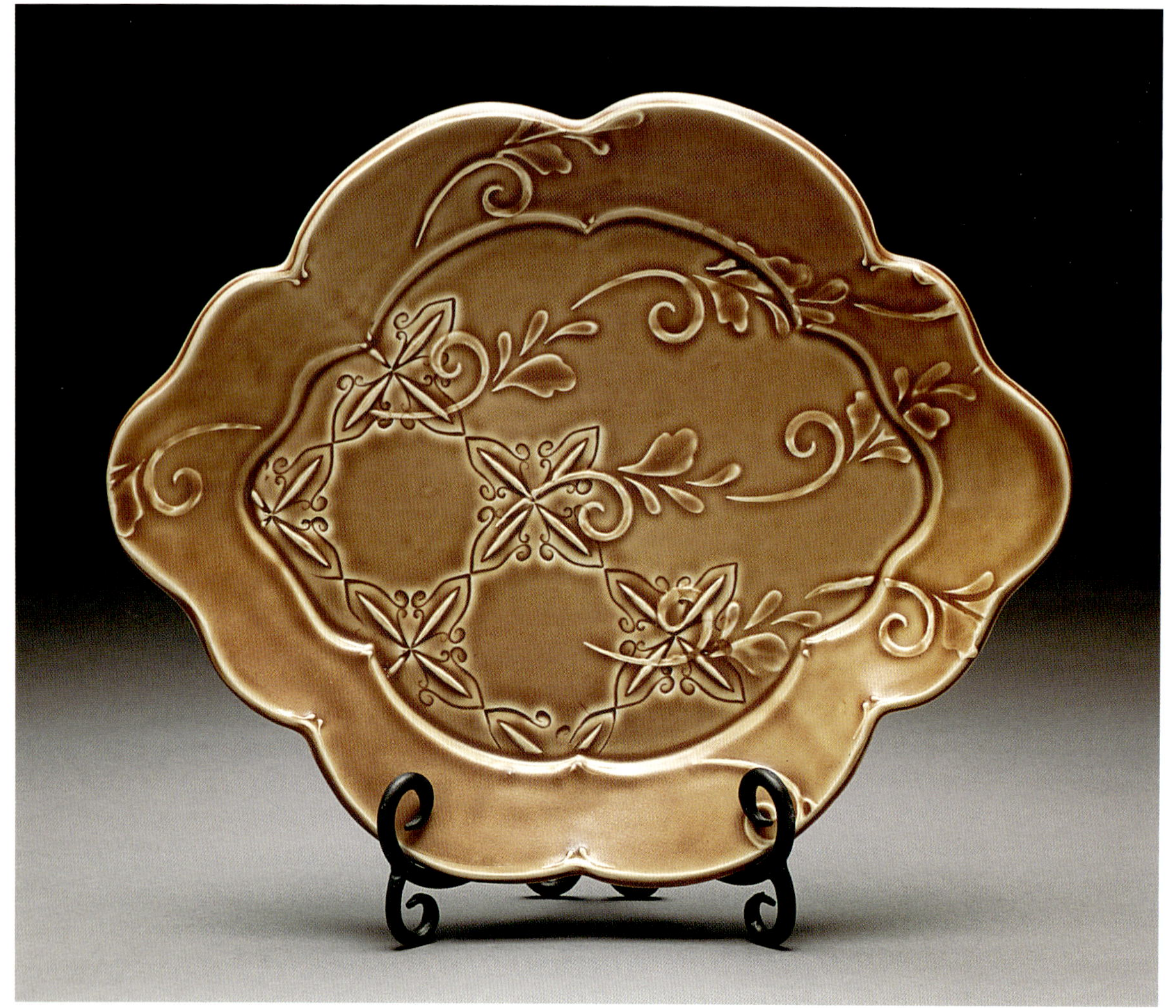

Kristen Kieffer

Small Platter, Salmon | 2007

2 X 14 X 11 INCHES (5.1 X 35.6 X 27.9 CM)

Drape-molded and altered mid-range porcelain; stamped, slip trailed; cone 7

PHOTO BY ARTIST

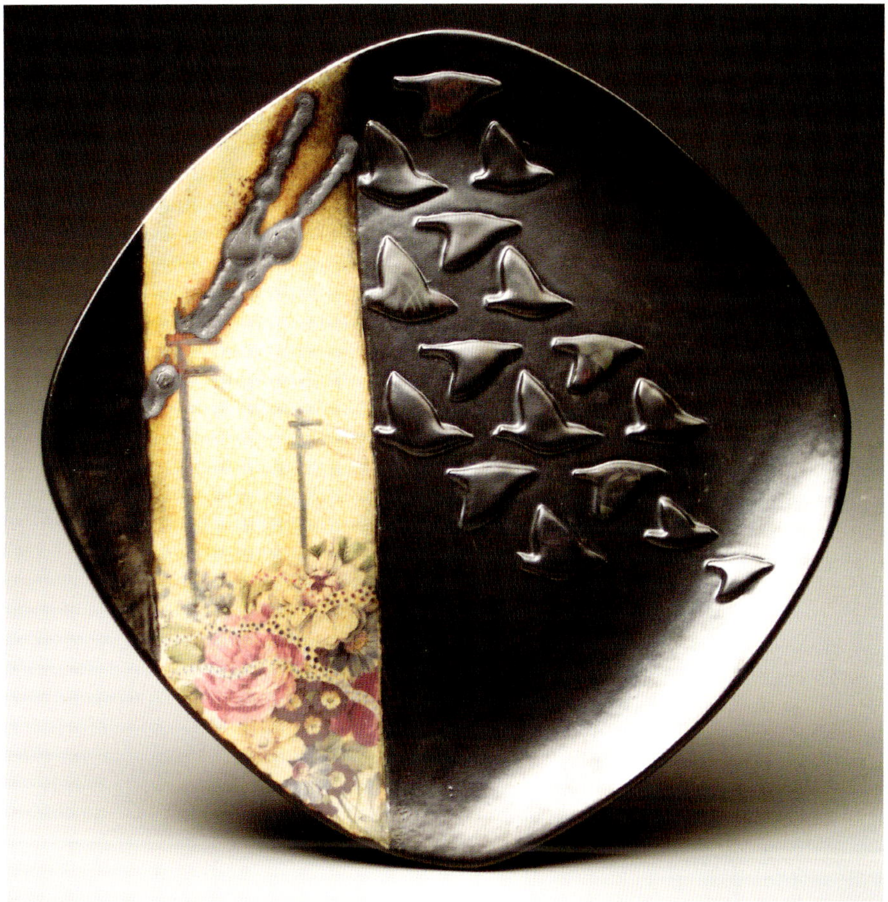

Shenny Phillips Cruces

Landscape and Memory | 2007

$1\frac{1}{2}$ X 10 INCHES (3.8 X 25.4 CM)

Hand-built and slump-molded porcelain; sprig details, copper wire; reduction glazes; updraft gas fired, cone 10; decals and china paint, cone 016

PHOTOS BY ARTIST

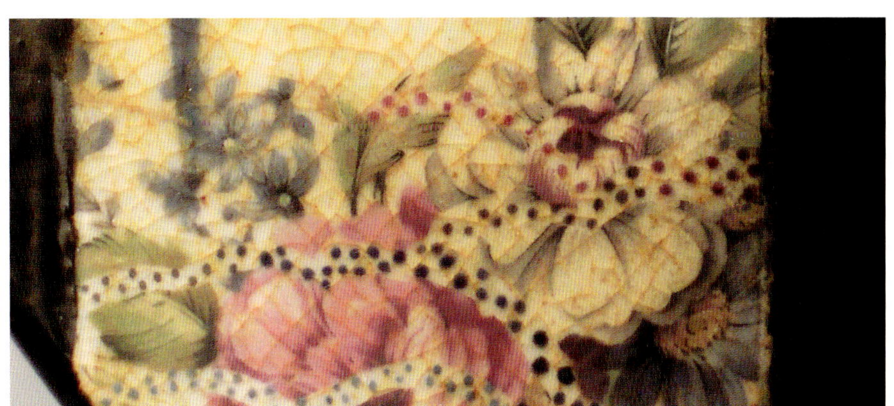

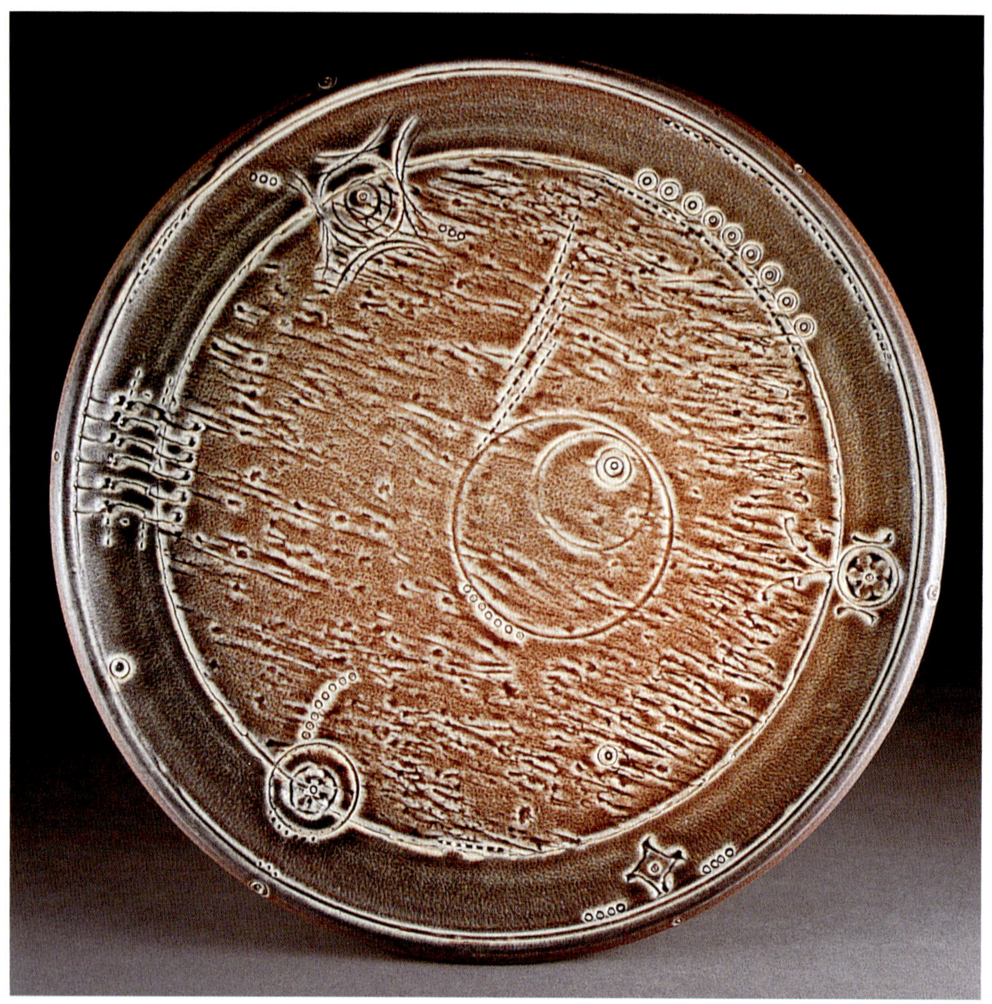

Jennifer Hill

Salad Plate, Deep Purple | 2007

3/4 X 10 INCHES (1.9 X 25.4 CM)

Wheel-thrown white stoneware; carved and stamped; sprayed glazes, electric fired, cone 5

PHOTO BY ARTIST

Mark Heimann

Shaman's Dance | 2003

4 X 21 INCHES (10.2 X 53.3 CM)

Drape-molded stoneware; carved, impressed; glaze, red iron-oxide band; gas fired in updraft reduction, cone 10

PHOTO BY BILL BACHHUBER

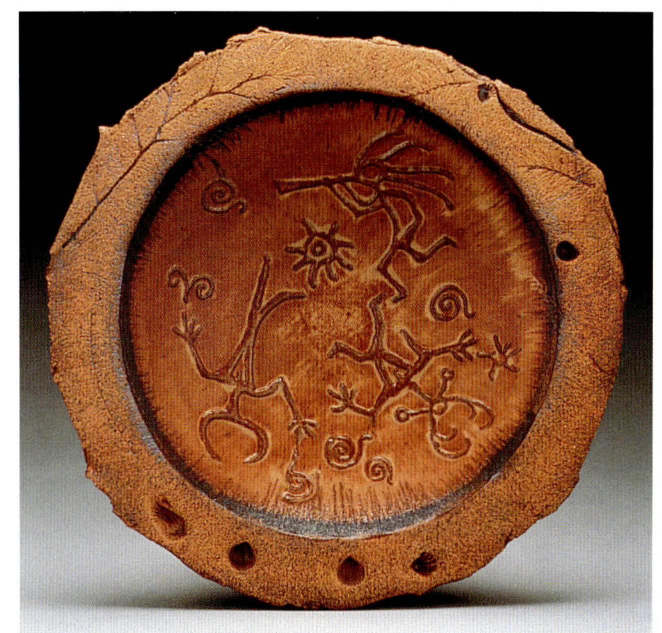

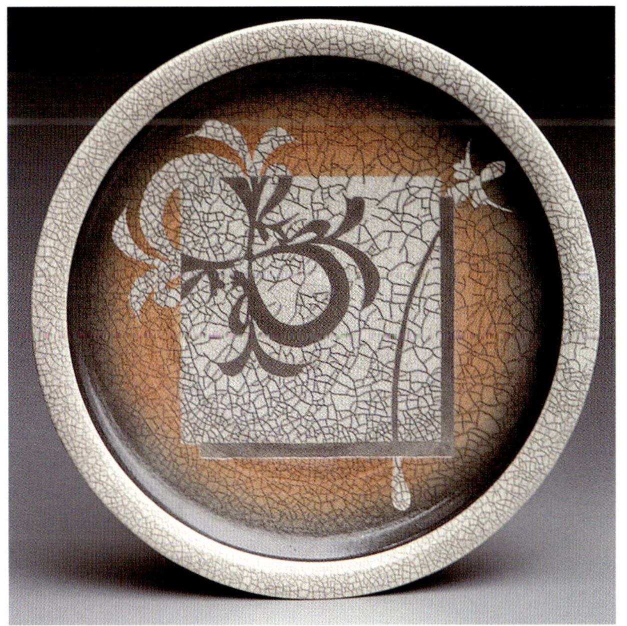

Phil Chapman

Platter | 2005

15 INCHES (38.1 CM) IN DIAMETER

Wheel-thrown raku porcelain; latex-resist brushwork; airbrushed underglazes, cone 06

PHOTO BY ARTIST

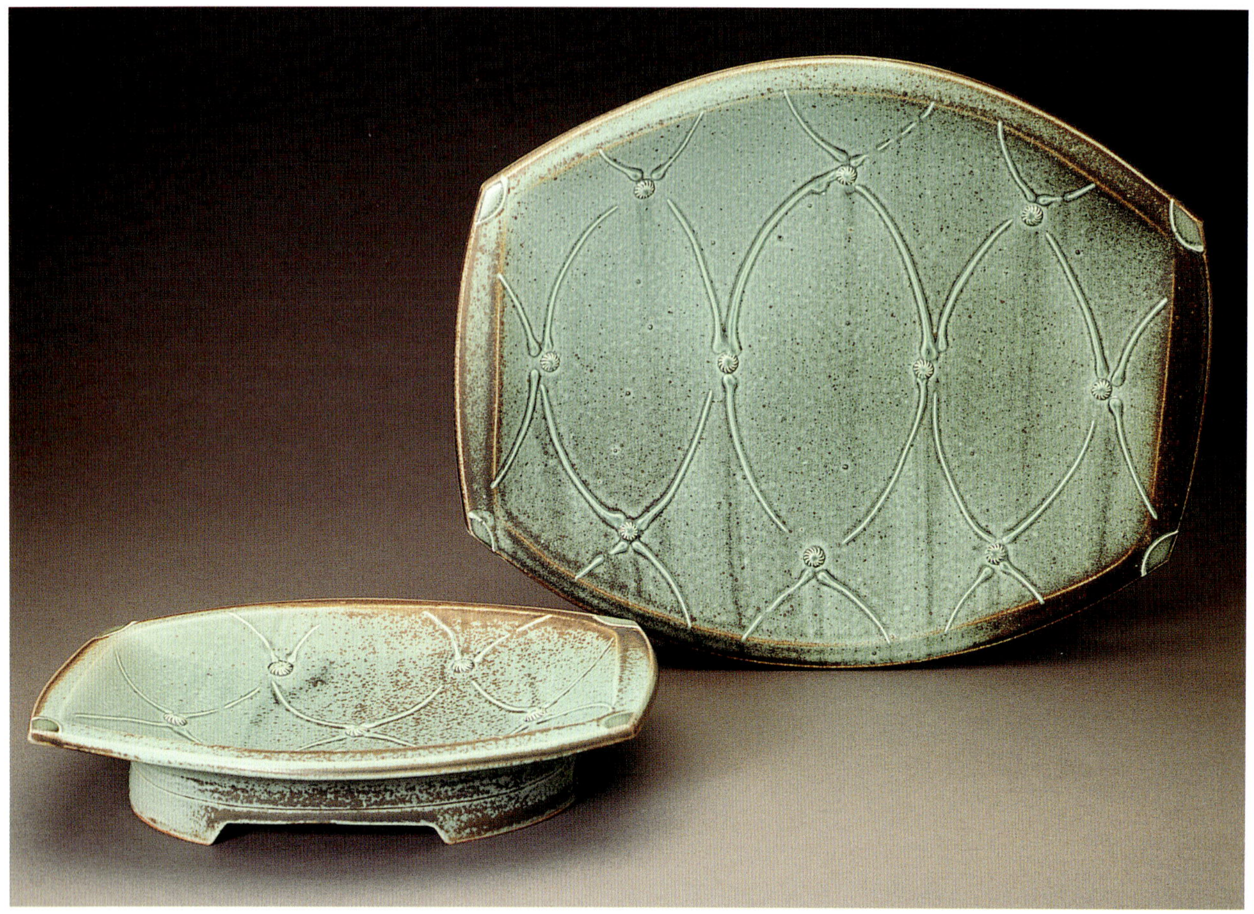

Marlene Jack

Pair of Rectangular Plates | 2006

LARGEST: 2 X 14 X 11 INCHES (5.1 X 35.6 X 27.9 CM)

Hand-constructed and wheel-thrown stoneware; slip trailed, press molded; soda fired, cone 10

PHOTO BY ARTIST

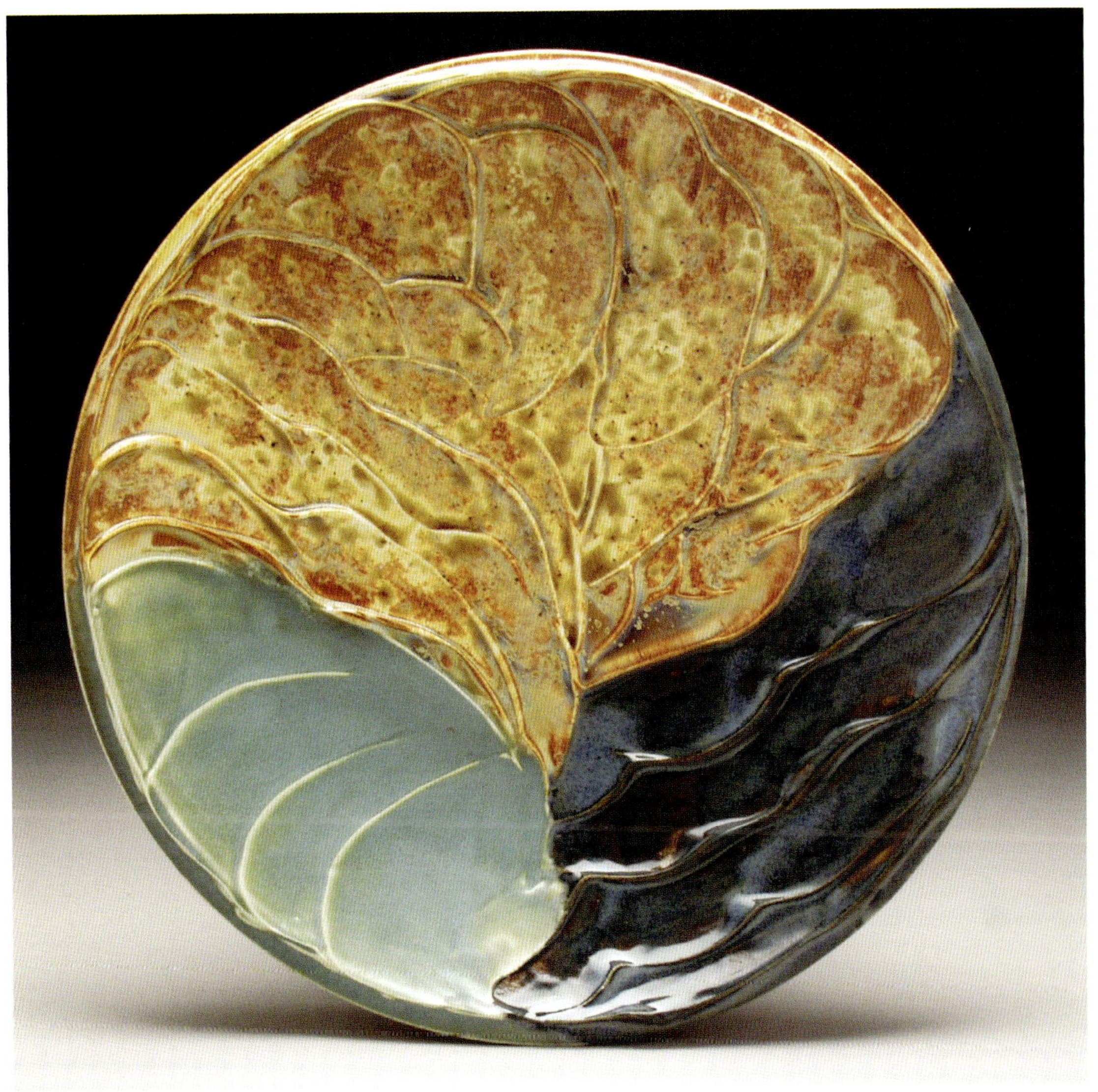

Helen J. Ryan

Earth, Wind, and Sea | 2007

1 1/2 X 11 INCHES (3.8 X 27.9 CM)

Wheel-thrown porcelain; porcelain slip; electric fired, cone 04; glazes with wood ash over gold, cone 6

PHOTO BY JED SCHLEGEL

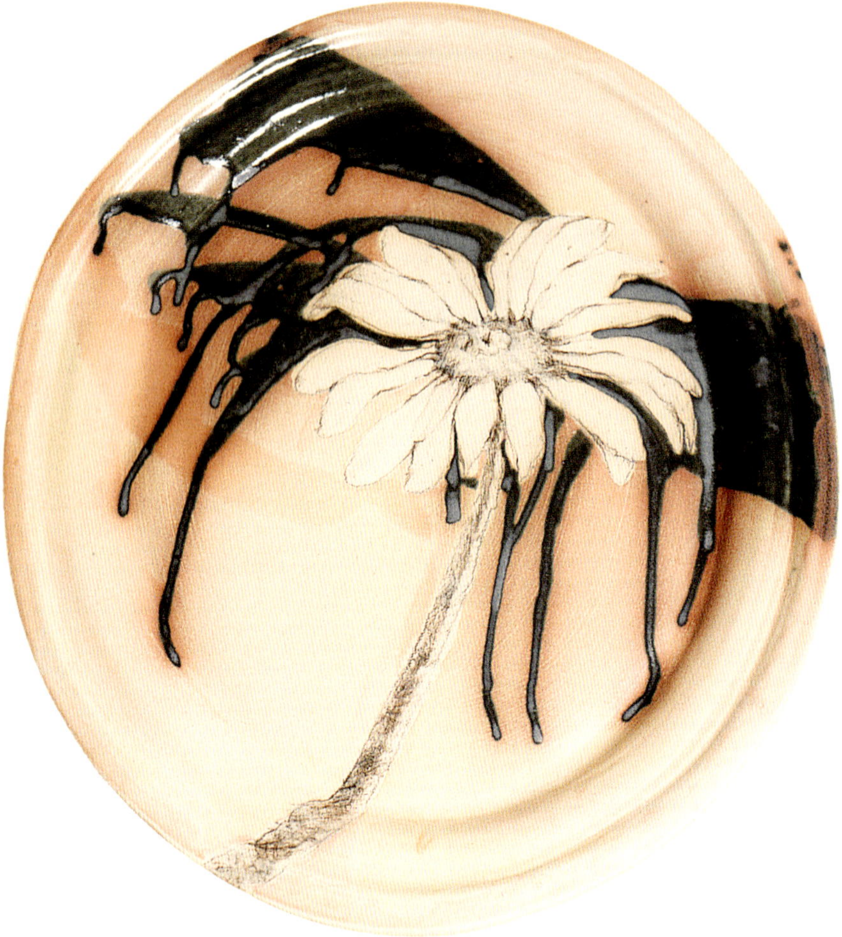

Grace Powers Fraioli

Daisy Platter | 1998

2 X 15 X 19 INCHES (5.1 X 38.1 X 48.3 CM)

Hand-built stoneware; underglaze pencil and glazes; oxidation fired, cone 9

PHOTOS BY ARTIST

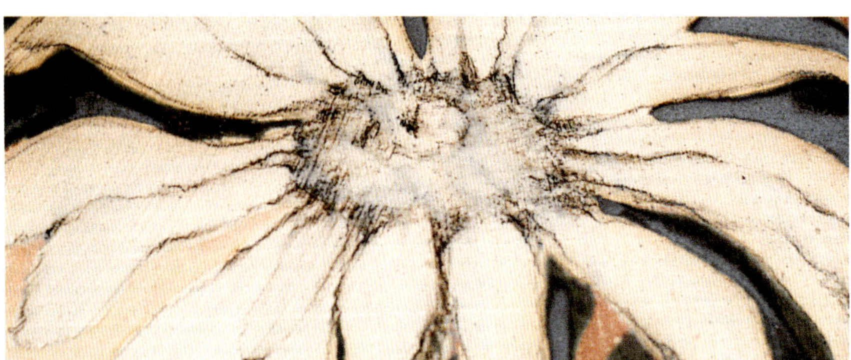

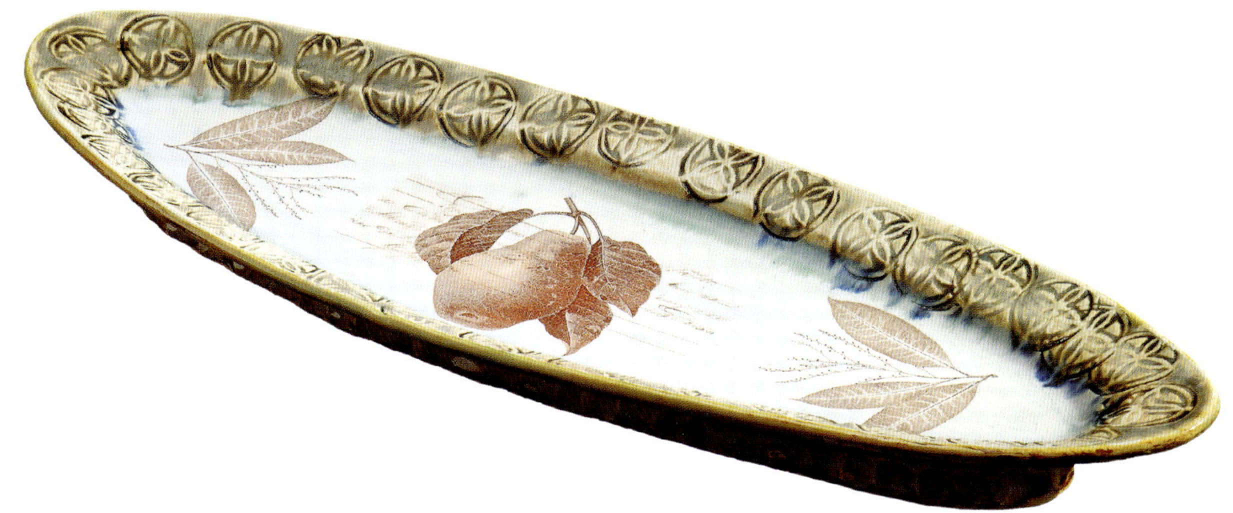

Maggie Mae Beyeler
Pear Platter | 2007
1 X 20 X 7 INCHES (2.5 X 50.8 X 17.8 CM)
Slab-built mid-range stoneware with wheel-thrown foot; embossed, image transfer; electric fired, cone 6
PHOTO BY CHAS MCGRATH

Susannah Lints
Yearning for Spring | 2007
3 X 13 1/2 X 13 1/2 INCHES (7.6 X 34.3 X 34.3 CM)
Slab, drape-molded terra cotta; black majolica; electric fired, cone 05
PHOTO BY COURTNEY FRISSE

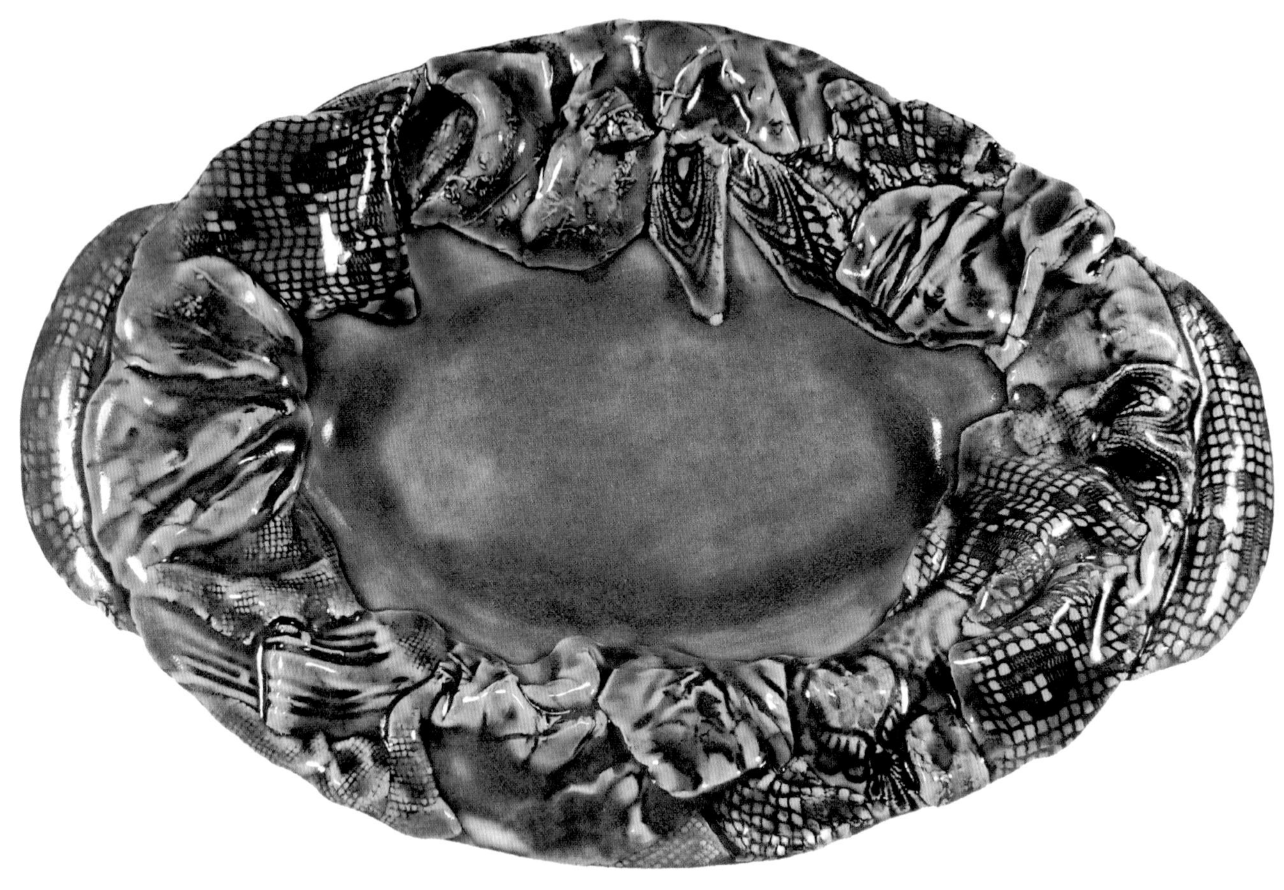

Ingrid Hogan

Oval Platter | 2006

2 X 16 X 11 INCHES (5.1 X 40.6 X 27.9 CM)

Hand-built porcelain; green celadon, gas fired, cone 10

PHOTO BY ARTIST

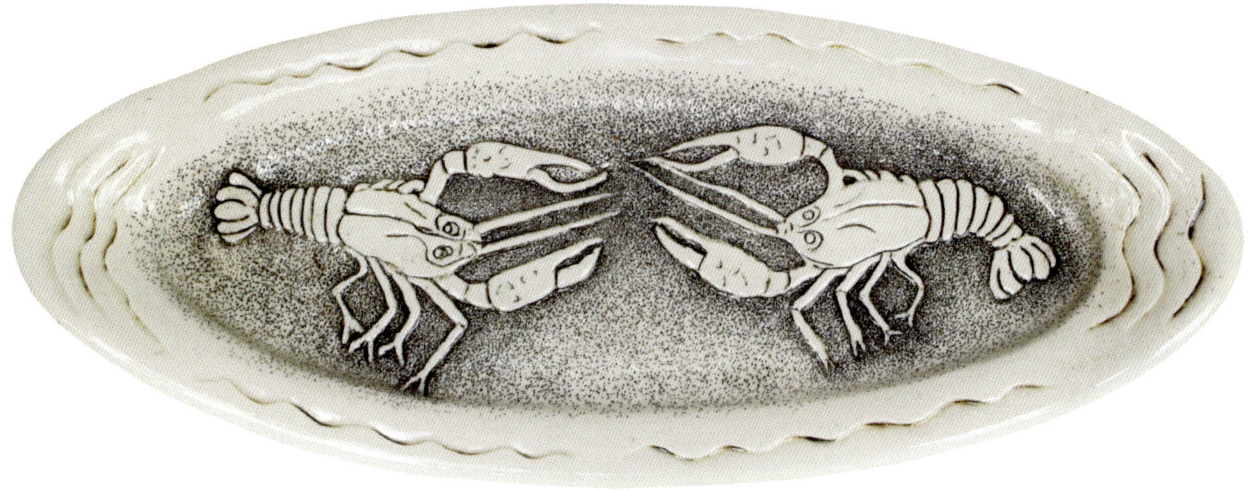

Wayne Horton

Crawfish Platter | 2007

$1\frac{1}{2}$ X 18 X 7 INCHES (3.8 X 45.7 X 17.8 CM)

Slab-built porcelain; carved; clear glaze, electric fired, cone 10

PHOTOS BY ERIN HORTON

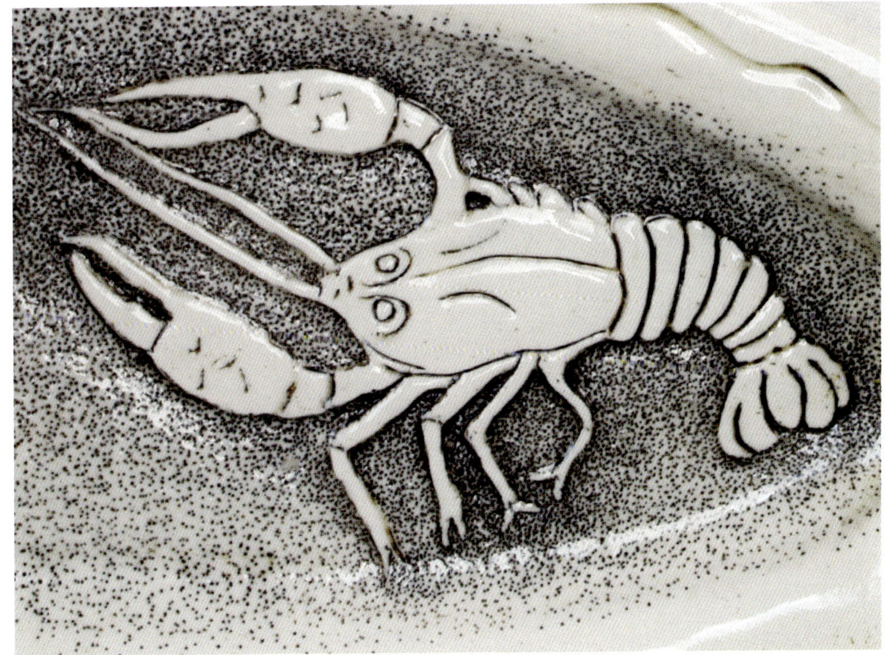

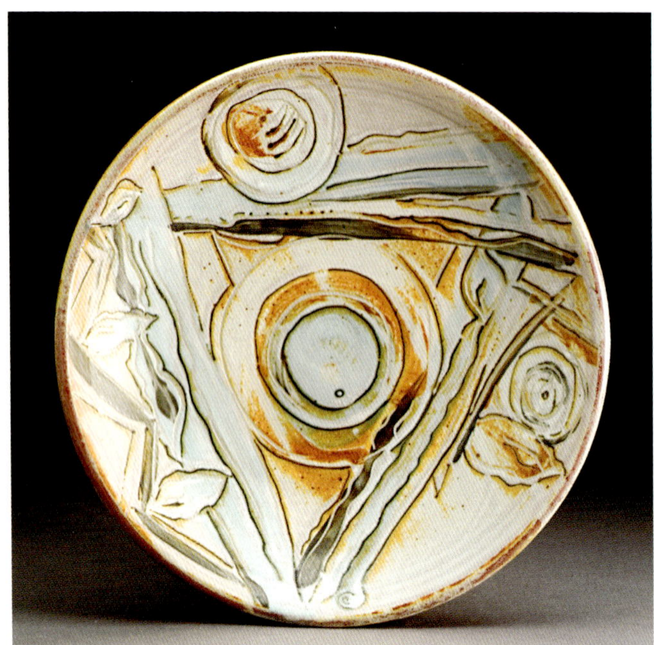

Claudia Dunaway

Home Free | 2007

13 INCHES (33 CM) IN DIAMETER

Wheel-thrown stoneware; colored slips; bisque fire; black wax detail; gas fired in reduction, cone 10–11

PHOTO BY TOM MILLS

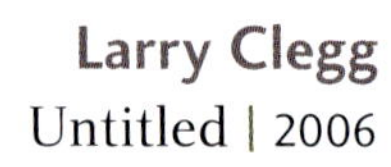

Larry Clegg

Untitled | 2006

$1\frac{1}{2}$ X 16 INCHES (3.8 X 40.6 CM)

Wheel-thrown porcelain; incised and impressed; airbrushed glazes; electric fired, 2320°F (1271°C)

PHOTO BY LARRY SANDERS

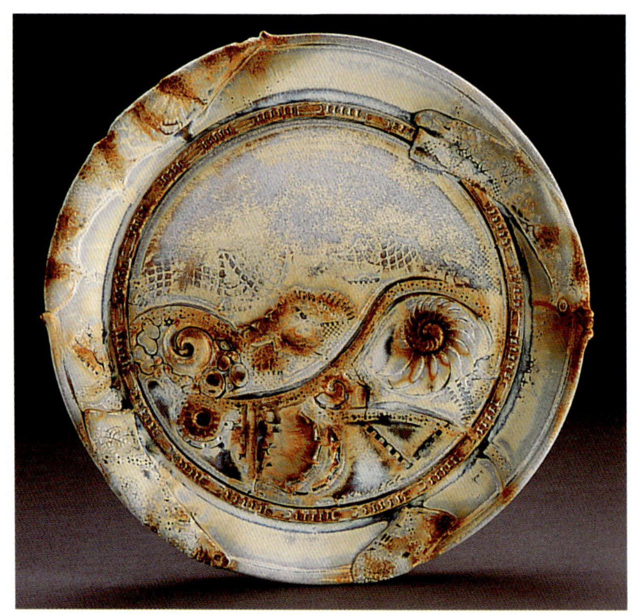

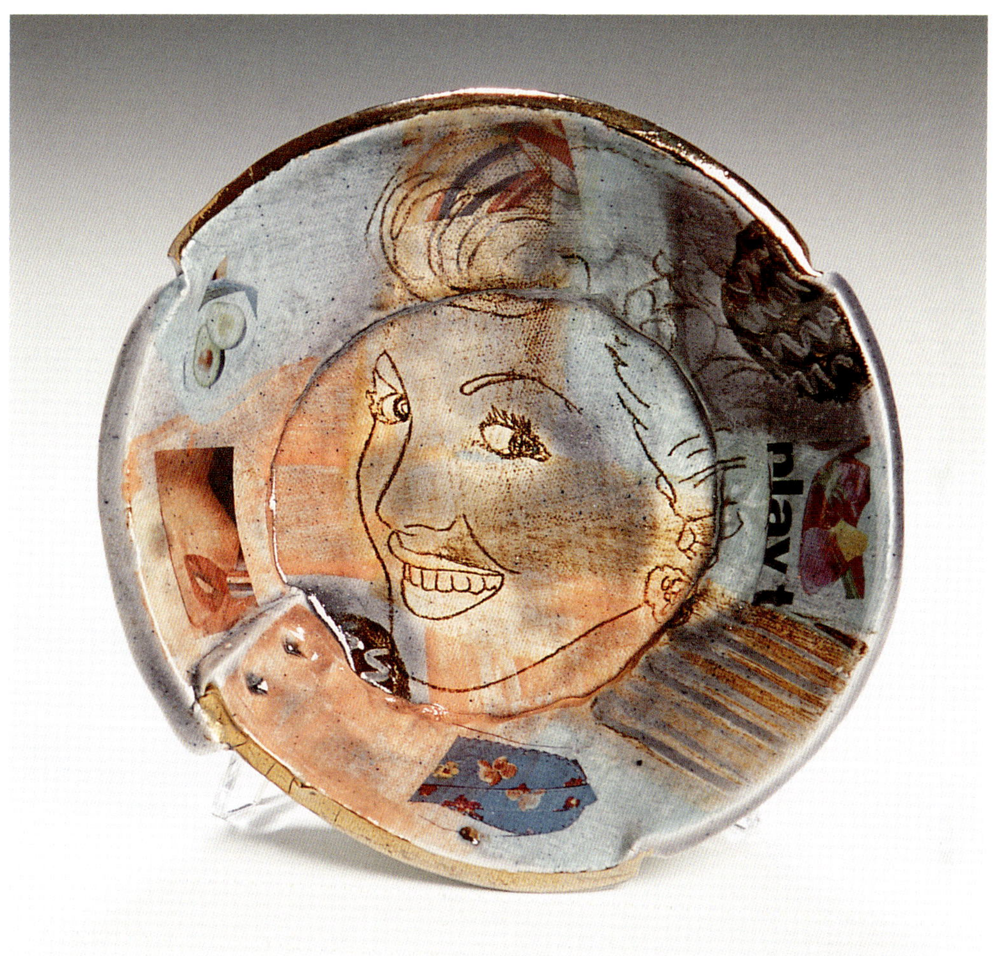

Philomena Pretsell

Blue Face Plate | 2006

$7\frac{1}{16}$ INCHES (18 CM) IN DIAMETER

Hand-built earthenware; slip, monoprint, decals, gold luster

PHOTO BY JOHN MCKENZIE

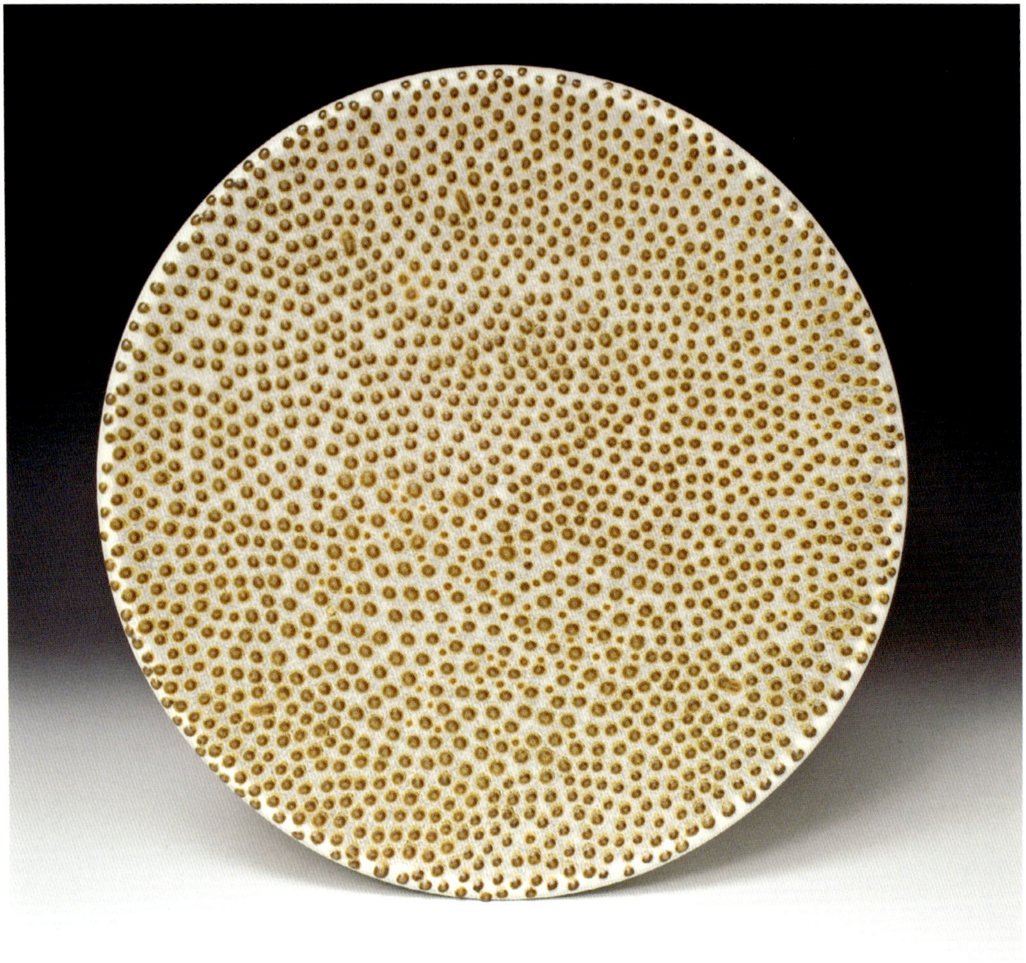

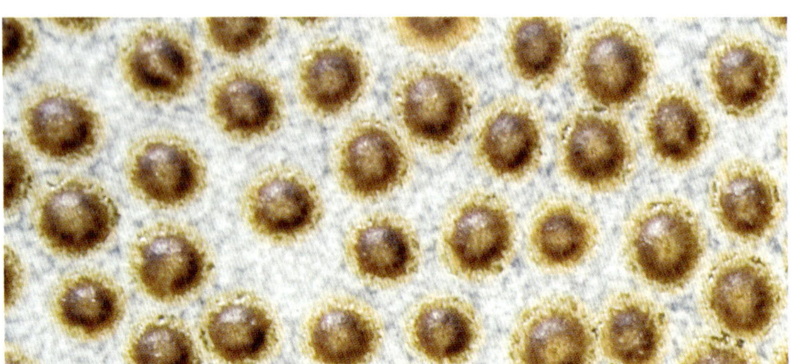

Samantha Henneke

Lots O' Dots | 2007

1 1/4 X 13 INCHES (3.2 X 33 CM)

Wheel-thrown white stoneware; iron slip dots; matte glaze, gas fired in reduction, cone 10

PHOTOS BY BULLDOG POTTERY

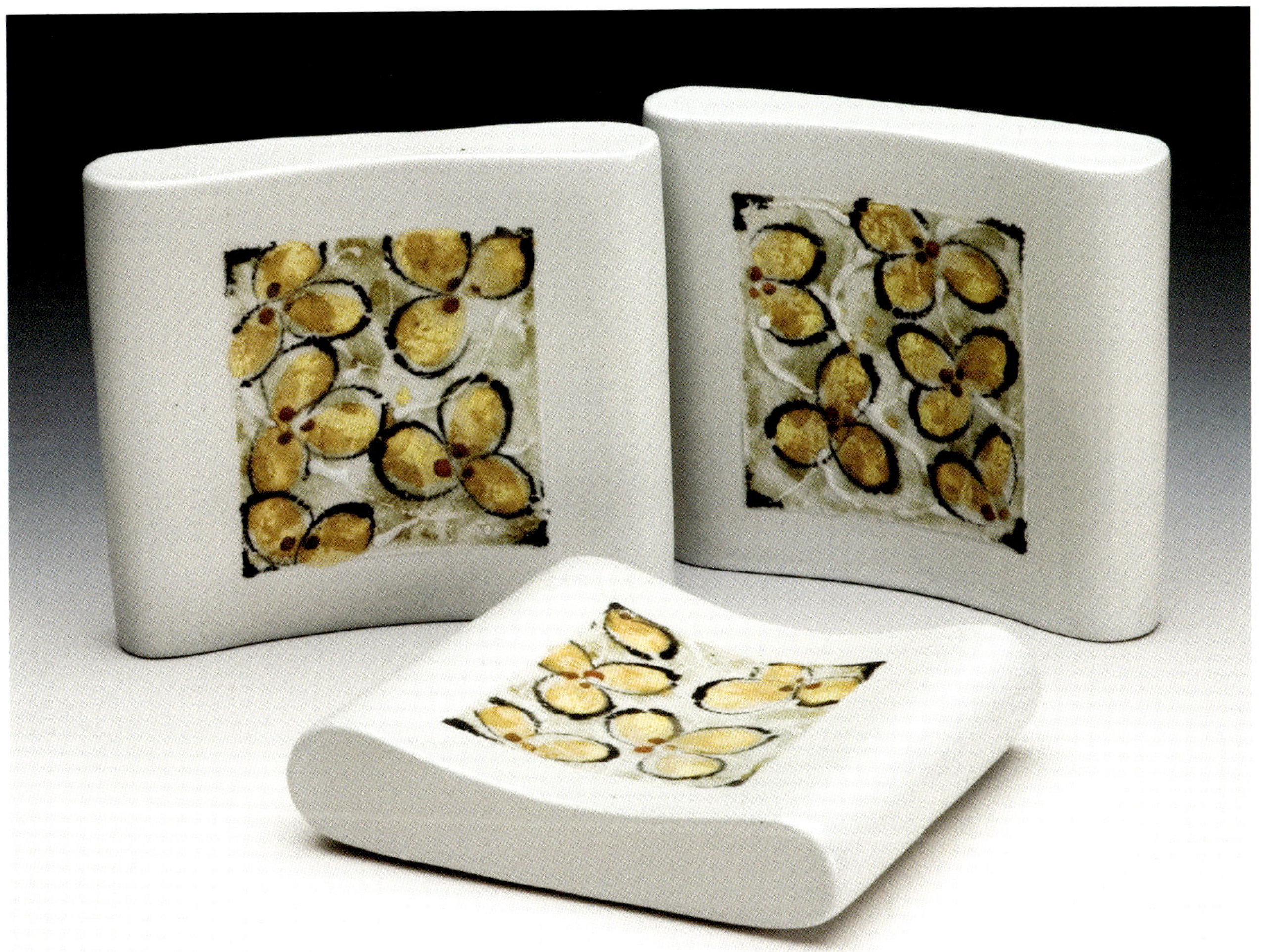

Karen Jennings

Glaze-on-Glaze Platters | 2007

EACH: 1 1/2 X 6 1/2 X 6 INCHES (3.8 X 16.5 X 15.2 CM)

Slab-built white stoneware; slip, glaze-on-glaze decoration; reduction fired, cone 10

PHOTO BY STEPHEN CUMMINGS

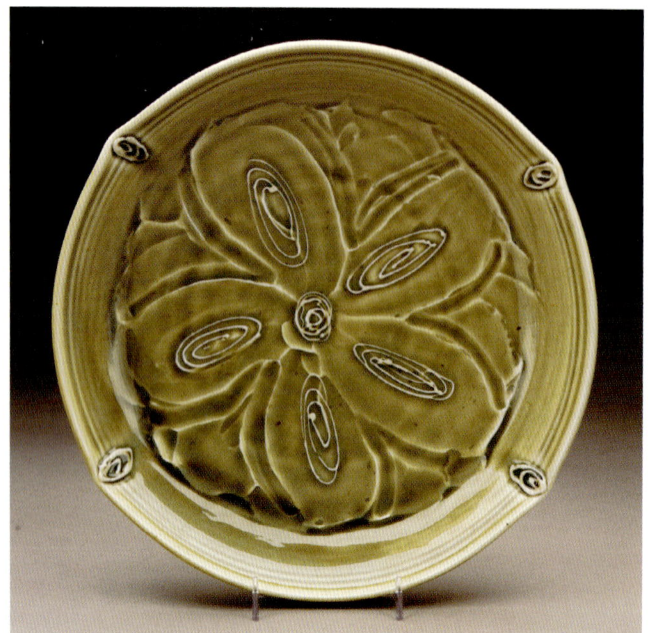

Debra Holiber

Flower Power Platter | 2006

1 7/8 X 11 3/4 INCHES (4.8 X 29.8 CM)

Wheel-thrown and altered porcelain; slip; celadon glaze; reduction fired, cone 10

PHOTO BY LOREN MARON

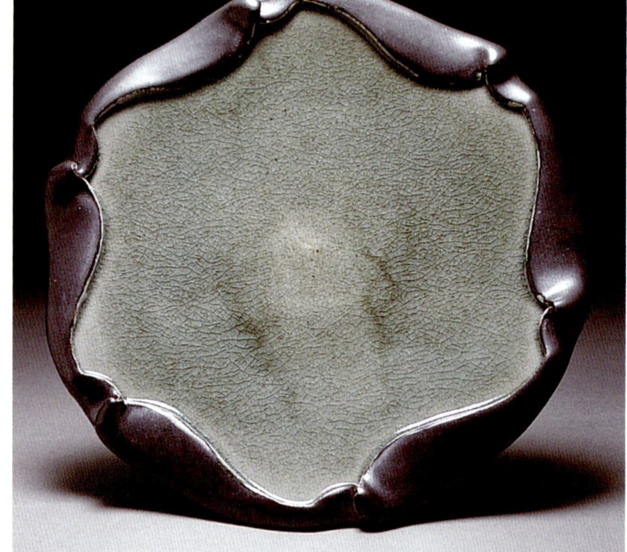

Chris Pickett

Untitled | 2005

1 X 11 INCHES (2.5 X 27.9 CM)

Thrown and altered stoneware; reduction fired, cone 10

PHOTO BY ARTIST

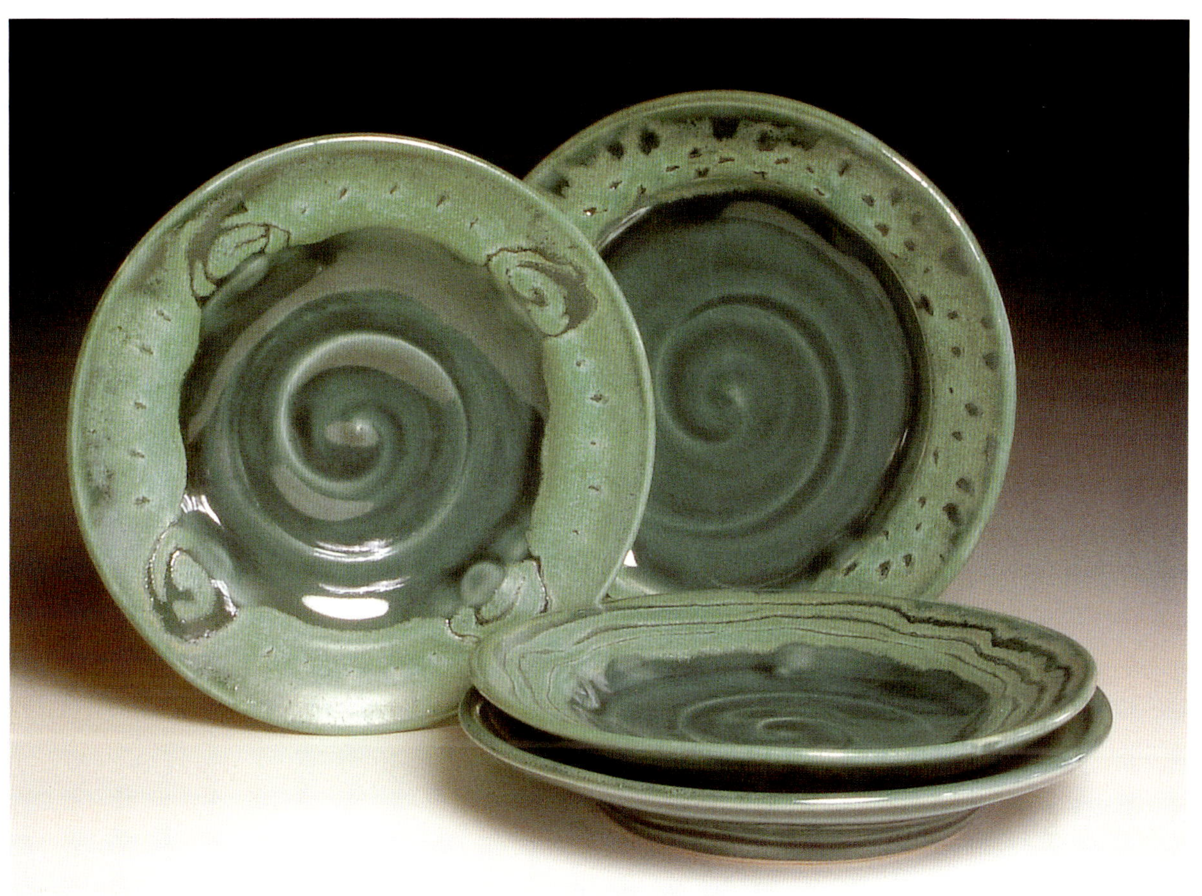

Marian Baker

Dessert Plates | 2007

EACH: 1 1/2 X 7 1/2 INCHES (3.8 X 19.1 CM)

Thrown and altered porcelain; wax-resist glaze technique; electric fired, cone 6

PHOTO BY ARTIST

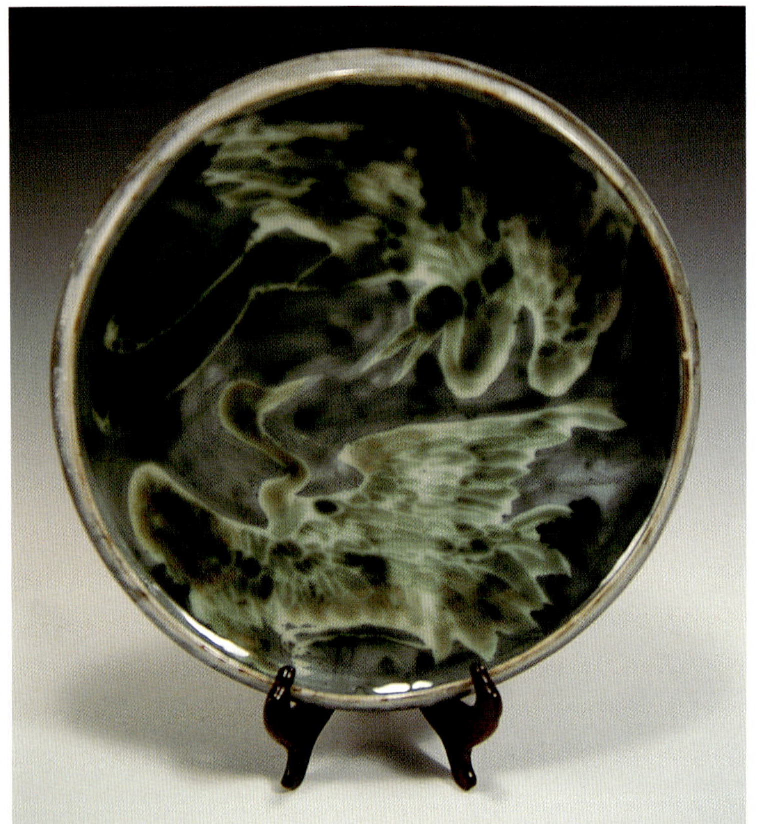

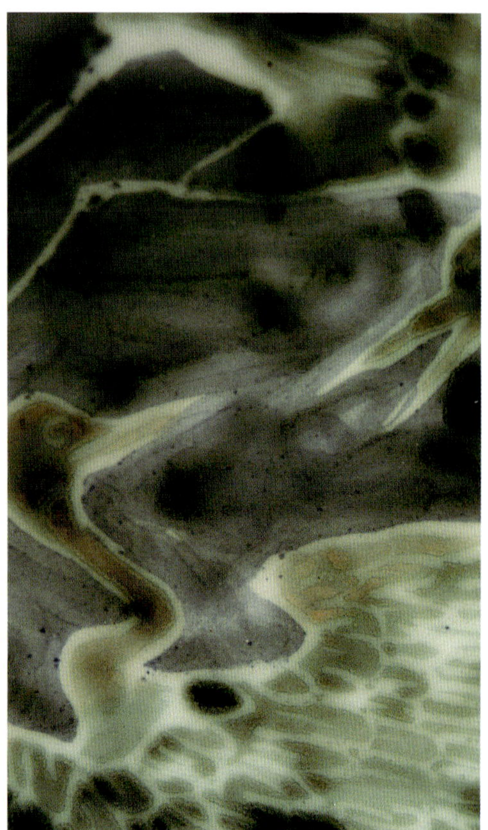

Lisa Ernst

Japanese Stylized Blue Herons | 2001

$2\frac{1}{2}$ X 14 INCHES (6.4 X 35.6 CM)

Thrown high-fire porcelain; wax resist, oxide wash; reduction fired, cone 10

PHOTOS BY ARTIST

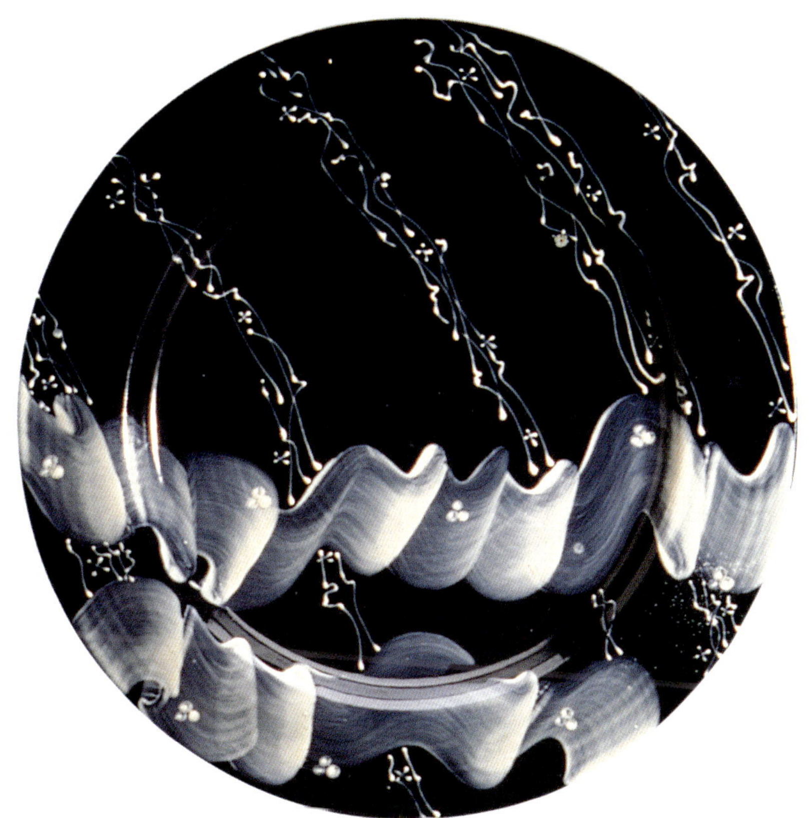

I.B. Remsen

Galaxy Platter | 1984

3 X 21 INCHES (7.6 X 53.3 CM)

Wheel-thrown stoneware; porcelain-based slips; reduction fired, cone 10

PHOTO BY BOB FORAN

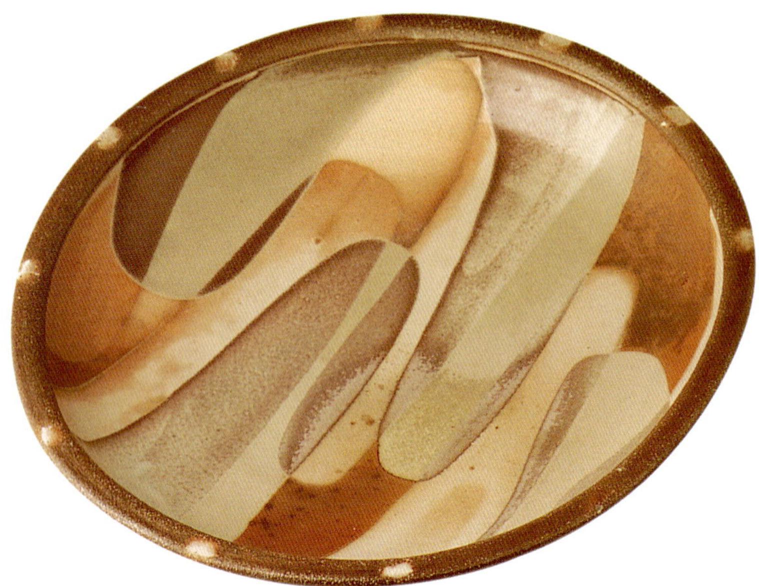

Alex Johnson

Serving Plate | 2006

5 X 18 X 18 INCHES (12.7 X 45.7 X 45.7 CM)

Wheel-thrown stoneware; kaolin slip; oribe and shino glazes; fired upside down over salt pack; wood fired, cone 10

PHOTO BY JEFF SAXMAN

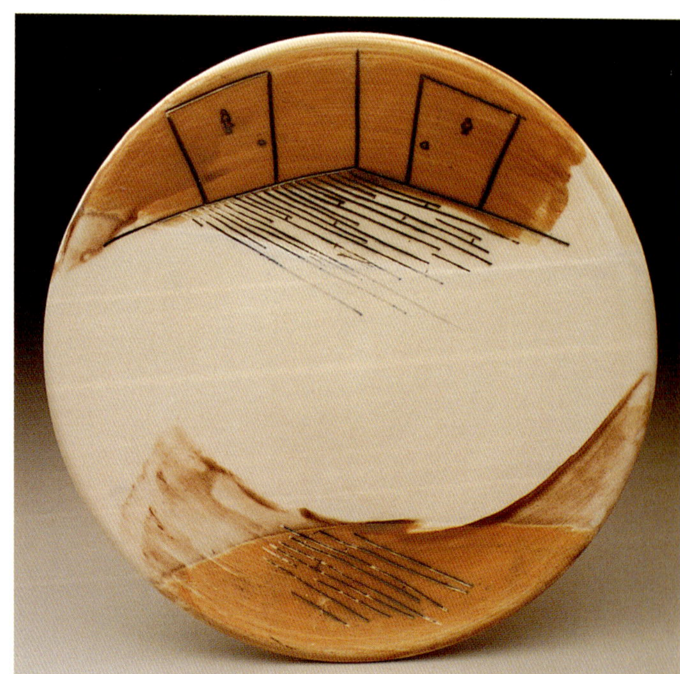

Kowkie Durst

Plate | 2005

1 X 10 INCHES (2.5 X 25.4 CM)

Wheel-thrown porcelain; sgraffito with terra sigillata and glaze; salt fired, cone 6

PHOTO BY ARTIST

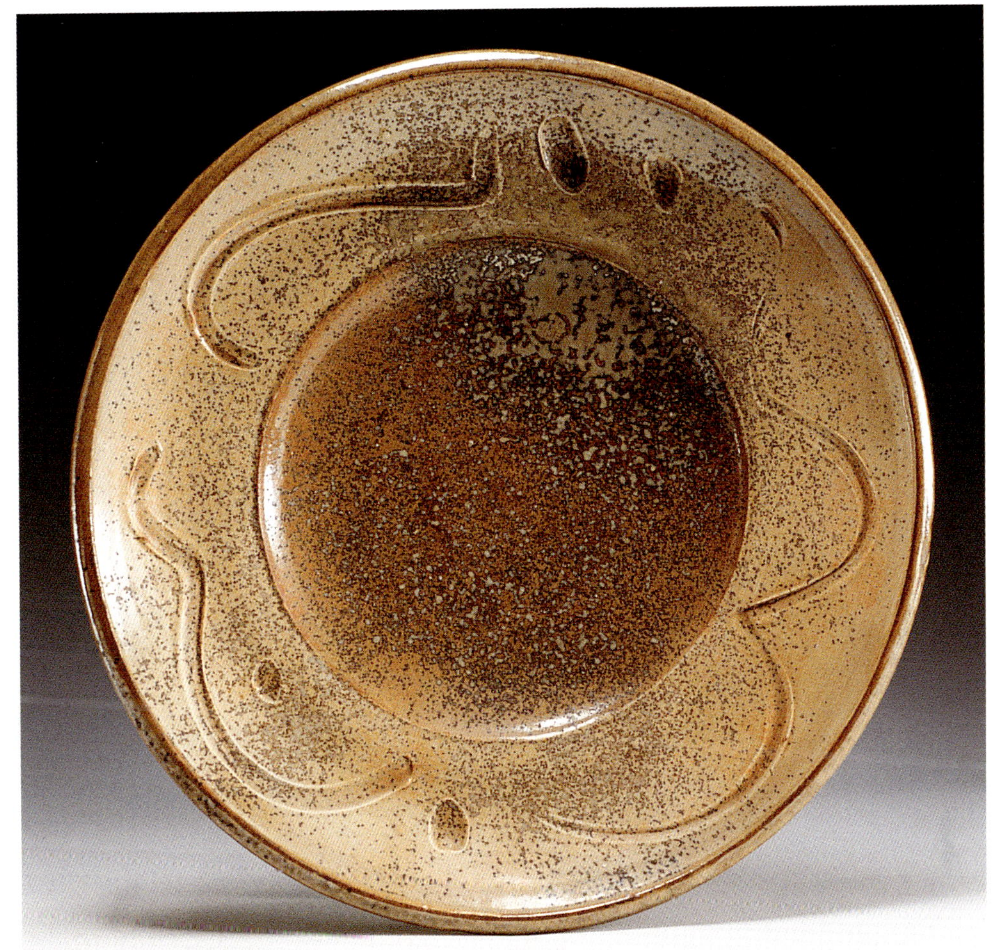

Sandra Daulton Shaughnessy

Movement Circle Platter | 2006

$2\frac{1}{2}$ X $14\frac{1}{4}$ INCHES (6.4 X 36.2 CM)

Wheel-thrown stoneware; porcelain slip; gas fired in reduction, cone 10; shino glaze with wood ash

PHOTO BY PETRONELLA J. YTSMA

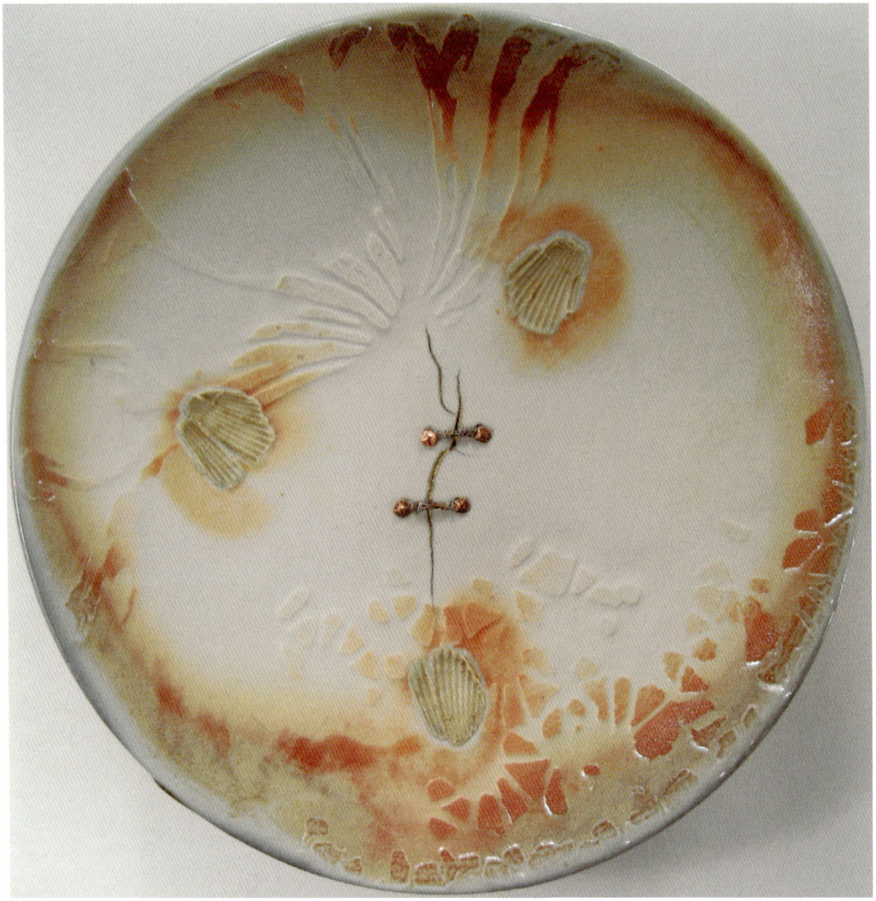

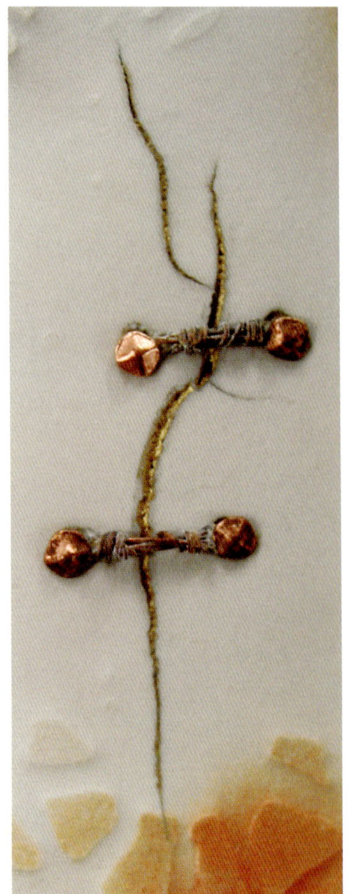

Enzien Kufeld

Stitching a Crack in the Ocean Floor | 2007

$2\frac{1}{2}$ X $9\frac{1}{4}$ X 9 INCHES (6.4 X 23.5 X 22.9 CM)

Wheel-thrown white stoneware; waxed and washed; natural ash glaze; wood fired, cone 11; cement mortar, gold leaf, patina copper wire, and copper

PHOTOS BY CHRISTIAN D. BARR

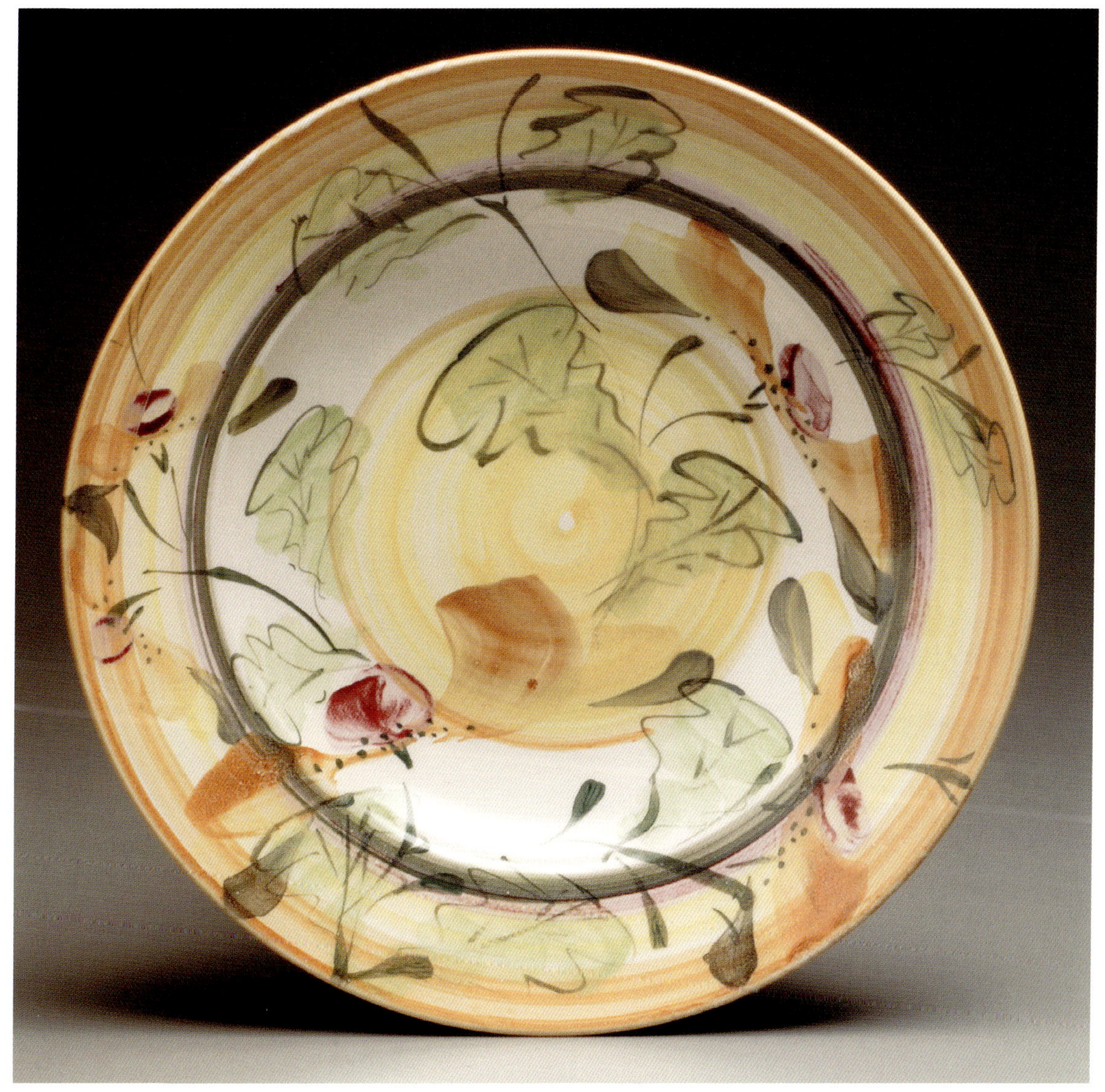

Charlotte Lindley Martin

Charger | 2006

3 X 15 INCHES (7.6 X 38.1 CM)

Wheel-thrown porcelain; painted majolica style; electric fired, cone 6

PHOTO BY JOHN CARLANO

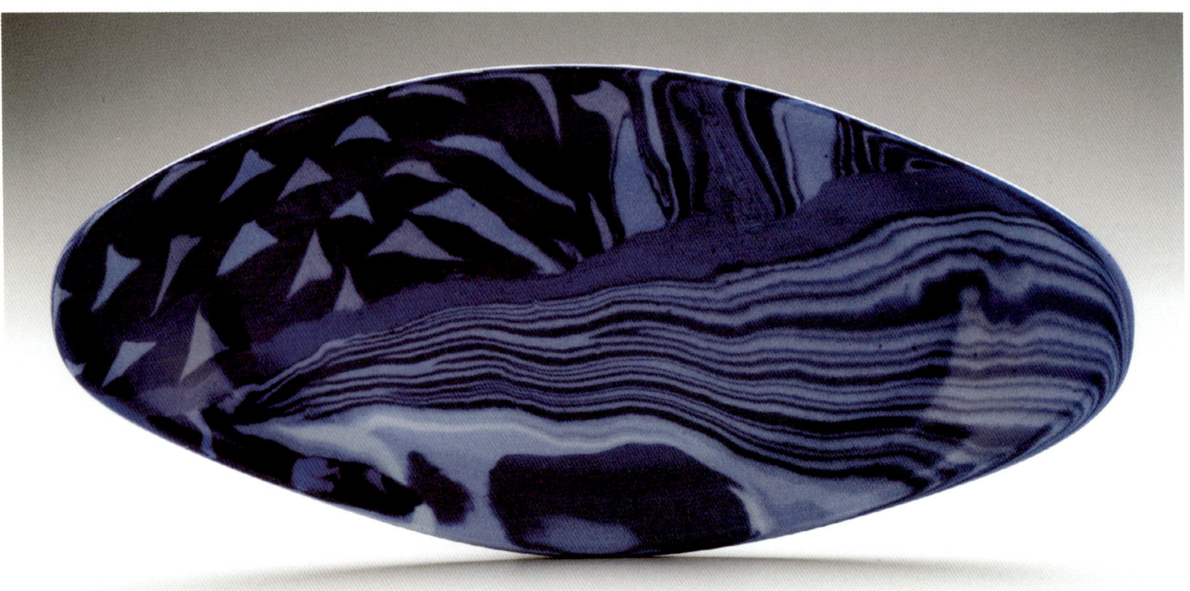

Jeanet Dreskin-Haig
Ocean Butter Plate | 2006
1 X 8 X 3¾ INCHES (2.5 X 20.3 X 9.5 CM)
Hand-built with laminated multi-colored porcelain; clear glaze, electric fired, cone 6
PHOTO BY HARRISON EVANS

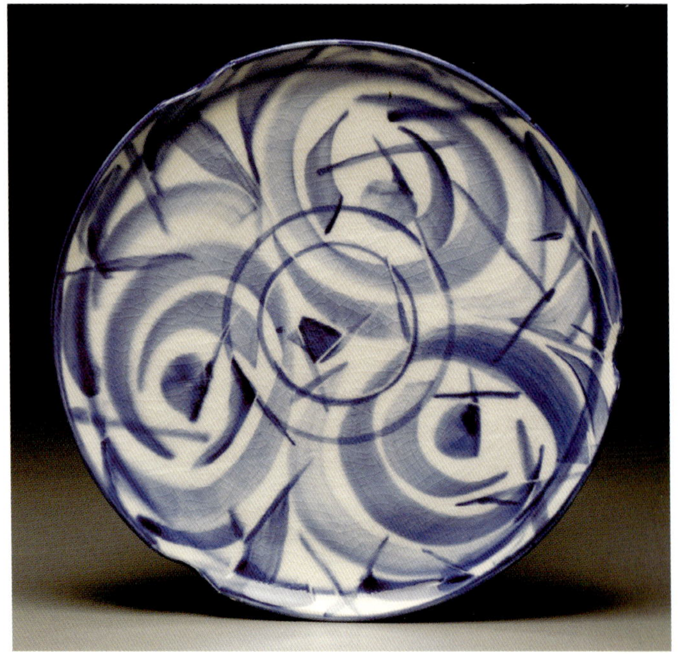

Maria Siskin
Untitled | 2007
¾ X 12 INCHES (1.9 X 30.5 CM)
Wheel-thrown and altered porcelain; green ware underglaze brushwork; glaze, electric fired, cone 6
PHOTO BY JOHN CARLANO

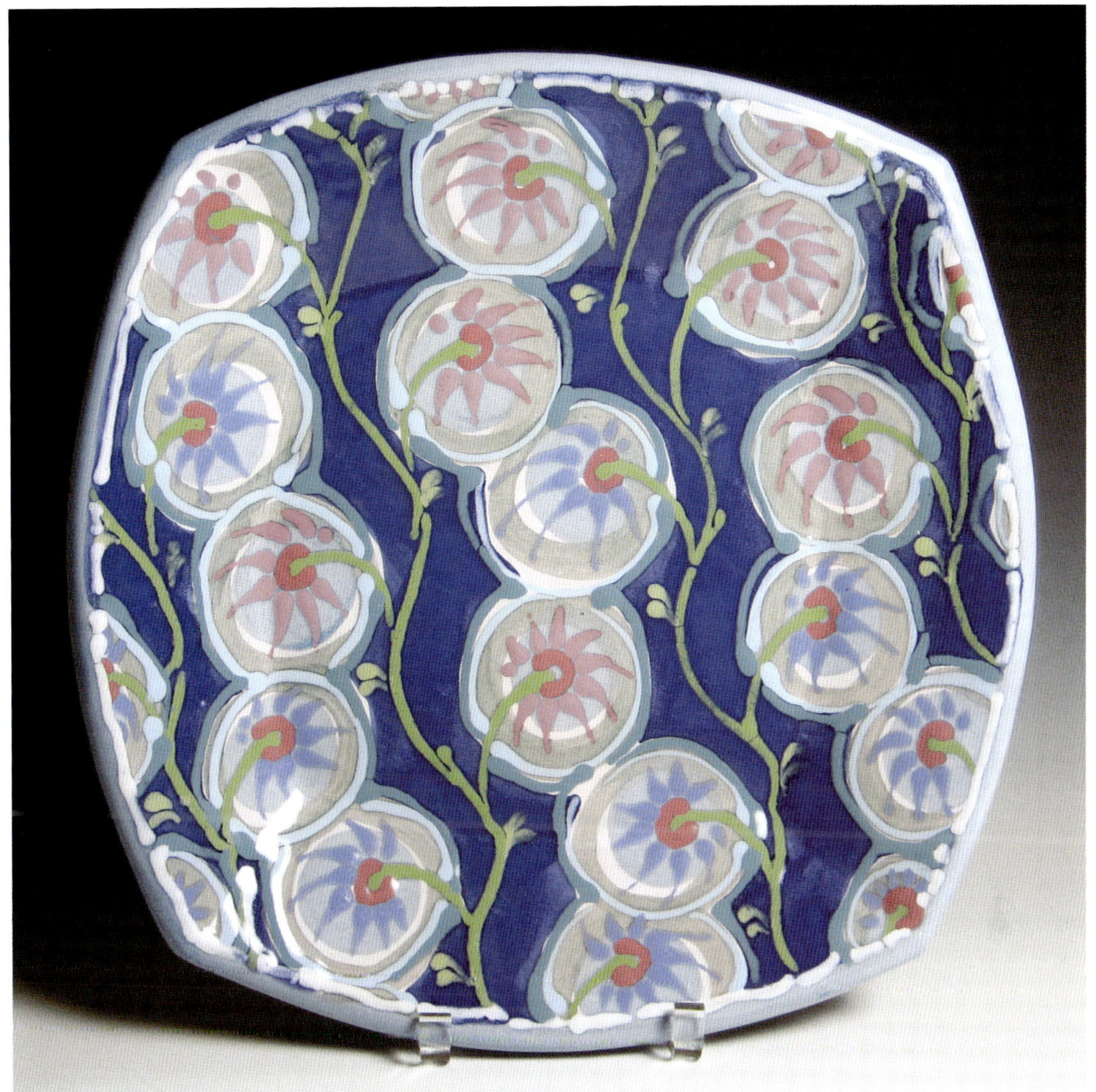

Kaitlyn Miller

Seacrest Platter | 2007

2 X 13 X 13 INCHES (5.1 X 33 X 33 CM)

Hand-built red earthenware;
majolica, stains, and glaze trailing;
electric fired, cone 04

PHOTO BY ARTIST

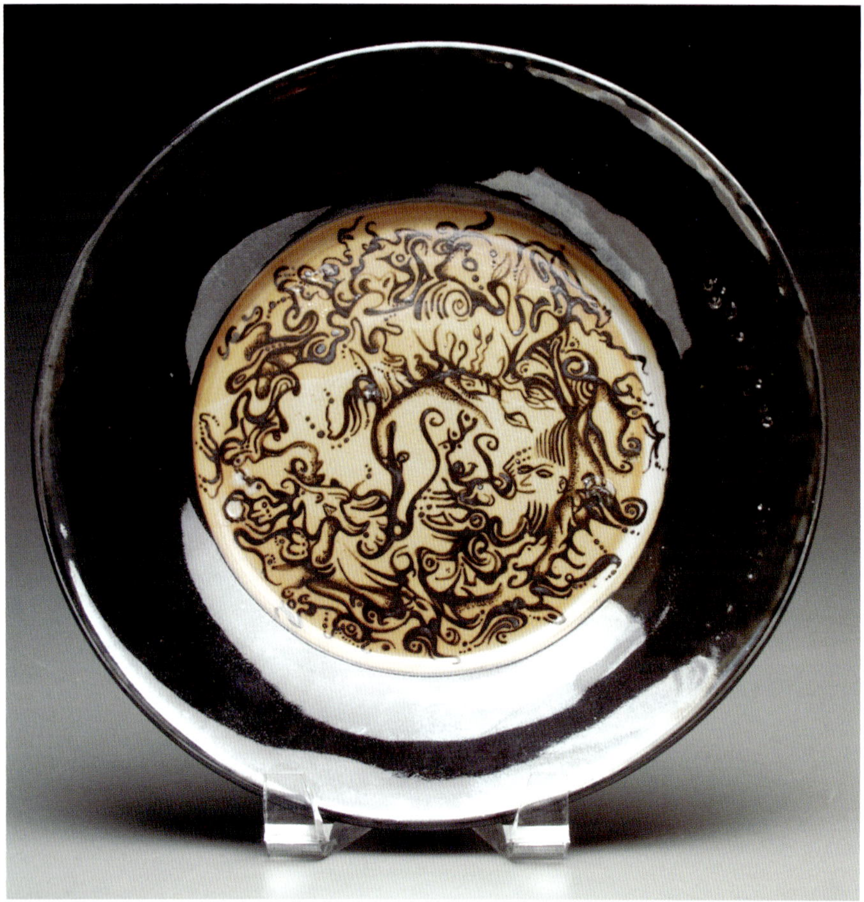

Char Applen

Untitled | 2007

$1\frac{1}{2}$ X 10 INCHES (3.8 X 25.4 CM)

Wheel-thrown porcelaneous stoneware; brushwork; shino, glossy black glaze; downdraft kiln, cone 10

PHOTOS BY DON RIDLEY

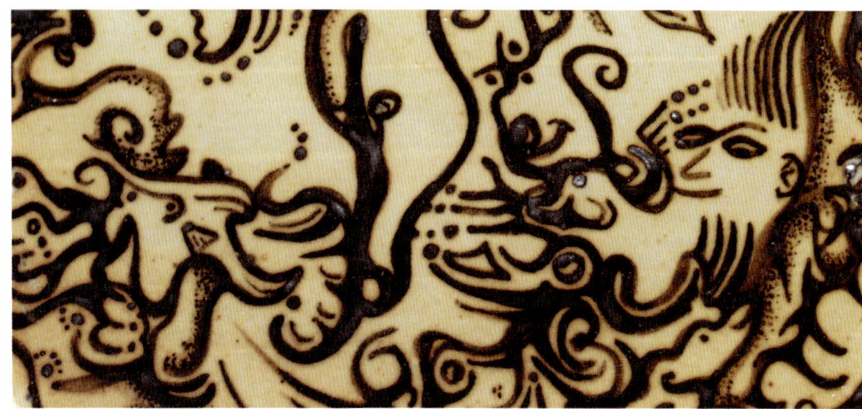

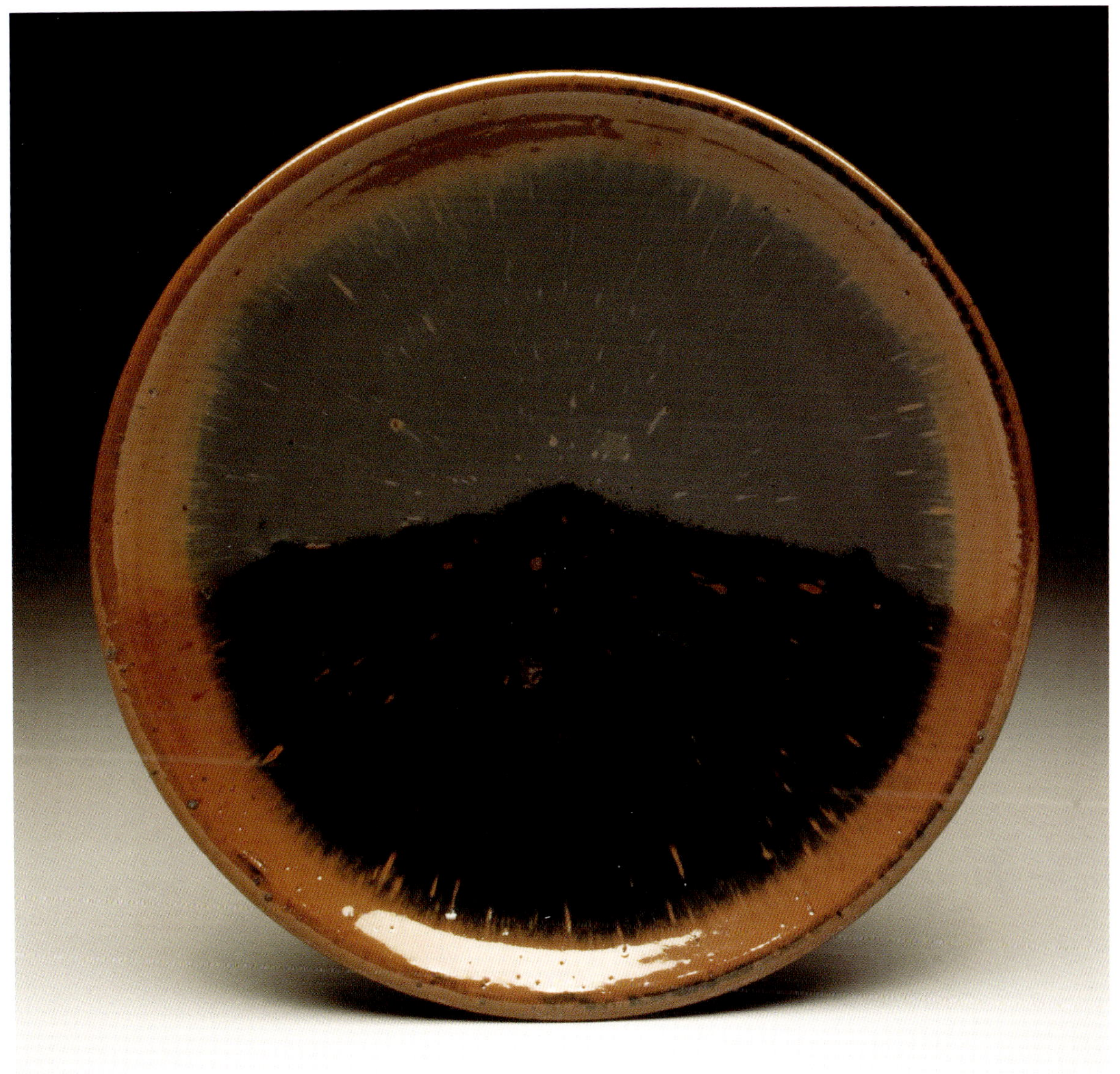

Ted Neal

Tianmu Shan Plate | 2007

$2^{1}/_{2}$ X 12 INCHES (6.4 X 30.5 CM)

Wheel-thrown stoneware; iron saturate glaze, gas fired in reduction, cone 10

PHOTO BY SERENA NANCARROW

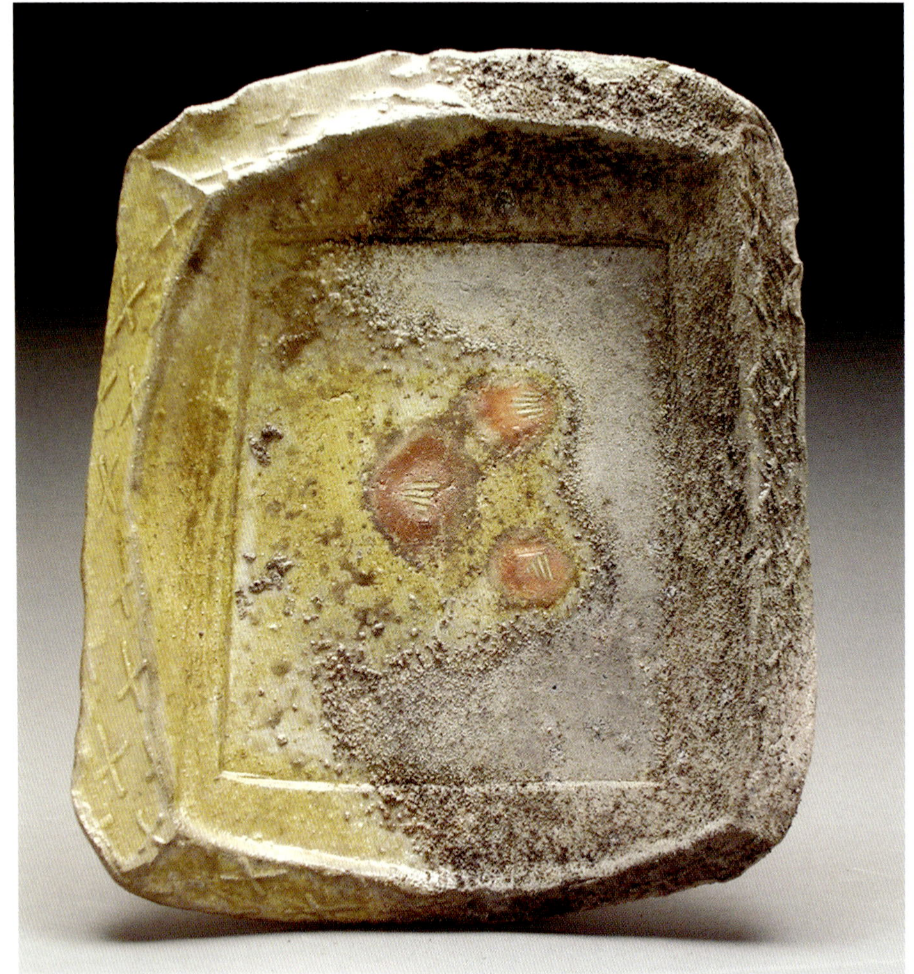

Ben Jensen

Firebox Tray | 2006

2 X 9 X 9 INCHES (5.1 X 22.9 X 22.9 CM)

Hand-built stoneware;
wood fired, cone 12

PHOTO BY ARTIST

Ruchika Madan

Square Platter with Fronds | 2006

2 X 16 X 16 INCHES (5.1 X 40.6 X 40.6 CM)

Hand-built white stoneware; sgraffito and carved; oxidation fired, cone 6

PHOTO BY ARTIST

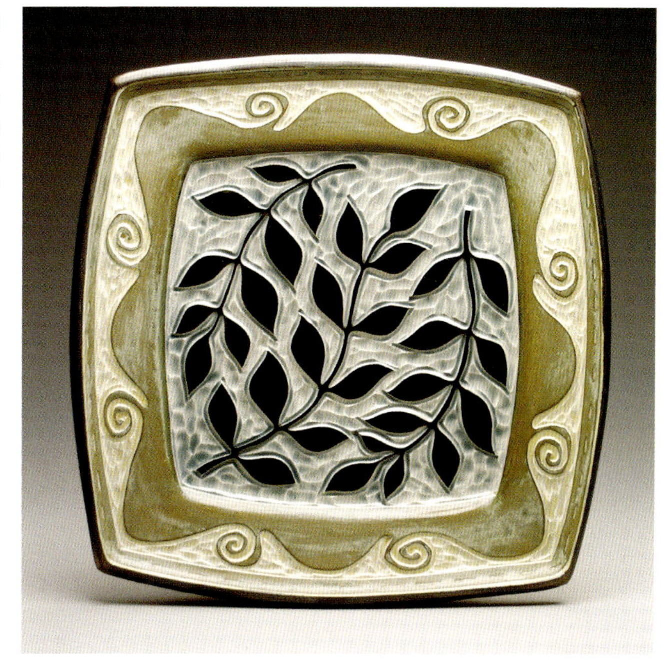

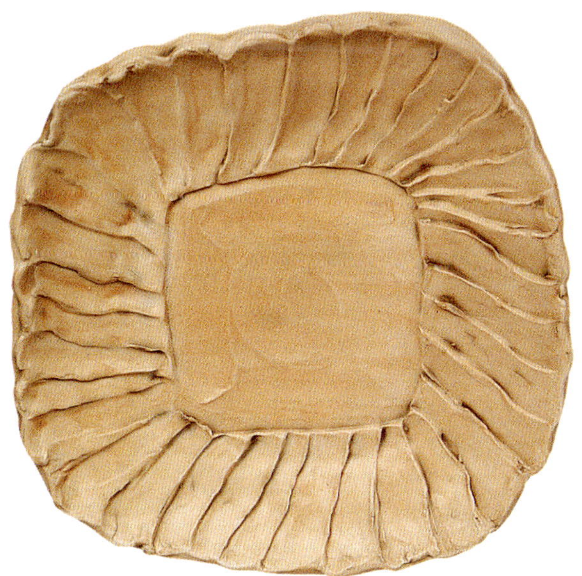

Carole Ann Fer

Pleated Serving Platter | 2006

$2^{1}/_{2}$ X 16 X 15 INCHES (6.4 X 40.6 X 38.1 CM)

Thrown and altered soft porcelain; electric fired, cone 08; copper patina wash, matte glaze; oxidation fired, cone 6

PHOTO BY ELLEN WIESKE

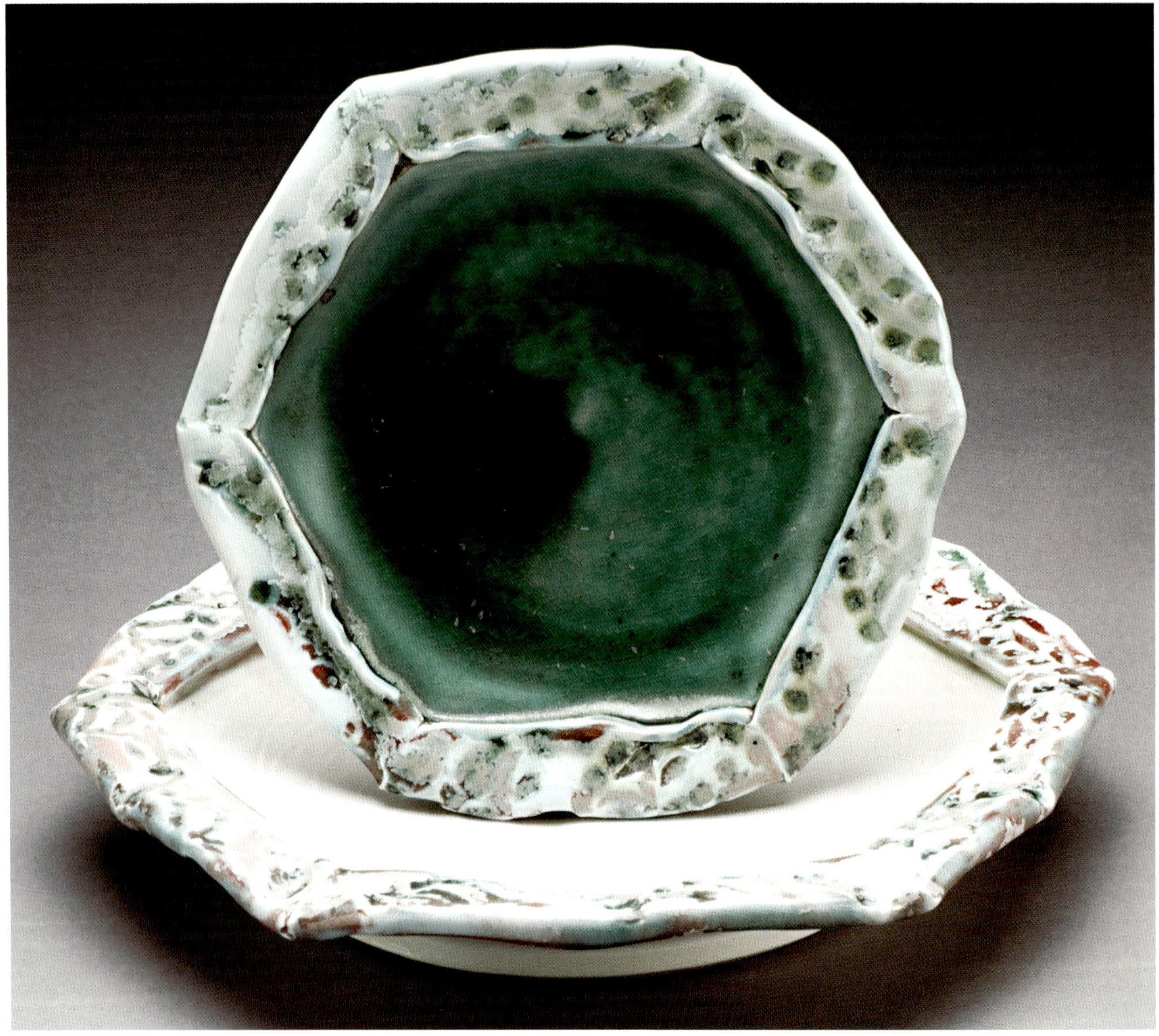

Gertrude Graham Smith

Cake Plates | 2006

EACH: $1\frac{1}{2}$ X $9\frac{1}{2}$ INCHES (3.8 X 24.1 CM)

Wheel-thrown porcelain;
soda fired, cone 10

PHOTO BY TOM MILLS

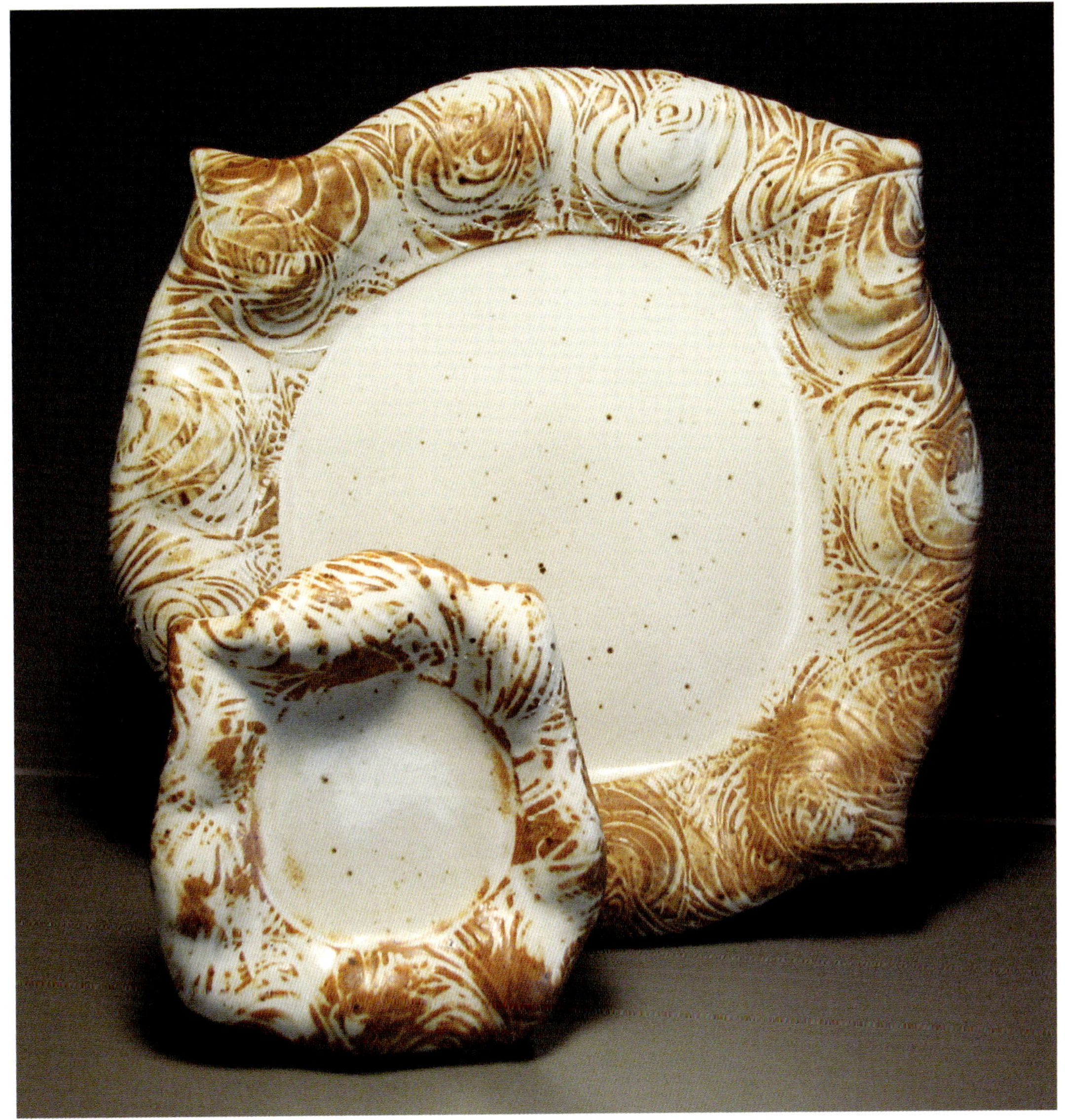

Lesli Wortham Bruce

Anna's Series | 2007

LARGEST: 1 1/2 X 11 1/2 X 11 1/2 INCHES (3.8 X 29.2 X 29.2 CM)

Hand-built slab stoneware; textured; gas fired in reduction, cone 10; glaze, cone 10

PHOTO BY ARTIST

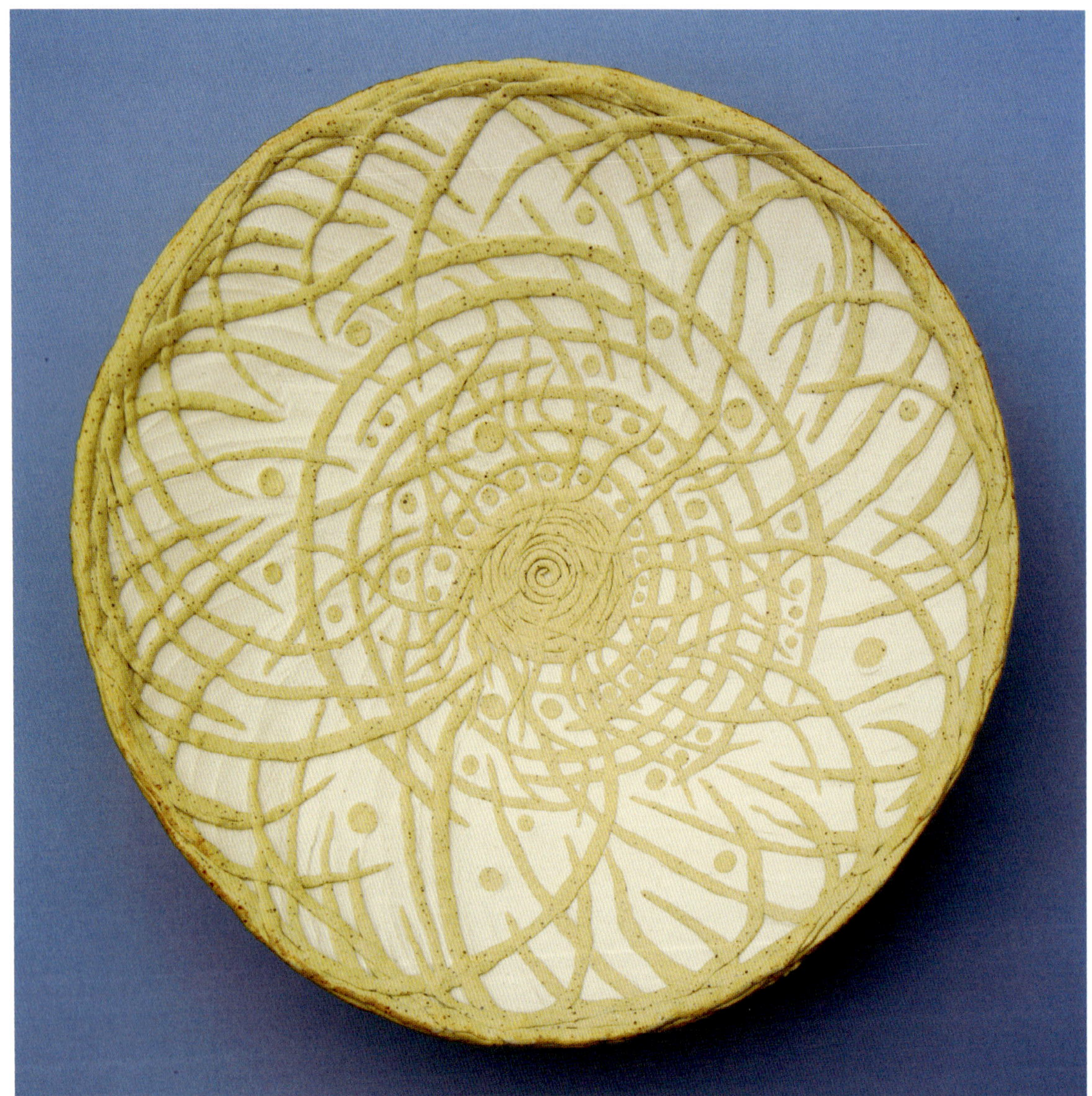

Danuta Tydor

Energy | 2006

13 INCHES (33 CM) IN DIAMETER

Hand-built porcelain stoneware; unglazed; electric fired, cone 6

PHOTO BY VLODEK TYDOR

Damian Grava

Expansion 1 | 2007

$3^1/_2$ X $18^1/_2$ X 18 INCHES (8.9 X 47 X 45.7 CM)

Wheel-thrown and altered stoneware; flashing slip; soda fired, cone 11

PHOTO BY BRET CORRINGTON

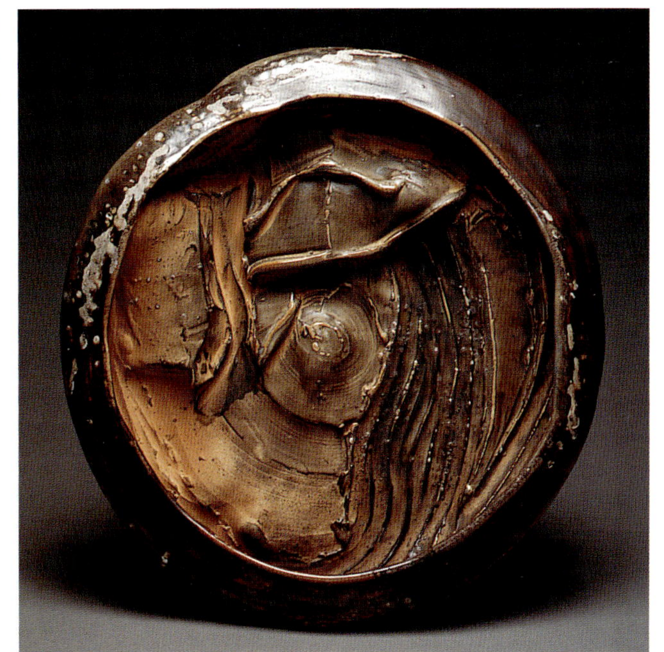

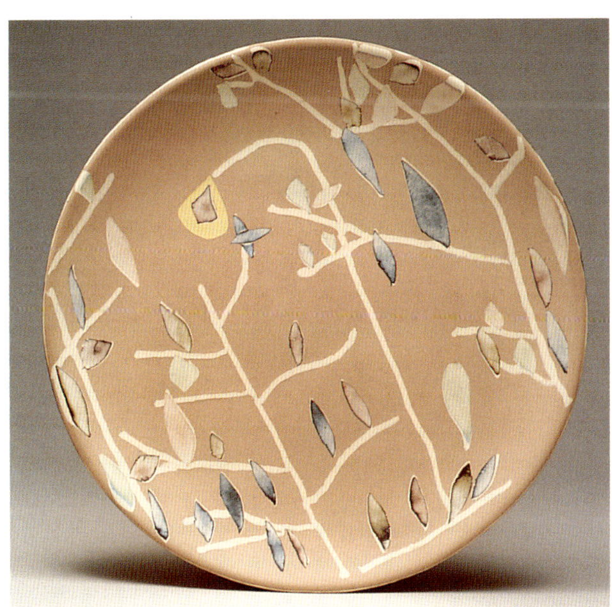

Susan Nemeth

Trees | 2003

1 X 12 INCHES (2.5 X 30.5 CM)

Press-molded porcelain; inlay using colored clays and slips; unglazed; electric fired, cone 9

PHOTO BY STEPHEN BRAYNE

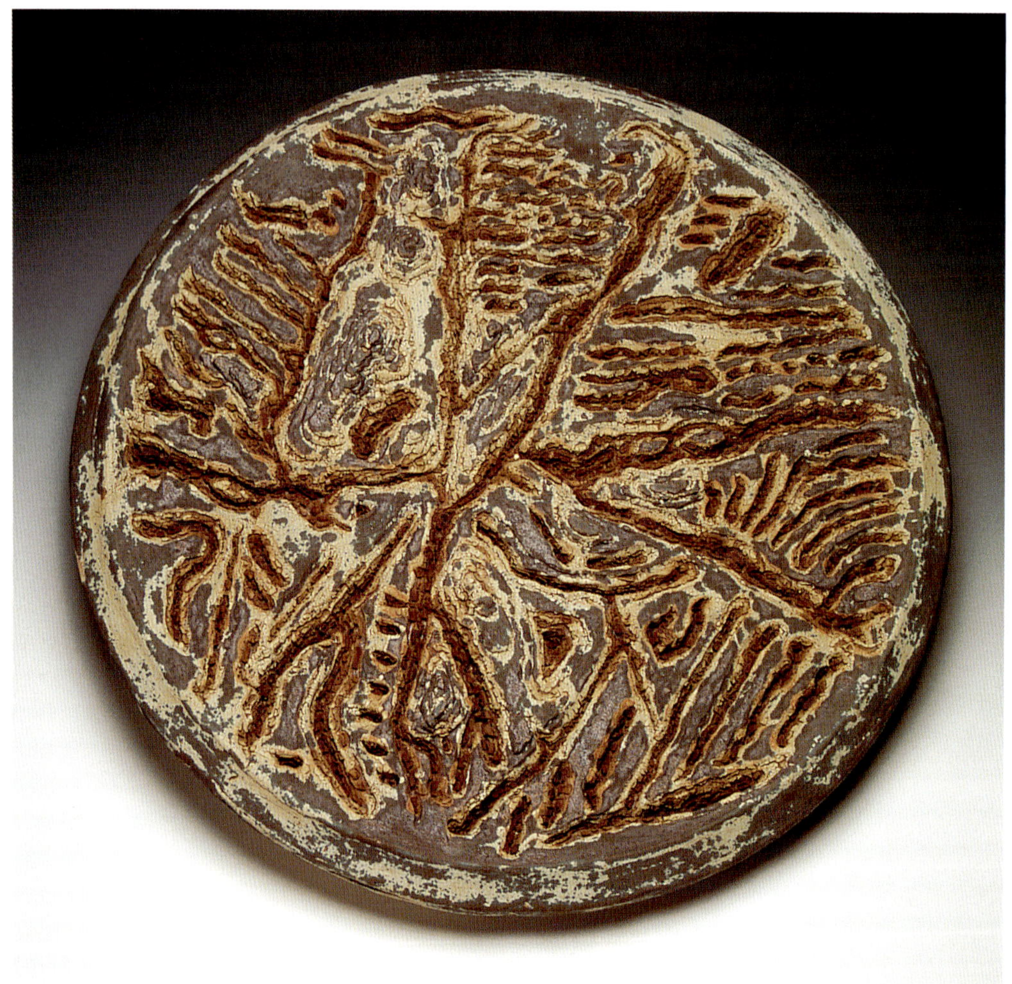

Steve Hilton

A Topographic Map of My Hand | 2005

3 X 29 INCHES (7.6 X 73.7 CM)

Thrown and carved earthenware;
cone 04 glaze, reduction

PHOTO BY ARTIST

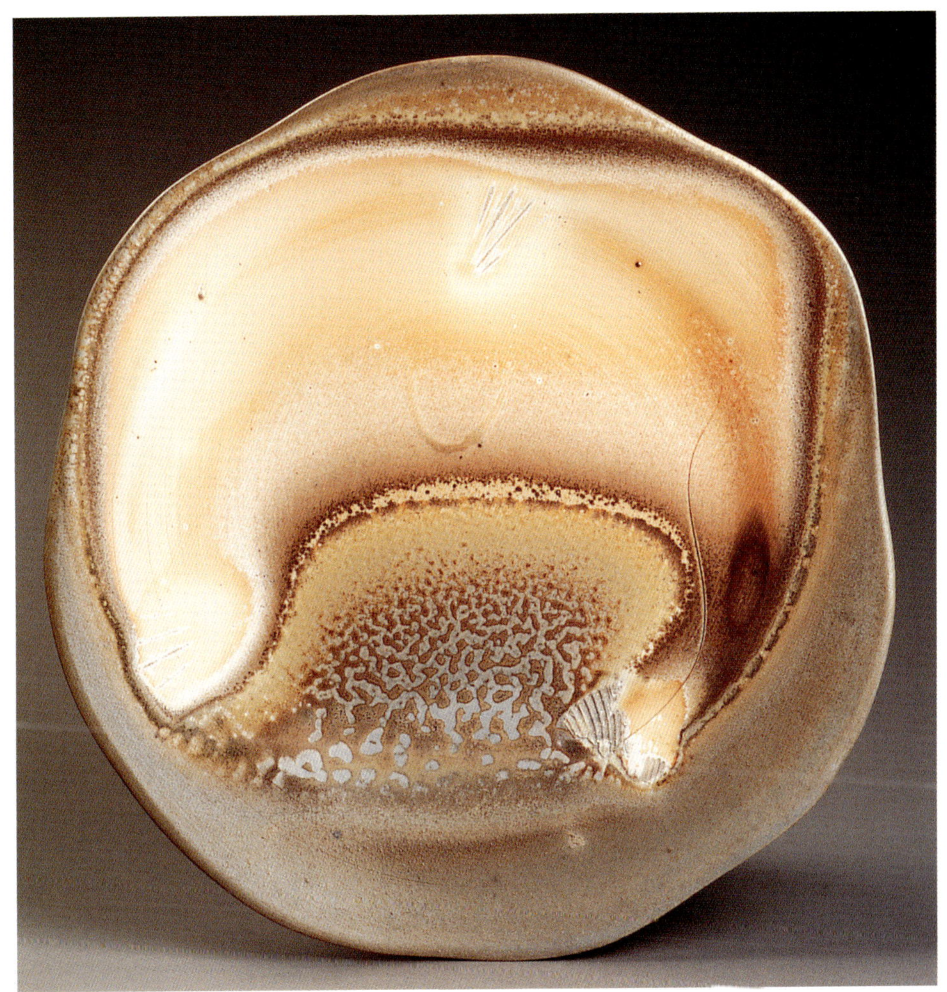

Liz Garrett

Unglazed Wood-Fired Platter | 2005

2 X 14 X 14 INCHES (5.1 X 35.6 X 35.6 CM)

Slab and wheel-constructed porcelain; anagama fired without glaze, cone 14

PHOTO BY ROGER SCHRIEBER

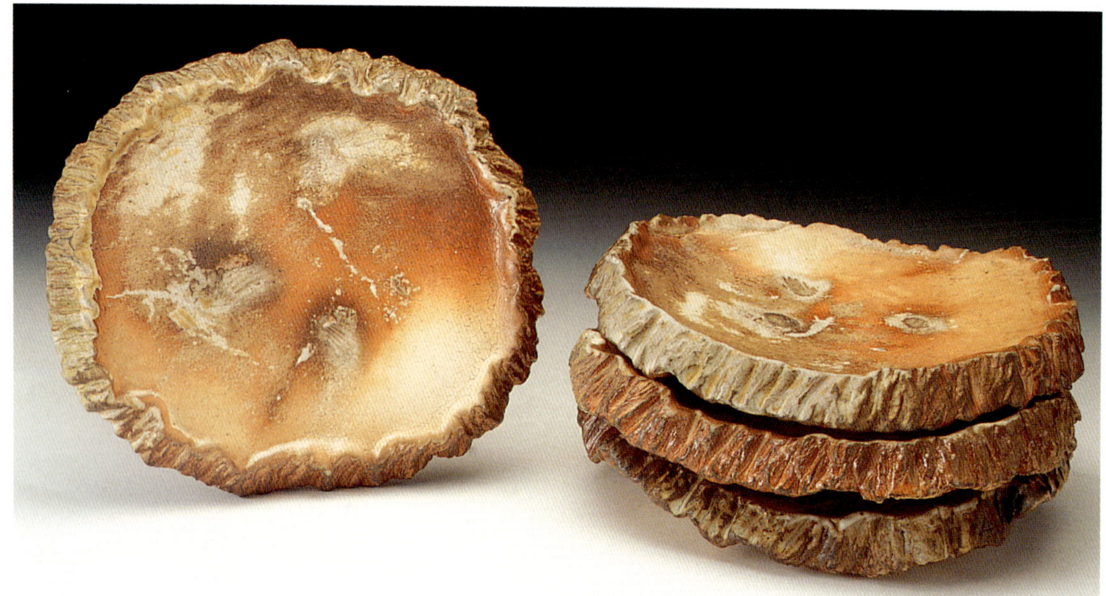

Joy Tanner

Bark Plates | 2006

EACH: 1 1/2 X 7 X 6 INCHES (3.8 X 17.8 X 15.2 CM)

Hand-built slab stoneware; impressed textures, flashing slips, sprayed; ash, salt, and soda fired, cone 10

PHOTO BY ARTIST

Jenni Brant

Salad Plates | 2007

EACH: 2 X 9 X 9 INCHES (5.1 X 22.9 X 22.9 CM)

Hand-built porcelain; electric fired, cone 6; luster, cone 018

PHOTO BY ARTIST

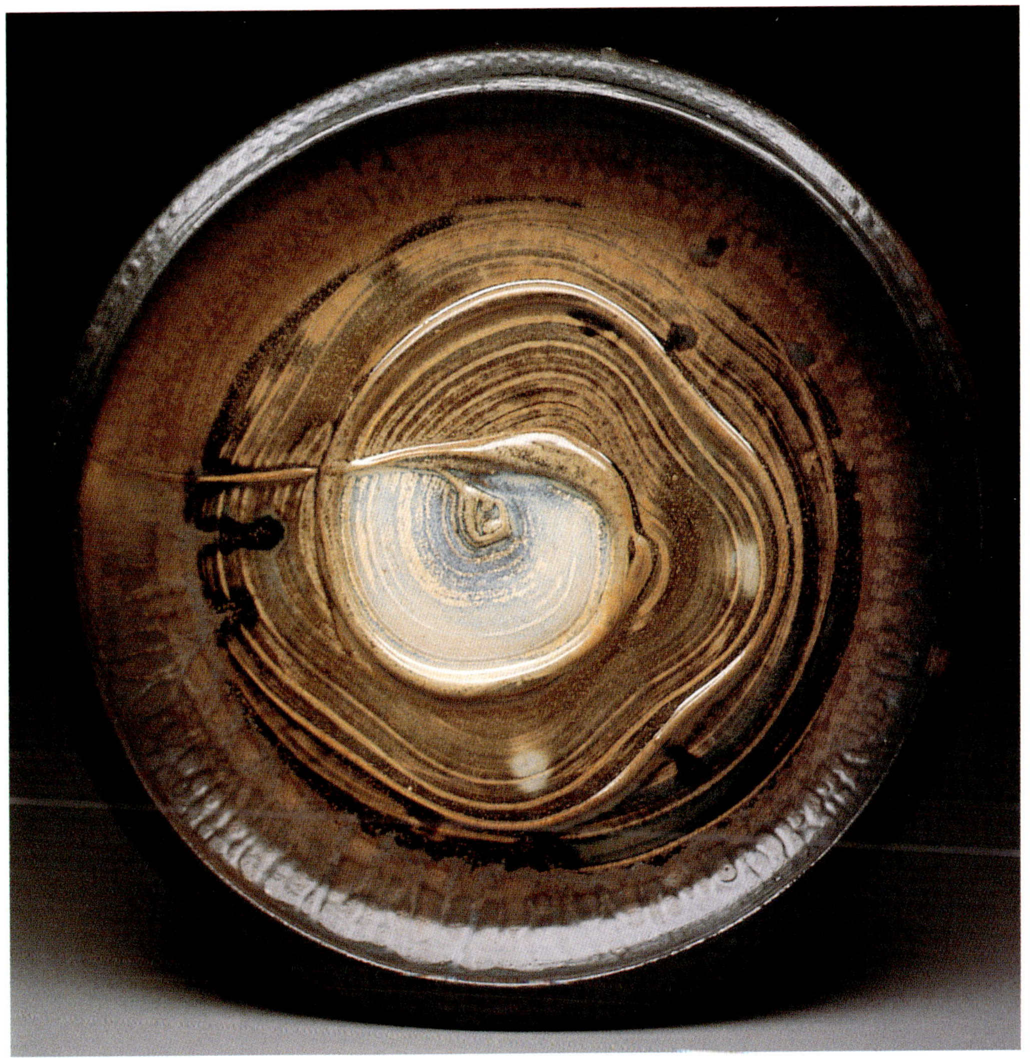

Chris Lively

Platter | 2007

2 X 15 INCHES (5.1 X 38.1 CM)

Wheel-thrown stoneware; brushed slip, sprayed glazes; natural gas updraft, cone 10 reduction

PHOTO BY ARTIST

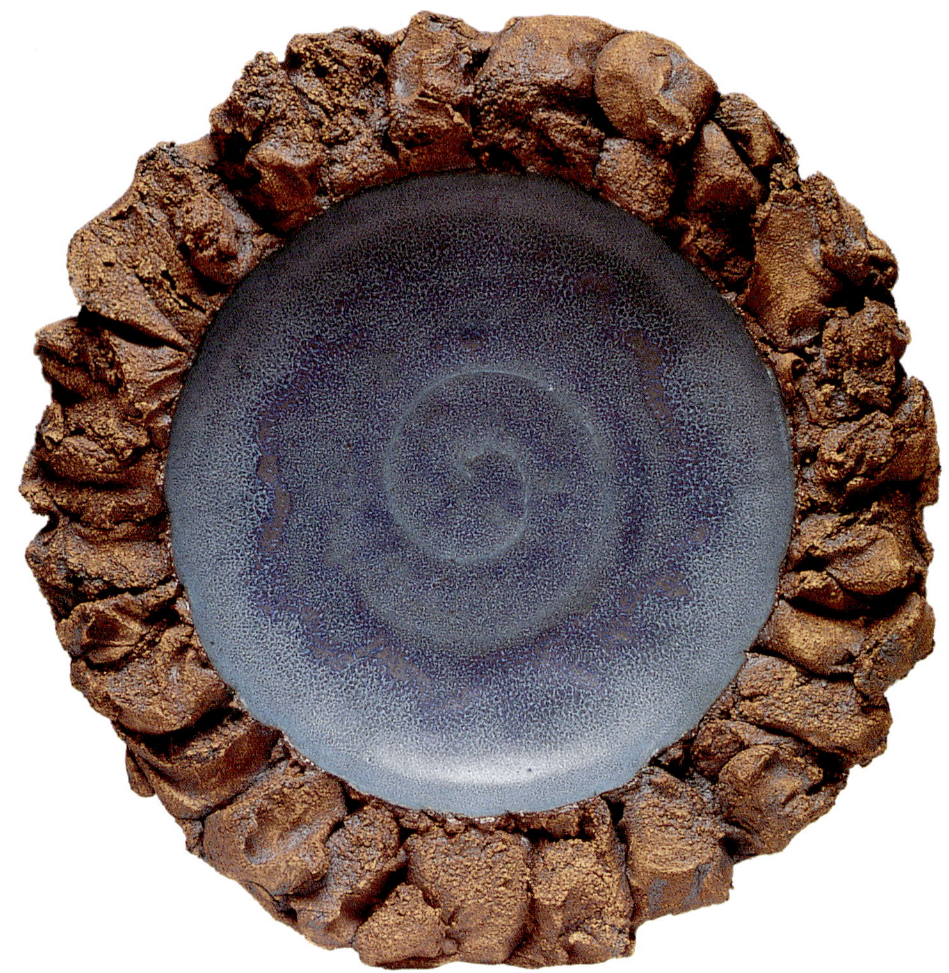

Ginny Marsh

Garden Platter | 2006

3 1/2 X 17 1/2 INCHES (8.9 X 44.5 CM)

Wheel-thrown stoneware; copper blue glaze, natural gas fired in reduction, cone 10

PHOTO BY ARTIST

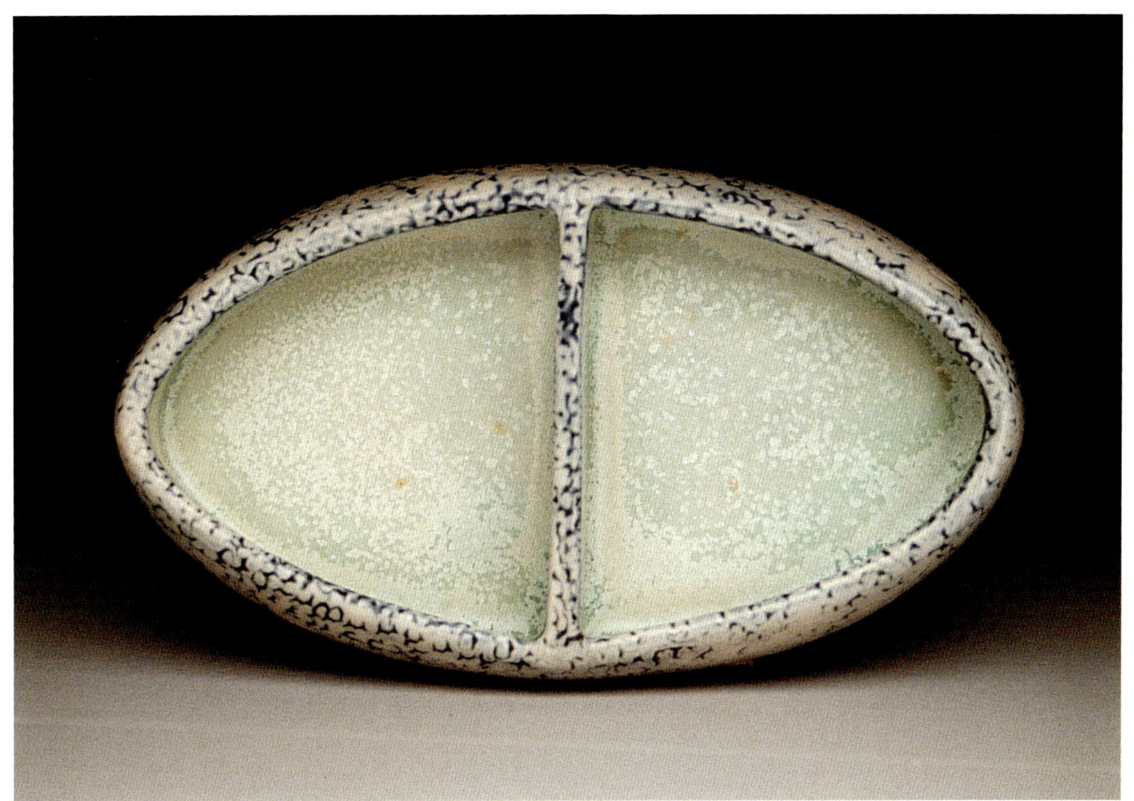

Karin Solberg

Split Snack Tray | 2006

1 X $6\frac{1}{2}$ X 4 INCHES (2.5 X 16.5 X 10.2 CM)

Wheel-thrown porcelain; salt fired, cone 10

PHOTO BY ARTIST

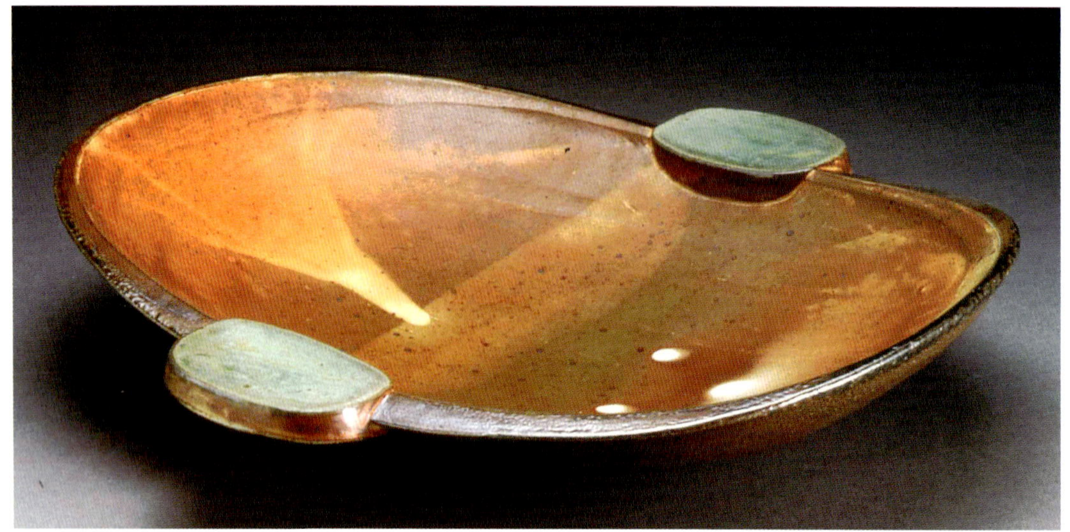

Matt Kelleher

Trencher with Two Green Ears | 2006

$2\frac{1}{2}$ X 16 X 12 INCHES (6.4 X 40.6 X 30.5 CM)

Slab-built stoneware over bisque mold; flashing slip; soda fired, cone 10

PHOTO BY TOM MILLS

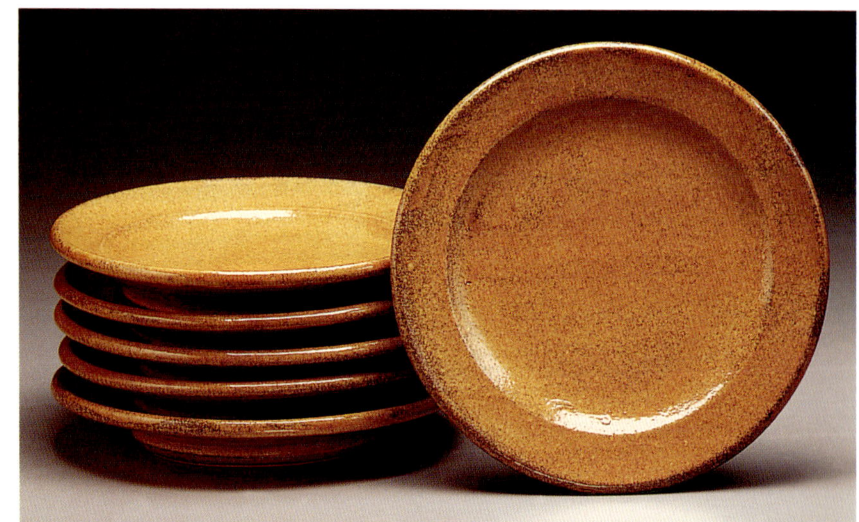

Lisa Buck

Set of Dinner Plates | 2005

EACH: $1\frac{1}{2}$ X 11 INCHES (3.8 X 27.9 CM)

Wheel-thrown earthenware; white slip and amber glaze; electric fired, cone 04

PHOTO BY STEVE SCHNEIDER

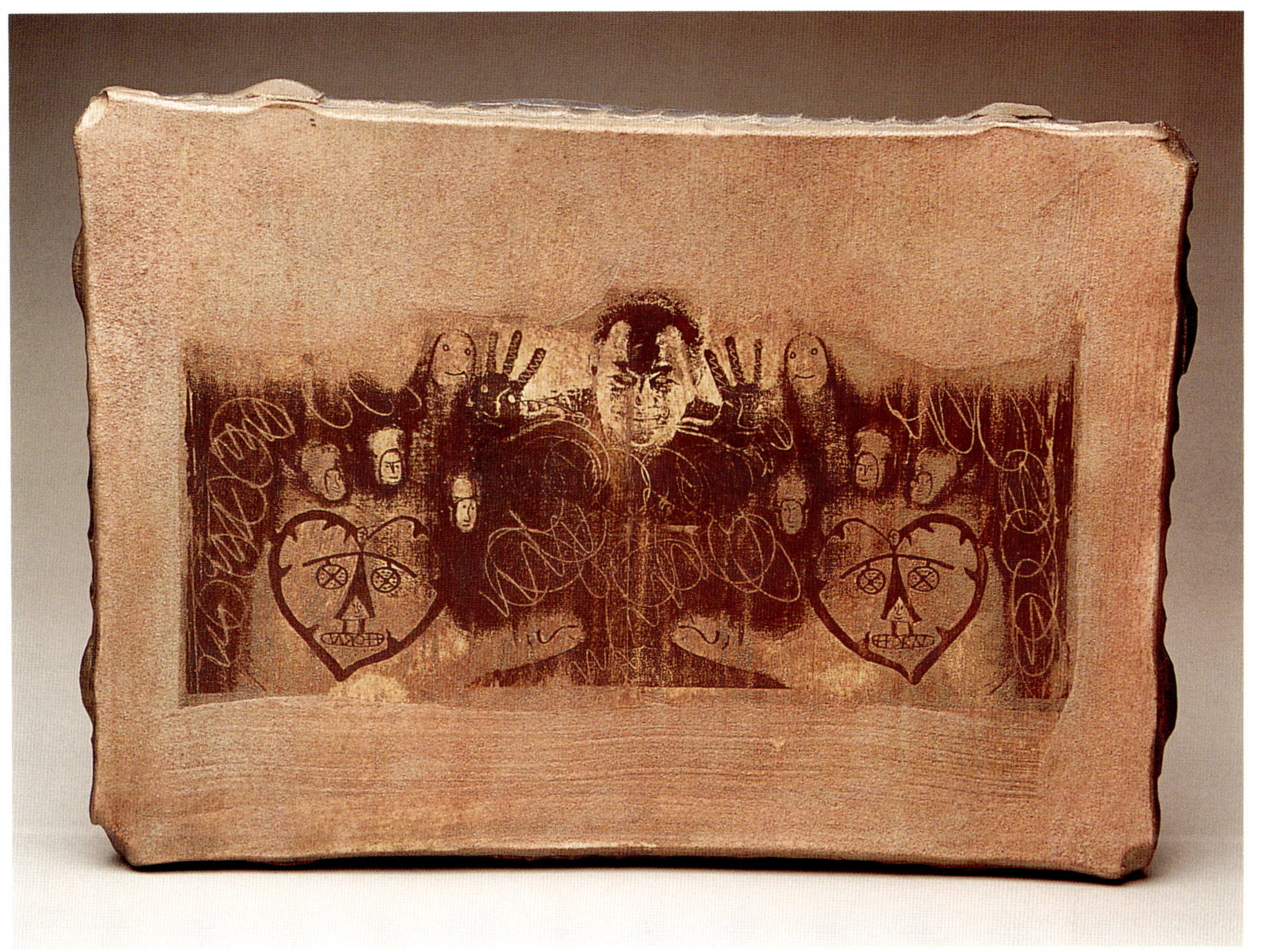

Stephen Horn

Pillow Plate with Self-Portrait | 2006

2 X 18 X 13 INCHES (5.1 X 45.7 X 33 CM)

Hand-built white stoneware; toner transfer print, flashing slip with copper wash; gas fired, cone 5

PHOTO BY SCOTT BRINEGAR

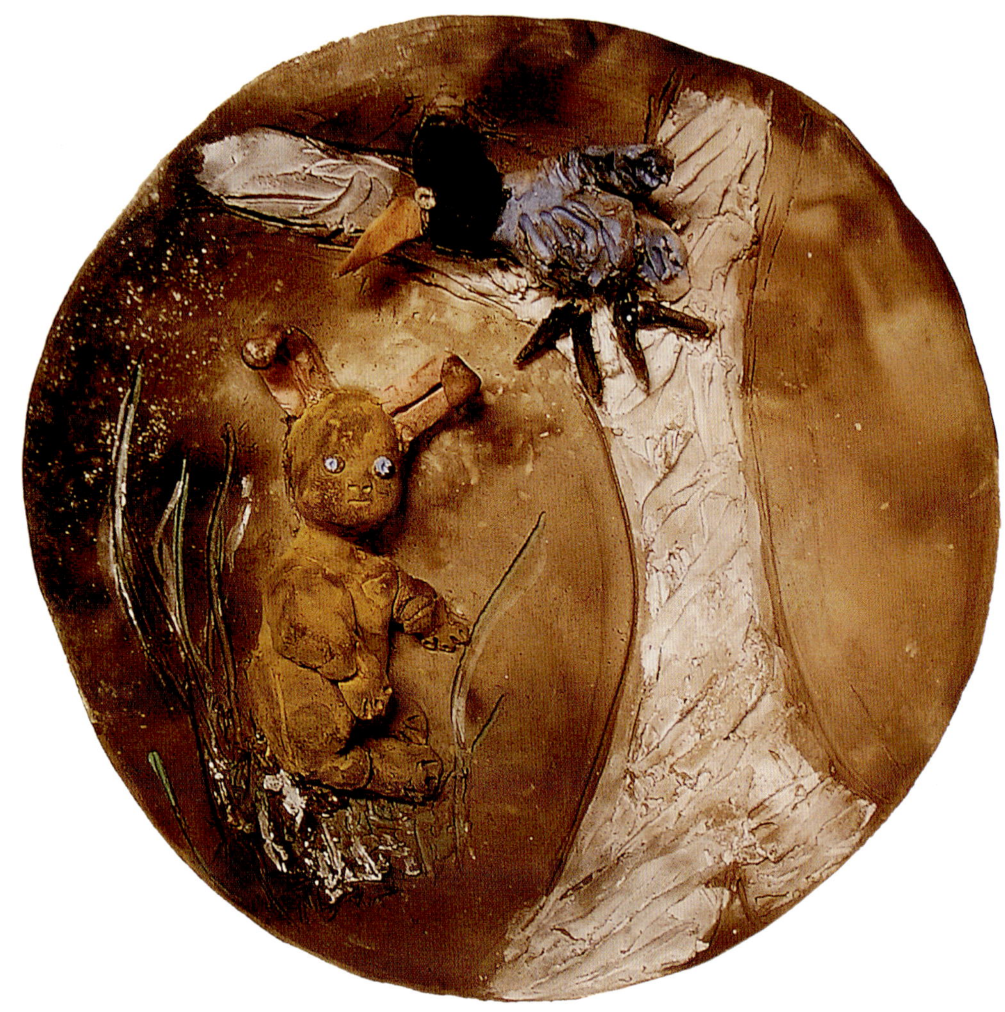

Kimberly Brennan

Plate Series #1 | 2007

3 X 10 INCHES (7.6 X 25.4 CM)

Hand-built stoneware; low-fire glazes, cone 05; pit fired; unfired glazes

PHOTO BY ARTIST

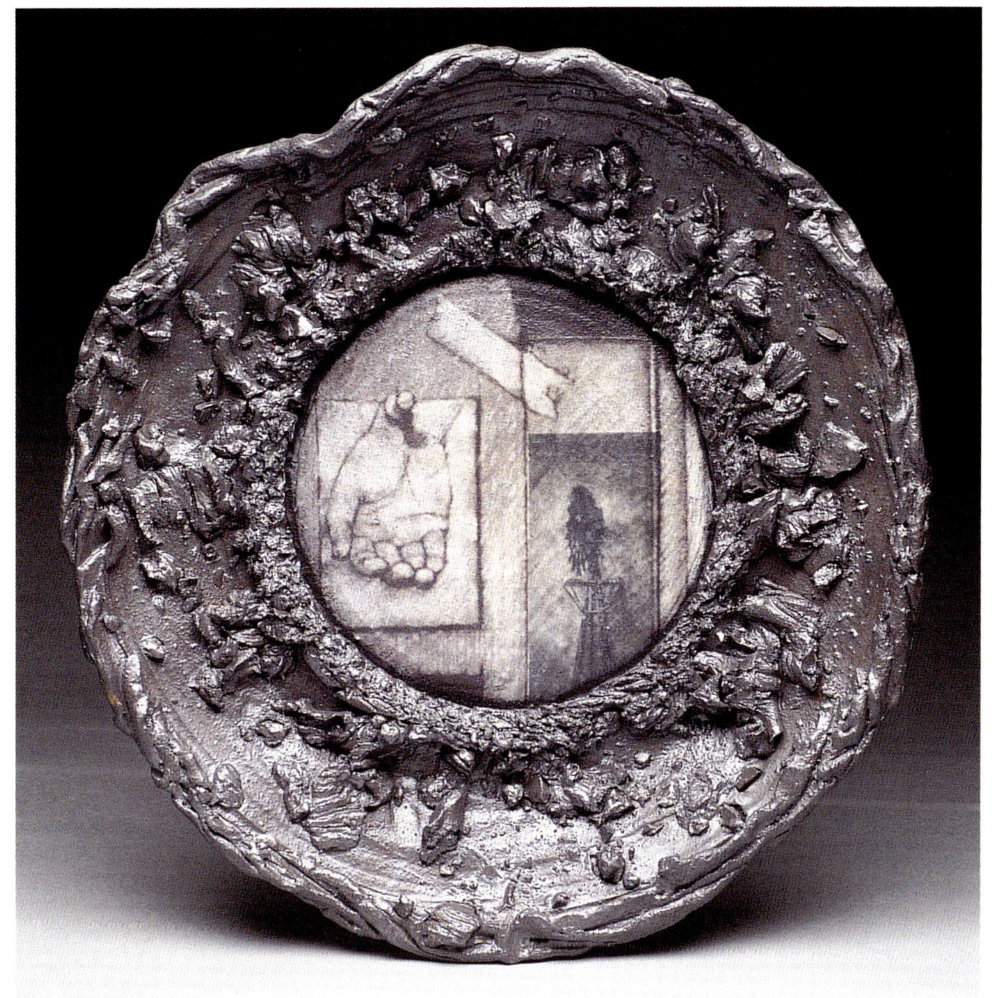

Andrew W. Martin
Juan Granados

Stray: Omission | 2007

3 1/2 X 18 1/4 X 18 INCHES (8.9 X 46.4 X 45.7 CM)

Wheel-thrown and altered stoneware; electric fired, cone 06; glaze, cone 6; image transfer

PHOTO BY JUAN GRANADOS

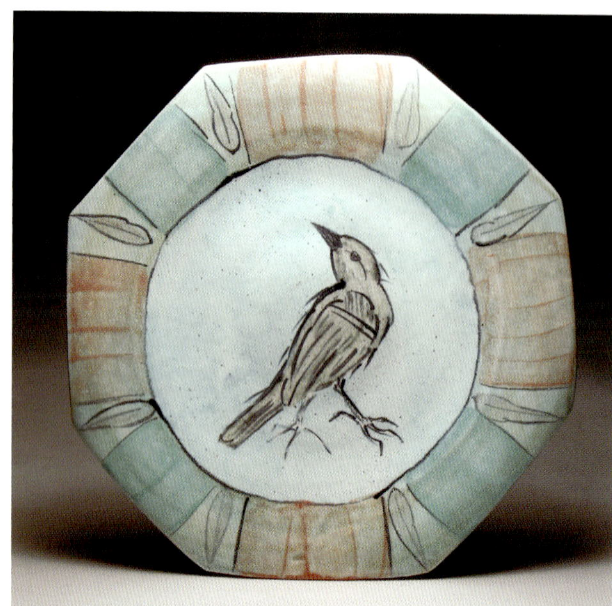

Scott Lykens

Blackbird | 2007

3 X 19 X 15 INCHES (7.6 X 48.3 X 38.1 CM)

Wheel-thrown red earthenware; majolica painted; electric fired, cone 3

PHOTO BY ARTIST

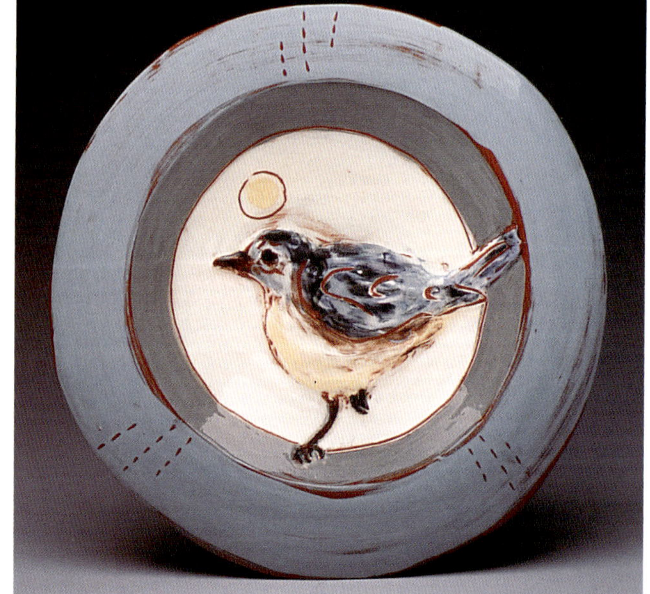

Shaunna Lyons

Dancing under the Full Moon Plate | 2006

10½ INCHES (26.7 CM) IN DIAMETER

Hand-built low-fire red clay; slips and stains; electric fired, cone 03; glazes, cone 04

PHOTO BY WALKER MONTGOMERY

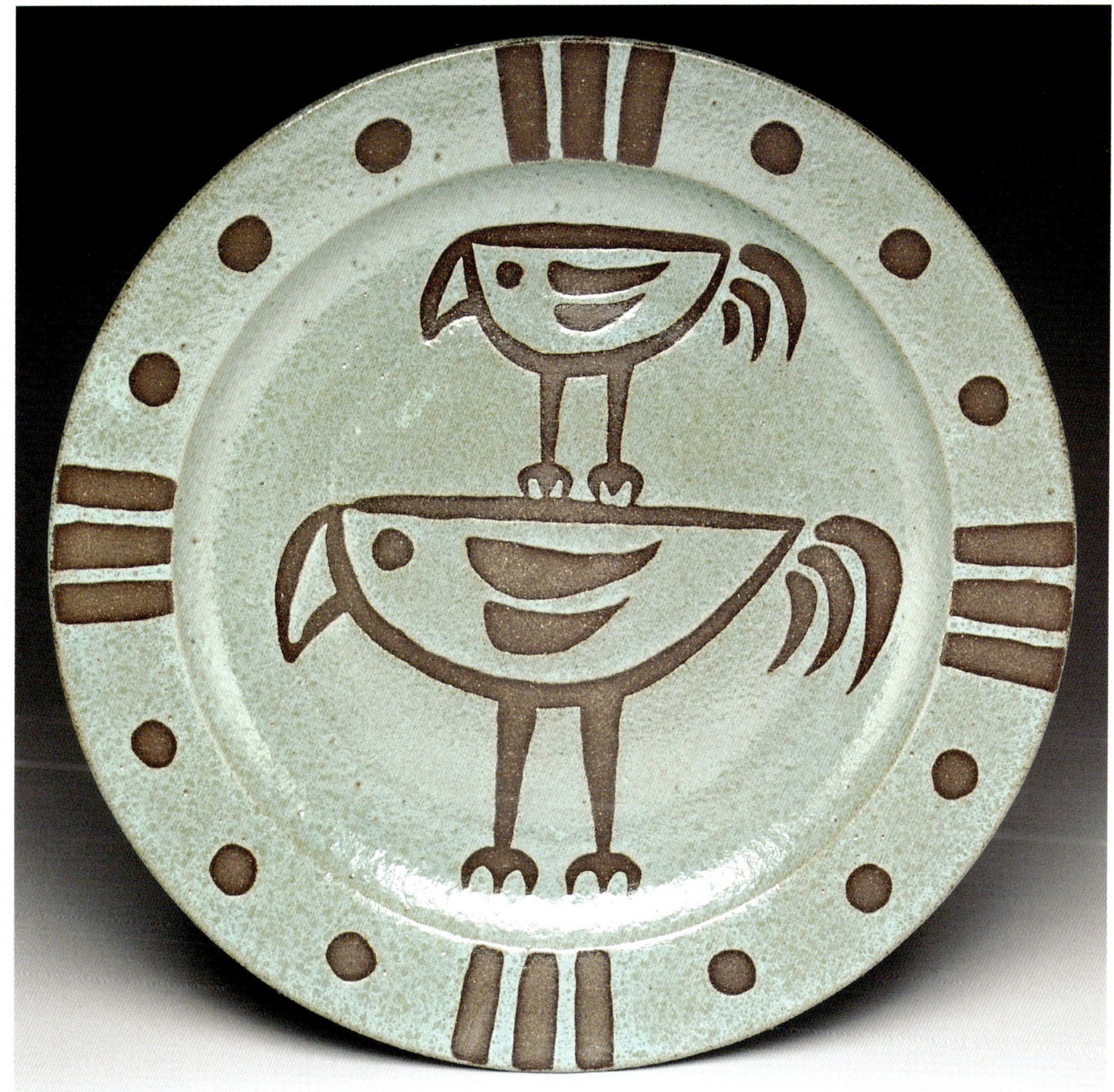

Vicki Paulet

Birds All the Way Down | 2006

1 X 14 INCHES (2.5 X 35.6 CM)

Wheel-thrown stoneware; electric fired, bisque, cone 04; glaze, cone 6

PHOTO BY ERIK HAAGENSEN

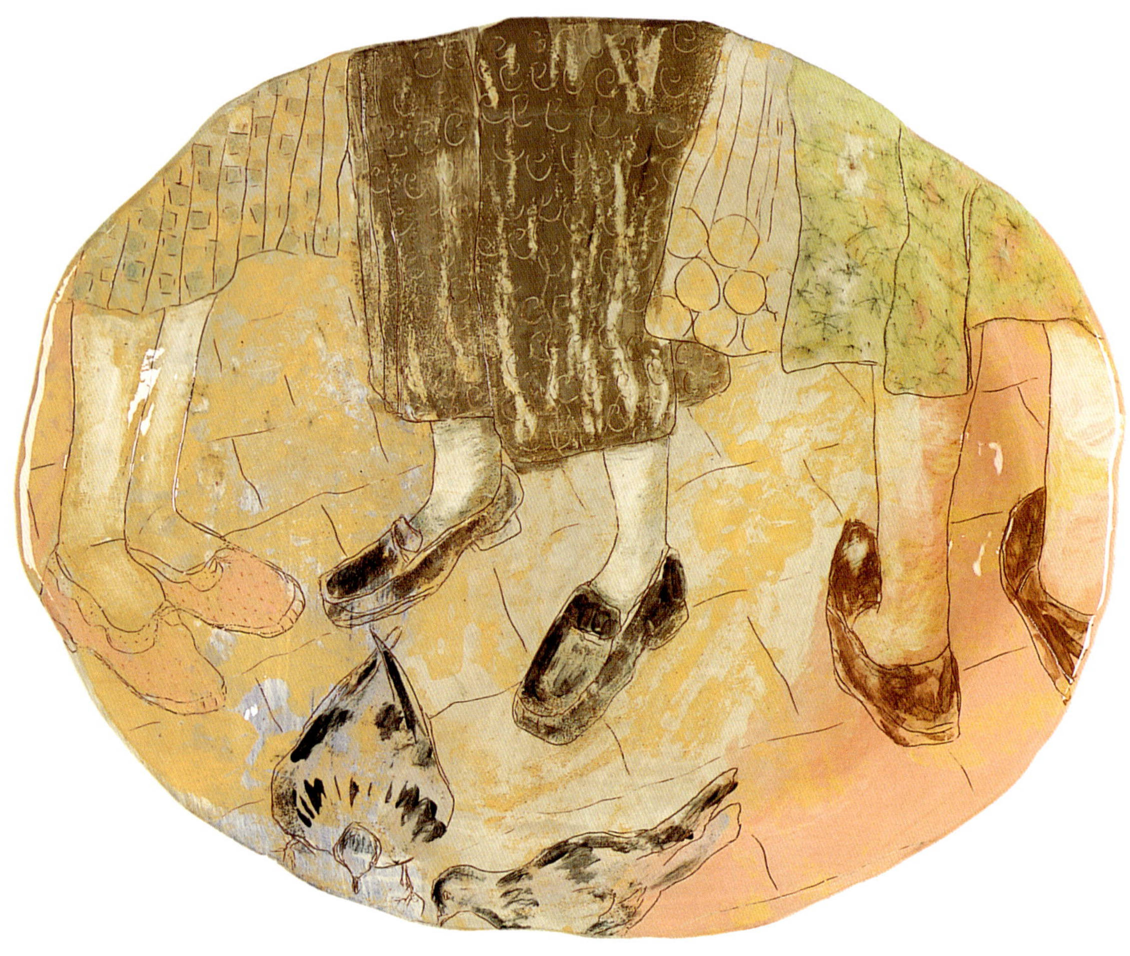

Linda Bristow

Untitled | 2007

2½ X 25 X 20 INCHES (6.4 X 63.5 X 50.8 CM)

Slab-built red earthenware; sgraffito, slips; clear glaze, electric fired, cone 01; glaze, cone 04

PHOTO BY ARTIST

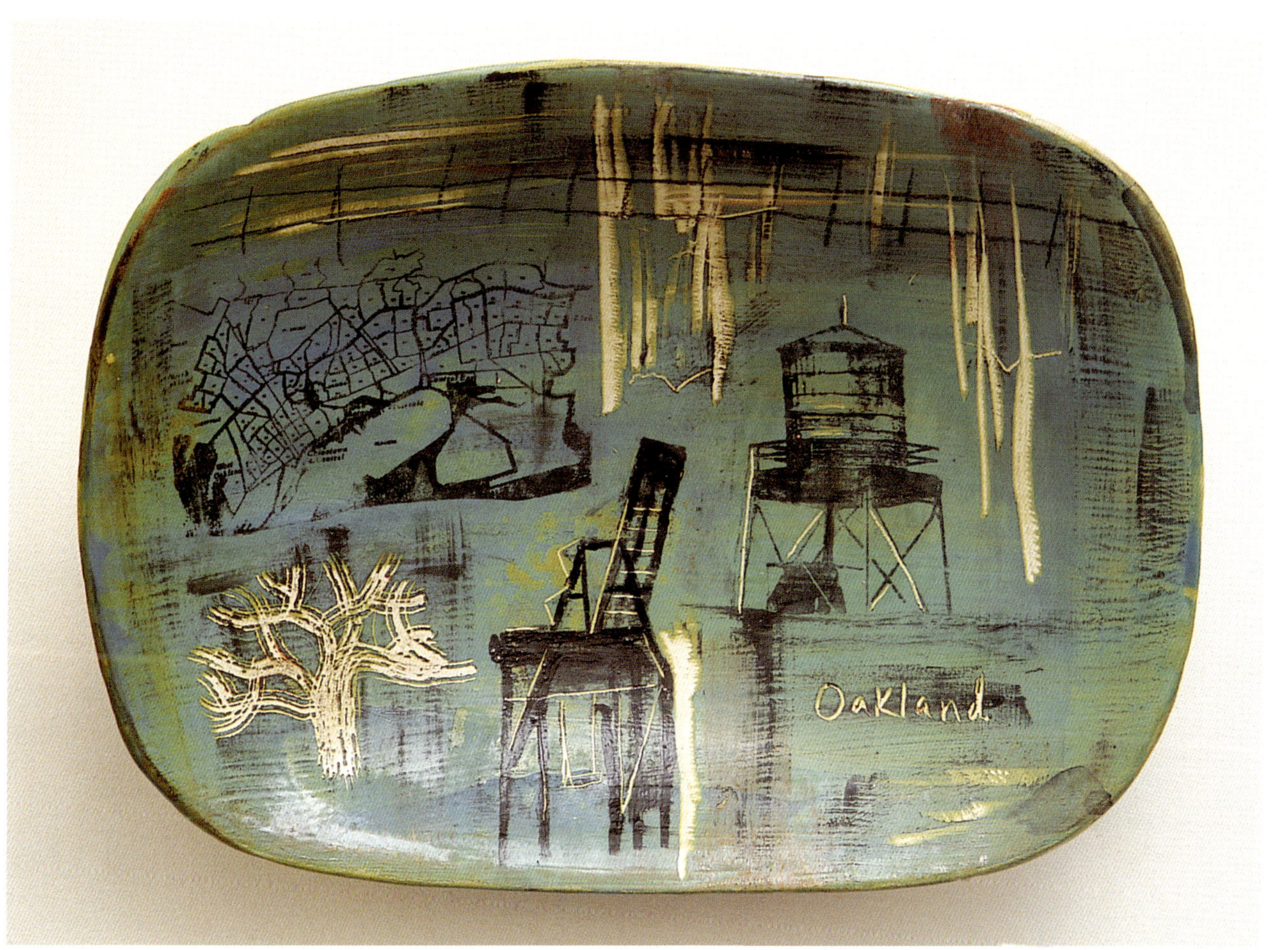

Tiffany Schmierer

Oakland Platter | 2007

4 X 15 X 10 INCHES (10.2 X 38.1 X 25.4 CM)

Hand-built earthenware; screen-printed and brushed underglazes; electric fired, cone 04; glaze, cone 06

PHOTO BY W. JAY JONES

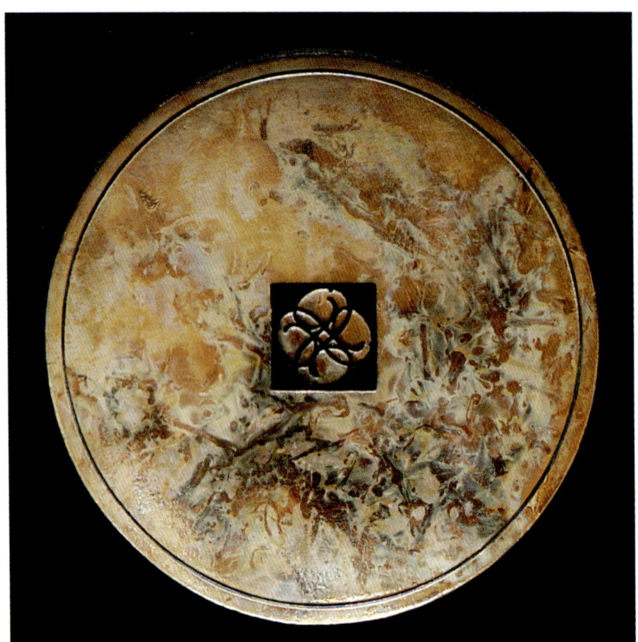

Leslie Green

Raku Round Plate—Gold | 2006

1 1/2 X 12 INCHES (3.8 X 30.5 CM)

Slab-built stoneware; painted glaze, raku fired, cone 06

PHOTO BY GARY G. GIBSON

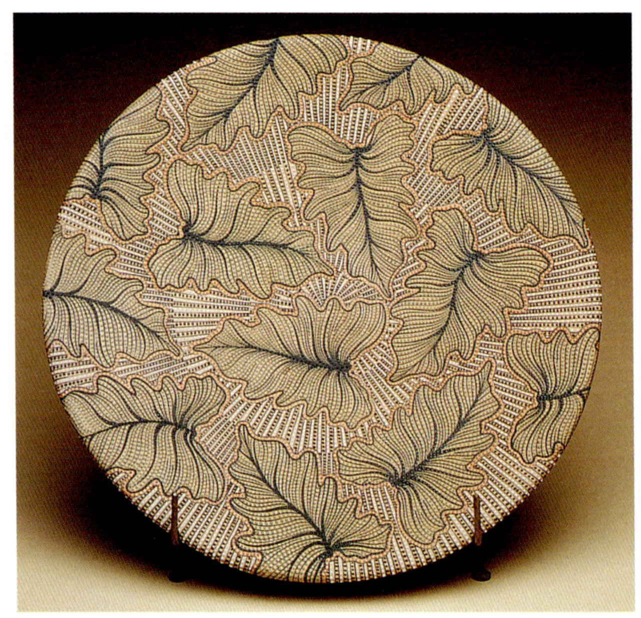

Ricky Maldonado

16 Leaves | 2004

1 1/2 X 18 INCHES (3.8 X 45.7 CM)

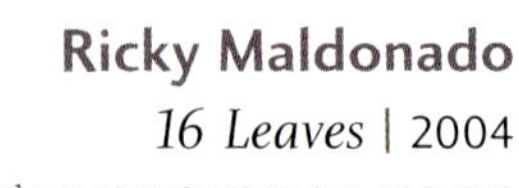

Slab earthenware; terra sigillata; cone 06 oxidation

PHOTO BY IMAGEINATION

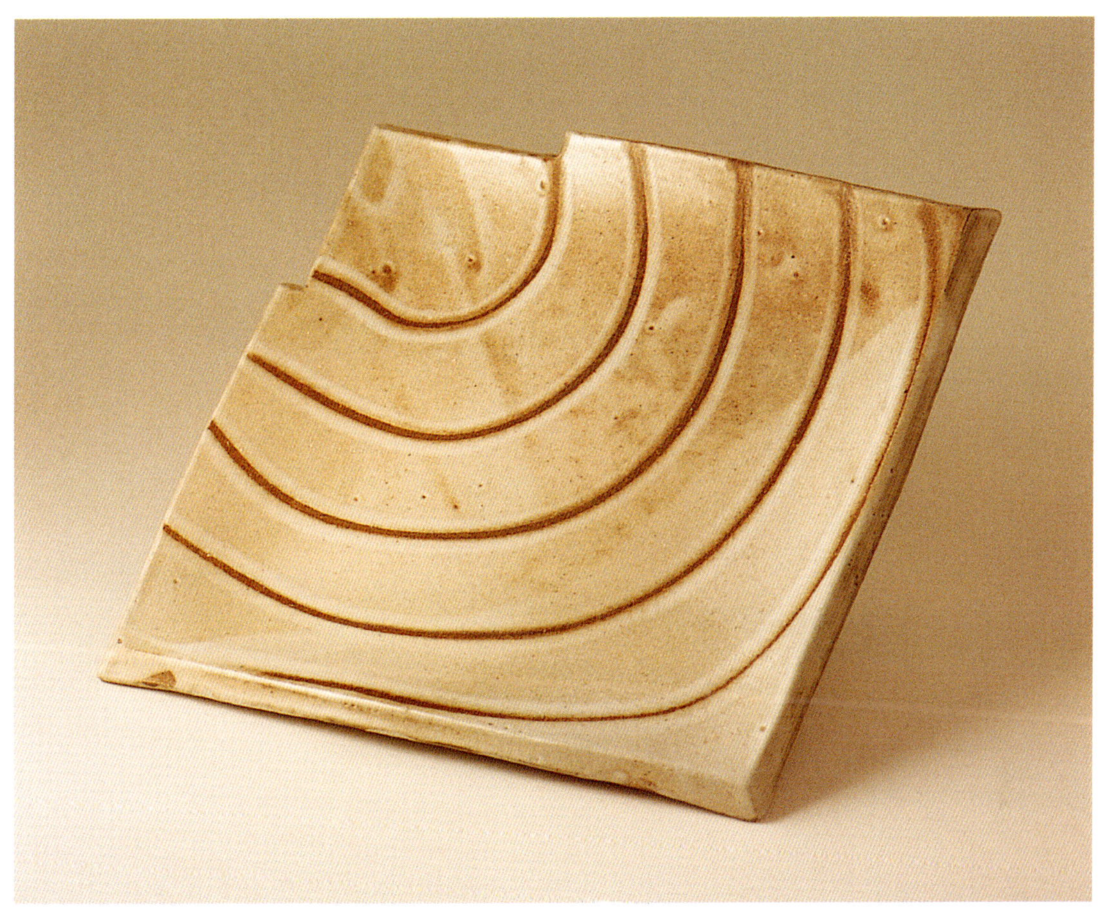

Alex Johnson

Square Serving Plate | 2006

2 X 13 X 13 INCHES (5.1 X 33 X 33 CM)

Slab-built stoneware with thrown foot; shino glaze with finger wipes; soda fired, cone 10

PHOTO BY JEFF SAXMAN

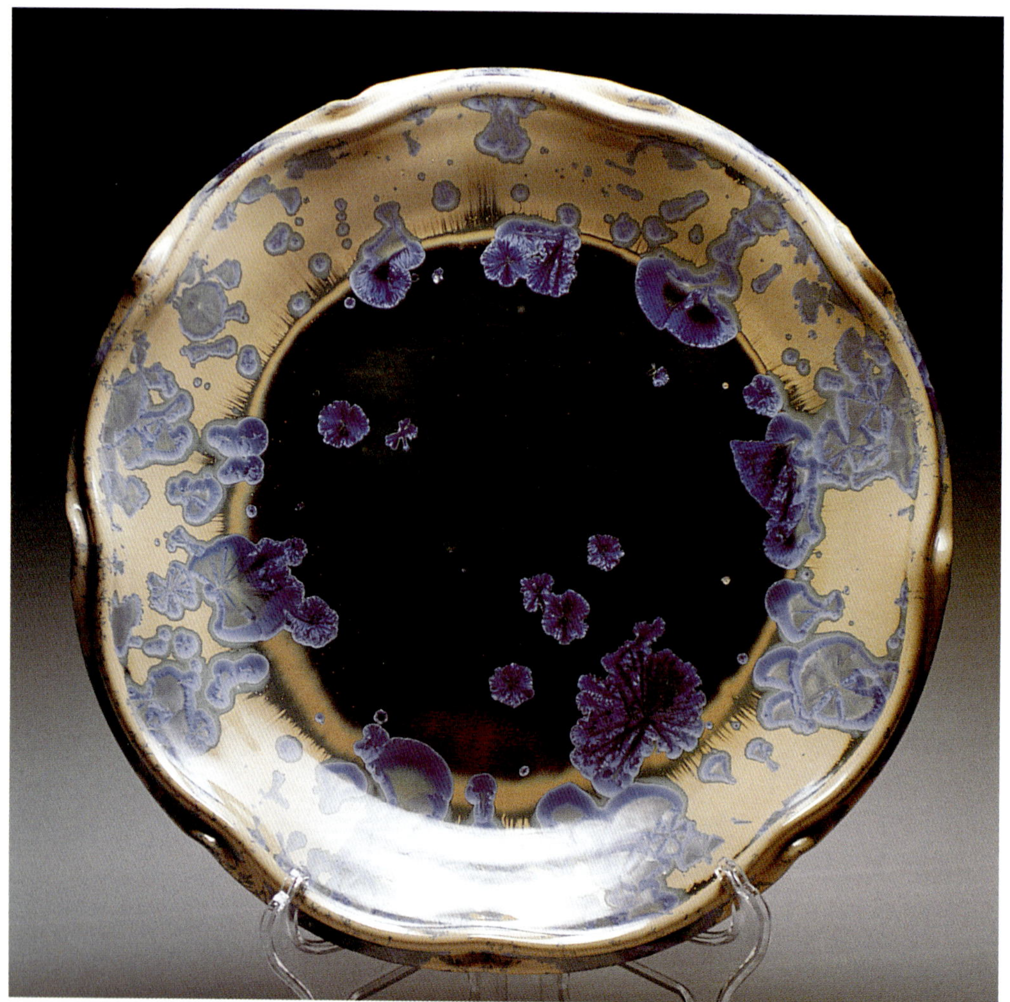

Laura Aultman

Pooling Mirror | 2003

2¼ X 15½ INCHES (5.7 X 39.4 CM)

Wheel-thrown porcelain; crystalline glaze; electric fired, cone 10 oxidation

PHOTO BY ARTIST

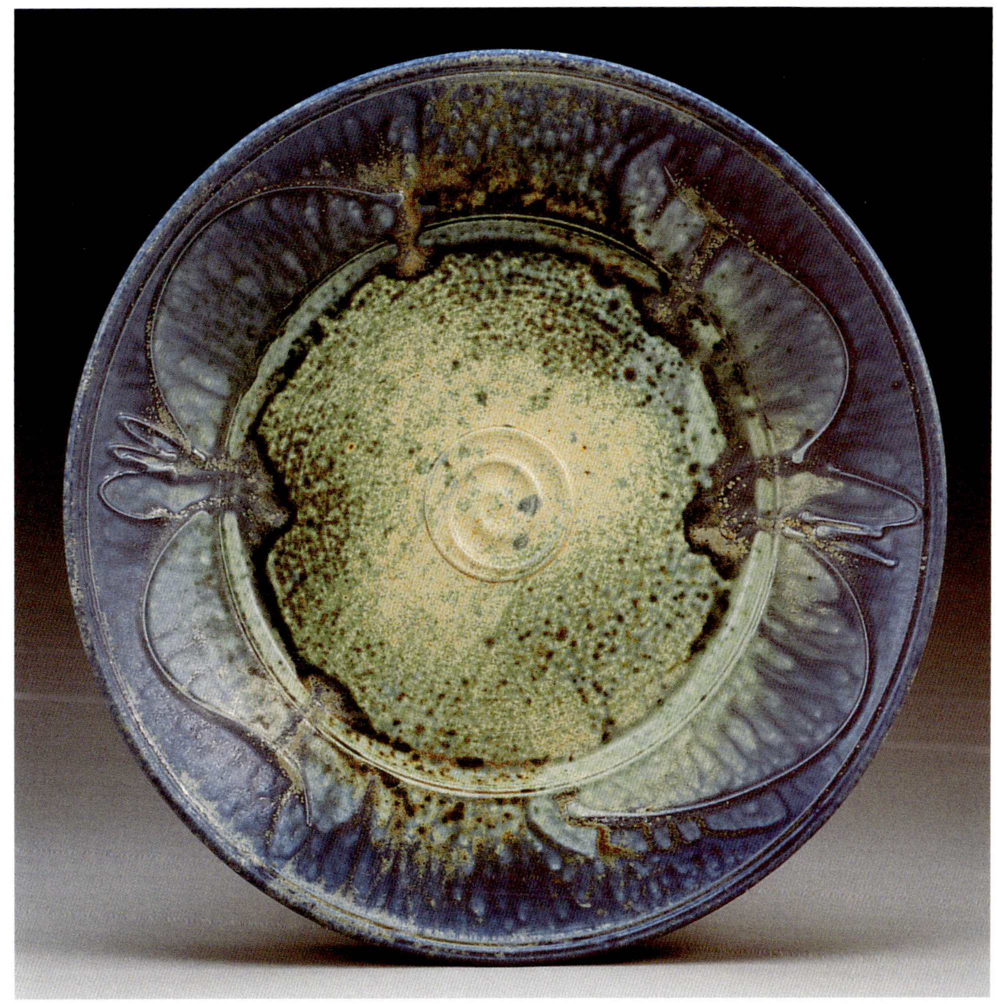

Karl Knudson

Platter | 2005

5 X 18 INCHES (12.7 X 45.7 CM)

Wheel-thrown stoneware; multiple matte and wood-ash glazes; reduction fired, cone 10

PHOTO BY BILL BACHHUBER

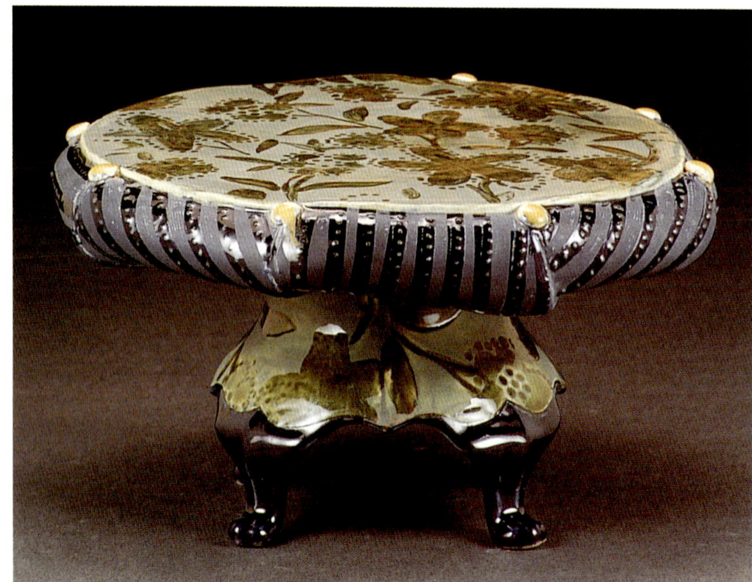

Valerie Duncan
Cake Plate | 2004
8 X 10 X 10 INCHES (20.3 X 25.4 X 25.4 CM)
Hand-built white stoneware;
glaze, electric fired, cone 6
PHOTOS BY ARTIST

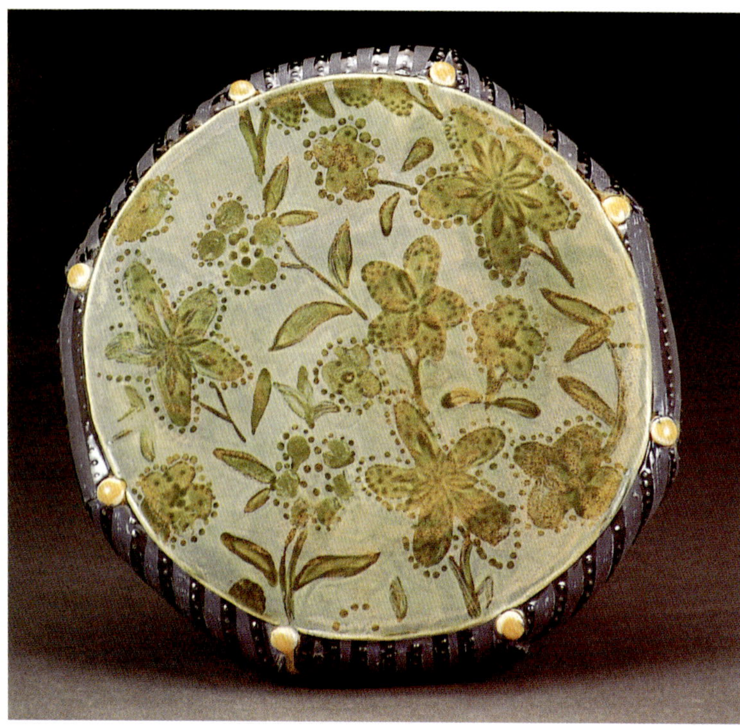

Valerie Metcalfe

Rosegold Platter | 2006

$4^{1}/_{2}$ X $18^{1}/_{2}$ INCHES (11.4 X 47 CM)

Carved and altered wheel-thrown porcelain; underglaze, iron-oxide painting; high fired in reduction, cone 11; luster fired electric, cone 019; soldered metal and glass accents

PHOTO BY BRUCE SPIELMAN

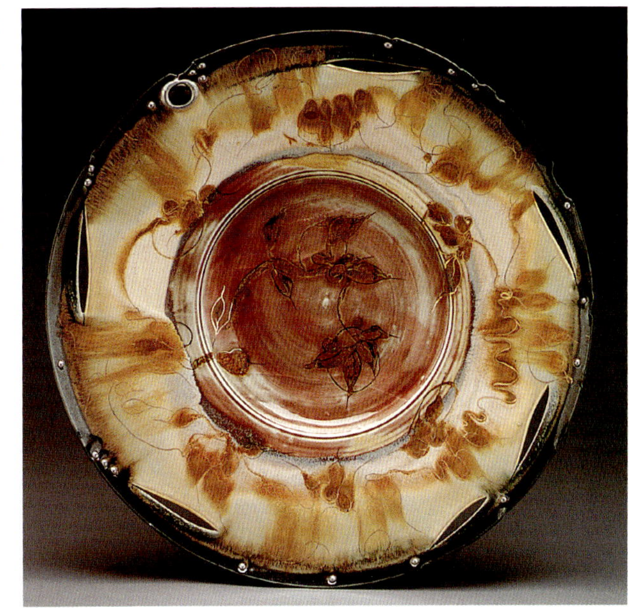

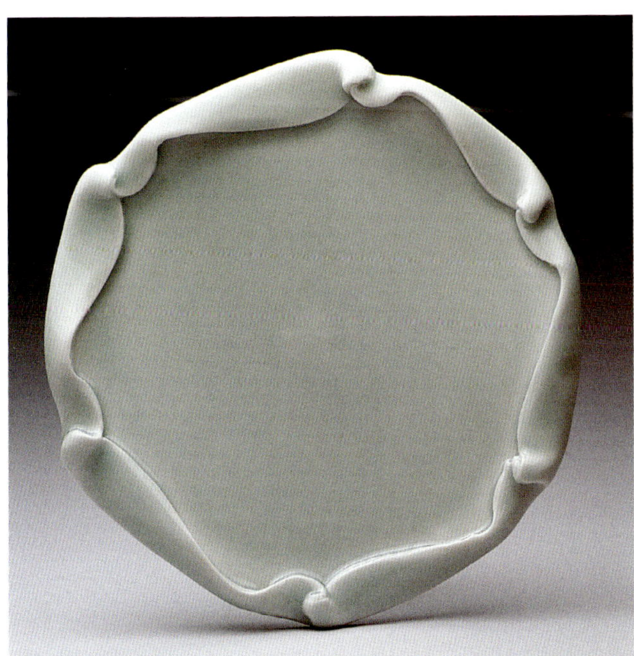

Chris Pickett

Untitled | 2005

1 X 11 INCHES (2.5 X 27.9 CM)

Thrown and altered porcelain; reduction fired, cone 10

PHOTO BY ARTIST

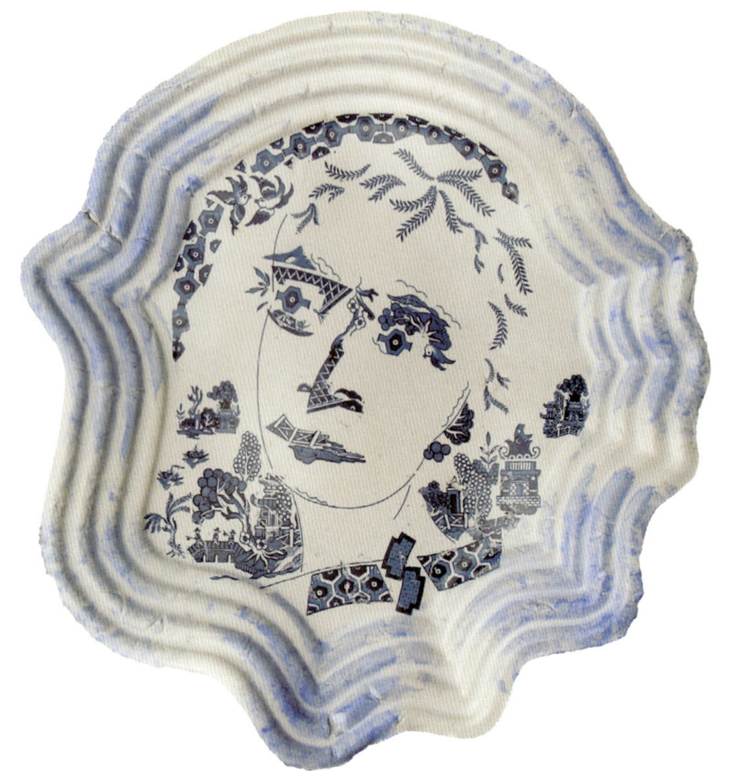

Rose Wallace

Willoware Plate | 2007

$2^{1}/_{2}$ X 16 INCHES (6.4 X 40.6 CM)

Slab-formed and distorted white earthenware; tin glaze, cobalt oxide; decals

PHOTOS BY ARTIST

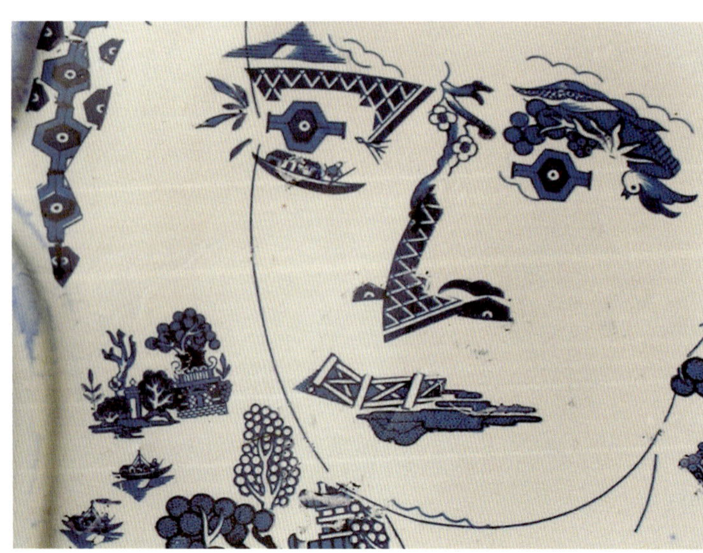

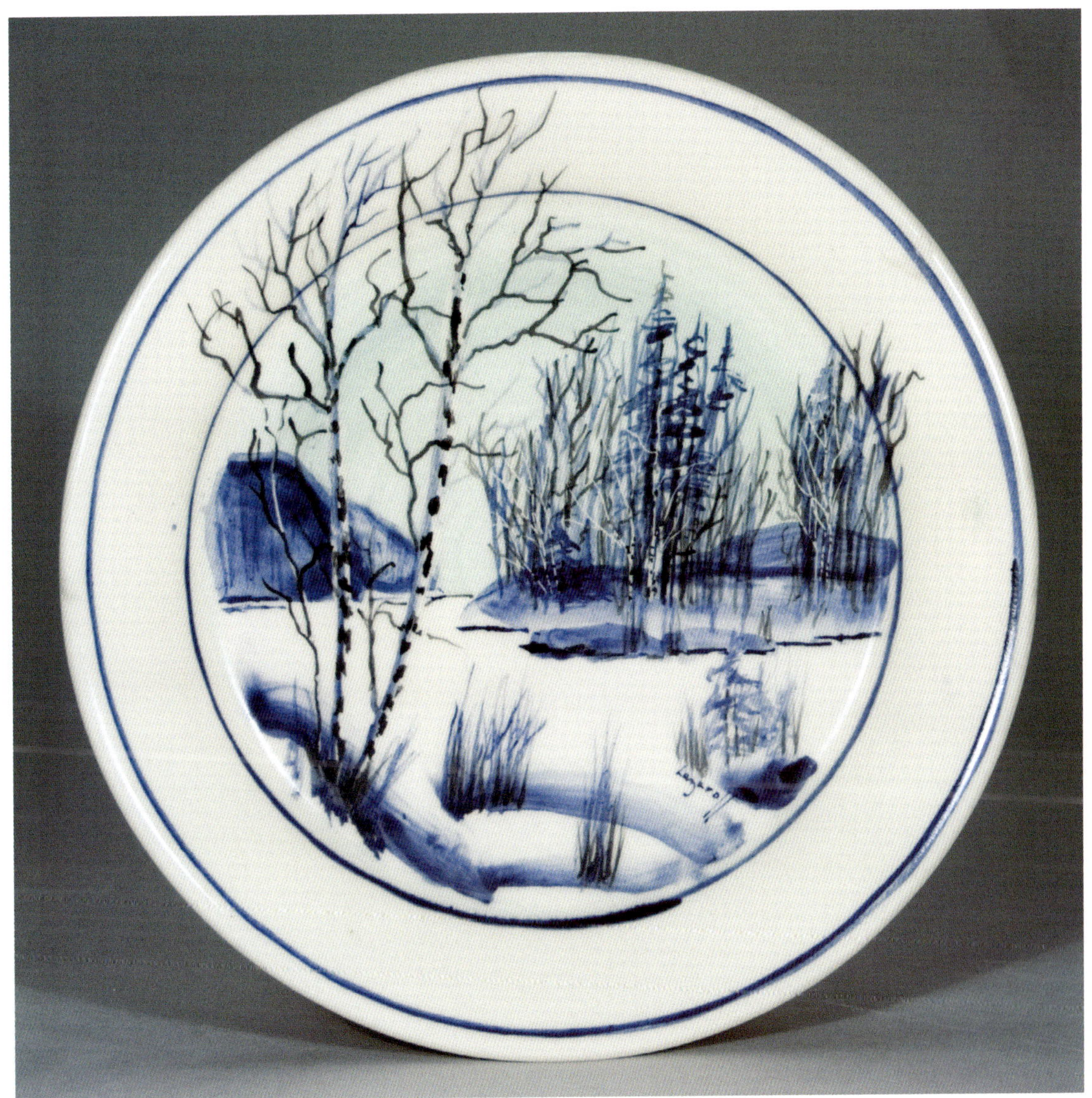

Terrance Frank Lazaroff

The Lake | 2006

1 1/4 X 12 INCHES (3.2 X 30.5 CM)

Wheel-thrown porcelain; transparent glaze, cobalt underglaze; electric fired, cone 6

PHOTO BY ARTIST

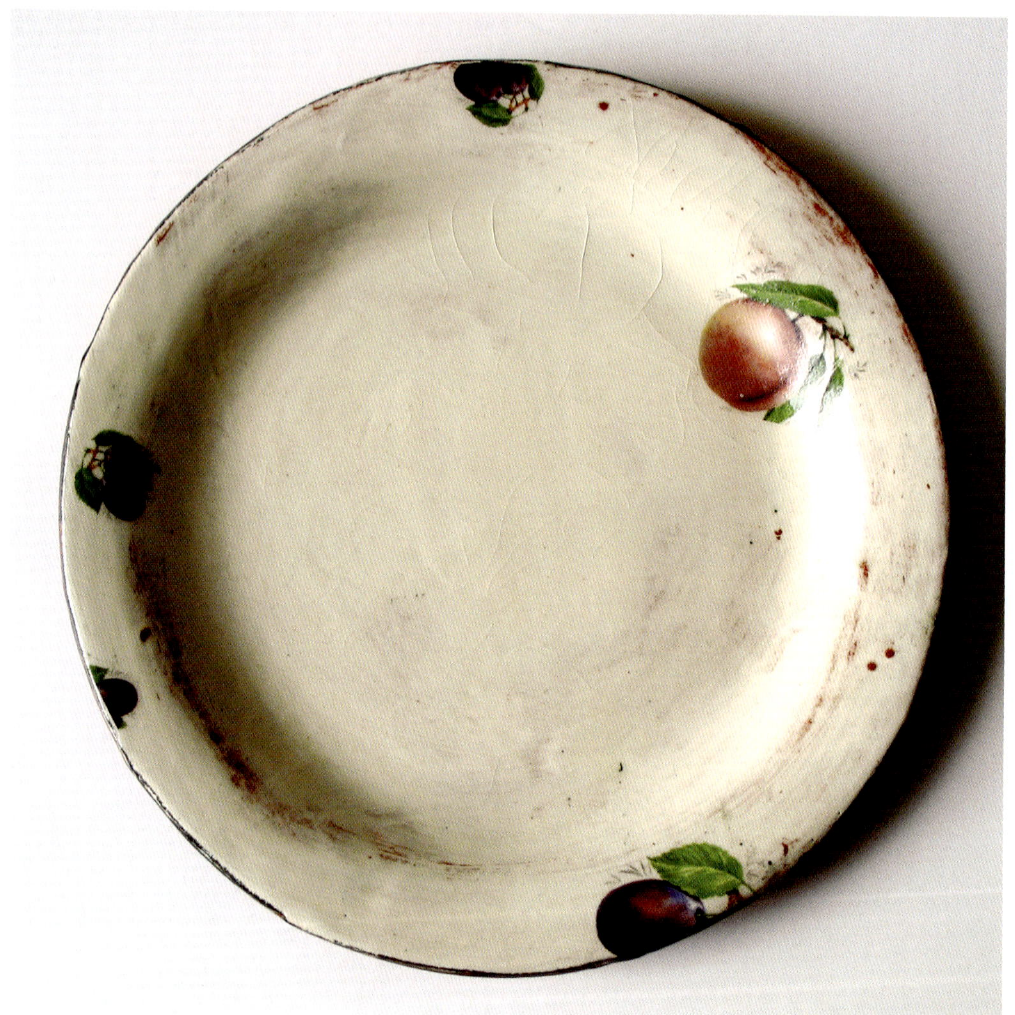

Maria Kristofersson

Retro II | 2007

5/8 X 6 5/16 INCHES (1.6 X 16 CM)

Hand-built on mold, earthenware; transfer; clear glaze, electric fired

PHOTO BY ARTIST

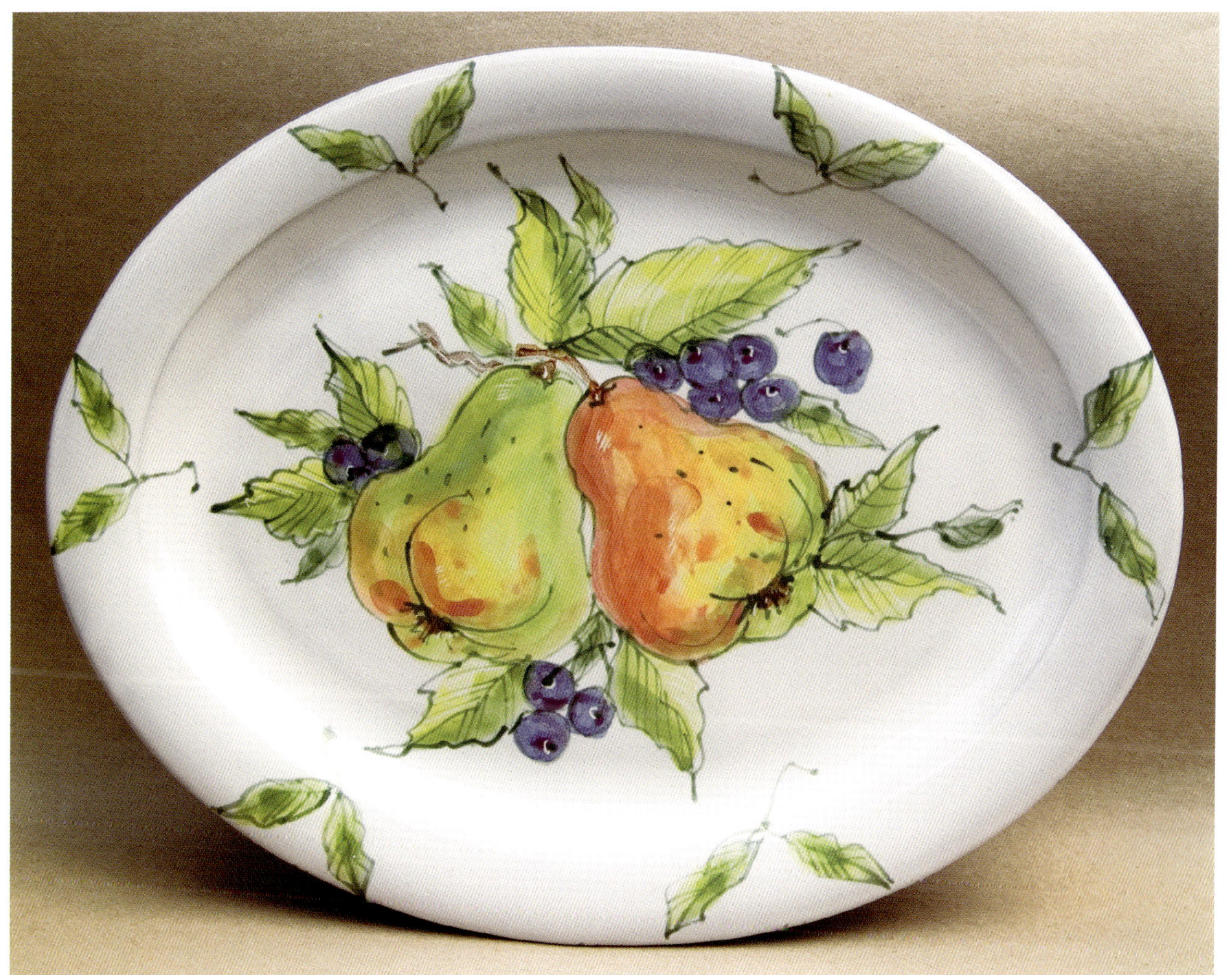

Amourentia Louisa Leibman

Prato com Pêras—Fruit Series | 1999

1 1/2 X 16 1/4 X 12 3/4 INCHES (3.8 X 41.3 X 32.4 CM)

Earthenware with mica; sgraffito; bisque, cone 06; tin glaze, stains and oxides; glost firing, cone 04

PHOTO BY ARTIST

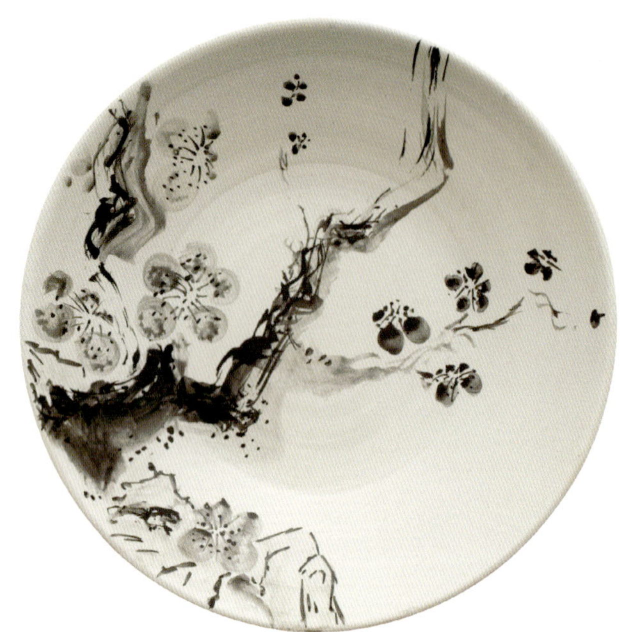

James P. Mitschmyer
Blossom #004 | 2007
$3\frac{1}{2}$ X 18 INCHES (8.9 X 45.7 CM)
Wheel-thrown white stoneware; black engobe; glaze fired in oxidation, cone 6
PHOTO BY ARTIST

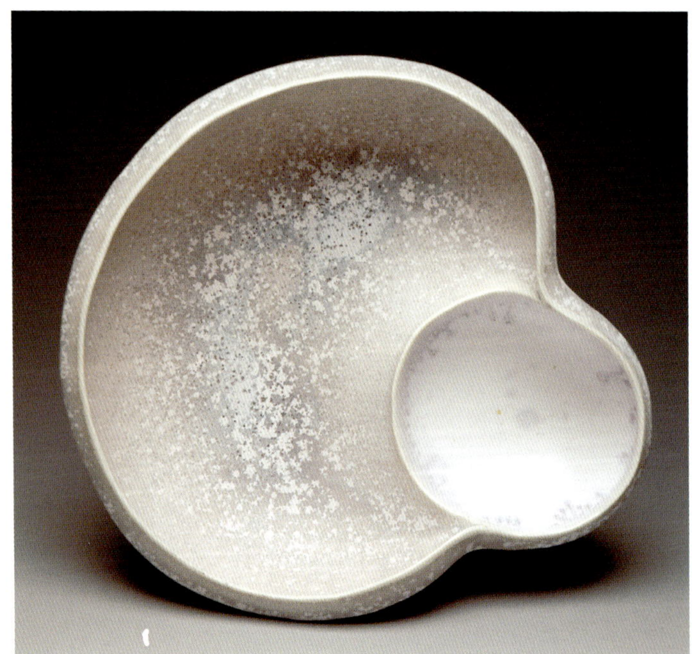

Gwendolyn Yoppolo
Plate Set | 2007
3 X 9 X 9 INCHES (7.6 X 22.9 X 22.9 CM)
Thrown and built porcelain; soda fired, cone 10
PHOTO BY ARTIST

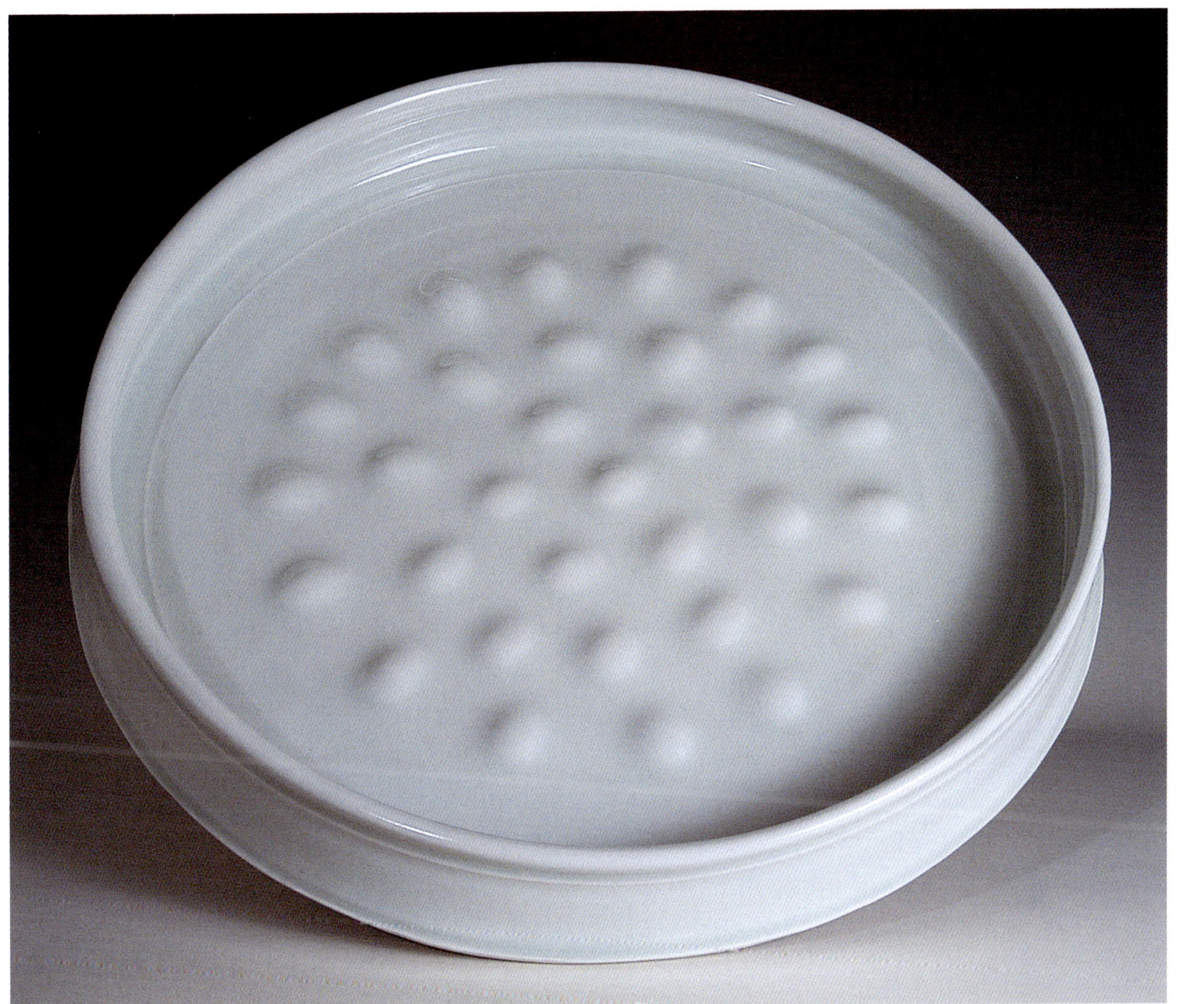

Antje Ernestus

Large Porcelain Platter | 2007

3 X 19 INCHES (7.6 X 48.3 CM)

Soft wheel-thrown and hand-built porcelain; textured; celadon glaze, gas fired in reduction, cone 10

PHOTO BY ARTIST

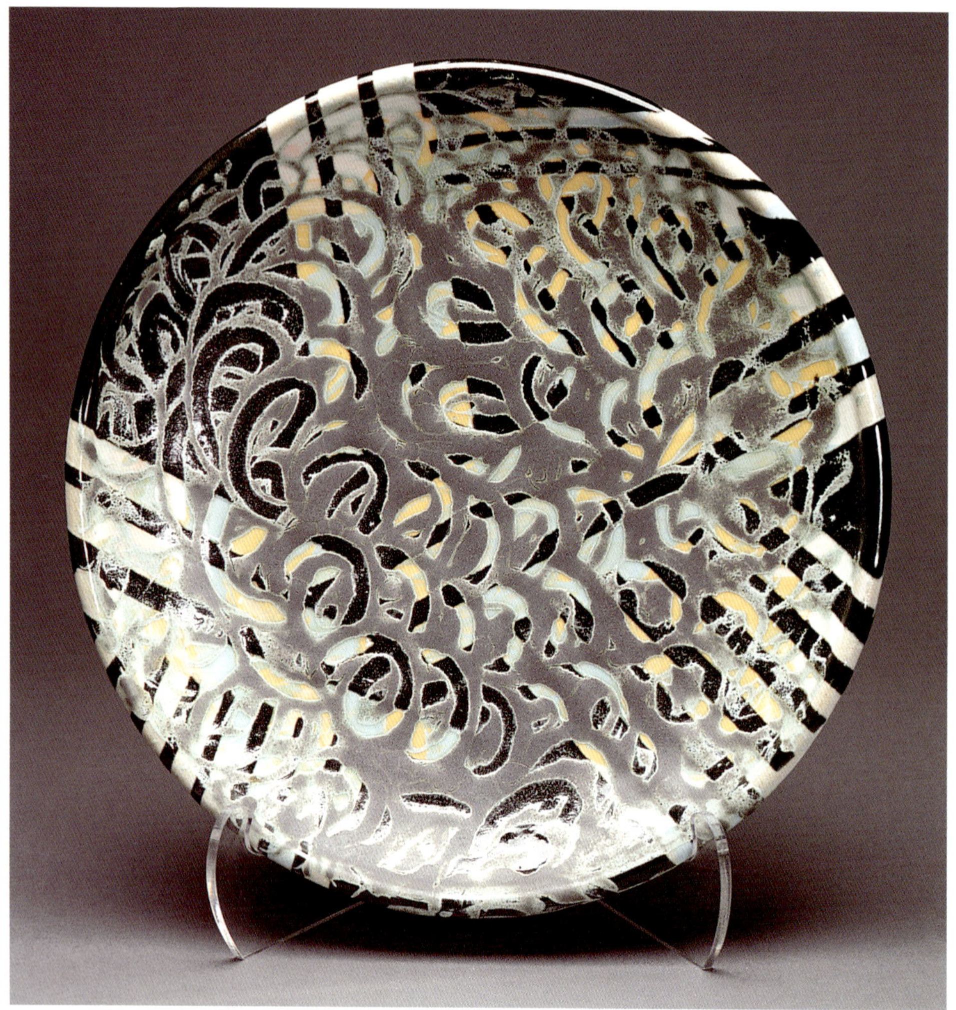

Linnis Blanton

Layers of Consciousness | 1995

2 X 15 INCHES (5.1 X 38.1 CM)

Wheel-thrown stoneware; electric fired, cone 04; glaze, cones 9–10

PHOTO BY PAUL GENNUSA

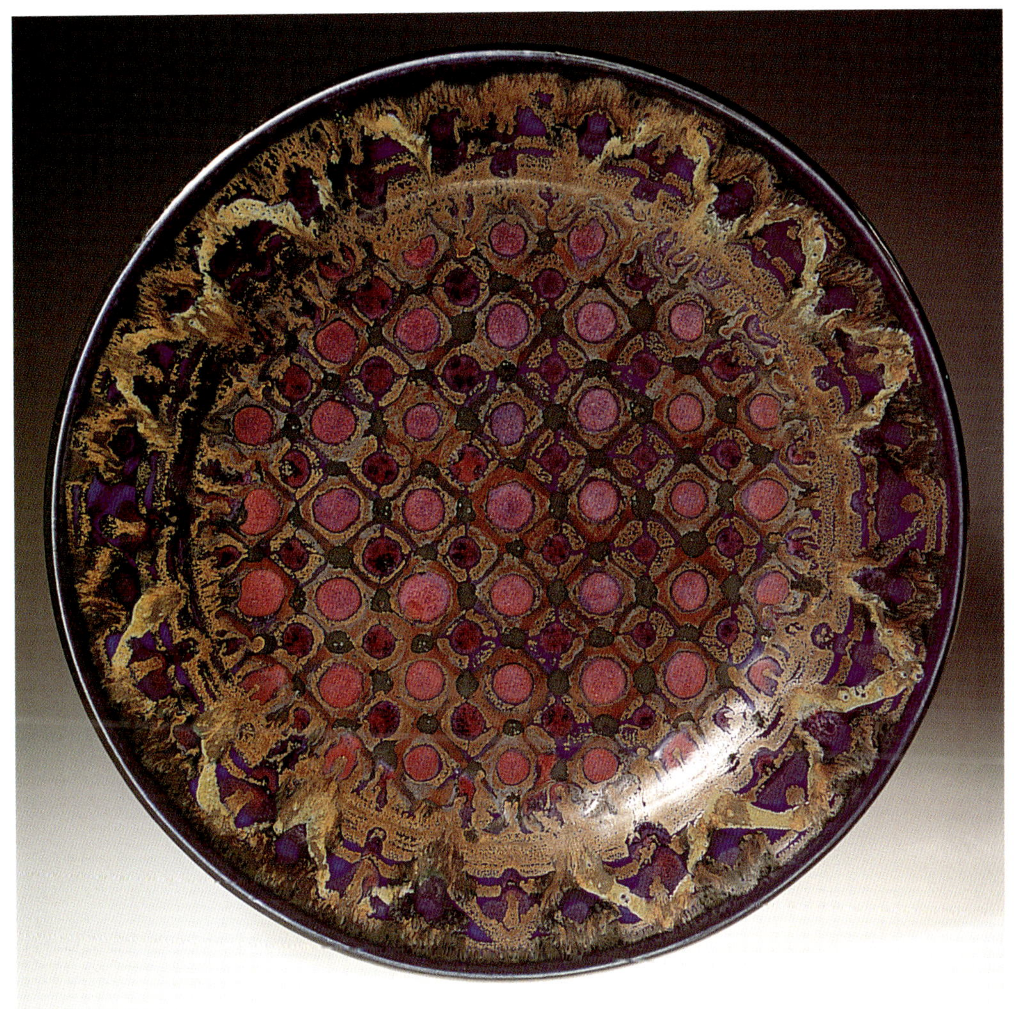

Mandy Wolpert

Geometric Printed Platter | 2002–2003

$15\frac{1}{2}$ INCHES (39.4 CM) IN DIAMETER

Wheel thrown; glaze-on-glaze printing and painting; reduction fired

PHOTO BY IAN HOBBS

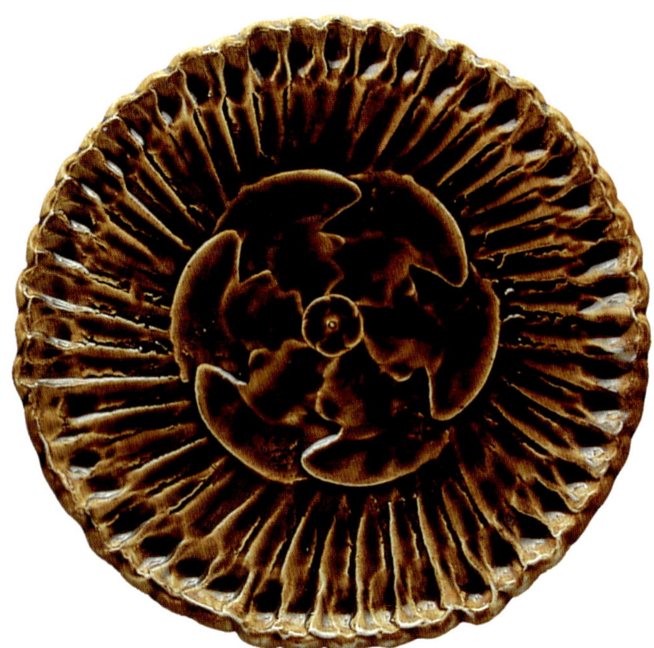

Ryan LaBar

Untitled | 2006

1 X 13 INCHES (2.5 X 33 CM)

Wheel-thrown porcelain; forming chatter, pinched; temmoku glaze; soda fired, cone 10

PHOTO BY ARTIST

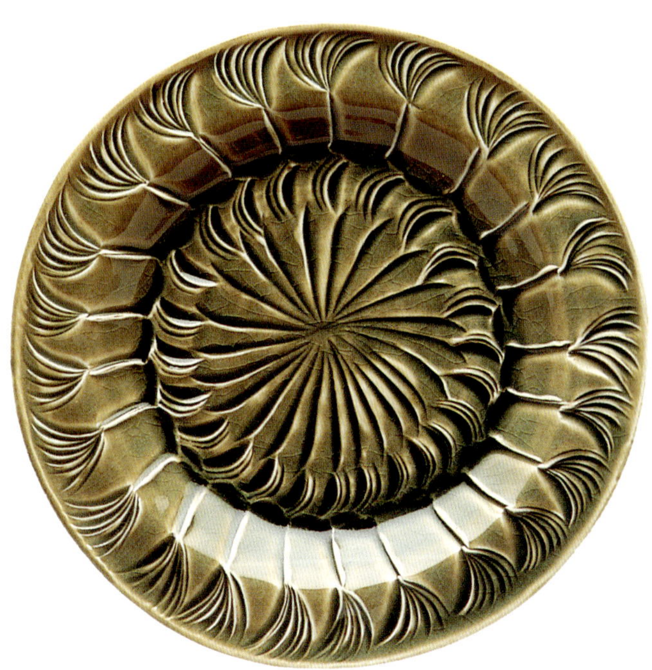

Lora Groton Rust

Pinwheel Plate | 2007

1 1/2 X 9 INCHES (3.8 X 22.9 CM)

Wheel-thrown porcelain; pinwheel texture; green celadon glaze; gas fired in reduction, cone 10

PHOTO BY WALKER MONTGOMERY

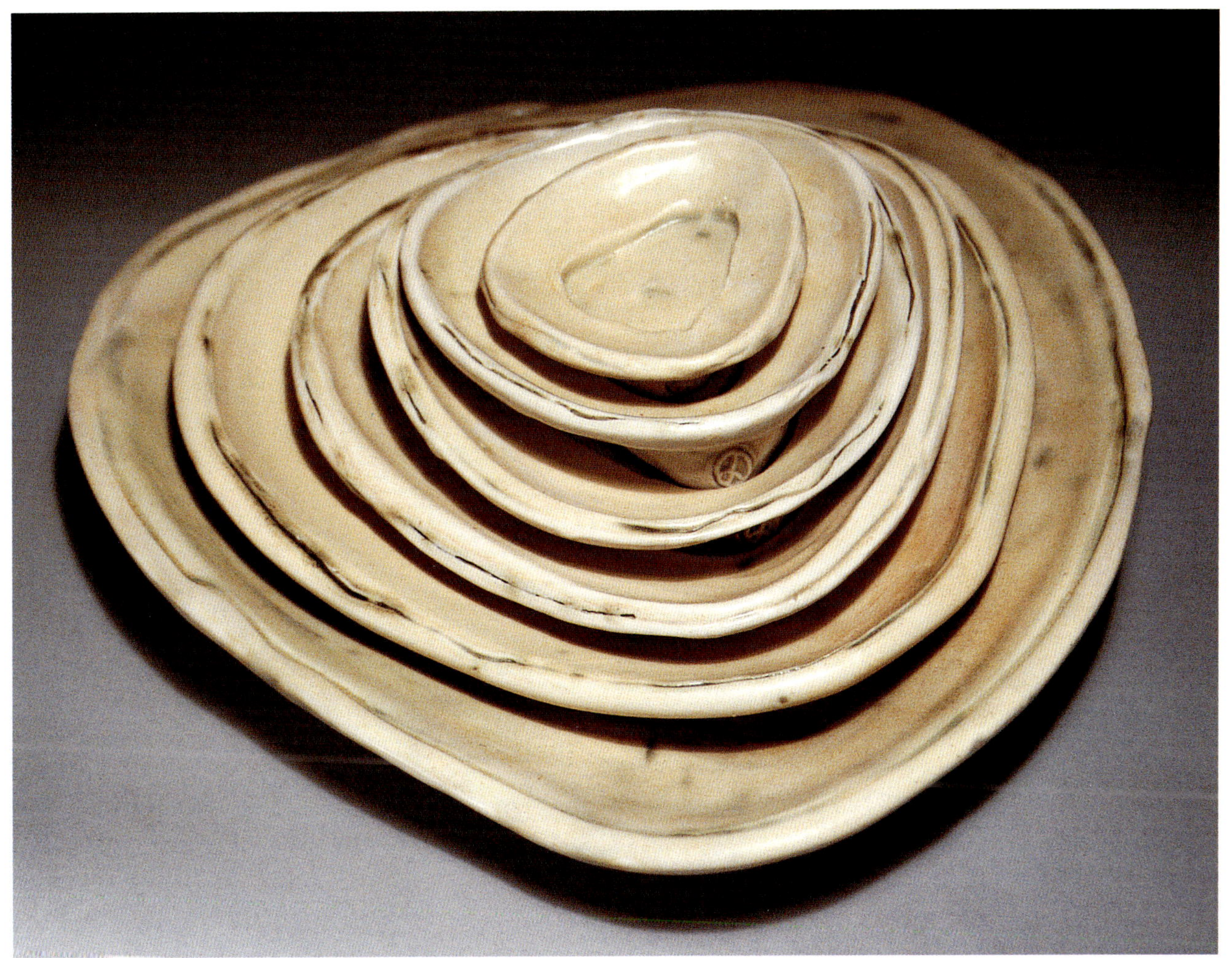

Carole Ann Fer

Nesting Set—Platters 'n Plates | 2006

5 X 14 X 13 INCHES (12.7 X 35.6 X 33 CM)

Thrown and altered soft porcelain; electric fired, cone 08; copper patina wash, matte glaze; oxidation fired, cone 6

PHOTO BY ELLEN WIESKE

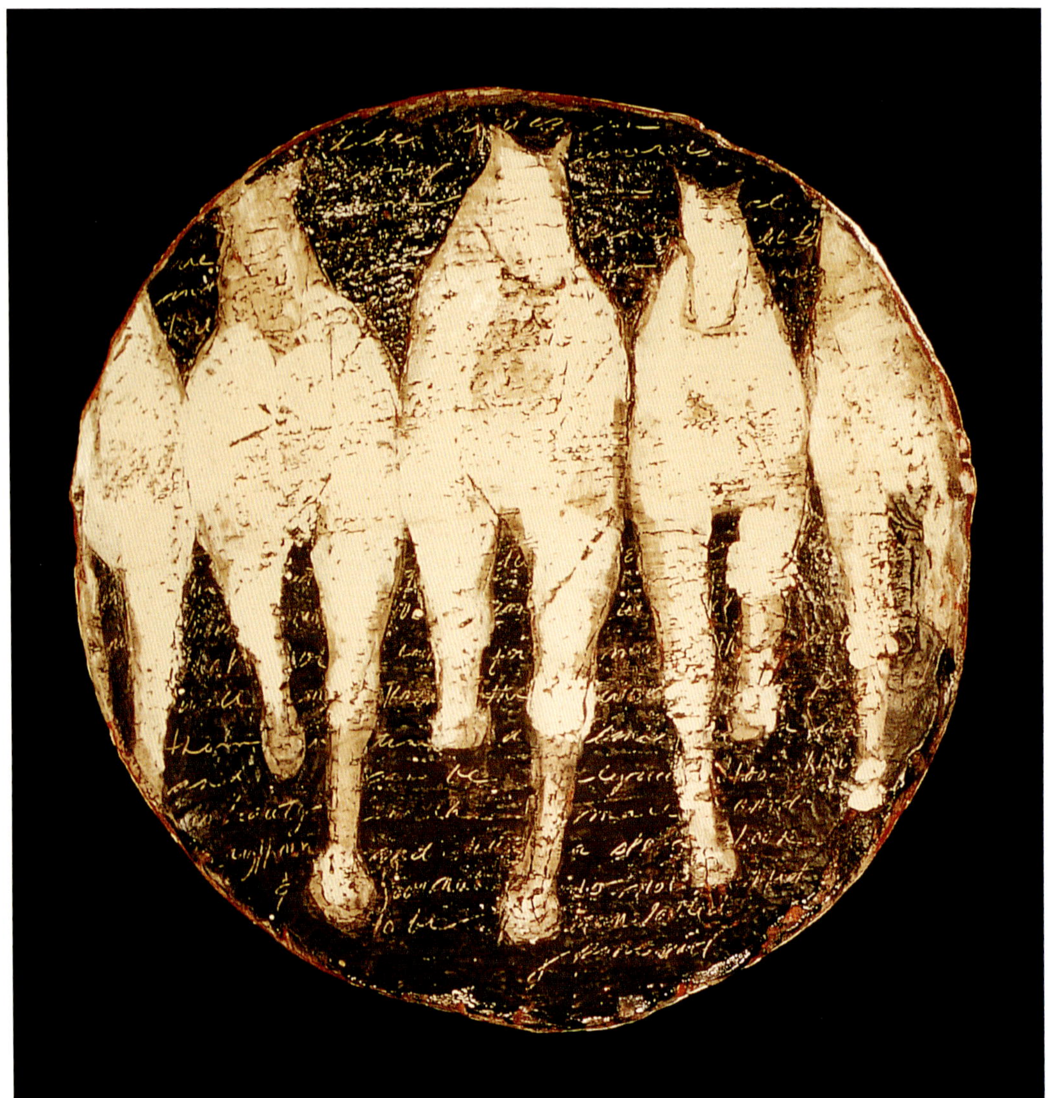

Jennifer Kincaid

Night Lyrics | 2006

3 X 22 INCHES (7.6 X 55.9 CM)

Slab and extruded earthenware; sgraffito; electric fired, cone 06; wash and glaze, cone 04

PHOTO BY BLACK BOX STUDIO

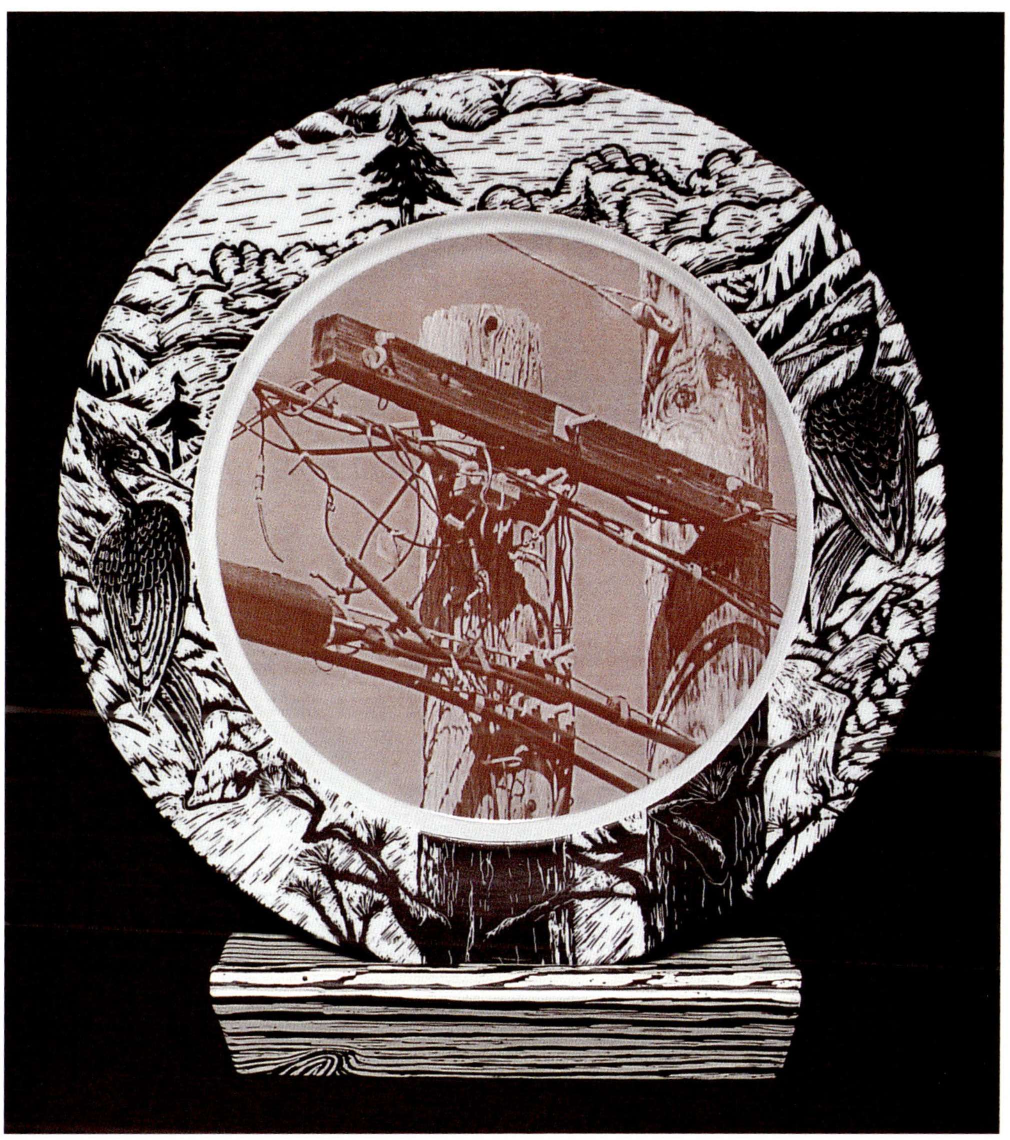

Jeff Irwin

Woodpeckers | 2005

2 X 13 X 11 INCHES (5.1 X 33 X 27.9 CM)

Found porcelain plate; laser decal, cone 03; black glaze, sgraffito; cone 03

PHOTO BY ARTIST

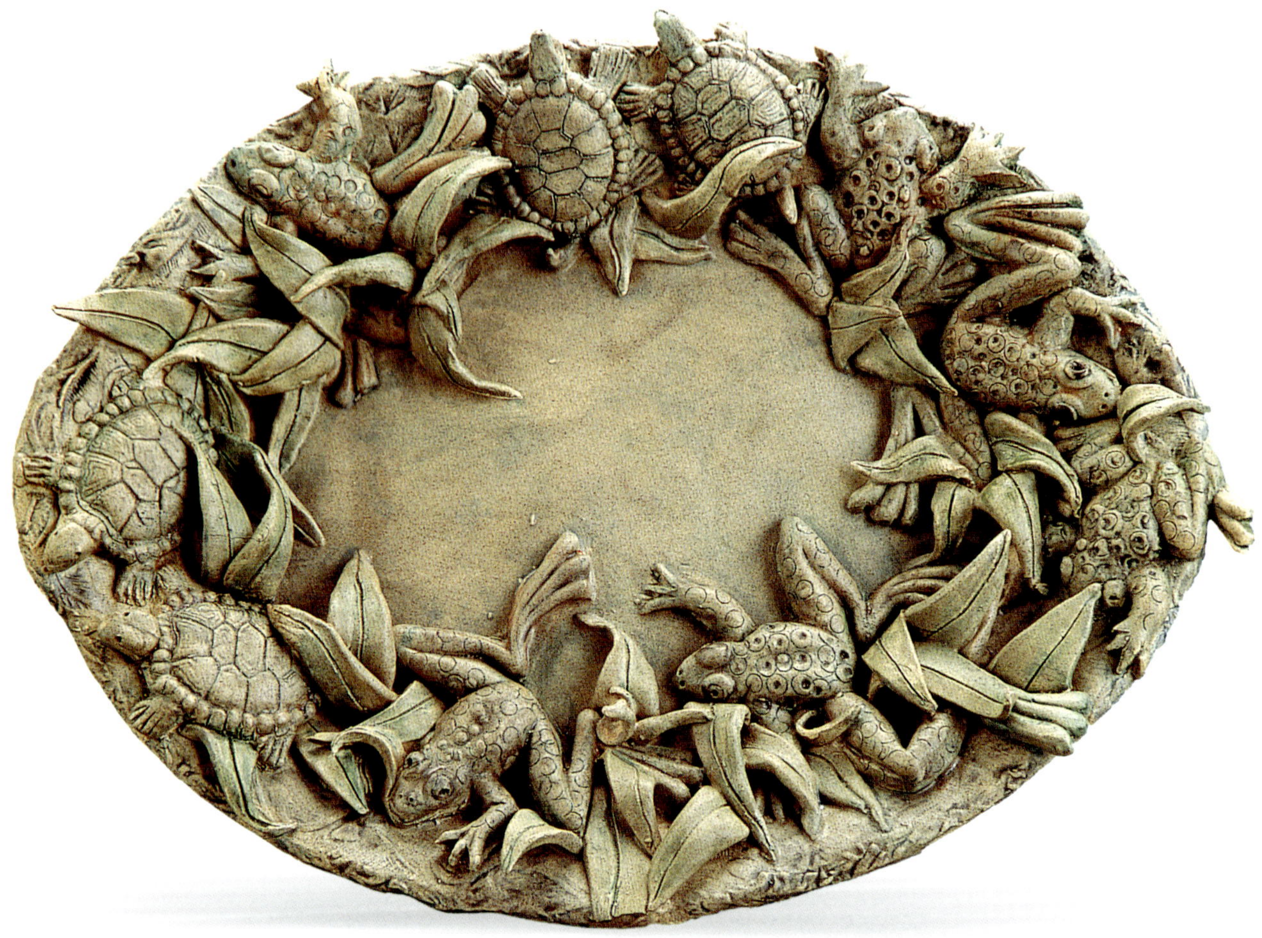

Mary Schulte

The Escape | 2007

2 X 16 X 10 INCHES (5.1 X 40.6 X 25.4 CM)

Hand-built stoneware; electric fired, cone 04, with low-fire glazes; china paints

PHOTO BY CHRIS MARCHETTI

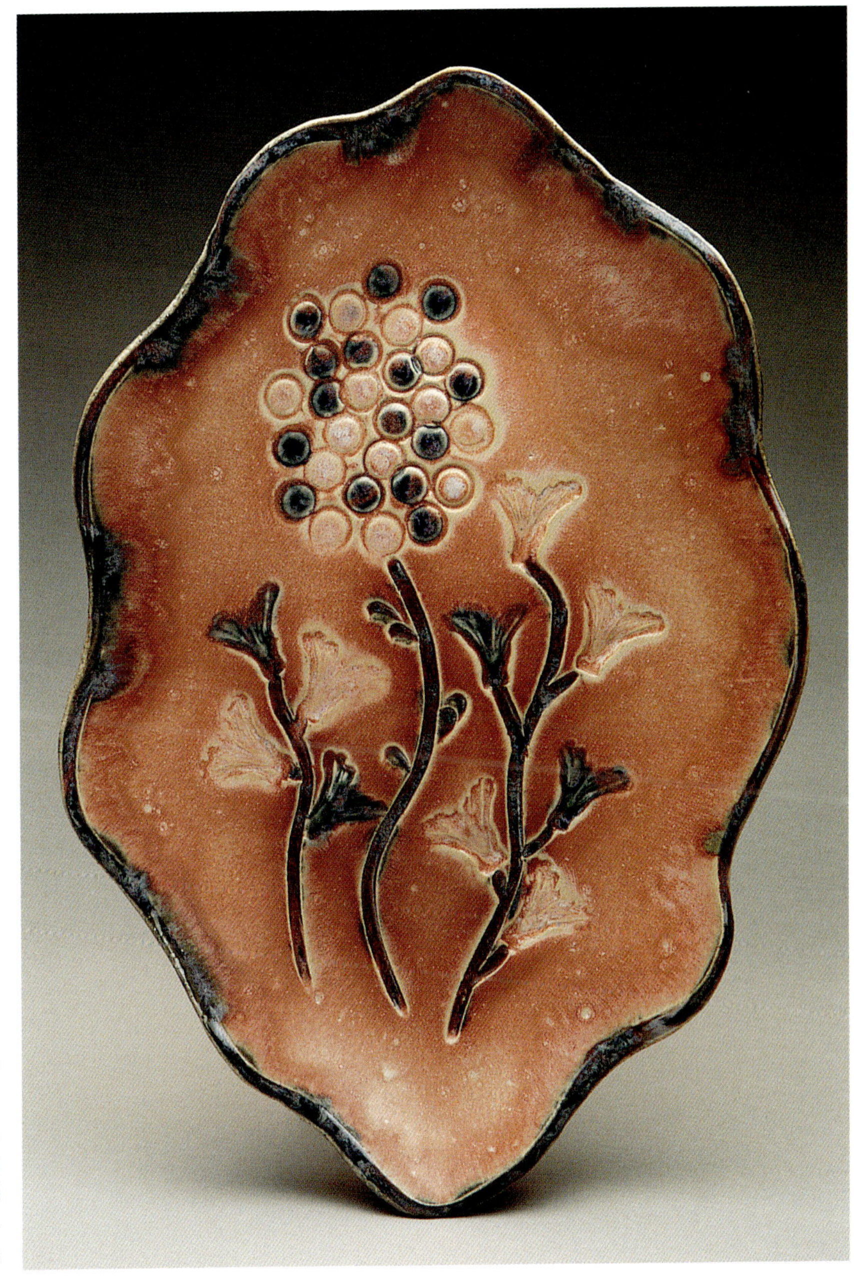

Michele Lyons

Platter | 2005

$3\frac{3}{8}$ X 10 X $15\frac{1}{2}$ INCHES (8.6 X 25.4 X 39.4 CM)

Hand-thrown and hump-molded stoneware; stamped, carved; brushed glazes, electric fired, cone 6

PHOTO BY NEIL ESTRICK

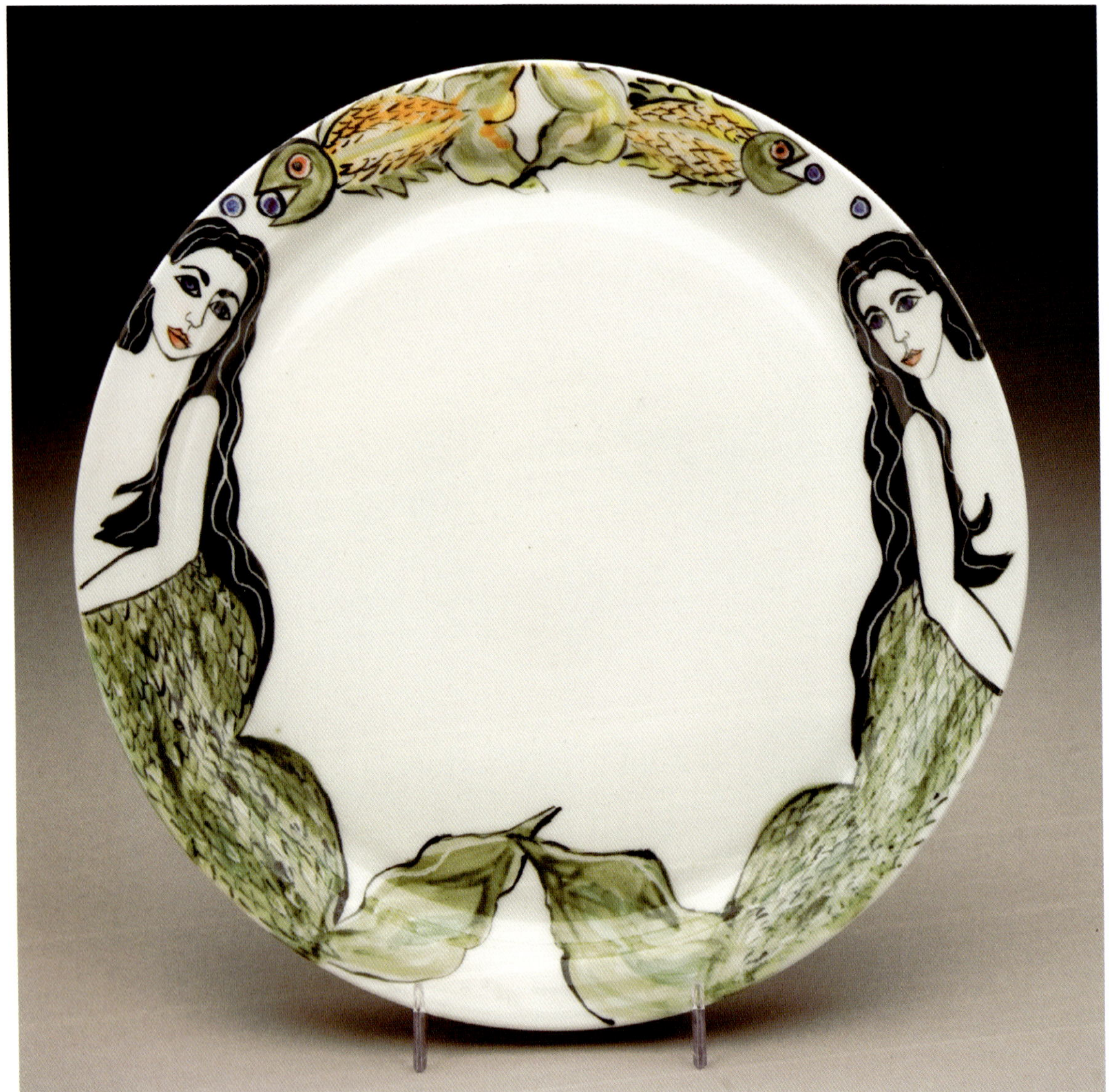

Roberta Shapiro

Mermaids and Fish Plate | 2007

11 1/2 INCHES (29.2 CM) IN DIAMETER

Wheel-thrown porcelain; stains, underglaze; clear glaze, gas fired, cone 10

PHOTO BY LOREN MARON

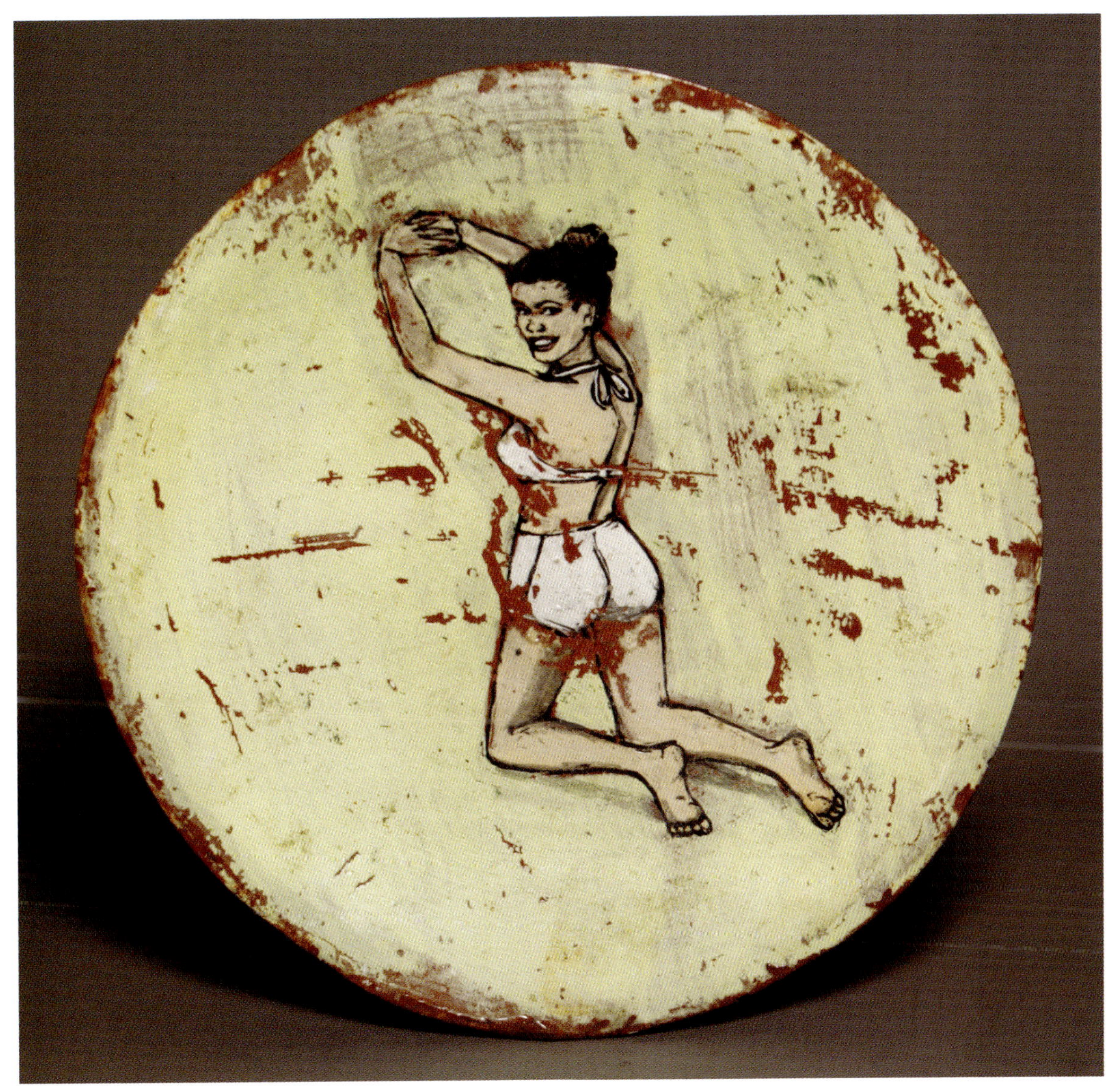

Shalene Valenzuela

White Bikini from Watershed Plate Series | 2004

1 1/4 X 8 INCHES (3.2 X 20.3 CM)

Slab-built earthenware; ceramic monoprint; electric fired, cone 04

PHOTO BY ARTIST

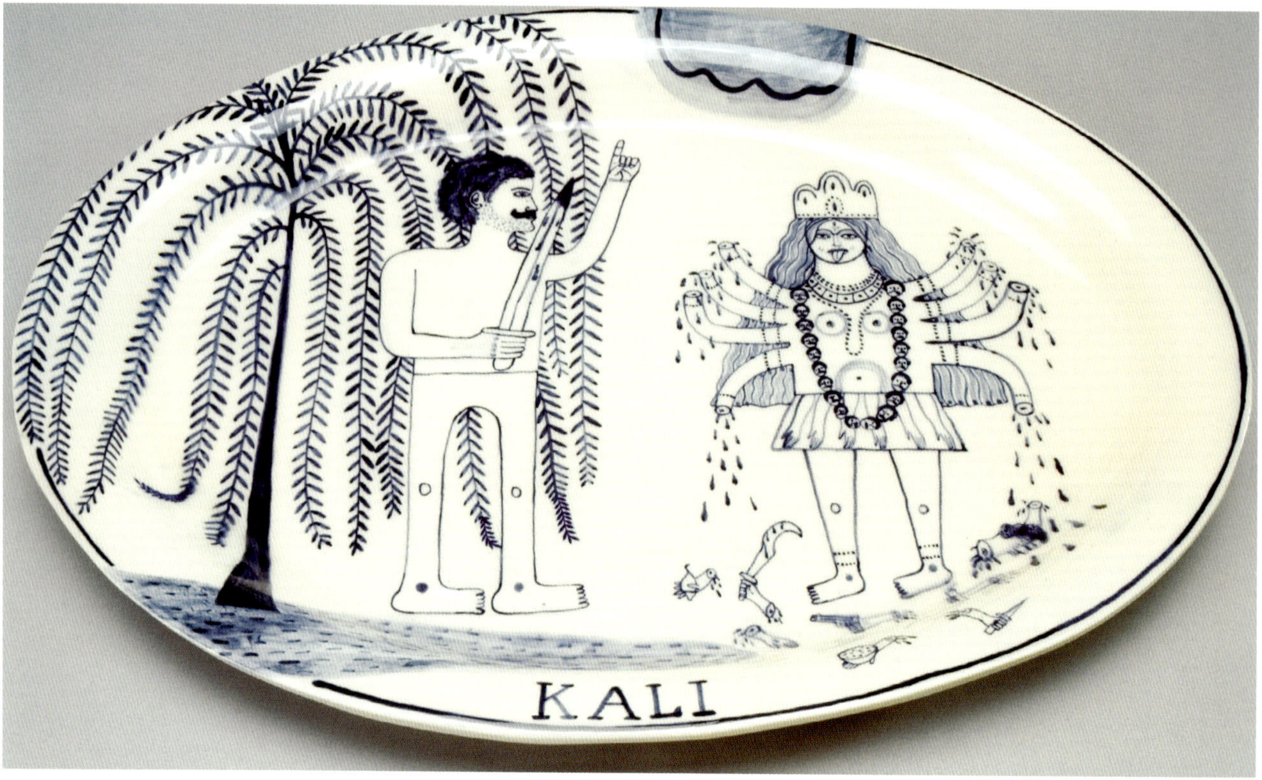

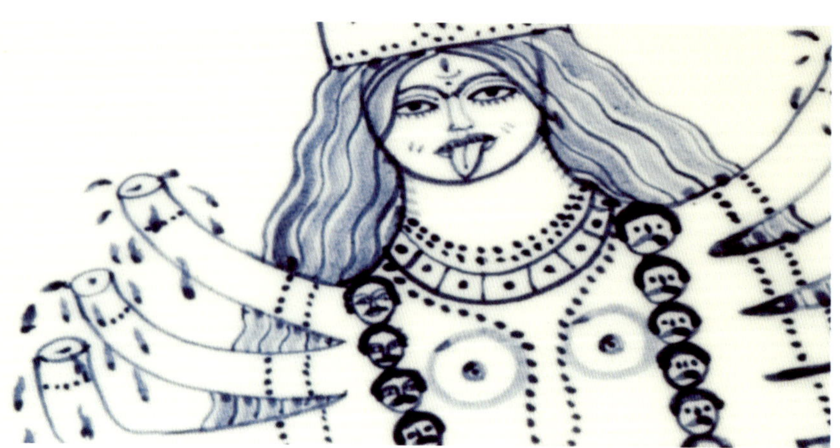

Stephen Bird

Kali | 2005

2 X 16 X 12 INCHES (5.1 X 40.6 X 30.5 CM)

White earthenware; underglaze; electric fired, cone 07; glaze, cone 1

PHOTOS BY GREG PIPER

Aaron M. Calvert

Glaze-Trailed Ant Head Plate | 2007

11 INCHES (27.9 CM) IN DIAMETER

Wheel-thrown stoneware; dipped blue glaze, trailed black glaze; gas fired, cone 10

PHOTO BY ARTIST

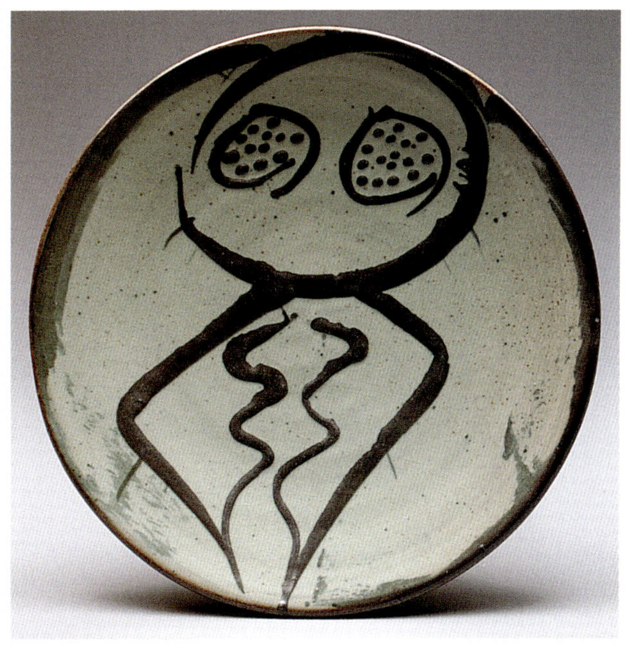

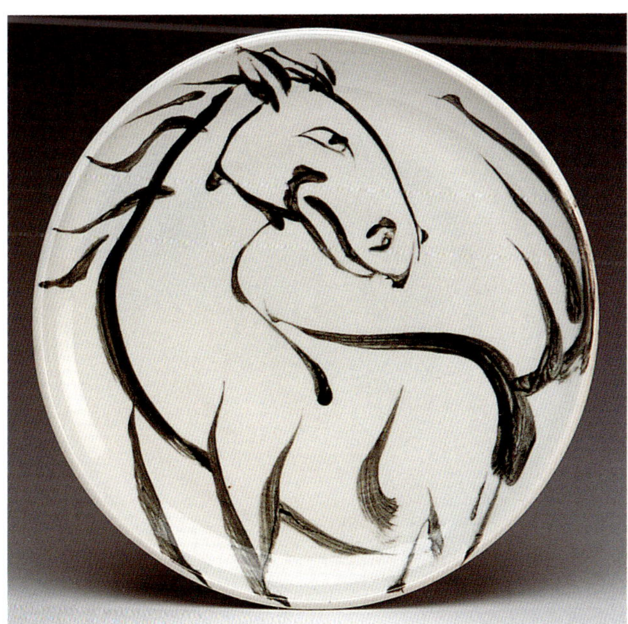

Andrew P. Linton

Horse Plate | 2003

1 5/8 X 10 3/4 INCHES (4.1 X 27.3 CM)

Wheel-thrown porcelain; black underglaze brushwork; Pete's Clear glaze, cone 10 reduction

PHOTO BY JIM KAMMER

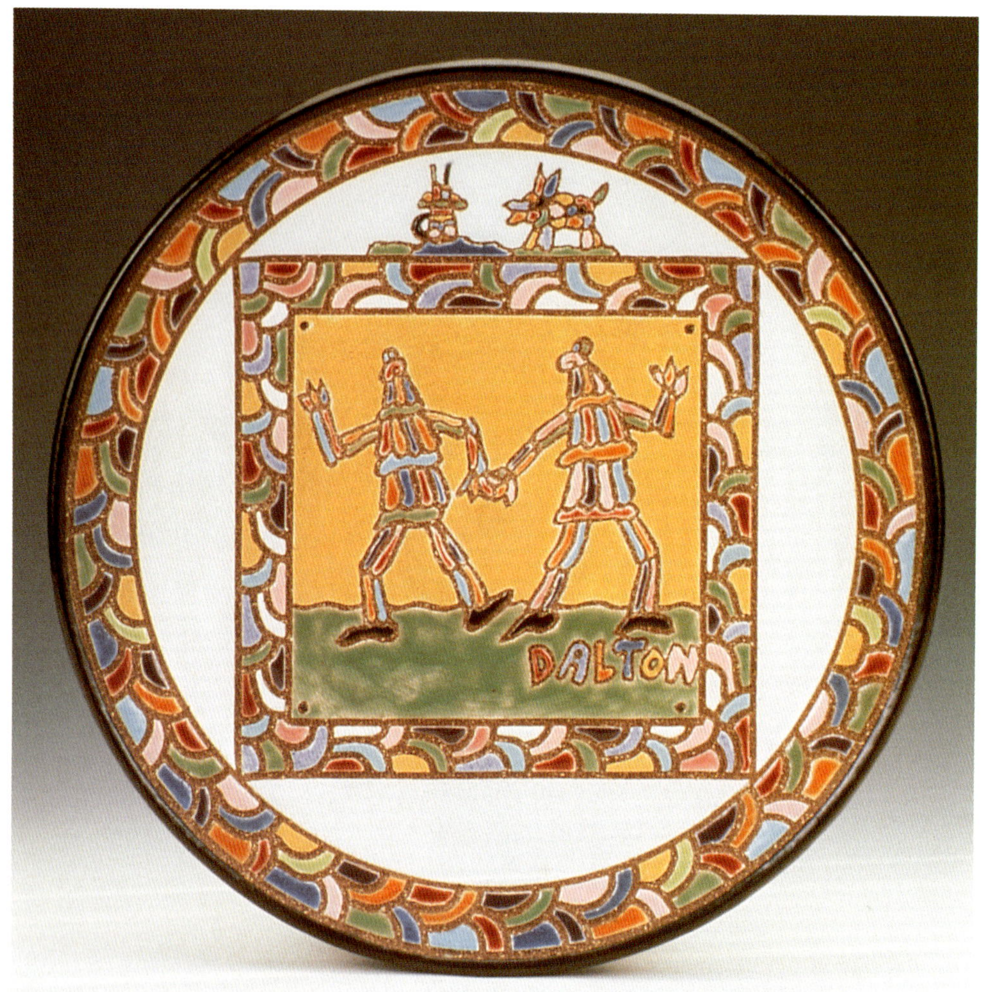

Norris Dalton

Dancing in the Sunlight | 1999

11 7/8 INCHES (30.2 CM) IN DIAMETER

Wheel-thrown mid-range black clay; sgraffito; electric fired, cone 5

PHOTO BY MICHAEL CROW

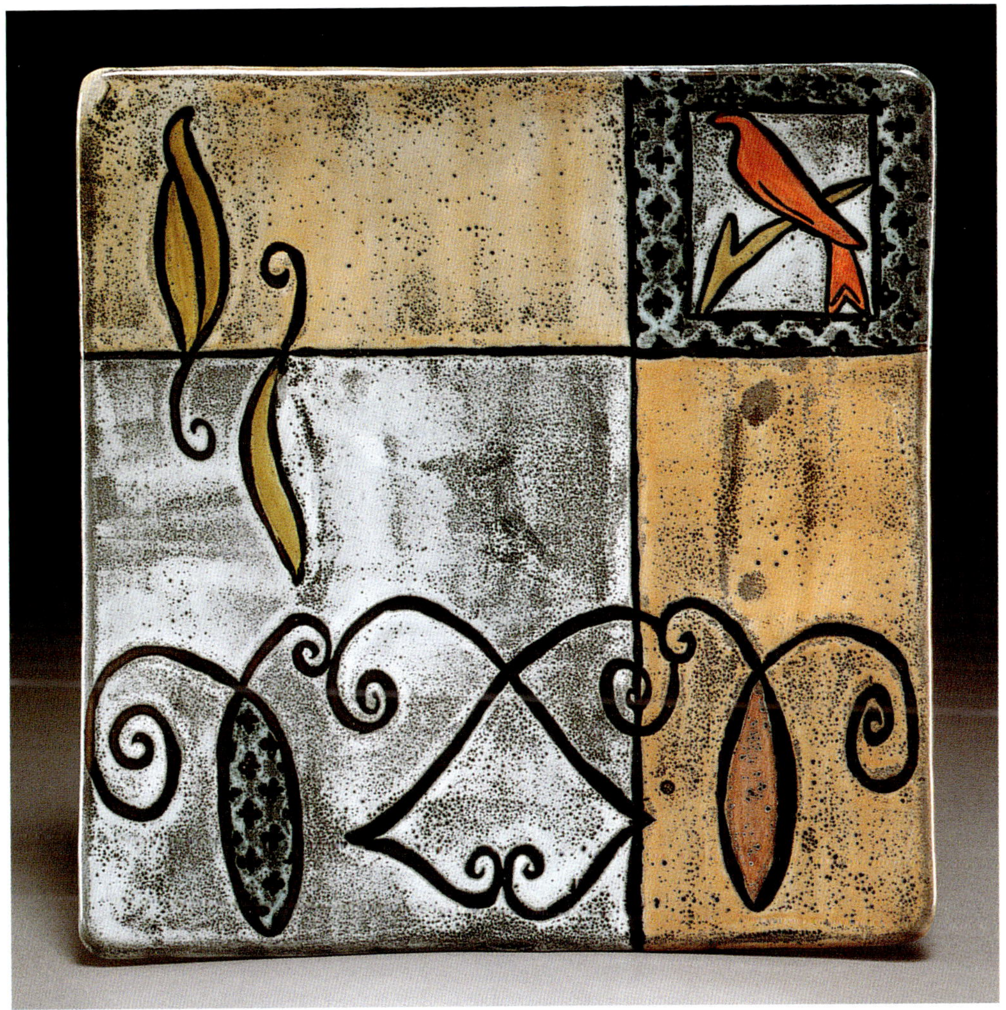

Susannah Lints

The littlest birds sing the prettiest songs | 2007

3 X 13 1/2 X 13 1/2 INCHES (7.6 X 34.3 X 34.3 CM)

Slab, drape-molded terra cotta;
black majolica; electric fired, cone 05

PHOTO BY COURTNEY FRISSEE

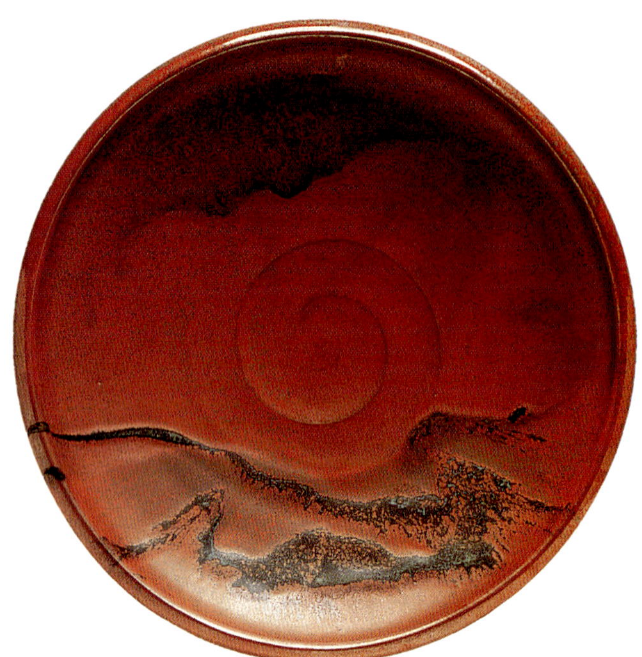

Ginny Marsh

Platter | 2006

3 X 16 INCHES (7.6 X 40.6 CM)

Wheel-thrown stoneware; iron red and celadon glazes, gas fired in reduction, cone 10

PHOTO BY ARTIST

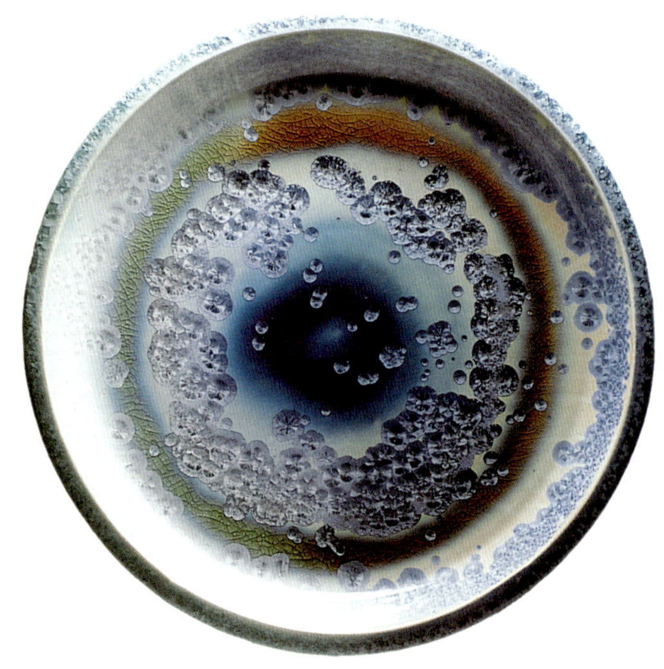

Laura Aultman

Crystal Galaxy | 2003

2 X 15½ INCHES (5.1 X 39.4 CM)

Wheel-thrown porcelain; crystalline glaze; electric fired, cone 10

PHOTO BY ARTIST

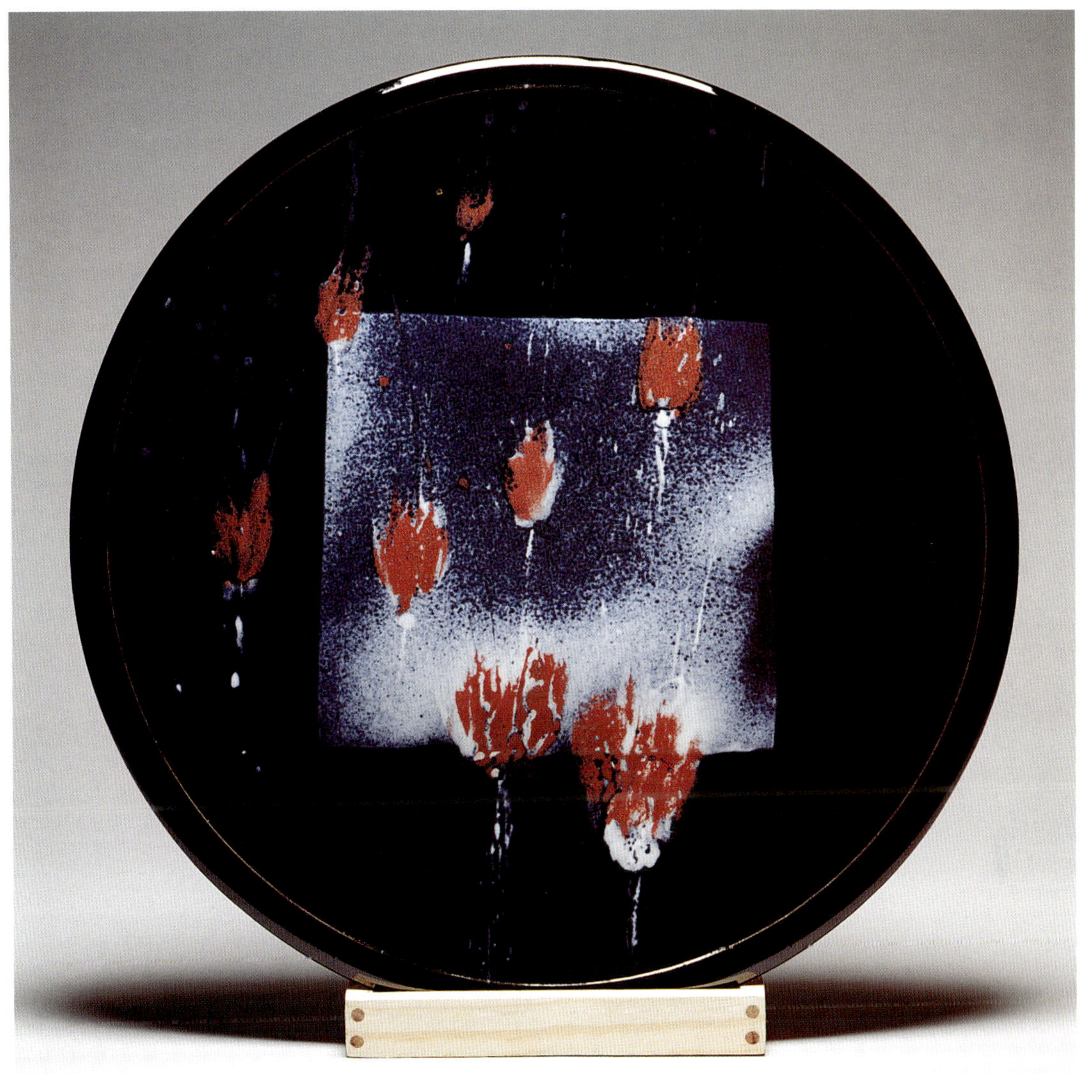

Willi Michalski

Bushfire | 2006

1 1/2 X 14 INCHES (3.8 X 35.6 CM)

Wheel-thrown stoneware; gas fired in reduction, cone 10; glaze-on-glaze, brushwork; cobalt glaze and copper red glaze

PHOTO BY WARWICK ORME

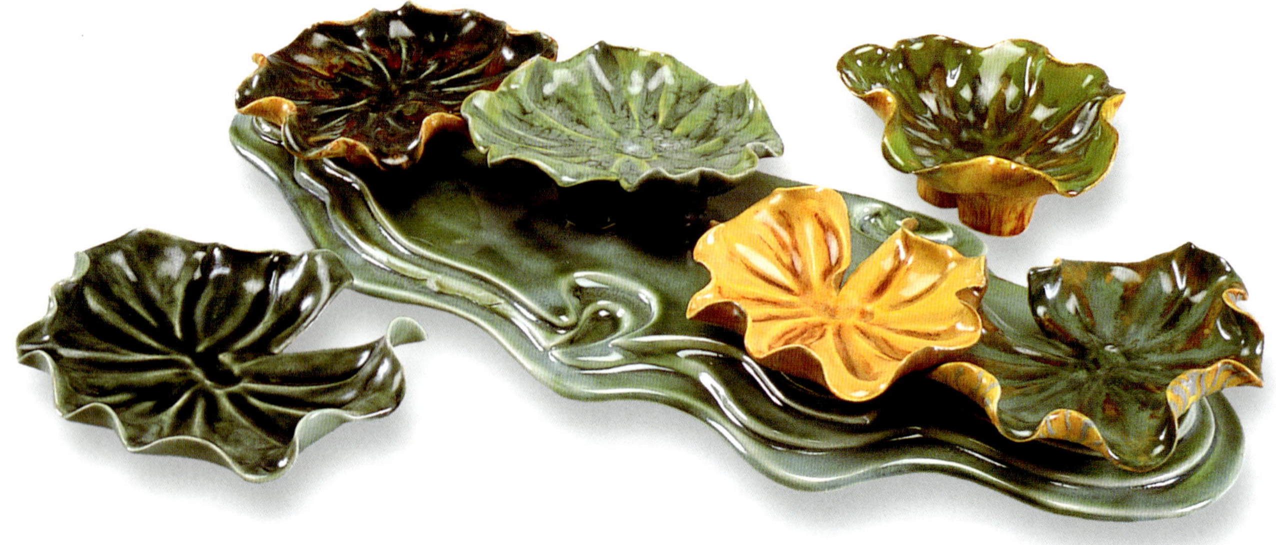

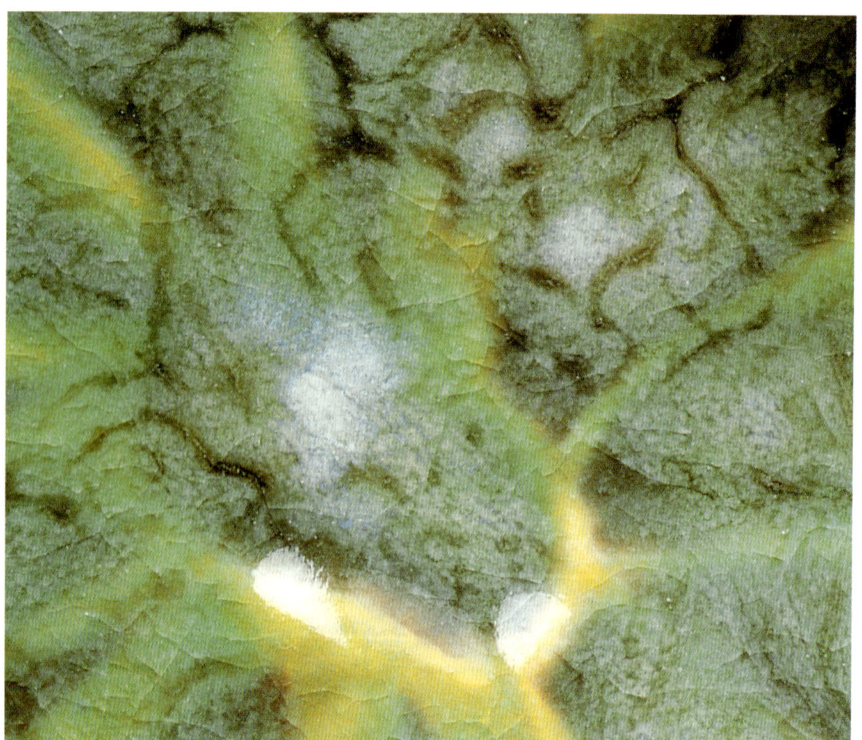

Sandra Lance

Lily Pond Serving Platter | 1998

LARGEST: 1 3/4 X 25 X 12 INCHES
(4.4 X 63.5 X 30.5 CM)

Hand-built porcelain; multi-color underglazes and glazes; multi-glaze, electric fired, cone 6

PHOTOS BY ARTIST

Kathryn E. Narrow

Wedding Plate | 1986

2 X 12 X 12 INCHES (5.1 X 30.5 X 30.5 CM)

Thrown porcelain; cut and carved; copper glaze, electric fired, cone 6

PHOTO BY ARTIST

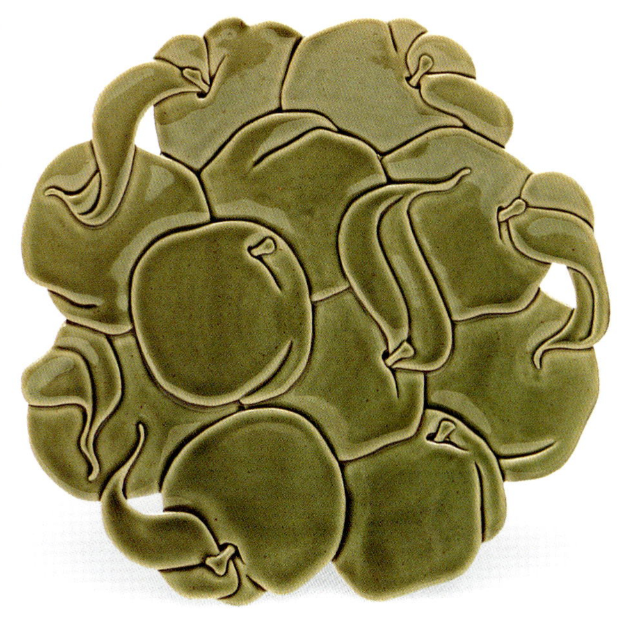

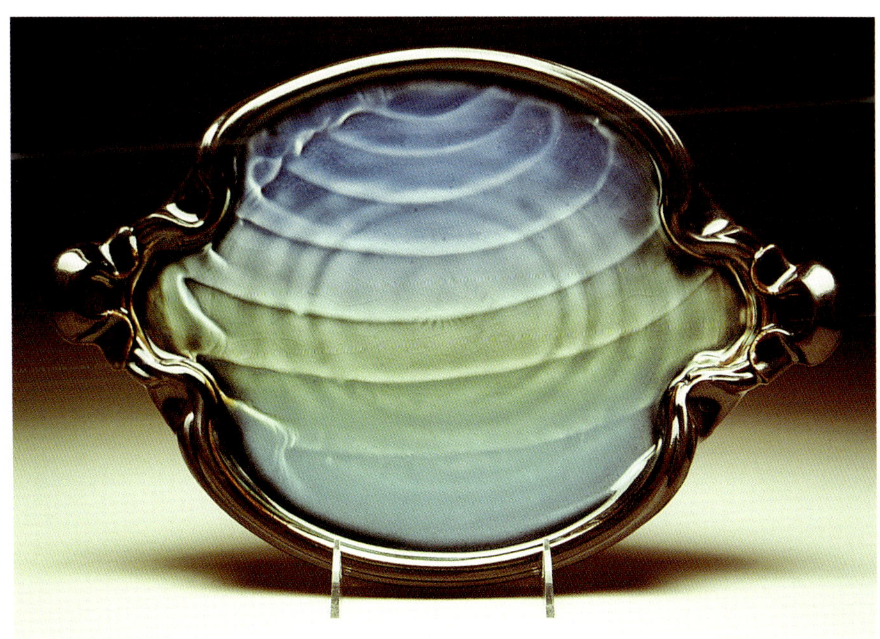

Sean O'Connell

Untitled | 2006

$1\frac{1}{2}$ X 15 X 11 INCHES (3.8 X 38.1 X 27.9 CM)

Thrown and altered porcelain; combed slip, sprayed glazes; gas fired in reduction, cone 10

PHOTO BY ARTIST

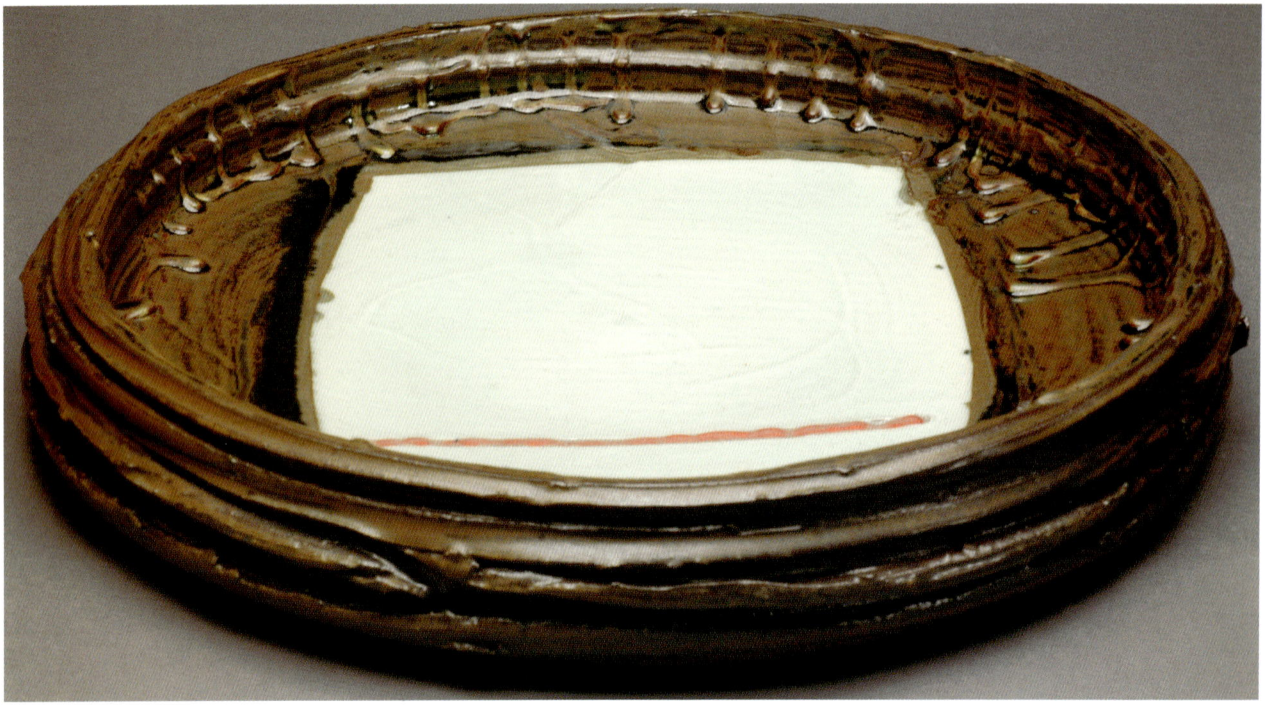

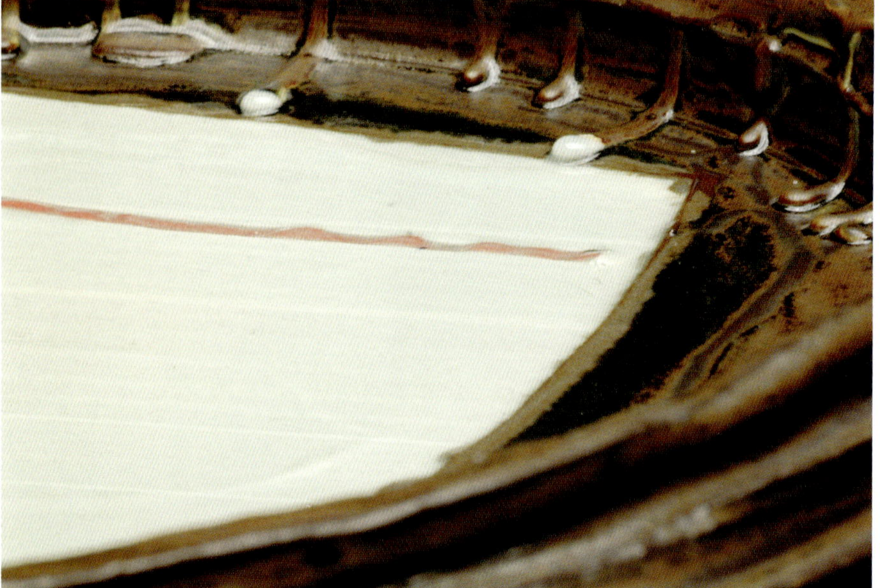

Benjamin Fiess

Untitled | 2006

3 X 16 INCHES (7.6 X 40.6 CM)

Wheel-thrown stoneware; porcelain slip; celadon and matte brown glazes; reduction fired, cone 10

PHOTOS BY ARTIST

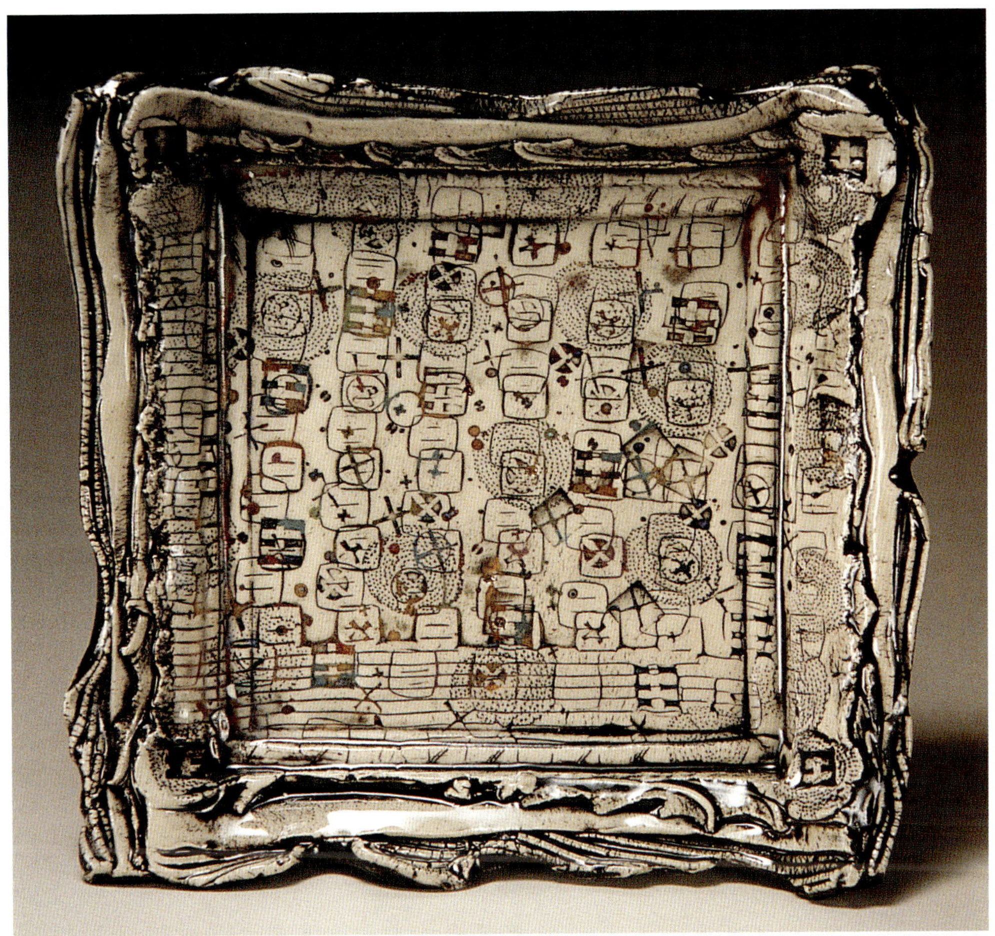

Lana Wilson

Plate | 2006

2½ X 11 X 10 INCHES (6.4 X 27.9 X 25.4 CM)

Slab-built white stoneware; textured, black and colored slips; clear glaze, electric fired, cone 6

PHOTO BY ARTIST

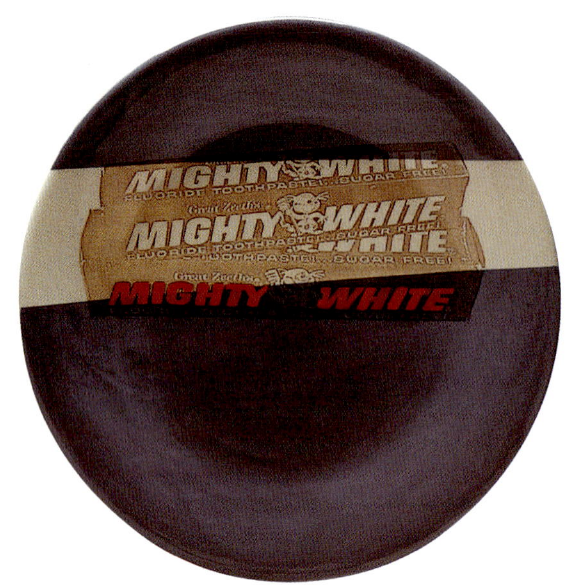

Christine Colby

Mighty White | 2004

1 X 10 INCHES (2.5 X 25.4 CM)

Slip-cast earthenware; electric fired, cone 04; glaze, cone 06; decal, cone 08; china paint, cone 018

PHOTO BY ARTIST

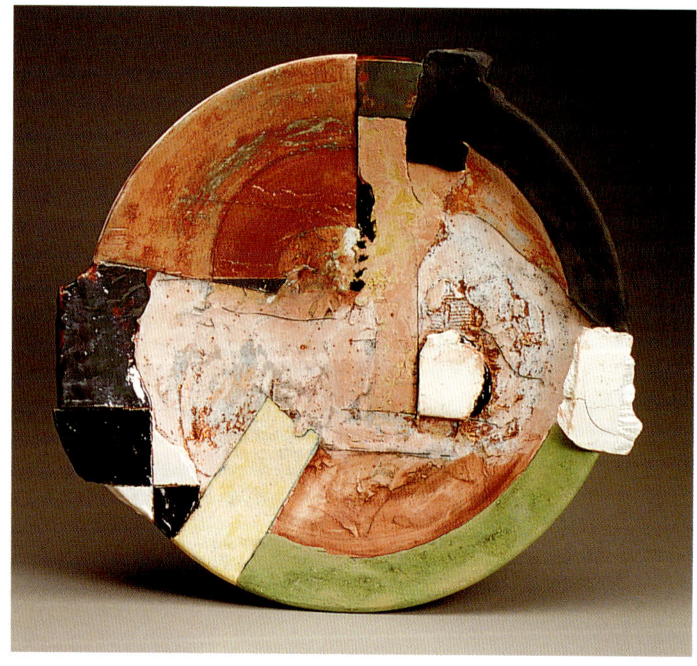

Eugene Lewis

The Way | 2001

24 INCHES (61 CM) IN DIAMETER

Wheel thrown and altered; gas low-fire reduction, cone 08

PHOTO BY ARTIST

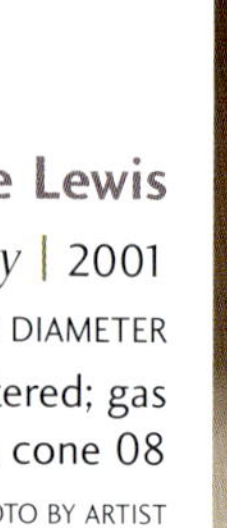

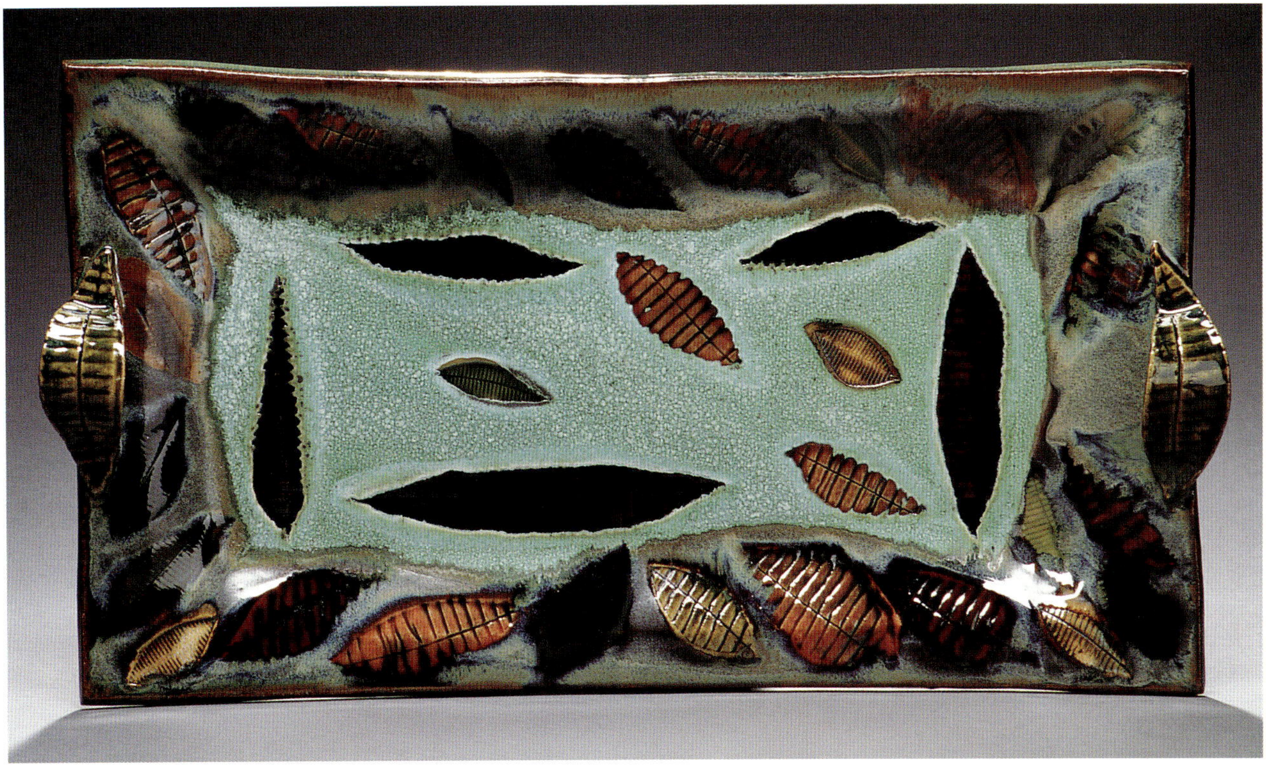

Susan DeMay

long leaf tray | 2005

3 X 24½ X 13 INCHES (7.6 X 62.2 X 33 CM)

Slab-built stoneware; impressed, stained; electric fired, cone 6; glaze, cone 6

PHOTOS BY JOHN LUCAS

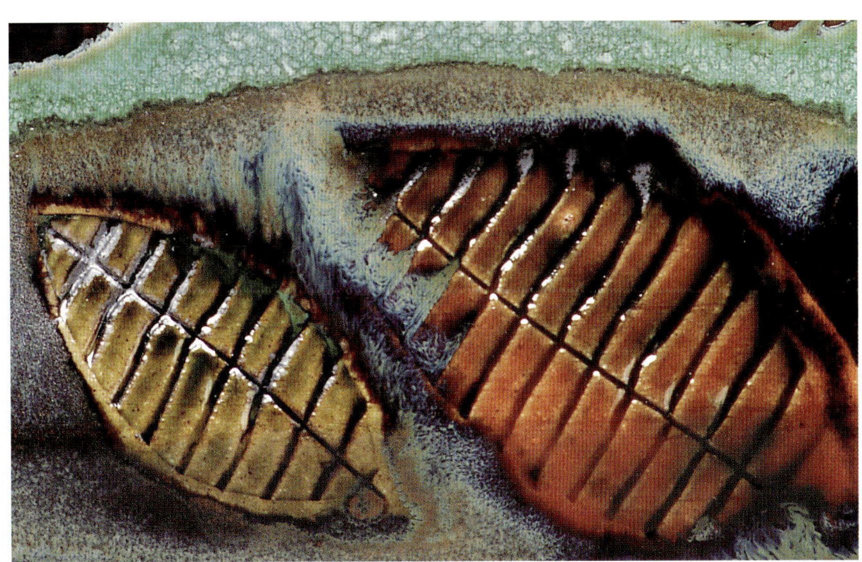

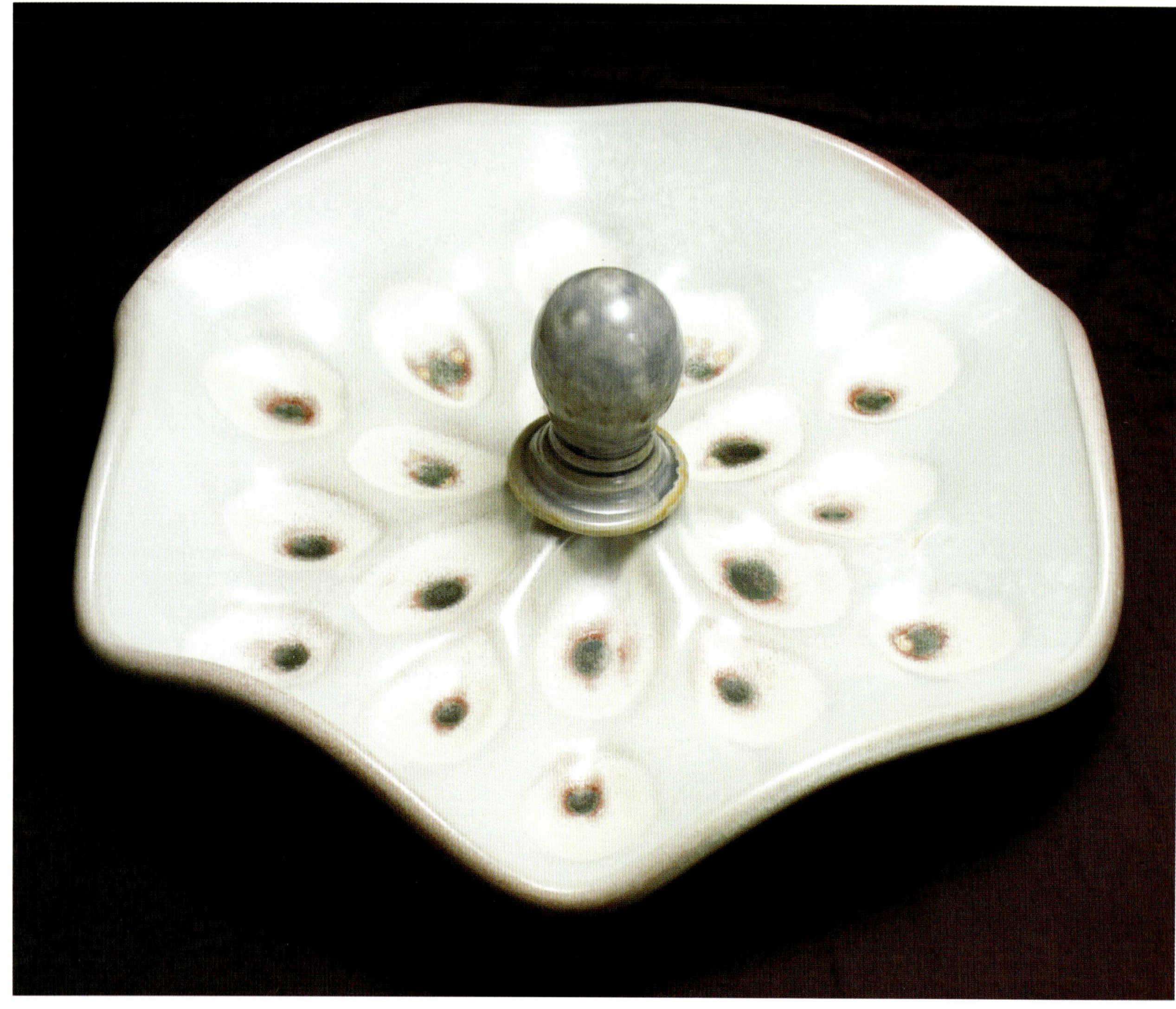

Jill J. Burns

Deviled Egg Platter | 2007

4 X 12 X 12 INCHES (10.2 X 30.5 X 30.5 CM)

Hand-built and wheel-thrown stoneware; soda fired, cone 10

PHOTO BY ARTIST

Jillian Higley

Seated Nude | 2007

1 X 9 INCHES (2.5 X 22.9 CM)

Hand-built porcelain; incised drawing; rutile wash, engobe; glaze, cone 6

PHOTO BY DAVE GULISANO

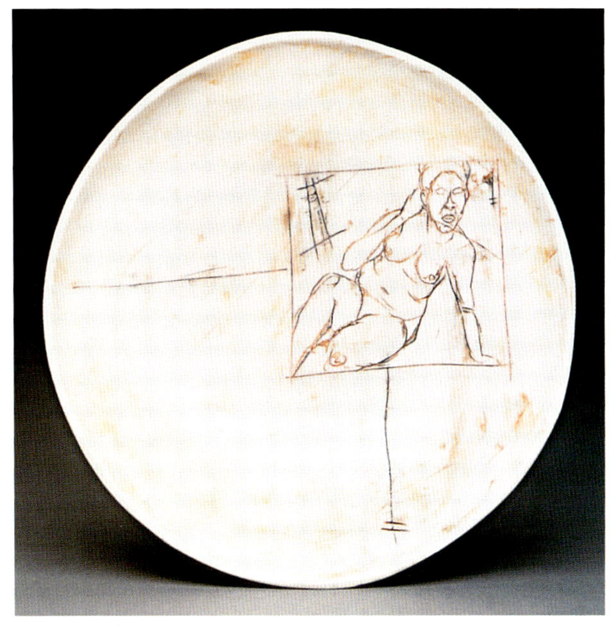

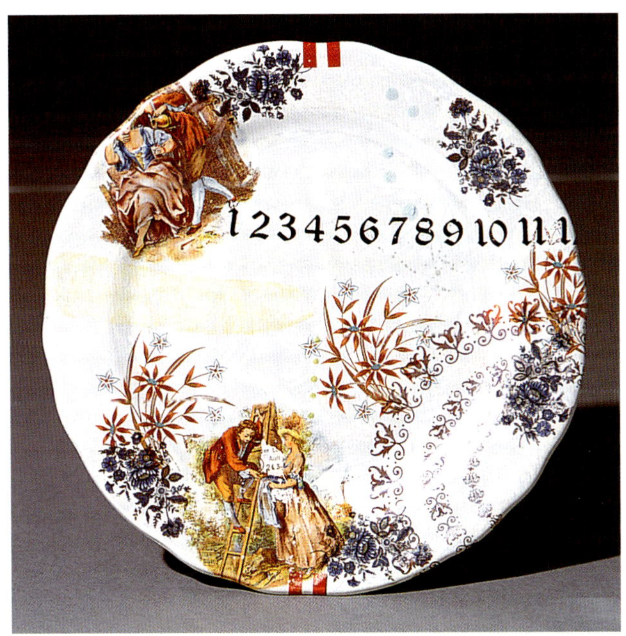

Julie Guyot

Decorative Plate #2 | 2007

1 X 11 INCHES (2.5 X 27.9 CM)

Slip-cast low-fire whiteware; underglaze transfers; laser and commercial decals; electric fired, cone 04; mother-of-pearl finish

PHOTO BY ANDREW ROSS

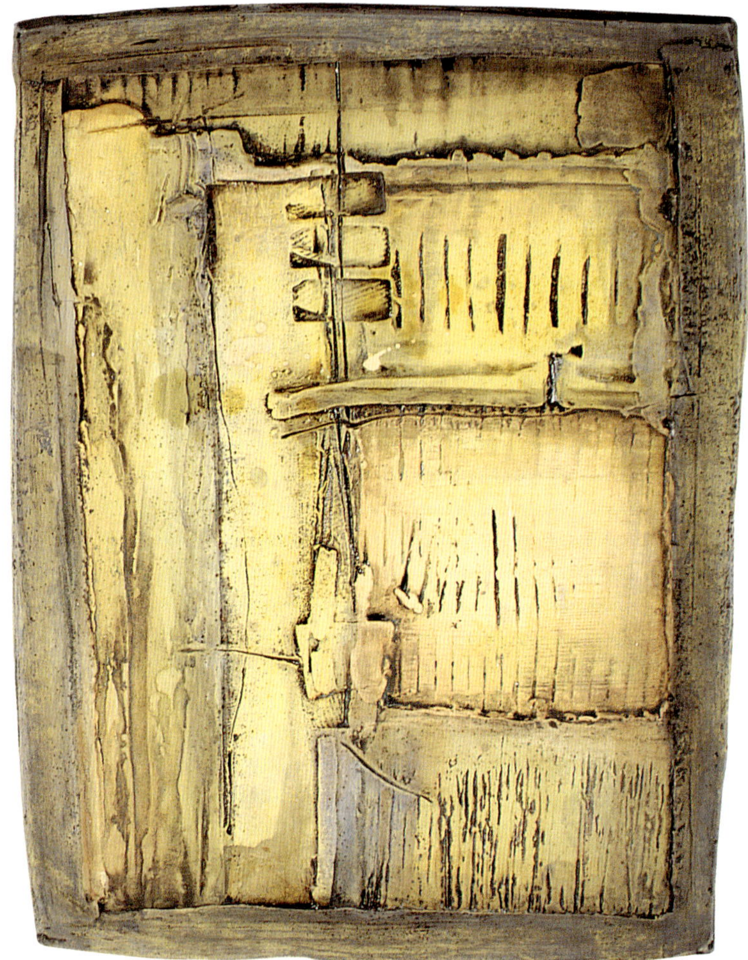

Una Mjurka

Exercises with Color (1) | 2004

$2^{1}/_{2}$ X 12 X $15^{1}/_{2}$ INCHES (6.4 X 30.5 X 39.4 CM)

Hand-built low-fire clay; multi-fired, cones 06 and 04; layered commercial underglazes, glaze washes

PHOTO BY ARTIST

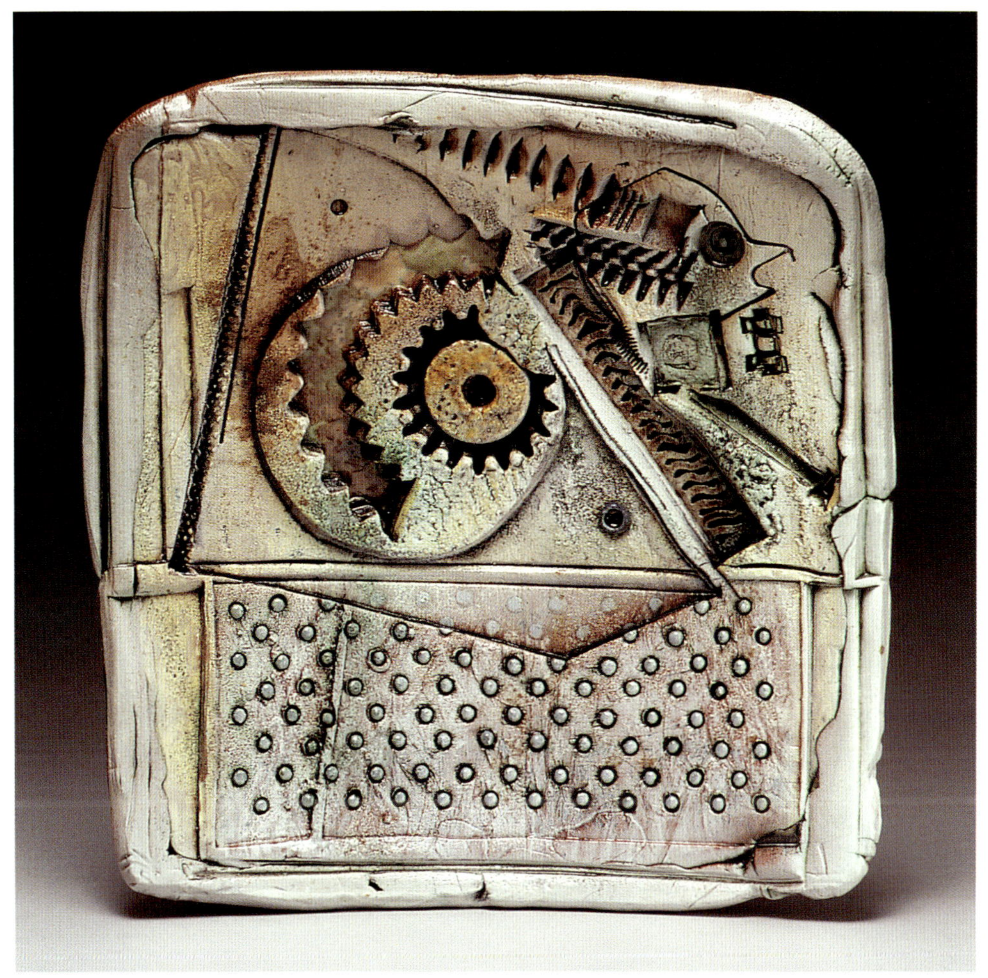

Sandra Blain

Centered | 2007

4½ X 15 X 15 INCHES (11.4 X 38.1 X 38.1 CM)

Slab and wheel-constructed earthenware; textured; slip, oxides; glazes, electric multi-fired, cone 04

PHOTO BY MICHAEL HEALY

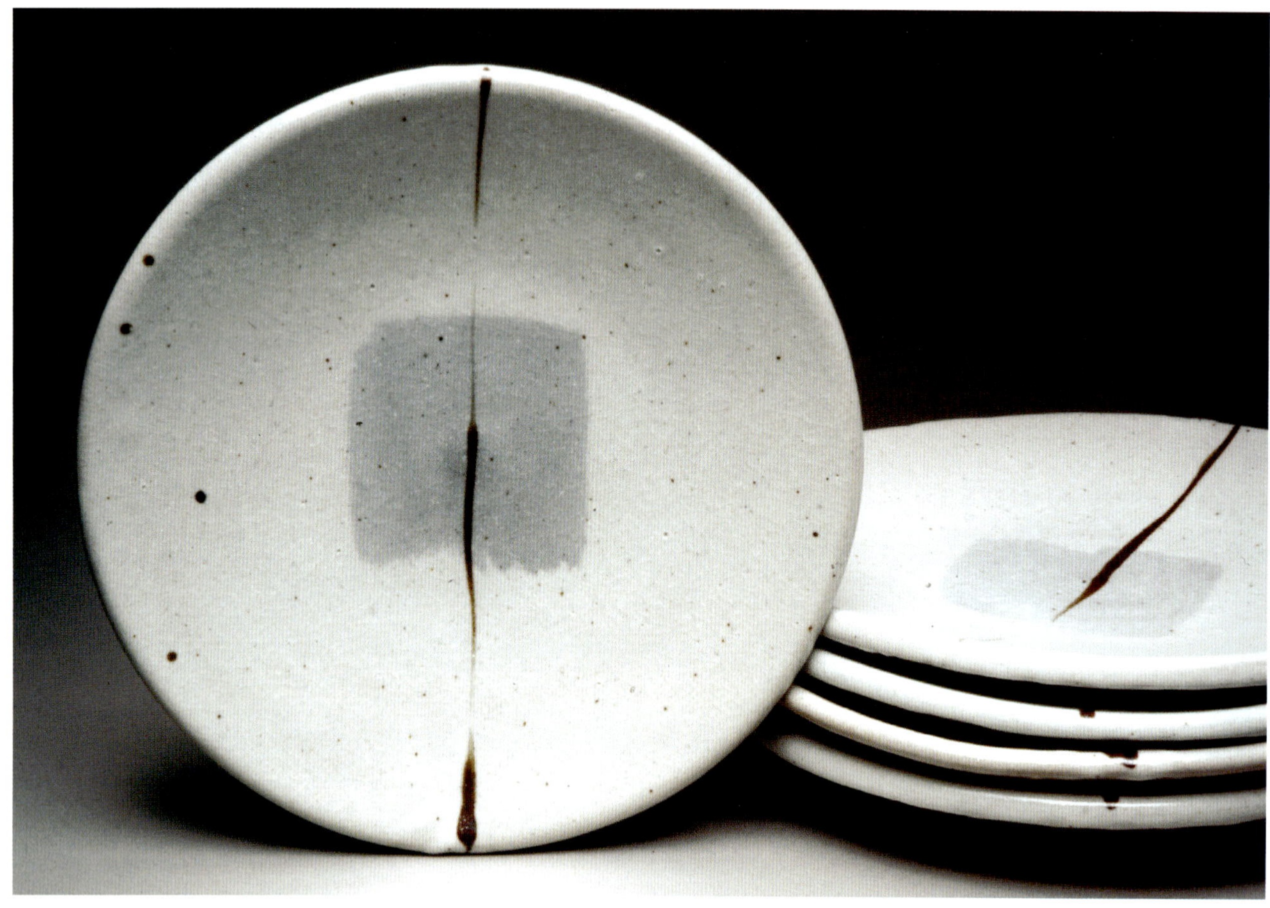

Joe Singewald

Set of Plates | 2005

EACH: 2 X 11 INCHES (5.1 X 27.9 CM)

Wheel-thrown stoneware;
gas fired, cone 10

PHOTO BY ARTIST

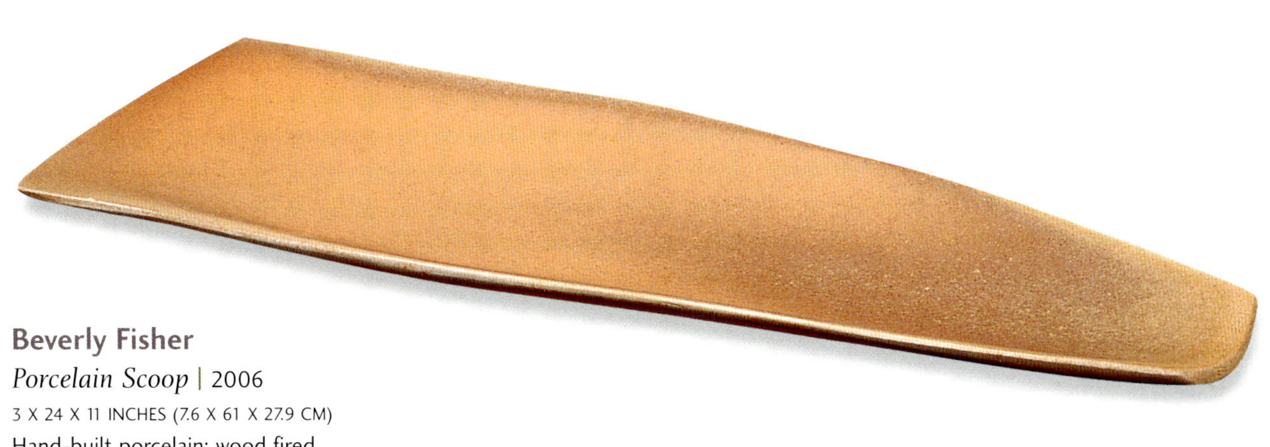

Beverly Fisher

Porcelain Scoop | 2006

3 X 24 X 11 INCHES (7.6 X 61 X 27.9 CM)

Hand-built porcelain; wood fired

PHOTO BY JOHN CARLANO

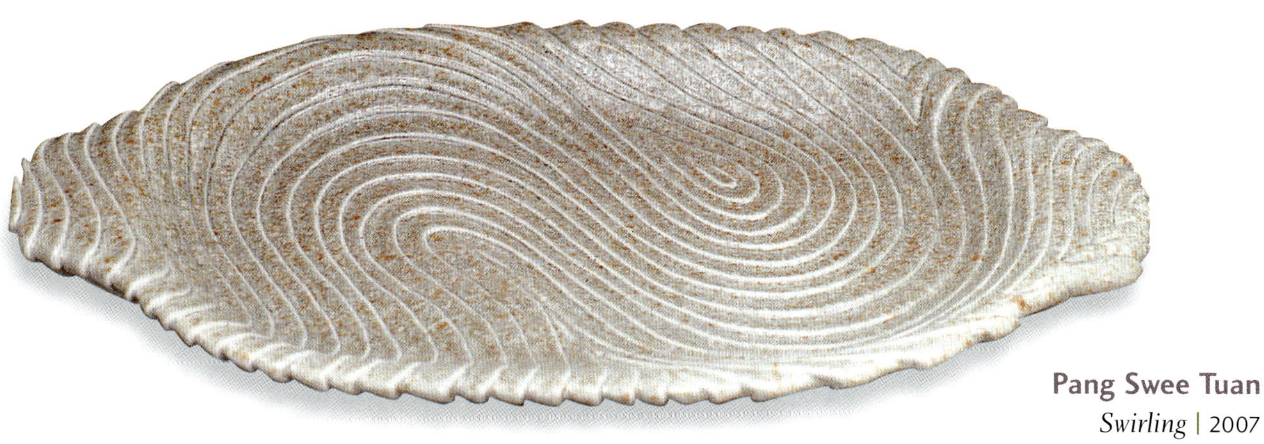

Pang Swee Tuan

Swirling | 2007

1 1/2 X 13 1/2 X 8 1/4 INCHES (3.8 X 34.3 X 21 CM)

Hand-built slab; carved details; electric fired, cone 6

PHOTO BY CHAN HON ONN

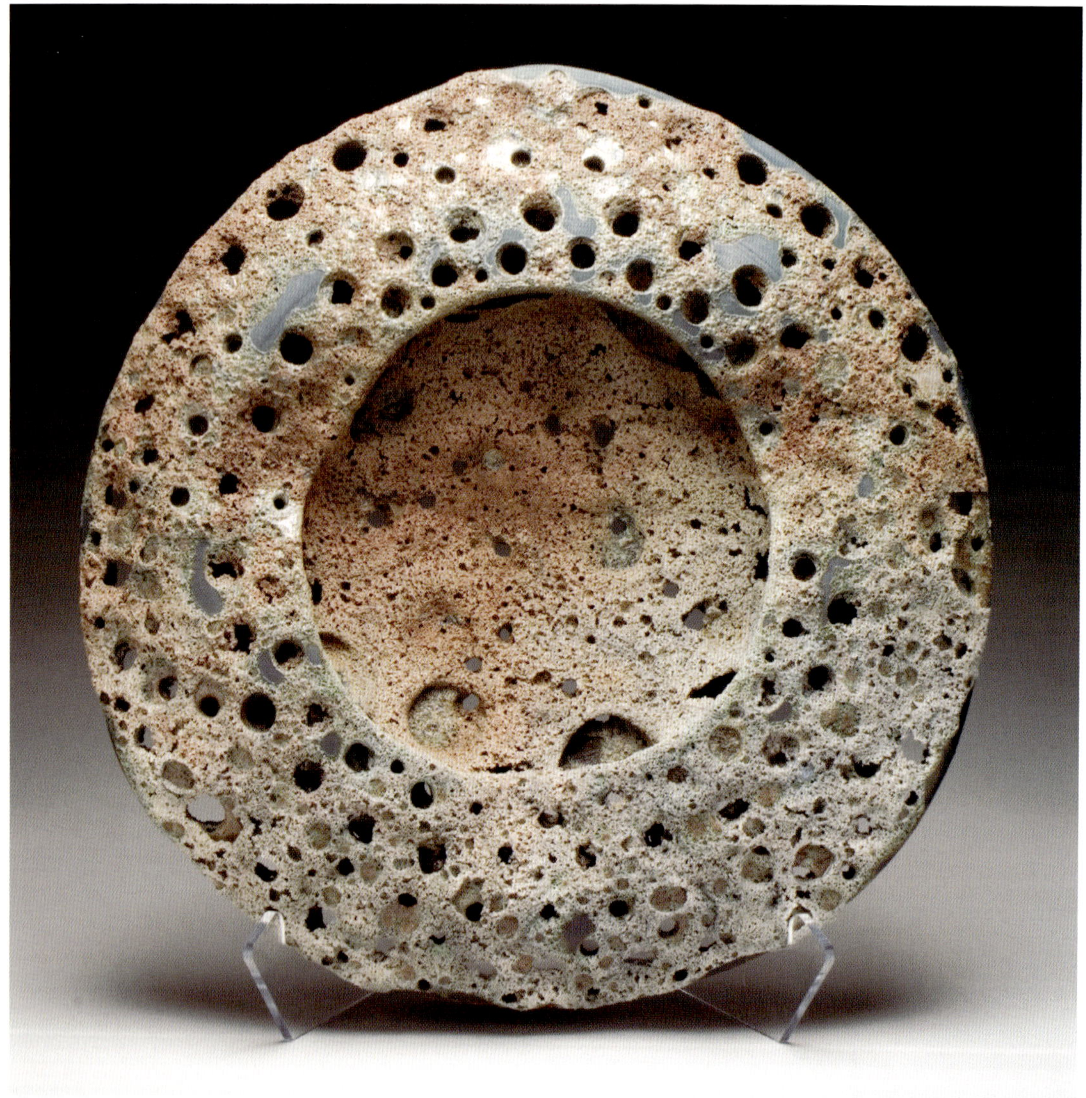

Todd Leech

red tide | 2007

4 X 19 INCHES (10.2 X 48.3 CM)

Wheel-thrown, hand-built, and drilled stoneware; foaming glaze, gas fired in reduction, cone 10

PHOTO BY ARTIST

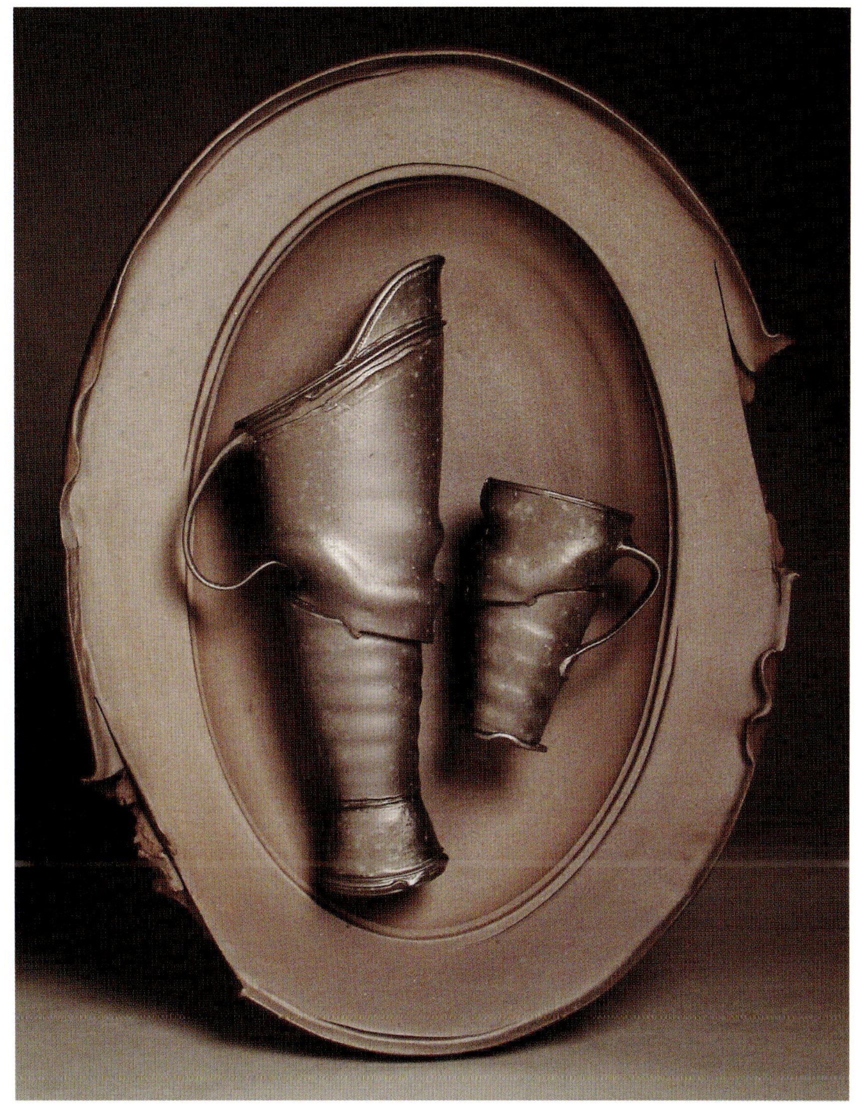

Robert Long

Cut Rim Platter with Pitcher | 2007

4 X 19 X 24 INCHES (10.2 X 48.3 X 61 CM)

Wheel-thrown, stretched, and assembled Aardvark Black Mountain clay; iron glaze, high-fire reduction, cone 10

PHOTO BY ARTIST

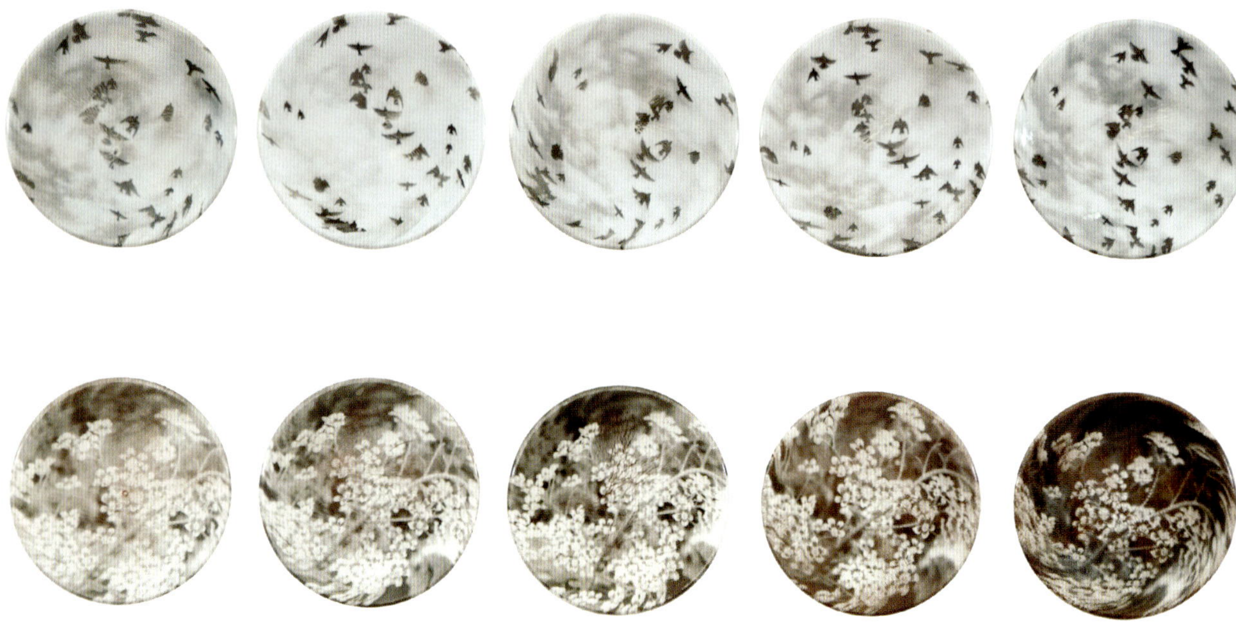

Heidi Parsons

Snapshot Plates: Brighton Birds Series (top); Blossom Series (bottom) | 2007

EACH: 2 X 13¾ INCHES (5 X 35 CM)

Red and white earthenware; screen printed; 1080 glaze

PHOTO BY ARTIST

Vince Pitelka

View on the Power Canal | 1993

2 1/2 X 19 INCHES (6.4 X 48.3 CM)

Slab-built white earthenware; colored clay inlay; clear glaze, electric fired, cone 03

PHOTO BY ARTIST

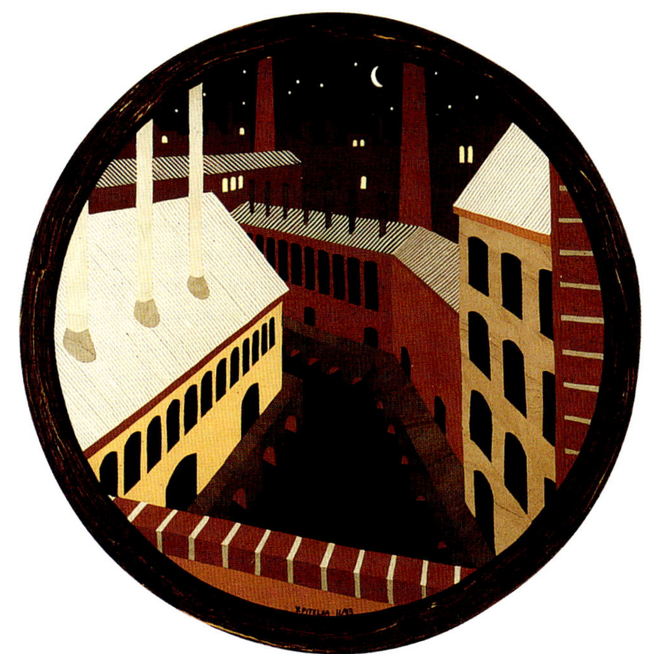

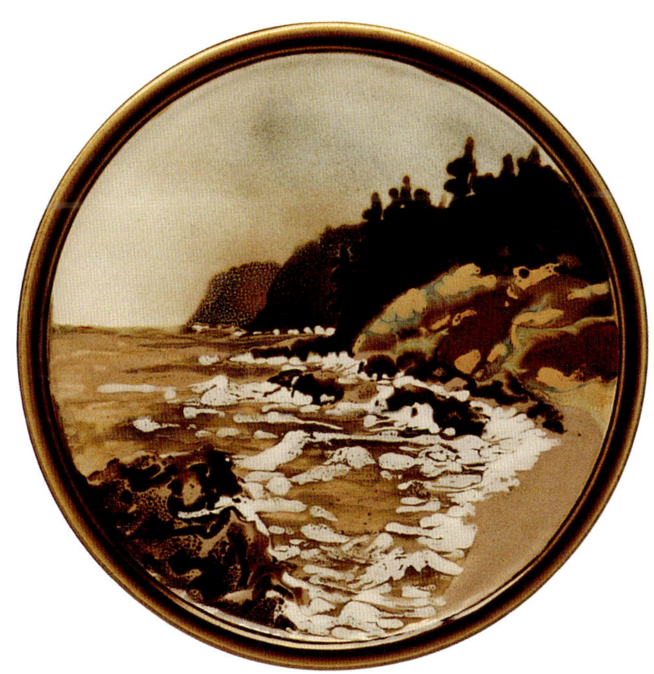

Paul Lewing

Glacier Point Platter | 1982

1 1/2 X 17 INCHES (3.8 X 43.2 CM)

Thrown porcelain; trailed glazes; gas fired in reduction, cone 10

PHOTO BY ROGER SCHREIBER

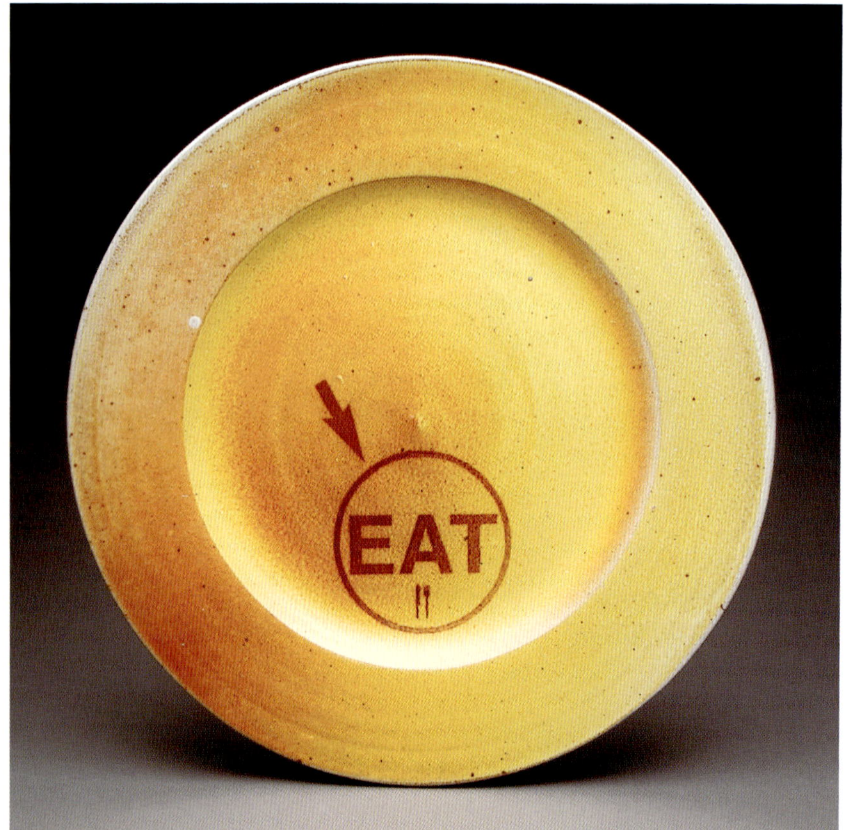

Michael T. Schmidt

Eat Platter | 2007

19 INCHES (48.3 CM) IN DIAMETER

Wheel-thrown stoneware; soda fired, cone 10; laser-print transfer

PHOTOS BY ARTIST

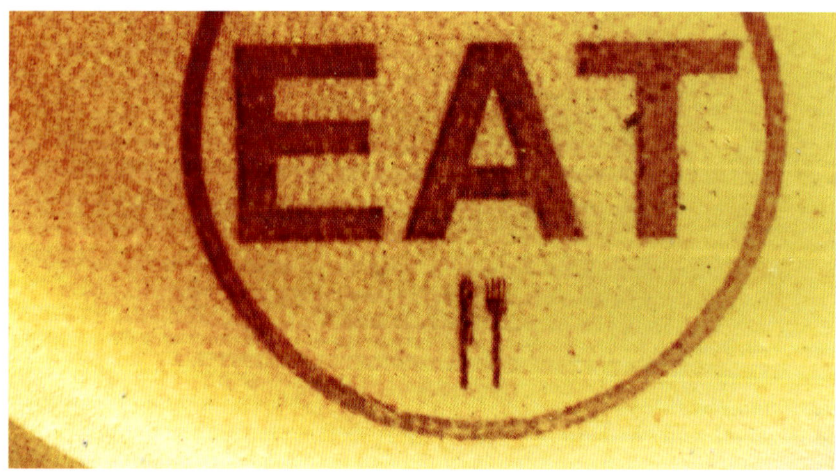

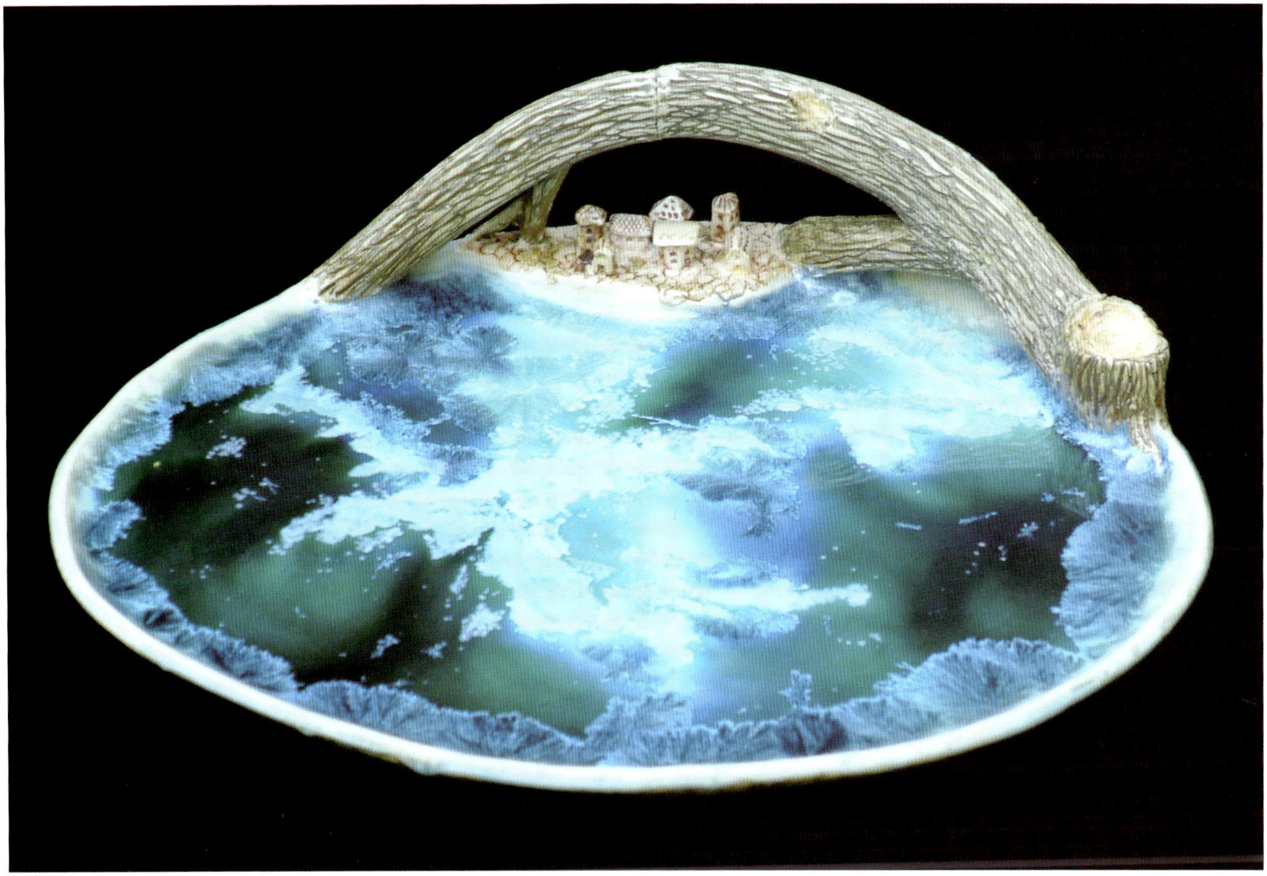

Tadeusz Walter

Untitled | 2007

$2\frac{1}{2}$ X $10\frac{3}{4}$ X $9\frac{3}{8}$ INCHES (6.4 X 27.3 X 23.8 CM)

Hand-built stoneware; electric tired, cone 9; glaze, crystalline glaze

PHOTOS BY ARTIST

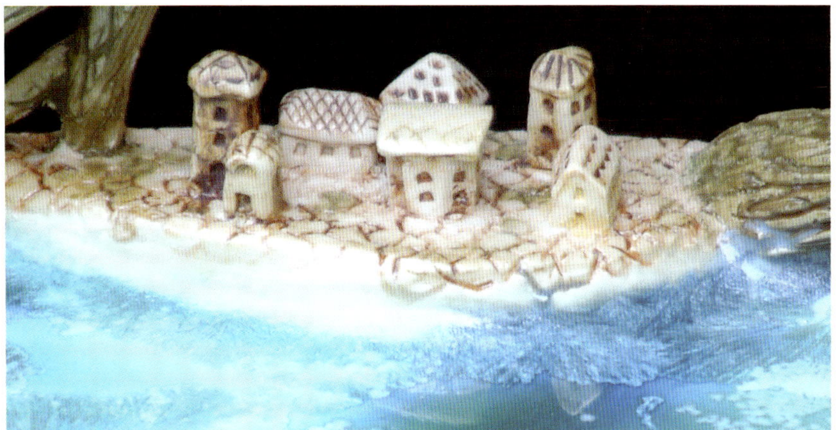

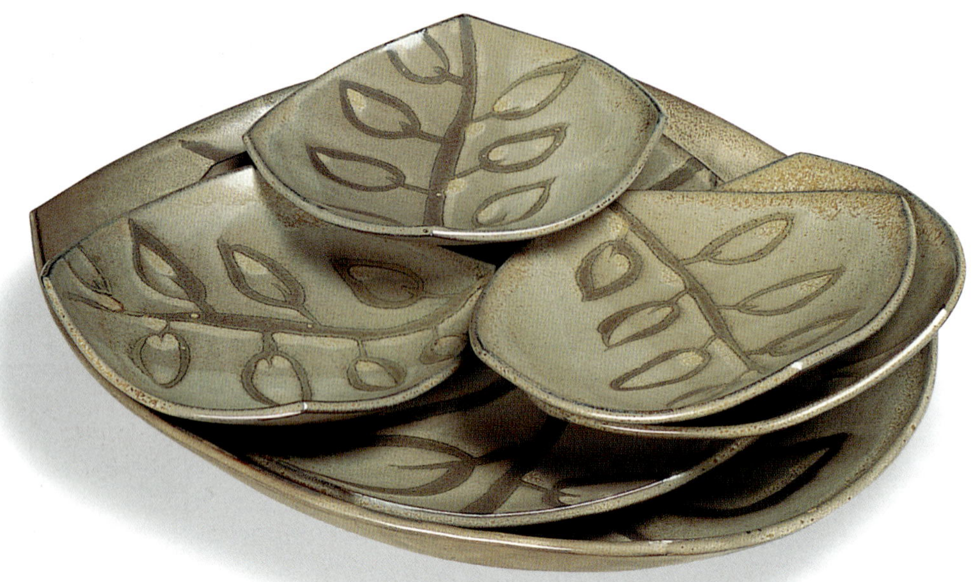

Teresa Gagne

Autumn—Pile of Leaves | 2007

LARGEST: 2 3/8 X 14 1/8 X 16 1/8 INCHES (6 X 36 X 41 CM)

Slab, hump-molded stoneware; rutile glaze over iron glaze, wax resist; electric fired, cone 5

PHOTO BY AK PHOTOS

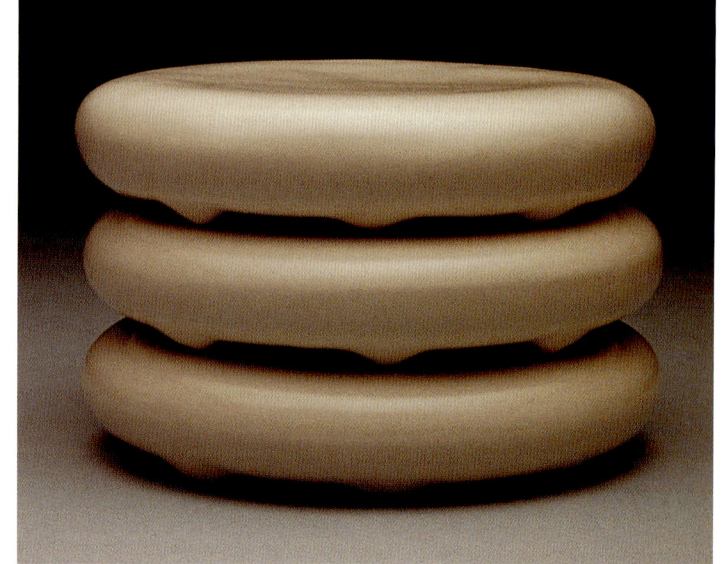

Karin Solberg

Stacked Sushi Plates | 2006

EACH: 1 1/2 X 6 X 6 INCHES (3.8 X 15.2 X 15.2 CM)

Wheel-thrown porcelain; salt fired, cone 10

PHOTO BY ARTIST

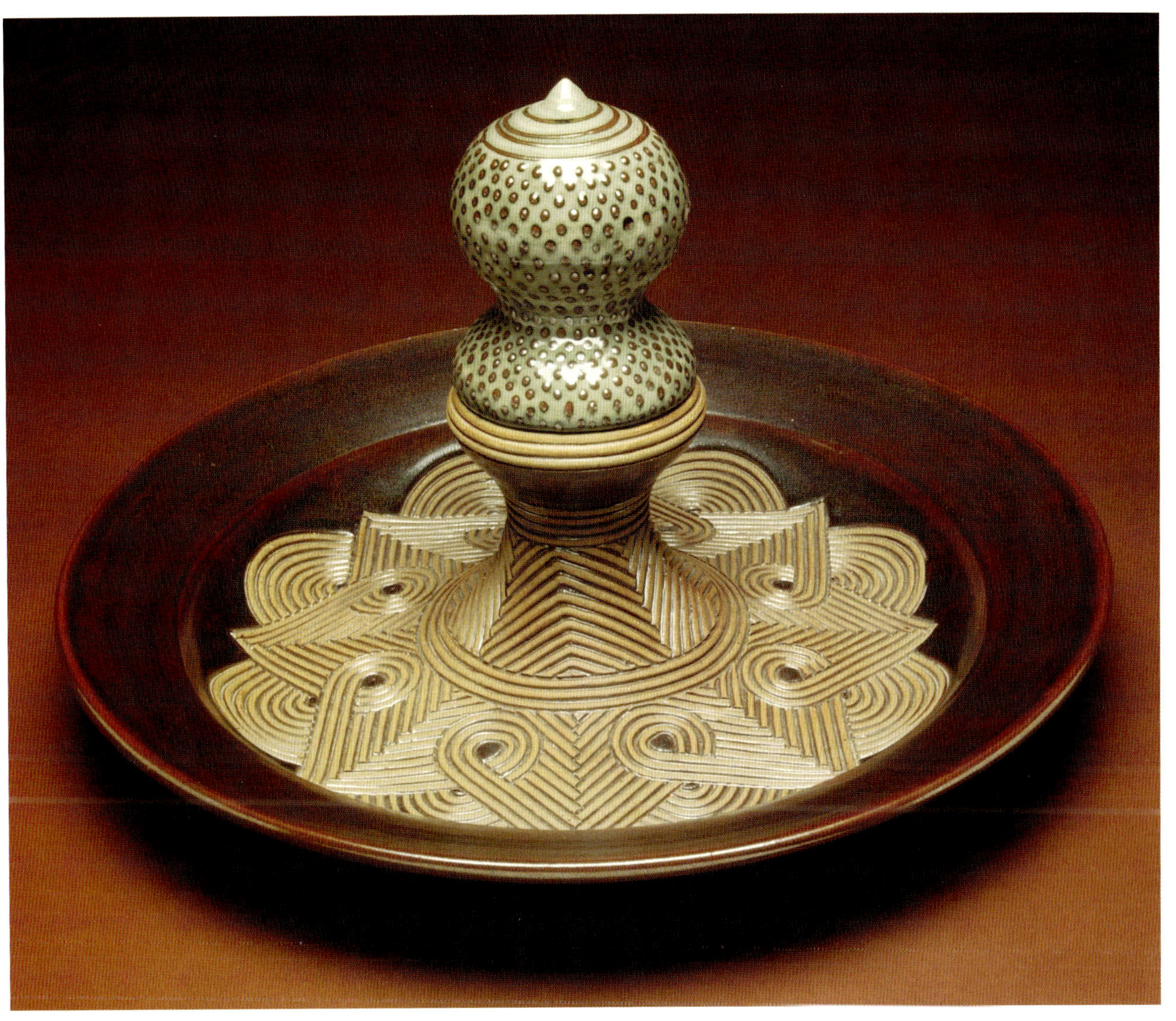

David R. MacDonald

Divination Series Plate | 2004

15 X 26 X 26 INCHES (38.1 X 66 X 66 CM)

Wheel-thrown stoneware, carved and slip trailed; gas fired, cone 10

PHOTO BY JOHN DOWLING

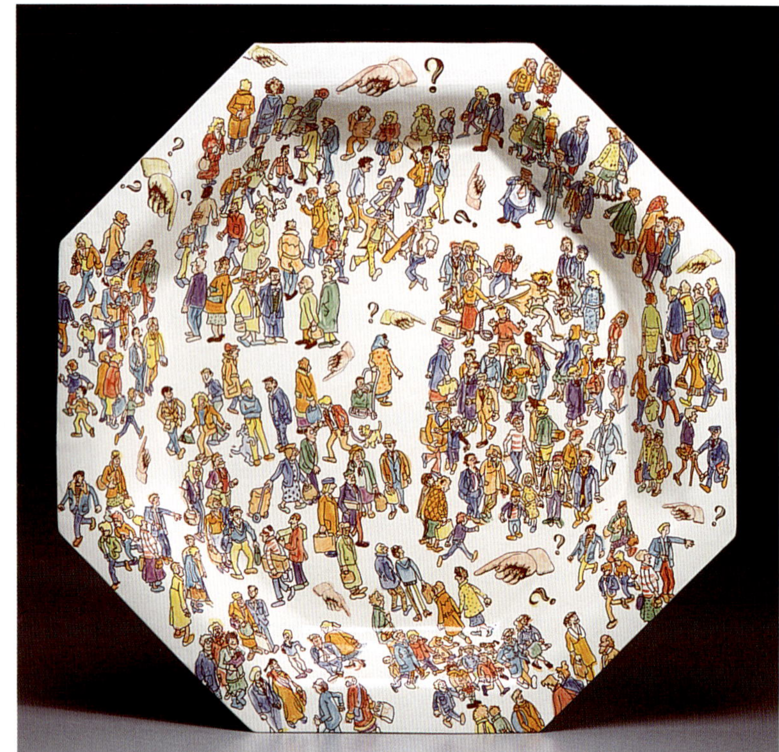

Paul Frehe

Where's Waldo? | 2005

$2^1/_2$ X 19 X 19 INCHES (6.4 X 48.3 X 48.3 CM)

Hand-built white earthenware; underglaze, clear glaze; electric fired, cone 05; laser decals, cone 08

PHOTOS BY STEVE MANN

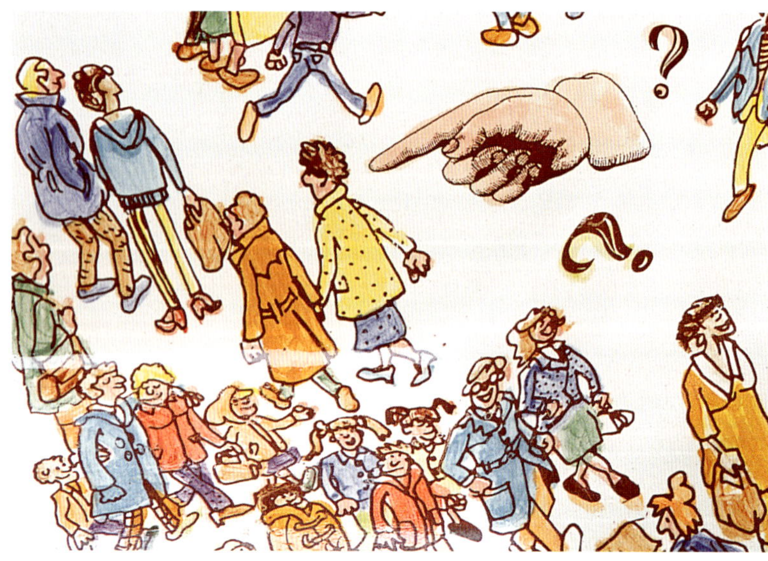

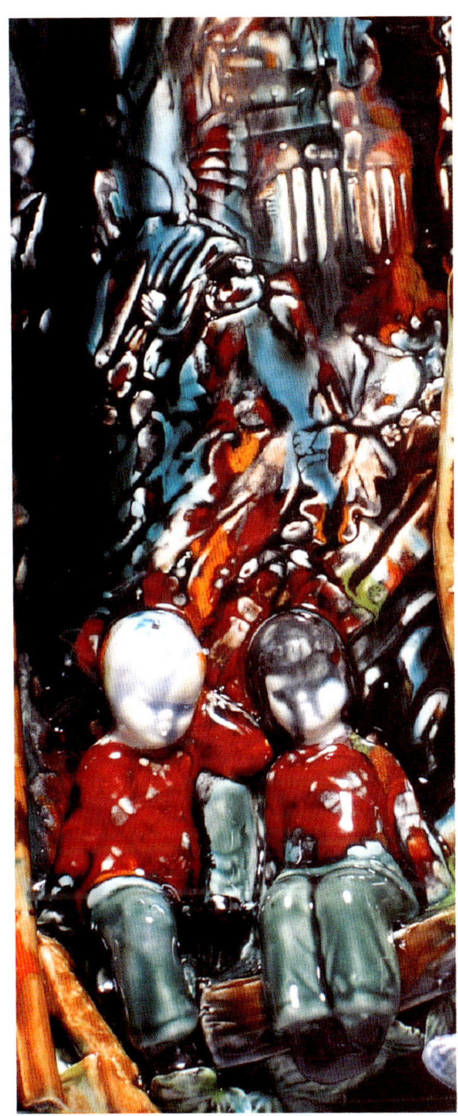

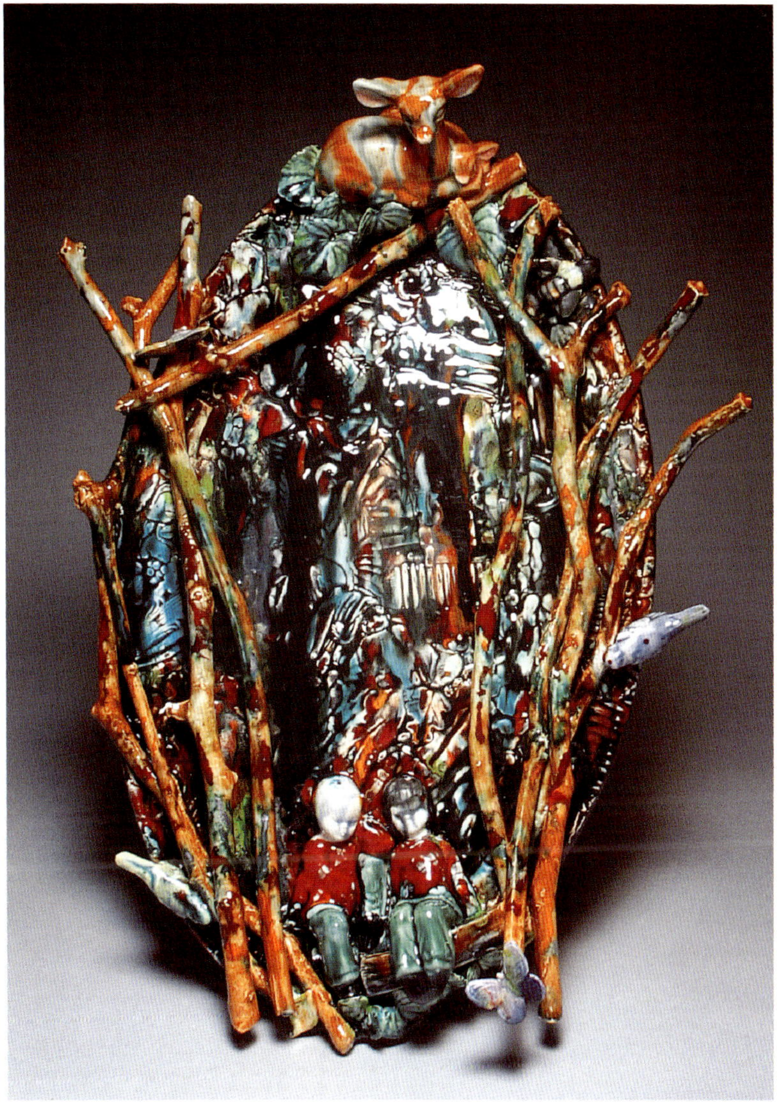

Craig Clifford

Watch Over Me | 2007

18 X 9 INCHES (45.7 X 22.9 CM)

Slip-cast and hand-built earthenware; low-fire commercial glaze, frit, copper, wood ash; electric fired, cone 04

PHOTOS BY DEBBIE KUPINSKY

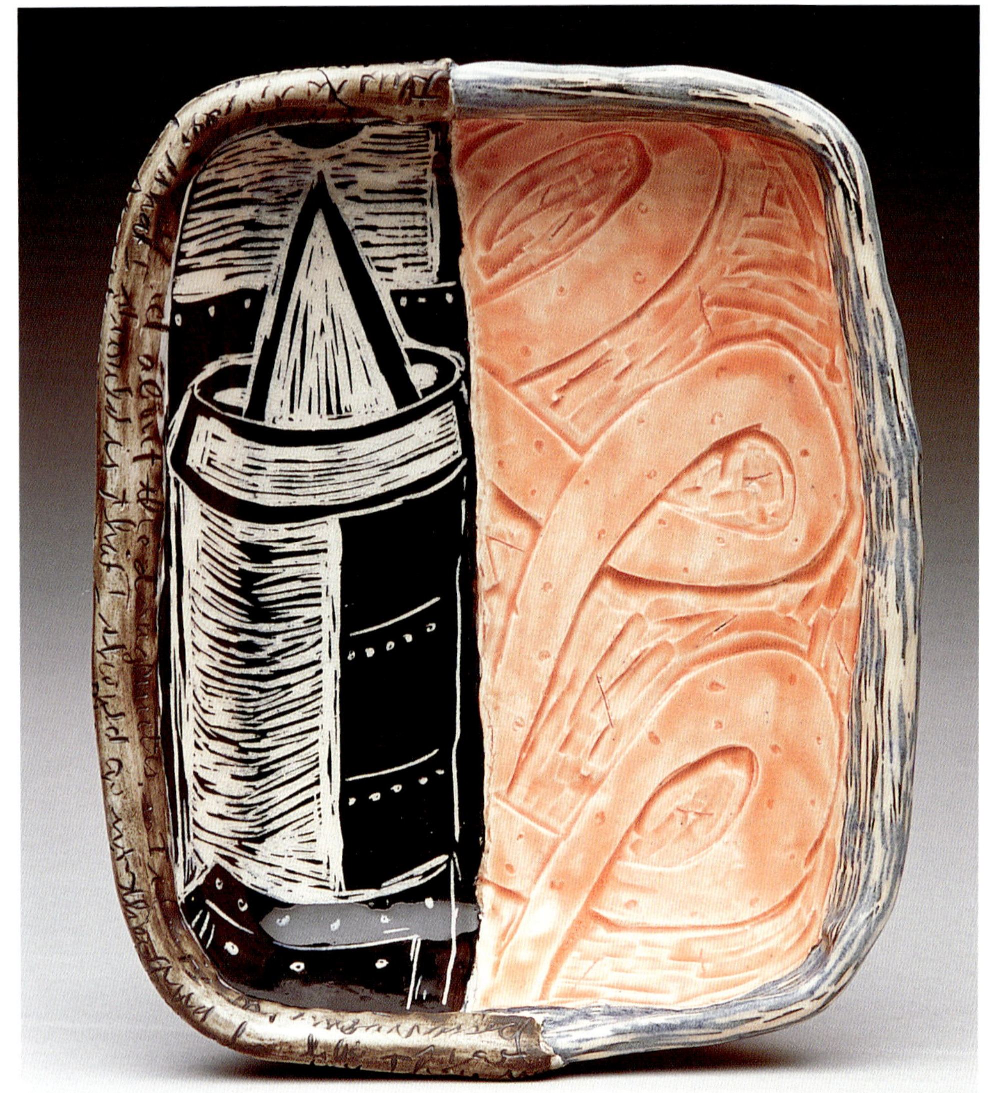

Susan Feagin

Turbine Dish | 2005

2 X 6 7/8 X 8 1/4 INCHES (5.1 X 17.5 X 21 CM)

Slab-built porcelain; carved and sgraffito; electric oxidation, cone 7

PHOTO BY WALKER MONTGOMERY

Steve Garcia

Don't Kill the Messenger | 2005

10 INCHES (25.4 CM) IN DIAMETER

Cast porcelain; multi-fired, cone 6; photo, onglaze decals, glaze

PHOTO BY ARTIST

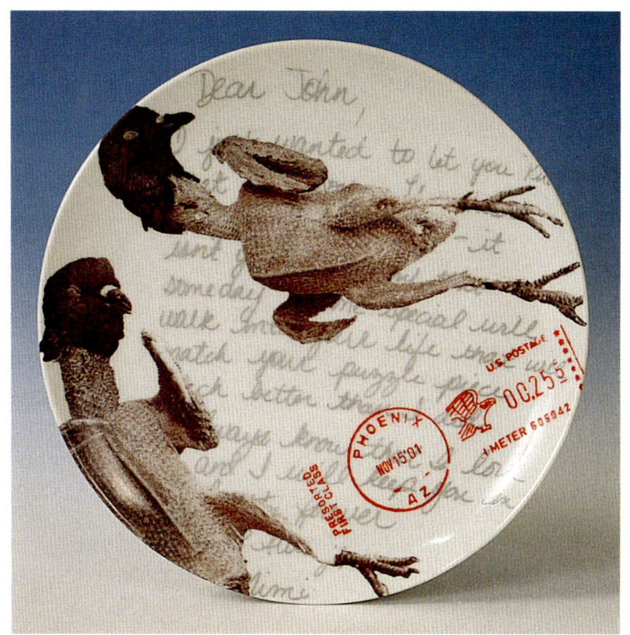

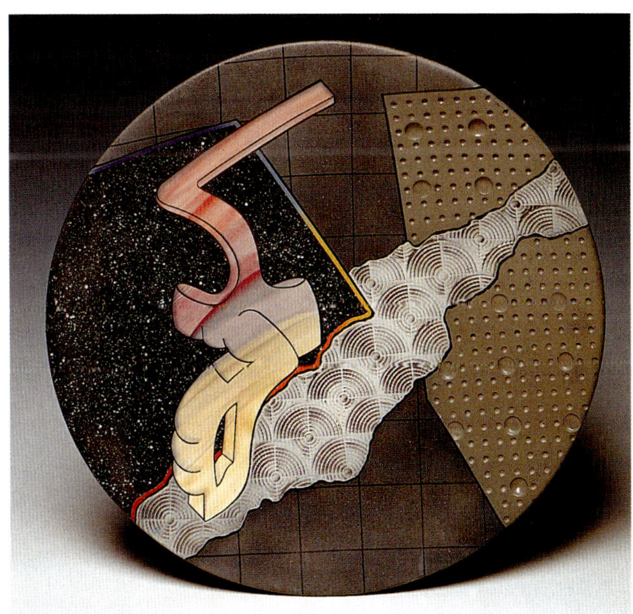

John W. Hopkins

Composition #59 | 2007

4 X 23 INCHES (10.2 X 58.4 CM)

Wheel-thrown earthenware; underglaze, overglaze; china paints, lusters; electric fired, cones 04, 06, 019, and 020; sandblasted

PHOTO BY ARTIST

About the Juror

Linda Arbuckle is well known nationally for her long career as an artist and teacher in ceramics. She received her Master of Fine Arts degree at Rhode Island School of Design in 1983, and she is currently a tenured professor at the University of Florida School of Art and Art History. She has taught workshops at many venues across the United States and in several international locations. Arbuckle was honored with a one-month residency in the People's Republic of China, awarded by the National Council on Education for the Ceramic Arts (NCECA), and she has received both a Visual Artist Fellowship from the National Endowment for the Arts and an Individual Artist Fellowship from the Florida Department of State.

Arbuckle has a chapter-length feature in *The Penland Book of Ceramics: Master Classes in Ceramic Techniques* (Lark, 2003). She has served as Director-at-Large on the NCECA board, and as juror for state arts grants in Louisiana and Florida and for the NCECA "Clay National" exhibition in 2004.

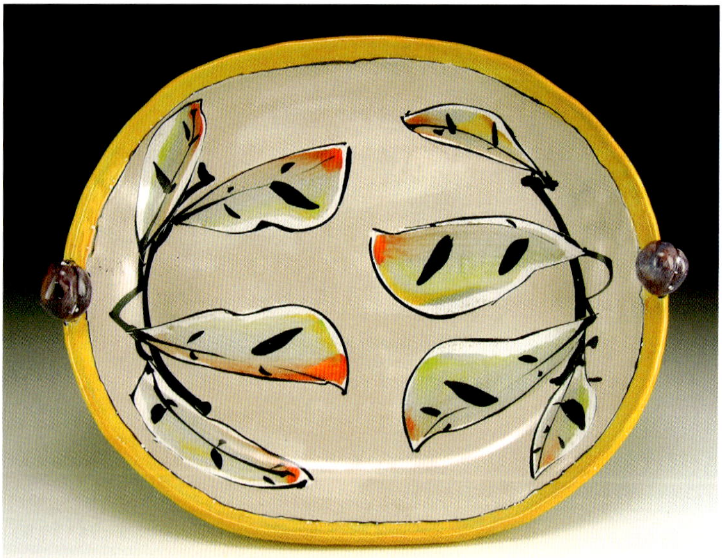

Linda Arbuckle

Oval: Winter Leaves, Plum Handles | 2007

2 1/4 X 12 X 9 1/2 INCHES (5.7 X 30.5 X 22.9 CM)

Hand-built terra cotta; majolica;
electric fired, cone 03

PHOTO BY ARTIST

Acknowledgments

To the hundreds and hundreds of wonderful ceramic artists who submitted work for consideration, our heartfelt gratitude. If only we could have chosen many more than 500! Juror Linda Arbuckle's remarkable eye and long experience made the selection process an enjoyable bit of teamwork. Special thanks also to Beth Sweet, whose first few days at Lark were spent in a dimly lit room, keeping the paperwork and records straight during the jury process and being a really good sport about it. Also providing essential support were Larry Shea, our very capable production editor, editorial assistant Dawn Dillingham, who never fails to deliver, plus our super-fab and hard-working art production folks: Shannon Yokeley, Jeff Hamilton, and Travis Medford. Amanda Carestio and Mark Bloom provided invaluable editorial assistance. Proofreader Chris Rich kept a sharp eye on hundreds of captions, and art director Matt Shay set a lovely table for all these wonderful photographs. A big thanks to all!

—Suzanne J.E. Tourtillott

Contributing Artists